Ellery H Clark

# A Treatise on Street Railway Accident Law

Salzwasser

**Ellery H Clark**

# A Treatise on Street Railway Accident Law

1. Auflage | ISBN: 978-3-84604-706-4

Erscheinungsort: Frankfurt, Deutschland

Erscheinungsjahr: 2020

Salzwasser Verlag GmbH

Reprint of the original, first published in 1904.

A TREATISE

ON

# STREET RAILWAY ACCIDENT LAW

BY

ELLERY H. CLARK

OF THE BOSTON BAR

SECOND EDITION

ST. PAUL, MINN.

KEEFE-DAVIDSON COMPANY

1904

Webb Publishing Co. Press, St. Paul.

TO V. M. M.
THIS BOOK IS DEDICATED
BY THE AUTHOR.

# PREFACE.

The recent development of our American street railway system has been little short of marvelous. Today our country is covered with hundreds and thousands of miles of track, designed for the use of horse, electric, and cable cars, dummy lines, and elevated trains. Great as have been the advantages attending the extension of the system, corresponding defects have not been lacking, and the appalling number of street railway accidents, instead of growing less year by year, as the public becomes more and more familiar with the dangers attending the operation of street cars, seems, on the contrary, to be steadily increasing. It is perhaps hardly necessary to add that these accidents are a most prolific source of litigation.

Believing that the tendency of the present day is towards specialization and concentration, the author, in 1902, published a book on the Street Railway Accident Law of Massachusetts. The kind reception accorded this work by the bench and bar has led to the production of the present volume, dealing with the street railway accident law of the entire country.

The author has endeavored to make thoroughness and system his watchwords. Every volume of the United States and state reports has been carefully searched, and the cases thus collected have been examined and classified with the most painstaking thoroughness. Of course, many cases in which a street railway company has figured merely by chance, as, for instance, cases involving points of pleading and practice, have been omitted as being outside the scope of the subject, but it is believed that practically every case of importance finds a place in this volume.

The author sincerely trusts that his endeavor to cover an important subject with thoroughness and system will prove of some value to the legal profession.

E. H. C.

Boston, May, 1904.

# TABLE OF CONTENTS.

## PART I.

## ACCIDENTS TO PASSENGERS.

### CHAPTER I.

WHO IS A PASSENGER.

I. Boarding the Car.

§ 1. Nature of the Relation.
2. Stations or Customary Stopping Places.
3. Boarding Car on Signal.
4. Boarding Car Without Signal.
5. Boarding Car in Violation of Rule.
6. Transfer.

II. Alighting from Car.

§ 7. In General.
8. Alighting Where There are Double Tracks.

III. On Car—Passenger, Trespasser, or Licensee.

§ 9. Payment of Fare.
10. Same—Children.
11. Same—Newsboys.
12. Position on Car.
13. Conduct.

IV. Passenger or Employe.

§ 14. Employe Off Duty.
15. Passenger Assisting Employe.
16. Passenger Allowed to Ride Free.

### CHAPTER II.

ACCIDENTS WHILE BOARDING THE CAR.

I. Due Care of Passenger.

§ 17. Due Care in Boarding Moving Car in General a Question of Fact.

18. Special Circumstances—Speed of Car.
19. Same—Age and Physical Condition.
20. Same—Incumbered with Bundles.
21. Same—Condition of Car.
22. Same—Condition of Track.
23. Same—Boarding Without Signal.
24. Same—Boarding Against Rule or Warning.
25. Same—Manner of Boarding Car.
26. Boarding Car not in Motion.

II. Negligence of Company.

§ 27. Reasonable Opportunity to Board.
28. Children.
29. Miscellaneous.

---

## CHAPTER III.

### ACCIDENTS WHILE ON CAR.

I. Unusual Conduct of Passenger.

§ 30. Riding on Front Platform—Due Care in General a Question of Fact.
31. Same—Consent of Those in Charge of the Car.
32. Same—Position on Platform.
33. Same—Intoxication.
34. Same—Children.
35. Riding on Rear Platform.
36. Riding on Step of Car.
37. Riding on Running Board.
38. Standing in Car.
39. Riding on Bumper.
40. Preparatory to Alighting.
41. Changing Position on Car.
42. Catching Dress.
43. Falling from Car.
44. Tripping in Car.
45. Putting Arm Outside Car.
46. Transferring.

II. Unusual Conduct of Company.

§ 47. Care Required of Company.

48. Running Cars on Sunday.
49. Crowding Cars.
50. Condition of Car.
51. Injury by Fellow Passenger.
52. Derailment.
53. Collision Between Two Street Cars.
54. Collision Between Street Car and Wagon.
55. Collision Between Street Car and Steam Railroad.
56. Jerk.
57. Speed of Car.
58. Miscellaneous Negligence in Operation.

## CHAPTER IV.

### ACCIDENTS WHILE ALIGHTING FROM CAR.

DUE CARE AND NEGLIGENCE.

§ 59. Due Care in Alighting from Moving Car in General a Question of Fact.
60. Reasonable Opportunity to Alight.
61. Speed of Car.
62. Manner of Alighting.
63. Age and Physical Condition of Passenger.
64. Sex of Passenger.
65. Incumbered with Bundles.
66. Place of Alighting.
67 Preparatory to Alighting.
68. Notice of Desire to Alight.
69. Alighting in Spite of Warning.
70. Condition of Car.
71. Injury by Fellow Passenger.
72. Miscellaneous.

## CHAPTER V.

### EJECTION.

I. WHAT RENDERS PASSENGER LIABLE TO EJECTION.

§ 73. Nonpayment of Fare.
74. Same—What is a Reasonable Tender.

75. Conduct.
76. Color.

II. MANNER, PLACE, AND TIME OF EJECTION.

§ 77. What Constitutes Ejection.
78. How Performed.

III. MASTER AND SERVANT.

§ 79. Responsibility for Acts of Servant.
80. Exemplary Damages.

IV. TICKETS AND TRANSFERS.

§ 81. Place of Transfer.
82. Time of Transfer.
83. Transfer Bad on Face.
84. Transfer Without Check.
85. Miscellaneous.

---

# PART II.

## ACCIDENTS TO TRAVELERS ON THE HIGHWAY.

---

## CHAPTER VI.

### PEDESTRIANS RUN OVER.

I. ADULTS.

§ 86. Due Care—General Considerations.
87. Same—Intoxicated and Infirm Persons.
88. Same—Crossing Tracks—Stopping, Looking and Listening.
89. Same—Walking on or near Track.
90. Same—Crossing Where There are Double Tracks.
91. Same—Laborer Working on or near Track.
92. Same—Miscellaneous.
93. Right of Way.
94. Negligence of Company—General Considerations.
95. Negligence in Operation—Lookout, Speed, Warning, etc.
96. Same—Laborer Working on or near Track.
97. Same—Miscellaneous.

II. CHILDREN.

§ 98. Capacity of Child.

99. Due Care of Child, for Jury.
100. Lack of Due Care of Child.
101. Due Care of Parent or Person in Charge of Child—Allowing Child in Street.
102. Same—Leaving Child Alone in or near the House.
103. Negligence of Company—Right of Way.
104. Same—General Considerations.
105. Same—Negligence in Operation.

---

## CHAPTER VII.

### ACCIDENTS TO DRIVERS OF WAGONS.

I. Collisions Between Car and Wagon.

§ 106. Due Care—Crossing Tracks—Stopping, Looking, and Listening.
107. Same—Driving on or near Tracks.
108. Same—Imputed Negligence.
109. Same—Age and Occupation.
110. Right of Way.
111. Negligence of Company—General Considerations.
112. Negligence in Operation—Lookout, Speed, Warning, etc.

II. Frightening Horses.

§ 113. Due Care of Driver of Horse.
114. Negligence of Company.

---

## CHAPTER VIII.

### BICYCLE RIDERS; HORSEBACK RIDERS; ANIMALS RUN OVER.

I. Bicycle Riders.

§ 115. Due Care.
116. Negligence.

II. Horseback Riders.

§ 117. In General.

III. Animals Run Over.

§ 118. In General.

## CHAPTER IX.

### ACCIDENTS FROM DEFECTS IN CONSTRUCTION AND OPERATION.

I. Electric Shock.

§ 119. Care of Company.
120. Presumption of Negligence.
121. Negligence in Operation.

II. Obstructions—Defects in Track—Defects in Operation.

§ 122. Liability of Company—City, Contractor, Lessee, etc.
123. Excavations between or near Tracks.
124. Obstruction near Track.
125. Defects in Tracks.
126. Wire.
127. Obstructing Tracks by Snow, Dirt, etc.
128. Miscellaneous.

---

# PART III.

## ACCIDENTS TO EMPLOYES.

---

## CHAPTER X.

### ACCIDENTS TO EMPLOYES.

I. Accidents to Conductors.

§ 129. Assumption of Risk and Lack of Due Care.
130. Due Care for Jury.
131. Who Are Fellow Servants.
132. Negligence of Company.

II. Accidents to Motormen, Gripmen, and Drivers.

§ 133. Assumption of Risk and Lack of Due Care.
134. Due Care for Jury.
135. Who are Fellow Servants.
136. Negligence of Company.

III. Accidents to Miscellaneous Employes.

§ 137. Assumption of Risk and Lack of Due Care.
138. Due Care, for Jury.
139. Who are Fellow Servants.
140. Negligence of Company.

# PART IV.

## EVIDENCE AND DAMAGES.

### CHAPTER XI.

THE VALUE OF EVIDENCE.

§ 141. Credibility of Witnesses in General.
142. Credibility as Affected by Interest or Bias.
143. Credibility as Affected by Corroboration.
144. Credibility as Affected by Contradictory Statements.

### CHAPTER XII.

ADMISSIBILITY OF EVIDENCE.

I. Evidence Bearing upon Plaintiff's Injuries.
§ 145. The Plaintiff Himself as Evidence.
146. Physical Examination of Plaintiff.
147. Exclamations and Statements of Plaintiff.
148. Medical Testimony.
149. Evidence of Other Witnesses.

II. Evidence Bearing on the Question of the Defendant's Negligence.
§ 150. Competency of Employes.
151. Starting and Stopping Cars.
152. Condition of Car.
153. Condition of Track.
154. Speed of Car.
155. General Negligence in Operation of Road.

### CHAPTER XIII.

DAMAGES.

§ 156. Excessive and Inadequate Damages.
157. Damages for Mental Suffering.
158. Special Damages.
159. Vindictive Damages.
160. Aggravation of Injuries.
161. Damages for Death.

# STREET RAILWAY ACCIDENT LAW.

## PART I.

## ACCIDENTS TO PASSENGERS.

### CHAPTER I.

### WHO IS A PASSENGER.

I. Boarding the Car.

§ 1. Nature of the Relation.
2. Stations or Customary Stopping Places.
3. Boarding Car on Signal.
4. Boarding Car Without Signal.
5. Boarding Car in Violation of Rule.
6. Transfer.

II. Alighting from Car.

§ 7. In General.
8. Alighting Where There are Double Tracks.

III. On Car—Passenger, Trespasser, or Licensee.

§ 9. Payment of Fare.
10. Same—Children.
11. Same—Newsboys.
12. Position on Car.
13. Conduct.

IV. Passenger or Employe.

§ 14. Employe Off Duty.
15. Passenger Assisting Employe.
16. Passenger Allowed to Ride Free.

#### I. Boarding the Car.

The relation of passenger and carrier is created by contract, express or implied, and begins when the passenger puts him-

**self in the care of the carrier with the intention of becoming a passenger, and is accepted as such by the carrier.**

**The relation may be established at a station or customary stopping place, but in the great majority of cases is established in the street itself.**

**Boarding a car without a signal is not enough to create the relation, nor is a mere unrecognized signal, or even a signal and answer, sufficient. But stopping a car when signaled is an invitation to all persons desiring to take passage to board the car, and, if a person is in the act of getting aboard, the relation is established. Slackening speed when signaled, without actually stopping, is also an invitation to board, and a person attempting to board in the exercise of due care is a passenger.**

**A person may be a passenger, although he violates a rule of the company in boarding the car.**

**A person transferring is a passenger while in the act of boarding, or even while on the way to board, the second car.**

### § 1. Nature of the relation.

It is a well-settled principle of law that the relation of passenger and carrier is a contractual one. The contract need not be express, but may be, and in the case of street railways usually is, implied from all the surrounding circumstances.[1] These must warrant the implication that the passenger has offered himself to be carried, and has been accepted as such by the carrier. The relation begins when the passenger puts himself in the care of the carrier, or

[1] North Birmingham Ry. Co. v. Liddicoat, 99 Ala. 545; North Chicago St. R. Co. v. Williams, 140 Ill. 275; Baltimore Traction Co. v. State, 78 Md. 409; Schepers v. Union Depot R. Co., 126 Mo. 665; Schaefer v. St. Louis & S. Ry. Co., 128 Mo. 64.

within his control, with the intention of becoming a passenger, and is accepted as such by the carrier.[2]

## § 2. Stations or customary stopping places.

Where a horse railroad company provided a waiting room for passengers close to a double track where incoming cars were shifted to the outgoing track by means of a movable section of the platform, and the plaintiff, who was waiting to take the cars, stepped from the waiting room, saw a car coming towards her sideways, and caught her foot in the movable section, it was held that she was a passenger.[3] The court said: "The counsel for the defendant insists that the relation of carrier and passenger did not exist between the parties at the time of the accident. This point, I think, cannot be maintained. Neither the entry into the cars nor the payment of the fare is essential to create that relation. Being within the waiting room, waiting to take the cars, was as effectual to make her a passenger as if she had been within the body of one of them. The waiting room is made for the purpose of receiving and accommodating the passengers until the car arrives."

In North Birmingham Ry. Co. v. Liddicoat[4] it was held that, if a person has the *bona fide* intention of taking passage by a train, and goes to a station at a reasonable time, he is entitled to protection as a passenger from the moment he enters the carrier's premises; and, further, that, if a common

2 North Birmingham Ry. Co. v. Liddicoat, 99 Ala. 545; Donovan v. Hartford St. Ry. Co., 65 Conn. 201; Schepers v. Union Depot R. Co., 126 Mo. 665; Schaefer v. St. Louis & S. Ry. Co., 128 Mo. 64.

3 Gordon v. Grand St. & N. R. Co., 40 Barb. (N. Y.) 546.

4 99 Ala. 545.

carrier is in the habit of receiving and discharging passengers at a place other than a regular station on its road, a person who knows of such custom and attempts to board a train at such place is as much justified in assuming that the carrier's cars are in a safe condition as he would be if he were attempting to board them at a regular station.

In the case of an elevated railway, where a car stopped, and a gate leading onto the platform was opened, the court said: "By permitting him to thus enter upon this space or platform, the plaintiff's husband at once became and was accepted as a passenger on said car, and defendant was bound to exercise the highest degree of care of a prudent person in similar circumstances for his safety, and be held to a strict responsibility therefor."[5] In Lake St. El. R. Co. v. Burgess,[6] a person on an elevated station platform was likewise held to be a passenger.

### § 3. Boarding car on signal.

The question of the relation of carrier and passenger usually arises, however, not at a station or fixed stopping place, but where the would-be passenger attempts to board the car in the street itself.

In Schepers v. Union Depot R. Co.[7] the court said: "It must be conceded that there is difficulty in many cases in determining when the relationship of carrier and passenger begins, and what acts of the parties are sufficient to create it. The difficulty is greater in case the carrier operates a street railway, having no regular stations or station agents

5 Barth v. Kansas City El. Ry. Co., 142 Mo. 535.
6 200 Ill. 628.
7 126 Mo. 665.

authorized to make contracts. In respect to such carriers, passage must be taken hastily, on the streets, at points prescribed by the rules of the carrier, or by the police regulations of the municipality."

The act of stopping a street car on being signaled is an invitation to the would-be passenger to board the car, and is an invitation not only to the person who has actually signaled the car to stop, but to others who desire to board the car.[8] Thus, in Joliet St. Ry. Co. v. Duggan,[9] the court said: "Where a street car has been stopped at a point usual for taking on passengers, the duty devolving upon those in charge of the car of giving ample opportunity for safely mounting is not limited to the person or persons who may have signaled the car. It is their duty to stop a sufficient time for others desiring to take passage to do so safely." And in Schepers v. Union Depot R. Co.[10] the court said: "When a street car has stopped at a usual place for receiving passengers, an acceptance of all persons who are waiting to take passage must be implied, as it may be impossible for each to be separately recognized."

It is well settled that a person does not have to be actually on a street car before he becomes entitled to the rights of a passenger. If the car has been stopped on being signaled, and he is in the act of getting aboard when the car

8 North Chicago St. R. Co. v. Cook, 43 Ill. App. 634; Joliet St. Ry. Co. v. Duggan, 45 Ill. App. 450; West Chicago St. R. Co. v. James, 69 Ill. App. 609; Citizens' St. R. Co. v. Jolly (Ind.) 67 N. E. 935; Davey v. Greenfield & T. F. St. Ry. Co., 177 Mass. 106; Gaffney v. St. Paul City Ry. Co., 81 Minn. 459; Schepers v. Union Depot R. Co., 126 Mo. 665.

9 45 Ill. App. 450.

10 126 Mo. 665.

starts, the relation of carrier and passenger is held to be established.[11] It is not necessary, moreover, to get further than to have one foot on the step of the platform or running board.[12]

It is not necessary that the car be actually stopped before the passenger attempts to board. The slackening of the speed of the car in response to a signal is an invitation from the driver to board the car;[13] and since boarding a moving street car is not necessarily lack of due care, as a matter of law,[14] it is held that, if a car slows up on being signaled, and a person in the exercise of due care is attempting to board when the car starts on again, he is a passenger.[15]

[11] Tucker v. Atlanta St. R. Co., 77 Ga. 61; North Chicago St. R. Co. v. Cook, 43 Ill. App. 634; West Chicago St. R. Co. v. James, 69 Ill. App. 609; Citizens' St. R. Co. v. Jolly (Ind.) 67 N. E. 935; Gordon v. West End St. Ry. Co., 175 Mass. 181; Davey v. Greenfield & T. F. St. Ry. Co., 177 Mass. 106; Smith v. St. Paul City Ry. Co., 32 Minn. 1; Miller v. St. Paul City Ry. Co., 66 Minn. 192; Gaffney v. St. Paul City Ry. Co., 81 Minn. 459; Schepers v. Union Depot R. Co., 126 Mo. 665; Barth v. Kansas City El. Ry. Co., 142 Mo. 535; Ganiard v. Rochester City & B. R. Co., 50 Hun, 22, affirmed 121 N. Y. 661; Reynolds v. Richmond & M. Ry. Co., 92 Va. 400.

[12] West Chicago St. R. Co. v. James, 69 Ill. App. 609; Gordon v. West End St. Ry. Co., 175 Mass. 181; Gaffney v. St. Paul City Ry. Co., 81 Minn. 459; Ganiard v. Rochester City & B. R. Co., 50 Hun, 22, affirmed 121 N. Y. 661.

[13] Finkeldey v. Omnibus Cable Co., 114 Cal. 28; Cicero & P. St. Ry. Co. v. Meixner, 160 Ill. 320; Conner v. Citizens' St. Ry. Co., 105 Ind. 62; Citizens' St. R. Co. v. Spahr, 7 Ind. App. 23; Citizens' St. Ry. Co. v. Merl, 26 Ind. App. 284; Sahlgaard v. St. Paul City Ry. Co., 48 Minn. 232; O'Mara v. St. Louis Transit Co. (Mo. App.) 76 S. W. 680; Savage v. Third Ave. R. Co., 29 App. Div. (N. Y.) 556; Reynolds v. Richmond & M. Ry. Co., 92 Va. 400.

[14] Infra, chapter 2, § 17.

[15] Citizens' St. Ry. Co. v. Merl, 26 Ind. App. 284; McDonough v. Metropolitan R. Co., 137 Mass. 210; Reynolds v. Richmond & M. Ry. Co., 92 Va. 400.

In McDonough v. Metropolitan R. Co.[16] there was evidence that the driver of a slowly moving horse car saw the signal of a boy of thirteen, and that, just as the boy was getting on the car, with one foot on the step of the front platform, and holding onto the railing with both hands, the car started with a sudden jerk, and the plaintiff was injured. The court said: "Upon the undisputed evidence, the plaintiff was traveling upon the defendant's car. The length of time he had been upon the car, and his position upon it, and the fact that he was changing his position, and had not assumed his seat or taken his stand upon the platform, are immaterial. He was on the car, and being carried by it on his journey. The instruction that, if he was there in the exercise of due care, he had the rights of a passenger, was correct, and, whether required by the facts or not, was sufficiently favorable to the defendant."

It is necessary, however, for the plaintiff to be in the exercise of due care. In Baltimore Traction Co. v. State,[17] in holding that one who attempts to board a street car moving six miles an hour cannot be regarded as a passenger, the court said: "There was no evidence that the gripman saw his signal, and, if he did, the deceased could not infer his tender to become a passenger had been accepted by the slowing of the car, provided it was still moving so rapidly as to make it obviously unsafe to attempt to board it. The relation of carrier and passenger may indeed be implied from slight circumstances, but one who attempts to take passage on a street car cannot be regarded as a passenger while he is in the act of entering it, unless he does so with a proper degree of care and

16 137 Mass. 210.
17 78 Md. 409.

prudence. The street was in no sense a passenger station, for the safety of which the company is responsible. So, until he had entered the car, or was in the act of prudently entering, he had not placed himself in the charge of the defendant; and if the attempt to enter was so obviously reckless and careless as to amount in itself to contributory negligence, it would be unreasonable to hold that such imprudent conduct entitled him to be regarded as a passenger while hanging onto the outside of the car."

Some very recent cases hold that slackening the speed of an electric car in response to a signal does not constitute an invitation to board, at least until the car has come to a standstill.[18]

A mere unrecognized signal is not sufficient to establish the relation of carrier and passenger.

In Reidy v. Metropolitan St. Ry. Co.,[19] the plaintiff, standing at a crossing, put up his hand as a signal to the car to stop. The car began to slow down, but did not stop, and, while he was attempting to board, the car suddenly started, and he was thrown to the ground and injured. There was no testimony to show that the car slowed down in response to the signal of the plaintiff, nor did it appear that either the gripman or the conductor knew that the plaintiff desired or was attempting to board the car. It was held that the plaintiff had no ground for assuming that the change in speed of the car was made for his benefit or convenience.

18 Monroe v. Metropolitan St. Ry. Co., 80 N. Y. Supp. 177; Powelson v. United Traction Co., 204 Pa. 474; Hunterson v. Union Traction Co. (Pa.) 55 Atl. 543. But see Mulligan v. Metropolitan St. Ry. Co., 85 N. Y. Supp. 791.

19 27 Misc. Rep. (N. Y.) 527.

So, in West Chicago St. R. Co. v. Binder,[20] a boy of twelve put up his hand as a signal for a cable car to stop. The gripman did not see the boy. The car slackened speed, but did not stop, and then resumed its course. The boy ran towards the car, and had caught hold of the rear platform, when there was a sudden increase in the speed of the car, and the boy was run over by the trailer car and killed. It was held that the boy was not a passenger.

In Schepers v. Union Depot R. Co.,[21] a man ran towards a car with his hand raised, but there was no evidence that his signal was seen by those in charge of the car. The court said: "He could not in this manner, by his own act alone, constitute himself a passenger, and thus secure the high degree of care due from a carrier to a passenger. Under the evidence, we think the relation of carrier and passenger was never created."

Even a signal and answer will not of itself be sufficient to establish the relation of passenger and carrier.

In Donovan v. Hartford St. Ry. Co.,[22] the plaintiff, intending to take an approaching street car, stepped out upon a cross walk and gave the usual signal, which the driver of the car saw and answered affirmatively. Just before the car reached the cross walk it was unexpectedly deflected to a side track, on which the plaintiff was standing, and struck and injured her. The court said: "A common carrier is bound to exercise a high degree of care towards those who have put themselves under his care as passengers, but not until they have thus put themselves under his care. Up to

[20] 51 Ill. App. 420.
[21] 126 Mo. 665.
[22] 65 Conn. 201.

that time, although they may have contracted with him for their future transportation, he owes no more care to them than to any third party. His special duty begins when, by coming upon his premises, or in the act of entering his vehicle, the actual relation of passenger to carrier is assumed."

Similarly, where the plaintiff stood on a cross walk awaiting an opportunity to board a stationary horse car, and, just before she did so, another car came by at high speed, causing a nervous shock, it was held that, as the plaintiff had not put her foot on the car, she had not become a passenger.[23]

In Carney v. Cincinnati St. Ry. Co.[24] it was somewhat loosely held that, if a car has stopped on a passenger's signal, he has virtually become a passenger.

## § 4. Boarding car without signal.

Of course, a mere attempt to board a car in motion, without a signal of any kind, is not enough to constitute the person thus attempting to board a passenger, since no steps have been taken to establish the relation of carrier and passenger between the parties.[25]

In Schaefer v. St. Louis & S. Ry. Co.,[26] the court said: "The plaintiff would have the court declare that, if he got on the step of the car for the purpose of getting upon the platform as a passenger, with the intention of paying his fare

[23] Mitchell v. Rochester Ry. Co., 4 Misc. Rep. (N. Y.) 575.

[24] 8 Ohio S. & C. P. Dec. 587.

[25] Basch v. North Chicago St. Ry. Co., 40 Ill. App. 583; Schepers v. Union Depot R. Co., 126 Mo. 665; Schaefer v. St. Louis & S. Ry. Co., 128 Mo. 64; Pitcher v. People's St. Ry. Co., 154 Pa. 560; Brooks v. Mt. Auburn Cable Co., 29 Wkly. Law Bul. (Ohio) 50.

[26] 128 Mo. 64.

when called upon, those acts made him a passenger, without regard to the fact as to how, when, and where he got upon the step of defendant's car. This instruction wholly ignores the fact as to whether or not defendant ever agreed to accept plaintiff as a passenger, or did any act indicating an intention to accept him as such. Without a contract for carriage on one part shown, and an acceptance on part of the other, either expressed or implied, the relation of passenger and carrier can never exist."

### § 5. Boarding car in violation of rule.

In North Chicago St. R. Co. v. Williams[27] there was evidence that the company had posted in the car a notice that passengers would not be allowed to get on or off the car while in motion. The conductor, standing on the back platform, did not warn the plaintiff not to get upon the car while it was in motion, but suffered him to step upon the platform without objection. The court held that it was a fair question for the jury whether, under all the circumstances, the plaintiff was invited to get on the car, and that, if he was so invited, he was a passenger, and said further: "But we are not prepared to hold that a party is a trespasser after he gets on a horse car, even though no fare has been collected of him before he meets with an injury, simply because he has violated a rule of the company as to the mode of his getting on."

In Smith v. Manhattan Ry. Co.,[28] the plaintiff, who had paid his fare, boarded an elevated railway train by the rear platform, in violation of a rule of the company. In an ac-

[27] 140 Ill. 275.
[28] 18 N. Y. Supp. 759.

tion for damages for an attempted ejection, the court held that his presence on the train was rightful, no matter what the irregularity in getting there.

## § 6. Transfer.

In Washington & G. R. Co. v. Patterson,[29] the plaintiff, who had obtained a transfer ticket from another car, which entitled her to ride on defendant's car, approached a car standing to receive passengers, and had placed her foot on the running board, and had taken hold of a stanchion for the purpose of raising herself to a seat, when the car suddenly started, and she was thrown to the ground and injured. It was held that she was entitled to the protection of a passenger in the car.

In North Chicago St. R. Co. v. Kaspers,[30] the appellee received a transfer ticket for a cable train, which started when he was about twenty feet away. Appellee ran after the train, and got upon the front platform of the third car from the rear, when there was a sudden jerk, and he was thrown off. It was held that he was a passenger, and entitled to the rights and protection due to a passenger.

In Keator v. Scranton Traction Company[31] it was held that, where a person is given a transfer ticket from one electric car to another, which is a block distant, to enable him to reach the destination for which he has paid, and, while in the cartway approaching the second car, which is the proper car for him to take under the terms of the transfer,

29 9 App. D. C. 423.

30 85 Ill. App. 316, affirmed 186 Ill. 246. And see Chicago City Ry. Co. v. Carroll (Ill.) 68 N. E. 1086.

31 191 Pa. 102.

he is struck, within five feet of the car, by a piece of the trolley pole, which broke while the conductor was turning it from one end of the car to the other, such person is a passenger, and is entitled to recover damages for the injuries sustained, if the railway company is unable to show the extraordinary care which it owes to a passenger.

Where a passenger was told to transfer from one car to another, and was obliged to cross a plank walk across a ravine, from which he fell, it was held that he was entitled to the high degree of care due a passenger.[32]

## II. Alighting from Car.

**The relation of carrier and passenger continues while the passenger is alighting, but, after the passenger has stepped from the car into the street, his rights are merely those of a traveler upon the highway, and not of a passenger. This is on the theory that the company has no control of the streets, and that its care should be coextensive with its control; and the same rule applies where the company operates double tracks, except where it has control of its premises, and can manage them as it chooses.**

**If a passenger alights for a mere temporary purpose, those in charge of the car must understand this if the relation of passenger and carrier is to continue.**

### § 7. In general.

Passengers upon street cars are entitled to sufficient time to get off, and the duty of the carrier is not discharged until the passenger is free from the car. The relation of passenger and carrier certainly exists while the passenger is in the act of alighting.[33] After the passenger has stepped from the car

[32] Jamison v. San Jose & S. C. R. Co., 55 Cal. 593.

[33] Atlanta Consolidated St. Ry. Co. v. Bates, 103 Ga. 333; Ft.

into the street, however, it is held that he is no longer upon the premises of the railway company, but upon a public place, where he has the same rights with every occupier, and over which place the company has no control. His rights are those of a traveler upon the highway, and not of a passenger, for the relation of carrier and passenger has ceased.[34]

If a passenger alights for a mere temporary purpose, this must be understood by those in charge of the car, if the relation of carrier and passenger is to be held to continue. Thus, in Central Ry. Co. v. Peacock,[35] the court said: "Whenever the passenger did alight, that contract was at an end, unless his alighting was well understood by the carrier's agent to be rightful and temporary, and that he was to resume his seat. He says he alighted for a purpose, and intended to resume his place in the car, and continue his journey, but this purpose was not communicated to or assented to by the driver and conductor. After he had alighted and walked a square, could he resume his place in the car without paying another fare, without the assent of the

Wayne Traction Co. v. Morvilius (Ind. App.) 68 N. E. 304; Louisville Ry. Co. v. Park, 96 Ky. 580; Jacobs v. West End St. Ry. Co., 178 Mass. 116; Finn v. Valley City St. & Cable Ry. Co., 86 Mich. 74; Fillingham v. St. Louis Transit Co. (Mo. App.) 77 S. W. 314.

[34] Hanson v. Urbana & C. Elec. St. Ry. Co., 75 Ill. App. 474; West Chicago St. R. Co. v. Walsh, 78 Ill. App. 595; Indianapolis St. Ry. Co. v. Tenner (Ind. App.) 67 N. E. 1044; Conway v. Lewiston & A. H. R. Co., 87 Me. 283, 90 Me. 199; Central Ry. Co. v. Peacock, 69 Md. 257; Creamer v. West End St. Ry. Co., 156 Mass. 320; Bigelow v. West End St. Ry. Co., 161 Mass. 393; Gargan v. West End St. Ry. Co., 176 Mass. 106; Platt v. Forty-second St. & G. St. Ferry R. Co., 2 Hun (N. Y.) 124; Wells v. Steinway Ry. Co., 18 App. Div. (N. Y.) 180; Smith v. City Ry. Co., 29 Or. 539; Finseth v. Suburban Ry. Co., 32 Or. 1; Buzby v. Philadelphia Traction Co., 126 Pa. 559; Street R. Co. v. Boddy, 105 Tenn. 666.

[35] 69 Md. 257.

conductor? Would the conductor be justified in omitting to demand another fare? We think not. * * * The carrier had a right to regard his contemplated trip as ended, and contract executed. He was no longer being carried as a passenger, but was walking on the street." A passenger who steps from the platform of an elevated train to the station platform to allow another passenger to alight does not cease to become a passenger.[36]

## § 8. Alighting where there are double tracks.

Where the company operates a double line of parallel tracks, there is some apparent conflict in the authorities as to whether the relation of carrier and passenger exists after the passenger has alighted from the car, and before he has had an opportunity of passing over and beyond the parallel track of the company's line.[37] The true rule would seem to be that the care of the carrier is coextensive with its control.

Thus, in Creamer v. West End St. Ry. Co.,[38] the court said: "We are of opinion that he was not a passenger when the accident occurred, and that he ceased to be a passenger when he alighted upon the street from his car. The street is in no sense a passenger station, for the safety of which a street railway company is responsible. When a passenger steps from the car upon the street, he becomes a traveler upon the highway, and terminates his relations and rights as a passenger, and the railway company is not responsible to him, as a carrier, for the condition of the

36 Graham v. Manhattan Ry. Co., 149 N. Y. 336.
37 Atlanta Consol. St. Ry. Co. v. Bates, 103 Ga. 333.
38 156 Mass. 320.

street, or for his safe passage from the car to the sidewalk. When a common carrier has the exclusive occupation of its tracks and stations, and can arrange and manage them as it sees fit, it may be properly held that persons intending to take passage upon or to leave a train have the relation and rights of passengers in leaving or approaching the cars at a station. But one who steps from a street railway car to the street is not upon the premises of the railway company, but upon a public place, where he has the same rights with every other occupier, and over which the company has no control. His rights are those of a traveler upon the highway, and not of a passenger."

In Street R. Co. v. Boddy[39] the court said: "On this question there is a conflict of authority, but we think the more reasonable view is that, where a man who has traveled on a street car steps from the car upon the street, this terminates his relation and rights as passenger, and the railway company is not responsible to him, as carrier, for the condition of the street, or for his safe passage from the car to the sidewalk. Where a common carrier has the exclusive control or occupation of its tracks and stations, and can arrange and manage them as it sees fit, it may be properly held that a person intending to take passage upon or leave a train sustains the relation of a passenger in leaving or approaching the car at a station, but 'one who steps from a street railway car to the street is not upon the premises of the railway company, but upon a public place, where he has the same rights with every other occupier, and over which the company has no control. His rights are those of a traveler upon the highway, and not of a passenger.'

[39] 105 Tenn. 666.

Creamer v. West End St. Ry. Co.[40] If the limitation indicated in the foregoing paragraph was not adopted, it would be difficult to suggest one resting upon a satisfactory basis. Take the case at bar. If the passenger relation did not determine when the defendant safely alighted from the car, when would it end? Would it continue only while he was crossing the parallel track, or until he had reached a point of comparative safety on the far side of the street? Or if, after reaching the ground, he had directed his steps to the other side of the street, would it have continued until he had reached the pavement? We think that the Massachusetts supreme court was wise in adopting the rule that this relation terminated the moment the passenger descended to the street. This is a fixed point, free from all speculation or uncertainty."

In Buzby v. Philadelphia Traction Co.[41] the court said: "The plaintiff had been carried to his destination, had alighted from the car in a place of safety, and his relation to the defendant as a passenger had ceased. The case, therefore, is the ordinary one of a traveler about to cross a public street, on which are two sets of railroad tracks, besides the usual space for wagons, etc., between the sidewalks."

The converse of this rule is shown in Burbridge v. Kansas City Cable R. Co.[42] Here the plaintiff was held to be a passenger after he had alighted from a car of the defendant, and was crossing a double track. The court said: "The uncontradicted evidence was that, at the time the plaintiff was injured, it was a rule then in force, for the management

40 156 Mass. 320.
41 126 Pa. 559.
42 36 Mo. App. 669.

and operation of defendant's trains, that its north track at the junction should be kept free of trains until the east-bound trains should not only leave the junction, but clear Main street, when only its west-bound trains, which should be held near Walnut street, a block east, should be permitted to approach the junction, so that the two trains would thus pass each other on the grade east of Main street. This was an assurance upon which the public had a right to rely. It was a well-devised and well-understood custom, the observance of which was alike beneficial to the defendant and the public. This was an approach to the defendant's trains at the junction, which the defendant gave assurance to the public that should be kept unobstructed and safe while its trains on the south track remained at the junction. The observance of the precaution was not inconsistent with the privilege granted the defendant by the City of Kansas, and under which it operated its railway. We think the facts of this case bring it within the rule declared by the supreme court of Iowa in McDonald v. Chicago & N. W. R. Co.[43] and approved by the St. Louis court of appeals in Chance v. St. Louis, I. M. & S. Ry. Co.,[44] to the effect that it is the duty of railway companies to keep in safe condition all portions of their platform and approaches thereto to which the public do or would naturally resort, and all portions of their station grounds reasonably near their platform, etc. We can perceive no reason why this statutory rule may not, to a certain extent, apply to street railways." Similarly, where the plaintiff was injured at a transfer station, the court said: "The passenger is entitled to this protective

[43] 26 Iowa, 145.
[44] 10 Mo. App. 351.

care of the railroad company until he or she is entirely free from danger from the movement of the cars on the tracks either way."[45]

Although some of the language in the cases of Evansville St. R. Co. v. Gentry[46] and Cincinnati St. Ry. Co. v. Snell[47] might seem to indicate that the court regarded the relation of passenger as still existing after a person had alighted from a street car, where there were double tracks, the point was not squarely presented for decision, and the care of the company was held to be only that of "reasonably protecting" such person from injury,—the same degree of care which it owed to persons who were merely travelers on the highway; and the only case in direct conflict with the rule above expressed is South Covington & C. St. Ry. Co. v. Beatty.[48] In this case the court held that there was no error in refusing to give the instruction that the appellee ceased to be a passenger when he alighted from the car, although the court seems to have misconceived the scope of the decision relied upon in their opinion.

A street car company is not under obligation to provide for its patrons cross ways from its stopping places in the street to the sidewalk; but if, for any reason, it does erect such passage ways, it must, at its peril, construct and maintain them in a reasonably safe condition.[49]

### III. On Car—Passenger, Trespasser, or Licensee.

**Actual payment of fare is not necessary to constitute the relation of passenger and carrier. A person allowed to ride**

45 Capital Traction Co. v. Lusby, 12 App. D. C. 295.

46 147 Ind. 408.

47 54 Ohio St. 197.

48 20 Ky. Law Rep. 1845.

49 Finseth v. Suburban Ry. Co., 32 Or. 1.

free under a rule of the company is a passenger; but one riding on a free pass limiting the liability of the carrier for negligence cannot recover damages for such negligence.

Where a child is invited to ride free by the employes in charge of a car, and accepts the invitation in good faith, according to the weight of authority, he is a passenger, and not a trespasser; but a child who is sui juris has been held not to be a passenger. A child attempting to steal a ride is a mere trespasser, but a child getting on a car without any intention of stealing a ride is not.

A newsboy who is permitted to jump on and off the cars to sell his papers is neither a passenger nor a trespasser, but a licensee. There is a conflict as to whether the company owes a newsboy the duty of using ordinary care, or is only liable for willful or wanton injury.

A person who assumes an unusual position on a part of a car not intended for passengers is not a passenger.

A passenger may forfeit his rights as such by refusing to pay fare, or by conduct or language which disturbs, or may reasonably be anticipated to disturb, his fellow passengers, or by refusing to obey the reasonable rules of the company; but a passenger who leaves his seat to protest against the conductor's treatment of a fellow passenger does not so forfeit his rights.

## § 9. Payment of fare.

Actual payment of fare is not necessary to constitute the relation of passenger and carrier.[50] An allegation that the plaintiff was on a car ready to pay fare is sufficient to show that he was a passenger, and, as such, lawfully upon the car;[51] and, similarly, when a person gets upon a car as a

[50] North Chicago St. R. Co. v. Williams, 140 Ill. 275; West Chicago St. R. Co. v. Manning, 70 Ill. App. 239, affirmed 170 Ill. 417; Gordon v. Grand St. & N. R. Co., 40 Barb. (N. Y.) 546.

[51] Barger v. North Chicago St. R. Co., 54 Ill. App. 284.

passenger, expecting and willing to pay fare, he becomes a passenger for hire, although the conductor fails to collect fare from him.[52]

In North Chicago St. R. Co. v. Williams,[53] the court said: "It is not necessary that there be an express contract in order to constitute the relation of carrier and passenger, nor that there should be a consummated contract. The contract may be implied from slight circumstances, and it need not be actually consummated by the payment of fare. * * * The whole matter seems to depend largely upon the intention of the person at the time he enters the car."

This last point is well brought out in the case of Myers v. Brooklyn Heights R. Co.[54] Here a person made repeated trips on a street railway line to its junction with another line, leased by the same corporation, with no desire to proceed beyond the junction, but for the purpose of seeing whether the company would give him a transfer upon the leased road. It was held that no action was maintainable under a statute for a refusal to carry "any passenger desiring to make one continuous trip between such points for one fare."

Where a passenger on a street car has been carried beyond his destination through the fault of the conductor, and is permitted by the conductor to remain upon the car without paying a second fare until the car has again reached his destination upon its return trip, it seems that his relation as

52 Wynn v. City & Suburban Ry. Co., 91 Ga. 344; Cogswell v. West St. & N. E. Electric Ry. Co., 5 Wash. 46.

53 140 Ill. 275.

54 10 App. Div. (N. Y.) 335.

a passenger continues during the return trip,[55] and if a passenger is carried beyond her destination because the conductor did not notice her signal to stop, she is still a passenger, and entitled to be treated as such.[56]

If a person expressly announces when he gets on a car that he will not pay his fare, he is nevertheless to be regarded as a passenger if he is allowed upon the car until demand is made for his fare, and he refuses to pay.[57]

Where a street railway company had a rule forbidding riding on the front platform, and the conductor took a ticket from the plaintiff, who rode there because of the crowded condition of the car, it was held that the plaintiff must be regarded as a passenger, and could not be ejected until his fare was tendered back to him.[58]

In Muldoon v. Seattle City Ry. Co.[59] it was held that a passenger riding upon a free pass, which contains conditions limiting the liability of the carrier on account of negligence, cannot recover for injuries received through the negligence of the carrier's servant; and, in a later trial of the same case, it was held that a public officer traveling upon a free pass is estopped from showing that the pass was void under the constitution.[60]

In Dickinson v. West End St. Ry. Co.[61] the defendant had made a rule "permitting policemen, firemen, advertising

[55] Rosenberg v. Third Ave. R. Co., 47 App. Div. (N. Y.) 323.

[56] Toledo Consol. St. Ry. Co. v. Fuller, 17 Ohio Cir. Ct. R. 562.

[57] Sanford v. Eighth Ave. R. Co., 23 N. Y. 343.

[58] Hanna v. Nassau Electric R. Co., 18 App. Div. (N. Y.) 137.

[59] 7 Wash. 528.

[60] Muldoon v. Seattle City Ry. Co., 10 Wash. 311.

[61] 177 Mass. 365.

agents, news agents, and employes of the defendant company in uniform to ride free at any time, such persons being required to ride upon the front platform, so far as practicable." Although apparently not necessary to the decision, in the course of the opinion the court said: "Persons riding gratuitously under this rule are passengers, as well as those who pay their fare. All members of the classes included in the rule stand alike in reference to the duty of care which the defendant owes them, whether they come within one part of the description or another."

## § 10. Same—Children.

The question of the relation established by riding without payment of fare has arisen very often when the driver, motorman, or conductor of a street car invites a child to ride free. It is almost universally held that such an invitation is an act within the scope of the employe's authority, and therefore binds the company, and that a child accepting such an invitation in good faith is not a trespasser. This ruling has been made in the case of a boy of eleven,[62] a boy of ten,[63] a boy of nine,[64] a boy of eight,[65] a boy of six,[66] a girl of ten,[67] and a girl of nine.[68]

[62] Hart v. West Side R. Co., 86 Wis. 483.

[63] Little Rock Traction & Electric Co. v. Nelson, 66 Ark. 494; Brennan v. Fair Haven & W. R. Co., 45 Conn. 284; Danbeck v. New Jersey Traction Co., 57 N. J. Law, 463.

[64] Metropolitan St. R. Co. v. Moore, 83 Ga. 453.

[65] Muehlhausen v. St. Louis R. Co., 91 Mo. 332.

[66] Buck v. People's St. Ry., E. L. & P. Co., 46 Mo. App. 555, 108 Mo. 179.

[67] Evansville St. Ry. Co. v. Meadows, 13 Ind. App. 155.

[68] Wilton v. Middlesex R. Co., 107 Mass. 108.

In Danbeck v. New Jersey Traction Co.[69] the court said: "The question is not as to the duty of the defendant towards persons of mature years, but what is that duty with respect to children? It might be quite reasonable to declare, as a rule of law, that a grown person has no right to enter a car except as a passenger, and, if he does so as the friend of the conductor, that such a situation creates no relationship between such person and the car company, and that the latter is under no obligation to see to his safety, while it might be unreasonable in the extreme to apply the same rule to a child under similar circumstances. Very few of the rules that regulate the conduct of a man with his fellows could be applied with the least show of reason to his intercourse with children."

A child of eleven has been held, however, to be on the same footing as an adult. In Marks v. Rochester Ry. Co.,[70] where it was adjudged on a previous trial that the plaintiff, a boy of eleven, procured by the driver to aid in taking a car back to a switch, was *sui juris,* it was held that the boy was not a passenger. The court said: "It is not believed that it is the law of this state that a railroad company may be made liable to a person who is *sui juris,* and who accepts a gratuitous ride upon the invitation of the company's conductor, in violation of his duty, for injuries sustained by him while occupying that relation. Whatever may be the rule as to the liability of a railroad company which, through its conductor or other employe, invites or induces helpless children to enter upon its cars for other purposes than to become passengers, who, while so situated,

69 57 N. J. Law, 463.
70 41 App. Div. (N. Y.) 66.

are injured through the negligence of such employes, it can have no applicability to a person who is *sui juris,* and fully knows and appreciates the nature of the invitation."

It is not necessary that the employe in charge of the car should actually invite the child to ride. If a child asks to be allowed to ride, and the request is assented to, this is sufficient,[71] and it has even been held to be enough if the driver of a car was aware of the presence of a child, and made no effort to remove him.[72] Although the cases agree that a child riding under these circumstances is not a trespasser, there seems to be some doubt as to whether the child should be regarded as possessing all the rights of any regular passenger for hire, and consequently entitled to the very high degree of care required of the carrier when the relation of passenger and carrier is shown to be established, or as occupying the middle position of a licensee entitled merely to the exercise of ordinary care on the part of the carrier. Some of the cases decide squarely that the child is on the same footing as any other passenger.[73] Thus, in Buck v. People's St. Ry., E. L. & P. Co.[74] the court said: "The plaintiff's son was received as a passenger. This fact cannot be affected by the omission of the driver to demand or collect fare. He was a full-fledged passenger, and, as such, was entitled to the same protection, and to have the

71 Buck v. People's St. Ry., E. L. & P. Co., 108 Mo. 179.

72 Muehlhausen v. St. Louis R. Co., 91 Mo. 332.

73 Little Rock Traction & Electric Co. v. Nelson, 66 Ark. 494; Metropolitan St. R. Co. v. Moore, 83 Ga. 453; Evansville St. Ry. Co. v. Meadows, 13 Ind. App. 155; Muehlhausen v. St. Louis R. Co., 91 Mo. 332; Buck v. People's St. Ry., E. L. & P. Co., 46 Mo. App. 555, 108 Mo. 179.

74 46 Mo. App. 555.

car managed with as much care, as if he had paid his fare." Other cases, by holding the company to the exercise of "ordinary care," or "reasonable care," would seem, at first sight, to place the child in a different position from other passengers, but it must be noted that violation of this duty was all that was necessary to a recovery in these cases, and that the question of the child's exact status beyond the fact that he was not a trespasser was not directly presented.[75]

In New York a different rule prevails. In Finley v. Hudson Electric Ry. Co.,[76] a boy was invited to ride free as payment for his services in opening a switch which it was the motorman's duty to open. The company had forbidden motormen to allow any one to ride upon such terms. It was held that the defendant owed the boy no duty as a passenger, since the motorman's act in inviting the boy to ride was not within the scope of his duty as employe, nor in furtherance of the company's interest, or for its benefit, and the law would not imply an assent on the part of the company to such an invitation.

The rule in Pennsylvania is like that in New York. A child of five, with another of eleven, got on the front platform of a street railway car, and the driver allowed them to continue there.[77] In commenting on this case in Biddle v. Hestonville, M. & F. P. Ry. Co.[78] the court said: "Both children here mentioned were trespassers; for although, in the first case, the child was on the car by invitation of the

[75] Brennan v. Fair Haven & W. R. Co., 45 Conn. 284; Wilton v. Middlesex R. Co., 107 Mass. 108; Danbeck v. New Jersey Traction Co., 57 N. J. Law, 463; Hart v. West Side R. Co., 86 Wis. 483.

[76] 64 Hun (N. Y.) 373.

[77] Pittsburg, A. & M. P. Ry. Co. v. Caldwell, 74 Pa. 421.

[78] 112 Pa. 551.

driver, yet, as he had no authority to give such invitation, according to the case of Duff v. Allegheny Valley R. Co.,[79] it was but as a trespasser."

The state of mind of the child, as has been mentioned, is of the greatest importance, and, in the common case of stealing a ride with no intention of paying fare, the child is held to be a trespasser. It has been so held in the case of a boy of twelve,[80] a boy of eleven,[81] one of ten,[82] one of eight,[83] and one of six.[84]

In North Birmingham Ry. Co. v. Liddicoat[85] the court said: "What has been said has no application to a person who, being at either a regular station or a place of customary use for receiving and discharging passengers, has not a *bona fide* intention of boarding a train as a passenger, but simply intends or attempts to obtain passage without the knowledge and consent of the carrier's servants or employes, and without paying fare. Such a person would in no sense be a passenger, but a trespasser, to whom the carrier would owe no higher duty than to refrain from wanton or willful negligence; or, upon discovering him to be in a position of peril, to employ such reasonable care as the facilities at hand would permit to avoid the threatened injury."

In Little Rock Traction & Electric Co. v. Nelson[86] the court said: "The employes of a street railway company

79 91 Pa. 458.

80 Hagestrom v. West Chicago St. Ry. Co., 78 Ill. App. 574; Biddle v. Hestonville, M. & F. P. Ry. Co., 112 Pa. 551.

81 North Birmingham Ry. Co. v. Liddicoat, 99 Ala. 545.

82 Little Rock Traction & Electric Co. v. Nelson, 66 Ark. 494.

83 Jackson v. St. Paul City Ry. Co., 74 Minn. 48.

84 Bishop v. Union R. Co., 14 R. I. 314.

85 99 Ala. 545.

86 66 Ark. 494.

are under no obligation to keep a lookout to prevent boys endeavoring to ride without permission and paying fare from entering its cars while in motion. Such a boy who does or attempts to do so is a trespasser, and the company owes him no duty save not to injure him wantonly."

There is, in addition, a class of cases where the child seems to have had no idea of paying fare, on the one hand, or of stealing a ride, on the other.

In Jackson v. St. Paul City Ry. Co.[87] it was held that, when a boy of eight got upon the car and sat down on the platform with his feet on the step, this was not *prima facie* evidence that he was a trespasser.

In Barre v. Reading City Passenger Ry. Co.,[88] a girl of eleven, and in Levin v. Second Ave. Traction Co.,[89] a boy of five, were held not to be "trespassers," in the legal signification of the word, on account of their youth. In Levin v. Second Ave. Traction Co.,[90] the court explained that they meant by this language that the children were not trespassers, to whom no duty was owed.

### § 11. Same—Newsboys.

A newsboy who is permitted to jump on and off the cars for the purpose of selling his papers, according to the weight of authority, is neither a passenger nor a trespasser, but occupies the position of a mere licensee.[91]

[87] 74 Minn. 48.

[88] 155 Pa. 170.

[89] 194 Pa. 156.

[90] 201 Pa. 58.

[91] North Chicago St. Ry. Co. v. Thurston, 43 Ill. App. 587; Raming v. Metropolitan St. Ry. Co., 157 Mo. 477; Padgitt v. Moll & C. Ry. Co., 159 Mo. 143; Fleming v. Brooklyn City R. Co., 1 Abb. N. C. 433, affirmed 74 N. Y. 618; Philadelphia Traction Co. v. Orbann, 119 Pa. 37; Blackmore v. Toronto St. Ry. Co., 38 U. C. Q. B. 172.

In Amato v. Sixth Ave. R. Co.,[92] nothing was said as to the custom of the railroad in allowing newsboys to sell their papers on their cars, but the court apparently recognized no middle ground, and said: "We assume that, in boarding the defendant's car, not intending to become a passenger, the plaintiff, for the time being, was a trespasser."

In Padgitt v. Moll & Citizens' Ry. Co.[93] the court said: "A newsboy jumping on and off a moving street car to sell his newspapers, not hailing to stop the car to receive him, nor signaling to stop to allow him to alight, not asking or receiving permission, either express or tacit, not asking or waiting for leave or license, but jumping on and off under circumstances that clearly indicate no purpose to pay fare, and no aim to be transported, but only to avail himself of the presence of persons on the car likely to buy his papers, is in no sense a passenger." It has also been held that he is in no better position if he is ready to pay fare if called upon.[94]

The cases are not in accord as to the degree of care required of the company under these circumstances.

In North Chicago St. Ry. Co. v. Thurston[95] it was held that the plaintiff could not recover unless he could prove that the company wantonly or willfully inflicted an injury upon him; and in Fleming v. Brooklyn City R. Co.[96] the court said: "The complaint proceeds upon the theory that, by permitting newsboys to traffic with the passengers on the

92 9 Misc. Rep. (N. Y.) 4.

93 159 Mo. 143.

94 Raming v. Metropolitan St. Ry. Co., 157 Mo. 477.

95 43 Ill. App. 587.

96 1 Abb. N. C. 433, affirmed 74 N. Y. 618.

cars, the defendant becomes charged with the duty of looking after their safety, of seeing that they do not run into danger, and of stopping and slackening the speed of the car for them to leave, whether requested to do so or not. I do not think the railroad company can fairly be said to have assumed any such obligation. Of course the driver had no right to do anything which would recklessly or needlessly expose this boy to danger."

In Padgitt v. Moll & Citizens' Ry. Co.[97] it was held that, while the plaintiff was in no sense a passenger, and the carrier was not under any obligation to observe towards him the same degree of care which it was obliged to show its passengers, nevertheless the law did require, under such circumstances, the exercise of ordinary care.

If a newsboy is allowed on a car, and is then ordered to get off where he can do so with safety, he is a trespasser if he remains on the car, and protected from willful injury only,[98] but he must hear the order.[99]

## § 12. Position on car.

The position which a person assumes may be a factor in determining his relation to the company. Thus, where a boy of twelve jumped upon the pipe which ran across a street car at the rear of the dashboard, and rode there without any intention of becoming a passenger or paying his fare, he was held to be a trespasser, and not a passenger;[100] and where a boy of eleven boards a car without intending to

97 159 Mo. 143.

98 Indianapolis St. Ry. Co. v. Hockett (Ind. App.) 64 N. E. 633.

99 Indianapolis St. Ry. Co. v. Hockett (Ind.) 67 N. E. 106.

100 Hagestrom v. West Chicago St. Ry. Co., 78 Ill. App. 574.

pay fare, but meaning to steal a ride, and hides himself to escape detection, he is a mere trespasser unless the driver or conductor assents to his riding, directly or by implication, and the mere fact that the driver knew of his presence is not enough to show assent.[101]

In Udell v. Citizens' St. R. Co.[102] the plaintiff, a boy eight and one-half years of age, being unable to get into an open, electric street car on account of the crowded condition thereof, stood on the side of the car not intended for passengers, and on which strips were placed to prevent the ingress or egress of passengers, with his feet on the boxing of the axle, and held onto a portion of a seat with his hands. He rode in a stooped position three-fourths of a mile, when, being unable to retain his hold, he fell, and was run over by the wheels of the car, and injured. None of the employes of the train saw the boy hanging on the car when it was in the act of starting, nor while under way, but might have seen him if they had made an examination of that part of the car. Plaintiff did not pay his fare, but intended to do so when called upon. Held, that plaintiff was not a passenger upon defendant's cars, to whom it owed a duty of safe carriage and immunity from injury. The court said: "Appellant was not in a place intended for passengers. He was not received as a passenger. His presence on the car was not made known to appellee's agents and servants. He did not conduct himself as a passenger. Appellee's servants were not required to search for trespassers before starting the cars, and appellee was not bound to discover appellant, and remove him from the perilous situation in which he had voluntarily placed himself."

101 Wynn v. City & Suburban Ry. Co., 91 Ga. 344.
102 152 Ind. 507.

In Weber v. Brooklyn, Q. C. & S. R. Co.[103] it was held that, when a passenger leaves his seat to protest to the conductor against his treatment of an intoxicated person, he does not thereby forfeit his rights as a passenger.

In Barlow v. Jersey City, H. & P. Ry. Co.,[104] a boy of twelve got on the step of the front platform of a moving electric car, meaning to become a passenger on the car. Access to the platform was barred by a closed door, the place provided for entering the car being at the rear platform. The boy rapped on the door, and the motorman saw him, but paid no attention to him. The car struck a wagon, and the boy was thrown off and injured. It was held that he was in no sense a passenger, and that the company owed him no duty except to abstain from willful injury.

## § 13. Conduct.

A passenger may forfeit his rights as such by his conduct. He may refuse to pay his fare on demand, and thus become liable to ejection,[105] and *a fortiori* he has no rights as a passenger after he has once been ejected, and is seeking to gain an entrance again.[106] Whether he has paid his fare or not, he forfeits his rights as a passenger by the use of abusive and insulting language calculated to disturb the other passengers,[107] or by conduct which is disorderly, and

103 47 App. Div. (N. Y.) 306.

104 67 N. J. Law, 364.

105 Chicago City Ry. Co. v. Pelletier, 134 Ill. 120; West Chicago St. R. Co. v. Luleich, 85 Ill. App. 643; Hudson v. Lynn & B. R. Co., 178 Mass. 64; Sanford v. Eighth Ave. R. Co., 23 N. Y. 343.

106 North Chicago St. R. Co. v. Olds, 40 Ill. App. 421, 64 Ill. App. 595.

107 Chicago City Ry. Co. v. Pelletier, 33 Ill. App. 455, 134 Ill. 120; Robinson v. Rockland, T. & C. St. Ry. Co., 87 Me. 387; Eads v. Met-

calculated to annoy his fellow passengers.[108] It is not necessary for those in charge of the car to wait until an actual disturbance takes place, but a reasonable anticipation of conduct that will prove offensive or annoying to other passengers is sufficient.[109] A passenger may lose his standing as such by refusing to obey a reasonable rule of the company, as, for instance, a rule requiring a passenger to deposit his fare in a box on entering a car,[110] a rule forbidding passengers to ride on the front[111] or rear platform,[112] a rule forbidding passengers to bring dogs upon the car,[113] or a rule that passengers must not take into street cars packages or goods that are cumbersome or dangerous.[114] A passenger who leaves his seat to protest to the conductor against his treatment of an intoxicated person does not thereby forfeit his rights as a passenger.[115]

ropolitan Ry. Co., 43 Mo. App. 536; Flynn v. Central Park, etc., R. Co., 49 N. Y. Super. Ct. 81.

108 West Chicago St. R. Co. v. Luleich, 85 Ill. App. 643; Vinton v. Middlesex R. Co., 11 Allen (Mass.) 304; Murphy v. Union Ry. Co., 118 Mass. 228; Edgerly v. Union St. R. Co., 67 N. H. 312; Higgins v. Watervliet Turnpike & R. Co., 46 N. Y. 23; Putnam v. Broadway & S. A. R. Co., 55 N. Y. 108; Flynn v. Central Park, etc., R. Co., 49 N. Y. Super. Ct. 81.

109 Lemont v. Washington & G. R. Co., 1 Mackey (D. C.) 180; Vinton v. Middlesex R. Co., 11 Allen (Mass.) 304; Murphy v. Union Ry. Co., 118 Mass. 228; Hudson v. Lynn & B. R. Co., 178 Mass. 64; Edgerly v. Union St. R. Co., 67 N. H. 312.

110 Nye v. Marysville & Y. C. St. R. Co., 97 Cal. 461; Curtis v. Louisville City Ry. Co., 94 Ky. 573.

111 Montgomery v. Buffalo Ry. Co., 165 N. Y. 139; McMillan v. Federal St. & P. V. P. Ry. Co., 172 Pa. 523.

112 Ft. Clark St. R. Co. v. Ebaugh, 49 Ill. App. 582.

113 Butler v. Steinway Ry. Co., 87 Hun (N. Y.) 10.

114 Dowd v. Albany Ry. Co., 47 App. Div. (N. Y.) 202.

115 Weber v. Brooklyn, Q. C. & S. R. Co., 47 App. Div. (N. Y.) 306.

## IV. Passenger or Employe.

**An employe off duty riding free under a rule or custom of the company is a passenger.**

**A passenger assisting a driver to push back a car is not a fellow servant of the driver of another car, which injures him.**

**A newsboy allowed on the cars to sell his papers is not an employe engaged or employed on or about the road or cars of the company, and a boy riding free to turn a switch is not a volunteer fellow servant.**

### § 14. Employe off duty.

In Dickinson v. West End St. Ry. Co.,[116] an action for personal injuries to a motorman, who was thrown from the front platform while riding on an electric car, in consequence of the negligence of the motorman in charge of it, it appeared that the plaintiff, at the time of the accident, was not on duty, but was riding home to dinner, and under a rule of the company, being in uniform, had not been required to pay a fare. It was held that the plaintiff was on the defondant's car as a passenger at the time of the accident, and was not at that moment in the service of the defendant in such a sense that the negligent motorman was his fellow servant.

A person who is employed by a railroad company as a day laborer, reporting daily for service, and subject to call, but allowed to attend to other business when not needed for the day, who gets on a train for his own purposes when "off duty," without being obliged to pay fare, according to a custom of the railroad, occupies the position of a passenger, and not of an employe, and a mere direction given him by the

116 177 Mass. 365.

conductor to do a single act, as to turn a switch, does not establish employment.[117]

A section man of a street car company which was in the habit of furnishing such employes transportation to and from their work is lawfully upon the train, and is not a mere trespasser while riding by order of his foreman, although no fare was collected or expected from him.[118]

A day laborer allowed to ride to and from work as part compensation is not a fellow servant of the employes operating a car on which he is riding home after work.[119]

## § 15. Passenger assisting employe.

Where a car went beyond a turnout on a single track, and it became necessary to push it back, it was held that a passenger assisting the driver of the car was not a fellow servant of the driver of another car, which injured him.[120]

## § 16. Passenger allowed to ride free.

In Philadelphia Traction Co. v. Orbann,[121] a newsboy allowed to board the cars of a street railway company to sell his papers was held to be a licensee, and not an employe engaged or employed on or about the road or cars of the company, under the act of April 4, 1868 (P. L. 58).

In Hart v. West Side R. Co.,[122] a boy of eleven was invited by the motorman to ride free to turn a switch for

117 McDaniel v. Highland Ave. & B. R. Co., 90 Ala. 64.

118 Denver & B. P. Rapid Transit Co. v. Dwyer, 20 Colo. 132.

119 Peterson v. Seattle Traction Co., 23 Wash. 615.

120 Street Ry. Co. v. Bolton, 43 Ohio St. 224.

121 119 Pa. 37.

122 86 Wis. 483.

him. The complaint alleged that it was the custom of the motorman to permit boys to ride upon the front platform for the purpose of inducing the boys to turn the switch, and that the plaintiff rode there for this purpose. It was held that the plaintiff was not a volunteer fellow servant; that even assuming that one who, at the request of those in charge of an electric car, temporarily assists in the operation of said car is to be regarded for the time being as a servant of the company, and the co-employe of those in charge of the car, the complaint failed to allege any such relationship.

# CHAPTER II.

## ACCIDENTS WHILE BOARDING THE CAR.

I. Due Care of Passenger.

§ 17. Due Care in Boarding Moving Car in General a Question of Fact.
18. Special Circumstances—Speed of Car.
19. Same—Age and Physical Condition.
20. Same—Incumbered with Bundles.
21. Same—Condition of Car.
22. Same—Condition of Track.
23. Same—Boarding Without Signal.
24. Same—Boarding Against Rule or Warning.
25. Same—Manner of Boarding Car.
26. Boarding Car not in Motion.

II. Negligence of Company.

§ 27. Reasonable Opportunity to Board.
28. Children.
29. Miscellaneous.

### I. Due Care of Passenger.

It is not lack of due care, as a matter of law, to board a moving street car, whether horse car, electric car, cable car, or car drawn by a dummy engine, and whether the attempt to board is made by the front platform, rear platform, or running board. Ordinarily it is a question of fact for the jury, depending on all the circumstances of each particular case.

Special circumstances, however, such as the speed of the car, the condition of the car and the track, the age and physical condition of the person making the attempt, whether or not he was incumbered with bundles, the manner of boarding, whether a signal was given, and whether the attempt was made contrary to a rule or warning, may justify the courts in holding a person guilty of lack of due care as a matter of law.

It is not lack of due care to board a stationary car by the front platform or by the rear platform without taking hold of the handles provided.

## § 17. Due care in boarding moving car in general a question of fact.

It is well settled that it is not lack of due care, as a matter of law, to board a moving street car.[1] This is so, wheth-

[1] North Birmingham Ry. Co. v. Liddicoat, 99 Ala. 545; Birmingham Electric Ry. Co. v. Clay, 108 Ala. 233; Finkeldey v. Omnibus Cable Co., 114 Cal. 28; Brown v. Washington & G. R. Co., 11 App. D. C. 37; West Chicago St. R. Co. v. Dudzik, 67 Ill. App. 681; West Chicago St. R. Co. v. Lups, 74 Ill. App. 420; North Chicago St. R. Co. v. Kaspers, 85 Ill. App. 316; North Chicago St. R. Co. v. Williams, 140 Ill. 275; Cicero & P. St. Ry. Co. v. Meixner, 160 Ill. 320; North Chicago St. R. Co. v. Wiswell, 168 Ill. 613; South Chicago City R. Co. v. Dufresne, 200 Ill. 456; Citizens' St. R. Co. v. Spahr, 7 Ind. App. 23; Citizens' St. Ry. Co. v. Merl, 26 Ind. App. 284; Conner v. Citizens' St. Ry. Co., 105 Ind. 62; Central Passenger Ry. Co. v. Rose, 15 Ky. Law Rep. 209; McDonough v. Metropolitan R. Co., 137 Mass. 210; Briggs v. Union St. Ry. Co., 148 Mass. 72; Corlin v. West End St. Ry. Co., 154 Mass. 197; Gordon v. West End St. Ry. Co., 175 Mass. 181; Davey v. Greenfield & T. F. St. Ry. Co., 177 Mass. 106; Sahlgaard v. St. Paul City Ry. Co., 48 Minn. 232; Schepers v. Union Depot R. Co., 126 Mo. 665; Schaefer v. St. Louis & S. Ry. Co., 128 Mo. 64; Sly v. Union Depot R. Co., 134 Mo. 681; Hansberger v. Sedalia Electric Ry., L. & P. Co., 82 Mo. App. 566; O'Mara v. St. Louis Transit Co. (Mo. App.) 76 S. W. 680; Omaha St. Ry. Co. v. Martin, 48 Neb. 65; Schmidt v. North Jersey St. Ry. Co., 66 N. J. Law, 424; Maher v. Central Park, N. & E. R. R. Co., 67 N. Y. 52; Eppendorf v. Brooklyn City & N. R. Co., 69 N. Y. 195; Moylan v. Second Ave. R. Co., 128 N. Y. 583; Morrison v Broadway & S. A. R. Co., 130 N. Y. 166; Savage v. Third Ave. R. Co., 29 App. Div. (N. Y.) 556; Wallace v. Third

er the car is a horse car,[2] an electric car,[3] a cable car,[4] or a car drawn by a dummy engine;[5] and whether the attempt

Ave. R. Co., 36 App. Div. (N. Y.) 57; Sexton v. Metropolitan St. Ry. Co., 40 App. Div. (N. Y.) 26; Valentine v. Broadway & S. A. R. Co., 14 Daly (N. Y.) 540; Seitz v. Dry Dock, E. B. & B. R. Co., 16 Daly (N. Y.) 264; Gilbert v. Third Ave. Ry. Co., 54 N. Y. Super. Ct. 270; McSwyny v. Broadway & S. A. R. Co., 7 N. Y. Supp. 456; Kimber v. Metropolitan St. Ry. Co., 69 App. Div. (N. Y.) 353; Lobsenz v. Metropolitan St. Ry. Co., 72 App. Div. (N. Y.) 181; Stager v. Ridge Ave. Passenger Ry. Co., 119 Pa. 70; Picard v. Ridge Ave. Passenger Ry. Co., 147 Pa. 195; Walters v. Philadelphia Traction Co., 161 Pa. 36; Woo Dan v. Seattle Electric Ry. & P. Co., 5 Wash. 466.

2 Finkeldey v. Omnibus Cable Co., 114 Cal. 28; Brown v. Washington & G. R. Co., 11 App. D. C. 37, North Chicago St. R. Co. v. Williams, 140 Ill. 275; Conner v. Citizens' St. Ry. Co., 105 Ind. 62; McDonough v. Metropolitan R. Co., 137 Mass. 210; Briggs v. Union St. Ry. Co., 148 Mass. 72; Maher v. Central Park, N. & E. R. R. Co., 67 N. Y. 52; Eppendorf v. Brooklyn City & N. R. Co., 69 N. Y. 195; Moylan v. Second Ave. R. Co., 128 N. Y. 583; Morrison v. Broadway & S. A. R. Co., 130 N. Y. 166; Sexton v. Metropolitan St. Ry. Co., 40 App. Div. (N. Y.) 26; Valentine v. Broadway & S. A. R. Co., 14 Daly (N. Y.) 540; Seitz v. Dry Dock, E. B. & B. R. Co., 16 Daly (N. Y.) 264; Stager v. Ridge Ave. Passenger Ry. Co., 119 Pa. 70; Picard v. Ridge Ave. Passenger Ry. Co., 147 Pa. 195.

3 Cicero & P. St. R. Co. v. Meixner, 160 Ill. 320; South Chicago City R. Co. v. Dufresne, 200 Ill. 456; Citizens' St. R. Co. v. Spahr, 7 Ind. App. 23; Citizens' St. Ry. Co. v. Merl, 26 Ind. App. 284; Central Passenger Ry. Co. v. Rose, 15 Ky. Law Rep. 209; Corlin v. West End. St. Ry. Co., 154 Mass. 197; Gordon v. West End St. Ry. Co., 175 Mass. 181; Davey v. Greenfield & T. F. St. Ry. Co., 177 Mass. 106; Schepers v. Union Depot R. Co., 126 Mo. 665; Schaefer v. St. Louis & S. Ry. Co., 128 Mo. 64; Sly v. Union Depot R. Co., 134 Mo. 681; Hansberger v. Sedalia Electric Ry., L. & P. Co., 82 Mo. App. 566; O'Mara v. St. Louis Transit Co. (Mo. App.) 76 S. W. 680; Omaha St. Ry. Co. v. Martin, 48 Neb. 65; Schmidt v. North Jersey St. Ry. Co., 66 N. J. Law, 424; Kimber v. Metropolitan St.

to board is made by the front platform,[6] or the rear platform,[7] although it is held to be more dangerous to enter by the front platform than by the rear,[8] or by the running board.[9]

Ry. Co., 69 App. Div. (N. Y.) 353; Lobsenz v. Metropolitan St. Ry. Co., 72 App. Div. (N. Y.) 181; Woo Dan v. Seattle Electric Ry. & P. Co., 5 Wash. 466.

4 West Chicago St. R. Co. v. Dudzik, 67 Ill. App. 681; West Chicago St. R. Co. v. Lups, 74 Ill. App. 420; North Chicago St. R. Co. v. Kaspers, 85 Ill. App. 316; North Chicago St. R. Co. v. Wiswell, 168 Ill. 613; Sahlgaard v. St. Paul City Ry. Co., 48 Minn. 232; Savage v. Third Ave. R. Co., 29 App. Div. (N. Y.) 556; Wallace v. Third Ave. R. Co., 36 App. Div. (N. Y.) 57; Walters v. Philadelphia Traction Co., 161 Pa. 36.

5 North Birmingham Ry. Co. v. Liddicoat, 99 Ala. 545.

6 Finkeldey v. Omnibus Cable Co., 114 Cal. 28; North Chicago St. R. Co. v. Kaspers, 85 Ill. App. 316; Cicero & P. St. Ry. Co. v. Meixner, 160 Ill. 320; McDonough v. Metropolitan R. Co., 137 Mass. 210; Sahlgaard v. St. Paul City Ry. Co., 48 Minn. 232; Hansberger v. Sedalia Electric Ry., L. & P. Co., 82 Mo. App. 566; Omaha St. Ry. Co. v. Martin, 48 Neb. 65; Maher v. Central Park, N. & E. R. R. Co., 67 N. Y. 52; Sexton v. Metropolitan St. Ry. Co., 40 App. Div. (N. Y.) 26; Stager v. Ridge Ave. Passenger Ry. Co., 119 Pa. 70; Woo Dan v. Seattle Electric Ry. & P. Co., 5 Wash. 466.

7 North Chicago St. R. Co. v. Wiswell, 168 Ill. 613; Conner v. Citizens' St. Ry. Co., 105 Ind. 62; Briggs v. Union St. Ry. Co., 148 Mass. 72; Corlin v. West End St. Ry. Co., 154 Mass. 197; Schepers v. Union Depot R. Co., 126 Mo. 665; Sly v. Union Depot R. Co., 134 Mo. 681; Morrison v. Broadway & S. A. R. Co., 130 N. Y. 166; Sexton v. Metropolitan St. Ry. Co., 40 App. Div. (N. Y.) 26; Kimber v. Metropolitan St. Ry. Co., 69 App. Div. (N. Y.) 353; Lobsenz v. Metropolitan St. Ry. Co., 72 App. Div. (N. Y.) 181.

8 Sahlgaard v. St. Paul City Ry. Co., 48 Minn. 232; Maher v. Central Park, N. & E. R. R. Co., 67 N. Y. 52; Paulson v. Brooklyn City R. Co., 13 Misc. Rep. (N. Y.) 387.

9 North Birmingham Ry. Co. v. Liddicoat, 99 Ala. 545; West Chicago St. R. Co. v. Lups, 74 Ill. App. 420; North Chicago St. R. Co. v. Williams, 140 Ill. 275; South Chicago City R. Co. v. Dufresne, 200

In Cicero & P. St. Ry. Co. v. Meixner[10] the court said: "In large and populous cities, where cars are constantly receiving and discharging passengers at crossings, it is a well-known fact that many of such passengers board cars and alight therefrom before such cars have come to a full stop, and that they do so usually with perfect safety. It is well known, also, that street car companies tacitly invite many passengers to board and alight from their cars by checking up to a slow rate of speed, and immediately starting up at a greater speed when the passenger is safely aboard or has alighted. It would be impossible for a court to lay down the rule as to what particular rate of speed would be sufficient notice to a passenger that, if he attempted to get on or off, he would be held guilty of contributory negligence. It would also be a great hardship, and unjust, to lay down a general rule that a passenger attempting to board a street car while in motion at all should be held in contributory negligence. Every person is supposed to know that the boarding of a moving train or car is attended with the danger of a misstep or fall, and a fall beside a moving car is liable to bring some part of the body or limbs in danger of being crushed. It is the duty of those having control and management of cars designated for traffic on the public streets to bring such cars to a full stop at such places as are convenient and necessary for the purpose of discharging and receiving passengers, and it is no less the duty of passengers,

Ill. 456; Citizens' St. Ry. Co. v. Merl, 26 Ind. App. 284; Gordon v. West End St. Ry. Co., 175 Mass. 181; Davey v. Greenfield & T. F. St. Ry. Co., 177 Mass. 106; Eppendorf v. Brooklyn City & N. R. Co., 69 N. Y. 195.

10 160 Ill. 320.

in getting on or off such cars, to observe due precaution for their own safety. We cannot say, however, that it is inconsistent with ordinary care and caution for a person to board a street car while in motion. Whether one has not exercised due care or caution in so doing is to be determined by the particular circumstances in each case, and is therefore a question of fact, to be submitted to the jury."

Ordinarily it is a question for the jury whether a person of ordinary prudence would, under the circumstances, have made the attempt. The age and physical condition of the person making the attempt, whether or not he is incumbered with packages, the rate of speed of the car, the nature of the car and place, and all the surrounding facts and circumstances must be taken into consideration.[11]

The strict rules as to boarding which are in force in the case of ordinary steam railroads are not applied in all their severity to street railroads, owing to the great difference in speed, method of propulsion, number of stops, etc.[12]

The question as to whether a different rule should be applied in the case of horse and electric cars has been frequently discussed. The general result seems to be that the difference in the agencies employed is not so great as to require the application of a different rule.

11 North Birmingham Ry. Co. v. Liddicoat, 99 Ala. 545; Finkeldey v. Omnibus Cable Co., 114 Cal. 28; McDonough v. Metropolitan R. Co., 137 Mass. 210; Sly v. Union Depot R. Co., 134 Mo. 681; Eppendorf v. Brooklyn City & N. R. Co., 69 N. Y. 195; Woo Dan v. Seattle Electric Ry. & P. Co., 5 Wash. 466.

12 North Chicago St. R. Co. v. Williams, 140 Ill. 275; Cicero & P. St. Ry. Co. v. Meixner, 160 Ill. 320; Citizens' St. R. Co. v. Spahr, 7 Ind. App. 23; Conner v. Citizens' St. Ry. Co., 105 Ind. 62; McDonough v. Metropolitan R. Co., 137 Mass. 210; Powelson v. United Traction Co., 204 Pa. 474.

In Citizens' St. R. Co. v. Spahr[13] the court said: "It is urged that here a different rule governs, because the motive power is different, being electricity, instead of horse power. No authority is cited to sustain the distinction, nor are we able to see any ground for any material difference in the rules of law to be applied, since the objects and general methods and purposes of the street railway remain the same, whatever be the motive power."

In Sahlgaard v. St. Paul City Ry. Co.[14] it was held that, as a rule, the attempt to board cable or electric trains may be more unsafe than horse cars, because of the greater speed of such trains.

In Pfeffer v. Buffalo Ry. Co.[15] the court, in speaking of the rule that starting a horse car suddenly is an act of negligence, said: "Stronger reasons exist for applying this rule to cars propelled by electricity than to horse cars, as the motive power is more sudden and powerful in its operation."

In Powelson v. United Traction Co.[16] the court held that to board an electric car is *per se* lack of due care, subject to some few exceptions.

In Cicero & P. St. Ry. Co. v. Meixner[17] the court said: "The cases heretofore cited, in which it has been held that it is not negligence *per se* for a person to board or alight from a street car while in motion, have reference, in a great

13 7 Ind. App. 23.

14 48 Minn. 232.

15 4 Misc. Rep. (N. Y.) 465.

16 204 Pa. 474. See, also, Hunterson v. Union Traction Co. (Pa.) 55 Atl. 543.

17 160 Ill. 320.

degree, to horse cars. Where such motive power is used, the act is not in itself negligence, while in the case of cars propelled by steam, the act is held to be negligence. Where the motive power is electricity, a question not entirely free from difficulty is presented. * * * Electricity as a motive power, while stronger and more powerful, and with possibilities of a greater speed, is at the same time more nearly under the control of the person in charge than horse power. * * * While in electric cars the possibilities of speed are greater than in the case of horse cars, yet the general operation and management of such cars so nearly approach that of horse cars that it must be held that the same rule of law which in the cases cited, and a long line of other cases, holds that it is not negligence *per se* to board or depart from such cars while in motion, is also applicable to electric cars."

In Corlin v. West End St. Ry. Co.[18] the court said: "There is nothing in the bill of exceptions to show that any different rule should be applied than if the car had been a horse car, moving at the same rate of speed. It is to be inferred that the car was designed for the transportation of passengers from place to place along the public streets, and was to take them up and leave them as requested. There were no platforms or other conveniences for getting on or off along the route, and, if there was a rule requiring the car to be stopped to receive and discharge passengers only at designated places, the bill of exceptions does not show it. On the question whether the plaintiff was using due care, such a rule would be immaterial, unless he knew it, or ought to have known it. It is probable that the car could be as

18 154 Mass. 197.

easily controlled as a horse car, and we see no reason for applying to it a rule of law which is not applicable to horse cars."

The rule applied to street cars whose motive power is electricity must, on principle, be applied to those whose motive power is cable.[19]

## § 18. Special circumstances—Speed of car.

In a number of cases the conduct of a person attempting to board a street car is so manifestly reckless that the courts have not hesitated to declare it a bar to recovery. The rate of speed at which the car is moving is, of course, a very important consideration. Thus it has been held that it is lack of due care to attempt to board a street car "in rapid motion,"[20] "while it was in motion,"[21] "moving quite rapidly,"[22] "moving at average speed, or faster,"[23] "moving seven or eight miles an hour,"[24] "moving ten miles an hour."[25] On the other hand, it has been held that it is not negligence, as matter of law, to board an electric car moving three or four miles an hour,[26] from three to seven miles an hour,[27] or even when it is moving eight miles an hour.[28]

19 North Chicago St. R. Co. v. Wiswell, 168 Ill. 613.

20 Chicago City Ry. Co. v. Delcourt, 33 Ill. App. 420; Hansberger v. Sedalia Electric Ry., L. & P. Co., 82 Mo. App. 566.

21 Chicago City Ry. Co. v. Hastings, 35 Ill. App. 434; Wolfkiel v. Sixth Ave. R. Co., 38 N. Y. 49.

22 Chicago City Ry. Co. v. Sullivan, 76 Ill. App. 505.

23 Sahlgaard v. St. Paul City Ry. Co., 48 Minn. 232.

24 Woo Dan v. Seattle Electric Ry. & P. Co., 5 Wash. 466.

25 Brooks v. Mt. Auburn Cable Co., 29 Wkly. Law Bul. (Ohio) 50.

26 Schepers v. Union Depot R. Co., 126 Mo. 665.

27 Sly v. Union Depot R. Co., 134 Mo. 681.

28 Citizens' St. R. Co. v. Spahr, 7 Ind. App. 23

In Birmingham R. & E. Co. v. Brannon,[29] a charge declaring that, as a matter of law, it is not negligence for a passenger to attempt to board a street car in slow motion, was held to be improper.

### § 19. Same—Age and physical condition.

The age of the plaintiff is another fact to be taken into consideration. The due care of a man of seventy, injured while boarding a moving car, was held to be a question for the jury;[30] and it has been held that an old man, boarding a crowded moving car while incumbered with a cane and an umbrella, is not in the exercise of due care.[31] The physical condition of the plaintiff also plays an important part. Where a cripple with a wooden leg attempted to board a moving car, it was held that he took the risk of the accident which ensued.[32] A person forty-five years old, five feet two inches in height, and weighing about two hundred pounds, who attempts to board a street car moving at the rate of six or more miles an hour, with a bottle in his right hand, and a basket on his left arm, is not in the exercise of due care.[33]

### § 20. Same—Incumbered with bundles.

Whether or not the plaintiff was incumbered with bundles, etc., has also been a factor which has influenced the courts. One who attempts to board a train, running from four to seven miles an hour, with his arms full of bundles, is not

29 132 Ala. 431.

30 Morrison v. Broadway & S. A. R. Co., 130 N. Y. 166.

31 Reynolds v. Richmond & M. Ry. Co., 92 Va. 400.

32 Holohan v. Washington & G. R. Co., 19 D. C. 316.

33 Baltimore Traction Co. v. State, 78 Md. 409.

in the exercise of due care.[34] Neither is a person about forty-five years of age, five feet two inches in height, and weighing about two hundred pounds, who attempts to board a street car moving at the rate of six or more miles an hour, with a bottle in his right hand, and a basket on his left arm;[35] or a man who attempts to board a moving street car with his coat and dinner bucket on his left arm;[36] or a man who attempts to board a moving car by the front platform, and is unable to use his right hand, his left being incumbered with a bundle of sash cord and a hammer.[37] An old man boarding a crowded moving car while incumbered with a cane and an umbrella is not in the exercise of due care.[38] It has, however, been held that boarding a moving car while incumbered with bundles,[39] or with an umbrella in one hand, and a handkerchief in the other, is not necessarily lack of due care;[40] and that a man incumbered with a plank, a cane, a bucket, and an ax must use more care than usual in boarding, but is not prevented from recovering, as matter of law.[41]

## § 21. Same—Condition of car.

The condition of the car is another circumstance to be considered. Thus, where a boy of fifteen boarded a moving car by the front step, which was obviously in an unsafe con-

34 Birmingham Electric Ry. Co. v. Clay, 108 Ala. 233.
35 Baltimore Traction Co. v. State, 78 Md. 409.
36 Reddington v. Philadelphia Traction Co., 132 Pa. 154.
37 Paulson v. Brooklyn City R. Co., 13 Misc. Rep. (N. Y.) 387.
38 Reynolds v. Richmond & M. Ry. Co., 92 Va. 400.
39 Birmingham R. & E. Co. v. Brannon, 132 Ala. 431.
40 White v. Atlanta Consol. St. Ry. Co., 92 Ga. 494.
41 Byrd v. New Orleans City & L. R. Co., 43 La. Ann. 822.

dition, this was held to be a bar to his recovery;[42] and a person injured by stepping upon a board which was clearly not intended to be used as a step was likewise held to be unable to maintain an action.[43]

## § 22. Same—Condition of track.

The character of the locality is another, and a very important, fact to be considered. Where there were two parallel street car tracks, it was held to be lack of due care for a person to stand between the tracks waiting to take passage on cars coming on one track, but paying no attention to see whether cars were approaching within dangerous proximity on the other track.[44]

Where there were parallel tracks, and a passenger saw a car coming on the adjacent track, but attempted to board between the two tracks, due care was held to be a question of fact for the jury;[45] but under almost exactly the same state of facts, he was held in two other cases to be guilty of lack of due care as matter of law.[46]

Where a person approaches a horse car which has stopped for him, and crosses another track, and attempts to enter on that side, he is not guilty of lack of due care as a matter of law.[47]

42 Dietrich v. Baltimore & H. S. Ry. Co., 58 Md. 347.

43 Keller v. Hestonville, M. & F. P. Ry. Co., 149 Pa. 65.

44 Miller v. St. Paul City Ry. Co., 42 Minn. 454; Schreiner v. St. Louis R. Co., 5 Mo. App. 596.

45 Schneider v. North Chicago St. R. Co., 80 Ill. App. 306.

46 Davenport v. Brooklyn City R. Co., 100 N. Y. 632; Halpin v. Third Ave. R. Co., 40 N. Y. Super. Ct. 175.

47 Dale v. Brooklyn City, H. P. & P. P. R. Co., 1 Hun (N. Y.) 146.

Where a man saw a truck standing in the street, got on the running board, and was almost immediately struck by the truck, it was held that he could not recover;[48] and the same ruling was made where the obstruction was a heap of railroad ties.[49]

Where a motorman stopped a car at a dangerous place beyond a crossing, the due care of a person attempting to board at such place was held to be for the jury.[50]

## § 23. Same—Boarding without signal.

Attempting to board a car without a signal does not establish any relation between the parties.[51] Thus it has been held that, when a person attempts to board a moving street car which has not been stopped for him, the company is liable only for a willful or wanton injury;[52] and where a car slackens speed, but there was no proof that it was in answer to the plaintiff's signal, it was held that he had no right to assume that such change in speed was made for his benefit.[53] Those in charge of a car are not negligent unless they knew a passenger wished to get on a car, or the situation was such that an attempt to board might naturally be expected, and are not bound to see a person boarding a moving street car.[54]

48 Moylan v. Second Ave. R. Co., 128 N. Y. 583.

49 Schmidt v. North Jersey St. Ry. Co., 66 N. J. Law, 424.

50 Vasele v. Grant St. Electric Ry. Co., 16 Wash. 602.

51 Supra, c. 1, § 4.

52 Basch v. North Chicago St. Ry. Co., 40 Ill. App. 583.

53 Reidy v. Metropolitan St. Ry. Co., 27 Misc. Rep. (N. Y.) 527.

54 Bachrach v. Nassau Electric R. Co., 54 N. Y. Supp. 958; Fremont v. Metropolitan St. Ry. Co., 82 N. Y. Supp. 307; Worthington v. Lindell Ry. Co., 72 Mo. App. 162.

### § 24. Same—Boarding car against rule or warning.

It has been held that a person who attempts to get upon a horse car while it is in motion, after being directed by the driver to wait until the car stops, and who persists in attempting to get on, and is injured by running against the arm of a passenger on the step of the car, is not in the exercise of due care, and cannot maintain an action against the company owning the car.[55]

In Baltimore City Passenger Ry. Co. v. Wilkinson[56] it was held that, if a person knowingly violates a rule against boarding a car by the front platform, he cannot recover, that the consent of the driver makes no difference, and that the fact that such notice was in the car, and that the plaintiff had often ridden in the car, was proof from which it might be inferred that he knew the rule.

In Maxey v. Metropolitan St. R. Co.[57] it was held that a conductor was not negligent in that respect if he warned a person not to board a crowded car, which had stopped to let a passenger off, in a reasonably loud voice, even though she did not hear.

### § 25. Same—Manner of boarding car.

In McSwyny v. Broadway & S. A. R. Co.[58] it was held that it was lack of due care for a woman to attempt to board a moving car by grasping the handle of the rear dashboard with her left hand, and placing her right foot on the step, and then raising her left foot to the step.

55 Gallagher v. West End St. Ry. Co., 156 Mass. 157.

56 30 Md. 224.

57 95 Mo. App. 303.

58 7 N. Y. Supp. 456.

In Birmingham R. & E. Co. v. Brannon[59] it was held that it was not lack of due care for a man to attempt to board a slowly-moving electric car, although he was incumbered with bundles, and got onto the step before grasping the handleholds on the body of the car or the platform, and though, after being on the step he caught the rear platform handlehold with his left hand, which was furthest from it, having to reach across his body to do so, his right hand being incapacitated by the packages he was carrying.

In Picard v. Ridge Ave. Passenger Ry. Co.,[60] a person facing the left-hand side of a car placed his left hand on the rail and his right foot on the step of the platform of a slowly-moving car, and, in an action for injuries received, was held not to be in the exercise of due care.

When a car starts suddenly as a passenger is boarding, it is not lack of due care to continue to hold onto the rail.[61]

### § 26. Boarding car not in motion.

Boarding a street car that is standing still is not lack of due care, whether the attempt is made by the front platform,[62] or by the rear; and in the latter case it is not lack of due care, as a matter of law, to board when the platform is unoccupied, without taking hold of the railings.[63]

59 132 Ala. 431.

60 147 Pa. 195.

61 Schoenfeld v. Metropolitan St. Ry. Co., 40 Misc. Rep. (N. Y.) 201.

62 Maher v. Central Park, N. & E. R. R. Co., 39 N. Y. Super. Ct. 155; Pfeffer v. Buffalo Ry. Co., 4 Misc. Rep. (N. Y.) 465.

63 Ganiard v. Rochester City & B. R. Co., 50 Hun (N. Y.) 22.

## II. Negligence of Company.

**If a car has been stopped for passengers to board, or has been slowed down to such an extent as to constitute an invitation to board, those in charge of the car must furnish a reasonable opportunity to intending passengers to board, and what is a reasonable opportunity depends to some extent on the age and agility of the persons making the attempt, and whether or not they are incumbered with bundles. Some cases hold that those in charge of a car must not only wait a reasonable time, but are bound to know that no one is in the act of boarding when they start the car. It is not negligence to start a car before a passenger is seated.**

**It is the duty of those in charge of the car to exercise ordinary care in selecting a suitable place for passengers to board, and to come to a full stop when signaled, although it is not negligence, as a matter of law, not to bring a car to a full stop, owing to the well-recognized custom on the part of both the company and the public.**

**It is no part of the duty of those in charge of the car to keep a lookout to prevent injury to boys endeavoring to ride without permission, and without paying fare.**

### § 27. Reasonable opportunity to board.

A street railway company, as a common carrier of passengers, while not an insurer of their safety,[64] is bound to use a high degree of care;[65] and it is universally held that,

[64] Citizens' St. R. Co. v. Jolly (Ind.) 67 N. E. 935; O'Connell v. St. Louis Cable & W. Ry. Co., 106 Mo. 482.

[65] Van de Venter v. Chicago City Ry. Co., 26 Fed. 32; North Chicago St. R. Co. v. Cook, 145 Ill. 551; Citizens' St. R. Co. v. Jolly (Ind.) 67 N. E. 935; Steeg v. St. Paul City Ry. Co., 50 Minn. 149; O'Connell v. St. Louis Cable & W. Ry. Co., 106 Mo. 482; Ganiard v. Rochester City & B. R. Co., 50 Hun, 22, affirmed 121 N. Y. 661.

after a car has once been stopped for persons wishing to board, those in charge of the car must allow such persons a reasonable time in which to reach a position of safety on the car, and to start a car while a person is thus boarding is negligence.[66] The rule is the same where a car runs off the track, and a passenger gets off to help put it back. The company is bound to furnish a reasonable opportunity to board the car again.[67]

What is a reasonable time depends to some extent on the

[66] Van de Venter v. Chicago City Ry. Co., 26 Fed. 32; Cohen v. West Chicago St. Ry. Co., 60 Fed. 698; Dudley v. Front St. Cable Ry. Co., 73 Fed. 128; Post v. Hartford St. Ry. Co., 72 Conn. 362; Anacostia & P. R. R. Co. v. Klein, 8 App. D. C. 75; Baltimore City Passenger Ry. Co. v. Baer, 90 Md. 97; Steeg v. St. Paul City Ry. Co., 50 Minn. 149; Miller v. St. Paul City Ry. Co., 66 Minn. 192; Sahlgaard v. St. Paul City Ry. Co., 48 Minn. 232; O'Connell v. St. Louis Cable & W. Ry. Co., 106 Mo. 482; Barth v. Kansas City El. Ry. Co., 142 Mo. 535; Meriwether v. Kansas City Cable Ry. Co., 45 Mo. App. 528; Wolfkiel v. Sixth Ave. R. Co., 38 N. Y. 49; Black v. Brooklyn City R. Co., 108 N. Y. 640; Akersloot v. Second Ave. R. Co., 131 N. Y. 599; Kellegher v. Forty-Second St., M. & St. N. Ave. R. Co., 171 N. Y. 309; Gaulard v. Rochester City & B. R. Co., 50 Hun, 22, affirmed 121 N. Y. 661; De Rozas v. Metropolitan St. Ry. Co., 13 App. Div. (N. Y.) 296; Wallace v. Third Ave. R. Co., 36 App. Div. (N. Y.) 57; Fay v. Metropolitan St. Ry. Co., 62 App. Div. (N. Y.) 51; McQuade v. Manhattan Ry. Co., 53 N. Y. Super. Ct. 91; Lamline v. Houston, W. St. & P. Ferry R. Co., 14 Daly (N. Y.) 144; Pfeffer v. Buffalo Ry. Co., 4 Misc. Rep. (N. Y.) 465; Kinkade v. Atlantic Ave. R. Co., 9 Misc. Rep. (N. Y.) 273, affirmed 149 N. Y. 615; Schalscha v. Third Ave. R. Co., 19 Misc. Rep. (N. Y.) 141; Schoenfeld v. Metropolitan St. Ry. Co., 40 Misc. Rep. (N. Y.) 201; Powelson v. United Traction Co., 204 Pa. 474; Shuart v. Traction Co., 15 Pa. Super. Ct. 26; McCurdy v. Traction Co., 15 Pa. Super. Ct. 29; Norfolk & A. Terminal Co. v. Morris' Adm'x (Va.) 44 S. E. 719.

[67] People's Passenger Ry. Co. v. Green, 56 Md. 84.

age and agility of the person making the attempt;[68] and the fact that a person's movements are somewhat incumbered by packages in his hands may reasonably require more delay and care in starting the train in order to assure his safety, as in the case of aged or infirm persons.[69]

It is not enough, in all cases, for the conductor or driver of a street car to wait a reasonable time for a passenger to board; but if he is busy about the car or inside the car, it is his duty to look and see that all intending passengers are safely on board before starting the car.[70] Thus, in Cohen v. West Chicago St. Ry. Co.[71] the court said: "The conductor of street cars, having the safety and even the lives of passengers in his keeping, has not discharged his whole duty to the public when he has stopped his train and waited what may appear, according to his schedule, a reasonable time for passengers to embark. * * * He is bound to know, when he starts his car suddenly and with full force, that no person attempting to embark is at that moment with one foot on the platform and the other on the ground, and with his hand upon the railing, in the act of getting on board, or is otherwise in a position of danger."

68 North Chicago St. R. Co. v. Cook, 43 Ill. App. 634; Bertram v. People's Ry. Co., 154 Mo. 639; Shuart v. Traction Co., 15 Pa. Super. Ct. 26.

69 Steeg v. St. Paul City Ry. Co., 50 Minn. 149.

70 Cohen v. West Chicago St. Ry. Co., 60 Fed. 698; Dudley v. Front St. Cable Ry. Co., 73 Fed. 128; Post v. Hartford St. Ry. Co., 72 Conn. 362; North Chicago St. R. Co. v. Cook, 145 Ill. 551; Schepers v. Union Depot R. Co., 126 Mo. 665; Meriwether v. Kansas City Cable Ry. Co., 45 Mo. App. 528; Wolfkiel v. Sixth Ave. R. Co., 38 N. Y. 49; McGill v. Central Crosstown R. Co., 84 N. Y. Supp. 477.

71 60 Fed. 698.

It is not necessary that the car be brought to an absolute standstill. If it is slowed down to such an extent as to constitute an invitation to board, it is negligence to start up again before the passenger has a chance to reach a place of safety;[72] but in Powelson v. United Traction Co.,[73] and in Monroe v. Metropolitan St. Ry. Co.,[74] the court held that slowing up was not an invitation to board until the car had stopped.

If a car is temporarily stopped by reason of an obstruction, it is for the jury to say whether the conductor should have seen a person about to board.[75]

It is not negligence, however, to start a street car before a passenger is seated,[76] although the court apparently took a different view in the case of Kinkade v. Atlantic Ave. R. Co.[77] In Picard v. Ridge Ave. Passenger Ry. Co.[78] the court said: "We would seriously inconvenience the traveling public were we to hold that the car should come to a

[72] Conner v. Citizens' St. Ry. Co., 105 Ind. 62; Citizens' St. R. Co. v. Spahr, 7 Ind. App. 23; Citizens' St. Ry. Co. v. Merl, 26 Ind. App. 284; Sahlgaard v. St. Paul City Ry. Co., 48 Minn. 232; O'Mara v. St. Louis Transit Co. (Mo. App.) 76 S. W. 680; Savage v. Third Ave. R. Co., 29 App. Div. (N. Y.) 556; Wallace v. Third Ave. R. Co., 36 App. Div. (N. Y.) 57; Walters v. Philadelphia Traction Co., 161 Pa. 36.

[73] 204 Pa. 474. See, also, Hunterson v. Union Traction Co. (Pa.) 55 Atl. 543.

[74] 80 N. Y. Supp. 177. But see Mulligan v. Metropolitan St. Ry. Co., 85 N. Y. Supp. 791.

[75] Dean v. Third Ave. R. Co., 34 App. Div. (N. Y.) 220.

[76] Miller v. St. Paul City Ry. Co., 66 Minn. 192; Barth v. Kansas City El. Ry. Co., 142 Mo. 535; Picard v. Ridge Ave. Passenger Ry. Co., 147 Pa. 195.

[77] 9 Misc. Rep. (N. Y.) 273, affirmed 149 N. Y. 615.

[78] 147 Pa. 195.

dead stop until every passenger who gets on is seated. It would delay travel on street cars very seriously. Regard must be had, in all such cases, to the habits of passengers and their reasonable convenience." Where the gates on an elevated car were closed before the plaintiff could board, and she was caught and injured, this was held to be evidence of negligence.[79]

The company must exercise ordinary care in selecting a suitable place to stop their car for the purpose of receiving a person as a passenger, and a street car company which was liable by statute for defects arising from its negligence in the highway occupied by its tracks may be held negligent in removing a fence near a ditch, and thus causing injury to a person seeking to board the car in the dark.[80] In Jackson Electric Ry., L. & P. Co. v. Lowry[81] it was held that a street railroad company owes a duty to the public to stop at its regular crossings, on a reasonable signal, to receive those desiring passage; and a rule of a street railroad company that, where its cars stop beyond the crossing, they should not be backed to receive a person who has properly signaled, is unreasonable when applied to a passenger on a rainy night, with a muddy road, the car forty feet beyond the crossing, and the passenger having seven blocks to walk unless he got passage.

It is negligence for a motorman to stop a car at a place beyond a crossing which is dangerous because of its elevation, and because of the fact that there are no lights there and no fence.[82]

79 Brown v. Manhattan Ry. Co., 81 N. Y. Supp. 755.

80 Call v. Portsmouth, K. & Y. St. Ry., 69 N. H. 562.

81 79 Miss. 431.

Numerous rulings have been made on the question of the duty of those in charge of a car to come to a stop when signaled. It has been held that a passenger has a right to insist that a car shall come to a full stop when he signals at a proper place,[83] and that those in charge of the car have an equal right to presume that the person signaling the car desires to have it stopped, and will not get on board while it is in motion.[84] On the other hand, it has been held that it is not negligence, as a matter of law, not to bring a car to a full stop before a person attempts to board,[85] since it is well recognized that it is the ordinary custom to merely slacken speed in order to take on passengers, and that this constitutes an invitation to them;[86] but the company will be liable if, by slowing down, it tacitly invites the passenger to board, and then injures him by starting with a sudden jerk.[87] Recent cases have held, however, that slowing down

82 Vasele v. Grant St. Electric Ry. Co., 16 Wash. 602.

83 Cicero & P. St. Ry. Co. v. Meixner, 160 Ill. 320; Sahlgaard v. St. Paul City Ry. Co., 48 Minn. 232; Savage v. Third Ave. R. Co., 30 App. Div. (N. Y.) 556.

84 Holohan v. Washington & G. R. Co., 19 D. C. 316.

85 Finkeldey v. Omnibus Cable Co., 114 Cal. 28; Cicero & P. St. Ry. Co. v. Meixner, 160 Ill. 320; Sahlgaard v. St. Paul City Ry. Co., 48 Minn. 232; Moylan v. Second Ave. R. Co., 128 N. Y. 583; Savage v. Third Ave. R. Co., 29 App. Div. (N. Y.) 556.

86 Conner v. Citizens' St. Ry. Co., 105 Ind. 62; Citizens' St. R. Co. v. Spahr, 7 Ind. App. 23; Citizens' St. Ry. Co. v. Merl, 26 Ind. App. 284; Sahlgaard v. St. Paul City Ry. Co., 48 Minn. 232; Savage v. Third Ave. R. Co., 29 App. Div. (N. Y.) 556.

87 Conner v. Citizens' St. Ry. Co., 105 Ind. 62; Citizens' St. R. Co. v. Spahr, 7 Ind. App. 23; Sahlgaard v. St. Paul City Ry. Co., 48 Minn. 232; O'Mara v. St. Louis Transit Co. (Mo. App.) 76 S. W. 680; Savage v. Third Ave. R. Co., 29 App. Div. (N. Y.) 556; Walters v. Philadelphia Traction Co., 161 Pa. 36.

in answer to a signal is not an invitation to board until the car has stopped.[88] One who signals a car at a usual stopping place, and sees the car stop, is justified in assuming the stop is for his benefit, even though in reality the stop is to let off a passenger; and if those in charge of the car do not intend to receive him, they must give notice to that effect.[89]

## § 28. Children.

It is not the duty of the employes of a street railway company to keep a lookout to prevent boys endeavoring to ride without permission and without paying fare from entering its cars while in motion;[90] and there was held to be no negligence on the part of the company when a boy of twelve boarded a moving train, and there was evidence that a brakeman had told him that he was young, and could run and jump on the car.[91] So, where a boy of seven unexpectedly tried to get on the front platform of a moving car while the driver, who was also the conductor, was on the rear platform, the company was held not to be responsible.[92] Where a boy of thirteen was injured while boarding a moving car, there was held to be no evidence of negligence on the part of the company.[93] The act of a driver or brake-

88 Powelson v. United Traction Co., 204 Pa. 474; Hunterson v. Union Traction Co. (Pa.) 55 Atl. 543; Monroe v. Metropolitan St. Ry. Co., 80 N. Y. Supp. 177. But see Mulligan v. Metropolitan St. Ry. Co., 85 N. Y. Supp. 791.

89 Maxey v. Metropolitan St. R. Co., 95 Mo. App. 303.

90 Jefferson v. Birmingham R. & E. Co., 116 Ala. 294; Little Rock Traction & Electric Co. v. Nelson, 66 Ark. 494.

91 Coller v. Frankford & S. Ry. Co., 9 Wkly. Notes Cas. (Pa.) 477.

92 Hestonville Passenger Ry. Co. v. Connell, 88 Pa. 520.

93 Omaha St. Ry. Co. v. Baker, 44 Neb. 511.

man of a horse car in assisting a boy of eight to get on board is in the course of his employment, and the company is liable for his negligence.[94] Where a car has stopped to let off a passenger, and a boy of seven attempts to board without signaling, there can be no recovery where it is not shown that the driver or conductor saw him.[95] Where a boy of thirteen signaled, and the driver slackened speed, and then started suddenly as the boy was boarding, it was held that, if the driver believed the boy was getting on the car, this was sufficient evidence of negligence.[96]

## § 29. Miscellaneous.

Where plaintiff, in boarding a car, caught his foot in an opening at the back of the step, it was held that the negligence of the defendant in having an open-back step was for the jury.[97] Where a conductor sees a truck ahead of his car standing close to the track, and starts his car while a passenger is trying to board, the negligence of the conductor is for the jury.[98] Where the plaintiff, who was putting her daughter on the car, told the conductor that she was not a passenger, and was injured, while alighting again, by the starting of the car, negligence of the conductor is for the jury.[99] Where a person put a child on a car, and there was evidence that she had done the same thing on previous

[94] Drew v. Sixth Ave. R. Co., 26 N. Y. 49.

[95] Pitcher v. People's St. Ry. Co., 154 Pa. 560, followed 174 Pa. 402.

[96] McDonough v. Metropolitan R. Co., 137 Mass. 210.

[97] Boehncke v. Brooklyn City R. Co., 3 Misc. Rep. (N. Y.) 49.

[98] Goldwasser v. Metropolitan St. Ry. Co., 32 Misc. Rep. (N. Y.) 682.

[99] Rott v. Forty-second St. & G. St. Ferry R. Co., 56 N. Y. Super. Ct. 151.

occasions, a nonsuit was held to be error.[100] Where the conductor shut the gate while the plaintiff was boarding, and caught his hand so that he was crushed to death, defendant's negligence is for the jury.[101] Whether the absence of the wheel guards required by a city ordinance on a street car is negligence is a question for the jury.[102] Even if the plaintiff has been negligent, he may nevertheless recover if the company, by the exercise of due care, could have prevented the accident.[103]

The fact that a starting signal was given by an unauthorized person will not exempt the company from liability if the conductor, by the exercise of due care, could have prevented the moving of the car.[104] Where the conductor of a crowded car remained inside, and started the car, on the information of a passenger on the back platform, while a passenger was trying to board, the question of negligence was held to be for the jury.[105]

The fact that the conductor of a street car is inside the car when it has slowed up at a street crossing to permit a passenger to board is no evidence of negligence on the part of the railroad company;[106] and it is not negligence not to

100 Houston v. Gate City St. R. Co., 89 Ga. 272.

101 Ericius v. Brooklyn Heights R. Co., 63 App. Div. (N. Y.) 353.

102 Finkeldey v. Omnibus Cable Co., 114 Cal. 28.

103 Central Passenger Ry. Co. v. Rose, 15 Ky. Law Rep. 209; Baltimore Traction Co. v. State, 78 Md. 409; Omaha St. Ry. Co. v. Martin, 48 Neb. 65; Christie v. Galveston City R. Co. (Tex. Civ. App.) 39 S. W. 638; Reynolds v. Richmond & M. Ry. Co., 92 Va. 400; Woodard v. West Side St. Ry. Co., 71 Wis. 625.

104 North Chicago St. R. Co. v. Cook, 145 Ill. 551.

105 McCurdy v. Traction Co., 15 Pa. Super. Ct. 29.

106 Picard v. Ridge Ave. Passenger Ry. Co., 147 Pa. 195.

have a conductor on a one-horse car.[107] A conductor is not necessary as a matter of law, but his absence may be considered by the jury as a fact bearing on the question of negligence.[108]

There is no negligence on the part of the company in a slight movement of the car while the plaintiff is in the act of boarding;[109] and in Stager v. Ridge Ave. Passenger Ry. Co.[110] it was held that there was no presumption of negligence from the mere happening of the accident, and that negligence could not be proved by mere conjecture as to how the accident happened.

Where a passenger received an electric shock as he took hold of the rail to board a car, this was held to raise a presumption of negligence.[111] Where a passenger was injured by a brake becoming unfastened in some unexplained manner while a crowd was boarding a car, there was held to be no evidence of negligence.[112] Mere proof that a passenger was injured by a banana peel on the stairway of an elevated station raises no presumption of negligence, and no recovery can be had.[113] An act relative to riding on the front platform does not apply to a person using the front platform as a means of entering the car.[114] In an action against

[107] Lamline v. Houston, W. St. & P. Ferry R. Co., 14 Daly (N. Y.) 144; Hestonville Passenger Ry. Co. v. Connell, 88 Pa. 520.

[108] Ganiard v. Rochester City & B. R. Co., 50 Hun (N. Y.) 22.

[109] Weber v. New Orleans & C. R. Co., 104 La. 367; Schmeltzer v. St. Paul City Ry. Co., 80 Minn. 50.

[110] 119 Pa. 70.

[111] Dallas Consol. Electric St. Ry. Co. v. Broadhurst (Tex. Civ. App.) 68 S. W. 315.

[112] Holt v. Southwest Electric Ry. Co., 84 Mo. App. 443.

[113] Benson v. Manhattan Ry. Co., 31 Misc. Rep. (N. Y.) 723.

[114] Morris v. Eighth Ave. R. Co., 68 Hun (N. Y.) 39.

a street railway company for the negligence of a servant, the test of the company's liability is whether the servant was engaged in the company's business, and was acting within the scope of his employment.[115] Where a passenger on an elevated station platform at night slipped into an opening between two cars, negligence was held to be for the jury,[116] but where a passenger was injured by a swinging door in an elevated station, there was held to be no negligence.[117] Where a person was injured by a runaway while attempting to board, there was held to be no evidence of negligence.[118] Where a car stopped at a platform built by a third party the company was held liable.[119]

[115] Lima R. Co. v. Little, 67 Ohio St. 91.

[116] Lake St. El. R. Co. v. Burgess, 200 Ill. 628.

[117] Fahner v. Brooklyn Heights R. Co., 86 App. Div. (N. Y.) 488.

[118] South Side Passenger Ry. Co. v. Trich, 117 Pa. 390.

[119] Leveret v. Shreveport Belt Ry. Co. (La.) 34 So. 579.

## CHAPTER III.

### ACCIDENTS WHILE ON CAR.

I. Unusual Conduct of Passenger.

§ 30. Riding on Front Platform—Due Care in General a Question of Fact.
31. Same—Consent of Those in Charge of the Car.
32. Same—Position on Platform.
33. Same—Intoxication.
34. Same—Children.
35. Riding on Rear Platform.
36. Riding on Step of Car.
37. Riding on Running Board.
38. Standing in Car.
39. Riding on Bumper.
40. Preparatory to Alighting.
41. Changing Position on Car.
42. Catching Dress.
43. Falling from Car.
44. Tripping in Car.
45. Putting Arm Outside Car.
46. Transferring.

II. Unusual Conduct of Company.

§ 47. Care Required of Company.
48. Running Cars on Sunday.
49. Crowding Cars.
50. Condition of Car.
51. Injury by Fellow Passenger.
52. Derailment.
53. Collision Between Two Street Cars.
54. Collision Between Street Car and Wagon.
55. Collision Between Street Car and Steam Railroad.
56. Jerk.
57. Speed of Car.
58. Miscellaneous Negligence in Operation.

## I. Unusual Conduct of Passenger.

**It is not lack of due care, as a matter of law, to ride upon the front or rear platform, steps, or running board of a street car. Each case must be determined according to its own circumstances, and important considerations are the consent of those in charge of the car, the crowded condition of the car, the age and physical condition of the passenger, whether he was holding onto anything, and the condition of the street.**

**Similarly, to stand in a car or to take a position on the platform, steps, or running board preparatory to alighting while the car is still in motion, or to change one's position on a car, is not lack of due care as a matter of law, but depends on the individual circumstances of each particular case; and the rule holds good in cases of a passenger falling from a car, tripping or catching dress in a car, putting his arm outside the window of a car, and transferring from one car to another.**

### § 30. Riding on front platform—Due care in general a question of fact.

It is not lack of due care, as a matter of law, to ride upon the front platform of a horse car,[1] an electric car,[2] a cable

[1] Augusta & S. R. Co. v. Renz, 55 Ga. 126; Meesel v. Lynn & B. R. Co., 8 Allen (Mass.) 234; Maguire v. Middlesex R. Co., 115 Mass. 239; Upham v. Detroit City Ry. Co., 85 Mich. 12; Archer v. Ft. Wayne & E. Ry. Co., 87 Mich. 101; Burns v. Bellefontaine Ry. Co., 50 Mo. 139; Ginna v. Second Ave. R. Co., 67 N. Y. 596; Nolan v. Brooklyn City & N. R. Co., 87 N. Y. 63; Vail v. Broadway R. Co., 147 N. Y. 377; Cattano v. Metropolitan St. R. Co., 173 N. Y. 565; Hastings v. Central Crosstown R. Co., 7 App. Div. (N. Y.) 312; Bradley v. Second Ave. R. Co., 34 App. Div. (N. Y.) 284; Cassidy v. Atlantic Ave. R. Co., 9 Misc. Rep. (N. Y.) 275; Seelig v. Metropolitan St. Ry. Co., 18 Misc. Rep. (N. Y.) 383; Hadencamp v. Second Ave. R. Co., 31 N. Y. Super Ct. 490; Ward v. Central Park, N. & E. R. R. Co., 33 N. Y. Super. Ct. 392; Schneider v. Second Ave. R. Co., 59 N. Y. Super. Ct. 536; Hourney v. Brooklyn City R. Co., 7 N. Y. Supp. 602; Sandford v. Hestonville, M. & F. P. R. Co., 136 Pa. 84.

car,[3] an elevated car,[4] or a car on a dummy line,[5] to sit on the front platform of an electric car,[6] or to sit on the outside seat of the "dummy" on a cable line.[7]

In Meesel v. Lynn & B. R. Co.[8] the court said: "The seats inside the car are not the only places where the managers of the train expect passengers to remain; but it is notorious that they stop habitually to receive passengers to stand inside till the car is full, and then to stand upon the platforms till they are full, and continue to stop and receive them even after there is no place for them to stand except on the steps of the platforms. Neither the officers of these corporations nor the managers of the cars nor the traveling public seem to regard this practice as hazardous, nor does experience thus far seem to require that it should be restrained upon the ground of its danger. There is, therefore, no basis upon which the court can decide, upon the evidence reported, that the plaintiff did not use ordinary care."

2 Watson v. Portland & C. E. Ry. Co., 91 Me. 584; Beal v. Lowell & D. St. Ry. Co., 157 Mass. 444; Sweetland v. Lynn & B. R. Co., 177 Mass. 574; East Omaha St. Ry. Co. v. Godola, 50 Neb. 906; Francisco v. Troy & L. R. Co., 88 Hun (N. Y.) 464; Taft v. Brooklyn Heights R. Co., 14 Misc. Rep. (N. Y. ) 390; Bailey v. Tacoma Traction Co., 16 Wash. 48.

3 Adams v. Washington & G. R. Co., 9 App. D. C. 26; Chicago West Div. Ry. Co. v. Klauber, 9 Ill. App. 613; Muldoon v. Seattle City Ry. Co., 7 Wash. 528.

4 Graham v. Manhattan Ry. Co., 149 N. Y. 336; Merwin v. Manhattan Ry. Co., 48 Hun (N. Y.) 608.

5 Highland Ave. & B. R. Co. v. Donovan, 94 Ala. 299.

6 Holloway v. Pasadena & P. Ry. Co., 130 Cal. 177; Denver & B. P. Rapid Transit Co. v. Dwyer, 20 Colo. 132; Seller v. Market St. Ry. Co. (Cal.) 72 Pac. 1006.

7 Hawkins v. Front St. Cable Ry. Co., 3 Wash. 592.

8 8 Allen (Mass.) 234.

It is evident that riding upon the platforms of steam railroads is more dangerous than riding upon the platforms of street cars, and the rules in force in the former cases do not apply to the latter.[9]

The question as to whether a different rule as to riding upon the front platform should be applied in the case of a horse car and an electric car, a horse car and a cable car, and a cable car and an electric car has been squarely met and discussed.

In Watson v. Portland & C. E. Ry. Co.[10] the court, after stating that the rule that riding on the front platform of a horse car is not lack of due care as a matter of law was not questioned, said: "But it is claimed upon the part of the defense that, while this is true in the case of a horse car, as to electric cars the rule laid down in this state, and generally with respect to trains of cars upon steam railroads, should apply. We do not think so. An electric street car is still a street car, and, in our opinion, the conditions, especially with respect to riding upon platforms, are more similar to those of the horse street car than those of a railroad train upon a steam railroad."

In Muldoon v. Seattle City Ry. Co.[11] the court said: "The nonsuit asked by appellant was properly refused. We do not think it can be said that it is negligence *per se* for a passenger to stand upon the front platform of the trail car in a moving cable train, in the absence of any rule of the company against it, and where it has been the custom

[9] Upham v. Detroit City Ry. Co., 85 Mich. 12; Vail v. Broadway R. Co., 147 N. Y. 377.

[10] 91 Me. 584.

[11] 7 Wash. 528.

for passengers to occupy that position. Doubtless there is more liability that accidents will occur where a car is propelled by cable than where horses are used, but common experience has not discriminated between the two to the extent of changing the rule of law. In most cases of this class the question of contributory negligence is one for the jury."

In Bailey v. Tacoma Traction Co.[12] the court said: "And it may be well said here that common experience has not discriminated between a car propelled by a cable and one propelled by electricity to the extent of changing the rule; for while it is probably a fact that electric cars are run at a greater rate of speed than cable cars, yet we think experience shows that accidents are as frequent upon the cable cars as upon the electric cars, owing, probably, to the lack of the facilities to easily control the cable cars which exist on the electric cars."

The provisions of the general railroad act in New York as to riding on the front platform do not apply to street railroads.[13]

## § 31. Same—Consent of those in charge of the car.

The consent of those in charge of the car, express or implied, is perhaps the most important consideration in determining the question of a passenger's due care in riding upon the front platform. Thus it has been held that it is not lack of due care, as a matter of law, for a passenger to stand upon the front platform of a crowded street car when his fare was taken,[14] or when no objection was made,[15] or

[12] 16 Wash. 48

[13] Vail v. Broadway R. Co., 147 N. Y. 377; Lax v. Forty-Second & G. St. Ferry R. Co., 46 N. Y. Super. Ct. 448.

[14] Highland Ave. & B. R. Co. v. Donovan, 94 Ala. 299; Ginna v.

to sit upon the front platform of a crowded street car without objection from those in charge.[16] Where there is no evidence as to whether the car was crowded or not, it is not lack of due care, as a matter of law, to stand upon the front platform when fare is collected,[17] or no objection is made;[18] and even if it appears that there was plenty of room inside the car, a passenger cannot be deemed guilty of lack of due care when he stands upon the front platform, and fare is collected of him,[19] or no objection is made to his so riding.[20] Even if there is a rule prohibiting riding on the front platform, taking fare from a passenger has been held to be a waiver of the rule,[21] and under such circumstances a conductor must return the passenger's fare before he is entitled to eject him for not complying with the rule of the company.[22]

In Hadencamp v. Second Ave. R. Co.[23] the court said: "But aside from this, even if the court must shut its eyes to

Second Ave. R. Co., 67 N. Y. 596; Graham v. Manhattan Ry. Co., 149 N. Y. 336; Merwin v. Manhattan Ry. Co., 48 Hun (N. Y.) 608; Hadencamp v. Second Ave. R. Co., 31 N. Y. Super. Ct. 490; McCaw v. Union Traction Co. (Pa.) 54 Atl. 893.

15 Adams v. Washington & G. R. Co., 9 App. D. C. 26; Augusta & S. R. Co. v. Renz, 55 Ga. 126; Archer v. Ft. Wayne & E. Ry. Co., 87 Mich. 101; East Omaha St. Ry. Co. v. Godola, 50 Neb. 906.

16 Holloway v. Pasadena & P. Ry. Co., 130 Cal. 177.

17 Bailey v. Tacoma Traction Co., 16 Wash. 48.

18 Muldoon v. Seattle City Ry. Co., 7 Wash. 528.

19 Nolan v. Brooklyn City & N. R. Co., 87 N. Y. 63.

20 Maguire v. Middlesex R. Co., 115 Mass. 239; Upham v. Detroit City Ry. Co., 85 Mich. 12; Burns v. Bellefontaine Ry. Co., 50 Mo. 139.

21 Highland Ave. & B. R. Co. v. Donovan, 94 Ala. 299; Hadencamp v. Second Ave. R. Co., 31 N. Y. Super. Ct. 490.

22 Hanna v. Nassau Electric R. Co., 18 App. Div. (N. Y.) 137.

23 31 N. Y. Super. Ct. 490.

the open, constant, every-day practice of the employes of street railways themselves in disregarding such notices, there is abundant evidence in this case that the employes of the defendant company do constantly and habitually disregard and disobey this notice, and so do with the consent and apparent encouragement of the company itself. * * * Surely they cannot complain if the court and jury construe their rules and notices in the same manner and meaning that their own officers and employes habitually do; nor can they expect the court to enforce rules which they habitually disregard in their own interest, and seek to enforce only when they could thereby shield themselves from liability. This would seem to be sufficient grounds upon which to sustain the ruling of the judge on circuit. But I am prepared to go further, and hold that, when a common carrier of passengers, by himself or his manager or conductor, accepts a person as a passenger, and receives from such person the full and established fare, without any restriction in the contract itself as to mode or place of carriage, he is bound to furnish such passenger with a safe and comfortable vehicle, and a safe and comfortable place or position in it or on it, and so to transport that passenger that he shall not sustain injury from any fault or neglect of the carrier, any rule, notice, or regulation of the carrier to the contrary notwithstanding, and is responsible for any injury the passenger may sustain by the fault or neglect of the carrier; provided, always, the passenger shall occupy as safe a place as he can, and conduct himself with proper care in the place where he is."

It has further been held that a rule prohibiting smoking except on the front platform might well be deemed to be a waiver of a rule forbidding riding on the front platform,[24] and that a notice forbidding riding on the front platform might well be waived by permitting passengers to so ride, without objection, and that the question of such waiver was rightly left to the jury.[25] The presence of other passengers on the platform is not enough to show a waiver.[26] Of course, on the other hand, where a passenger rides on the front platform, with the knowledge of the conductor, according to custom, this will not justify an instruction that he is not guilty of lack of due care as a matter of law.[27]

While it is held that riding upon the front platform is not lack of due care as matter of law, the custom of the street railway company in allowing passengers to ride in this manner is one circumstance to be considered.[28] Thus, where it appears that the company permitted smoking upon the front platform, it was held that riding there on a slippery day when snow had been falling was not lack of due care as a matter of law;[29] and the custom of requiring passengers to smoke on the front platform has been held to be an express permission to allow them to so ride.[30]

Of course, where a passenger is directed to ride upon the front platform by an employe in charge of the car, there is still stronger reason for holding that he is not guilty of lack of due care as a matter of law than when he is merely permitted to ride in this manner. Such a holding has

24 Vail v. Broadway R. Co., 147 N. Y. 377.

25 Sweetland v. Lynn & B. R. Co., 177 Mass. 574.

26 Burns v. Boston El. Ry. Co. (Mass.) 66 N. E. 418.

27 Chicago West Div. Ry. Co. v. Klauber, 9 Ill. App. 613.

28 Muldoon v. Seattle City Ry. Co., 7 Wash. 528.

29 Bradley v. Second Ave. R. Co., 34 App. Div. (N. Y.) 284.

30 Nolan v. Brooklyn City & N. R. Co., 87 N. Y. 63.

been made where a passenger was directed to go upon the front platform simply because the car was full,[31] where a passenger was directed to go upon the front platform to smoke,[32] and where one was directed to go upon the front platform because he was incumbered with bundles.[33] On the other hand, a rule forbidding passengers to ride on the front platform,[34] a rule forbidding passengers to ride on the front platform if there is room inside,[35] and a notice forbidding riding on the front platform[36] are all reasonable, and a passenger cannot complain of the enforcement of such a reasonable rule unless he shows some good reason for its suspension.[37] Thus, where a passenger sat on the front platform of a moving horse car with his feet on the steps, against the rule of the corporation and the warning of the driver of the car, without any reasonable excuse therefor, he was held not to be in the exercise of due care.[38] A rule prohibiting drivers from letting intoxicated persons ride on the front platform has also been held to be reasonable.[39] A passenger who could read, but did not read a plainly posted notice forbidding riding on the front platform, was

31 Meesel v. Lynn & B. R. Co., 8 Allen (Mass.) 234.

32 Francisco v. Troy & L. R. Co., 88 Hun (N. Y.) 464; Hastings v. Central Crosstown R. Co., 7 App. Div. (N. Y.) 312; Seelig v. Metropolitan St. Ry. Co., 18 Misc. Rep. (N. Y.) 383.

33 Schneider v. Second Ave. R. Co., 59 N. Y. Super. Ct. 536.

34 Wills v. Lynn & B. R. Co., 129 Mass. 351.

35 McMillan v. Federal St. & P. V. P. Ry. Co., 172 Pa. 523.

36 Baltimore & Y. Turnpike Road v. Cason, 72 Md. 377; O'Neill v. Lynn & B. R. Co., 155 Mass. 371; Burns v. Boston El. Ry. Co. (Mass.) 66 N. E. 418.

37 McMillan v. Federal St. & P. V. P. Ry. Co., 172 Pa. 523.

38 Wills v. Lynn & B. R. Co., 129 Mass. 351.

39 O'Neill v. Lynn & B. R. Co., 155 Mass. 371.

held bound to know the notice.[40] In a very recent case it was held that knowledge of a notice that passengers riding on the front platform did so at their own risk barred recovery;[41] but a boy of ten is not precluded from recovery, even if he knew of a notice forbidding riding on the front platform.[42]

## § 32. Same—Position on platform.

Whether or not the plaintiff was holding onto anything at the time of the accident is another circumstance to be considered as bearing upon the question of his due care. Thus, due care has been held to be for the jury where a passenger was holding onto the railing with both hands,[43] and where a passenger had both hands in his pockets on a cold night.[44] It is not lack of due care, as a matter of law, to omit to take hold of an iron bar to prevent being thrown from the platform.[45] Where a passenger knew that the street was in bad condition, and held onto the railing, but let go in order to pay the conductor his fare, due care was held to be for the jury;[46] but where a passenger knew that the street was in bad condition, and stood on the very edge of the front platform without holding onto anything, he was held guilty of lack of due care as a matter of law.[47] It is

40 Baltimore & Y. Turnpike Road v. Cason, 72 Md. 377.

41 Burns v. Boston El. Ry. Co. (Mass.) 66 N. E. 418.

42 Brennan v. Fair Haven & W. R. Co., 45 Conn. 284.

43 Francisco v. Troy & L. R. Co., 88 Hun (N. Y.) 464.

44 Adams v. Washington & G. R. Co., 9 App. D. C. 26.

45 Kean v. West Chicago St. R. Co., 75 Ill. App. 38; Ginna v. Second Ave. R. Co., 67 N. Y. 596; Cornish v. Toronto St. Ry. Co., 23 U. C. C. P. 355.

46 Hastings v. Central Crosstown R. Co., 7 App. Div. (N. Y.) 312.

47 Ward v. Central Park, N. & E. R. R. Co., 33 N. Y. Super. Ct. 392.

not lack of due care for a passenger to give up his seat on the front platform to a lady, and remain standing there.[48]

Where the only passenger on a horse car rode on the driver's high stool on the front platform without invitation from the driver, it was held that he was guilty of lack of due care as matter of law.[49] On the other hand, in Bailey v. Tacoma Traction Co.,[50] where riding on the driver's stool was customary, and the conductor collected fares from passengers so riding, it was held not to be lack of due care to so ride; but it is lack of due care for a passenger to sit on the driving bar on a street car when there is room inside the car, although he is invited to do so by the driver.[51]

Where a passenger left his seat, where he was protected by a wire screen, rushed to the front platform at night, and leaned out to see a fire, and was struck by a tree five or six inches from a car, he was held not to be in the exercise of due care.[52] Where a boy of thirteen sat on the front platform with his knees projecting, so that he was struck by a mortar box standing near the track, it was held that a compulsory nonsuit was properly entered.[53]

It is well settled that a passenger riding upon the front platform assumes the risk of the ordinary dangers incident to such a position,[54] as, for instance, an increase in speed caused by the driver's whipping up his horses,[55] or the jolt-

48 Still v. Nassau Electric R. Co., 32 App. Div. (N. Y.) 276.

49 Mann v. Philadelphia Traction Co., 175 Pa. 122.

50 16 Wash. 48.

51 Downey v. Hendrie, 46 Mich. 498.

52 Sias v. Rochester Ry. Co., 18 App. Div. (N. Y.) 506.

53 Butler v. Pittsburgh & B. P. Ry. Co., 139 Pa. 195.

54 Lax v. Forty-Second & G. St. Ferry R. Co., 46 N. Y. Super. Ct. 448.

55 Cassidy v. Atlantic Ave. R. Co., 9 Misc. Rep. (N. Y.) 275.

ing or swaying of the car,[56] but he does not assume an unusual risk from the negligence of those in charge of the car.[57] It cannot be said that a passenger riding on the front platform does not assume any increased risk as a matter of law.[57a]

It is lack of due care, as a matter of law, for a passenger to get upon the front platform of a street car on a very stormy night, when the platform is so crowded that he cannot ride in safety.[58] It must be remembered, however, that, when the company allows the front platform to be crowded, it must assume the duty of using greater care than usual;[59] and the jury is warranted in finding negligence where a car went around a curve at such speed that a passenger's hands were wrenched from the rail to which he was holding, and he was thrown from the car.[60] Where a horse fell from negligent driving, and in getting up kicked a passenger standing on the front platform, there was held to be no causal connection.[60a]

## § 33. Same—Intoxication.

The mere fact that a passenger was intoxicated at the time of the accident will not prevent his maintaining an

[56] Moser v. South Covington & C. St. Ry. Co. (Ky.) 74 S. W. 1090; Watson v. Portland & C. E. Ry. Co., 91 Me. 584; Baltimore & Y. Turnpike Road v. Cason, 72 Md. 377.

[57] Graham v. Manhattan Ry. Co., 149 N. Y. 336.

[57a] Zimmer v. Fox River Valley Elec. Ry. Co. (Wis.) 95 N. W. 957.

[58] Tregear v. Dry Dock, E. B. & B. R. Co., 14 Abb. Pr. (N. S.; N. Y.) 49.

[59] Archer v. Ft. Wayne & E. Ry. Co., 87 Mich. 101; Sandford v. Hestonville, M. & F. P. R. Co., 136 Pa. 84.

[60] Lucas v. Metropolitan St. Ry. Co., 56 App. Div. (N. Y.) 405.

[60a] Roedecker v. Metropolitan St. Ry. Co., 84 N. Y. Supp. 300.

action for being thrown from the front platform of a horse car, unless his intoxication contributed to the injury.[61] But where there was evidence that the plaintiff was drunk at the time of the accident, and had been in that condition for the preceding twenty-four hours; that he had no recollection of taking the car, or of any of the facts connected with the accident, and first came to a realization of his injuries at the hospital; that, shortly before the accident, he was standing on the front platform, with his hands on the guard rail, and his body swaying back and forth; that the rate of speed was moderate, being four miles an hour; and that, although the up and down motion of the car was such, at the time the plaintiff went off, as to throw another passenger towards the driver, his face striking the driver's shoulder, there was no evidence of any defect in the rails or in the roadbed,—it was held that the jury would not have been warranted in finding that the plaintiff exercised due care, or that his intoxication did not contribute to the injury.[62]

## § 34. Same—Children.

The age and capacity of a child must be taken into account in determining the question of his due care;[63] and whether a child is guilty of lack of due care in riding on the front platform of a street car is generally a question for

61 Adams v. Washington & G. R. Co., 9 App. D. C. 26; Maguire v. Middlesex R. Co., 115 Mass. 239.

62 Holland v. West End St. Ry. Co., 155 Mass. 387.

63 Wynn v. City & Suburban Ry. Co., 91 Ga. 344; East Saginaw City Ry. Co. v. Bohn, 27 Mich. 503; Connolly v. Knickerbocker Ice Co., 114 N. Y. 104; Crissey v. Hestonville, M. & F. P. Ry. Co., 75 Pa. 83; Sandford v. Hestonville, M. & F. P. R. Co., 136 Pa. 84.

the jury.[64] Negligence cannot be imputed to a child of five.[65] It has been held that riding upon the front platform is *prima facie* evidence of lack of due care, and that the presumption is not rebutted when it appears that a boy of nine sat upon the front platform.[66] Where a boy of thirteen sat on the front platform with his knees projecting, so that he was struck by a mortar box standing near the track, it was held that a compulsory nonsuit was properly entered;[67] but the due care of a boy of thirteen sitting on the front platform with his feet on the steps, and injured by a collision with a wagon, has been held to be for the jury.[67a] In an action against a defendant other than the street railway company, it has been held that the due care of a boy of seven is for the jury, although there is a municipal ordinance forbidding riding on the front platform.[68]

The duty of the carrier towards children is even greater than towards other passengers;[69] and it is generally held to be negligence to allow children to ride upon the front platform, if those in charge of the car knew of it, or, in the ex-

64 Evansville St. Ry. Co. v. Meadows, 13 Ind. App. 155; Wynn v. City & Suburban Ry. Co., 91 Ga. 344; Wilton v. Middlesex R. Co., 125 Mass. 130; Crissey v. Hestonville, M. & F. P. Ry. Co., 75 Pa. 83.

65 Pittsburg, A. & M. P. Ry. Co. v. Caldwell, 74 Pa. 421; Levin v. Second Ave. Traction Co., 194 Pa. 156.

66 Solomon v. Central Park, N. & E. R. R. Co., 31 N. Y. Super. Ct. 298.

67 Butler v. Pittsburgh & B. P. Ry. Co., 139 Pa. 195.

67a Seller v. Market St. Ry. Co. (Cal.) 72 Pac. 1006.

68 Connolly v. Knickerbocker Ice Co., 114 N. Y. 104.

69 Wynn v. City & Suburban Ry. Co., 91 Ga. 344; Sheridan v. Brooklyn City & N. R. Co., 36 N. Y. 39; Pittsburg, A. & M. P. Ry. Co. v. Caldwell, 74 Pa. 421.

ercise of due care, should have known of it.[70] In other cases the negligence of those in charge of the car, under these circumstances, was held to be a question for the jury.[71] The company has been held guilty of negligence where a driver left the platform while a boy of nine was riding there,[72] and where those in charge of a car made a boy of nine stand on the front platform of a crowded car, and he was pushed off by a passenger alighting.[73]

### § 35. Riding on rear platform.

A passenger riding on the rear platform is governed by much the same rules as one riding on the front platform, and riding on the rear platform of a horse car[74] or an electric car[75] is not lack of due care as a matter of law; but it has been held that riding on the platform outside the city

[70] Saare v. Union Ry. Co., 20 Mo. App. 211; Danbeck v. New Jersey Traction Co., 57 N. J. Law, 463; Pittsburg, A. & M. P. Ry. Co. v. Caldwell, 74 Pa. 421; Philadelphia City Passenger Ry. Co. v. Hassard, 75 Pa. 367; Levin v. Second Ave. Traction Co., 194 Pa. 156, 201 Pa. 58.

[71] Wynn v. City & Suburban Ry. Co., 91 Ga. 344; East Saginaw City Ry. Co. v. Bohn, 27 Mich. 503; Buck v. People's St. Ry., E. L. & P. Co., 46 Mo. App. 555; Jensen v. Barbour, 15 Mont. 582; Crissey v. Hestonville, M. & F. P. Ry. Co., 75 Pa. 83.

[72] Metropolitan St. R. Co. v. Moore, 83 Ga. 453.

[73] Sheridan v. Brooklyn City & N. R. Co., 36 N. Y. 39.

[74] Seigel v. Eisen, 41 Cal. 109; Metropolitan R. Co. v. Snashall, 3 App. D. C. 420; Fleck v. Union Ry. Co., 134 Mass. 480; Matz v. St. Paul City Ry. Co., 52 Minn. 159; Hunt v. Missouri R. Co., 14 Mo. App. 160; Dickson v. Ridge Ave. Passenger Ry. Co., 19 Phila. (Pa.) 430.

[75] Marion St. R. Co. v. Shaffer, 9 Ind. App. 486; Terre Haute Electric Ry. Co. v. Lauer, 21 Ind. App. 466; Sutherland v. Standard L. & A. Ins. Co., 87 Iowa, 505.

limits is governed by the same rules as in the case of steam railroads, and is lack of due care.[76]

The consent of those in charge of the car, and the crowded condition of the car, are two very important facts to be considered. It is not lack of due care to ride upon the rear platform of a crowded street car without objection from those in charge of the car;[77] or when there is no evidence as to the crowded condition of the car, but the conductor allowed the passenger to ride, and there was not shown to be any rule forbidding it.[78] When there is plenty of room inside a car, the authorities are in conflict. It has been held that, on the one hand, riding on the rear platform under these conditions is not lack of due care, at least in the absence of any rule forbidding it,[79] and, on the other, that the rear platform of an electric car is a place of known danger, and that, if a passenger who could have found a seat inside the car is injured while riding there, he is guilty of contributory negligence, and cannot recover for injuries arising from a collision caused by the negligence of the company.[80] A rule forbidding passengers to ride on the rear platform is a reasonable one,[81] and a passenger runs the risk of the ordinary dangers incidental to such a position,

76 Cincinnati, L. & A. Electric St. R. Co. v. Lohe (Ohio) 67 N. E. 161.

77 Metropolitan R. Co. v. Snashall, 3 App. D. C. 420; Reber v. Pittsburg & B. Traction Co., 179 Pa. 339.

78 Cincinnati Omnibus Co. v. Kuhnell, 11 Wkly. Law Bul. (Ohio) 189.

79 Matz v. St. Paul City Ry. Co., 52 Minn. 159.

80 Thane v. Scranton Traction Co., 191 Pa. 249.

81 Ft. Clark St. R. Co. v. Ebaugh, 49 Ill. App. 582.

such as rounding a curve at ordinary speed,[82] or a slight jerk.[83]

It is the duty of passengers to follow the reasonable instructions of those in charge of the car, and a request to give up seats to lady passengers is not unreasonable.[84]

Omitting to take hold of the rail on the rear platform is not of itself lack of due care.[85]

The negligence of a street railway company in not providing guards of sufficient height to prevent passengers from falling from the rear platform has been held to be a question for the jury;[86] and where both platforms were filled to their utmost capacity, it was held that the negligence of the company both as to the condition of the platform and the permitting such a large number of passengers to ride was for the jury.[87] Where a contractor allowed a derrick rope to hang too low, and a horse car was negligently driven into it, both the contractor and the company were held liable;[88] and it is negligence for a conductor to bring a woman out onto the rear platform when the truck of a hook and ladder company is rapidly approaching.[89] Where a boy of eight rode on the rear platform with his feet on the step, it was held that his due care and the negligence of the com-

82 Andrews v. Capitol, N. O. St. & S. W. R. Co., 2 Mackey (D. C.) 137.

83 Byron v. Lynn & B. R. Co., 177 Mass. 303; Timms v. Old Colony St. Ry. Co. (Mass.) 66 N. E. 797.

84 Terre Haute Electric Ry. Co. v. Lauer, 21 Ind. App. 466.

85 North Chicago St. R. Co. v. Baur, 179 Ill. 126; Fleck v. Union Ry. Co., 134 Mass. 480; Matz v. St. Paul City Ry. Co., 52 Minn. 159.

86 Matz v. St. Paul City Ry. Co., 52 Minn. 159.

87 Norris v. Brooklyn City R. Co., 4 Misc. Rep. (N. Y.) 294.

88 Hunt v. Missouri R. Co., 14 Mo. App. 160.

89 Maverick v. Eighth Ave. R. Co., 36 N. Y. 378.

pany were questions for the jury.[90] Electric cars occupy a position midway between steam cars and horse cars, and their great speed causes increased danger.[91] Whether intoxication contributed to the accident is a question for the jury.[92]

## § 36. Riding on step of car.

As in the case of riding upon the front or rear platform of a street car, it cannot be said, as matter of law, that riding upon the steps of a street car is of itself lack of due care. This is so, whether the car is a horse car[93] or an electric car,[94] although it has been held that, in the absence of explanation, riding upon the steps of the front platform of a horse car is *prima facie* evidence of negligence.[95] A passenger who rides upon the step of the front platform of a crowded horse car with the assent of the conductor or driver is not guilty of lack of due care as matter of law;[96] and the same ruling has been made in the case of an electric car.[97]

90 Jackson v. St. Paul City Ry. Co., 74 Minn. 48.

91 Thane v. Scranton Traction Co., 191 Pa. 249; Reber v. Pittsburg & B. Traction Co., 179 Pa. 339.

92 Donoho v. Metropolitan St. Ry. Co., 30 Misc. Rep. (N. Y.) 433.

93 Huelsenkamp v. Citizens' Ry. Co., 37 Mo. 537; Seymour v. Citizens' Ry. Co., 114 Mo. 266; Lehr v. Steinway & H. P. R. Co., 118 N. Y. 556; Saltzman v. Brooklyn City R. Co., 73 Hun (N. Y.) 567; Germantown Passenger Ry. Co. v. Walling, 97 Pa. 55; West Philadelphia Passenger Ry. Co. v. Gallagher, 108 Pa. 524.

94 Wilde v. Lynn & B. R. Co., 163 Mass. 533; Pray v. Omaha St. Ry. Co., 44 Neb. 167; Schaefer v. Union Ry. Co., 29 App. Div. (N. Y.) 261; Schwartz v. Cincinnati St. Ry. Co., 1 Ohio Dec. 197.

95 Ashbrook v. Frederick Ave. Ry. Co., 18 Mo. App. 290; Pray v. Omaha St. Ry. Co., 44 Neb. 167; Clark v. Eighth Ave. R. Co., 36 N. Y. 135.

96 Huelsenkamp v. Citizens' Ry. Co., 37 Mo. 537; Seymour v. Citi-

There is a conflict of authority as to what constitutes assent on the part of those in charge of a car. Where a passenger rode on a step of a crowded car, it was held, in Huelsenkamp v. Citizens' Ry. Co.,[98] that consent could not be inferred; but in Pray v. Omaha St. Ry. Co.[99] it was held that a person so riding is presumed to be there with the consent of the servants of the company.

Where a passenger rode on the step of a dummy car because the platform was crowded, although there was plenty of room inside the car, and was struck by a post, with the position of which he was familiar, he was held not to be in the exercise of due care.[100] It has been held that, if a person riding in the daytime on the front steps or platform of a closed street car, moving at the rate of four miles an hour, casually or momentarily turns his head, or leans his body out beyond the line of the car as incident to an effort to secure a more comfortable or a safer position, he is not necessarily precluded from recovering in an action against the railway corporation for injuries occasioned by his head striking a post standing about three feet from the nearer rail of the car track, and visible from the car for a quarter of

zens' Ry. Co., 114 Mo. 266; Clark v. Eighth Ave. R. Co., 36 N. Y. 135; Lehr v. Steinway & H. P. R. Co., 118 N. Y. 556; Saltzman v. Brooklyn City R. Co., 73 Hun (N. Y.) 567; Germantown Passenger Ry. Co. v. Walling, 97 Pa. 55; West Philadelphia Passenger Ry. Co. v. Gallagher, 108 Pa. 524.

97 Wilde v. Lynn & B. R. Co., 163 Mass. 533; Pray v. Omaha St. Ry. Co., 44 Neb. 167; Schaefer v. Union Ry. Co., 29 App. Div. (N. Y.) 261.

98 34 Mo. 45.

99 44 Neb. 167.

100 Aikin v. Frankford & S. P. C. P. R. Co., 142 Pa. 47.

a mile as the car approached; but, if he deliberately leans out beyond the car with his face turned in the direction opposite to that in which the car is moving, he cannot recover for such injury.[101]

It is not lack of due care, as matter of law, to stand on the step of an electric car, although the entrance on that side is barred by a chain[102] or by a gate.[103] If a passenger is forced to ride upon the step of a crowded car, the company is bound to use greater care;[104] but where a man was unnecessarily on the step, and was injured by a collision with a wagon, there was held to be no evidence of the company's negligence.[105] A passenger riding on the step of a street car assumes the risk arising from the ordinary motion of the car, but not the risk arising from the negligence of the company.[106] A passenger riding on the front step is not subject to the provisions of an act regulating the liability of the company to persons getting on or off at the front end of the car.[107]

## § 37. Riding on running board.

Although riding on the running board has apparently been attended with rather more danger than riding on the platforms or steps, it is nevertheless held that riding in this position is not of itself lack of due care as a matter of law;

101 Cummings v. Worcester, L. & S. St. Ry. Co., 166 Mass. 220.

102 Schwartz v. Cincinnati St. Ry. Co., 1 Ohio Dec. 197.

103 Seymour v. Citizens' Ry. Co., 114 Mo. 266.

104 Kinkade v. Atlantic Ave. R. Co., 9 Misc. Rep. (N. Y.) 273, affirmed 149 N. Y. 615.

105 Ashbrook v. Frederick Ave. Ry. Co., 18 Mo. App. 290.

106 Willmott v. Corrigan Consol. St. Ry. Co., 106 Mo. 535.

107 Seymour v. Citizens' Ry. Co., 114 Mo. 266.

and the rule is the same, whether the car is a horse car,[108] a cable car,[109] an electric car,[110] or a stage sleigh,[111] although electric cars have been held to require more care in operation than horse cars,[112] and to occupy a position midway between that of horse cars and steam cars.[113]

Whether or not the car is crowded is perhaps the most important consideration in determining the question of the passenger's due care. Where the car is crowded, and the passenger rides on the running board without objection from those in charge of the car, he is held not to be guilty of lack of due care as matter of law,[114] while, if there is plenty

[108] Harbison v. Metropolitan R. Co., 9 App. D. C. 60; North Chicago St. R. Co. v. Williams, 140 Ill. 275; Topeka City Ry. Co. v. Higgs, 38 Kan. 375; City Ry. Co. v. Lee, 50 N. J. Law, 435; Bruno v. Brooklyn City R. Co., 5 Misc. Rep. (N. Y.) 327; Herdt v. Rochester City & B. R. Co., 20 N. Y. Supp. 346; Geitz v. Milwaukee City Ry. Co., 72 Wis. 307.

[109] West Chicago St. R. Co. v. McNulty, 64 Ill. App. 549; West Chicago St. R. Co. v. Marks, 82 Ill. App. 185; Pomaski v. Grant, 119 Mich. 675.

[110] Hesse v. Meriden, S. & C. Tramway Co. (Conn.) 54 Atl. 299; McGrath v. Brooklyn, Q. C. & S. R. Co., 87 Hun (N. Y.) 310; Hassen v. Nassau Electric R. Co., 34 App. Div. (N. Y.) 71; Brainard v. Nassau Electric R. Co., 44 App. Div. (N. Y.) 613; Henderson v. Nassau Electric R. Co., 46 App. Div. (N. Y.) 280; Sheeron v. Coney Island & B. R. Co., 78 App. Div. (N. Y.) 476; Anderson v. City & Suburban Ry. Co. (Or.) 71 Pac. 659; Bumbear v. United Traction Co., 198 Pa. 198; Elliott v. Newport St. Ry. Co., 18 R. I. 707; Cogswell v. West St. & N. E. Electric Ry. Co., 5 Wash. 46.

[111] Spooner v. Brooklyn City R. Co., 54 N. Y. 230.

[112] Cogswell v. West St. & N. E. Electric Ry. Co., 5 Wash. 46.

[113] Bumbear v. United Traction Co., 198 Pa. 198.

[114] Hesse v. Meriden, S. & C. Tramway Co. (Conn.) 54 Atl. 299; West Chicago St. R. Co. v. McNulty, 64 Ill. App. 549; West Chicago St. R. Co. v. Marks, 82 Ill. App. 185; Topeka City Ry. Co. v. Higgs, 38 Kan. 375; Pomaski v. Grant, 119 Mich. 675; City Ry. Co. v. Lee,

of room inside, it has been held that the passenger assumes all the risks arising from the position which he chooses to take;[115] and in any event, a passenger riding on the running board assumes the risk of the ordinary perils incident to the position.[116] To give up one's seat to a woman passenger, and stand on the running board, is not lack of due care as matter of law.[117]

If a passenger rides on the running board when there is room inside the car, and is injured by the breaking of a handle bar as he swings out from the car, and it appears that the handle bar was meant to help passengers in boarding and leaving the car, and was strong enough for that purpose, the passenger cannot recover.[118]

50 N. J. Law, 435; Flynn v. Consolidated Traction Co., 64 N. J. Law, 375; McGrath v. Brooklyn, Q. C. & S. R. Co., 87 Hun (N. Y.) 310; Hassen v. Nassau Electric R. Co., 34 App. Div. (N. Y.) 71; Brainard v. Nassau Electric R. Co., 44 App. Div. (N. Y.) 613; Bruno v. Brooklyn City R. Co., 5 Misc. Rep. (N. Y.) 327; Herdt v. Rochester City & B. R. Co., 20 N. Y. Supp. 346; Sheeron v. Coney Island & B. R. Co., 78 App. Div. (N. Y.) 476; Anderson v. City & Suburban Ry. Co. (Or.) 71 Pac. 659; Bumbear v. United Traction Co., 198 Pa. 198; Elliott v. Newport St. Ry. Co., 18 R. I. 707; Cogswell v. West St. & N. E. Electric Ry. Co., 5 Wash. 46; Geitz v. Milwaukee City Ry. Co., 72 Wis. 307.

115 Bumbear v. United Traction Co., 198 Pa. 198.

116 Harbison v. Metropolitan R. Co., 9 App. D. C. 60; Citizens' St. R. Co. v. Hoffbauer, 23 Ind. App. 614; Whalen v. Consolidated Traction Co., 61 N. J. Law, 606; Nies v. Brooklyn Heights R. Co., 68 App. Div. (N. Y.) 259; Herdt v. Rochester City & B. R. Co., 20 N. Y. Supp. 346; Bumbear v. United Traction Co., 198 Pa. 198; Bainbridge v. Union Traction Co. (Pa.) 55 Atl. 836; Elliott v. Newport St. Ry. Co., 18 R. I. 707.

117 Brainard v. Nassau Electric R. Co., 44 App. Div. (N. Y.) 613.

118 Brightwood Ry. Co. v. Carter, 12 App. D. C. 155.

A very common case is where the passenger, while riding on the running board, comes into collision with a wagon, a post, or another car. It has been held that a passenger who is moving along the running board, and is struck by a wagon standing near the track, is not guilty of lack of due care as a matter of law.[119] On the other hand, it has been held that a passenger cannot recover when he was riding on the running board, when he could have ridden upon the rear platform, and came into collision with a truck, which he saw as soon as he got on board the car;[120] and a similar ruling has been made where it did not appear that the passenger actually saw the wagon, but where it was clear that he should have done so.[121] Where a motorman signaled to the driver of a wagon to get off the track, and he did so, and stopped within two feet of the track, it was held that the motorman was bound to take notice of its position, and to take great care to avoid injury to passengers;[122] and where it appeared that a conductor knew of the position of a truck near the track, and started his car ahead, there was held to be evidence of negligence for the jury,[123] and in a number of cases of collision with a wagon negligence was held to be

[119] Faris v. Brooklyn City & N. R. Co., 46 App. Div. (N. Y.) 231; Henderson v. Nassau Electric R. Co., 46 App. Div. (N. Y.) 280.

[120] Caspers v. Dry Dock, E. B. & B. R. Co., 22 App. Div. (N. Y.) 156; Littman v. Dry Dock, E. B. & B. R. Co., 6 Misc. Rep. (N. Y.) 34. And see Moody v. Springfield St. Ry. Co., 182 Mass. 158.

[121] Moylan v. Second Ave. R. Co., 128 N. Y. 583; Flynn v. Consolidated Traction Co., 64 N. J. Law, 375.

[122] Henderson v. Nassau Electric R. Co., 46 App. Div. (N. Y.) 280.

[123] Goldwasser v. Metropolitan St. Ry. Co., 32 Misc. Rep. (N. Y.) 682.

for the jury.[124] A person placed in sudden peril is not held to the usual standard of care.[125] Where a newsboy got on the running board to sell his papers, and was struck by a wagon standing near the track, there was held to be no negligence on the part of the company.[126]

The following rulings have been made where the passenger was injured by a collision with another car. The case was held to be for the jury where the plaintiff was injured by a collision with another car, and there was evidence that the tracks were nearer together than at any other place, and slanted inwards.[127] The space of four feet between the inner rails of a double track—the smallest space allowed by law—cannot be said to be dangerous to passengers as a matter of law; and where a passenger on the running board was struck by another car, and there was no evidence of a defect in the tracks or a lurch of the car, there was held to be no presumption of negligence.[128] There was held to be no negligence where a passenger on the running board was struck by a closed car, and it appeared that there was a space of seventeen inches between the outside step and the body of the other car;[129] but where a passenger on the running board was injured by a collision with a car passing in the opposite direction, and it appeared that the posts of the

124 West Chicago St. R. Co. v. McNulty, 64 Ill. App. 549; Sweeney v. Kansas City Cable Ry. Co., 150 Mo. 385; Bumbear v. United Traction Co., 198 Pa. 198.

125 West Chicago St. R. Co. v. McNulty, 64 Ill. App. 549.

126 Padgitt v. Moll & Citizens' Ry. Co., 159 Mo. 143.

127 Gray v. Rochester City & B. R. Co., 61 Hun (N. Y.) 212; Herdt v. Rochester City & B. R. Co., 20 N. Y. Supp. 346.

128 Harbison v. Metropolitan R. Co., 9 App. D. C. 60.

129 Craighead v. Brooklyn City R. Co., 123 N. Y. 391.

cars were twenty-five inches apart when standing still, negligence was held to be for the jury.[130] It is gross negligence for a street car company to allow its cars to become overcrowded, and then to run them so near another track that they cannot pass another car without injury to passengers.[131]

Where a car took the wrong track, and the plaintiff, discovering this, stepped out on the running board to find the conductor, and was struck by a trolley pole, and it appeared that it was after dark, it was held that due care and negligence were for the jury.[132] Where a passenger, while on the running board of a crowded car, was struck by a trolley pole ten and one-half inches from the running board, due care and negligence were held to be for the jury;[133] but in Sibley v. New Orleans City & L. R. Co.,[134] where a passenger was injured by a pole fourteen inches from the running board, the court held, on all the evidence, that the plaintiff must have leaned out into the darkness, and could not recover. Where there were poles between a double track, and a passenger got on the running board to attract the conductor's attention, and was struck by one of these poles, it was held that he could not recover.[135] A passenger who walked along the running board without reasonable cause, and, swinging out, struck an elevated column, was held not entitled to recover.[136] Where there was plenty of space be-

130 Geltz v. Milwaukee City Ry. Co., 72 Wis. 307.

131 Topeka City Ry. Co. v. Higgs, 38 Kan. 375.

132 Citizens' St. R. Co. v. Hoffbauer, 23 Ind. App. 614.

133 Hesse v. Meriden, S. & C. Tramway Co. (Conn.) 54 Atl. 299; Elliott v. Newport St. Ry. Co., 18 R. I. 707.

134 49 La. Ann. 588.

135 State v. Lake Roland El. Ry. Co., 84 Md. 163.

136 Coleman v. Second Ave. R. Co., 114 N. Y. 609.

tween a car and a pole, and a passenger leaned out and was struck, he was held not to be in the exercise of due care.[137]

The fact that a passenger riding on the running board of a crowded car is intoxicated does not necessarily prevent his recovering. His due care is a question for the jury, and the conductor, knowing of his intoxication, must exercise care in passing by him.[138]

To run a car so near an obstruction that a passenger may, in the ordinary course of things, be hurt, is evidence of negligence for the jury.[139] Where a passenger was riding on the running board, and his hand slipped from the upright, which was slippery with rain, and there was no unusual motion of the car, it was held that there was no evidence of negligence.[140] Where a passenger on a street car was walking along the running board, and struck his head against one of the elevated columns, the street car company was held to be guilty of no negligence.[141] It is not unusual or dangerous to have trolley poles between a double track, and it is not negligence not to have a bar on the side of the car nearest the poles.[142] Where a conductor called to a passenger to come forward on the running board, and, in passing around the conductor, the passenger was struck by an elevated column, it was held that the conductor's invitation did not relieve the passenger from the duty of using due

137 Nugent v. New Haven St. Ry. Co., 73 Conn. 139.

138 Kingston v. Ft. Wayne & E. Ry. Co., 112 Mich. 40.

139 North Chicago St. R. Co. v. Williams, 40 Ill. App. 590, 140 Ill. 275; West Chicago St. R. Co. v. Marks, 82 Ill. App. 185.

140 Johnson v. Brooklyn Heights R. Co., 63 App. Div. (N. Y.) 374.

141 Murphy v. Ninth Ave. R. Co., 6 Misc. Rep. (N. Y.) 298; Vroman v. Houston, W. St. & P. Ferry R. Co., 7 Misc. Rep. (N. Y.) 234.

142 State v. Lake Roland El. Ry. Co., 84 Md. 163.

care.[143] Where a passenger on the running board was struck by a barrier[144] near the track, due care and negligence were held to be for the jury. Where a passenger on the running board was injured by contact with a bridge, and the space between the running board and the bridge was only eighteen inches, it was held that, owing to plaintiff's position, both plaintiff and defendant were bound to use more care than usual, and that plaintiff's due care was for the jury, even if he leaned back to look for a friend, or to replace money in his pocket.[145]

Where a passenger testified that he was thrown off the running board because the conductor stumbled against him, it was held error to grant a nonsuit.[146] Where a boy of eight rode on the running board at the side of the car not meant for passengers, where strips were placed to prevent their getting on or off, and fell off and was injured, it was held that he exposed himself to evident peril, and could not recover.[147] Even if a passenger is not in the exercise of due care, the defendant may be liable if it could have avoided the accident.[148]

## § 38. Standing in car.

It is not contributory negligence for a woman to stand in a crowded street car.[149] When a woman enters a crowded

143 Third Ave. R. Co. v. Barton, 107 Fed. 215.

144 North Chicago St. R. Co. v. Polkey (Ill.) 67 N. E. 793; Citizens' St. Ry. Co. v. Merl, 26 Ind. App. 284; Berry v. Utica Belt Line St. R. Co., 76 App. Div. (N. Y.) 490.

145 Anderson v. City & Suburban Ry. Co. (Or.) 71 Pac. 659.

146 Whalen v. Consolidated Traction Co., 61 N. J. Law, 606.

147 Udell v. Citizens' St. R. Co., 152 Ind. 507.

148 Denver & B. P. Rapid Transit Co. v. Dwyer, 20 Colo. 132.

149 Griffith v. Utica & M. R. Co., 17 N. Y. Supp. 692.

car, she must hold onto the straps provided for the purpose if she reasonably can, and, if she cannot, and takes hold of a friend's hand for support, her due care is for the jury.[150] Where the conductor did not stop, and a passenger stood up to hail him, and was thrown off by a jerk of the car on a curve, the case was held to be for the jury.[151] It is not lack of due care to go to the door to make inquiries of the conductor as to the destination of the car.[152]

Where a passenger standing in the gripman's aisle was struck by the brake, it was held that a street railway company allowing its cars to be crowded must use a high degree of care, and is not excused because a passenger lightly disobeys a rule, unless he is warned of the danger, so that he appreciates it.[153]

A person who enters an open horse car, the seats of which are all occupied by passengers, and, without objection by the conductor of the car, who collects a fare of him, stands in the space between the passengers occupying one seat and the back of the next seat, holding onto the latter with his hands, is not precluded, by reason of having taken such a position, from maintaining an action against the corporation owning the car for injuries occasioned by being thrown from the car while it is being driven around a curve in the street.[154] Where a woman was standing because she could

150 Whipple v. West Philadelphia Passenger Ry. Co., 2 Wkly. Notes Cas. (Pa.) 559; West Philadelphia Passenger Ry. Co. v. Whipple, 5 Wkly. Notes Cas. (Pa.) 68.

151 Ripley v. Second Ave. R. Co., 8 Misc. Rep. (N. Y.) 449.

152 Farrell v. Houston, W. St. & P. Ferry R. Co., 4 N. Y. Supp. 597.

153 West Chicago St. R. Co. v. Johnson, 77 Ill. App. 142, affirmed 180 Ill. 285.

154 Lapointe v. Middlesex R. Co., 144 Mass. 18.

find no seat or strap, and the car started suddenly, the negligence of the company was held to be for the jury.[155] Where a passenger lost his hat, got up to signal the conductor, and was struck by a post less than two feet from the floor of the car, it was held that he was not to blame for rising, and that the negligence of the company was for the jury.[156] Where a passenger stood in a crowded coach, the degree of care which the company owed to her was held to be increased.[157] Where a woman stood at the end of a seat in an open car with a market basket on her arm, although she was warned to keep her seat, she cannot recover.[158]

## § 39. Riding on bumper.

Where the car is so full that there is no room in the car or on the platform, standing on the bumper outside of the platform is lack of due care as matter of law;[159] and the case is still stronger against the passenger when the conductor warns him that he is occupying a dangerous position.[160] Where a passenger was allowed to ride on the bumper, the company was held liable for gross negligence in a rear-end collision.[161]

## § 40. Preparatory to alighting.

Standing in a car, which is still moving, preparatory to alighting, is held not to be lack of due care as matter of

155 Continental Passenger Ry. Co. v. Swain, 13 Wkly. Notes Cas. (Pa.) 41.

156 Schmidt v. Coney Island & B. R. Co., 26 App. Div. (N. Y.) 391.

157 Geddes v. Metropolitan R. Co., 103 Mass. 391.

158 Jackson v. Philadelphia Traction Co., 182 Pa. 104.

159 Bard v. Pennsylvania Traction Co., 176 Pa. 97.

160 Nieboer v. Detroit Electric Ry. Co., 128 Mich. 486.

161 Grieve v. North Jersey St. Ry. Co., 65 N. J. Law, 409.

law. For a passenger to signal a street car to stop, and then to walk to a place where he expects to alight, and stand there waiting for the car to stop, is so common that such conduct cannot be said to be lack of ordinary care.[162] Thus, the plaintiff has been held not to be barred from recovery where he stood, preparatory to alighting, on the rear platform,[163] or the running board,[164] or step of rear platform,[165] or inside the car,[166] or with one foot on the rear platform and one on the step,[167] or with one foot in the car and one on the running board.[168]

There is no rule of law which requires a passenger in a street car to retain his seat or other position until the car has actually stopped, and it is a matter of universal ob-

162 North Chicago St. R. Co. v. Southwick, 66 Ill. App. 241.

163 North Chicago St. R. Co. v. Southwick, 66 Ill. App. 241; North Chicago St. R. Co. v. Baur, 79 Ill. App. 121; Fleck v. Union Ry. Co., 134 Mass. 480; Etson v. Ft. Wayne & B. I. Ry. Co., 110 Mich. 494; Blondel v. St. Paul City Ry. Co., 66 Minn. 284; Scott v. Bergen County Traction Co., 63 N. J. Law, 407.

164 Armstrong v. Montgomery St. Ry. Co., 123 Ala. 233; Sweeney v. Kansas City Cable Ry. Co., 150 Mo. 385; Omaha St. Ry. Co. v. Craig, 39 Neb. 601; Medler v. Atlantic Ave. R. Co., 12 N. Y. Supp. 930.

165 Washington & G. R. Co. v. Harmon's Adm'r, 147 U. S. 571; Birmingham R. & E. Co. v. James, 121 Ala. 120; Watkins v. Birmingham R. & E. Co., 120 Ala. 147; Currie v. Mendenhall, 77 Minn. 179; Bowie v. Greenville St. Ry. Co., 69 Miss. 196; Linch v. Pittsburgh Traction Co., 153 Pa. 102; Foster v. Union Traction Co., 199 Pa. 498.

166 Demann v. Eighth Ave. R. Co., 10 Misc. Rep. (N. Y.) 191; Sweeney v. Union Traction Co., 199 Pa. 293; Consolidated Traction Co. v. Thalheimer, 59 N. J. Law, 474.

167 Mitchell v. Electric Traction Co., 12 Pa. Super. Ct. 472.

168 Springfield Consolidated Ry. Co. v. Hoeffner, 71 Ill. App. 162; Bradley v. Ft. Wayne & E. Ry. Co., 94 Mich. 35.

servation that thousands every day leave their seats to get off before the car has stopped without sustaining any injury.[169]

A passenger on a street car, who goes out upon the platform after the conductor has called the name of a street, and is standing upon the step when the car stops, is justified in alighting.[170]

In Dresslar v. Citizens' St. R. Co.[171] it was held that where a passenger, in attempting to change his position from the platform to the step below, preparatory to alighting, was injured by the gradual increase in speed, there was no negligence on the part of the company; and the same ruling has been made where the passenger fell off, but there was no unusual motion of the car.[172] Where a passenger testified that, as the car slowed down in answer to his signal, he went onto the rear platform, and "the car went right from under him," but there was no proof of any jolt or jerk, there is no evidence of negligence on the part of the company.[173] Where a passenger's signal was not heeded, and he stood up on the extreme edge of the car, and was thrown off when the car stopped with a jar, there was held to be a lack of due care.[173a]

In Lacas v. Detroit City Ry. Co.[174] it was held that, where a passenger was just about to put her foot upon the

169 Babcock v. Los Angeles Traction Co., 128 Cal. 173; Nichols v. Sixth Ave. R. Co., 38 N. Y. 131.

170 North Chicago St. R. Co. v. Brown, 178 Ill. 187.

171 19 Ind. App. 383.

172 Philips v. St. Charles St. R. Co., 106 La. 592.

173 Armstrong v. Metropolitan St. Ry. Co., 23 App. Div. (N. Y.) 137.

173a Jennings v. Union Traction Co. (Pa.) 55 Atl. 765.

174 92 Mich. 412.

running board, and it would have been difficult for her to turn back, she was not guilty of lack of due care in continuing her descent from the car as it started. Where a passenger placed his hand on the door of an elevated railroad car to steady himself before alighting, and a guard opened the door just before the train stopped, there was held to be no negligence.[175]

## § 41. Changing position on car.

Where an employe not on duty tried to pass from the tender to a car on a dummy train while the train was in rapid motion on a short curve, it was held that he was not in the exercise of due care.[176] When a passenger attempts to pass from the running board of an open car to the steps of a closed car on a dummy line while the car is in motion, he is guilty of contributory negligence, and proof of a custom of passengers to do this will not help him, since the act is obviously dangerous.[177] When a passenger is injured in consequence of passing from the running board of one car to that of another because of the ordinary vibration, or failure to get a firm foothold or grasp, or by losing his hold on the car, or a misstep, or losing his balance, his own negligence will prevent recovery.[178]

It has been held that it is lack of due care to pass from the platform of one open car to that of the next while the train is in motion;[179] but on the other hand it has been

175 Hannon v. Boston El. Ry. Co., 182 Mass. 425.

176 McDaniel v. Highland Ave. & B. R. Co., 90 Ala. 64.

177 Hill v. Birmingham Union Ry. Co., 100 Ala. 447.

178 Eickhof v. Chicago North Shore St. Ry. Co., 77 Ill. App. 196.

held that, where it is customary for conductors and passengers to pass from the platform of one car to that of another on an electric train, it is not lack of due care, as a matter of law, to do so;[180] and walking on the upper deck of a horse car for the purpose of descending to the lower platform while the car is in motion is not lack of due care as matter of law.[181]

Where a passenger walked along the running board without any necessity, and leaned out and struck an elevated column, he was held not to be in the exercise of due care;[182] and where a passenger went from the rear platform along the running board and struck a column,[183] and one got on at one side of the car and crossed to the opposite side, where the columns were,[184] it was held in both cases that there was no evidence of the company's negligence. There was likewise held to be no negligence where a passenger changing his position on the running board was struck by another car.[185] Where there were poles between a double track, and a passenger got out on the running board to attract the conductor's attention, and struck a pole, it was held that he could not recover.[186] Even if the conductor calls a passenger to come forward on the running board, and, in going

179 Bemiss v. New Orleans City & L. R. Co., 47 La. Ann. 1671.

180 Burt v. Douglas County St. Ry. Co., 83 Wis. 229.

181 Baltimore & Y. Turnpike Road v. Leonhardt, 66 Md. 70.

182 Coleman v. Second Ave. R. Co., 114 N. Y. 609.

183 Vroman v. Houston, W. St. & P. Ferry R. Co., 7 Misc. Rep. (N. Y.) 234.

184 Murphy v. Ninth Ave. R. Co., 6 Misc. Rep. (N. Y.) 298.

185 Harbison v. Metropolitan R. Co., 9 App. D. C. 60.

186 State v. Lake Roland El. Ry. Co., 84 Md. 163.

around the conductor, he is struck by an elevated column, the invitation does not relieve the passenger from the duty of using due care.[187]

## § 42. Catching dress.

Where a passenger caught her dress on a bolt on the floor of a car, even if she knew, or, by the exercise of ordinary care, might have known, that the bolt was there, she is not guilty of lack of due care as matter of law;[188] and where a passenger caught her dress on a bolt extending three-eighths of an inch above the floor of the car, it was held that the jury could find, without direct proof, that such a bolt was dangerous, and that the due care of the passenger was a question of fact.[189] Where a passenger caught her dress on a broken curtain hook, and the company proved that such hooks were used on all its cars, that such an accident had never occurred before, and that, at the end of each trip, the cars were inspected, and the broken hooks, if discovered, replaced, there was held to be no evidence of negligence;[190] and where a passenger caught her dress upon the catch of the door, a finding that the company was not guilty of any negligence was held to be correct.[191]

## § 43. Falling from car.

Where a boy of seven, who was in the habit of boarding street cars to sell water, fell from the platform and was killed, it was held that a nonsuit was properly entered on

[187] Third Ave. R. Co. v. Barton, 107 Fed. 215.
[188] North Chicago St. R. Co. v. Eldridge, 151 Ill. 542.
[189] Chartrand v. Southern Ry. Co., 57 Mo. App. 425.
[190] Kelly v. New York & S. B. Ry. Co., 109 N. Y. 44.
[191] Atwood v. Metropolitan St. R. Co., 25 Misc. Rep. (N. Y.) 758.

the ground of contributory negligence.[192] Where a conductor called a boy onto the platform, and he fell off through his own imprudence, it was held that he could not recover.[193] In Chicago City Ry. Co. v. Burrell,[194] where an adult, and in Bishop v. Union R. Co.,[195] where a child of six, fell from a moving car, there was held to be no evidence of negligence on the part of the company. The fact that a sidebar meant to prevent passengers from boarding or leaving the car on that side, and not to prevent them from falling out, was up when the defendant fell out, will not justify the jury in finding negligence.[196] But where a passenger falls off a street car in full motion in front of the wheels, and the servants in charge of the car know that he has fallen, and is holding onto the iron rail to save himself from being run over, it is culpable negligence if they do not stop the car.[197]

Where a boy of four fell through an open space in an open street car, the due care of the child and the negligence of the company were held to be questions for the jury.[198] Where a boy of eight sat on the platform with his feet on the step, and became dizzy and fell off, negligence was held to be for the jury.[199] Where a passenger stood near a door of a transfer car, and the door was suddenly opened by an employe of the company, so that she fell out, it was held

192 Smith v. Passenger Ry. Co., 13 Phila. (Pa.) 6.

193 Cronan v. Crescent City R. Co., 49 La. Ann. 65.

194 70 Ill. App. 60.

195 14 R. I. 314.

196 Whitaker v. Staten Island Midland R. Co., 65 App. Div. (N. Y.) 451.

197 Chicago West Div. Ry. Co. v. Hughes, 69 Ill. 170.

198 Metropolitan R. Co. v. Falvey, 5 App. D. C. 176.

199 Jackson v. St. Paul City Ry. Co., 74 Minn. 48.

that, if she stood where she did under an order from the employe, she had the right to assume that the place was a safe one.[200] In Mt. Adams & E. P. I. Ry. Co. v. Reul there was held to be no evidence of negligence.[201] Where a passenger rose to feel in his pocket for his fare, and fell from the car, it was held that the company was not liable.[202] Where it was uncertain how a passenger fell from a car, there was held to be insufficient evidence of negligence.[203]

## § 44. Tripping in car.

In Farley v. Philadelphia Traction Co.[204] a passenger fell over the box placed over the wheel of an open car, which was in plain sight, and was held not to be in the exercise of due care, and therefore unable to recover. In a similar case, where it appeared that the company had used such a guard for a long time without injury, there was held to be no evidence of negligence on the part of the company.[205] Where a passenger sued the company on the double ground that he fell over a wheel guard and fell over a basket, it was held that there was no negligence in regard to the wheel guard, and that there was no negligence in allowing a passenger in an open car to place a basket between his feet, and that a passenger who attempted to get over the basket assumed the risk.[206] Where a passenger tripped over a hose lying in

200 Prothero v. Citizens' St. Ry. Co., 134 Ind. 431.

201 4 Ohio Cir. Ct. R. 362.

202 Witherington v. Lynn & B. R. Co., 182 Mass. 596.

203 Payne v. Forty-Second St. & G. St. Ferry R. Co., 40 N. Y. Super. Ct. 8.

204 6 Pa. Co. Ct. R. 347.

205 Thompson v. Metropolitan St. Ry. Co., 140 Mo. 125.

206 Van Winkle v. Brooklyn City R. Co., 46 Hun (N. Y.) 564.

plain sight on a wharf maintained by the company, there was held to be lack of due care.[207]

### § 45. Putting arm outside car.

Where a passenger was sitting with his arm resting on the window sill, but wholly within the car, and it was thrown out by a jolt of the car while rounding a curve, it was held that occupying such a position was not lack of due care as matter of law.[208] Even if a passenger does allow his elbow or his hand to project from a window of a street car, his due care is still a question for the jury;[209] and the rule is the same where a passenger stood on the rear platform of a street car with his hands over the dasher.[210] But it has been held that, where a passenger puts his elbow or arm outside of a street car window voluntarily without any qualifying circumstances impelling him to do it, this is lack of due care as matter of law.[211] It is negligence to allow cars to run so closely together as to injure a passenger whose elbow is projecting a few inches outside the car.[212] Where an electric car is crossing a bridge, and the conductor sees that a passenger is in danger because his arm is projecting from the car window, it is negligence not to warn him of his peril, and contributory

207 Strutt v. Brooklyn & R. B. R. Co., 18 App. Div. (N. Y.) 134.

208 People's Passenger Ry. Co. v. Lauderbach, 4 Penny. (Pa.) 406; Germantown Passenger Ry. Co. v. Brophy, 105 Pa. 38.

209 Summers v. Crescent City R. Co., 34 La. Ann. 139; Dahlberg v. Minneapolis St. Ry. Co., 32 Minn. 404; Miller v. St. Louis R. Co., 5 Mo. App. 471; Francis v. New York Steam Co., 114 N. Y. 380; Tucker v. Buffalo Ry. Co., 53 App. Div. (N. Y.) 571.

210 Seigel v. Eisen, 41 Cal. 109.

211 People's Passenger Ry. Co. v. Lauderbach, 4 Penny. (Pa.) 406.

212 Summers v. Crescent City R. Co., 34 La. Ann. 139; Tucker v. Buffalo Ry. Co., 53 App. Div. (N. Y.) 571.

negligence is no excuse.[213] A motorman has a right to assume that no part of a passenger's person will project beyond the lines of the car.[213a]

## § 46. Transferring.

In Jamison v. San Jose & S. C. R. Co.,[214] where a passenger had to transfer across a plank bridge, without a railing, in the dark, it was held that there was no contributory negligence as a matter of law, and that a verdict for the plaintiff would not be disturbed.

## II. Unusual Conduct of Company.

**A street railway company is not an insurer of the safety of its passengers, but it owes them a very high degree of care.**

**Where a passenger is injured through the negligence of the company, the fact that he was traveling on Sunday is no defense.**

**Negligence in overcrowding cars is generally a question for the jury, but it may be held negligent as a matter of law. On the other hand, a passenger may be guilty of lack of due care in riding on a crowded car.**

**The company must use a high degree of care in regard to electricity, and an accident from the electrical apparatus of a car usually raises a presumption of negligence. In accidents arising from ordinary defects in the condition of a car, negligence is usually held to be for the jury.**

**The company must do what they reasonably can to protect passengers against injury from fellow passengers.**

**Derailment raises a presumption of negligence, as does a**

213 South Covington & C. St. Ry. Co. v. McCleave, 18 Ky. Law Rep. 1036.

213a Zeliff v. North Jersey St. Ry. Co. (N. J. Sup.) 55 Atl. 96.

214 55 Cal. 593.

collision between two street cars of the same line. Where there is a collision between two cars of different lines, no presumption arises with respect to the car on which the plaintiff is not a passenger; and the same ruling is made where the collision is between a street car and a steam railroad. In all these cases of collisions, it is held that the negligence of the employe in charge of a car cannot be imputed to a passenger.

An unusual or extraordinary jerk establishes a prima facie case of negligence, but the jerk must be unusual, and not one ordinarily made in the management of a car.

The question of excessive speed is usually left to the jury.

## § 47. Care required of company.

While a street railway company is not an insurer of the safety of its passengers, it is almost universally held that it does owe them a high degree of care.[215] Just what this degree of care is it is difficult to define, since different courts have used different phraseology; but it is sufficient to state that it is an extraordinary degree of care,—something more than the ordinary care owed to people who do not occupy the relation of passengers.[216]

[215] West Chicago St. Ry. Co. v. Craig, 57 Ill. App. 411; Louisville & P. R. Co. v. Smith, 2 Duv. (Ky.) 556; Baltimore & Y. Turnpike Road v. Leonhardt, 66 Md. 70; Baltimore City Passenger Ry. Co. v. Nugent, 86 Md. 349; Huelsenkamp v. Citizens' Ry. Co., 37 Mo. 537; Gilson v. Jackson County Horse Ry. Co., 76 Mo. 282; O'Connell v. St. Louis Cable & W. Ry. Co., 106 Mo. 482; Hite v. Metropolitan St. Ry. Co., 130 Mo. 132; Thompson v. Metropolitan St. Ry. Co., 140 Mo. 125; City Ry. Co. v. Lee, 50 N. J. Law, 435; Stierle v. Union Ry. Co., 156 N. Y. 70.

[216] Metropolitan R. Co. v. Falvey, 5 App. D. C. 176; Bosqui v. Sutro R. Co., 131 Cal. 390; Holly v. Atlanta St. R. Co., 61 Ga. 215; Macon Consolidated St. R. Co. v. Barnes, 113 Ga. 212; West Chicago

In Topeka City Ry. Co. v. Higgs,[217] the court held that a street railway company must exercise all possible skill,

St. R. Co. v. Johnson, 180 Ill. 285; West Chicago St. R. Co. v. Kromshinsky, 185 Ill. 92; Chicago City Ry. Co. v. Engel, 35 Ill. App. 490; West Chicago St. Ry. Co. v. Craig, 57 Ill. App. 411; West Chicago St. R. Co. v. Nash, 64 Ill. App. 548; Citizens' St. Ry. Co. v. Twiname, 111 Ind. 587; Prothero v. Citizens' St. Ry. Co., 134 Ind. 431; Hammond, W. & E. C. Electric Ry. Co. v. Spyzchalski, 17 Ind. App. 7; Douglass v. Sioux City Ry. Co., 91 Iowa, 94; Topeka City Ry. Co. v. Higgs, 38 Kan. 375; Louisville City Ry. Co. v. Weams, 80 Ky. 420; Louisville Ry. Co. v. Park, 96 Ky. 580; Central Passenger Ry. Co. v. Bishop, 8 Ky. Law Rep. 781; Louisville & P. R. Co. v. Smith, 2 Duv. (Ky.) 556; Baltimore & Y. Turnpike Road v. Leonhardt, 66 Md. 70; Baltimore City Passenger Ry. Co. v. Nugent, 86 Md. 349; Watson v. St. Paul City Ry. Co., 42 Minn. 46; Hamilton v. Great Falls St. Ry. Co., 17 Mont. 334; Huelsenkamp v. Citizens' Ry. Co., 37 Mo. 537; Gilson v. Jackson County Horse Ry. Co., 76 Mo. 282; O'Connell v. St. Louis Cable & W. Ry. Co., 106 Mo. 482; Willmott v. Corrigan Consolidated St. Ry. Co., 106 Mo. 535; Jackson v. Grand Ave. Ry. Co., 118 Mo. 199; Hite v. Metropolitan St. Ry. Co., 130 Mo. 132; Haderlein v. St. Louis R. Co., 3 Mo. App. 601; Wilkerson v. Corrigan Consolidated St. Ry. Co., 26 Mo. App. 144; Jacquin v. Grand Ave. Cable Co., 57 Mo. App. 320; Powers v. Union Ry. Co., 60 Mo. App. 481; Parker v. Metropolitan St. Ry. Co., 69 Mo. App. 54; Posch v. Southern Electric R. Co., 76 Mo. App. 601; Freeman v. Metropolitan St. Ry. Co., 95 Mo. App. 94; East Omaha St. Ry. Co. v. Godola, 50 Neb. 906; Lincoln St. Ry. Co. v. McClellan, 54 Neb. 672; City Ry. Co. v. Lee, 50 N. J. Law, 435; Consolidated Traction Co. v. Thalheimer, 59 N. J. Law, 474; Whalen v. Consolidated Traction Co., 61 N. J. Law, 606; Hansen v. North Jersey St. Ry. Co., 64 N. J. Law, 686; Maverick v. Eighth Ave. R. Co., 36 N. Y. 378; Coddington v. Brooklyn Crosstown R. Co., 102 N. Y. 66; Lansing v. Coney Island & B. R. Co., 16 App. Div. (N. Y.) 146; Poulsen v. Nassau Electric R. Co., 18 App. Div. (N. Y.) 221; Koehne v. New York & Q. C. Ry. Co., 32 App. Div. (N. Y.) 419, affirmed 165 N. Y. 603; Keegan v. Third Ave. R. Co., 34 App. Div. (N. Y.) 297, affirmed 165 N. Y. 622; Schuler v. Third Ave. R. Co., 1 Misc.

[217] 38 Kan. 375.

foresight, and care in the running of its cars, and that "all possible skill and care" meant every reasonable precaution in the management and operation of the cars to prevent injuries to passengers, and meant good tracks, safe cars, experienced drivers, careful management, and judicious operation in every respect. The utmost care of prudent men must be exercised in approaching a place of danger, as, for instance, guiding a car through a mob.[217a]

In New York an exception appears to have been made to this general rule. In Stierle v. Union Ry. Co.[218]—an action to recover for the negligence of a driver in switching his car from one track to another—it was held that the general rule as to a high degree of care did not apply, and that the driver was bound to use only the care of the ordinarily prudent man. On a rehearing of the case[219] the court said that they did not intend to change the general rule, but merely that that rule was not applicable under the circumstances of this particular case. In Merrill v. Metropolitan St. Ry. Co.,[220] where

Rep. (N. Y.) 351; Hadencamp v. Second Ave. R. Co., 31 N. Y. Super. Ct. 490; Dlabola v. Manhattan Ry. Co., 8 N. Y. Supp. 334; Dussell v. Akron St. R. Co., 10 Ohio S. & C. P. Dec. 631; Brooklyn St. R. Co. v. Kelley, 6 Ohio Cir. Ct. R. 155; Philadelphia & R. R. Co. v. Boyer, 97 Pa. 91; Smedley v. Hestonville, M. & F. P. Ry. Co., 184 Pa. 620; People's Passenger Ry. Co. v. Weiller, 17 Wkly. Notes Cas. (Pa.) 306; Elliott v. Newport St. Ry. Co., 18 R. I. 707; Citizens' Ry. Co. v. Craig (Tex. Civ. App.) 69 S. W. 239; Dallas Consolidated Traction Ry. Co. v. Randolph, 8 Tex. Civ. App. 213; Reynolds v. Richmond & M. Ry. Co., 92 Va. 400; Payne v. Spokane St. Ry. Co., 15 Wash. 522; Heucke v. Milwaukee City Ry. Co., 69 Wis. 401.

217a Bosworth v. Union R. Co. (R. I.) 55 Atl. 490.

218 156 N. Y. 70.

219 156 N. Y. 684.

220 73 App. Div. (N. Y.) 401.

a passenger was injured by a jolt while rounding a curve, the court held, on the authority of the Stierle Case, that reasonable care under the circumstances was the measure of the duty of the defendant's servants; and the Stierle Case was approved in Regensburg v. Nassau Electric R. Co.,[221] where the court charged that a motorman must use a very high degree of care to avoid a runaway, but not the very highest degree of care; and was also approved in Conway v. Brooklyn Heights R. Co.[222]

Where a street railway company used hacks to carry its passengers from its terminus, they were held to the same high degree of care required of common carriers.[223]

Children and infirm or sick passengers are entitled to still greater care;[224] but those in charge of the car must have a reasonable opportunity of knowing of their infirmity.[225]

### § 49. Running cars on Sunday.

The court will not say that running street cars on Sunday in and near cities is not a work of necessity, and that it is not lawful to so run them.[226] A passenger riding in a street car on Sunday for pleasure may maintain an action for the negligence of the company.[227]

In Stanton v. Metropolitan R. Co.[228] it was held that a

[221] 58 App. Div. (N. Y.) 566.

[222] 81 N. Y. Supp. 878.

[223] Bonce v. Dubuque St. Ry. Co., 53 Iowa, 278.

[224] Newark & S. O. R. Co. v. McCann, 58 N. J. Law, 642; Sheridan v. Brooklyn City & N. R. Co., 36 N. Y. 39.

[225] Jacksonville St. Ry. Co. v. Chappell, 21 Fla. 175.

[226] Augusta & S. R. Co. v. Renz, 55 Ga. 126.

[227] Horton v. Norwalk Tramway Co., 66 Conn. 272; Knowlton v. Milwaukee City Ry. Co., 59 Wis. 278.

[228] 14 Allen (Mass.) 485. (See R. L. c. 98, § 17.)

person cannot legally travel on the Lord's Day from one city to another, a distance of several miles, for the purpose of visiting a stranger, if no occasion of necessity or charity is shown for him to pay such visit, and cannot maintain an action against a street railway company to recover damages for a personal injury received by him, while so traveling in one of their cars, in consequence of their negligence.

In Doyle v. Lynn & B. R. Co.[229] it was held that one who travels from one town to another on the Lord's Day for the sole purpose of visiting a friend whom he knows to be sick, and thinks may be in need of assistance, and of rendering such assistance as on inquiry he might find to be necessary, is traveling for charity; and in an action against a railroad corporation for injuries sustained while a passenger on that day, on putting in evidence that he was traveling for the purpose above stated, he is entitled to go to the jury on the question whether he was traveling lawfully or not, although he offers no evidence of the ground of his belief that his friend was in need of assistance.

In Feital v. Middlesex R. Co.[230]—an action by a passenger on a street railway for personal injuries—it was held that the facts that the exercises of a spiritualist camp meeting included a show to which an admittance fee was charged, and that some of the speakers declared that they would throw away their Bibles in their search after truth, are not conclusive that a person who traveled on the Lord's Day to attend the meeting did so unlawfully, and the question whether he traveled except from necessity or charity is for the jury.

[229] 118 Mass. 195.
[230] 109 Mass. 398.

## § 49. Crowding cars.

It is not negligence, as a matter of law, to crowd street cars or the platforms of street cars, but the question is generally left to the jury.[231] In Meesel v. Lynn & B. R. Co.[232] the court said: "The seats inside the car are not the only places where the managers of the train expect passengers to remain; but it is notorious that they stop habitually to receive passengers to stand inside until the car is full, and then to stand upon the platforms till they are full, and continue to stop and receive them even after there is no place for them to stand except on the steps of the platform. Neither the officers of these corporations nor the managers of the cars nor the traveling public seem to regard this practice as hazardous, nor does experience thus far seem to require that it should be restrained upon the ground of its danger."

Where a woman with a child on her arm alighted when there was ice on the steps, and a passenger stood so that she could not get hold of the rail, the case was held to be for the jury.[233] In an action for negligent overcrowding of a car, evidence that the plaintiff stood alone on the platform, and was pushed off by passengers leaving, will not support the

231 Holloway v. Pasadena & P. Ry. Co., 130 Cal. 177; Chicago City Ry. Co. v. Young, 62 Ill. 238; Burns v. Boston El. Ry. Co. (Mass.) 66 N. E. 418; Brusch v. St. Paul City Ry. Co., 52 Minn. 512; Pray v. Omaha St. Ry. Co., 44 Neb. 167; East Omaha St. Ry. Co. v. Godola, 50 Neb. 906; Lehr v. Steinway & H. P. R. Co., 118 N. Y. 556; Graham v. Manhattan Ry. Co., 149 N. Y. 336; Cattano v. Metropolitan St. Ry. Co., 173 N. Y. 565; Mt. Adams & E. P. I. Ry. Co. v. Reul, 4 Ohio Cir. Ct. R. 362; Anderson v. City & Suburban Ry. Co. (Or.) 71 Pac. 659.

232 8 Allen (Mass.) 234.

233 Neslie v. Second & Third Sts. Passenger Ry. Co., 113 Pa. 300.

action.[234] Where a passenger testified that he stood with one foot on the platform and one on the step, with articles in both hands, and that he was crowded between two men and fell from the car while it was in ordinary motion, there was held to be no evidence of negligence.[235]

It is lack of due care, as a matter of law, for a passenger to get upon the front platform on a very stormy night, when the car is too crowded for him to ride in safety;[236] and where a passenger who made his way from the car onto the crowded platform was pushed off, it was held that, even assuming negligence on the part of the company in permitting such crowding, nevertheless the passenger knew that the crowd was there, and could not recover for the injury.[237]

Where the company allows its cars to be greatly overcrowded without objection, and then runs a car so near the intersection of a switch of the main track that cars cannot pass without injury to passengers, it is gross negligence.[238] Where a passenger in a crowded car stood in the gripman's aisle, and was struck by a brake, it was held that, when a street railway company allows its cars to be crowded, they are not to be relieved from using the high degree of care required of them because a passenger lightly disobeys a rule, unless he is warned of the danger so that he appreciates it.[239] It has

234 Randall v. Frankford & S. Passenger Ry. Co., 8 Pa. Co. Ct. R. 277.

235 Barry v. Union Traction Co., 194 Pa. 576.

236 Tregear v. Dry Dock, E. B. & B. R. Co., 14 Abb. Pr. (N. S.; N. Y.) 49.

237 Chicago City R. Co. v. Considine, 50 Ill. App. 47.

238 Topeka City Ry. Co. v. Higgs, 38 Kan. 375.

239 West Chicago St. R. Co. v. Johnson, 77 Ill. App. 142, affirmed 180 Ill. 285.

been held that a street railway company must use greater care than usual when it allows its cars to become crowded.[240]

### § 50. Condition of car.

Where an electric car burst into flames, the company must explain the cause of the fire. Proof that a fuse blew out will not exempt them from the imputation of negligence, since there is usually only a flash of light when a fuse blows out.[241] A fuse burning out raises no presumption of negligence, but where there is evidence of a more serious defect, negligence is for the jury.[241a] Where a passenger became frightened at the flash of the controller, and jumped from the car, and there was evidence that the flashing was of an unusual character, that the controller was out of order, which could easily have been discovered, and the car had not been inspected before it left the station, it was held that negligence was properly submitted to the jury, and that the jury might have imputed negligence to the company from the fact that the motorman, after the flashing began, allowed the car to continue on its course until the fuse burned out.[242] Where an inspector was examining a controller which was out of order, and the car suddenly started forward, and struck a railroad train, it was held that the

240 Geddes v. Metropolitan R. Co., 103 Mass. 391; Archer v. Ft. Wayne & E. Ry. Co., 87 Mich. 101; Kinkade v. Atlantic Ave. R. Co., 9 Misc. Rep. (N. Y.) 273; Anderson v. City & Suburban Ry. Co. (Or.) 71 Pac. 659; Sandford v. Hestonville, M. & F. P. R. Co., 136 Pa. 84; McCaw v. Union Traction Co. (Pa.) 54 Atl. 893.

241 Poulsen v. Nassau Electric R. Co., 18 App. Div. (N. Y.) 221.

241a Cassady v. Old Colony St. Ry. Co. (Mass.) 68 N. E. 10.

242 Poulsen v. Nassau Electric R. Co., 30 App. Div. (N. Y.) 246.

company was negligent, and the plaintiff was not.[243] The company must use a very high degree of care in regard to such a powerful force as electricity; and where flames leaped from the controller box, and a passenger received a shock while leaving the car, this was held to be a *prima facie* case of negligence.[244] Where the controller exploded, negligence in operating the car, and negligence in the motorman's leaving his post on a crowded car, and causing a panic, were held to be for the jury.[245] Where the handles on the dashers of an electric car became charged with electricity and injured a passenger, the company was held chargeable with notice thereof.[246] Overheating of a wheel plate by friction caused by overloading a car raises a presumption of negligence.[246a]

Where a spliced cable broke eight days after it had been mended, negligence is for the jury, although there is evidence that a splice would last five or six weeks, and the employes who made it testified that the work was done thoroughly, where the defendant fails to produce the watcher who was inspecting the cable on the day of the accident.[247]

In Richmond R. & E. Co. v. Bowles[248]—a case of an accident from a broken trolley wire—it was held that electricity is an agency no less powerful and dangerous than steam, and

243 Willis v. Second Ave. Traction Co., 189 Pa. 430.

244 Leonard v. Brooklyn Heights R. Co., 57 App. Div. (N. Y.) 125.

245 Buckbee v. Third Ave. R. Co., 64 App. Div. (N. Y.) 360.

246 D'Arcy v. Westchester Electric Ry. Co., 81 N. Y. Supp. 952; Denver Tramway Co. v. Reid, 4 Colo. App. 53; Dunlay v. United Traction Co., 18 Pa. Super. Ct. 206; Burt v. Douglas County St. Ry. Co., 83 Wis. 229.

246a Powell v. Hudson Valley Ry. Co., 84 N. Y. Supp. 337.

247 Smith v. Metropolitan St. Ry. Co., 59 App. Div. (N. Y.) 60.

248 92 Va. 738.

imposes equal obligations upon those who use it; and in Baltimore City Passenger Ry. Co. v. Nugent [249] it was held that, where a passenger was injured by the breaking of a trolley wire, this was a *prima facie* case of negligence, but that the presumption could be rebutted if the accident occurred from a hidden defect, which could not reasonably have been discovered, and if competent contractors used proper material and a proper method of construction. In Louisville Ry. Co. v. Russell's Adm'r,[250] where the trolley wire broke, and a passenger was killed by coming in contact with a live wire, the question of an unavoidable accident on the ground that the trolley wire broke by reason of crystallization, which could not have been expected, was properly left to the jury.

In accidents arising from a defective brake, the question of the defendant's negligence is usually for the jury.[251] It has been held in such a case that, where an accident is caused by a thing controlled or managed by the defendant, and is such as would not have happened in the ordinary course of things if those in control had used reasonable care, this gives rise to a presumption of negligence.[252] In Sharp v. Kansas City Cable Ry. Co.[253] it was held that proof that the brake would not hold the car made out a *prima facie* case for the plaintiff, and that the company was bound to an-

249 86 Md. 349.

250 20 Ky. Law Rep. 1246.

251 Etson v. Ft. Wayne & B. I. Ry. Co., 114 Mich. 605; Feary v. Metropolitan St. Ry. Co., 162 Mo. 75; Schneider v. Second Ave. R. Co., 133 N. Y. 583; Wynn v. Central Park, N. & E. R. R. Co., 133 N. Y. 575.

252 Gilmore v. Brooklyn Heights R. Co., 6 App. Div. (N. Y.) 117.

253 114 Mo. 94.

ticipate such weather and condition of the track as might reasonably be expected. Where a driver put on the brake while a car was going down hill, it was held that, even if he used more force than was necessary, this did not authorize the submission of the question of his due care to the jury.[254] Where the plaintiff stopped to pick up a bundle on the front platform, and was hit in the head by the brake, the case was held to be for the jury.[255] Where a driver put on the brake when the car was going down hill seven miles an hour, and caused the car to give a sudden jerk, negligence was held to be for the jury.[256] Where a passenger had gone on the front platform to leave the car, and was struck by the brake, it was held that the case did not come within a statute providing that the company should not be liable for injuries occasioned to passengers while leaving the car by the front platform.[257] It is negligence to have a snap switch closed so that an air brake will not work.[257a]

A street railway company is not liable for using old cars, but it must keep them in good repair.[258] Where a drunken man broke the glass in a door, so that it was ready to fall, there was no conductor on the car, and the driver knew that the injury had been done, but did not examine into the extent of it, this was held to be negligence.[259] Where it was the custom to keep a gate on a platform nearest a parallel track closed, and it was left open, negligence was held to be for the

254 Wynn v. Central Park, N. & E. R. R. Co., 133 N. Y. 575.

255 Schuler v. Third Ave. R. Co., 1 Misc. Rep. (N. Y.) 351.

256 Murray v. Brooklyn City R. Co., 7 N. Y. Supp. 900.

257 Nissen v. Missouri R. Co., 19 Mo. App. 662.

257a McAllister v. People's Ry. Co. (Del.) 54 Atl. 743.

258 Wormsdorf v. Detroit City Ry. Co., 75 Mich. 472.

259 Allen v. Dry Dock, E. B. & B. R. Co., 2 N. Y. Supp. 738.

jury;[260] and whether a street railway company should have guards on the platforms to prevent passengers from falling off was likewise held to be a question for the jury.[261] Where a gate gave way, and the conductor, whose duty it was to see that it was fastened, knew that it could not be fastened, this was held to be sufficient evidence of negligence.[262] The fact that a passenger saw a trapdoor in a car raised and lowered again is no defense in an action for falling through the trapdoor.[263] Where a curtain rod broke while a high wind was blowing, and one end of the rod struck a passenger, the company was held not to be liable;[264] and where a passenger caught her dress on a curtain hook, and it appeared that such hooks were in use on all the company's cars, that such an accident had never happened before, and that the cars were inspected at the end of each trip, and broken hooks repaired, there was held to be no negligence.[265] Where a ring in the floor of a car rises when the car stops, this is negligence, although the ring is a customary device, and the car was built by a reputable builder.[266] Where a fire extinguisher in a car fell and injured a passenger, this was held to be *prima facie* negligence.[267] Whether failure to provide fenders or gates is negligence is a question for the jury.[268] Where a strap

[260] Adams v. Washington & G. R. Co., 9 App. D. C. 26.

[261] Archer v. Ft. Wayne & E. Ry. Co., 87 Mich. 101.

[262] Pendergast v. Union Ry. Co., 10 App. Div. (N. Y.) 207.

[263] Washington v. Spokane St. Ry. Co., 13 Wash. 9.

[264] Leyh v. Newburgh Electric Ry. Co., 41 App. Div. (N. Y.) 218.

[265] Kelly v. New York & S. B. Ry. Co., 109 N. Y. 44.

[266] Kingman v. Lynn & B. R. Co., 181 Mass. 387.

[267] Allen v. United Traction Co., 67 App. Div. (N. Y.) 363.

[268] North Chicago St. R. Co. v. Wrixon, 51 Ill. App. 307; Philadelphia City Passenger Ry. Co. v. Hassard, 75 Pa. 367; Hestonville Passenger Ry. Co. v. Connell, 88 Pa. 520; West Philadelphia Passenger Ry. Co. v. Gallagher, 108 Pa. 524.

broke, negligence was held to be for the jury.[269] Where a suspension bar broke, the presumption of negligence was held to be rebutted by proof that the bar was purchased from a reputable dealer, and was inspected daily.[269a]

## § 51. Injury by fellow passenger.

It is a general rule that those in charge of a street car must do all that they reasonably can to protect passengers against injury from their fellow passengers,[270] and whether this duty was performed or not was held to be a question for the jury, where three drunken passengers began a fight,[271] and where a passenger was injured during a fight between his fellow passengers, and it appeared that there was no conductor on the car.[272]

Where a manifestly intoxicated and quarrelsome man was allowed to ride in a street car because the driver said he was "too full" to ride on the front platform, the company is liable for an unprovoked assault upon a passenger;[273] and the company was held negligent where its employes allowed a drunk and disorderly man, who had been ejected once, to get upon the car again, and he struck and killed another passenger.[274] On the other hand, it has been held that the company is not liable for conduct of its passengers

269 Grotsch v. Steinway Ry. Co., 19 App. Div. (N. Y.) 130.

269a Murray v. Pawtuxet Valley St. Ry. Co. (R. I.) 55 Atl. 491.

270 Holly v. Atlanta St. R. Co., 61 Ga. 215; Cross v. Detroit Citizens' St. Ry. Co., 120 Mich. 137; Putnam v. Broadway & S. A. R. Co., 55 N. Y. 108; Randall v. Frankford, S. & P. C. P. R. Co., 139 Pa. 464.

271 Cross v. Detroit Citizens' St. Ry. Co., 120 Mich. 137.

272 Holly v. Atlanta St. R. Co., 61 Ga. 215.

273 Hendricks v. Sixth Ave. R. Co., 44 N. Y. Super. Ct. 8.

274 United R. & E. Co. v. State, 93 Md. 619.

unless it was unusual and disorderly, and could have been prevented by those in charge of the car;[275] and there was held to be no evidence of negligence where an intoxicated passenger remained quiet for some time, and then suddenly killed a fellow passenger with a car hook.[276] In Sullivan v. Jefferson Ave. Ry. Co.,[277] where a fellow passenger threw a lighted match on plaintiff's dress, and the driver stopped the car, but was unable to render any assistance, it was held that the defendant was not liable. Where a child was compelled to ride on the platform of a crowded car, and was thrown off by the carelessness of a fellow passenger, the company was nevertheless held responsible.[278] In Lott v. New Orleans City & L. R. Co.,[279] where some boys were allowed to ride free, and one pushed another off, it was held that the company was not liable.

Where a crowd was invited to a park by a street railway company, and collected to take a car, with no one to check their movements, negligence was held to be for the jury.[280] Where a passenger was pushed off the front platform of a crowded car by his fellow passengers, it was held that he was not guilty of lack of due care, and that negligence was for the jury.[281] Where a company continued to run its cars during a strike, and a passenger was injured by a stone thrown by a striker, the company was held not liable.[282]

[275] Randall v. Frankford, S. & P. C. P. R. Co., 139 Pa. 464.

[276] Putnam v. Broadway & S. A. R. Co., 55 N. Y. 108.

[277] 133 Mo. 1.

[278] Sheridan v. Brooklyn City & N. R. Co., 36 N. Y. 39.

[279] 37 La. Ann. 337.

[280] Muhlhause v. Monongahela St. Ry. Co., 201 Pa. 237.

[281] Merwin v. Manhattan Ry. Co., 48 Hun (N. Y.) 608.

[282] Fewings v. Mendenhall (Minn.) 93 N. W. 127.

## § 52. Derailment.

It is almost universally held that the derailment of a street car furnishes *prima facie* evidence of negligence;[283] and this is so, notwithstanding the use of a high degree of care and skill on the part of the defendant and its agents.[284]

In Elgin City Ry. Co. v. Wilson[285] the court said: "The presumption is that the overturning of the car resulted from the defective condition of the track or the mismanagement of the car, or both combined, and the *onus* was upon the company to show that the accident resulted from a cause for which it was not responsible."

In Bergen County Traction Co. v. Demarest[286] the court said: "In the ordinary operation of the defendant's railroad, its cars would not have left the rails. It is a matter of common knowledge that the roadbed of a street railroad is so built, and the cars so constructed, that, when there is no defect in either, and the cars are run with due care, the

283 Bosqui v. Sutro R. Co., 131 Cal. 390; Bassett v. Los Angeles Traction Co., 133 Cal. xiv, 65 Pac. 470; Electric Ry. Co. v. Carson, 98 Ga. 652; Elgin City Ry. Co. v. Wilson, 56 Ill. App. 364; Calumet Electric St. Ry. Co. v. Jennings, 83 Ill. App. 612; Louisville & P. R. Co. v. Smith, 2 Duv. (Ky.) 556; Feital v. Middlesex R. Co., 109 Mass. 398; Harriman v. Reading & L. St. Ry. Co., 173 Mass. 28; Bishop v. St. Paul City Ry. Co., 48 Minn. 26; Haderlein v. St. Louis R. Co., 3 Mo. App. 601; Wilkerson v. Corrigan Consolidated St. Ry. Co., 26 Mo. App. 144; Spellman v. Lincoln Rapid Transit Co., 36 Neb. 890; Bergen County Traction Co. v. Demarest, 62 N. J. Law, 755; Dusenbury v. North Hudson County Ry. Co., 66 N. J. Law, 44; Pollock v. Brooklyn & C. T. R. Co., 15 N. Y. Supp. 189; Cincinnati St. Ry. Co. v. Kelsey, 2 Ohio Dec. 440; Reading City Passenger Ry. Co. v. Eckert, 1 Sup. Ct. Dig. (Pa.) 55.

284 Cincinnati St. Ry. Co. v. Kelsey, 2 Ohio Dec. 440.

285 56 Ill. App. 364.

286 62 N. J. Law, 755.

latter will remain upon the track; and consequently, proof of the derailment of a car, in the absence of evidence to the contrary, justifies the conclusion that it resulted either from improper construction, failure to keep in proper repair, or negligence in operation."

In Brooklyn St. R. Co. v. Kelley[287] the rule is less strongly stated to be that "negligence may be established by the accident itself, and the circumstances surrounding it under which it occurred, from which you may infer negligence to have been the cause of the injury."

The law in New York was at one time apparently in conflict with the weight of authority, but it seems probable that a recent decision has practically overruled the previous cases. In Hastings v. Central Crosstown R. Co.[288] the court said: "Counsel for the plaintiff insists that negligence is to be imputed to the defendant from the mere fact that the car left the track, upon the authority of Edgerton v. New York & H. R. Co.[289] and subsequent cases to the same effect; but the rule applied in that case refers altogether to steam railways, and to cases where not only the vehicles, but the tracks, are within the entire control of the defendant. It would be grossly unjust to extend that rule to street railway companies, which have not exclusive control over their tracks or the roadway, but whose tracks are daily used by thousands of other vehicles, and are placed in public streets under the control of the city authorities, and in which work is constantly being done on or under the roadways and tracks."

[287] 6 Ohio Cir. Ct. R. 155.
[288] 7 App. Div. (N. Y.) 312.
[289] 39 N. Y. 227.

In Stevenson v. Second Ave. R. Co. [290] the court explained that the Hastings Case did not decide that the mere derailment of a street car is not sufficient proof *prima facie* of negligence, and that what the court said merely had reference to the claim made by counsel that the Edgerton Case was in point, and was merely meant to illustrate that the rule applicable to steam railroads should not in every case, and as a matter of law, be applied to street railroads; but in Hollahan v. Metropolitan St. Ry. Co.[291] the court apparently followed the Hastings Case, and in Ramson v. Metropolitan St. R. Co.[292] the court, while holding that derailment from a collision with a barrel justified an inference of negligence, cited the Stevenson Case as authority for the proposition that mere derailment is not enough to justify such inference. In Adams v. Union Ry. Co.[292a] the court went over all the cases, and decided that, whatever the rule may be in cases of horse cars, in cases of cars moved by electricity or mechanical power derailment does raise a presumption of negligence, as in the case of steam railroads, distinguishing the previous cases on the ground that they were cases of horse cars.

Proof of a latent defect in a wheel is not necessarily a defense where the jury might have found the derailment occurred from the unlawful speed of the car.[293] Where the company was negligent, and the car ran off the tracks, riding upon the platform was held not to be the proximate cause.[294]

290 35 App. Div. (N. Y.) 474.

291 73 App. Div. (N. Y.) 164.

292 78 App. Div. (N. Y.) 101.

292a 80 App. Div. (N. Y.) 136.

293 Johnsen v. Oakland, S. L. & H. Electric Ry. Co., 127 Cal. 608.

294 Vail v. Cincinnati Inclined Plane Ry. Co., 7 Ohio Circ. Dec. 28.

Where a car going in the wrong direction hit a frog, and ran off the track, there was held to be no negligence in the construction of the tracks, but negligence in driving too fast was for the jury.[295] Evidence of high speed and the presence of crushed rock on the track justifies the jury in finding negligence.[295a]

The company must adopt and use all approved appliances which are in general use, and necessary for the safety of passengers, and need not provide "all known and approved machinery necessary to protect passengers."[296]

Any presumption of negligence is rebutted by testimony that there was a perfect track, car, and harness in good repair, gentle horses, and a skillful driver, alert and at his post, but that a man with a bundle jumped suddenly from an express wagon, and frightened the horses.[297] Whether a stone wholly or partly covered with snow and slush, and lying between the tracks, could have been discovered in time to prevent derailment, is for the jury.[298] Where the horses on a car became frightened, and the car was derailed, negligence was held to be for the jury.[298a] Running a car down hill at high speed when there is a curve and a ravine at the bottom is negligence.[298b]

[295] White v. Milwaukee City Ry. Co., 61 Wis. 536.

[295a] Smith v. Milwaukee Elec. Ry. & Light Co. (Wis.) 96 N. W. 823.

[296] Witsell v. West Asheville & S. S. Ry. Co., 120 N. C. 557.

[297] Perry v. Malarin, 107 Cal. 363.

[298] Dusenbury v. North Hudson County Ry. Co., 66 N. J. Law, 44.

[298a] Doolin v. Omnibus Cable Co. (Cal.) 73 Pac. 1060.

[298b] South Covington & C. St. Ry. Co. v. Constans (Ky.) 74 S. W. 705.

The company is responsible for a latent defect discoverable during manufacture, but not after the car came into their hands.[299]

### § 53. Collision between two street cars.

A collision on the same track between two street cars of the same line establishes a *prima facie* case of negligence;[300] and the rule is the same where a car collided with another, which was being shifted from one track to another.[301] Where a collision occurs between cars of different lines, the presumption of negligence does not arise in respect to the car on which the plaintiff is not a passenger;[302] for the company owning the car on which the plaintiff is a passenger is held to a high degree of care, while the owners of the other car owe to the plaintiff only the duty of ordinary care.[303] The presumption of negligence does arise, however, against the owner of the car on which the plaintiff is a passenger, as in the case of cars of the same line.[304]

Numerous rulings have been made as to the right of way of cars at the intersection of the tracks. Where an electric

[299] Siemsen v. Oakland, S. L. & H. Electric Ry. Co., 134 Cal. 494.

[300] Carter v. Kansas City Cable Ry. Co., 42 Fed. 37; North Chicago St. Ry. Co. v. Cotton, 140 Ill. 486; North Chicago St. Ry. Co. v. Cotton, 41 Ill. App. 311; North Chicago St. R. Co. v. Boyd, 57 Ill. App. 535; Smith v. St. Paul City Ry. Co., 32 Minn. 1; Hamilton v. Great Falls St. Ry. Co., 17 Mont. 334; Anderson v. Brooklyn Heights R. Co., 32 App. Div. (N. Y.) 266; Madara v. Shamokin & M. C. Electric Ry. Co., 192 Pa. 542; Palmer v. Warren St. Ry. Co. (Pa.) 56 Atl. 49.

[301] Kay v. Metropolitan St. Ry. Co., 29 App. Div. (N. Y.) 466.

[302] Tompkins v. Clay St. R. Co., 66 Cal. 163; Falke v. Third Ave. R. Co., 38 App. Div. (N. Y.) 49.

[303] O'Rourke v. Lindell Ry. Co., 142 Mo. 342.

[304] Osgood v. Los Angeles Traction Co., 137 Cal. 280.

car and a cable car collided at a crossing, and it appeared that the companies jointly employed a flagman to direct the crossing of the cars by signals, it was held error to instruct the jury that if the flagman signaled the cable car to come forward, it had the right to proceed, although the gripman could see that the electric car was approaching the crossing.[305] In Metropolitan R. Co. v. Hammett[306] it was held that, where two street car lines intersect, the last car should stop, and let the other pass; that an electric car has no right of way over a horse car, and that the driver of the horse car has a right to suppose that the electric car is moving at lawful speed, and will look out for him if he gets to the crossing first. Even though one car, from its position prior to the collision, has the right of way, it must nevertheless sacrifice it to avoid the danger of a collision.[307] A carrier of passengers has no right to experiment at the risk of those whom he carries,[308] and great care is required of street railway companies in the operation of parallel lines within a few feet of each other.[309]

In Wynne v. Atlantic Ave. R. Co.,[310] where a passenger was injured in a collision, there was held to be sufficient evidence of negligence on the part of the driver of the car colliding with that on which he was a passenger.

305 Taylor v. Grand Ave. Ry. Co., 137 Mo. 363.

306 13 App. D. C. 370.

307 Loudoun v. Eighth Ave. R. Co., 16 App. Div. (N. Y.) 152; Zimmer v. Third Ave. R. Co., 36 App. Div. (N. Y.) 265.

308 Barrett v. Third Ave. R. Co., 45 N. Y. 628.

309 West Chicago St. R. Co. v. Yund, 68 Ill. App. 609.

310 14 Misc. Rep. (N. Y.) 394.

In Snediker v. Nassau Electric R. Co.,[311] where a car collided with a car which had just come into collision with a wagon, and there was evidence that the motorman did all in his power to avoid a collision, the jury were held to be justified in finding no negligence.

In Blanchette v. Holyoke St. Ry. Co.,[312] where there were frequent curves, and a conductor, when his trolley came off, gave no warning to a car which he knew was approaching from the rear, there was held to be sufficient evidence of negligence.

A passenger in sudden peril is not held to the usual standard of care; but if a passenger acts rashly, thinking there is danger when there is none, he cannot recover.[313] In the case of a collision it was held that the fact that a passenger rode on the rear platform with his hand over the dasher did not contribute to the injury as a matter of law;[314] and in Thirteenth & F. St. Passenger Ry. v. Boudrou[315] it was held that the fact that a passenger was riding on the rear platform when struck by the pole of another car was a condition, and not the cause of the injury. The negligence of a driver of a street car cannot be imputed to a passenger.[316]

311 41 App. Div. (N. Y.) 628.

312 175 Mass. 51.

313 Birmingham R. & E. Co. v. Butler, 135 Ala. 388; Quinn v. Shamokin & M. C. Electric Ry. Co., 7 Pa. Super. Ct. 19; Palmer v. Warren St. Ry. Co. (Pa.) 56 Atl. 49; Wade v. Columbia Electric St. Ry. L. & P. Co., 51 S. C. 296.

314 Seigel v. Eisen, 41 Cal. 109.

315 92 Pa. 475.

316 Newport St. R. Co. v. Johnson, 2 Ky. Law Rep. 225; Taylor v. Grand Ave. Ry. Co., 137 Mo. 363; Kuttner v. Lindell Ry. Co., 29 Mo. App. 502.

Evidence that the driver of a street car was driving rapidly on a foggy morning, and heard the bell of another car twenty-five or thirty feet from the street crossing, warrants the submission of negligence to the jury.[317] A street car company is negligent where the trolley came off, the lights went out, the motorman and conductor did not look for an approaching car, and a collision ensued.[318]

If a street car company used all reasonable care in the manufacture and inspection of the machinery of its cars, it is not liable for a latent defect in a grip.[319]

In a number of cases negligence has been held to be a question for the jury.[320]

Where a collision results from the negligence of both companies, they can be sued jointly.[321]

## § 54. Collision between street car and wagon.

Where a team and a car each tried to reach a bridge ahead of the other, the fact that a city ordinance gave the car the right of way as against a private team is no excuse for the company, since it was its duty to avoid a collision, and then to seek a remedy for violation of the ordinance.[322]

317 Hourney v. Brooklyn City R. Co., 7 N. Y. Supp. 602.

318 Kehoe v. Allentown & L. V. Traction Co., 187 Pa. 474.

319 Carter v. Kansas City Cable Ry. Co., 42 Fed. 37.

320 Kuttner v. Lindell Ry. Co., 29 Mo. App. 502; Schneider v. Second Ave. R. Co., 59 N. Y. Super. Ct. 536; Goorin v. Allegheny Traction Co., 179 Pa. 327; Quinn v. Shamokin & M. C. Electric Ry. Co., 7 Pa. Super. Ct. 19.

321 Tompkins v. Clay St. R. Co., 66 Cal. 163; West Chicago St. R. Co. v. Piper, 165 Ill. 325; West Chicago St. R. Co. v. Yund, 68 Ill. App. 609; Barrett v. Third Ave. R. Co., 45 N. Y. 628; Schneider v. Second Ave. R. Co., 59 N. Y. Super. Ct. 536.

322 Rend v. Chicago West Div. Ry. Co., 8 Ill. App. 517.

A hook and ladder on the way to a fire has a right of way over a street car, and a collision establishes a *prima facie* case of negligence on the part of the company.[323] It has been held that the mere fact of a collision between a street car and a wagon raises no presumption of negligence against the company.[324]

The negligence of the driver of a car cannot be imputed to a passenger.[325] Lack of due care cannot be imputed to a passenger because he assumes an attitude to which the construction of the car invites him, and it is not his duty to look out for collisions with passing teams.[326] A passenger placed in sudden peril is not held to the usual standard of care.[327]

It is well settled that a gripman or a motorman must do all that he reasonably can to avoid collision,[328] and a gripman is liable not only for what he saw and heard, but for what he should have seen and heard.[329] Where a street car was being driven at unlawful speed, and was struck by the pole of a truck, which penetrated the front of the car, there was held to be evidence of negligence;[330] and where a passenger on a cable car whose curtains were drawn down

323 Olsen v. Citizens' Ry. Co., 152 Mo. 426.

324 Chicago City Ry. Co. v. Rood, 163 Ill. 477; Federal St. & P. V. Ry. Co. v. Gibson, 96 Pa. 83.

325 Transfer Co. v. Kelly, 36 Ohio St. 86.

326 Chicago City Ry. Co. v. Rood, 62 Ill. App. 550.

327 West Chicago St. R. Co. v. McNulty, 166 Ill. 203; Wanzer v. Chippewa Valley Electric R. Co., 108 Wis. 319.

328 West Chicago St. R. Co. v. Williams, 87 Ill. App. 548; Memphis St. R. Co. v. Norris, 108 Tenn. 632; Sears v. Seattle Consol. St. Ry. Co., 6 Wash. 227.

329 Parker v. Metropolitan St. Ry. Co., 69 Mo. App. 54.

330 Hill v. Ninth Ave. R. Co., 109 N. Y. 239.

to keep out the rain was injured by the shaft of a wagon coming into the car, the negligence of the gripman was held to be for the jury;[331] but where the driver of a wagon suddenly turned, so that projecting lumber went through a window and injured the plaintiff, there was held to be no negligence, even assuming unusual speed.[332] Where a trunk fell from a truck and injured a passenger, negligence was held to be for the jury.[333]

In a number of cases negligence was held to be for the jury.[334] The negligence of a third person will not excuse the company,[335] and the company is not necessarily excused because of a wagon striking a car instead of a car striking a wagon.[336] The company was held, in West Chicago St. R. Co. v. Tuerk,[337] not to be entitled to an instruction that failure to ring a gong was not negligence as a matter of law.

331 Potts v. Chicago City Ry. Co., 33 Fed. 610.

332 Alexander v. Rochester City & B. R. Co., 128 N. Y. 13.

333 Suse v. Metropolitan St. Ry. Co., 80 App. Div. (N. Y.) 24.

334 Mt. Adams & E. P. I. Ry. Co. v. Lowery, 74 Fed. 463; Cook v. Clay St. Hill R. Co., 60 Cal. 604; Chicago City Ry. Co. v. Anderson, 80 Ill. App. 71; West Chicago St. R. Co. v. Carr, 170 Ill. 478; Watkins v. Atlantic Ave. R. Co., 20 Hun (N. Y.) 237; Seidlinger v. Brooklyn City R. Co., 28 Hun (N. Y.) 503; Hurley v. New York & B. Brew. Co., 13 App. Div. (N. Y.) 167; Coulahan v. Metropolitan St. Ry. Co., 28 App. Div. (N. Y.) 394; Fox v. Brooklyn City R. Co., 7 Misc. Rep. (N. Y.) 285; Devlin v. Atlantic Ave. R. Co., 57 Hun (N. Y.) 591; Kreuzen v. Forty-Second St., M. & St. N. Ave. R. Co., 13 N. Y. Supp. 588; Heucke v. Milwaukee City Ry. Co., 69 Wis. 401; Wanzer v. Chippewa Valley Electric R. Co., 108 Wis. 319.

335 West Chicago St. R. Co. v. Tuerk, 90 Ill. App. 105.

336 Keegan v. Third Ave. R. Co., 34 App. Div. (N. Y.) 297.

337 193 Ill. 385.

Where a motorman did all in his power to avoid a sudden collision, there was held to be no negligence.[338] In Regensburg v. Nassau Electric R. Co.[339] it was held that a motorman must use a very high degree of care to avoid a collision with a runaway. Where a conductor injured a passenger to avoid a suddenly threatened collision, it was held that, as he was confronted with a sudden emergency, there was no negligence.[340]

## § 55. Collision between street car and steam railroad.

The negligence of the driver of a car cannot be imputed to a passenger.[341] A person placed in sudden peril is not held to the usual standard of care;[342] and where the gripman of a car tried to cross ahead of a railroad train, and a passenger jumped to avoid injury, the question of proximate cause was held to be for the jury.[343] A passenger on a street car approaching a railroad crossing is under no obligation to look and listen for an approaching locomotive, and to jump off the car in fear of a collision.[344]

338 Cleveland City Ry. Co. v. Osborn, 66 Ohio St. 45.

339 58 App. Div. (N. Y.) 566.

340 Kantrowitz v. Metropolitan St. Ry. Co., 63 App. Div. (N. Y.) 65.

341 Georgia Pac. Ry. Co. v. Hughes, 87 Ala. 610; Railway Co. v. Harrell, 58 Ark. 454; Woodley v. Baltimore & P. R. Co., 19 D. C. 542; Holzab v. New Orleans & C. R. Co., 38 La. Ann. 185; Bennett v. New Jersey R. & T. Co., 36 N. J. Law, 225; Downey v. Philadelphia Traction Co., 14 Pa. Co. Ct. R. 251.

342 Selma St. & Suburban Ry. Co. v. Owen, 132 Ala. 420; Shankenbery v. Metropolitan St. Ry. Co., 46 Fed. 177; Kleiber v. People's Ry. Co., 107 Mo. 240.

343 Bischoff v. People's Ry. Co., 121 Mo. 216; Twomley v. Central Park, N. & E. R. R. Co., 69 N. Y. 158; Robson v. Nassau Electric R. Co., 80 App. Div. (N. Y.) 301.

344 O'Toole v. Pittsburgh & L. E. R. Co., 158 Pa. 99.

A collision between a street car and a steam railroad is held to raise a presumption of negligence against the street railroad company,[345] but not against the steam railroad.[346]

Where the view of the crossing is obstructed, it is the duty of the driver to stop his car and go ahead, when there is no conductor on board.[347] The direction of a flagman at a crossing is not enough if the motorman of an electric car should have suspected danger; and where a statute provided that a street car should stop before crossing a steam railroad track, and that some one should go ahead and see that the track was clear, the fact that the gates were not down, and that a watchman signaled the car to come ahead, will not excuse the company for not sending a man ahead.[348] It is negligence for the driver of a street car not to stop before crossing a steam railroad track, as required by ordinance,[349] and not to look and listen before crossing.[350] Where the driver of a horse car saw a steam railroad train approaching at a crossing, but attempted to cross, and was caught between the gates, there was held to be no negligence on the part of the company.[351] The company is not liable where a motorman attempts to cross in front of a steam rail-

345 Railway Co. v. Harrell, 58 Ark. 454; West Chicago St. R. Co. v. Martin, 154 Ill. 523; Chicago City Ry. Co. v. Engel, 35 Ill. App. 490; Central Passenger Ry. Co. v. Kuhn, 86 Ky. 578; Central Passenger Ry. Co. v. Bishop, 9 Ky. Law Rep. 348; People's Passenger Ry. Co. v. Weiller, 17 Wkly. Notes Cas. (Pa.) 306.

346 Railway Co. v. Harrell, 58 Ark. 454.

347 Central Passenger Ry. Co. v. Kuhn, 86 Ky. 578.

348 Philadelphia & R. R. Co. v. Boyer, 97 Pa. 91.

349 Cincinnati St. Ry. Co. v. Murray, 53 Ohio St. 570.

350 Selma St. & Suburban Ry. Co. v. Owen, 132 Ala. 420.

351 Washington & G. R. Co. v. Hickey, 166 U. S. 521.

road train at a crossing, if there would have been no danger except for the unforeseen obstruction of the car by a wagon.[352] The company is not liable for injuries caused by a sudden lurch of the car, when the motorman was doing all in his power to avoid a collision.[353] The company was held liable where there was a steep grade near a crossing, and there was only a motorman in charge of the car.[354]

If a street car and a steam railroad are both negligent, they can be sued jointly.[355] In Schneider v. Second Ave. R. Co.,[356] negligence was held to be for the jury. The fact that the driver of a street car has been ordered to obey the signals of the flagman at the crossing, and he does so, does not make the flagman an agent of the street railroad company.[357] Whether it is negligence not to have a flagman at a crossing is a question for the jury.[358] Where a locomotive gives no signal, those in charge of an electric car have no right to assume it will stop, and thus risk the lives of the passengers by keeping on.[359]

352 Shankenbery v. Metropolitan St. Ry. Co., 46 Fed. 177.

353 Corkhill v. Camden & S. Ry. Co. (N. J. Law) 54 Atl. 522.

354 Russell v. Shreveport Belt Ry. Co., 50 La. Ann. 501; Flournoy v. Shreveport Belt Ry. Co., 50 La. Ann. 635.

355 Washington & G. R. Co. v. Hickey, 12 App. D. C. 269; Matthews v. Delaware, L. & W. R. Co., 56 N. J. Law, 34; O'Toole v. Pittsburgh & L. E. R. Co., 158 Pa. 99; Downey v. Philadelphia Traction Co., 14 Pa. Co. Ct. R. 251.

356 133 N. Y. 583.

357 Chicago Ry. Co. v. Volk, 45 Ill. 175.

358 Jacquin v. Grand Ave. Cable Co., 57 Mo. App. 320.

359 Hammond, W. & E. C. Electric Ry. Co. v. Spyzchalski, 17 Ind. App. 7.

## § 56. Jerk.

Where a passenger is injured by an unusual or extraordinary jerk, this has been held to establish a *prima facie* case of negligence on the part of the company,—as, for instance, where a cable car was stopped so suddenly that it threw a passenger from her seat, and broke the glass in the car windows;[360] where a car gave such a jerk that the plaintiff was thrown from her seat;[361] where there was an unusual movement of the car, which threw the passengers first forward and then backwards;[362] where a car was started with an unusual jerk, which threw a passenger against a car window;[363] and where the jerk was sufficient to throw off a passenger who had gone to the rear door preparatory to alighting.[364] In Dougherty v. Missouri R. Co.[365] the rule was held to be that, where the conveyance is shown to be under the control of the carrier, and an accident is such as does not happen in the ordinary course of things if those in charge use proper care, it affords reasonable evidence, in the absence of explanation, that the accident arose from want of care; and in West Chicago St. R. Co. v. Kennelly[366] the rule was more broadly stated to be that, where a passenger on a train, while exercising ordinary care for his own

360 Clow v. Pittsburgh Traction Co., 158 Pa. 410.

361 North Chicago St. R. Co. v. Schwartz, 82 Ill. App. 493; Murphy v. Coney Island & B. R. Co., 36 Hun (N. Y.) 199; Smedley v. Hestonville, M. & F. P. Ry. Co., 184 Pa. 620.

362 Dixey v. Philadelphia Traction Co., 180 Pa. 401.

363 Dougherty v. Missouri Pac. R. Co., 9 Mo. App. 478.

364 Birmingham Union Ry. Co. v. Hale, 90 Ala. 8; Consolidated Traction Co. v. Thalheimer, 59 N. J. Law, 474.

365 81 Mo. 325.

366 66 Ill. App. 244.

safety, is injured by the operation of the road, the burden of showing that the injury was not due to negligence is upon the defendant.

To establish such a *prima facie* case of negligence, however, it must appear that the jerk was an unusual or extraordinary one.[367] In Bartley v. Metropolitan St. Ry. Co.[368] the court said: "It is a matter of common knowledge, of which even the court is not ignorant, as well as a matter of physics, that the rope of a cable railroad cannot be kept taut, and that the jerks, which are common and unavoidable to such roads, are caused by a slack in the rope being taken up. In order to recover from the cable railroad, it is not enough to show that there was a jerk, but it must affirmatively appear that the jerk was an extraordinary or unusual one, or attributable to a defect in the track, an imperfection in the car or apparatus, or to a dangerous rate of speed, or to unskillful handling of the car by the gripman." Similarly, it has been held that there must be some jerk when a horse car is started, and that there is no negligence in a sudden movement of the car under these circumstances,[369] and that it is not negligence to whip the horses in starting a car, unless there is something unusual in the process.[370]

A passenger on a street car takes the risk of the usual and necessary movements of an electric car,[371] and the com-

367 Adams v. Washington & G. R. Co., 9 App. D. C. 26; Jacksonville St. Ry. Co. v. Chappell, 21 Fla. 175; Pryor v. Metropolitan St. Ry. Co., 85 Mo. App. 367.

368 148 Mo. 124.

369 Hayes v. Forty-Second St. & G. St. Ferry R. Co., 97 N. Y. 259.

370 Rochat v. North Hudson County Ry. Co., 49 N. J. Law, 445.

371 Byron v. Lynn & B. R. Co., 177 Mass. 303; Timms v. Old Colony St. Ry. Co. (Mass.) 66 N. E. 797; Bruce v. Brooklyn Heights R.

pany is not liable for an injury to a passenger on an electric car while rounding a curve, unless the speed is excessive, and more power is used than necessary.[372] The fact that a passenger was so violently twisted as to be injured does not of itself show an excessive use of electric power;[373] and the mere fact that a passenger is injured by another passenger being thrown upon him as the car rounds a curve is not enough to justify a recovery.[374] In the case of a cable car there was held to be no negligence where a passenger was injured by a jerk which was a necessary incident in rounding a curve because of the slack of the rope.[375] Where a street car stops suddenly for some unknown reason, this raises no presumption of negligence;[376] and where a passenger was jerked from a car and run over, it was held that even if the conductor was negligent, this was not the proximate cause of the injury.[377]

Where the driver was the only person in charge of a car, and he left the platform to collect fares, and the horses started suddenly, and jerked a boy of ten off the front platform, this was held to be the grossest negligence.[378] The rate of speed of a car is immaterial where it is acknowledged

Co., 68 App. Div. (N. Y.) 242; Nies v. Brooklyn Heights R. Co., 68 App. Div. (N. Y.) 259.

372 Brennan v. Brooklyn Heights R. Co., 12 Misc. Rep. (N. Y.) 570; Zimmer v. Fox River Valley Electric Ry. Co. (Wis.) 95 N. W. 957.

373 Ayers v. Rochester Ry. Co., 156 N. Y. 104.

374 Merrill v. Metropolitan St. Ry. Co., 73 App. Div. (N. Y.) 401.

375 Hite v. Metropolitan St. Ry. Co., 130 Mo. 132.

376 Hoffman v. Third Ave. R. Co., 45 App. Div. (N. Y.) 586.

377 South Side Passenger Ry. Co. v. Trich, 117 Pa. 390.

378 Saare v. Union Ry. Co., 20 Mo. App. 211.

to be improper;[379] and if a method of starting a street car is in fact unsafe, the custom of the company in starting their cars, or what they think is a reasonably safe method in such starting, will not constitute a defense.[380]

There have been numerous cases where the negligence of the company in causing the car to give a sudden jerk has been held to be for the jury. Such cases are where the jerk is due to the management of the brake,[381] where the car strikes a switch,[382] where there is something unusual about the method of starting, as, for instance, where a horse plunged under the blows of the whip,[383] where a team of eight mules was employed to start a balky horse,[384] and where the jerk was such as to disturb the equilibrium of the passengers.[385]

## § 57. Speed of car.

There has been held to be sufficient evidence of negligence to go to the jury in the following cases: Where there was

379 Gidionsen v. Union Depot R. Co., 129 Mo. 392.

380 Dickert v. Salt Lake City R. Co., 20 Utah, 394.

381 Etson v. Ft. Wayne & B. I. Ry. Co., 114 Mich. 605; Bradley v. Second Ave. R. Co., 34 App. Div. (N. Y.) 284; Murray v. Brooklyn City R. Co., 7 N. Y. Supp. 900; Medler v. Atlantic Ave. R. Co., 12 N. Y. Supp. 930.

382 Holloway v. Pasadena & P. Ry. Co., 130 Cal. 177; Sweetland v. Lynn & B. R. Co., 177 Mass. 574; Seelig v. Metropolitan St. Ry. Co., 18 Misc. Rep. (N. Y.) 383.

383 Eberhardt v. Metropolitan St. Ry. Co., 69 App. Div. (N. Y.) 560; Nolan v. Brooklyn City & N. R. Co., 87 N. Y. 63.

384 Continental Passenger Ry. Co. v. Swain, 13 Wkly. Notes Cas. (Pa.) 41.

385 Samuels v. California St. Cable Ry. Co., 124 Cal. 294; Francisco v. Troy & L. R. Co., 88 Hun (N. Y.) 464; Lansing v. Coney Island & B. R. Co., 16 App. Div. (N. Y.) 146; Grotsch v. Steinway Ry. Co.,

evidence that a car was running around a curve at from seven to fifteen miles an hour, and the conductor admitted that it was not safe to run more than five miles an hour;[386] where a car was running at from twelve to fifteen miles an hour,[387] and there was a rule that it must not cross a switch at more than four miles an hour; where a driver ran a car down hill at unusual speed while approaching a switch which he knew to be dangerous;[388] where a car was being driven rapidly when moving in a direction opposite from the usual one;[389] and where a car was running fifteen or twenty miles an hour around a sharp curve.[390] Where an electric car was rocking and pitching at a fearful rate, the court held that, upon all the evidence, the car was moving at a reckless rate of speed.[391] The speed at which a car is going is immaterial where it is acknowledged to be improper;[392] but the fact that horses were going at unusual but not dangerous speed does not tend to prove negligenee;[393] and while excessive and unlawful speed shows negligence, it does not of itself show that sueh rate of speed was the proximate cause of the

19 App. Div. (N. Y.) 130; Dillon v. Forty-Second St., M. & St. N. Ave. Ry. Co., 28 App. Div. (N. Y.) 404; Dochtermann v. Brooklyn Heights R. Co., 32 App. Div. (N. Y.) 13, affirmed 164 N. Y. 586; Hassen v. Nassau Electric R. Co., 34 App. Div. (N. Y.) 71; Ripley v. Second Ave. R. Co., 8 Misc. Rep. (N. Y.) 449; Sheeron v. Coney Island & B. R. Co., 78 App. Div. (N. Y.) 476.

386 East Omaha St. Ry. Co. v. Godola, 50 Neb. 906.

387 Sweetland v. Lynn & B. R. Co., 177 Mass. 574.

388 Seelig v. Metropolitan St. Ry. Co., 18 Misc. Rep. (N. Y.) 383.

389 White v. Milwaukee City Ry. Co., 61 Wis. 536.

390 Reber v. Pittsburg & B. Traction Co., 179 Pa. 339.

391 Elgin City Ry. Co. v. Wilson, 56 Ill. App. 364.

392 Gidionsen v. Union Depot R. Co., 129 Mo. 392.

393 Perry v. Malarin, 107 Cal. 363.

accident.[394] In an action for running a car at too great speed, there must be some evidence that the rate of speed is unusual, improper, or dangerous, and the jury cannot fix such rate of speed without evidence.[395] To run a train faster than an ordinance allows has been held negligence *per se*.[396] To run at high speed on a down grade when there is snow on the tracks is negligence.[397] It is evidence of negligence to run fifteen miles an hour in the fog.[397a]

## § 58. Miscellaneous, negligence in operation.

Where a driver, while frightening away some boys, broke a window and injured a passenger, his negligence was held to be for the jury.[398] It is negligence to shut the door so as to cut off the finger of a passenger leaving the car.[399] Where a conductor pulled a woman from a car, and her hand caught in the door, there was held to be sufficient evidence of negligence.[400] A city ordinance requiring a street railway company to have both a driver and a conductor on each of its cars is a proper regulation.[401]

In Valentine v. Middlesex R. Co.,[402] and in Edlund v. St. Paul City Ry. Co.,[403]—cases of accidents during repairs on the track,—negligence was held to be for the jury. Where

[394] Johnsen v. Oakland, S. L. & H. Electric Ry. Co., 127 Cal. 608.
[395] Francisco v. Troy & L. R. Co., 78 Hun (N. Y.) 13.
[396] Weber v. Kansas City Cable Ry. Co., 100 Mo. 194.
[397] Danville St. Car. Co. v. Payne (Va.) 24 S. E. 904.
[397a] Fisher v. Union Ry. Co., 86 App. Div. (N. Y.) 365.
[398] Allen v. Galveston City Ry. Co., 79 Tex. 631.
[399] McGlynn v. Brooklyn Crosstown R. Co., 6 N. Y. State Rep. 51.
[400] Mackin v. People's St. Ry. & E. L. & P. Co., 45 Mo. App. 82.
[401] South Covington & C. St. Ry. Co. v. Berry, 93 Ky. 43.
[402] 137 Mass. 28.
[403] 78 Minn. 434.

a city placed a cable across the company's tracks, and allowed it to slacken, so that it caught the trolley, and killed a passenger, it was held that there was no negligence on the part of the company, and that it was immaterial that the conductor was inside the car, when he should have been on the rear platform.[404] Where the track was torn up, and a motorman invited a woman to leave by the front door, and she fell within a few steps of the car, negligence was held to be for the jury, where it appeared that the ground was broken, and that it was a dark night.[405] In Smedley v. Hestonville, M. & F. P. Ry. Co.,[406] where a street was dug up, and the wheels of a car dropped when the car was passing from the new to the old rails, a verdict for the plaintiff was held to be justified. In the case of an injury from an iron manhole cover between the tracks, it was held that, in cases of latent defects, the question is not whether the company did know of such defects, but whether it should have known of them.[407] It is negligent to run cars over a palpably defective place, and a plaintiff has a right to presume that all due precautions have been taken.[408] Where a motorman ran a car into a pile of bricks in spite of the warning of a man in the street, there was held to be evidence of negligence, and a judgment of nonsuit was reversed;[409] and to drive into an excavation in spite of a warning has been held to be negligence.[410] Where a passenger fell off a car, and the

404 Baltimore Consol. Ry. Co. v. State, 91 Md. 506.

405 Sowash v. Consolidated Traction Co., 188 Pa. 618.

406 184 Pa. 620.

407 West Chicago St. R. Co. v. Stephens, 66 Ill. App. 303.

408 Citizens' St. Ry. Co. v. Twiname, 111 Ind. 587.

409 Buehler v. Union Traction Co., 200 Pa. 177.

410 Daub v. Yonkers R. Co., 69 Hun (N. Y.) 138.

servants in charge of the car knew that he was holding onto an iron rail to save himself from being run over, it is culpable negligence not to stop the car.[411] Where a passenger was injured by a runaway, there was held to be no evidence of negligence.[412]

A street railway company must use reasonable care in selecting its horses, and the company is responsible for whatever the driver finds out about them.[413] Where a pair of horses, which had worked satisfactorily for six weeks, ran away, there was held to be no negligence.[414] The mere fact that a horse had once run away does not show negligence.[415] In Lynch v. Brooklyn City R. Co.[416] it was held that, whether the horses were frightened by a blast, or because the driver let the whiffle-tree fall on their ankles, was a question for the jury. Where the driver left a car in the street without tying the mules, and they ran away, the company was held liable for an injury to a passenger trying to alight;[417] and where a passenger jumped from a car while the horses were running away, due care was held to be for the jury.[418] Excitement caused by a car backing suddenly down hill is proper to be considered on the question of due care.[419] Where, in passing a switch, one man is needed at each end of the car, and only one man is put in charge of the car, this is

411 Chicago West Div. Ry. Co. v. Hughes, 69 Ill. 170.
412 Hamilton v. West End St. Ry. Co., 163 Mass. 199.
413 Noble v. St. Joseph & B. H. St. R. Co., 98 Mich. 249.
414 Quinlan v. Sixth Ave. R. Co., 4 Daly (N. Y.) 487.
415 Perry v. Malarin, 107 Cal. 363.
416 1 Silv. Sup. (N. Y.) 361.
417 Texarkana St. Ry. Co. v. Hart (Tex. Civ. App.) 26 S. W. 435.
418 Dimmey v. Wheeling & E. G. R. Co., 27 W. Va. 32.
419 Joliet St. Ry. Co. v. McCarthy, 42 Ill. App. 49.

conclusive evidence of negligence; and where the man in charge did not stop the car in adjusting the trolley while going around a curve, and fell off, this was held negligence.[420] Where a runaway ran into a car and injured a passenger, there was held to be no negligence on the part of the company.[421]

The company has been held liable, where a conductor insulted a passenger, on the ground of breach of contract, although it did not authorize or ratify, but promptly repudiated, the act.[422] Where a passenger asked a conductor to stop the car, as she felt sick, he refused, and she fell unconscious through the door, due care and negligence were held to be for the jury.[423] A driver who, on being relieved, is leaving the car to get a meal, is engaged in business of the company, and they are liable for the death of a passenger caused by his gross negligence.[424]

It has been held that a municipal ordinance is not binding on the company without proof of its assent thereto,[425] but see the late cases of Gebhardt v. St. Louis Transit Co.[426] and McLain v. St. Louis & S. Ry. Co.[427]

Where two companies jointly operated a line partly owned by each, it was held that each was liable for the negligent

420 Redfield v. Oakland Consol. St. Ry. Co., 110 Cal. 277.

421 Hamilton v. West End St. Ry. Co., 163 Mass. 199.

422 Knoxville Traction Co. v. Lane, 103 Tenn. 376.

423 Newark & S. O. R. Co. v. McCann, 58 N. J. Law, 642.

424 Commonwealth v. Brockton St. Ry. Co., 143 Mass. 501.

425 Fath v. Tower Grove & L. Ry. Co., 105 Mo. 537; Byington v. St. Louis R. Co., 147 Mo. 673; Day v. Citizens' Ry. Co., 81 Mo. App. 471; Hitchcock v. Brooklyn City R. Co., 3 N. Y. Supp. 218.

426 (Mo. App.) 71 S. W. 448.

427 (Mo. App.) 73 S. W. 909.

operation of the other;[428] but in Anderson v. Des Moines St. Ry. Co.[429] it was held that, where two lines were operated separately, there was no evidence to hold the defendant. In Howard v. Union Traction Co.[430] it was held that a street railway company and a gas company could not be sued as joint tort feasors, when the plaintiff, in alighting, tripped over a block of wood belonging to the gas company, on the ground that there was no community of fault. Where an accident occurred on a bridge built and maintained by the state, there was held to be no negligence on the part of the street railway company.[431] A resident of a city must know of an ordinance as to the stopping of cars.[432] If two tort feasors are both negligent, they are jointly liable;[433] but if a plaintiff accepts satisfaction from one joint tort feasor, he cannot sue the other.[434]

Lessees of a road have been held liable for an injury to a passenger,[435] even though the road was leased unlawfully,[436] and, on the other hand, the lessor company has been held liable.[437]

428 Richard v. Detroit R., R. & L. O. Ry. Co. (Mich.) 89 N. W. 52; Messenger v. St. Paul City Ry. Co., 77 Minn. 34.

429 97 Iowa, 739.

430 195 Pa. 391.

431 Birmingham v. Rochester City & B. R. Co., 137 N. Y. 13.

432 Pryor v. Metropolitan St. Ry. Co., 85 Mo. App. 367.

433 McGary v. West Chicago St. R. Co., 85 Ill. App. 610; Douglass v. Sioux City Ry. Co., 91 Iowa, 94; Taylor v. Grand Ave. Ry. Co., 137 Mo. 363; Schneider v. Second Ave. R. Co., 59 N. Y. Super. Ct. 536; Texas & P. Ry. Co. v. Doherty, 4 Willson, Civ. Cas. Ct. App. § 164.

434 Spurr v. North Hudson County R. Co., 56 N. J. Law, 346.

435 Quested v. Newburyport & A. Horse R. Co., 127 Mass. 204.

436 Feital v. Middlesex R. Co., 109 Mass. 398.

437 Braslin v. Somerville Horse R. Co., 145 Mass. 64.

# CHAPTER IV.

## ACCIDENTS WHILE ALIGHTING FROM CAR.

I. Due Care and Negligence.

§ 59. Due Care in Alighting from Moving Car in General a Question of Fact.
60. Reasonable Opportunity to Alight.
61. Speed of Car.
62. Manner of Alighting.
63. Age and Physical Condition of Passenger.
64. Sex of Passenger.
65. Incumbered with Bundles.
66. Place of Alighting.
67. Preparatory to Alighting.
68. Notice of Desire to Alight.
69. Alighting in Spite of Warning.
70. Condition of Car.
71. Injury by Fellow Passenger.
72. Miscellaneous.

### Due Care and Negligence.

It is not lack of due care, as a matter of law, to alight from a moving car, whether it is a horse car, an electric car, a cable car, or a car on a dummy line, and whether the attempt is made from the rear platform, the front platform, or the running board. Various circumstances, however, may tend to make the attempt to alight lack of due care as a matter of law, and among these are the speed of the car, the manner of making the attempt, the age, sex, and physical condition of the passenger, whether or not he is incumbered with bundles, his position upon the car, whether or not he gave notice of his desire to alight, whether or not he was warned not to make the attempt, and the condition of the street and car.

**If a street car has stopped for a passenger to alight, or has been slowed up to such an extent as to constitute an invitation to alight, a passenger must be given a reasonable opportunity to do so, and to start the car while he is alighting is negligence.**

**The company is not liable for the acts of fellow passengers unless it could reasonably have prevented them.**

### § 59. Due care in alighting from moving car in general a question of fact.

It is well settled that it cannot be said, as matter of law, that alighting from a moving street car is lack of due care. It is ordinarily left to the jury to say whether or not the passenger acted as a reasonably prudent and cautious man would have acted under like circumstances. This ruling has been made in the case of a horse car,[1] an electric car,[2]

[1] Brennan v. Fair Haven & W. R. Co., 45 Conn. 284; Chicago City Ry. Co. v. Mumford, 97 Ill. 560; Ober v. Crescent City R. Co., 44 La. Ann. 1059; Schacherl v. St. Paul City Ry. Co., 42 Minn. 42; Fortune v. Missouri R. Co., 10 Mo. App. 252; Duncan v. Wyatt Park Ry. Co., 48 Mo. App. 659; Wyatt v. Citizens' Ry. Co., 55 Mo. 485; New Jersey Traction Co. v. Gardner, 60 N. J. Law, 571; Maisels v. Dry Dock, E. B. & B. St. R., 16 App. Div. (N. Y.) 391; Munroe v. Third Ave. R. Co., 50 N. Y. Super. Ct. 114; Crissey v. Hestonville, M. & F. P. Ry. Co., 75 Pa. 83.

[2] Denver Tramway Co. v. Reid, 22 Colo. 349; Posten v. Denver Consol. Tramway Co., 11 Colo. App. 187; Betts v. Wilmington City Ry. Co. (Del.) 53 Atl. 358; Springfield Consol. Ry. Co. v. Hoeffner, 175 Ill. 634; Indianapolis St. Ry. Co. v. Hockett, 159 Ind. 677; Root v. Des Moines City Ry. Co., 113 Iowa, 675; Creamer v. West End St. Ry. Co., 156 Mass. 320; Kelly v. Third Ave. R. Co., 25 App. Div. (N. Y.) 603; Patterson v. Westchester Electric Ry. Co., 26 App. Div. (N. Y.) 336; Willis v. Metropolitan St. Ry. Co., 63 App. Div. (N. Y.) 332; Harris v. Union Ry. Co., 69 App. Div. (N. Y.) 385; Cunningham v. Dry Dock, E. B. & B. R. Co., 29 Misc. Rep. (N. Y.) 772; Kuhlman v. Metropolitan St. Ry. Co., 30 Misc. Rep. (N. Y.) 417.

a cable car,[3] and a car on a dummy line.[4] The rule is the same, whether the passenger alights from the rear platform,[5] the front platform,[6] or the running board.[7]

There are, however, many cases where the court has felt justified in declaring that, under all the circumstances of the case, an attempt to alight from a moving street car is lack of due care as matter of law.

In Watkins v. Birmingham R. & E. Co.[8] the court said: "There may be, it is true, exceptional circumstances attending the attempt thus to alight, such as the great speed of the train, the age or infirmity of the passenger, or his being incumbered with bundles or children, or other facts which render the attempt so obviously dangerous that the court may, where the testimony is undisputed, declare, as matter of law,

3 Chicago City Ry. Co. v. Meehan, 77 Ill. App. 215; Weber v. Kansas City Cable Ry. Co., 100 Mo. 194; Brown v. Seattle City Ry. Co., 16 Wash. 465.

4 Watkins v. Birmingham R. & E. Co., 120 Ala. 147; Birmingham R. & E. Co. v. James, 121 Ala. 120.

5 Watkins v. Birmingham R. & E. Co., 120 Ala. 147; Birmingham R. & E. Co. v. James, 121 Ala. 120; Posten v. Denver Consol. Tramway Co., 11 Colo. App. 187; Chicago City Ry. Co. v. Mumford, 97 Ill. 560; Root v. Des Moines City Ry. Co., 113 Iowa, 675; Fortune v. Missouri R. Co., 10 Mo. App. 252; Duncan v. Wyatt Park Ry. Co., 48 Mo. App. 659; Weber v. Kansas City Cable Ry. Co., 100 Mo. 194; Willis v. Metropolitan St. Ry. Co., 63 App. Div. (N. Y.) 332; Munroe v. Third Ave. R. Co., 50 N. Y. Super. Ct. 114.

6 New Jersey Traction Co. v. Gardner, 60 N. J. Law, 571; Maisels v. Dry Dock, E. B. & B. St. R., 16 App. Div. (N. Y.) 391; Crissey v. Hestonville, M. & F. P. Ry. Co., 75 Pa. 83; Brown v. Seattle City Ry. Co., 16 Wash. 465.

7 Denver Tramway Co. v. Reid, 22 Colo. 349; Chicago City Ry. Co. v. Meehan, 77 Ill. App. 215; Creamer v. West End St. Ry. Co., 156 Mass. 320.

8 120 Ala. 147.

that the passenger's conduct was reckless and negligent;" and in Posten v. Denver Consol. Tramway Co.[9] the court said: "Chief among these circumstances necessary and important to be considered are the manner in which the act was attempted to be performed, and the rate of speed at which the car was moving at the time. If the evidence should disclose that the passenger was heavily incumbered with packages or bundles, so as to palpably impede his movements, and it could be reasonably inferred that, by reason of this, the accident happened, or, if his manner of alighting—by jumping, for instance—was such as to clearly indicate that it was the direct cause of the injury, or if the car was running at such a high rate of speed as to make it manifest that the act would probably result in personal injury, it is obvious that a state of facts would have been shown stamping the act as unmistakably negligent, and there would be no necessity for submitting it to a jury for its determination."

### § 60. Reasonable opportunity to alight.

It is well settled that, while a street car company is not an insurer of its passengers against accident,[10] it does owe them a very high degree of care.[11] Consequently, a pas-

[9] 11 Colo. App. 187.

[10] West Chicago St. R. Co. v. Luka, 72 Ill. App. 60; Gilbert v. West End St. Ry. Co., 160 Mass. 403; New Jersey Traction Co. v. Gardner, 58 N. J. Law, 176.

[11] Washington & G. R. Co. v. Harmon's Adm'r, 147 U. S. 571; City & Suburban Ry. v. Findley, 76 Ga. 311; Atlanta Ry. Co. v. Randall (Ga.) 43 S. E. 412; North Chicago St. R. Co. v. Wrixon, 51 Ill. App. 307; West Chicago St. R. Co. v. Lyon, 57 Ill. App. 536; West Chicago St. R. Co. v. Luka, 72 Ill. App. 60; Conner v. Citizens' St. R. Co., 146 Ind. 430; Ft. Wayne Traction Co. v. Morvilius (Ind. App.) 68 N.

senger is entitled to a reasonable opportunity to alight, if a street car has stopped for him to do so,[12] or has been slowed up to such an extent as to constitute an invitation

E. 304; Root v. Des Moines City Ry. Co., 113 Iowa, 675; Leavenworth Electric R. Co. v. Cusick, 60 Kan. 590; Metropolitan St. Ry. Co. v. Hanson (Kan.) 72 Pac. 773; Louisville City Ry. v. Weams, 80 Ky. 420; Louisville Ry. Co. v. Park, 96 Ky. 580; Lutz v. Louisville Ry. Co., 20 Ky. Law Rep. 1163; Gilbert v. West End St. Ry. Co., 160 Mass. 403; Weber v. Kansas City Cable Ry. Co., 100 Mo. 194; Cobb v. Lindell Ry. Co., 149 Mo. 135; Grace v. St. Louis R. Co., 156 Mo. 295; Chase v. Jamestown St. Ry. Co., 15 N. Y. Supp. 35; Richmond City Ry. Co. v. Scott, 86 Va. 902; Richmond Traction Co. v. Williams (Va.) 46 S. E. 292; Brown v. Seattle City Ry. Co., 16 Wash. 465.

12 Denver Consol. Tramway Co. v. Rush (Colo. App.) 73 Pac. 664; Rouser v. Washington & G. R. Co., 13 App. D. C. 320; Atlanta Ry. Co. v. Randall (Ga.) 43 S. E. 412; Chicago West Div. Ry. Co. v. Mills, 105 Ill. 63; West Chicago St. R. Co. v. Waniata, 68 Ill. App. 481; West Chicago St. R. Co. v. Manning, 70 Ill. App. 239; West Chicago St. R. Co. v. Luka, 72 Ill. App. 60; Belt Electric Line Co. v. Tomlin, 19 Ky. Law Rep. 433; Lutz v. Louisville Ry. Co., 20 Ky. Law Rep. 1163; Paducah St. Ry. Co. v. Walsh, 22 Ky. Law Rep. 532; Henning v. Louisville Ry. Co. (Ky.) 74 S. W. 209; Wardle v. New Orleans City R. Co., 35 La. Ann. 202; Conway v. New Orleans & C. R. Co., 46 La. Ann. 1429; Finn v. Valley City St. & Cable Ry. Co., 86 Mich. 74; Werbowlsky v. Ft. Wayne & E. Ry. Co., 86 Mich. 236; Britton v. Street Ry. Co., 90 Mich. 159; Selby v. Detroit Ry., 122 Mich. 311; Skelton v. St. Paul City Ry. Co. (Minn.) 92 N. W. 960; Weber v. Kansas City Cable Ry. Co., 100 Mo. 194; Ridenhour v. Kansas City Cable Ry. Co., 102 Mo. 270; Scamell v. St. Louis Transit Co. (Mo. App.) 76 S. W. 660; Fenig v. North Jersey St. Ry. Co., 64 N. J. Law, 715; Mulhado v. Brooklyn City R. Co., 30 N. Y. 370; Poulin v. Broadway & S. A. R. Co., 61 N. Y. 621; Losee v. Watervliet Turnpike & R. Co., 63 Hun (N. Y.) 404; Smith v. Kingston City R. Co., 55 App. Div. (N. Y.) 143; Willis v. Metropolitan St. Ry. Co., 63 App. Div. (N. Y.) 332; Colt v. Sixth Ave. R. Co., 33 N. Y. Super. Ct. 189; Murphy v. Metropolitan St. Ry. Co., 19 Misc. Rep. (N. Y.) 194; Weiss v. Metropolitan St. Ry.

to alight,[13] and to start the car before the passenger has had a reasonable opportunity to alight is negligence as a matter of law.

The rule as to furnishing a reasonable opportunity for alighting is not altered when the car stops, but not at a customary stopping place;[14] and it has been held that those in charge of a street car, when signaled to stop, must not only give a reasonable time for passengers to alight, but must see and know, before starting again, that no one is alighting, or in any other dangerous position,[15] and this rule has

Co., 29 Misc. Rep. (N. Y.) 332; Schaefer v. Central Crosstown R. Co., 30 Misc. Rep. (N. Y.) 114; Flanagan v. Metropolitan St. Ry. Co., 31 Misc. Rep. (N. Y.) 820; Brady v. Metropolitan St. Ry. Co., 33 Misc. Rep. (N. Y.) 793; Koues v. Metropolitan St. Ry. Co., 83 N. Y. Supp. 380; Ashtabula Rapid Transit Co. v. Holmes, 67 Ohio St. 153; Mt. Adams & E. P. Ry. Co. v. Wysong, 2 Ohio Dec. 65; Dussel v. Akron St. R. Co., 10 Ohio S. & C. P. Dec. 631; Fairmount & A. S. P. Ry. Co. v. Stutler, 54 Pa. 375; Jagger v. People's St. Ry. Co., 180 Pa. 436.

13 Chicago City Ry. Co. v. Mumford, 97 Ill. 560; Springfield Consol. Ry. Co. v. Hoeffner, 175 Ill. 634; Currie v. Mendenhall, 77 Minn. 179; Cobb v. Lindell Ry. Co., 149 Mo. 135; Munroe v. Third Ave. R. Co., 50 N. Y. Super. Ct. 114; Rapid Transit Ry. Co. v. Lusk (Tex. Civ. App.) 66 S. W. 799.

14 Betts v. Wilmington City Ry. Co. (Del.) 53 Atl. 358; Washington & G. R. Co. v. Grant, 11 App. D. C. 107; West Chicago St. R. Co. v. Manning, 170 Ill. 417; West Chicago St. R. Co. v. Luka, 72 Ill. App. 60; Root v. Des Moines City Ry. Co., 113 Iowa, 675; Beringer v. Dubuque St. Ry. Co. (Iowa) 91 N. W. 931; United Rys. & Elec. Co. v. Hertel (Md.) 55 Atl. 428; United Rys. & Elec. Co. v. Woodbridge (Md.) 55 Atl. 444; Jackson v. Grand Ave. Ry. Co., 118 Mo. 199.

15 Birmingham Union Ry. Co. v. Smith, 90 Ala. 60; Highland Ave. & B. R. Co. v. Burt, 92 Ala. 291; Metropolitan R. Co. v. Jones, 1 App. D. C. 200; Washington & G. R. Co. v. Grant, 11 App. D. C. 107; Chicago City Ry. Co. v. Mumford, 97 Ill. 560; Chicago West Div.

been held to apply to electric cars running on schedule time outside the city limits, and stopping only at regular stations.[16]

In Gardner v. Detroit St. Ry. Co.[17] it was held that the fact that a car is started while a passenger is alighting does not shift the burden of proof; but in Martin v. Second Ave. R. Co.[18] it was held that the passenger need not prove what caused the jerk, and that the defendant must show that it was not responsible for it, in order to escape liability. Where a passenger was injured while alighting from a moving street car, it was held that he was not obliged to prove whether he was thrown backwards or forwards;[19] and a passenger is not prevented from recovering because he was unnecessarily on the front platform, where the driver started the car negligently while he was alighting.[20] It is not necessary to prove that the car started forward,—that it gave a sudden jerk, causing the accident, is sufficient.[21] In two instances it has been held that starting a car while a passenger is alighting is not negligence as matter of law.[22] Where a passenger had a reasonable time in which to change

Ry. Co. v. Mills, 105 Ill. 63; Anderson v. Citizens' St. R. Co., 12 Ind. App. 194; Conner v. Citizens' St. R. Co., 146 Ind. 430; Leavenworth Electric R. Co. v. Cusick, 60 Kan. 590; Asbury v. Charlotte Electric Ry. & Power Co., 125 N. C. 568; Omaha & C. B. R. & B. Co. v. Levinston, 49 Neb. 17; Memphis St. Ry. Co. v. Shaw (Tenn.) 75 S. W. 713.

16 Birmingham R. & E. Co. v. Wildman, 119 Ala. 547.

17 99 Mich. 182.

18 3 App. Div. (N. Y.) 448.

19 Guntzer v. Yonkers R. Co., 51 App. Div. (N. Y.) 222.

20 Lax v. Forty-Second & G. St. Ferry R. Co., 46 N. Y. Super. Ct. 448.

21 Citizens' St. Ry. Co. v. Huffer, 26 Ind. App. 575.

22 West End & A. St. Ry. Co. v. Mozely, 79 Ga. 463; Chicago City Ry. Co. v. Dinsmore, 162 Ill. 658.

his position from the front to the rear platform, but did not, and stepped off just as the car started, he was held unable to recover.[23]

Where a passenger requests a conductor to wait a moment until a rapidly moving team has passed, he has a right to expect that the conductor will wait a reasonable time.[24] Testimony that, as a woman was alighting holding onto the rail, she heard the bell ring, and that, when she regained consciousness, she found her arm pulled from its socket, warrants the jury in finding that the car started as she was alighting.[25] Where a car came to a full stop, and the conductor announced a transfer point, the negligence of the motorman in starting ahead without a signal and without looking around was held to be for the jury.[26]

### § 61. Speed of car.

As previously mentioned, the speed of the car is one of the primary considerations in determining the question of the passenger's due care.

Where a passenger jumped off a car running twenty miles an hour, although he did not know the car was running so fast, and did know of a city ordinance restricting the speed of the car to seven miles an hour, it was held that a nonsuit was properly ordered; and it is no excuse that the conductor would not stop when requested, and kept silent when he heard another passenger tell the plaintiff that the car was not going to stop, and that he had better jump.[27]

23 Brown v. Congress & B. St. Ry. Co., 49 Mich. 153.

24 Hutchins v. Macomber, 68 N. H. 473.

25 Bartle v. Houghton County St. Ry. Co. (Mich.) 93 N. W. 620.

26 Bessenger v. Metropolitan St. R. Co., 79 App. Div. (N. Y.) 32.

27 Masterson v. Macon City & S. St. R. Co., 88 Ga. 436.

A woman's stepping from a cable car while it was moving at any such speed as eleven miles an hour has been characterized as "gross contributory negligence";[28] and a woman alighting from a street car moving "fast enough to throw her" was held negligent, and not entitled to recover.[29] Where a passenger stepped off a street car which was running at its usual rate of speed,—from seven to twelve miles an hour,—he was held guilty of such contributory negligence as would bar his recovery.[30] When a passenger was in the habit of jumping off a moving car, and the conductor and motorman knew of this, and would slow down the car to the speed of four or five miles an hour on his signal, it was held that a nonsuit was properly granted on the ground of contributory negligence.[31] In Neff v. Harrisburg Traction Co.[32] the court went so far as to declare, apparently against the overwhelming weight of authority, that it is negligent for a passenger to leave an electric car while it is in motion.

The refusal of the driver or motorman of a street car to stop the car will not justify a passenger in leaving it while it is in motion,[33] even in the case of a child six and one-half years old,[34] or a man of seventy.[35]

28 Denver Tramway Co. v. Owens, 20 Colo. 107.

29 Calderwood v. North Birmingham St. Ry. Co., 96 Ala. 318.

30 Saiko v. St. Paul City Ry. Co., 67 Minn. 8.

31 Jagger v. People's St. Ry. Co., 180 Pa. 436.

32 192 Pa. 501.

33 Denver Tramway Co. v. Owens, 20 Colo. 107; Masterson v. Macon City & S. St. R. Co., 88 Ga. 436; Rouser v. Washington & G. R. Co., 13 App. D. C. 320; North Chicago St. R. Co. v. Wrixon, 51 Ill. App. 307; Dresslar v. Citizens' St. R. Co., 19 Ind. App. 383; Duncan v. Wyatt Park Ry. Co., 48 Mo. App. 659; White v. West End

It has been held that a person who voluntarily jumps from a moving car assumes the risk of the accident which ensues,[36] and that it is no part of the duty of a street railway company to prevent a passenger, much less a trespasser, from leaving a car while it is in motion.[37]

When a passenger has signaled a car to stop, and it is slowing down in response to his signal, if he chooses to get off before it has stopped, it has been held that this is such lack of due care as will bar a recovery, the court proceeding on the theory that passengers have a right to have the car brought to a stand before alighting, and, if they choose to alight while the car is still in motion, they assume the risk of what may happen;[38] and in Harmon v. Washington & G. R. Co.[39] it was held that, in such a case, it would be irrelevant to inquire whether the plaintiff was in the exercise of due care or not, since the defendant, being in the actual performance of its duty, could not be held negligent.

In a number of cases it has been held that the defendant was entitled to a ruling that, if a passenger alights from a car which is slowing down, he cannot recover; but these

St. Ry. Co., 165 Mass. 522; Maisels v. Dry Dock, E. B. & B. St. R., 16 App. Div. (N. Y.) 391; Mettlestadt v. Ninth Ave. R. Co., 27 N. Y. Super. Ct. 377; Hagan v. Philadelphia & G. Ferry Ry. Co., 10 Wkly. Notes Cas. (Pa.) 360.

34 Cram v. Metropolitan R. Co., 112 Mass. 38.

35 Outen v. North & South St. R. Co., 94 Ga. 662.

36 McDonald v. Montgomery St. Ry., 110 Ala. 161; Jones v. Canal & C. R. Co., 109 La. 214; White v. West End St. Ry. Co., 165 Mass. 522; Werbowlsky v. Ft. Wayne & E. Ry. Co., 86 Mich. 236.

37 Brightman v. Union St. Ry. Co., 167 Mass. 113.

38 Philips v. St. Charles St. R. Co., 106 La. 592; Saffer v. Dry Dock, E. B. & B. R. Co., 5 N. Y. Supp. 700.

39 6 Mackey (D. C.) 57.

were cases where the plaintiff's right of recovery was based upon a claim that the car had been stopped and started again, so that the question was in reality more one of pleading than of substantive law.[40]

Rules applicable to steam railways are not applicable to horse cars;[41] and in Denver Tramway Co. v. Reid[42] the court said: "In the last few years, horses have been almost entirely displaced as a motive power on street car lines in cities by cables and electricity, and the operation of cars and trains correspondingly accelerated. As transit becomes more rapid, the dangers incident to street railway travel are correspondingly augmented, and, as the danger is increased, the law exacts greater care on the part of both the passenger and the carrier. For this reason, many of the decisions applicable to passengers on horse cars are inapplicable to the newer methods of transportation. The cable and electric service today more nearly resembles the ordinary railway train, and the case law which has grown up with reference to the latter is more in point."

§ 62. **Manner of alighting.**

It is generally held that a person stepping off a moving street car backwards is not entitled to recover, although this is not lack of due care as matter of law.[43]

40 De Foe v. St. Paul City Ry. Co., 65 Minn. 319; Patterson v. Westchester Electric Ry. Co., 26 App. Div. (N. Y.) 336; Kelly v. Third Ave. R. Co., 25 App. Div. (N. Y.) 603; Kuhlman v. Metropolitan St. Ry. Co., 30 Misc. Rep. (N. Y.) 417; Coleman v. Metropolitan St. Ry. Co., 81 N. Y. Supp. 836.

41 Ober v. Crescent City R. Co., 44 La. Ann. 1059.

42 22 Colo. 349.

43 Chicago City Ry. Co. v. Meehan, 77 Ill. App. 215.

In Purtell v. Ridge Ave. Passenger Ry. Co.[44] it was held that a boy of eleven, jumping backwards from the front platform of a moving street car, is guilty of lack of due care as a matter of law; and in Colgan v. West Philadelphia Passenger Ry. Co.[45] the same rule was made in the case of a boy of sixteen, and it was further held that the plaintiff could not make the excuse that he was a child of tender years. In Wrasse v. Citizens' Traction Co.,[46] a boy of ten, who attempted to jump off a moving car backwards, was likewise held unable to recover, but on the ground that there was no evidence of negligence on the part of the company; and similarly it has been held that there is no negligence on the part of the company where a passenger steps off the front platform of a moving car backwards, without notice.[47] In Richmond v. Second Ave. R. Co.[48] it was held that to step off a moving street car backwards is lack of due care unless the passenger is induced to do so by the negligence of the company.

In Rouser v. Washington & G. R. Co.[49] it was held that, when a car is negligently started while a passenger is alighting, her right to recover is not impaired by the fact that she may have stepped off with her back to the front of the train, and without holding onto the car. The court said: "When the car has been stopped, the passenger has the right to presume that it will not be started while he is in the act of stepping off. Consequently, while it would be prudent to

[44] 3 Pa. Co. Ct. R. 273.

[45] 4 Wkly. Notes Cas. (Pa.) 400.

[46] 146 Pa. 417.

[47] Steuer v. Metropolitan St. Ry. Co., 46 App. Div. (N. Y.) 500.

[48] 76 Hun (N. Y.) 233.

[49] 13 App. D. C. 320.

provide against possible negligence of the carrier by grasping the handle-bar and getting off with face to the front, we cannot say that he is under any legal obligation to do so. We think that he has the right to step off with or without grasping the car, and facing in any direction that he chooses."

Getting off the front platform of a street car which is not in motion is not lack of due care;[50] and in Hope v. West Chicago St. R. Co.[51] it was held that an instruction was erroneous which gave the impression that it was dangerous to alight from an electric car while it is not in motion. In Missouri, by statute, however, lack of due care is presumed when a passenger is injured while alighting from the front platform.[52] Where a passenger was injured while alighting, but there was no proof that the car moved, there was held to be no negligence.[53]

Where a car started while a crippled passenger was alighting, it was held that, as the passenger was placed in a sudden emergency, to hold onto the rail was not negligence.[54] Similarly, it is not lack of due care for an aged and infirm passenger to hold onto the running board in falling, when a car is prematurely started,[55] or for a woman to try to get back onto the car.[55a]

Getting over an immovable guard on the front platform in order to alight is lack of due care as matter of law,[56] and

[50] Mulhado v. Brooklyn City R. Co., 30 N. Y. 370.

[51] 82 Ill. App. 311.

[52] McKeon v. Citizens' Ry. Co., 42 Mo. 79.

[53] Gretzner v. New Orleans & C. R. Co., 105 La. 266.

[54] Knowlton v. Milwaukee City Ry. Co., 59 Wis. 278.

[55] Indiana Ry. Co. v. Maurer (Ind.) 66 N. E. 156.

[55a] Brazis v. St. Louis Transit Co. (Mo. App.) 76 S. W. 708.

[56] Fry v. People's Passenger Ry. Co., 17 Phila. (Pa.) 61.

the fact that the conductor told a passenger to do so is no excuse.[57]

Omitting to take hold of handles or handle rails while in the act of alighting is held not to be lack of due care as a matter of law. Thus, in Scott v. Bergen County Traction Co.,[58] the due care of a passenger who omitted to take hold of a handle rail on the rear platform while standing there preparatory to alighting was held to be a question for the jury; and in Chase v. Jamestown St. Ry. Co.[59] the trial court was sustained in declining to hold, as matter of law, that a passenger who did not take hold of the arms of the seat while alighting from an open street car was guilty of lack of due care. So it has been held that whether omitting to grasp the handle holds on the uprights of the seats of an open car is lack of due care or not is a question for the jury,[60] and that it is not lack of due care, as matter of law, for a passenger, while alighting, not to use the handles provided for the purpose, particularly when it appears that, in order to use them, the passenger must turn around and get off backwards.[61] Where a woman got off the car with a child on her left arm, and there was ice on the platform, and a passenger stood so that she could not get hold of the rail, due care and negligence were held to be for the jury.[62] In Schaefer v. Central Crosstown R. Co.[63] it was held that

57 Reilly v. Green & C. St. P. Ry. Co., 4 Wkly. Notes Cas. (Pa.) 273.

58 63 N. J. Law, 407.

59 15 N. Y. Supp. 35.

60 Omaha St. Ry. Co. v. Craig, 39 Neb. 601.

61 Martin v. Second Ave. R. Co., 3 App. Div. (N. Y.) 448.

62 Neslie v. Second & Third Sts. Passenger Ry. Co., 113 Pa. 300.

63 30 Misc. Rep. (N. Y.) 114.

it was not lack of due care, as matter of law, for a washerwoman with a large bundle of linen to descend the steps of a street car without taking hold of the rail.

## § 63. Age and physical condition of passenger.

Due care has been held to be for the jury where, on the one hand, a boy of eight,[64] one of nine,[65] one of ten,[66] one of thirteen,[67] and one of seventeen,[68] jumped from a street car while it was in rapid motion, and where, on the other, a man over sixty,[69] one of seventy-four,[70] and one of seventy-eight,[70a] jumped from a moving car. Where a boy of thirteen jumped off a moving car, it was held that, under all the circumstances of the case, the accident was due to his own imprudence.[71]

The refusal of a conductor to stop a car will not justify a boy six and one-half years old in alighting.[72] Where a boy of six was stealing a ride, and, being told by the conductor to get off, jumped from the car without waiting for it to stop, it was held that he could not recover.[73] Where a boy of eight was stealing a ride, and voluntarily jumped

64 Moran v. Versailles Traction Co., 188 Pa. 557.

65 Ridenhour v. Kansas City Cable Ry. Co., 102 Mo. 270.

66 Brennan v. Fair Haven & W. R. Co., 45 Conn. 284.

67 Pueblo Electric St. Ry. Co. v. Sherman, 25 Colo. 114; Crissey v. Hestonville, M. & F. P. Ry. Co., 75 Pa. 83.

68 Wyatt v. Citizens' Ry. Co., 55 Mo. 485.

69 Denver Tramway Co. v. Reid, 22 Colo. 349.

70 Munroe v. Third Ave. R. Co., 50 N. Y. Super. Ct. 114.

70a Dawson v. St. Louis Transit Co. (Mo. App.) 76 S. W. 689.

71 Cronan v. Crescent City R. Co., 49 La. Ann. 65.

72 Cram v. Metropolitan R. Co., 112 Mass. 38.

73 Feingold v. Philadelphia Traction Co., 21 Pa. Co. Ct. R. 183.

from a moving car, it was held that he could not recover, and that a street car company was under no obligation to prevent a passenger, much less a trespasser, from leaving a car while it was in motion.[74]

More attention should be paid to an aged or infirm passenger than to one in ordinary health;[75] but an instruction that a carrier must use reasonable care towards women and children in their alighting was held objectionable, as likely to be understood to mean that he must assist them to alight.[76]

Where a driver was helping a small boy off the car, and the brake became loose and injured him, the driver's negligence was held to be for the jury.[77] When a driver permits a boy of seven to ride, he cannot order him off without giving him an opportunity to alight in safety, and, if he tells him to get off while the car is in motion, negligence is for the jury.[78] It is not negligence for a conductor to call a boy to the platform when his destination is reached, and the boy falls off the platform by his own imprudence.[79]

It is the duty of a street railway company to prevent children from getting off the front platform, and the negligence of the company is for the jury when a boy of ten

74 Brightman v. Union St. Ry. Co., 167 Mass. 113.

75 Anderson v. Citizens' St. R. Co., 12 Ind. App. 194; Furgason v. Citizens' St. Ry. Co., 16 Ind. App. 171; Wardle v. New Orleans City R. Co., 35 La. Ann. 202; Ridenhour v. Kansas City Cable Ry. Co., 102 Mo. 270; Colt v. Sixth Ave. R. Co., 33 N. Y. Super. Ct. 189; Schiller v. Dry Dock, E. B. & B. R. Co., 26 Misc. Rep. (N. Y.) 392; Memphis St. Ry. Co. v. Shaw (Tenn.) 75 S. W. 713.

76 Selby v. Detroit Ry., 122 Mich. 311.

77 Buck v. People's St. Ry. & E. L. & P. Co., 108 Mo. 179.

78 McCahill v. Detroit City Ry. Co., 96 Mich. 156.

79 Cronan v. Crescent City R. Co., 49 La. Ann. 65.

got off the front platform because of the crowded condition of the car,[80] and one of thirteen was allowed to jump off a moving car to turn the trolley.[81]

### § 64. Sex of passenger.

The sex of the passenger is one circumstance to be considered.

In Chicago City Ry. Co. v. Meehan[82] the court said: "We do not say that it is always negligence for a person to alight from a car with the back towards the front end of the train; but by the modifications made by the court, the manner of getting off the car is ignored. Even if it be considered that, under such circumstances, it would not be negligence or want of ordinary care for a young man in sound physical condition and vigor to jump or step from a car while it is in motion, and not at a regular stopping place, yet it might be negligence, and show an absolute want of ordinary care, for a woman, under the same circumstances, to step or jump from a moving car with her back towards the front end of the train. In alighting from a moving car in the manner indicated, a woman would usually be laboring under a serious disadvantage by reason of her mode of dress."

It is not lack of due care, as matter of law, for a woman to wear a dress so long that it would be likely to catch upon such appliances as necessarily extend above the platform of a street car;[83] and it has been held that it cannot be

80 Philadelphia City Passenger Ry. Co. v. Hassard, 75 Pa. 367.

81 Pueblo Electric St. Ry. Co. v. Sherman, 25 Colo. 114.

82 77 Ill. App. 215.

83 Smith v. Kingston City R. Co., 55 App. Div. (N. Y.) 143.

said, as matter of law, that a hoop skirt is an unnecessary article of female apparel, or that an extra degree of care is required on the part of the wearer.[84] A passenger is not guilty of contributory negligence in allowing her dress to trail while she is leaving a street car, unless she has some reason to apprehend danger in so doing.[85] When a conductor assisted a woman to alight, and, in getting back on the car, stepped on her skirt, which had not been removed from the step, causing her to fall, this states a cause of action.[86] A woman alighting from a street car should be given time enough to step off, and also to clear her skirts from any obstruction on the platform upon which they may have caught.[87] If it is the custom to wear hoop skirts, the carrier must look out for the safety of passengers wearing them.[88]

There is no negligence on the part of the company where a woman's skirt caught in some unexplained manner while she was alighting;[89] but where a woman's dress caught on a threaded bolt extending three-eighths of an inch above the floor, it was held that the jury were authorized in finding negligence from the physical facts, without direct proof.[90]

84 Colt v. Sixth Ave. R. Co., 33 N. Y. Super. Ct. 189; Poulin v. Broadway & S. A. R. Co., 34 N. Y. Super. Ct. 296.

85 Colt v. Sixth Ave. R. Co., 33 N. Y. Super. Ct. 189; Paterson v. Inclined Plane Ry. Co., 5 Ohio S. & C. P. Dec. 665.

86 Citizens' St. R. Co. v. Shepherd, 29 Ind. App. 412, 65 N. E. 765.

87 Smith v. Kingston City R. Co., 55 App. Div. (N. Y.) 143; Colt v. Sixth Ave. R. Co., 33 N. Y. Super. Ct. 189.

88 Poulin v. Broadway & S. A. R. Co., 34 N. Y. Super. Ct. 296.

89 Doyle v. Metropolitan St. Ry. Co., 29 Misc. Rep. (N. Y.) 331.

90 Chartrand v. Southern Ry. Co., 57 Mo. App. 425.

**§ 65. Incumbered with bundles.**

It has been held that a passenger alighting from the front steps of a moving street car with a fifty-pound keg of lead in his hands is not in the exercise of due care;[91] and likewise that alighting from a moving car with a large package weighing fifteen pounds in one hand is lack of due care as matter of law.[92]

On the other hand, where a passenger was carrying two bundles of chair bottoms, weighing fifty pounds, but had the free use of both hands, the court held that whether it is lack of due care to alight from a moving car while incumbered with bundles is a question for the jury, depending on the speed of the car, and all the surrounding circumstances;[93] and it has been held that it is not lack of due care, as matter of law, for a washerwoman with a large bundle of linen to descend the steps of a street car without taking hold of the rail.[94] Where a woman got off a car with a child on her left arm, and there was ice on the platform, and a passenger stood so that she could not get hold of the rail, due care and negligence were held to be for the jury.[95]

Passengers incumbered with bundles must be given a reasonable opportunity to alight;[96] and where a car is negligently started, it is no excuse that a passenger was so incumbered with packages that she could not avail herself fully of the means provided for alighting.[97]

91 Ricketts v. Birmingham St. Ry. Co., 85 Ala. 600.
92 Kirchner v. Detroit City Ry., 91 Mich. 400.
93 Richmond v. Second Ave. R. Co., 76 Hun (N. Y.) 233.
94 Schaefer v. Central Crosstown R. Co., 30 Misc. Rep. (N. Y.) 114.
95 Neslie v. Second & Third Sts. Passenger Ry. Co., 113 Pa. 300.
96 Machen v. Railway Co., 13 Pa. Super. Ct. 642.
97 Cawfield v. Asheville St. Ry. Co., 111 N. C. 597.

## § 66. Place of alighting.

The authorities are in conflict as to the duty of a street railway company in selecting a stopping place. It is stated, on the one hand, that the company must furnish its passengers with a reasonably safe place at which to alight;[98] on the other, that if it uses ordinary care in selecting a stopping place, it is not liable if the place is in fact unsafe, since the company has no control over the streets.[99] Of course, under the latter holding, the company would be liable at its *termini* or regular stops, where it had control.[100]

Where a street railway company dug a trench, it was held bound to use reasonable care to guard the trench and warn passengers alighting.[101] Where an embankment or an excavation was made by the city, the same duty to warn passengers was held to exist;[102] and where a passenger was carried by his station on a dark night, and, alighting, fell into a trench, the company was held liable.[103] Where a train went by a station on a dark night, and the conductor lighted a passenger off the car with a lantern, and the passenger was

98 Montgomery St. Ry. Co. v. Mason, 133 Ala. 508; West Chicago St. Ry. Co. v. Cahill, 64 Ill. App. 539; Jagger v. People's St. Ry. Co., 180 Pa. 436.

99 Conway v. Lewiston & A. H. R Co., 87 Me. 283, 90 Me. 199; Stewart v. St. Paul City Ry. Co., 78 Minn. 85; Foley v. Brunswick Traction Co., 66 N. J. Law, 637; Flack v. Nassau Electric R. Co., 41 App. Div. (N. Y.) 399.

100 Flack v. Nassau Electric R. Co., 41 App. Div. (N. Y.) 399.

101 Wolf v. Third Ave. R. Co., 67 App. Div (N. Y.) 605. And see Joslyn v. Milford, H. & F. St. Ry. Co. (Mass.) 67 N. E. 866.

102 Ft. Wayne Traction Co. v. Morvilius (Ind. App.) 68 N. E. 304; Flack v. Nassau Electric R. Co., 41 App. Div. (N. Y.) 399.

103 Richmond City Ry. Co. v. Scott, 86 Va. 902; Henry v. Grant St. Electric Ry. Co., 24 Wash. 246.

run over, it was held that to induce a passenger to get off at a dangerous place was negligence, and that this was a question for the jury.[104] Where a passenger stepped into an excavation in broad daylight, it was held that those in charge of the car had a right to assume she would pay heed to her steps;[105] but in a precisely similar case exactly the opposite conclusion was reached.[106] A petition alleging that a street railway company, bound to keep the street in repair, stopped at a dangerous hole in a crossing, states a cause of action.[107]

Where a car stopped, apparently in answer to a passenger's signal, but not at a usual stopping place, her due care in alighting is a question for the jury.[108]

Where a passenger was injured while alighting by stepping on a ridge of earth at some pleasure grounds maintained by the company, due care and negligence are questions for the jury.[109]

When the place where the passenger is about to alight is rendered dangerous because of an approaching truck, she is entitled to a reasonable time in which to alight and select a safe position on the street, and is not obliged to proceed on the car to some other safe point.[110]

104 McDonald v. Kansas City & I. Rapid Transit Ry. Co., 127 Mo. 38.

105 Bigelow v. West End St. Ry. Co., 161 Mass. 393; Lee v. Boston El. Ry. Co., 182 Mass. 454.

106 Bass v. Concord St. Ry. Co., 70 N. H. 170.

107 Ober v. Crescent City R. Co., 44 La. Ann. 1059.

108 North Birmingham St. Ry. Co. v. Calderwood, 89 Ala. 247.

109 Poole v. Consolidated St. Ry. Co., 100 Mich. 379.

110 Norton v. Third Ave. R. Co., 26 App. Div. (N. Y.) 60.

## § 67. Preparatory to alighting.

Standing in a car, which is still moving, preparatory to alighting, is held not to be lack of due care as matter of law. For a passenger to signal a street car to stop, and then to walk to a place where he expects to alight, and stand there waiting for the car to stop, is so common that such conduct cannot be said to be lack of ordinary care.[111] Thus, the plaintiff has been held not to be barred from recovery where he stood, preparatory to alighting, on the rear platform,[112] or the running board,[113] or the step of the rear platform,[114] or inside the car,[115] or with one foot on the rear platform and one on the step,[116] or with one foot in the car and one on the running board.[117]

There is no rule of law which requires a passenger in a street car to retain his seat or other position until the car has actually stopped, and it is matter of universal ob-

111 North Chicago St. R. Co. v. Southwick, 66 Ill. App. 241.

112 North Chicago St. R. Co. v. Southwick, 66 Ill. App. 241; North Chicago St. R. Co. v. Baur, 79 Ill. App. 121; Etson v. Ft. Wayne & B. I. Ry. Co., 110 Mich. 494; Blondel v. St. Paul City Ry. Co., 66 Minn. 284; Scott v. Bergen County Traction Co., 63 N. J. Law, 407.

113 Armstrong v. Montgomery St. Ry. Co., 123 Ala. 233; Sweeney v. Kansas City Cable Ry. Co., 150 Mo. 385; Omaha St. Ry. Co. v. Craig, 39 Neb. 601; Medler v. Atlantic Ave. R. Co., 12 N. Y. Supp. 930.

114 Washington & G. R. Co. v. Harmon's Adm'r, 147 U. S. 571; Birmingham R. & E. Co. v. James, 121 Ala. 120; Watkins v. Birmingham R. & E. Co., 120 Ala. 147; Currie v. Mendenhall, 77 Minn. 179; Bowie v. Greenville St. Ry. Co., 69 Miss. 196; Linch v. Pittsburgh Traction Co., 153 Pa. 102; Foster v. Union Traction Co., 199 Pa. 498.

115 Demann v. Eighth Ave. R. Co., 10 Misc. Rep. (N. Y.) 191; Sweeney v. Union Traction Co., 199 Pa. 293; Consolidated Traction Co. v. Thalheimer, 59 N. J. Law, 474.

116 Mitchell v. Electric Traction Co., 12 Pa. Super. Ct. 472.

117 Springfield Consolidated Ry. Co. v. Hoeffner. 71 Ill. App. 162; Bradley v. Ft. Wayne & E. Ry. Co.. 94 Mich. 35.

servation that thousands every day leave their seats to get off before the car has stopped without sustaining any injury.[118]

A passenger on a street car who goes out upon the platform after the conductor has called the name of a street, and is standing upon the step when the car stops, is justified in alighting.[119]

In Dresslar v. Citizens' St. R. Co.[120] it was held that where a passenger, in attempting to change his position from the platform to the step below, preparatory to alighting, was injured by the gradual increase in speed, there was no negligence on the part of the company; and the same ruling has been made where the passenger fell off, but there was no unusual motion of the car.[121] Where a passenger testified that, as the car slowed down in answer to his signal, he went onto the rear platform, and "the car went right from under him," but there was no proof of any jolt or jerk, there is no evidence of negligence on the part of the company.[122] In Lacas v. Detroit City Ry. Co.[123] it was held that, where the passenger was just about to put her foot upon the running board, and it would have been difficult for her to turn back, she was not guilty of lack of due care in continuing her descent from the car as it started; and the same ruling was made in Piper v. Minneapolis St. Ry. Co.,[124]

118 Babcock v. Los Angeles Traction Co., 128 Cal. 173; Nichols v. Sixth Ave. R. Co., 38 N. Y. 131.

119 North Chicago St. R. Co. v. Brown, 178 Ill. 187; Indianapolis St. Ry. Co. v. Hockett, 159 Ind. 677.

120 19 Ind. App. 383.

121 Philips v. St. Charles St. R. Co., 106 La. 592.

122 Armstrong v. Metropolitan St. Ry. Co., 23 App. Div. (N. Y.) 137.

123 92 Mich. 412.

124 52 Minn. 269.

and in Indianapolis St. Ry. Co. v. Lawn.[125] Where a passenger jumped from a car in fear of an apparent collision, it was held that a person placed in sudden peril is not held to the usual standard of care.[126] Where a passenger placed his hand on the door of a car on an elevated railroad to steady himself before alighting, and a guard opened the door just before the train stopped, there was held to be no negligence.[127]

### § 68. Notice of desire to alight.

Whether or not a passenger gave notice of his desire to alight from a street car is an important point in determining the question of due care and negligence.[128] Although such notice need not be express, but may be implied from the conduct of the passenger,[129] a passenger has no right to assume, after he has signaled the conductor, that a reduction of speed is for his benefit, in the absence of any knowledge that the conductor communicated his signal to the gripman, and that the reduction in speed was in answer to that signal.[130] Where the conductor, on a passenger's signal, raised his hand towards the bell rope, and, as the passenger stepped off, the car started suddenly, due care and negligence were held to be for the jury.[131] Where one passenger gives notice of a desire to alight, and the car stops, or is about to stop, another passenger, who wishes to alight,

125 (Ind. App.) 66 N. E. 508.

126 South Covington & C. St. Ry. Co. v. Ware, 84 Ky. 267.

127 Hannon v. Boston El. Ry. Co., 182 Mass. 425.

128 McDonald v. Kansas City Cable Ry. Co., 32 Mo. App. 70.

129 West Chicago St. R. Co. v. Stiver, 69 Ill. App. 625.

130 Armstrong v. Metropolitan St. Ry. Co., 36 App. Div. (N. Y.) 525.

131 Harris v. Union Ry. Co., 69 App. Div. (N. Y.) 385.

need not give notice of his desire to do so as a matter of law.[132] If a street car is stopped at a customary place, a passenger has the right to alight without notice, and the driver must allow him a reasonable time to alight, and is liable if he knew or should have known that the passenger was alighting, even if he had reason to believe the passenger was not going to get off, or was expressly so notified.[133] Actual or express notice is not required if the conductor knew or ought to have known that the passenger was in the act of alighting.[134]

Where a conductor went ahead to a crossing, and then signaled the car to come on, and a passenger, who had given no notice of his intention to alight, was injured, while the motorman gave no notice of starting, it was held that due care and negligence were for the jury.[135]

While a passenger is thus not always guilty of lack of due care in alighting without giving notice, it is equally true that the passenger is always bound to show that the negligence of the company contributed to the injury; and where a passenger gave a signal to stop, the car slowed up and she gave a second signal, and was injured while alighting, the company was held not liable when it did not appear that her second signal was not a regular starting signal, nor that the motorman might have known that she was in a dangerous position.[136] It may be stated, as a general proposi-

132 Schaefer v. Central Crosstown R. Co., 30 Misc. Rep. (N. Y.) 114; Rathbone v. Union R. Co., 13 R. I. 709.

133 Chicago West Div. Ry. Co. v. Mills, 105 Ill. 63.

134 Washington & G. R. Co. v. Grant, 11 App. D. C. 107; Louisville Ry. Co. v. Rammaker, 21 Ky. Law Rep. 250.

135 Bensing v. People's Electric St. Ry. Co., 9 Pa. Super. Ct. 142.

tion, that, where a passenger is injured while alighting without giving notice to those in charge of the car, and it does not appear that they had a reasonable opportunity of knowing that the passenger was alighting, there is no negligence on the part of the company.[137] A conductor is not absolutely bound to remember the notice which a passenger gives him of her desire to alight.[138] It is the duty of those in charge of the car to bring it to a full stop when a passenger signifies his intention to alight.[139] If the conductor is not in his place, and a passenger alights when the car stops apparently in answer to her signal, due care is for the jury.[140]

136 Sirk v. Marion St. Ry. Co., 11 Ind. App. 680.

137 Chicago West Div. Ry. Co. v. Mills, 91 Ill. 39; Ackerstadt v. Chicago City Ry. Co., 194 Ill. 616; Chicago City Ry. Co. v. Gregg, 69 Ill. App. 77; Nichols v. Middlesex R. Co., 106 Mass. 463; Gilbert v. West End St. Ry. Co., 160 Mass. 403; Jacobs v. West End St. Ry Co., 178 Mass. 116; Oddy v. West End St. Ry. Co., 178 Mass. 341; Spaulding v. Quincy & B. St. Ry. Co. (Mass.) 69 N. E. 217; Lee v. Elizabeth, P. & C. J. Ry. Co. (N. J. Sup.) 55 Atl. 106; Hogan v. Central Park, N. & E. R. R. Co., 124 N. Y. 647; Losee v. Watervliet Turnpike & R. Co., 63 Hun (N. Y.) 404; Steuer v. Metropolitan St. Ry. Co., 46 App. Div. (N. Y.) 500; Sims v. Metropolitan St. Ry Co., 65 App. Div. (N. Y.) 270; Dickson v. Broadway & S. A. R. Co. 33 N. Y. Super. Ct. 330; Grabenstein v. Metropolitan St. Ry. Co. 84 N. Y. Supp. 261; Ashtabula Rapid Transit Co. v. Holmes, 67 Ohio St. 153; Clutzbeher v. Union Passenger Ry. Co. (Pa.) 1 Atl 597; Blakney v. Seattle Electric Co., 28 Wash. 607.

138 Robinson v. Northampton St. Ry. Co., 157 Mass. 224.

139 Rouser v. Washington & G. R. Co., 13 App. D. C. 320; Crissey v. Hestonville, M. & F. P. Ry. Co., 75 Pa. 83.

140 North Birmingham St. Ry. Co. v. Calderwood, 89 Ala. 247; Gillespie v. Yonkers R. Co., 83 N. Y. Supp. 1043.

## § 69. Alighting in spite of warning.

Where a passenger was about to alight at a place where the car had stopped to await a signal from a flagman before passing over the crossing, and was told by the conductor not to get off, but insisted on so doing, and was injured, she cannot recover.[141] If a passenger alights from a car in disregard of the conductor's[142] or motorman's[143] request to await until it stops, the company is not liable.

## § 70. Condition of car.

A street car company must exercise the highest degree of care to keep its platforms and steps in safe condition as far as practicable, considering the climate, the temperature, and the condition of the air and ground with respect to snow, moisture, and frost;[144] and in Neslie v. Second & Third Sts. Passenger Ry. Co.[145] the question whether ice was allowed to remain on the steps an unreasonable length of time was held to be for the jury.

When a passenger testified that, as he was alighting, he caught his foot in the step of the car, and, as he pulled to get it loose, fell and was injured, there was held to be no evidence of negligence.[146]

One who alights from a moving car assumes the risk of the accident, and the construction of a car cannot be said to be defective when it is dangerous only in view of such conduct.[147]

141 Jackson v. Grand Ave. Ry. Co., 118 Mo. 199.

142 Duncan v. Wyatt Park Ry. Co., 48 Mo. App. 659.

143 Campbell v. Los Angeles Ry. Co., 135 Cal. 137.

144 Herbert v. St. Paul City Ry. Co., 85 Minn. 341.

145 113 Pa. 300.

146 Howell v. Union Traction Co., 202 Pa. 338.

In Hitchcock v. Brooklyn City R. Co.[148] there was held to be no evidence of a defective step. Where there are parallel tracks, it is a question for the jury whether it is negligence not to have guards to prevent passengers from alighting on the side next to the parallel track.[149]

Where a passenger was injured by catching her clothing on a broken curtain hook, and the company proved that it used these hooks on all its cars, that such an accident had never occurred before, that the cars were inspected at the end of each trip, and, if a broken hook was found, it was replaced, there was held to be no negligence.[150] The crowded condition of a car is no excuse for the conductor's lack of attention towards a passenger who is alighting.[151]

Where it was claimed that a step was worn, and was allowed to become slippery by an accumulation of mud, negligence was held to be for the jury;[152] and where a passenger was injured by a slippery step while alighting during a snow storm, a verdict for the plaintiff was held to be justified.[153]

## § 71. Injury by fellow passenger.

If a passenger is injured by a fellow passenger stepping on her dress while she is alighting, the company is not liable.[154]

147 Werbowlsky v. Ft. Wayne & E. Ry. Co., 86 Mich. 236.

148 3 N. Y. Supp. 218.

149 Atlanta Consol. St. Ry. Co. v. Bates, 103 Ga. 333.

150 Kelly v. New York & S. B. Ry. Co., 109 N. Y. 44.

151 West Chicago St. R. Co. v. Waniata, 68 Ill. App. 481.

152 Louisville Ry. Co. v. Park, 96 Ky. 580.

153 Foster v. Old Colony St. Ry. Co., 182 Mass. 378.

154 Poole v. Consolidated St. Ry. Co., 100 Mich. 379.

In Bowdle v. Detroit St. Ry. Co.[155] it was held that, when a passenger's dress caught in a hook while she was alighting, the defendant would not be liable if the hook were but recently displaced by a passenger, and that was the sole cause of the accident.

Where there is a rush of passengers when a car has stopped for them to alight, the conductor must do what he reasonably can to prevent injuries to the passengers; but it is not his duty to assist any passenger in particular, unless he sees that one is in special danger.[156]

If a passenger is injured in a crowd at a transfer station, and such place is dangerous because of the hurried efforts of the passengers to change cars, so that a conductor is necessary on each car, the company is liable if a conductor left his car before reaching the transfer station.[157]

The company is not liable for injuries by fellow passengers while a passenger was alighting, when the conductor was assisting a child in her care to alight.[158]

Where a fellow passenger rang the bell to start while a passenger was alighting, there was held to be no evidence of negligence of the company.[159]

The company is not liable for the act of an intermeddler in giving the signal to start, when its employes could not guard against it; but where the conductor makes no attempt to stop the car, it will be held to ratify the act.[160]

155 103 Mich. 272.

156 Jarmy v. Duluth St. Ry. Co., 55 Minn. 271.

157 Baldwin v. Fair Haven & W. R. Co., 68 Conn. 567.

158 Furgason v. Citizens' St. Ry. Co., 16 Ind. App. 171.

159 O'Neil v. Lynn & B. R. Co., 180 Mass. 576; Krone v. Southwest Missouri Electric Ry. Co. (Mo. App.) 71 S. W. 712.

160 Leavenworth Electric R. Co. v. Cusick, 60 Kan. 590.

Where a passenger was injured, while alighting, by other passengers crowding onto the car, negligence was held to be for the jury.[161]

## § 72. Miscellaneous.

Where a passenger got off a car to get his hat, and was run over by another car, due care and negligence were held to be for the jury.[162] In determining what is due care, the instinct of self-preservation must be considered;[163] and when a woman got off a moving car for fear of being insulted, the reasonableness of her belief was held to be for the jury.[164]

The mere fact that an accident happens to a passenger while he is alighting from a car is not enough to raise a presumption of negligence;[165] and even when there is a sudden jerk, but the cause is unexplained, this is not sufficient to show negligence.[166] If the injury to a passenger is caused by apparatus wholly under the control of the carrier, and furnished and applied by it, a presumption of negligence arises.[167] In City & Suburban Ry. v. Findley[168] it was somewhat loosely stated that the presumption is always against the carrier.

161 Buck v. Manhattan Ry. Co., 15 Daly (N. Y.) 550.

162 Thomas v. Union Ry. Co., 18 App. Div. (N. Y.) 185.

163 Slaughter v. Metropolitan St. Ry. Co., 116 Mo. 269.

164 Ashton v. Detroit City Ry. Co., 78 Mich. 587.

165 Chicago City Ry. Co. v. Catlin, 70 Ill. App. 97; Dresslar v. Citizens' St. R. Co., 19 Ind. App. 383; Olfermann v. Union Depot R. Co., 125 Mo. 408.

166 Bradley v. Ft. Wayne & E. Ry. Co., 94 Mich. 35; Etson v. Ft. Wayne & B. I. Ry. Co., 110 Mich. 494.

167 Chicago City Ry. Co. v. Catlin, 70 Ill. App. 97.

168 76 Ga. 311.

Where one employe was both motorman and conductor, it was held that the test of negligence was not whether an injury could have been prevented if two men had been employed, but that the expense of a second man, the amount of traffic, and the danger in operating the car should all be taken into consideration.[169]

Where a passenger was injured while alighting, and there was no conductor, and the driver knew nothing of the accident, a verdict against the company was held to be supported by the evidence;[170] but where there was an ordinance forbidding conductors to allow women to leave a moving car, and a woman was injured while so alighting when the conductor was temporarily absent from the car, the plaintiff was held to have established a *prima facie* case.[171]

Where a cripple was carried by his usual stopping place, and the train stopped, and then backed while he was getting off, the negligence of the company is for the jury.[172]

Where a car was negligently started, and the conductor tried to save a passenger from falling, and, instead, accelerated her fall, it was held that the company was liable for both acts.[173]

In Posten v. Denver Consol. Tramway Co.[174] it was held error to sustain a nonsuit where a passenger was alighting from a slowly moving car, and the conductor seized him and caused him to fall, and it is negligence for a conductor

169 Palmer v. Winona Ry. & Light Co., 78 Minn. 138.

170 City & Suburban Ry. v. Findley, 76 Ga. 311.

171 Fortune v. Missouri R. Co., 10 Mo. App. 252.

172 Gadsden & A. U. Ry. Co. v. Causler, 97 Ala. 235.

173 Macer v. Third Ave. R. Co., 47 N. Y. Super. Ct. 461.

174 11 Colo. App. 187.

to get on the steps of the rear platform and throw a passenger off.[174a]

A passenger is chargeable with knowledge of an ordinance requiring cars to stop at the further side of a street.[175]

174a Fleming v. St. Louis & S. Ry. Co. (Mo. App.) 74 S. W. 382.

175 North Birmingham St. Ry. Co. v. Calderwood, 89 Ala. 247.

# CHAPTER V.

## EJECTION.

I. What Renders Passenger Liable to Ejection.

§ 73. Nonpayment of Fare.
74. Same—What is a Reasonable Tender.
75. Conduct.
76. Color..

II. Manner, Place, and Time of Ejection.

§ 77. What Constitutes Ejection.
78. How Performed.

III. Master and Servant.

§ 79. Responsibility for Acts of Servant.
80. Exemplary Damages.

IV. Tickets and Transfers.

§ 81. Place of Transfer.
82. Time of Transfer.
83. Transfer Bad on Face.
84. Transfer Without Check.
85. Miscellaneous.

### I. What Renders Passenger Liable to Ejection.

**A passenger may be ejected for a refusal to pay fare, or for making a tender of fare unreasonable in quality or amount, and may be ejected for language or conduct which causes, or is reasonably certain to cause, offense or annoyance to other passengers, or for a refusal to obey the reasonable rules of the company. A passenger may not be ejected on account of his color.**

## § 73. Nonpayment of fare.

Those in charge of a street car may eject a passenger for refusal to pay fare,[1] and may in like manner eject trespassers who have no intention of paying fare,[2] and may prevent access to a car by a trespasser,[3] or prevent passengers from boarding a car before it has reached its usual stopping place.[4] *A fortiori* they may eject one who has just been rightfully ejected, and is seeking to gain an entrance a second time.[5] A statute providing for ejection from street cars in case fare is not paid applies to electric cars, though enacted before their introduction.[6]

A rule requiring a passenger to deposit his fare in a box upon entering a car is a reasonable one,[7] and a passenger who will not comply with the rule can be ejected with the use of reasonable force;[8] but where a driver, who is authorized to make change, gives a passenger five cents too little, the passenger must be regarded as having paid his fare, and the driver cannot eject him for his refusal to put an ad-

1 Chicago City Ry. Co. v. Pelletier, 134 Ill. 120; West Chicago St. R. Co. v. Luleich, 85 Ill. App. 643; Hudson v. Lynn & B. R. Co., 178 Mass. 64; Sanford v. Eighth Ave. R. Co., 23 N. Y. 343; Lynch v. Metropolitan El. Ry. Co., 90 N. Y. 77.

2 North Chicago City Ry. Co. v. Gastka, 128 Ill. 613; Amato v. Sixth Ave. R. Co., 9 Misc. Rep. (N. Y.) 4; Ansteth v. Buffalo Ry. Co., 9 Misc. Rep. (N. Y.) 419.

3 Amato v. Sixth Ave. R. Co., 9 Misc. Rep. (N. Y.) 4; Ansteth v. Buffalo Ry. Co., 9 Misc. Rep. (N. Y.) 419.

4 Lesser v. St. Louis & S. Ry. Co., 85 Mo. App. 326.

5 North Chicago St. R. Co. v. Olds, 40 Ill. App. 421, 64 Ill. App. 595.

6 Hudson v. Lynn & B. R. Co., 178 Mass. 64.

7 Nye v. Marysville & Y. C. St. R. Co., 97 Cal. 461; Curtis v. Louisville City Ry. Co., 94 Ky. 573.

8 Nye v. Marysville & Y. C. St. R. Co., 97 Cal. 461.

ditional fare in the box.[9] Where the company posts a rule requiring passengers to drop their fares in a box, a passenger cannot be expected to know of private directions given to drivers to go through the cars and collect fares when the cars are crowded, and a passenger who has put his fare into the box is wrongfully ejected for refusing to pay another fare.[10] In Corbett v. Twenty-Third St. Ry. Co.,[11] a passenger put one fare too many into the box, and the driver told him he must go to the office of the company to get it back. In the meantime a lady entered the car, and gave her fare to the plaintiff, who put it in his pocket, and on refusal to give it up, was arrested. It was held that the rule of the company requiring a passenger to go to the office was unreasonable, that the plaintiff's conduct was entirely reasonable, and that the company was liable for his removal from the car and his detention in the station house.

A statute declaring that railroad companies shall not charge more than three cents a mile does not apply to a horse railroad where the passenger pays one fixed sum, whether he goes the entire distance or not.[12] In Forman v. New Orleans & C. R. Co.[13] it was held that a discrimination in the rate of fare, allowing residents on a certain street to ride for a less sum under certain conditions, was not unreasonable.

A passenger may not enter a car, and make a continuous round trip over a given route for one fare, under a statutory provision, but, after passing the usual terminus where the

9 Curtis v. Louisville City Ry. Co., 94 Ky. 573.

10 Perry v. Pittsburgh Union Passenger Ry., 153 Pa. 236.

11 42 Hun (N. Y.) 587.

12 Hoyt v. Sixth Ave. R. Co., 1 Daly (N. Y.) 528.

13 40 La. Ann. 446.

return trip begins, another fare must be paid, and for such refusal the passenger may be ejected.[14] Where a conductor tells a passenger that he will carry him between two points for a certain fare, the company is bound by this representation; and if the conductor demands a higher fare and the passenger refuses to pay it, and is ejected, he may maintain an action for such ejection.[15] Where a passenger drops a piece of money in the straw on the bottom of a street car, he is entitled to a reasonable length of time to search for his money.[16] Where there was a controversy between the conductor and the passenger as to whether the passenger had paid his fare, the fact that the passenger could have prevented his ejection by giving the conductor another ticket will not reduce the damages to the sum represented by the value of the ticket, where the conductor, with the delay of a few minutes, could have made an investigation which would have definitely determined whether or not the plaintiff had paid his fare.[17] After the ejection has commenced, it is proper to continue it, notwithstanding a tender of the fare.[17a]

If a passenger in an open car chooses to change to a closed car attached to it, he is rightly ejected for refusing to pay a second fare.[18] A rule that a passenger shall pay a larger sum in cash than that needed for a ticket is unreasonable where the passenger is taken on where tickets are not

14 Wimmer v. Union Traction Co., 12 Pa. Super. Ct. 467.

15 Wright v. Glens Falls, S. H. & F. E. St. R. Co., 24 App. Div. (N. Y.) 617.

16 Hall v. Second & Third Sts. Passenger Ry. Co., 14 Wkly. Notes Cas. (Pa.) 242.

17 Sprenger v. Tacoma Traction Co., 15 Wash. 660.

17a Garrison v. United Rys. & Elec. Co. (Md.) 55 Atl. 371.

18 Lasker v. Third Ave. R. Co., 27 Misc. Rep. (N. Y.) 824.

for sale.[18a] Where a passenger asked if a car was an M. P. car, and the conductor said that it was, the fact that the car was coming from and not going towards M. P. was held not to relieve the passenger from paying another fare after reaching the terminus.[18b]

### § 74. Same—What is a reasonable tendeı

The question as to what is legal tender for car fare, both as to the quality and the amount of the sum offered, has arisen several times. A genuine silver coin of the United States (a half dollar of 1824), distinguishable as such, though somewhat rare, and differing in appearance from other coins of this government of like denomination and of later dates, is nevertheless a legal tender for car fare, and a passenger ejected for refusal to make payment otherwise than by tendering such a coin is entitled to an action for damages.[19] Similarly, a genuine silver coin worn smooth by use, not appreciably diminished in weight, and distinguishable, is a legal tender for car fare, and a passenger ejected for refusal to make other payment can maintain an action for such ejection.[20] Where a passenger tenders the exact fare in legal coin, he is wrongfully ejected, even though the coin is so worn that the conductor honestly believes it is not good.[21] A dollar bill, however, from the upper left-hand corner of which a piece one inch and a half by one inch and a quarter has been torn, is not a legal tender for car fare, and the

18a Kennedy v. Birmingham Ry., L. & P. Co. (Ala.) 35 So. 108.

18b McGarry v. Holyoke St. R. Co., 182 Mass. 123.

19 Atlanta Consol. St. Ry. Co. v. Keeny, 99 Ga. 266.

20 Mobile St. Ry. Co. v. Watters, 135 Ala. 227; Jersey City & B. R. Co. v. Morgan, 52 N. J. Law, 60.

21 Ruth v. St. Louis Transit Co. (Mo. App.) 71 S. W. 1055.

conductor may eject a passenger who refuses to make other payment. He is not bound to accept a bill which is substantially mutilated.[22]

A passenger upon a street railroad is not bound to tender the exact fare, but must tender a reasonable sum, and the carrier must accept such tender, and furnish change to a reasonable amount.[23]

The authorities are not in harmony as to what is a reasonable sum. In California it has been held that the tender of a five-dollar gold piece is reasonable.[24] The court said: "It does not follow, if it be established as a rule that five dollars in a reasonable amount to be tendered to a conductor, that twenty dollars or fifty dollars is also a reasonable amount, and must be accepted. The fears of the appellant are based upon the assumption that passengers generally will contumaciously, to avoid the payment of fare, and require the companies to carry them free, offer coin of a large denomination; but these fears, we think, can safely be set aside upon the theory that a question like this will settle itself by a spirit of mutual accommodation between carrier and passenger. It is a well-known fact that the five-dollar gold piece is practically the lowest gold coin in use in this section of the country."

In New York, on the contrary, it has been held that a rule of a street car company in a large city, requiring its conductors to furnish change to passengers to the amount of two dollars, is reasonable, and a tender of a five-dollar

22 North Hudson County Ry. Co. v. Anderson, 61 N. J. Law, 248.

23 Barrett v. Market St. Ry. Co., 81 Cal. 296; Barker v. Central Park, N. & E. R. R. Co., 151 N. Y. 237; Muldowney v. Pittsburg & B. Traction Co., 8 Pa. Super. Ct. 335.

24 Barrett v. Market St. Ry. Co., 81 Cal. 296.

bill is unreasonable, and need not be accepted.[25] In commenting upon the California case just cited, the court said: "It is quite possible that there existed local reasons for the decision in California, as the judge writing the opinion suggested that the five-dollar gold piece was practically the lowest gold coin in use in that section of the country."

In Pennsylvania, also, it has been held that the tender of a five-dollar bill for a five-cent fare is unreasonable as matter of law, and that the conductor is not bound to receive it.[26]

## § 75. Conduct.

Ejection may also be made for misconduct. A passenger may offend by his language, as by calling the conductor a liar in the presence and hearing of other passengers, without having been reasonably provoked to the use of such language by the improper conduct of the conductor, and in such a case he is rightfully ejected.[27] So, if his language to the conductor is abusive and insulting.[28] In Chicago City Ry. Co. v. Pelletier[29] the court said: "Undoubtedly, if he was using profane, vulgar, and indecent language, having a tendency to offend and annoy passengers, the conductor would have the right to stop the car and order him off, and, on his refusal to go, might eject him, using such force as might be necessary for that purpose. A person who will not behave with ordinary decency upon a car,

25 Barker v. Central Park, N. & E. R. R. Co., 151 N. Y. 237.

26 Muldowney v. Pittsburg & B. Traction Co., 8 Pa. Super. Ct. 335.

27 Eads v. Metropolitan Ry. Co., 43 Mo. App. 536.

28 Flynn v. Central Park, &c., R. Co., 49 N. Y. Super. Ct. 81.

29 33 Ill. App. 455.

and will not leave it at the command of the conductor, may be treated as a trespasser thereon, whether he has paid fare or not, and, as such, ejected." In affirming the judgment of the appellate court,[30] the court took pains to bring out the point that the duty of the company in preventing the use of offensive language on its cars was for the protection of its passengers, and arose out of its duty to them. Thus it was held that the conductor has no right to put a passenger off his car for the use of vulgar and indecent language in a tone loud enough to attract the attention of other passengers, and refusing to desist, unless such language is calculated to annoy and disturb them. The court said: "It seems to be contended that the fact that the attention of the passengers, or any number of them, was attracted by the language, whether it was calculated to annoy or disturb them or not, would justify the ejection of a passenger. Such is not the rule. Railway companies are not conservators of the public or of private morals. * * * However strongly the use of indecent language in a public conveyance should be condemned, it is apparent that the use of such language, attracting a few persons on the rear platform or seat, might create neither annoyance nor disturbance, while the same language used at other times, in the presence of others, or under different circumstances, would be highly offensive, and justly subject the passenger who persists in using the same to ejection from the car."

In Maine, by statute, the use of indecent or profane language in a street railroad car is a breach of the peace, and the conductor of the car may remove a person guilty

30 Chicago City Ry. Co. v. Pelletier, 134 Ill. 120.

of such breach of peace from the car, or may arrest him.[31] The court said: "It is the opinion of the court that he may rightfully be removed from the car, not as a punishment for his insult to the conductor as an individual, but to vindicate the authority of the law, which forbids the use of such language in a street car or any other public place where women and children have a right to be."

Besides the use of profane and indecent language, a passenger may be guilty of other misconduct which will justify expulsion. As in the case of improper language, the comfort and convenience of the other passengers is the test to be kept in mind; and the rule as usually stated is that the company not only have the power, but it is their duty, to expel from their cars persons who are disorderly to the inconvenience and annoyance of other passengers.[32] It is not necessary for those in charge of the car to wait until some actual disturbance takes place, but a reasonable anticipation of conduct that will prove offensive or annoying to other passengers is sufficient.[33]

The fact that a passenger is drunk will not in every case justify his expulsion. It is rather the degree of intoxica-

31 Robinson v. Rockland, T. & C. St. Ry., 87 Me. 387.

32 West Chicago St. R. Co. v. Luleich, 85 Ill. App. 643; Vinton v. Middlesex R. Co., 11 Allen (Mass.) 304; Murphy v. Union Ry. Co., 118 Mass. 228; Higgins v. Watervliet Turnpike & R. Co., 46 N. Y. 23; Putnam v. Broadway & S. A. R. Co., 55 N. Y. 108; Flynn v. Central Park, &c., R. Co., 49 N. Y. Super. Ct. 81; Edgerly v. Union St. R. Co., 67 N. H. 312.

33 Lemont v. Washington & G. R. Co., 1 Mackey (D. C.) 180; Vinton v. Middlesex R. Co., 11 Allen (Mass.) 304; Murphy v. Union Ry. Co., 118 Mass. 228; Hudson v. Lynn & B. R. Co., 178 Mass. 64; Cobb v. Boston El. Ry. Co., 179 Mass. 212; Edgerly v. Union St. R. Co., 67 N. H. 312.

tion, its effect upon the passenger, and the fact that, by reason of the intoxication, he is dangerous or annoying to other passengers, that gives the right of expulsion.[34] A conductor has the right to eject a passenger who is intoxicated, and has vomited upon the floor of the car,[35] and a passenger who, although sober, is afflicted with severe vomiting.[36] A conductor should remove a drunken passenger, who is vomiting profusely, at once, and need not wait until a passenger who is entering has taken her seat, and the aisle is clear.[37]

Where a conductor ejected a passenger afflicted with St. Vitus' dance, it was held to be no excuse that there was a rule of the company forbidding intoxicated persons to ride, and that the involuntary motions of the plaintiff resembled those of an intoxicated man.[38] Where a passenger troubled with heart disease was taken sick on a car, and, when removed, died within a few minutes, there was held to be no evidence that the company caused the passenger's death.[39]

A rule of a street railway company forbidding passengers to stand on the platform when there is room inside the car is a reasonable regulation, and a passenger who refuses to obey it is rightfully ejected;[40] but where there is a rule forbidding riding on the front platform, and fare is collected from a passenger who rides on the front platform when the

[34] Putnam v. Broadway & S. A. R. Co., 55 N. Y. 108.

[35] Converse v. Washington & G. R. Co., 2 MacArthur (D. C.) 504.

[36] Conolly v. Crescent City R. Co., 41 La. Ann. 57.

[37] Cobb v. Boston El. Ry. Co., 179 Mass. 212.

[38] Regner v. Glens Falls, S. H. & F. E. St. R. Co., 74 Hun (N. Y.) 202.

[39] Briggs v. Minneapolis St. Ry. Co., 52 Minn. 36.

[40] Ft. Clark St. R. v. Ebaugh, 49 Ill. App. 582; McMillan v. Federal St. & P. V. Passenger Ry. Co., 172 Pa. 523.

car is crowded, he cannot be ejected unless his fare is returned.[41] The fact that a passenger feels sick is no excuse for his violating this rule.[42]

Where a passenger goes on a car with a dog, and refuses to leave when told that he is violating a rule of the company, he is rightfully ejected;[43] and the reasonableness of a rule of the company forbidding the carrying of live animals in the cars is for the court, not for the jury.[44]

A rule that passengers must not take into street cars packages or goods that are cumbersome or dangerous is reasonable as a matter of law; and where a passenger with a valise and two rifles, with bayonets attached, boarded a closed street car, in which there were several passengers, he was rightfully ejected.[45]

In Morris v. Atlantic Ave. R. Co.,[46] whether two packages were so large as to inconvenience other passengers, within a rule of the company, and thus necessitate the payment of an extra fare, was held to be a question for the jury, and the decision of the conductor not conclusive.

A conductor has a right to eject a pasenger who is attempting to get on the car at an unreasonable place, forbidden by the rules of the company.[47]

A passenger who refuses to remove his muddy boots from the cushions of the seats is rightly ejected.[48]

41 Hanna v. Nassau Electric R. Co., 18 App. Div. (N. Y.) 137.

42 Montgomery v. Buffalo Ry. Co., 165 N. Y. 139.

43 Butler v. Steinway Ry. Co., 87 Hun (N. Y.) 10.

44 Daniel v. North Jersey St. Ry. Co., 64 N. J. Law, 603.

45 Dowd v. Albany Ry. Co., 47 App. Div. (N. Y.) 202.

46 116 N. Y. 552.

47 Lesser v. St. Louis & S. Ry. Co., 85 Mo. App. 326.

48 Davis v. Ottawa Electric Ry. Co., 28 Ont. 654.

### § 76. Color.

A conductor cannot eject a passenger on account of color,[49] and a regulation of the company will not justify him in such ejection.[50] A law providing for separate but equal accommodations for white and colored passengers is constitutional.[50a]

## II. Manner, Place and Time of Ejection.

**It does not require the use of "force," in the general acceptance of the term, to constitute an ejection. Mere contact is enough, and even this is not always necessary.**

**Leaving a car under protest is enough, and forcing a child, by threats or gestures, to jump from a moving car, constitutes an ejection.**

**Ejection must be performed in a reasonable manner, and at a reasonable place and time.**

### § 77. What constitutes ejection.

"Force," in its legal significance, may mean merely contact. Thus, in Watson v. Oswego St. Ry. Co.,[51] the conductor ordered the plaintiff, who was weak from the effect of drugs, to leave the car, and placed his hand on his arm. The plaintiff complied with the order, being assisted by the conductor and a friend, he being helpless at the time. It was held that, if the physical contact of the conductor was in the slightest degree a constraining power in

40 Pleasants v. North Beach & M. R. Co., 34 Cal. 586; Turner v. North Beach & M. R. Co., 34 Cal. 594; Derry v. Lowry, 6 Phila. (Pa.) 30.

50 Derry v. Lowry, 6 Phila. (Pa.) 30.

50a State v. Pearson (La.) 34 So. 575.

51 7 Misc. Rep. (N. Y.) 562.

causing the plaintiff to act and leave the car, it constituted "force," in the legal acceptance of the term. Where a conductor took a girl by the arm, intending to remove her from the car against her will, this was held to be forcible removal.[52] Personal injury is not essential to a recovery.[53]

It is even held that actual physical contact is not necessary to constitute an ejection. It is enough to show that a passenger left the car, under protest, in obedience to the orders of the conductor.[54] Forcing a child, by threats or gestures, to jump from a moving car, constitutes an ejection.[55]

### § 78. How performed.

The right of ejection must be exercised in a reasonable manner. No more force than is necessary must be used in ejecting a passenger[56] or a trespasser.[57]

[52] Curtis v. Sioux City & H. P. Ry. Co., 87 Iowa, 622.

[53] Light v. Harrisburg & M. Electric Ry. Co., 4 Pa. Super. Ct. 427.

[54] Highland Ave. & B. R. Co. v. Winn, 93 Ala. 306; Consolidated Traction Co. v. Taborn, 58 N. J. Law, 1; Ray v. Cortland & H. Traction Co., 19 App. Div. (N. Y.) 530; Eddy v. Syracuse Rapid Transit R. Co., 50 App. Div. (N. Y.) 109; Laird v. Pittsburg Traction Co., 166 Pa. 4.

[55] Bay Shore R. Co. v. Harris, 67 Ala. 6; Indianapolis St. Ry. Co. v. Hockett (Ind.) 67 N. E. 106; Ansteth v. Buffalo Ry. Co., 9 Misc. Rep. (N. Y.) 419; Mt. Adams & E. P. Inclined Ry. Co. v. Doherty, 8 Ohio. Cir. Ct. R. 349; Sandford v. Hestonville, M. & F. P. Ry., 153 Pa. 300; Washington, A. & M. V. Electric Ry. Co. v. Quayle, 95 Va. 741; Richmond Traction Co. v. Wilkinson (Va.) 43 S. E. 622.

[56] Nye v. Marysville & Y. C. St. R. Co., 97 Cal. 461; Converse v. Washington & G. R. Co., 2 MacArthur (D. C.) 504; Chicago City Ry. Co. v. Pelletier, 134 Ill. 120; Ft. Clark St. R. v. Ebaugh, 49 Ill. App. 582; Nussbaum v. Louisville Ry. Co., 22 Ky. Law Rep. 271; Eads v. Metropolitan Ry. Co., 43 Mo. App. 536; Lesser v. St. Louis & S. Ry. Co., 85 Mo. App. 326; Haman v. Omaha Horse Ry. Co., 35 Neb. 74; Jackson v. Second Ave. R. Co., 47 N. Y. 274; Lynch v.

Indecent or insulting language used by a passenger will not justify a conductor in assaulting him.[58] If, however, the passenger uses the language with the intention of provoking the assault, he cannot recover.[59]

The court, in Weber v. Brooklyn, Q. C. & S. R. Co.,[60] regarded the decision in Scott v. Central Park, N. & E. R. R. Co.[61] as holding that language calculated or likely to bring about an assault will excuse the conductor, and refused to sanction this doctrine; but it seems probable that, in the Scott Case, language intended to provoke an assault was meant, the court saying: "If he suceeds in his efforts to bring about such a result."

So, where a passenger refuses to alight, insultingly challenges the conductor to put him off, and then violently assaults the conductor upon his proceeding in a lawful manner to make the expulsion, the company is not liable for great and unnecessary violence used by the conductor;[62] and in Wise v. South Covington & C. Ry.[63] it was held that a passenger who brought about an encounter by abusive

Metropolitan El. Ry. Co., 90 N. Y. 77; Butler v. Steinway Ry. Co., 87 Hun (N. Y.) 10; Dowd v. Albany Ry., 47 App. Div. (N. Y.) 202; Caldwell v. Central Park, N. & E. R. R. Co., 7 Misc. Rep. (N. Y.) 67.

57 North Chicago City Ry. Co. v. Gastka, 128 Ill. 613; Amato v. Sixth Ave. R. Co., 9 Misc. Rep. (N. Y.) 4.

58 Hanson v. Urbana & C. Electric St. Ry. Co., 75 Ill. App. 474; Weber v. Brooklyn, Q. C. & S. R. Co., 47 App. Div. (N. Y.) 306; Haman v. Omaha Horse Ry. Co., 35 Neb. 74.

59 Weber v. Brooklyn, Q. C. & S. R. Co., 47 App. Div. (N. Y.) 306; Scott v. Central Park, N. & E. R. R. Co., 53 Hun (N. Y.) 414.

60 47 App. Div. (N. Y.) 306.

61 53 Hun (N. Y.) 414.

62 City Electric Ry. Co. v. Shropshire, 101 Ga. 33.

63 17 Ky. Law Rep. 1359.

language, and by an assault upon the conductor, was not entitled to recover, even if the conductor used excessive force. If a passenger provokes an assault by his own violence, he cannot recover.[64]

To sustain an action for trespass, it is not necessary to show malice.[65]

The ejection must also be at a reasonable place, not dangerous to life and limb.[66] A conductor has no right to eject a passenger from a moving car where there is an embankment of snow and ice on each side of the track,[67] or place a passenger, helpless from an apoplectic attack, in the open street on a bleak, drizzling December day,[68] or leave a helpless passenger in a dark road on a wet night, far from houses, near railroad tracks and marshy lands.[69]

Ejection must also be at a reasonable time. It is negligence for the conductor to throw a passenger who refuses to pay his fare from the front platform of a street car in the nighttime, when there is a high bank of snow on each side of the track, and the passenger has a right to resist to save his life.[70] To justify throwing a passenger from a swiftly moving car, the defendant must show circumstances proving an unusual act of this kind to be necessary, and it is not enough to show that plaintiff was a trespasser, and that

64 Sonnen v. St. Louis Transit Co. (Mo. App.) 76 S. W. 691; James v. Metropolitan St. Ry. Co., 80 N. Y. Supp. 710.

65 Kirton v. North Chicago St. R. Co., 91 Ill. App. 554.

66 Chicago City Ry. Co. v. Pelletier, 134 Ill. 120; Edgerly v. Union St. R. Co., 67 N. H. 312; Lynch v. Metropolitan El. Ry. Co., 90 N. Y. 77; Light v. Harrisburg & M. Electric Ry. Co., 4 Pa. Super. Ct. 427.

67 Sanford v. Eighth Ave. R. Co., 23 N. Y. 343.

68 Conolly v. Crescent City R. Co., 41 La. Ann. 57.

69 Hudson v. Lynn & B. R. Co., 178 Mass. 64.

70 Sanford v. Eighth Ave. R. Co., 23 N. Y. 343.

only reasonable force was used.[71] A passenger may recover for ejection from a moving train, although he is not injured.[72]

The company has no right to seize a boy of ten, although he is a trespasser, and throw him from the car while it is in motion,[73] or to so violently assault or frighten him as to cause him to fall from the car, or to jump from the car;[74] and pushing a child from a moving car is negligence, whether the child be regarded as a passenger or merely as a trespasser.[75] A pedestrian has a right to cross over a street car platform to avoid a block, and is wrongfully ejected for so doing.[76]

Where a driver put his hand on the shoulder of a boy of nine or ten, and told him to get off a moving car, the due care of the boy in getting off was held to be for the jury.[77] Where a driver ordered a newsboy to get off the car, and reached for his whip, it cannot be said that the plaintiff was negligent in alighting from the car while in motion, since it was not his voluntary act.[78] Negligence in ordering

71 Wright v. Union R. Co., 21 R. I. 554.

72 Oppenheimer v. Manhattan Ry. Co., 18 N. Y. Supp. 411.

73 Mt. Adams & E. P. Inclined Ry. Co. v. Doherty, 8 Ohio Cir. Ct. R. 349.

74 Lovett v. Salem & S. D. R. Co., 9 Allen (Mass.) 557; Ansteth v. Buffalo Ry. Co., 9 Misc. Rep. (N. Y.) 419, affirmed 145 N. Y. 210; Richmond Traction Co. v. Wilkinson (Va.) 43 S. E. 622.

75 Biddle v. Hestonville, M. & F. P. Ry. Co., 112 Pa. 551, followed 1 Mona. 553; Barre v. Reading City Passenger Ry., 155 Pa. 170; Hart v. West Side R. Co., 86 Wis. 483.

76 Shea v. Sixth Ave. R. Co., 62 N. Y. 180.

77 Hestonville, M. & F. P. R. Co. v. Gray, 3 Wkly. Notes Cas. (Pa.) 421.

78 Baber v. Broadway & S. A. R. Co., 10 Misc. Rep. (N. Y.) 109.

a newsboy to get off a car running five miles an hour is for the jury.[79]

In Healey v. City Passenger R. Co.,[80] and in Murphy v. Union Ry. Co.,[81] negligence in removing a passenger from a moving street car was held to be a question for the jury; and where a boy of seven jumped from a moving car, in obedience to the conductor's orders, negligence was held to be for the jury.[82]

Where a passenger used abusive language to the conductor, and threatened to report him, and the conductor shoved him from the car while it was moving fast, the case was held to be rightly submitted to the jury;[83] and a conductor may push a passenger, who violently assaults him, off the car while it is in motion, without rendering the company liable for the injury, if he had reason to believe, at the time, that this action was necessary to his protection.[84]

It has been held that a passenger must leave the car when ordered to by the conductor, even though the order is unwarranted, and look to the company for damages, and that, if a struggle ensues, he can recover only for wanton injuries;[85] and in North Chicago St. R. Co. v. Olds,[86] and in Kiley v. Chicago City Ry. Co.,[87] it was held that a passenger's right to ride cannot be enforced by resistance, but by a civil action.

79 Indianapolis St. Ry. Co. v. Hockett (Ind.) 67 N. E. 106.
80 28 Ohio St. 23.
81 118 Mass. 228.
82 Richmond Traction Co. v. Wilkinson (Va.) 43 S. E. 622.
83 Flynn v. Central Park, etc., R. Co., 49 N. Y. Super. Ct. 81.
84 Hayes v. St. Louis R. Co., 15 Mo. App. 584.
85 Schaefer v. North Chicago St. R. Co., 82 Ill. App. 473.
86 40 Ill. App. 421.
87 189 Ill. 384.

On the other hand, it has been held that, where a driver maliciously orders a passenger to leave the car, a failure to obey the order should not prevent recovery for injuries incurred during its enforcement;[88] and in Denver Tramway Co. v. Reed,[89] the court inclined to the view that passengers have a right to defend their privileges when they are illegally and unjustly assailed. Where a conductor seeks to throw a passenger from a moving car in the nighttime, when there is an embankment of snow and ice on each side of the track, the passenger has a right to resist to save his life.[90]

## III. Master and Servant.

**The company is liable for the acts of its employes done in the course of their employment, whether such acts are negligent or willful, but for acts outside the scope of their employment the company is not liable.**

**There is a conflict of authority in those jurisdictions where exemplary damages are allowed on the question of holding the company liable for the wanton acts of its servants, without proof of authorization or ratification.**

### § 79. Responsibility for acts of servant.

A street car company is generally held liable for the acts of its employes performed in the course of their employment, whether such acts are merely negligent, or are wanton and reckless.[91]

88 Louisville City Ry. Co. v. Mercer, 11 Ky. Law Rep. 810.

89 4 Colo. App. 500.

90 Sanford v. Eighth Ave. R. Co., 23 N. Y. 343.

91 Converse v. Washington & G. R. Co., 2 MacArthur (D. C.) 504; Savannah St., &c., R. Co. v. Bryan, 86 Ga. 312; North Chicago City Ry. Co. v. Gastka, 128 Ill. 613; Citizens' St. R. Co. v. Willoeby, 134 Ind. 563; Winnegar's Adm'r v. Central Passenger Ry. Co., 85 Ky.

In Stewart v. Brooklyn & C. R. Co.[92] the court said: "By the defendant's contract with the plaintiff it had undertaken to carry him safely and to treat him respectfully; and while a common carrier does not undertake to insure against injury from every possible danger, he does undertake to protect the passenger against any injury arising from the negligence or willful misconduct of its servants while engaged in performing a duty which the carrier owes to the passenger. * * * It is the injury that was suffered by the plaintiff while in the defendant's car, and not the motive which induced it, that constitutes the gist of the action. No reason exists for holding a master liable for the negligence of servants in his employment which does not with equal force preclude him from alleging intentional default of the servant as an excuse for not performing a duty which he has undertaken. In the former case the negligence

547; Eads v. Metropolitan Ry. Co., 43 Mo. App. 536; Tanger v. Southwest Missouri Electric Ry. Co., 85 Mo. App. 28; Higgins v. Watervliet Turnpike & R. Co., 46 N. Y. 23; Isaacs v. Third Ave. R. Co., 47 N. Y. 122; Jackson v. Second Ave. R. Co., 47 N. Y. 274; Shea v. Sixth Ave. R. Co., 62 N. Y. 180; Schultz v. Third Ave. R. Co., 89 N. Y. 242; Stewart v. Brooklyn & C. R. Co., 90 N. Y. 588; Palmeri v. Manhattan Ry. Co., 133 N. Y. 261; Rown v. Christopher & T. St. R Co., 34 Hun (N. Y.) 471; Burns v. Glens Falls, S. H. & F. E. St. R Co., 4 App. Div. (N. Y.) 426; Luhrs v. Brooklyn Heights R. Co. 11 App. Div. (N. Y.) 173; Franklin v. Third Ave. R. Co., 52 App Div. (N. Y.) 512; Meyer v. Second Ave. R. Co., 8 Bosw. (N. Y.) 305; White v. Twenty-Third St. R. Co., 20 N. Y. Wkly. Dig. 510; Lyons v. Broadway & S. A. R. Co., 10 N. Y. Supp. 237; Moritz v Interurban St. Ry. Co., 84 N. Y. Supp. 162; Passenger R. Co. v Young, 21 Ohio St. 518; Pittsburg, A. & M. P. Ry. Co. v. Donahue, 70 Pa. 119; Smith v. Hestonville, M. & F. R. Co., 17 Phila (Pa.) 184.

92 90 N. Y. 588.

of the servant is that of the master, and that is the ground of the master's liability; in the latter, the act of the servant is the act of the master, the motive of the servant making no difference in regard to the legal character of the master's default in doing his duty." Thus, the company has been held liable for an unprovoked assault on a passenger,[93] and for a forcible and malicious ejection from the car.[94]

In Isaacs v. Third Ave. R. Co.[95] it was held that such ejection was a wanton and willful trespass, not in the performance of the conductor's duty, and that the company was not liable therefor; but this case was distinguished and practically overruled in Stewart v. Brooklyn & C. R. Co.[96]

The company is liable for the act of a driver[97] or a gate keeper[98] in summoning a policeman, and having a passenger, with whom he had a dispute, arrested and locked up in the station house, although it has been held, on the con-

93 Savannah St., &c., R. Co. v. Bryan, 86 Ga. 312; Stewart v. Brooklyn & C. R. Co., 90 N. Y. 588; Luhrs v. Brooklyn Heights R. Co., 11 App. Div. (N. Y.) 173; Franklin v. Third Ave. R. Co., 52 App. Div. (N. Y.) 512, Smith v. Hestonville, M. & F. R. Co., 17 Phila. (Pa.) 184.

94 North Chicago City Ry. Co. v. Gastka, 128 Ill. 613; Citizens' St. R. Co. v. Willoeby, 134 Ind. 563; Winnegar's Adm'r v. Central Passenger Ry. Co., 85 Ky. 547; Tanger v. Southwest Missouri Electric Ry. Co., 85 Mo. App. 28; Burns v. Glens Falls, S. H. & F. E. St. R. Co., 4 App. Div. (N. Y.) 426; Lyons v. Broadway & S. A. R. Co., 10 N. Y. Supp. 237; Meyer v. Second Ave. R. Co., 8 Bosw. (N. Y.) 305.

95 47 N. Y. 122.

96 90 N. Y. 588.

97 West Chicago St. R. Co. v. Luleich, 85 Ill. App. 643; Rown v. Christopher & T. St. R. Co., 34 Hun (N. Y.) 471; White v. Twenty-Third St. R. Co., 20 N. Y. Wkly. Dig. 510.

98 Lynch v. Metropolitan El. Ry. Co., 90 N. Y. 77.

trary, that the company is not liable for the arrest of a passenger unless it ratifies the act, since the act is not within the scope of the conductor's authority.[99] The company is liable for the act of a ticket agent in forcibly detaining a passenger.[100] But if the employe goes outside of his employment, and without regard to his service, in order to effect some purpose of his own, wantonly commits a trespass, the company is not liable;[101] and a passenger cannot recover when he is ejected as the result of a dispute between himself and the conductor, wholly unconnected with the business of the company.[102] So it has been held that a trespass committed by a servant merely to prevent an annoyance to himself is not an act for which the master is liable, and that a driver's telling boys, who were running alongside of a car, to keep off, and his striking at them with the reins, are not enough to show that the driver was acting within the scope of his employment;[103] and the company is not liable for the act of an employe in arresting and prosecuting a passenger for passing counterfeit money, or violating an ordinance requiring payment of fare, unless the act was authorized or ratified, since such an act is not within the scope of the employe's authority.[104] *A fortiori,* the com-

99 Lezinsky v. Metropolitan St. Ry. Co., 88 Fed. 437; Cunningham v. Seattle Electric Ry. & Power Co., 3 Wash. 471.

100 Palmeri v. Manhattan Ry. Co., 133 N. Y. 261.

101 North Chicago City Ry. Co. v. Gastka, 128 Ill. 613; Winnegar's Adm'r v. Central Passenger Ry. Co., 85 Ky. 547; Isaacs v. Third Ave R. Co., 47 N. Y. 122.

102 Burns v. Glens Falls, S. H. & F. E. St. R. Co., 4 App. Div (N. Y.) 426; Flynn v. Central Park, &c., R. Co., 49 N. Y. Super. Ct. 81.

103 Mogk v. Chicago City Ry. Co., 80 Ill. App. 411.

104 Lafitte v. New Orleans, C. & L. R. Co., 43 La. Ann. 34; Central Ry. Co. v. Brewer, 78 Md. 394.

pany is not liable in the absence of authorization or direction for an assault on one who is not a passenger.[104a]

A conductor's authority to eject a passenger from a car gives him no implied authority to arrest and prosecute a passenger for attempting to ride without paying fare.[105]

The fact that it is the conductor's duty to eject trespassers does not necessarily rebut the inference that the driver was acting within the scope of his employment in directing a passenger to leave the car,[106] but in Coll v. Toronto Ry. Co.[107] it was held that the company was not liable where the motorman pushed a newsboy off the car. An action for malicious prosecution will not lie where there is no proof of judicial proceedings.[108]

The company is not liable for the acts of one passenger to another, simply because such acts were done in the presence of the conductor, and he knew they were done.[109]

Where a rule of the company directs a conductor to call a policeman in case of trouble, the company is liable, in an action for malicious prosecution, when a conductor had a passenger arrested.[110]

A passenger may recover for being carried by her destination against her will, and threatened by the conductor.[111]

104a Birmingham Ry. & Elec. Co. v. Mason (Ala.) 34 So. 207.

105 Little Rock Traction & Electric Co. v. Walker, 65 Ark. 144.

106 Baber v. Broadway & S. A. R. Co., 13 Misc. Rep. (N. Y.) 169.

107 25 Ont. App. 55.

108 Barry v. Third Ave. R. Co., 51 App. Div. (N. Y.) 385.

109 Springfield Consol. Ry. Co. v. Flynn, 55 Ill. App. 600.

110 Ruth v. St. Louis Transit Co. (Mo. App.) 71 N. W. 1055.

111 San Antonio Traction Co. v. Crawford (Tex. Civ. App.) 71 S. W. 306.

## § 80. Exemplary damages.

In some cases it is held that a street car company is not liable in exemplary damages for the misconduct of its employes in wrongfully ejecting passengers, unless it authorizes or ratifies their acts,[112] while, in other cases, exemplary damages are allowed without any discussion of the question of authorization or ratification.[113] The mere act of ejection is not enough to warrant the recovery of exemplary damages, but there must be something more.[114] On the other hand, the good faith of an employe in ejecting a passenger is not necessarily a bar in an action for exemplary damages,[115] while it has been held to be a bar in a criminal prosecution.[116]

Knowingly keeping an employe after he has wantonly assaulted a passenger is a ratification of the act, and renders

112 Redwood v. Metropolitan R. Co., 6 D. C. 302; Rouse v. Metropolitan St. Ry. Co., 41 Mo. App. 298; Muckle v. Rochester Ry. Co., 79 Hun (N. Y.) 32; Wright v. Glens Falls, S. H. & F. E. St. R. Co., 24 App. Div. (N. Y.) 617; Eddy v. Syracuse Rapid Transit Ry. Co., 50 App. Div. (N. Y.) 109; Murphy v. Central Park, N. & E. R. R. Co., 48 N. Y. Super. Ct. 96; Donivan v. Manhattan Ry. Co., 49 N. Y. State Rep. 722.

113 City & Suburban Ry. v. Brauss, 70 Ga. 368; Atlanta Consol. St. Ry. Co. v. Keeny, 99 Ga. 266; Citizens' St. R. Co. v. Willoeby, 134 Ind. 563; Kiley v. Chicago City Ry. Co., 90 Ill. App. 275; Louisville City Ry. Co. v. Mercer, 11 Ky. Law Rep. 810; Lexington Ry. Co. v. Cozine, 23 Ky. Law Rep. 1137, 64 S. W. 848; Baltimore & Yorktown Turnpike Road v. Boone, 45 Md. 344; Nashville St. Ry. v. Griffin, 104 Tenn. 81; Vassau v. Madison Electric Ry. Co., 106 Wis. 301.

114 Denver Tramway Co. v. Cloud, 6 Colo. App. 445; Pine v. St. Paul City Ry. Co., 50 Minn. 144; Hamilton v. Third Ave. R. Co., 53 N. Y. 25; Vassau v. Madison Electric Ry. Co., 106 Wis. 301.

115 Malecek v. Tower Grove & L. R. Co., 57 Mo. 17.

116 State v. McDonald, 7 Mo. App. 510.

the company liable in exemplary damages;[117] but mere retention of an employe without knowledge of his guilt will not authorize an inference of ratification.[118] Where a conductor assaulted a passenger, the attorney of the road defended him when he was arrested, and the managers of the railroad paid his fine, and he was retained, this justifies a finding of ratification.[119]

## IV. Tickets and Transfers.

**A passenger must conform to all reasonable regulations of the company as to place and time of transfer.**

**Where a transfer bad upon its face is given to a passenger, or he is transferred without any evidence of his right to ride, the authorities are in conflict as to the rights and duties of the conductor on the car to which he has been transferred. Some cases justify the ejection of the passenger who does not present proper evidence of his right to ride, while others hold that the company is to blame for failing to provide proper evidence, and that the passenger may recover for his ejection.**

### § 81. Place of transfer.

A street car company cannot change its rules requiring a transfer ticket without due notice.[120] A rule that the conductor shall detach the coupon on a ticket is a reasonable one, and if a passenger tears off the coupon, and refuses to show the main ticket, he is rightfully ejected.[121]

A rule requiring a transfer check is not unreasonable, and

117 Tanger v. Southwest Missouri Electric Ry. Co., 85 Mo. App. 28.
118 Donivan v. Manhattan Ry. Co., 49 N. Y. State Rep. 722.
119 Denison & S. Ry. Co. v. Randell (Tex. Civ. App.) 69 S. W. 1013.
120 Consolidated Traction Co. v. Taborn, 58 N. J. Law, 1.
121 Walker v. Dry Dock, E. B. & B. R. Co., 33 How. Pr. (N. Y.) 327.

a passenger must comply with the conditions thereof, so that, when a passenger enters the car at a point other than that prescribed by the transfer check, which he has accepted, it is the duty of the conductor not to receive the ticket, and to require the payment of fare, and, if the passenger refuses to pay, the company is not liable for ejecting him.[122]

A municipal ordinance provided that the fare on a street railway should not exceed five cents, where a company operated a single line of its cars running between the same *termini*. Afterwards the company constructed other lines running to different *termini*, and it was held that a passenger had no right to ride on a car bound for one *terminus*, and then, at the junction, get upon another car, and ride to a different *terminus* all for one fare, and could be rightfully ejected for refusal to pay additional fare on the second car.[123]

It is a reasonable regulation to require transfer passengers to enter the cars within the prescribed limits of a station, but it is an unreasonable enforcement of this rule to eject a passenger, who the company knew had paid fare, because he entered the car a few feet beyond the station line.[124]

A transfer ticket plainly marked for one line is good only for that line, but, where good on several lines, passengers may choose either.[125]

A rule of a street railway company carrying passengers over two sections of its line for one fare, which requires a passenger to keep and show, undetached by him, a coupon ticket as proof of his right to continue on the car beyond a

122 Percy v. Metropolitan St. Ry. Co., 58 Mo. App. 75.

123 Ellis v. Milwaukee City Ry. Co., 67 Wis. 135.

124 Nashville St. Ry. v. Griffin, 104 Tenn. 81.

125 Pine v. St. Paul City Ry. Co., 50 Minn. 144.

given point, is reasonable as a matter of law, and a passenger refusing to obey such rule is rightfully ejected.[126]

### § 82. Time of transfer.

In Muckle v. Rochester Ry. Co. [127] the court seemed to regard a rule that a transfer check must be used within ten minutes after arrival at the place of transfer as reasonable; but in Jenkins v. Brooklyn Heights R. Co.[128] the court expressly declared that a rule requiring a transfer ticket to be used within ten minutes, regardless of the condition of the cars which the street railway company supplies during that time, is arbitrary and illegal.

It is a reasonable rule that a transfer ticket must be used within fifteen minutes, and it is a passenger's duty to read such ticket; but if he has to wait more than fifteen minutes for his car, his ticket is good.[129] It has been held, however, that when the time limit set upon the transfer has expired, it is valueless, even if no car has come along.[129a]

It seems that a passenger upon a car of an electric railroad, which is unreasonably delayed, has no right to insist upon riding, without the payment of another fare, upon another car of the same road, in order to sooner reach his destination. If the railroad company refuses to make the desired transfer, he must find his redress in damages for the breach of its contract with him.[130]

126 De Lucas v. New Orleans & C. R. Co., 38 La. Ann. 930.

127 79 Hun (N. Y.) 32.

128 29 App. Div. (N. Y.) 8.

129 Heffron v. Detroit City Ry. Co., 92 Mich. 406.

129a Garrison v. United Rys. & Elec. Co. (Md.) 55 Atl. 371.

130 Taylor v. Nassau Electric R. Co., 32 App. Div. (N. Y.) 486.

A transferred passenger has no right to take the first car that comes along, and force himself into a dangerous or improper position upon the car. His duty is to wait until a car approaches in proper condition to receive him, and, should no such car appear, he can maintain an action against the company for breach of its contract to carry him.[131]

## § 83. Transfer bad on face.

Where a passenger on a street car presents to the conductor, as an evidence of his right to ride, a ticket or a transfer check which shows upon its face that he has no such right, the authorities are in irreconcilable conflict as to the propriety of ejecting such passenger. One class of cases treats the face of the ticket as the important consideration, and justifies the ejection of the holder of the defective ticket upon his refusal to pay fare, allowing him, as his only remedy, an action for breach of the carrier's contract, and not for his ejection.[132] The other and the more numerous class of cases holds that the passenger has a right to rely on the acts and statements of the ticket agent or conductor, and that, if he is ejected on account of a defective ticket, when he has acted in good faith and without fault, the carrier is liable for such ejection.[133]

[131] Hanna v. Nassau Electric R. Co., 18 App. Div. (N. Y.) 137.

[132] Kiley v. Chicago City Ry. Co., 189 Ill. 384; Bradshaw v. South Boston R. Co., 135 Mass. 407; Keen v. Detroit Electric Ry., 123 Mich. 247; Woods v. Metropolitan St. Ry. Co., 48 Mo. App. 125; Anderson v. Union Traction Co., 7 Pa. Dist. R. 41.

[133] Carpenter v. Washington & G. R. Co., 121 U. S. 474; Indianapolis St. Ry. Co. v. Wilson (Ind.) 66 N. E. 950; Rouser v. North Park St. Ry. Co., 97 Mich. 565; Hayter v. Brunswick Traction Co., 66 N. J. Law, 575; Perrine v. North Jersey St. Ry. Co. (N. J. Law) 54

Where a passenger presented a wrong transfer check, it was held that a street car conductor cannot be expected to listen to and decide upon the passenger's account of a disputed transaction relating to the sale of a transfer ticket by a conductor on another line, and the passenger should either pay his fare or get off the car quietly, and then sue the company for breach of contract.[134] In a similar case[135] the court said: "The conductor of a street railway car cannot reasonably be required to take the mere word of a passenger that he is entitled to be carried by reason of having paid a fare to the conductor of another car, or even to receive and decide upon the verbal statements of others as to the fact. The conductor has other duties to perform, and it would often be impossible for him to ascertain and decide upon the right of the passenger, except in the usual, simple, and direct way. The checks used upon the defendant's road were transferable, and a proper check, when given, might be lost or stolen, or delivered to some other person. It is no great hardship upon the passenger to put upon him the duty of seeing to it, in the first instance, that he receives and presents to the conductor the proper ticket or check, or, if he fails to do this, to leave him to his remedy against the company for a breach of its contract. Other-

Atl. 799; Muckle v. Rochester Ry. Co., 79 Hun (N. Y.) 32; Ray v. Cortland & H. Traction Co., 19 App. Div. (N. Y.) 530; Eddy v. Syracuse Rapid Transit Ry. Co., 50 App. Div. (N. Y.) 109; McMahon v. Third Ave. R. Co., 47 N. Y. Super. Ct. 282; Jacobs v. Third Ave. R. Co., 71 App. Div. (N. Y.) 199; Laird v. Pittsburg Traction Co., 166 Pa. 4; O'Rourke v. Street Ry. Co., 103 Tenn. 124; Lawshe v. Tacoma Ry. & Power Co., 29 Wash. 681.

134 Anderson v. Union Traction Co., 7 Pa. Dist. R. 41.

135 Bradshaw v. South Boston R. Co., 135 Mass. 407.

wise, the conductor must investigate and determine the question, as best he can, while the car is on its passage. The circumstances would not be favorable for a correct decision in a doubtful case. A wrong decision in favor of the passenger would usually leave the company without remedy for the fare. The passenger disappears at the end of the trip; and, even if it should be ascertained by subsequent inquiry that he had obtained his passage fraudulently, the legal remedy against him would be futile. A railroad company is not expected to give credit for the payment of a single fare. A wrong decision against the passenger, on the other hand, would subject the company to liability in an action at law, and perhaps with substantial damages. The practical result would be, either that the railroad company would find itself obliged, in common prudence, to carry every passenger who should claim a right to ride in its cars, and thus to submit to frequent frauds, or else, in order to avoid this wrong, to make such stringent rules as greatly to incommode the public, and deprive them of the facilities of transfer from one line to another, which they now enjoy."

Where a passenger on a street car is given a wrong transfer check, and the conductor on the second car will not take it, the passenger must pay his fare or leave the car at the conductor's request, and hold the company liable for the consequences.[136]

A passenger on an F. avenue street car, who was given a transfer stamped as good on "C." cars only, cannot recover damages against the company for the refusal of a conductor on a "B." car to accept the transfer, and his ejection of

136 Kiley v. Chicago City Ry. Co., 189 Ill. 384.

plaintiff from such car, though transfers from the F. avenue line had theretofore been good on both cars; the transfer, as between the last conductor and the passenger, being conclusive against the latter's right to travel on "B." cars, and his remedy, if any, being for the failure of the first conductor to furnish a proper transfer.[137]

Where a passenger offered a transfer check which in some manner had been torn in two, and the company offered evidence that it was the custom of many passengers to tear checks in two, and throw them down at the place of transfer, so that any one could pick them up, and also that the defendant had a rule requiring a "proper transfer check," it was held that this evidence should have been admitted, and, if established, the conductor would be justified in ejecting plaintiff on his refusal to pay fare.[138]

In O'Rourke v. Street Ry. Co.[139] a passenger was ejected on the assumption that the time during which his transfer could be used had expired, when, as a matter of fact, the transfer tickets were wrongly punched nearly an hour earlier than the time when they were actually issued. The court held that the plaintiff could recover for his ejection, and said: "It may be true, as suggested in some of the authorities, that the carrier can dispatch its business more conveniently and expeditiously, and can avoid losses through fraud and imposition more readily, by treating the ticket as conclusive evidence of the passenger's right to be carried, than by taking and adopting his *ex parte* statement of the

137 Keen v. Detroit Electric Ry. Co., 123 Mich. 247.

138 Woods v. Metropolitan St. Ry. Co., 48 Mo. App. 125.

139 103 Tenn. 124.

real contract, when claimed to be different from the ticket; yet such ends, desirable as they may be and are, afford no legal sanction for the expulsion of the passenger who is without fault, and whose ticket fails alone through the mistake or negligence of the carrier's agent, nor does the undesirability render the expulsion of such person any the less a tortious breach of the contract. Every expulsion of a rightful passenger is wrongful." This case is cited and approved in the recent cases of Lawshe v. Tacoma Ry. & Power Co.[140] and Memphis St. Ry. Co. v. Graves.[140a]

A passenger on a street car, desiring to be transferred to another line, received a transfer ticket, on the margin of which the 9 o'clock a. m. hour was punched. The hour of 7:30 o'clock was also punched. On the back of the transfer ticket was this sentence: "It is the duty of the person receiving it, and one of the conditions upon which this check is accepted, that the passenger examine date and time, and see that the same are correct." Plaintiff made a timely request for the transfer check, but it was not given him until he was in the act of leaving the car. The conductor of the car to which plaintiff was transferred refused to take the ticket, alleging that it was "two hours old." Plaintiff assured him that he had received the check from the conductor of the other car at 9 o'clock a. m.,—immediately before entering the second car,—and refused to pay an additional fare. Plaintiff was ejected from the car. Held, that plaintiff was entitled to recover.[141]

140 29 Wash. 681.

140a (Tenn.) 75 S. W. 729.

141 Laird v. Pittsburg Traction Co., 166 Pa. 4.

The company had a rule that a transfer ticket must be used within ten minutes after the arrival at the place of connection. A passenger took such a transfer, and took the first car which passed, but the transfer check was wrongly punched, so that the time for its use appeared to have expired, and the conductor of the second car ejected the plaintiff. It was conceded that the passenger might have a remedy for breach of contract; but the court held, further, that the passenger might maintain an action for ejection, saying: "Although the conductor personally may have been justified, by his instructions, to do so, the defendant was put in the wrong by the act of the other conductor, and was no more justified in the attempted act of ejection than it would have been if the plaintiff had at the time had and presented the evidence of his right to remain as a passenger in the car without further payment."[142]

When the time on a transfer ticket was wrongfully punched, and the passenger was not negligent in not discovering this, his ejection from a second car is wrongful.[143] In this case the court said: "To hold that the plaintiff's only remedy is an action for breach of the contract for transportation might encourage the employment of negligent or incompetent conductors, to the serious annoyance and inconvenience of the traveling public, and would not afford passengers reasonable protection or security in their rights." To the same effect is Perrine v. North Jersey St. Ry. Co.[144]

A street railway company is liable for ejecting a person who presents a transfer ticket from a connecting road, not

[142] Muckle v. Rochester Ry. Co., 79 Hun (N. Y.) 32.

[143] Eddy v. Syracuse Rapid Transit Ry. Co., 50 App. Div. (N. Y.) 109.

[144] (N. J. Law) 54 Atl. 799.

acceptable under the rules of the company because not properly punched, though the mistake was made by an employe of a connecting road, there being a traffic agreement between the two roads, whereby transfers were used from one to the other. Where one is ejected from a street car because his transfer ticket was not properly punched, he is not to be charged with contributory negligence in receiving the same, he not understanding the ticket, and being ignorant of whether it was correctly punched.[145]

A transfer ticket of peculiar color and print consisted of two parts, the upper of which gave the passenger a right to ride on the second road. A conductor tore off part of the upper portion, and the conductor of the second road refused to accept this fragment, and ejected the passenger for his refusal to pay fare. It was held, as matter of law, that the conductor was bound to know that the fragment was a portion of a genuine ticket.[146]

So, when a passenger paid a through fare, and received a ticket from the conductor which the latter said was good for a stopover, although he had no right to issue any stopover tickets to be used upon the same line, the passenger may recover for being ejected when his ticket was refused on the next car, and he refused to pay additional fare.[147]

In Hayter v. Brunswick Traction Co.,[148] a passenger was transferred, and the conductor of the first car told him which car to take, but the conductor of the second car told plaintiff that transfer was not good, and ejected him. It

[145] Jacobs v. Third Ave. R. Co., 71 App. Div. (N. Y.) 199.
[146] Rouser v. North Park St. Ry. Co., 97 Mich. 565.
[147] Ray v. Cortland & H. Traction Co., 19 App. Div. (N. Y.) 530.
[148] 66 N. J. Law, 575.

was held that the company was liable for such ejection. The conductor of the second car must accept the reasonable explanations of the passenger.[149]

Plaintiff, having paid for passage over defendant's route of street railway, was given, at an intermediate point thereon, in return for an additional sum paid by him, a ticket, on which were these words: "Third Ave. Rd. Co.; good only from Sixty-Fifth street up to Yorkville and Harlem for a continuous ride. By order of the President." The ticket was indorsed: "Conductor's check, July 6, 1878." Plaintiff did not then use the ticket, but afterwards, and on the same day, he entered one of defendant's cars below, and paid fare to such intermediate point, and, at a place above said point, tendered the conductor the ticket. It was not accepted, and, on his refusal to again pay fare, he was ejected from the car. Held that, in the absence of knowledge by the plaintiff of any rule limiting his rights under said ticket, the company was liable for the above act of its servant.[150]

A charge that a passenger could recover if he was given a wrong transfer ticket, and that the plaintiff could recover exemplary damages for malicious and wanton injury, was held eminently favorable to the plaintiff.[151]

### § 84. Transfer without check

In Wakefield v. South Boston R. Co.,[152]—an action for an assault and battery by an agent of the defendant,—it was

149 Indianapolis St. Ry. Co. v. Wilson (Ind.) 66 N. E. 950.
150 McMahon v. Third Ave. R. Co., 47 N. Y. Super. Ct. 282.
151 Carpenter v. Washington & G. R. Co., 121 U. S. 474.
152 117 Mass. 544.

held that the provision of Gen. St. 1871, c. 381, § 36, that a passenger upon a horse car in the city of Boston shall, upon paying a sum in addition to the regular fare, receive a check entitling him to a passage, on the same day only, in any car run in the city between any two points therein, without paying more than a sum named "for both of the passages aforesaid," does not entitle one who has received such a check, and who has once changed cars and surrendered his check in the second car at the request of the conductor, to a passage in a third car, proceeding farther upon the same line, although he is told by the conductor of the second car that he may ride on the third car without further payment of fare. In the course of the opinion, Colt, J., said: "The conductor of that car, whose duty it was to collect the fare, had no authority to give him a free passage upon his statement that the conductor of another car had promised it to him without any consideration. Conductors have no authority so to bind the corporation by which they are employed."

A passenger paid his fare, intending to go to T. street. The car did not go the whole distance, and the conductor told him he could get off and take the next car. The conductor on the next car told him he must pay or get off, and he was ejected. It was held that the passenger ought to have had evidence of the payment of his fare, and that the conductor was under no legal obligation to accept his statement; that the passenger should have paid his fare on demand, and sought redress from the company for a violation of the contract.[153] The court said: "Counsel has cited no authority, nor have I found one, which holds that a stranger

[153] Mahoney v. Detroit St. Ry. Co., 93 Mich. 612.

may enter the car of either a railway or street car company without any evidence that he has paid his fare, and secure passage by his own statement to the conductor that he has previously paid it to some other authorized agent. It is the duty of the passenger to secure evidence of such payment, or to pay when his fare is demanded. The business of such companies cannot be carried on upon any other basis. This certainly is common sense and experience."

Plaintiff paid his fare on one of the defendant's cars. The car stopped for some reason, and he was transferred to another car. Upon his refusal to pay another fare, he was ejected by the conductor, who honestly supposed that fare had not been paid. It was held that the plaintiff could recover for compensatory damages.[154]

Where a passenger told the conductor where he wanted to go, and was transferred, but given no transfer ticket, and he did not know that one was necessary, the company was held liable when the conductor of the second car ejected plaintiff for not having a transfer ticket, and refusing to pay fare.[155]

A passenger was transferred, and the conductor took up his transfer check. Then the car was taken off. The conductor disappeared, and the driver told the plaintiff to take the next car. He did so, but was ejected because he had no transfer check, and refused to pay fare. It was held that the plaintiff showed, *prima facie,* a right to recover for the conduct of the defendant's agents, leading to and including the expulsion.[156]

154 Hamilton v. Third Ave. R. Co., 53 N. Y. 25.
155 City & Suburban Ry. v. Brauss, 70 Ga. 368.
156 Appleby v. St. Paul City Ry. Co., 54 Minn. 169.

### § 85. Miscellaneous.

A company cannot change its rules not requiring a transfer ticket without due notice.[157]

Where a conductor threatened to eject a woman for not paying fare, whether she was negligent or not in not getting a transfer is for the jury.[158]

Where a plaintiff was transferred, but made to pay a second fare,[159] and where a conductor wrongfully refused to accept a transfer, and demanded additional fare, but before the passenger left the car, offered to return the fare, and take the transfer,[160] it was held that the company was not liable under the general railroad act, which makes allowances for a mistake not amounting to gross negligence.

A city may require that a street railway operated under its control shall keep tickets for sale on each car,—six for twenty-five cents.[161] Where a franchise from a village provided that tickets should be kept on sale on the cars, they must be ready at any point on the line, and not only in the village.[162]

One holding a street railway ticket good from L. to D. is entitled to carriage upon presentation of the ticket, although he has paid his fare to L. from a point farther out on the line, from which point the regular through fare exceeds the sum of the fare paid and the price of the ticket.[163]

157 Consolidated Traction Co. v. Taborn, 58 N. J. Law, 1.

158 Little Rock Traction & Electric Co. v. Trainer, 68 Ark. 106.

159 Stewart v. Metropolitan St. Ry. Co., 20 Misc. Rep. (N. Y.) 605.

160 Tullis v. Brooklyn Heights R. Co., 71 App. Div. (N. Y.) 494. And see Goodspeed v. Ithaca St. Ry. Co., 84 N. Y. Supp. 383.

161 Sternberg v. State, 36 Neb. 307.

162 Rice v. Detroit, Y. & A. A. Ry., 122 Mich. 677.

163 Kissane v. Detroit, Y. & A. A. Ry., 121 Mich. 175.

In Cronin v. Highland St. Ry. Co.,[164]—an action for being expelled from a car of the defendant corporation,—it was held that, under Pub. St. c. 113, § 47, providing that a commutation check issued by a street railway in Boston shall entitle the holder "to a passage on the same day only in any car run by any other company between any two points in said city, but not to a passage over the same route on which the check was issued, or a route parallel thereto, and between and including two common points," the holder of such a check, in returning towards his starting point, is not entitled to be carried upon the check in the car of another company, whose route is substantially parallel to the route of the company issuing the check, and is between and includes two common points, although a wide detour is made at one place in the route of the latter company between the two common points.

[164] 144 Mass. 249.

# PART II.

## ACCIDENTS TO TRAVELERS ON THE HIGHWAY.

---

## CHAPTER VI.

### PEDESTRIANS RUN OVER.

I. ADULTS.

§ 86. Due Care—General Considerations.
87. Same—Intoxicated and Infirm Persons.
88. Same—Crossing Tracks—Stopping, Looking, and Listening.
89. Same—Walking on or near Track.
90. Same—Crossing Where There are Double Tracks.
91. Same—Laborer Working on or near Track.
92. Same—Miscellaneous.
93. Right of Way.
94. Negligence of Company—General Considerations.
95. Negligence in Operation—Lookout, Speed, Warning, etc.
96. Same—Laborer Working on or near Track.
97. Same—Miscellaneous.

II. CHILDREN.

§ 98. Capacity of Child.
99. Due Care of Child, for Jury.
100. Lack of Due Care of Child.
101. Due Care of Parent or Person in Charge of Child—Allowing Child in Street.
102. Same—Leaving Child Alone in or near the House.
103. Negligence of Company—Right of Way.
104. Same—General Considerations.
105. Same—Negligence in Operation.

### I. Adults.

**A pedestrian must use ordinary care, under the circumstances, in approaching and crossing a street railway track, and in walking near or upon the track. A street railway company does not owe to pedestrians the same high degree of care which it owes to its passengers, but is bound to exercise ordinary care towards them; and even if a pedestrian is guilty of lack of due care, the company is nevertheless liable if it could have prevented the accident by the use of ordinary care.**

**Between crossings, a street car has a superior right of way, since it cannot leave its tracks, and is run for the benefit and convenience of the public, but at street crossings, the rights of street cars and pedestrians are equal.**

**A pedestrian is not required to stop, look, and listen before crossing a street railway track, and there is a conflict of authority as to whether he must look and listen or look before crossing, as a matter of law. If a pedestrian goes suddenly in front of a car without looking, he is almost invariably held unable to recover.**

**In determining the questions of due care and negligence, all the surrounding circumstances in each particular case are taken into consideration. The chief considerations are the character of the locality, the speed of the car, and its distance from the pedestrian, whether a warning was given, the obstruction of the view or of the track, and the occupation of the plaintiff.**

## § 86. Due care—General considerations.

Ordinary care is all that is required of a traveler in approaching and crossing street railway tracks,[1] although a

[1] Driscoll v. Market St. Cable Ry. Co., 97 Cal. 553; Kernan v. Market St. R. Co., 137 Cal. 326; West Chicago St. R. Co. v. Nilson, 70 Ill. App. 171; Baltimore Consol. Ry. Co. v. Rifcowitz, 89 Md. 338; Bunyan v. Citizens' Ry. Co., 127 Mo. 12; Newark Passenger Ry. Co. v. Block, 55 N. J. Law, 605; Connelly v. Trenton Passenger Ry. Co., 56 N. J. Law, 700; Consolidated Traction Co. v. Chenowith, 58 N. J. Law, 416; Consolidated Traction Co. v. Glynn, 59 N. J. Law, 432; McGrath v. North Jersey St. Ry. Co., 66 N. J. Law, 312.

higher degree of care is necessary in crossing the tracks of an electric railway than in crossing the tracks of a horse railway.[2] The consideration of the question of a person's due care is not limited to his conduct after he becomes aware that he is in danger;[3] and even if the company is negligent, the plaintiff cannot recover if he should have become aware of such negligence, and could have avoided it by the use of ordinary care.[4] Thus, failure to ring a gong does not excuse a person about to cross the track from the exercise of proper care.[5]

It is almost universally held that, even if a person is guilty of lack of due care, the company is nevertheless liable if they could have prevented the accident by the use of the ordinary care required of them;[6] although, in Scott v. Third Ave. R. Co.,[7] it was held that an instruction to this effect

[2] Hawthorne v. Cincinnati St. Ry. Co., 2 Ohio Dec. 548.

[3] Chicago West Div. Ry. Co. v. Haviland, 12 Ill. App. 561.

[4] Macon & I. S. St. Ry. Co. v. Holmes, 103 Ga. 655.

[5] McQuade v. Metropolitan St. Ry. Co., 17 Misc. Rep. (N. Y.) 154.

[6] Oliver v. Denver Tramway Co., 13 Colo. App. 543; Atlanta Ry. & Power Co. v. Walker, 112 Ga. 725; Floyd v. Paducah Ry. & Light Co. (Ky.) 73 S. W. 1122; Baltimore Traction Co. v. Wallace, 77 Md. 435; North Baltimore Passenger Ry. Co. v. Arnreich, 78 Md. 589; Baltimore Consol. Ry. Co. v. Rifcowitz, 89 Md. 338; Werner v. Citizens' Ry. Co., 81 Mo. 368; Bunyan v. Citizens' Ry. Co., 127 Mo. 12; Watson v. Mound City St. Ry. Co., 133 Mo. 246; Holwerson v. St. Louis & S. Ry. Co., 157 Mo. 216; Meyer v. Lindell Ry. Co., 6 Mo. App. 27; Davies v. People's R. Co., 67 Mo. App. 598; O'Keefe v. St. Louis & S. R. Co., 81 Mo. App. 386; Aldrich v. St. Louis Transit Co. (Mo. App.) 74 S. W. 141; Shanks v. Springfield Traction Co. (Mo. App.) 74 S. W. 386; Parkinson v. Concord St. Ry., 71 N. H. 28; McKeon v. Steinway Ry. Co., 20 App. Div. (N. Y.) 601; Healey v. Dry Dock, E. B. & B. R. Co., 46 N. Y. Super. Ct. 473; Richmond Passenger & Power Co. v. Steger (Va.) 43 S. E. 612.

[7] 59 Hun (N. Y.) 456.

was erroneous. In some cases, although the correctness of the rule is not questioned, it is held not applicable to the state of facts presented.[8] Conduct of travelers which becomes dangerous only when those in charge of street cars neglect to observe the usual precautions should not be treated as contributory negligence defeating the right of recovery.[9] Where a woman crosses the street at an unusual place, she must use greater care than if she had used the customary crossing.[10] A person placed in sudden peril is not held to the usual standard of care.[11]

## § 87. Same—Intoxicated and infirm persons.

Intoxication does not relieve a man from the degree of care required of a sober man under the same circumstances;[12] and if a traveler is intoxicated, and would not have been injured if he had been sober, he cannot recover.[13] While the fact that a man is intoxicated is no excuse for him, and

8 Ries v. St. Louis Transit Co. (Mo.) 77 S. W. 734; Trauber v. Third Ave. R. Co., 80 App. Div. (N. Y.) 37; Phelan v. Forty-Second St., M. & St. N. Ave. Ry. Co., 79 App. Div. (N. Y.) 548; Poole v. Metropolitan St. Ry. Co., 83 App. Div. (N. Y.) 235.

9 Wahlgren v. Market St. Ry. Co., 132 Cal. 656; Lang v. Houston, W. S. & P. Ferry R. Co., 75 Hun (N. Y.) 151; Walls v. Rochester Ry. Co., 92 Hun (N. Y.) 581; Schwarzbaum v. Third Ave. R. Co., 54 App. Div. (N. Y.) 164, 60 App. Div. 274; Frank v. Metropolitan St. Ry. Co., 58 App. Div. (N. Y.) 100; Dallas Rapid Transit Ry. Co. v. Elliott, 7 Tex. Civ. App. 216; Dallas Consol. Traction Ry. Co. v. Hurley, 10 Tex. Civ. App. 246.

10 Henry v. Grand Ave. Ry. Co., 113 Mo. 525.

11 North Chicago St. R. Co. v. Louis, 35 Ill. App. 477.

12 Chicago City Ry. Co. v. Lewis, 5 Ill. App. 242; Bageard v. Consolidated Traction Co., 64 N. J. Law, 316.

13 Bradley v. Second Ave. R. Co., 8 Daly (N. Y.) 289.

does not require the company to use greater care,[14] a drunken man is as much entitled to the exercise of due care on the part of the company as a sober man, and much more in need of it.[15]

The fact that a plaintiff was an old man over seventy, with his hearing very considerably impaired, is a material circumstance bearing on his due care;[16] and it has been held that a deaf man is held to the degree of care which a prudent man under his disabilities would use,[17] and that it is incumbent upon a deaf man to be more alert in the use of his other senses.[18]

### § 88. Same—Crossing tracks—Stopping, looking, and listening.

Perhaps the most important consideration bearing upon the question of the due care of a traveler who attempts to pass in front of a street car, and is run over, is whether or not he looked for an approaching car. It is well settled that a person who goes directly in front of a street car, where there is evidence either that he did not look or that there was an unobstructed view, so that he might have looked, is not in the exercise of due care.[19]

14 Weeks v. New Orleans & C. R. Co., 32 La. Ann. 615.

15 West Chicago St. R. Co. v. Ranstead, 70 Ill. App. 111.

16 Chicago West Div. Ry. Co. v. Haviland, 12 Ill. App. 561.

17 Buttelli v. Jersey City, H. & R. Electric Ry. Co., 59 N. J. Law, 302.

18 Beem v. Tama & T. Electric Ry. & Light Co., 104 Iowa, 563; Hall v. West End St. Ry. Co., 168 Mass. 461.

19 Schwartz v. Crescent City R. Co., 30 La. Ann. 15; Mathes v. Lowell, L. & H. St. Ry., 177 Mass. 416; Dooley v. Greenfield & T. F. St. Ry. Co. (Mass.) 68 N. E. 203; Kelly v. Hendrie, 26 Mich. 255; McGee v. Consolidated St. Ry. Co., 102 Mich. 107; Hickey v. St. Paul City Ry. Co., 60 Minn. 119; Terien v. St. Paul City Ry. Co.,

This is the general rule, but certain phases of the mental or physical condition of the plaintiff, and the general conditions existing at the time of the accident, remain to be considered as bearing in favor of or against the plaintiff's case. A traveler who walks upon the track without stopping to look or listen, with his eyes on the ground, apparently absorbed in thought, is not in the exercise of due care,[20] nor is one who starts to cross a street railway track looking upon the ground "in a brown study," and not looking up or down the street.[21] An elderly man, a little deaf, who heedlessly attempts to cross a street car track, and is run over, is not in the exercise of due care;[22] and the same ruling was made in the case of a man who had good eyesight, but was very deaf, and who walked onto a street car track, where he had

70 Minn. 532; Baly v. St. Paul City Ry. Co. (Minn.) 95 N. W. 757; Bunyan v. Citizens' Ry. Co., 127 Mo. 12; Watson v. Mound City St. Ry. Co., 133 Mo. 246; Moore v. Lindell Ry. Co. (Mo.) 75 S. W. 672; McGrath v. North Jersey St. Ry. Co., 66 N. J. Law, 312; Doller v. Union Ry. Co., 7 App. Div. (N. Y.) 283; Curry v. Rochester Ry. Co., 90 Hun (N. Y.) 230; Harnett v. Bleecker St. & F. Ferry R. Co., 49 N. Y. Super. Ct. 185, Cowan v. Third Ave R. Co., 1 N. Y. Supp. 612; Enk v. Brooklyn City R. Co., 19 N. Y. Supp. 130; Muessman v. Metropolitan St. Ry. Co., 76 App. Div. (N. Y.) 1; McKinley v. Metropolitan St. Ry. Co., 77 App. Div. (N. Y.) 256; Smith v. City Ry. Co., 29 Or. 539; Wolf v. City & Suburban Ry. Co. (Or.) 72 Pac. 329; Kappus v. Metropolitan St. Ry. Co., 82 App. Div. (N. Y.) 13; Du Frane v. Metropolitan St. Ry. Co., 83 App. Div. (N. Y.) 298; Warner v. People's St. Ry. Co., 141 Pa. 615; Watkins v. Union Traction Co., 194 Pa. 564; Sullivan v. Consolidated Traction Co., 198 Pa. 187; McCauley v. Philadelphia Traction Co., 13 Pa. Super. Ct. 354; Richmond Traction Co. v. Hildebrand, 98 Va. 22.

20 Martin v. Third Ave. R. Co., 27 App. Div. (N. Y.) 52.

21 Cain v. Macon Consol. St. R. Co., 97 Ga. 298.

22 Webster v. New Orleans City & L. R. Co., 51 La. Ann. 299.

an unobstructed view, without looking;[23] and in the very similar case of a man seventy-one years old, and quite deaf, who walked across a street railway track without looking, when he could have seen an approaching car for a distance of over five hundred feet.[24]

In Driscoll v. Market St. Cable Ry. Co.[25] it was held that a street railway company is not liable to a traveler who walked suddenly in front of a moving car in a careless, reckless, or absent-minded way; and where a man saw an electric car approaching for a long distance, and had plenty of time to get out of the way, but jumped in front of the car, he was held unable to recover.[26] Where a woman looked up and down a suburban street, and saw no car, and then, wearing a sunbonnet which projected beyond her face, crossed without looking either to the right or left, and was run over by an electric car, which was sounding its gong, and was seen by several other persons several blocks before it reached the place of the accident, she was held not to be in the exercise of due care.[27] Similarly, where a woman started to cross a street car track on a cold night with her head bundled up, and collided with the middle of a car, it was held that she was not entitled to recover;[28] and a woman who saw a car, but walked against it with her umbrella raised, is not in the exercise of due care;[29] but the due

23 Hall v. West End St. Ry. Co., 168 Mass. 461; Aldrich v. St. Louis Transit Co. (Mo. App.) 74 S. W. 141.

24 Beem v. Tama & T. Electric Ry. & Light Co., 104 Iowa, 563.

25 97 Cal. 553.

26 Jager v. Coney Island & B. R. Co., 84 Hun (N. Y.) 307.

27 Hickman v. Nassau Electric R. Co., 36 App. Div. (N. Y.) 376.

28 McQuade v. Metropolitan St. Ry. Co., 17 Misc. Rep. (N. Y.) 154.

29 Holmes v. Union Traction Co., 199 Pa. 229.

care of a woman who crossed a street car track at night during a severe storm, and ventured on the track with her umbrella raised, without looking for an approaching car, was held to be for the jury.[30] Where the plaintiff turned up his coat collar and pulled down his hat to protect himself from the rain, and walked directly in front of a car coming on a track parallel to the one occupied by the car he had just left, he was held not to be in the exercise of due care.[31] A traveler who crossed immediately in front of an electric car in the nighttime was held not to be in the exercise of due care;[32] and the same was held where a man stood near a street car track by night without showing any indication of his intention to cross, and then crossed when a car was so near that it could not be stopped.[33] Because a traveler could have looked, it cannot be legally inferred that he did so.[34]

The authorities are in hopeless conflict as to whether a traveler should be required, as a matter of law, to "stop, look, and listen," "look and listen," or even "look," before crossing a street railway track. It is generally held that the rules as to "stopping, looking, and listening," which are in force in the case of steam railroads, are not applicable in all their strictness to street railroads.[35]

30 Conley v. Albany Ry., 22 App. Div. (N. Y.) 321.

31 Macleod v. Graven, 73 Fed. 627.

32 Hoelzer v. Crescent City R. Co., 49 La. Ann. 1302.

33 Knoker v. Canal & C. R. Co., 52 La. Ann. 806.

34 O'Reilly v. Brooklyn Heights R. Co., 81 N. Y. Supp. 572.

35 Driscoll v. Market St. Cable Ry. Co., 97 Cal. 553; Capital Traction Co. v. Lusby, 12 App. D. C. 295; Terien v. St. Paul City Ry. Co., 70 Minn. 532; Brown v. Twenty-Third St. Ry. Co., 56 N. Y. Super. Ct. 356; McCauley v. Philadelphia Traction Co., 13 Pa. Super. Ct. 354.

In Hoelzel v. Crescent City R. Co.[36] it was held that the rule that a person about to cross a railroad track should "stop, look, and listen" applied to an electric car; but in Farrar v. New Orleans & C. R. Co.[37] the court held that it was too much to expect a traveler to "stop, look, and listen," and the same ruling was made in Evansville St. R. Co. v. Gentry,[38] while in McCauley v. Philadelphia Traction Co.[39] it was held that the rule requiring a traveler to "stop, look, and listen" before crossing a steam railroad track applied only in part to street railways. In Baltimore Traction Co v. Helms,[40] and in Baltimore Consol. Ry. Co. v. Rifcowitz,[41] it was held that a failure to stop and look before crossing a street railway track will not always be contributory negligence.

Some jurisdictions hold that it is a traveler's duty to "look and listen" before crossing a street railway track, and that, if he does not do this, he is not in the exercise of due care.[42] In other jurisdictions the exact opposite is held, namely, that failure to look and listen is not always lack of due care as matter of law.[43] A rule midway between these

[36] 49 La. Ann. 1302.

[37] 52 La. Ann. 417.

[38] 147 Ind. 408.

[39] 13 Pa. Super. Ct. 354.

[40] 84 Md. 515.

[41] 89 Md. 338.

[42] Young v. Citizens' St. R. Co., 148 Ind. 54; Farrar v. New Orleans & C. R. Co., 52 La. Ann. 417; Canedo v. New Orleans & C. R Co., 52 La. Ann. 2149; McGee v. Consolidated St. Ry. Co., 102 Mich 107; Wolf v. City & Suburban Ry. Co. (Or.) 72 Pac. 329.

[43] Terien v. St. Paul City Ry. Co., 70 Minn. 532; Peterson v. Minneapolis St. Ry. Co. (Minn.) 95 N. W. 751; Mitchell v. Third Ave. R Co., 62 App. Div. (N. Y.) 371.

two is suggested in Smith v. City Ry. Co.[44] This case holds that to cross an electric car track without looking or listening is presumptively lack of due care. In Terien v. St. Paul City Ry. Co.[45] it was held that, while there is not the same absolute duty to look and listen as there is in the case of a steam railroad, there is still some duty to look and listen, and that this may be greater in the case of electric cars than in the case of horse cars.

Whether it is lack of due care, as a matter of law, not to look before crossing a street railway track, is another disputed point. Some cases affirm this proposition,[46] while others hold that failure to look is merely one circumstance to be considered in determining the question of the plaintiff's due care.[47]

Some jurisdictions prefer not to lay down any absolute rule as to the duty of a traveler who is crossing a street railway track to stop, look, and listen, but prefer to adopt the broad general rule that he must use his powers of observation, and that his care should be that which a prudent man would exercise under the circumstances.[48]

44 29 Or. 539.

45 70 Minn. 532.

46 Bailey v. Market St. Cable Ry. Co., 110 Cal. 320.

47 North Chicago St. R. Co. v. Nelson, 79 Ill. App. 229; Brown v. Twenty-Third St. R. Co., 56 N. Y. Super. Ct. 356.

48 Kernan v. Market St. Ry. Co., 137 Cal. 326; Louisville R. Co. v. Poe, 24 Ky. Law Rep. 1700, 72 S. W. 6; Baltimore Consol. Ry. Co. v. Rifcowitz. 89 Md. 338; Bunyan v. Citizens' Ry. Co., 127 Mo. 12; Newark Passenger Ry. Co. v. Block, 55 N. J. Law, 605; Connelly v. Trenton Passenger Ry. Co., 56 N. J. Law, 700; Consolidated Traction Co. v. Chenowith, 58 N. J. Law, 416; Consolidated Traction Co. v. Glynn, 59 N. J. Law, 432; McGrath v. North Jersey St. Ry. Co., 66 N. J. Law, 312

While the fact that a person looks and listens before crossing a track will not excuse his want of ordinary care while crossing it,[49] on the other hand, if his attention is diverted by a runaway at a street railway crossing, he cannot be said not to be in the exercise of due care because he omits to look up and down the street for an approaching car.[50] Where a traveler does look before crossing a street railway track, this is generally enough to carry the question of his due care to the jury,[51] even though, after seeing a car, he goes upon the track without looking again;[52] although a traveler was held unable to recover when he gave one hasty glance, and then went forward without looking or listening again.[53] The question of due care is especially apt to be left to the jury where there are other circumstances, such as evidence that the car was traveling at high speed, or with-

49 McGee v. Consolidated St. Ry. Co., 102 Mich. 107; Rauscher v. Philadelphia Traction Co., 176 Pa. 349; Nugent v. Philadelphia Traction Co., 181 Pa. 160.

50 City Electric Ry. Co. v. Jones, 61 Ill. App. 183; Peterson v. Minneapolis St. Ry. Co. (Minn.) 95 N. W. 751.

51 Wells v. Brooklyn City R. Co., 58 Hun (N. Y.) 389; Mills v. Brooklyn City R. Co., 10 Misc. Rep. (N. Y.) 1; Killen v. Brooklyn Heights R. Co., 31 Misc. Rep. (N. Y.) 290; Cowan v. Third Ave. Ry. Co., 9 N. Y. Supp. 610; Mauer v. Brooklyn Heights R. Co., 87 App. Div. (N. Y.) 119; McGovern v. Union Traction Co., 192 Pa. 344.

52 Consolidated Traction Co. v. Glynn, 59 N. J. Law, 432; Hickman v. Nassau Electric R. Co., 41 App. Div. (N. Y.) 629; Killen v. Brooklyn Heights R. Co., 48 App. Div. (N. Y.) 557, 31 Misc. Rep. (N. Y.) 290; Curtin v. Metropolitan St. Ry. Co., 22 Misc. Rep. (N. Y.) 83; Copeland v. Metropolitan St. Ry. Co., 78 App. Div. (N. Y.) 418.

53 Metz v. St. Paul City Ry. Co. (Minn.) 92 N. W. 502.

out giving warning of its approach,[54] or that the traveler had his attention distracted by other vehicles,[55] or that a traveler and a street car both stopped, each apparently expecting the other to wait, and then started so near together that a collision was inevitable.[56] Where a man with a push cart called to the driver of the car to stop, but did not stop himself, and a collision ensued, he was held not to be in the exercise of due care.[57]

If there are any obstacles in the way, a traveler should wait before crossing.[58] In Doherty v. Detroit Citizens' St. Ry. Co.,[59] a traveler who looked when he was twelve feet from the track, and did not see a car because of a covered wagon in the way, was held not to be in the exercise of due care, when he could have seen the car if he had looked again when within two or three feet of the track.

Where a traveler saw a car, and chose to take the risk of being able to cross ahead of it, and was mistaken in his cal-

54 Consolidated Traction Co. v. Glynn, 59 N. J. Law, 432; Chicago City R. Co. v. Fennimore, 199 Ill. 1; Wells v. Brooklyn City R. Co., 58 Hun (N. Y.) 389; Gildea v. Metropolitan St. Ry. Co., 58 App. Div. (N. Y.) 528; Halliday v. Brooklyn Heights R. Co., 59 App. Div. (N. Y.) 57; Mitchell v. Third Ave. R. Co., 62 App. Div. (N. Y.) 371; Sesselmann v. Metropolitan St. Ry. Co., 65 App. Div. (N. Y.) 484; Faurot v. Brooklyn Heights R. Co., 14 Misc. Rep. (N. Y.) 398; Curtin v. Metropolitan St. Ry. Co., 22 Misc. Rep. (N. Y.) 83; Stillings v. Metropolitan St. Ry. Co., 84 App. Div. (N. Y.) 201; Henderson v. United Traction Co., 202 Pa. 527.

55 Mulligan v. Third Ave. R. Co., 87 App. Div. (N. Y.) 320; Connelly v. Trenton Passenger Ry. Co., 56 N. J. Law, 700.

56 Cleary v. Pittsburgh, A. & M. Traction Co., 179 Pa. 526.

57 Thal v. Metropolitan St. Ry. Co., 76 N. Y. Supp. 918.

58 Newark Passenger Ry. Co. v. Block, 55 N. J. Law, 605; Ames v. Waterloo & C. F. Rapid Transit Co. (Iowa) 95 N. W. 161.

59 118 Mich. 209.

culation, he was held not to be in the exercise of due care;[60] and where a traveler attempted to cross directly in front of a car, and tripped on the rail, he was held not to be in the exercise of due care.[61]

Conduct of travelers which becomes dangerous only when those in charge of street cars neglect to observe the usual precautions should not be treated as contributory negligence defeating the right of recovery. Thus, in Newark Passenger Ry. Co. v. Block[62] it was held that, while one crossing a street must look out for passing vehicles, he need not look beyond the distance within which vehicles moving at lawful speed would endanger him. A traveler has a right to assume that a street car is presumably under control,[63] and it is not lack of due care for him to fail to observe that it is moving at more than twice its usual speed,[64] or to assume that the driver will obey the customary signal of a person wishing to board a car.[65]

It is not lack of due care, as a matter of law, to cross a street car track which runs across the sidewalk into the car house, where no warning was given, and no lookout kept;[66] nor is a traveler guilty of lack of due care where a car came down a grade at a street crossing at a speed greater than

60 Griffith v. Denver Consol. Tramway Co., 14 Colo. App. 504; North Chicago St. R. Co. v. Martin, 51 Ill. App. 247; Brown v. Elizabeth P. & C. J. R. Co., 68 N. J. Law, 618; Walsh v. Atlantic Ave. R. Co., 23 App. Div. (N. Y.) 19; Freeman v. Brooklyn Heights R. Co., 81 N. Y. Supp. 828.

61 Gilliland v. Middlesex & S. Traction Co., 67 N. J. Law, 542.

62 55 N. J. Law, 605.

63 Dallas Rapid Transit Ry. Co. v. Elliott, 7 Tex. Civ. App. 216.

64 Frank v. Metropolitan St. Ry. Co., 58 App. Div. (N. Y.) 100.

65 Lang v. Houston, W. St. & P. Ferry R. Co., 75 Hun (N. Y.) 151.

66 Wahlgren v. Market St. Ry. Co., 132 Cal. 656.

that allowed by city ordinance, when the tracks were wet and muddy.[67] Where a man was run over on a dark night by a car driven at great speed, without lights and without warning, he was held not to be guilty of contributory negligence;[68] and where a traveler crossed a track on a dark and rainy night, and was struck by a car approaching at high speed, it was held that it could not be said that he was guilty of lack of due care as a matter of law.[69]

Where the plaintiff was transferring, and the custom was for the car to remain standing, it was held not to be lack of due care to walk near the track between the track and a bank of snow, even without looking or listening;[70] and where a man sixty-seven years old attempted to cross in front of a car coming at an unusually rapid rate of speed down a grade, and crossed the track, but, in attempting to get over a snowbank, fell and was run over, it was held that due care was for the jury.[71] If there is plenty of time to cross in front of a car, a passenger need not wait because of the possible danger of falling.[72]

### § 89. Same—Walking on or near track.

Although a traveler has a right to walk on the tracks if he uses due care,[73] walking on a street car track is necessarily dangerous, and a traveler who does so and is injured

[67] Walls v. Rochester Ry. Co., 92 Hun (N. Y.) 581.

[68] Dallas Consol. Traction Ry. Co. v. Hurley, 10 Tex. Civ. App. 246.

[69] Schwarzbaum v. Third Ave. R. Co., 54 App. Div. (N. Y.) 164, 60 App. Div. 274; Frank v. Metropolitan St. Ry. Co., 58 App. Div. (N. Y.) 100.

[70] Cameron v. Union Trunk Line, 10 Wash. 507.

[71] Friedman v. Dry Dock, E. B. & B. R. Co., 11 N. Y. Supp. 429.

[72] Baxter v. Second Ave. R. Co., 3 Rob. (N. Y.) 510.

[73] Infra, § 93.

is usually held unable to recover. Thus, in Johnson v. Canal & C. R. Co.,[74] and in Smith v. Crescent City R. Co.,[75] it was held that one who walks on a street car track of his own choice in the nighttime, and is run over, is not in the exercise of due care. Where a man walked along a narrow space between two street car tracks, without looking for a car, to pick up a shoe cast by one of his horses, and was struck while stooping to pick it up, he was held not to be in the exercise of due care.[76] It is not lack of due care to walk along the street by the side of a street railway track unless a traveler places himself in such a position as to be run over or injured by a car.[77] Where a traveler looked for a car, and saw none, and there was evidence that he saw for a distance of four hundred feet, and then walked for twenty-five feet beside the tracks without looking again, and was struck by a car, it was held that the plaintiff failed to show that he was free from contributory negligence;[78] and where there was no path on a street, but a ditch at the side, and street car tracks were laid two feet from the ditch, the due care of a man walking on the track, or in the space between the track and the ditch, is for the jury.[79] Where a traveler walking near the track on a dark night listened, but was struck by a car running at high speed without warning, due care was held to be for the jury.[80] Where an in-

[74] 27 La. Ann. 53.

[75] 47 La. Ann. 833.

[76] Dix v. Railway Co., 15 Pa. Super. Ct. 350. And see Judge v. Elkins (Mass.) 66 N. E. 708.

[77] Brooks v. Lincoln St. Ry. Co., 22 Neb. 816.

[78] Young v. Citizens' St. R. Co., 148 Ind. 54.

[79] Buttelli v. Jersey City, H. & R. Electric Ry. Co., 59 N. J. Law, 302.

[80] Carlson v. Lynn & B. R. Co., 172 Mass. 388.

toxicated man was run over while walking on the track on a dark, hazy night, he was held not to be in the exercise of due care;[81] and in Kramer v. New Orleans, C. & L. R. Co.[82] it was held that a drunken man lying near the side of a street car track with his legs across the track was not in the exercise of due care. Where a man was walking near the track, and there was no evidence as to what happened between that time and the time when he was seen lying on the track directly in front of the car, there was held to be no evidence of due care.[83]

The fact that a woman stood near the sidewalk over which street cars ran on a curve to enter into the station does not constitute lack of due care;[84] but where a man was run over, and there was evidence that he stood near the track when the car was ten or fifteen feet away, and the car would have passed him safely if he had remained standing there, there was held to be no evidence of due care.[85] A blind man who stopped in the middle of the track at the call of some one on the street was held unable to recover.[86] A deaf man who does not look back frequently is not in the exercise of due care.[86a] Where a post of an elevated railroad made it necessary for a woman to stand within two feet of the street car tracks to see whether cars were approaching a crossing, and she was run down, while in this position, by

81 Chicago City Ry. Co. v. Lewis, 5 Ill. App. 242; Weeks v. New Orleans & C. R. Co., 32 La. Ann. 615.

82 51 La. Ann. 1689.

83 Cox v. South Shore & B. St. Ry. Co., 182 Mass. 497.

84 O'Toole v. Central Park, N. R. & E. R. R. Co., 12 N. Y. Supp. 347.

85 McDermott v. Third Ave. R. Co., 44 Hun (N. Y.) 107.

86 Webb v. Chicago City Ry. Co., 83 Ill. App. 565.

86a Shanks v. Springfield Traction Co. (Mo. App.) 74 S. W. 386.

a car coming very rapidly without warning, due care was held to be for the jury;[87] and due care is for the jury where a woman stood, with her back to the car, near the track.[87a]

## § 90. Same—Crossing where there are double tracks.

A very common state of facts is where a passenger alights from a car where there are double tracks, and, crossing in the rear of the car, is struck by a car coming on the other track. Under these circumstances, the plaintiff was held unable to recover, where it appeared that he started to cross without looking,[88] and, of course, the case was stronger against the plaintiff where he was warned of his danger.[89] In Stowers v. Citizens' St. Ry. Co.,[90] a passenger who alighted from a car at midnight, and, crossing in the rear of the car, was struck by a car coming on the other track, five feet away, which he could readily have seen, was held not to be in the exercise of due care; and in Cincinnati St. Ry. Co. v. Snell,[91] where there was no evidence as to whether the plaintiff looked or not, it was held that it could not be said, as a matter of law, that he was in the exercise of due care.

87 G'Sell v. Metropolitan St. Ry. Co., 35 Misc. Rep. (N. Y.) 387.

87a Loder v. Metropolitan St. Ry. Co., 84 App. Div. (N. Y.) 591.

88 Thorsell v. Chicago City Ry. Co., 82 Ill. App. 375; Indianapolis St. Ry. Co. v. Tenner (Ind. App.) 67 N. E. 1044; Baltimore Traction Co. v. Helms, 84 Md. 515; Casper v. Metropolitan St. Ry. Co., 84 App. Div. (N. Y.) 639; Toledo Consol. St. Ry. Co. v. Lutterbeck, 11 Ohio Cir. Ct. R. 279; Landrigan v. Brooklyn Heights R. Co., 23 App. Div. (N. Y.) 43; Buzby v. Philadelphia Traction Co., 126 Pa. 559; Burgess v. Salt Lake City R. Co., 17 Utah, 406.

89 Gray v. Ft. Pitt Traction Co., 198 Pa. 184.

90 21 Ind. App. 434.

91 54 Ohio St. 197.

The question of due care under these circumstances is, however, often left to the jury,[92] especially where there is further evidence to be considered, as, for instance, that the car was approaching without warning at a high rate of speed,[93] that the accident occurred in a thinly populated suburban district at 10 o'clock at night,[94] or that the night was a very stormy one, and the plaintiff was a stranger, who had never seen a double track or an electric car.[95]

Where a passenger jumped from a moving horse car onto a parallel track, and was run over, he was held not to be in the exercise of due care;[96] and when a man stepped from a car onto a parallel track without looking, and was run over by a car which was approaching slowly, with the gong ringing, he was likewise held not to be entitled to recover.[97] In Creamer v. West End St. Ry. Co.[98] it was held that, while it may not be, as matter of law, negligent for one to leave a street car while in motion or to attempt to cross a street car track without looking to see whether a car is approaching, yet neither of these acts is evidence of due care; and where

92 West Chicago St. R. Co. v. Nilson, 70 Ill. App. 171; Omaha St. Ry. Co. v. Loehneisen, 40 Neb. 37; Reed v. Metropolitan St. Ry. Co., 84 N. Y. Supp. 454; Beers v. Metropolitan St. Ry. Co., 84 N. Y. Supp. 785.

93 Dobert v. Troy City Ry. Co., 91 Hun (N. Y.) 28; Sesselmann v. Metropolitan St. Ry. Co., 65 App. Div. (N. Y.) 484; Pelletreau v. Metropolitan St. Ry. Co., 74 App. Div. (N. Y.) 192; Stevens v. Union Ry. Co., 75 App. Div. (N. Y.) 602; Smith v. Union Trunk Line, 18 Wash. 351.

94 Wise v. Brooklyn Heights R. Co., 46 App. Div. (N. Y.) 246.

95 Boyer v. St. Paul City Ry. Co., 54 Minn. 127.

96 Maloney v. Brooklyn City R. Co., 18 N. Y. Wkly. Dig. 152.

97 Baltimore Consol. Ry. Co. v. Armstrong, 92 Md. 554.

98 156 Mass. 320.

the undisputed evidence showed that, in spite of warnings from those in his immediate vicinity, a passenger on a street railway car suddenly, without precaution, alighted therefrom, and was struck by another car and killed, no action is maintainable against the company.

Equally common is the very similar state of facts where one who is a traveler upon the highway to begin with, and who does not change his *status* from that of a passenger to a traveler by alighting, seeks to cross behind a car, and is run over by a car approaching on the other track. In a number of cases the traveler was held, under these circumstances, not to be in the exercise of due care;[99] and the same ruling was made where a traveler stepped from behind a wagon, and was waiting to see whether a car was coming or not,[100] when he stepped back while crossing a double track,[101] and where he was caught between two cars.[102]

In Fonda v. St. Paul City Ry. Co.,[103] and in McClain v. Brooklyn City R. Co.,[104] the due care of the traveler under these circumstances was held to be for the jury, where it appeared that he looked, and the car approached the crossing at high speed.

99 McCarthy v. Detroit Citizens' St. Ry. Co., 120 Mich. 400; Greengard v. St. Paul City Ry. Co., 72 Minn. 181; Scott v. Third Ave. R. Co., 16 N. Y. Supp. 350; Little v. Third Ave. R. Co., 83 App. Div. (N. Y.) 330; Blaney v. Electric Traction Co., 184 Pa. 524.

100 Bethel v. Cincinnati St. Ry. Co., 8 Ohio Circ. Dec. 310.

101 Jackson v. Union Ry. Co., 77 App. Div. (N. Y.) 161; Trauber v. Third Ave. R. Co., 80 App. Div. (N. Y.) 37.

102 Nugent v. Philadelphia Traction Co., 181 Pa. 160; Meyer v. Pittsburgh, A. & M. Traction Co., 189 Pa. 414.

103 71 Minn. 438.

104 116 N. Y. 459.

A traveler is not in the exercise of due care when he goes on the track to board a car knowing that another car may move towards a switch behind the car which he intends to take, as he voluntarily assumes a position of danger.[105] One who attempted to cross a street car track between two cars coming from opposite directions was held guilty of lack of due care under all the circumstances of the case,[106] as was a man who was run over while walking after dark in a narrow space between double tracks in spite of a warning,[107] and one who stood in a narrow space between two tracks waiting to board a car.[108] Where a traveler stood between the tracks, and stepped back upon one of the tracks without seeing a car approaching in plain view ten feet away, this was held to be lack of due care as matter of law;[109] and where there were double tracks, and a man looked for a car, but saw none, went onto the second track, and saw a car coming, and then stepped back on the first track, and was run over, his due care was held to be for the jury.[110]

### § 91. Same—Laborer working on or near track.

A laborer working on or near the tracks of a street railway company must necessarily have his attention somewhat distracted from keeping a constant outlook for approaching cars. Therefore, in many cases, the due care of a person so situated has been held to be for the jury. The circum-

105 Malpass v. Hestonville, M. & F. P. R. Co., 189 Pa. 599.

106 Hurdle v. Washington & G. R. Co., 8 App. D. C. 120.

107 Childs v. New Orleans City R. Co., 33 La. Ann. 154.

108 Halpin v. Third Ave. R. Co., 40 N. Y. Super. Ct. 175.

109 Bailey v. Market St. Cable Ry. Co., 110 Cal. 320.

110 McCormick v. Brooklyn City R. Co., 10 Misc. Rep. (N. Y.) 8.

stances under which such a ruling has been made are varied, as, for instance, where a laborer was working in a trench near a street railway track, and the horses attached to a car fell into the trench and injured him,[111] where a laborer was working between the tracks,[112] and where a laborer in a ditch was struck by a street car, and there was evidence that he looked for a car, and that there were street noises which deadened the sound of the car as it approached.[113] Similarly, where a contractor stood near a trench, and did not hear the call of the driver of an approaching car, his attention being occupied by a workman in the trench;[114] where the foreman of a gang engaged in opening a drain between the street car tracks stooped down to remove a plank, and was struck by a car;[115] and where a workman was run over while moving a heavy iron beam from a street car track,—due care in all of these cases was held to be for the jury.[116] Where a laborer was stooping over between the tracks of a street railway company, and was struck by a car, due care was held to be for the jury;[117] and the same ruling was made where three men were working with

111 Fernandes v. Sacramento City Ry. Co., 52 Cal. 45; Burns v. Second Ave. R. Co., 21 App. Div. (N. Y.) 521.

112 Pittsburg Electric Ry. Co. v. Kelly, 57 Kan. 514; McCooey v. Forty-Second St. & G. St. Ferry R. Co., 79 Hun (N. Y.) 255; Lahey v. Central Park, etc., R. Co., 2 Misc. Rep. (N. Y.) 537.

113 Little v. Street Ry. Co., 78 Mich. 205.

114 Farrell v. Waterbury Horse R. Co., 60 Conn. 239.

115 Morrissey v. Westchester Electric Ry. Co., 18 App. Div. (N. Y.) 67.

116 Weingarten v. Metropolitan St. Ry. Co., 62 App. Div. (N. Y.) 364.

117 Third Ave. Ry. Co. v. Krausz, 112 Fed. 379.

a hose near a street railway track, and a bolt on a car caught the hose and injured them.[118]

Since, as has been said, the attention of a laborer is necessarily somewhat distracted, the question of a warning on the part of those in charge of an approaching car is an important one. Where a laborer was pouring hot asphalt between the rails, and, as he got out of the way of one car, was struck by another, which gave no signal of its approach;[119] where a laborer was pouring tar into the cracks in a street, and, while stooping over after looking for a car, was struck by one which approached without signaling;[120] and where a workman was laying cement between the rails, and stopped, looked, and listened before stooping over his work, but was struck by a car running at a high speed without any warning,—due care in each case was held to be for the jury.[121] Where a laborer was working in a ditch, and was compelled to stand with his back towards approaching cars, and, contrary to custom, no warning was given of the approach of the car;[122] where a laborer working on the pavement near a street railway track was run over, and there was evidence that no warning was given until the car was very near him;[123] and where a flagman in the performance of his duty was run over by a horse car, although

118 Laschinger v. St. Paul City Ry. Co., 84 Minn. 333.

119 Bengivenga v. Brooklyn Heights R. Co., 48 App. Div. (N. Y.) 515.

120 Lewis v. Binghamton R. Co., 35 App. Div. (N. Y.) 12; Hennessey v. Forty-Second St., M. & St. N. Ave. Ry. Co., 84 N. Y. Supp. 158.

121 O'Malley v. Scranton Traction Co., 191 Pa. 410.

122 Daum v. North Jersey St. Ry. Co. (N. J. Law) 54 Atl. 221; Owens v. Peoples' Passenger Ry., 155 Pa. 334.

123 Hennessy v. Brooklyn Heights R. Co., 57 App. Div. (N. Y.) 27.

the driver could see him for several hundred feet,[124]—due care in all of these cases was likewise held to be for the jury. Where a workman looked and listened before stepping between the rails, and was struck by a car coming without warning, the court ruled that there was no lack of due care on the part of the workman.[125]

In spite of the fact that a laborer working on or near street railway tracks is thus often placed at a disadvantage, his conduct may nevertheless show such plain disregard of ordinary care that he is held unable to recover as a matter of law. Thus while the general rules applying to travelers on foot approaching a railway track do not apply to a street sweeper, whose duties require him to work between rails of the car tracks, where cars are constantly passing,[126] a crossing sweeper, who kept no lookout for cars, and, when warned by a policeman, stepped back to avoid a car coming from one direction, and was struck by another coming in the other direction, was held not to be in the exercise of due care;[127] and a deaf street sweeper who was struck by an electric car which approached him in plain sight for nearly two thousand feet was held not to be in the exercise of due care.[128]

As usual, the plaintiff's failure to look is a circumstance counting strongly against him. Thus, where a regular re-

124 D'Oro v. Atlantic Ave. R. Co., 13 N. Y. Supp. 789.

125 Houston City St. Ry. Co. v. Woodlock (Tex. Civ. App.) 29 S. W. 817.

126 Smith v. Bailey, 14 App. Div. (N. Y.) 283; Dipaolo v. Third Ave. R. Co., 55 App. Div. (N. Y.) 566; O'Connor v. Union Ry. Co., 67 App. Div. (N. Y.) 99.

127 Daly v. Detroit Citizens' St. Ry. Co., 105 Mich. 193.

128 Lyons v. Bay Cities Consol. Ry. Co., 115 Mich. 114.

pairer of crossings stood with his back towards approaching cars, leaned over, and was struck, it was held that he was guilty of contributory negligence, even though the motorman gave no signal.[129] Similarly where a laborer stooped over to fix a plank near the track, and did not look for a car, he was held guilty of lack of due care.[130] Where a man unloading a wagon stood near the track, and did not notice an approaching car, although he had a clear view, he was held not to be in the exercise of due care;[131] and a workman who voluntarily placed himself in a position of danger in a narrow path between an obstruction and a car track was held unable to recover.[132] Where a man was working in the rear of a coal wagon which stood near a track, leaving plenty of room for cars to pass, he was held not to be in the exercise of due care.[133] Where a man with a push cart called to a driver to stop, but did not stop himself, and a collision ensued, he was held not to be in the exercise of due care,[134] but in a similar case, where the car came at high speed, due care was held to be for the jury.[134a] Where a workman in a trench saw a car, and had plenty of room to keep out of the way, but raised his head and was struck, he was held unable to recover;[135] and the same ruling was made where a workman instinctively put his

129 Eddy v. Cedar Rapids & M. C. Ry. Co., 98 Iowa, 626.

130 Hafner v. St. Paul City Ry. Co., 73 Minn. 252.

131 Davies v. People's Ry. Co., 159 Mo. 1. And see Gleason v. Worcester Consol. St. Ry. Co. (Mass.) 68 N. E. 223.

132 Furguson v. Philadelphia Traction Co., 20 Phila. (Pa.) 249.

133 McKelvey v. Twenty-Third St. Ry. Co., 5 Misc. Rep. (N. Y.) 424.

134 Thal v. Metropolitan St. Ry. Co., 76 N. Y. Supp. 918.

134a Greenbaum v. Interurban St. Ry. Co., 84 N. Y. Supp. 588.

135 Riddle v. Forty-Second St., M. & St. N. Ave. R. Co., 173 N. Y. 327.

hand on the track.[136] Where a workman looked for four hundred feet, but saw no car, and walked by the track for twenty-five feet without looking again, he was held guilty of lack of due care.[137]

## § 92. Same—Miscellaneous.

Where a traveler was injured while attempting to lead a frightened horse across a street railway track, his due care was held to be for the jury.[138] Whether a mother was justified in thinking she could save her child from being run over without danger to herself was held, in West Chicago St. R. Co. v. Liderman,[139] to be a question for the jury, and, on appeal, it was further held that contributory negligence would not be imputed to her unless her action was clearly rash, but that there would be an exception to the rule when the rescuer was responsible for the dangerous position of the person to be rescued.[140] In Camden, G. & W. Ry. Co. v. Young[141] it was held that, where a passenger was carried beyond his destination, and the conductor told him to walk back on the track, and he was run over on a trestle, due care was for the jury, but that, if he was warned not to go on the trestle, he was not in the exercise of due care. Where a woman was crossing a trestle, it was held that the only duty of the company was to use reasonable care after her peril was discovered, as she was a tres-

136 Nolan v. Metropolitan St. Ry. Co., 65 App. Div. (N. Y.) 184.

137 Young v. Citizens' St. R. Co., 148 Ind. 54.

138 Deuster v. Milwaukee St. Ry. Co., 89 Wis. 191.

139 87 Ill. App. 638.

140 West Chicago St. R. Co. v. Liderman, 187 Ill. 463.

141 60 N. J. Law, 193.

passer.[141a] A policeman cannot order a motorman to push a coal truck ahead under a law allowing him to "regulate the movements of teams and vehicles in the street," and cannot recover for injuries received in the process.[141b]

## § 93. Right of way.

A street railway company does not owe to travelers the high degree of care which it owes to passengers. It is bound, however, to use reasonable care in operating its lines.[142] While the authorities are not in absolute harmony, the rule as generally stated is that, between crossings, the street car has a superior or paramount, but not an exclusive, right of way,[143] since the street car cannot turn out from the line of its tracks.[144]

141a Richmond Passenger & P. Co. v. Rack's Adm'r (Va.) 44 S. E. 709.

141b Connelly v. Metropolitan St. Ry. Co., 84 N. Y. Supp. 305.

142 Third Ave. Ry. Co. v. Krausz, 112 Fed. 379; Shea v. Potrero & B. V. R. Co., 44 Cal. 414; Driscoll v. Market St. Cable Ry. Co., 97 Cal. 553; West Chicago St. R. Co. v. Coit, 50 Ill. App. 640; West Chicago St. R. Co. v. Binder, 51 Ill. App. 420; Isackson v. Duluth St. Ry. Co., 75 Minn. 27; Omaha St. Ry. Co. v. Loehneisen, 40 Neb. 37; Pendleton St. R. Co. v. Shires, 18 Ohio St. 255; San Antonio St. Ry. Co. v. Renken, 15 Tex. Civ. App. 229.

143 Hot Springs St. Ry. Co. v. Johnson, 64 Ark. 420; Shea v. Potrero & B. V. R. Co., 44 Cal. 414; Bailey v. Market St. Cable Ry. Co., 110 Cal. 320; Buttelli v. Jersey City, H. & R. Electric Ry. Co., 59 N. J. Law, 302; Lahey v. Central Park, &c., R. Co., 2 Misc. Rep. (N. Y.) 537; McKelvey v. Twenty-Third St. Ry. Co., 5 Misc. Rep. (N. Y.) 424; Schulman v. Houston, W. St. & P. Ferry R. Co., 15 Misc. Rep. (N. Y.) 30; Warner v. Peoples' St. Ry. Co., 141 Pa. 615; Street R. Co. v. Howard, 102 Tenn. 474.

144 Hot Springs St. Ry. Co. v. Johnson, 64 Ark. 420; Shea v. Potrero & B. V. R. Co., 44 Cal. 414; Bailey v. Market St. Cable Ry. Co., 110 Cal. 320; Fonda v. St. Paul City Ry. Co., 77 Minn. 336; But-

In Bailey v. Market St. Cable Ry. Co.,[145] the additional reason was given that street cars are run for the benefit and convenience of the public, and should not be unnecessarily delayed; and in Fandel v. Third Ave. R. Co.,[146]—the case of a cable car,—it was held that, as street cars are large and heavy vehicles, moved by machinery, they necessarily have, to a considerable extent, the right of way. It is therefore clear that an instruction that a street car has an absolute right of way under all the circumstances should not be given,[147] and cars cannot be run at any speed the public demands, so that others must look out for them.[148]

As the right of the street car is not exclusive, travelers have a right to use the streets of a city for travel, and may cross the street at any point they see fit, so long as they use reasonable care, and do not materially interfere with the progress of the cars.[149] One case has gone so far as to hold that the public can use any part of the street on terms of per-

telli v. Jersey City, H. & R. Electric Ry. Co., 59 N. J. Law, 302; Fandel v. Third Ave. R. Co., 15 App. Div. (N. Y.) 426; McKelvey v. Twenty-Third St. Ry. Co., 5 Misc. Rep. (N. Y.) 424; Warner v. Peoples' St. Ry. Co.; 141 Pa. 615

145 110 Cal. 320.

146 15 App. Div. (N. Y.) 426.

147 Chicago West Div. Ry. Co. v. Ingraham, 33 Ill. App. 351.

148 Newark Passenger Ry. Co. v. Block, 55 N. J. Law, 605; Consolidated Traction Co. v. Glynn, 59 N. J. Law, 432.

149 Hot Springs St. Ry. Co. v. Johnson, 64 Ark. 420; Shea v. Potrero & B. V. R. Co., 44 Cal. 414; Bailey v. Market St. Cable Ry. Co., 110 Cal. 320; Baltimore Traction Co. v. Helms, 84 Md. 515; Liddy v. St. Louis R. Co., 40 Mo. 506; Henry v. Grand Ave. Ry. Co., 113 Mo. 525; Buttelli v. Jersey City, H. & R. Electric Ry. Co., 59 N. J. Law, 302; Warner v. People's St. R. Co., 141 Pa. 615; Street R. Co. v. Howard, 102 Tenn. 474.

fect equality with the street railway company, but this is contrary to the weight of authority.[150]

At street crossings, street cars must be kept under control, and they have no greater rights than travelers on foot crossing their tracks.[151]

## § 94. Negligence of company—General considerations.

While a street railway company is bound to use only ordiary care towards travelers,[152] it is almost universally held that, even if a traveler is guilty of lack of due care, the company is nevertheless liable if they could have prevented the accident by the use of the ordinary care required of them,[153]

150 San Antonio St. Ry. Co. v. Renken, 15 Tex. Civ. App. 229.

151 Mitchell v. Third Ave. R. Co., 62 App. Div. (N. Y.) 371; Sesselmann v. Metropolitan St. Ry. Co., 65 App. Div. (N. Y.) 484; Schulman v. Houston, W. St. & P. Ferry R. Co., 15 Misc. Rep. (N. Y.) 30; Street R. Co. v. Howard, 102 Tenn. 474.

152 Third Ave. Ry. Co. v. Krausz, 112 Fed. 379; Shea v. Potrero & B. V. R. Co., 44 Cal. 414; Driscoll v. Market St. Cable Ry. Co., 97 Cal. 553; West Chicago St. R. Co. v. Coit, 50 Ill. App. 640; West Chicago St. R. Co. v. Binder, 51 Ill. App. 420; Isackson v. Duluth St. Ry. Co., 75 Minn. 27; Omaha St. Ry. Co. v. Loehneisen, 40 Neb. 37; Pendleton St. R. Co. v. Shires, 18 Ohio St. 255; San Antonio St. Ry. Co. v. Renken, 15 Tex. Civ. App. 229; Norfolk Ry. & Light Co. v. Corletto (Va.) 41 S. E. 740.

153 Oliver v. Denver Tramway Co., 13 Colo. App. 543; Floyd v. Paducah Ry. & Light Co. (Ky.) 73 S. W. 1122; Atlanta Ry. & Power Co. v. Walker, 112 Ga. 725; Baltimore Traction Co. v. Wallace, 77 Md. 435; North Baltimore Passenger Ry. Co. v. Arnreich, 78 Md. 589; Baltimore Consol. Ry. Co. v. Rifcowitz, 89 Md. 338; Werner v. Citizens' Ry. Co., 81 Mo. 368; Bunyan v. Citizens' Ry. Co., 127 Mo. 12; Watson v. Mound City St. Ry. Co., 133 Mo. 246; Holwerson v. St. Louis & S. Ry. Co., 157 Mo. 216; Meyer v. Lindell Ry. Co., 6 Mo. App. 27; Davies v. People's R. Co., 67 Mo. App. 598; O'Keefe v. St. Louis & S. R. Co., 81 Mo. App. 386; Aldrich v. St. Louis Transit Co. (Mo. App.) 74 S. W. 141; Shanks v. Springfield Traction Co. (Mo. App.)

although, in Scott v. Third Ave. R. Co.,[154] it was held that an instruction to this effect was erroneous. In some cases, although the correctness of the rule is not questioned, it is held not applicable to the state of facts presented.[155] The fact that a passenger left the car in violation of a rule of the company will not excuse the company for injuries inflicted after the passenger had left the car, and was clearly a traveler on the highway.[156]

## § 95. Negligence in operation—Lookout, speed, warning, etc.

The rules as to the care which should be exercised by those in control of street cars in keeping a lookout and in giving warning are expressed in different language in the various cases which have arisen. A driver or motorman must keep a vigilant watch for persons who may be approaching the tracks,[157] but a rule of the company which requires a higher degree of care than this is inoperative.[158] While approach-

74 S. W. 386; Parkinson v. Concord St. Ry. Co., 71 N. H. 28; McKeon v. Steinway R. Co., 20 App. Div. (N. Y.) 601; Healey v. Dry Dock, E. B. & B. R. Co., 46 N. Y. Super. Ct. 473; Richmond Passenger & Power Co. v. Steger (Va.) 43 S. E. 612.

154 59 Hun (N. Y.) 456.

155 Trauber v. Third Ave. R. Co., 80 App. Div. (N. Y.) 37; Phelan v. Forty-Second St., M. & St. N. Ave. Ry. Co., 79 App. Div. (N. Y.) 548.

156 Platt v. Forty-Second St. & G. St. Ferry R. Co., 2 Hun (N. Y.) 124.

157 Owensboro City R. Co. v. Hill, 21 Ky. Law Rep. 1638; Baltimore Traction Co. v. Wallace, 77 Md. 435; Baltimore Traction Co v. Helms, 84 Md. 515; Bunyan v. Citizens' Ry. Co., 127 Mo. 12; Brooks v. Lincoln St. Ry. Co., 22 Neb. 816; Wells v. Brooklyn City R. Co., 58 Hun (N. Y.) 389; Harvey v. Nassau Electric R. Co., 35 App. Div. (N. Y.) 307.

158 Isackson v. Duluth St. Ry. Co., 75 Minn. 27.

ing a street crossing he must have his car well under control,[159] and failure to ring a bell from a point twenty-five feet away from a crossing is negligence, both because it violates a reasonable ordinance, and is in itself careless.[160] Similarly, a failure to sound a gong near a street crossing has been held evidence of negligence.[161] A motorman should always be at his post, and it is negligence to require him to collect fares.[162]

It is not true, as a matter of law, that a motorman must observe the track in front of the car, and that portion of the street contiguous to the track on either side,[163] and those in charge of a street car do not have to slow up, ring a bell, or give some warning every time they meet another car.[164]

In general it is held that a driver or motorman has a right to assume that a person standing near the track or approaching the track will not undertake to cross suddenly in front of the car;[165] therefore the driver need not check his car because a man is on the track sixty feet away,[166] and a driver

159 Wallen v. North Chicago St. R. Co., 82 Ill. App. 103; Owensboro City R. Co. v. Hill, 21 Ky. Law Rep. 1638; Little v. Boston & M. R. R. (N. H.) 55 Atl. 190; Martin v. Third Ave. R. Co., 27 App. Div. (N. Y.) 52; Harvey v. Nassau Electric R. Co., 35 App. Div. (N. Y.) 307.

160 Driscoll v. Market St. Cable Ry. Co., 97 Cal. 553.

161 Schwarzbaum v. Third Ave. R. Co., 54 App. Div. (N. Y.) 164.

162 City Electric Ry. Co. v. Jones, 61 Ill. App. 183.

163 Macon & I. S. St. Ry. Co. v. Holmes, 103 Ga. 655.

164 West Chicago St. R. Co. v. Coit, 50 Ill. App. 640.

165 Daly v. Detroit Citizens' St. Ry. Co., 105 Mich. 193; Bunyan v. Citizens' Ry. Co., 127 Mo. 12; Wolf v. City & Suburban Ry. Co. (Or.) 72 Pac. 329.

166 Beem v. Tama & T. Electric Ry. & Light Co., 104 Iowa, 563; Farrar v. New Orleans & C. R. Co., 52 La. Ann. 417; McQuade v. Metropolitan St. Ry. Co., 17 Misc. Rep. (N. Y.) 154.

need not check or stop his car on seeing a pedestrian approaching the track.[167] The fact that a woman runs towards a car waving a handkerchief is not enough to charge the motorman with knowledge that she will cross in front of the car.[168] It is held, however, that it is the duty of a driver to see that the track is clear,[169] and that the fact that he did not see a person cross the tracks in time to prevent an accident will not necessarily excuse the company.[170] Even if a motorman uses due care after he sees a person on the track, but does not use due care in discovering him, the company is nevertheless liable.[171] If a motorman sees that a person is in a position of peril, he must use reasonable care to prevent an accident,[172] and, if he sees that a man does not heed his signal, and runs him down, this is evidence of negligence.[173] A motorman running a car over a trestle on private property is under no obligation to look out for travelers.[174]

In many cases the conduct of a traveler is so reckless and so entirely unexpected that it is held that those in charge of the street cars are free from imputation of any negligence as a matter of law. Thus, there was held to be no negligence on the part of the company where a boy of twelve was run

167 Driscoll v. Market St. Cable Ry. Co., 97 Cal. 553; Hickman v. Nassau Electric R. Co., 36 App. Div. (N. Y.) 376.

168 Meyer v. Lindell Ry. Co., 6 Mo. App. 27.

169 Griffiths v. Metropolitan St. Ry. Co., 63 App. Div. (N. Y.) 86.

170 Baltimore Traction Co. v. Wallace, 77 Md. 435.

171 Birmingham Ry. & Elec. Co. v. Jackson, 136 Ala. 279; Louisville City Ry. Co. v. Wood, 2 Ky. Law Rep. 387; San Antonio St. Ry. Co. v. Renken, 15 Tex. Civ. App. 229.

172 O'Keefe v. St. Louis & S. R. Co., 81 Mo. App. 386.

173 Buttelli v. Jersey City, H. & R. Electric Ry. Co., 59 N. J. Law, 302.

174 Camden, G. & W. Ry. Co. v. Young, 60 N. J. Law, 193.

over while attempting to board a moving car, when the gripman had not seen his signal;[175] where a man was run over at night by a dummy engine;[176] where a woman started to cross a street without paying any attention to a car, and the driver called to her, and used every possible effort to stop the car;[177] where a woman stood at a street crossing, and allowed herself to be struck by a car passing at ordinary speed;[178] and where a traveler started to cross a double track, and suddenly stepped back in front of a car.[179]

A street railway company is not responsible for conduct of third persons, and, where the horses on a street car ran away through the conduct of two drunken men, without any fault on the part of the driver, there was held to be no negligence.[180]

Where a traveler was running to take a car, and tripped and was struck by the car, there was held to be no negligence.[181]

The fact that the accident occurred at night is an additional circumstance to be considered. Where a passenger was killed by an electric car in the nighttime it was held that negligence was for the jury;[182] and where the driver of a horse car saw an object fifteen feet ahead of the car on a dark

175 West Chicago St. R. Co. v. Binder, 51 Ill. App. 420.

176 Dougherty v. Frankford & S. Passenger Ry. Co., 5 Wkly. Notes Cas. (Pa.) 14.

177 Ewing v. Atlantic Ave. R. Co., 11 N. Y. Supp. 626.

178 Widmer v. West End St. Ry. Co., 158 Mass. 49.

179 Aldrich v. St. Louis Transit Co. (Mo. App.) 74 S. W. 141; Jackson v. Union Ry. Co., 77 App. Div. (N. Y.) 161; Trauber v. Third Ave. R. Co., 80 App. Div. (N. Y.) 37.

180 Unger v. Forty-Second St. & G. St. Ferry R. Co., 51 N. Y. 497.

181 Winchell v. St. Paul City Ry. Co. (Minn.) 90 N. W. 1050.

182 Coll v. Easton Transit Co., 180 Pa. 618.

night, and could have stopped the car, but did not, and ran over a human being, negligence was held to be for the jury.[183] Evidence that a street car was driven at an unlawful rate of speed on a dark night, without lights, and without a careful watch being kept, warrants a finding of negligence;[184] and negligence is also a jury question where a woman was struck by a car coming at full speed, without lights and without warning, in the nighttime.[185]

Where a man lying on a street car track was run over about midnight, it was held that the driver could not have anticipated that any one would be lying on the track, and that there was no evidence of negligence on his part.[186] A similar ruling was made where a motorman, coming around a curve seventy-five feet away, ran over a drunken man lying near the side of the track, with his legs across the track;[187] and where a car coming four miles an hour on a dark, hazy night ran over an intoxicated traveler midway between two streets, and it appeared that the driver, hearing some one shout, stopped the car as soon as possible.[188]

A motorman running in a thinly settled district saw an object on the track at night which he thought was a dog. He applied the brakes and sounded the gong, and, on approaching a little nearer, reversed. The object on the track was a

183 Werner v. Citizens' Ry. Co., 81 Mo. 368.

184 Dallas Consol. Traction Ry. Co. v. Hurley, 10 Tex. Civ. App. 246.

185 Gildea v. Metropolitan St. Ry. Co., 58 App. Div. (N. Y.) 528.

186 Murray v. Forty-Second St., M. & St. N. Ave. R. Co., 9 App. Div. (N. Y.) 610.

187 Kramer v. New Orleans, C. & L. R. Co., 51 La. Ann. 1689.

188 Chicago City Ry. Co. v. Lewis, 5 Ill. App. 242.

man, and the car ran over him and killed him. It was held that there was no negligence.[189]

Negligence has been held to be for the jury where there was evidence of high speed at a crossing;[190] where a car was run through the fog at the rate of eighteen miles an hour;[191] where a car was coming very swiftly down a declivity;[192] where a car was running fifteen miles an hour;[193] where the speed of the car was constantly increased up to within a short distance of the point where the accident occurred, and the motorman was talking to some one inside the car;[194] where a car suddenly increased its speed as it approached a street crossing;[195] where a car rounded a curve at the rate of five or six miles an hour, when there was an ordinance forbidding any greater speed than three miles an hour;[196] where a man over seventy years of age saw a car about sixty feet away, and was struck before he could cross the track, which was twelve feet distant;[197] where a grip car was run six miles an hour in a crowded city street;[198] and where a car was driven by a boy fifteen at a speed greater than that allowed

189 Stelk v. McNulta, 99 Fed. 138.

190 Welty v. St. Charles St. R. Co., 109 La. 733; Hoyt v. Metropolitan St. R. Co., 73 App. Div. (N. Y.) 249.

191 Denton v. Brooklyn Heights R. Co., 78 N. Y. Supp. 157.

192 Mulhair v. West Philadelphia Passenger Ry. Co., 5 Wkly. Notes Cas. (Pa.) 190; West Philadelphia Passenger Ry. Co. v. Mulhair, 6 Wkly. Notes Cas. (Pa.) 508.

193 Faurot v. Brooklyn Heights R. Co., 14 Misc. Rep. (N. Y.) 398.

194 Killen v. Brooklyn Heights R. Co., 48 App. Div. (N. Y.) 557.

195 West Chicago St. R. Co. v. McCallum, 169 Ill. 240.

196 Brown v. Twenty-Third St. R. Co., 56 N. Y. Super. Ct. 356.

197 Mills v. Brooklyn City R. Co., 10 Misc. Rep. (N. Y.) 1.

198 Chicago City Ry. Co. v. Roach, 76 Ill. App. 496.

by ordinance.[199] Any speed beyond that allowed by ordinance tends to show negligence.[200]

Evidence that no warning was given at a street crossing has been held sufficient to take the question of negligence to the jury;[201] but it is not the duty of a street railway company to ring a gong between crossings.[202] Failure to have a car under control has been held to justify a verdict for the plaintiff.[203]

The general rule is that, where a street railway company operates a double line of tracks, they must use such care at crossings in regulating the speed of their cars and giving warning of their approach as will reasonably protect travelers from injury.[204] Thus there is evidence of negligence for the jury where it did not appear that the speed of a car was checked, or that it gave any signal of its approach,[205] and where there was evidence that a car came at a high rate of speed without warning.[206] Where a woman who was crossing a double track stepped back immediately in front of a car, there was held to be no evidence of negligence.[207]

199 Wall v. Helena St. Ry. Co., 12 Mont. 44.

200 Liddy v. St. Louis R. Co., 40 Mo. 506.

201 Chicago City R. Co. v. Loomis, 201 Ill. 118.

202 Kuhnen v. Union Ry. Co., 10 App. Div. (N. Y.) 195.

203 Horgan v. Jones, 131 Cal. 521.

204 Capital Traction Co. v. Lusby, 12 App. D. C. 295; Evansville St. R. Co. v. Gentry, 147 Ind. 408; Pelletreau v. Metropolitan St. Ry. Co., 74 App. Div. (N. Y.) 192; Stevens v. Union Ry. Co., 75 App. Div. (N. Y.) 602; Cincinnati St. Ry. Co. v. Snell, 54 Ohio St. 197; Bethel v. Cincinnati St. Ry. Co., 8 Ohio Circ. Dec. 310.

205 Dobert v. Troy City Ry. Co., 91 Hun (N. Y.) 28.

206 McClain v. Brooklyn City R. Co., 116 N. Y. 459; Sesselmann v. Metropolitan St. Ry. Co., 65 App. Div. (N. Y.) 484.

207 Mulligan v. Third Ave. R. Co., 61 App. Div. (N. Y.) 214.

In Lundy v. Second Ave. R. Co.,[208] where a driver, after alighting, attempted to cross in the rear of a car, and was struck by the car suddenly moving backwards, negligence was held to be for the jury; and in Cameron v. Union Trunk Line,[209] where a car to which passengers were being transfered suddenly backed while the conductor was on the forward end, and ran over a woman who was being transferred, and it appeared that the custom was for the car to remain stationary, it was held proper to instruct the jury that the company should have had an employe at the rear end of the car. Where a driver was caught between two cars which passed only eleven inches apart, both defendants were held negligent.[210] Where a traveler was crushed between two cars on a curve at a street crossing, the company was held negligent.[210a]

Where there is evidence of great speed, combined with evidence that no warning was given, there is still more reason for submitting the question of negligence to the jury. This general ruling, undor the varying circumstances of each particular set of facts, has been made in a number of cases.[211]

208 1 Misc. Rep. (N. Y.) 100.

209 10 Wash. 507.

210 West Chicago St. Ry. Co. v. Annis, 62 Ill. App. 180.

210a Schwartz v. New Orleans & C. R. Co. (La.) 34 So. 667.

211 Wahlgren v. Market St. Ry. Co., 132 Cal. 656; Chicago City R. Co. v. Fennimore, 199 Ill. 1; Louisville Ry. Co. v. Will's Adm'x (Ky.) 66 S. W. 628; Conway v. New Orleans, C. & L. R. Co., 51 La. Ann. 146; Peterson v. Minneapolis St. Ry. Co. (Minn.) 95 N. W. 751; Fandel v. Third Ave. R. Co., 15 App. Div. (N. Y.) 426; Halliday v. Brooklyn Heights R. Co., 59 App. Div. (N. Y.) 57; Copeland v. Metropolitan St. Ry. Co., 67 App. Div. (N. Y.) 483; G'Sell v. Metropolitan St. Ry. Co., 35 Misc. Rep. (N. Y.) 387; Cosgrove v. Metropolitan St. Ry. Co., 74 App. Div. (N. Y.) 166; Henderson v. United Traction Co., 202 Pa. 527.

It is not negligence, as a matter of law, not to have a headlight on a car,[212] and the mere fact that a man walking in a city street is run over raises no presumption of negligence.[213]

In certain miscellaneous cases, negligence has been held to be for the jury, as where a driver was injured while attempting to lead a frightened horse across a street railway track,[214] where a man about to board a car was struck by another passing car,[215] and where a passenger was carried beyond his destination, and the conductor told him to walk back on the track, and he was run over on a trestle.[216]

Where a passenger was boarding a car, and was thrown off by its sudden start, and was run over by another car, there was held to be no negligence on the part of the driver of the second car;[217] and where a passenger who was drunk or sick was helped from a car at a terminus, and twenty minutes later was run over by another car, there was held to be no causal connection, and therefore no cause for action.[218] Where a traveler saw the car, it is error to charge that the failure of the gripman to warn crossing pedestrians of the car's approach would make the company liable.[219] Where a woman was struck by a runaway team of horses, and no excuse was offered, it was held that a verdict for the plaintiff would not be disturbed.[220]

212 Omaha St. Ry. Co. v. Clair, 39 Neb. 454.

213 Chicago City Ry. Co. v. Lewis, 5 Ill. App. 242.

214 Deuster v. Milwaukee St. Ry. Co., 89 Wis. 191.

215 West Chicago St. R. Co. v. Shiplett, 85 Ill. App. 683.

216 Camden, G. & W. Ry. Co. v. Young, 60 N. J. Law, 193.

217 Black v. Brooklyn City R. Co., 108 N. Y. 640.

218 Bageard v. Consolidated Traction Co., 64 N. J. Law, 316.

219 Schulman v. Houston, W. St. & P. Ferry R. Co., 15 Misc. Rep (N. Y.) 30.

220 North Chicago St. R. Co. v. Louis, 35 Ill. App. 477.

## § 96. Same—Laborer working on or near track.

In almost every case where a laborer has been injured while working on or near a street railway track, no definite ruling has been made on the question of negligence, owing to the almost necessarily complicated state of facts, but negligence is left to the jury, as where the horse of a car fell into a trench and injured a workman;[221] where a horse car ran over a laborer working between the tracks;[222] and where a laborer working near the track,[223] and one working in a ditch under the track,[224] was struck by a car approaching without warning. Where a laborer pouring tar into cracks in the street looked for a car, and then stooped down, and was struck by a car which approached without signaling, it was held that negligence was for the jury, and that the custom of the laborer not to get out of the way until the car was very close was no excuse for the motorman's not giving a signal.[225] Where a flagman, in the performance of his duty, was run over by a horse car, although the driver could see him for several hundred feet, negligence was held to be for the jury.[226] Where the conductor of a car thought that there was room to pass a pipe, and the foreman in charge of the work signaled to the driver to come on, and the driver pro-

221 Burns v. Second Ave. R. Co., 21 App. Div. (N. Y.) 521.

222 Pittsburg Electric Ry. Co. v. Kelly, 57 Kan. 514; McCooey v. Forty-Second St. & G. St. Ferry R. Co., 79 Hun (N. Y.) 255; Lahey v. Central Park, &c., R. Co., 2 Misc. Rep. (N. Y.) 537; Morrissey v. Westchester Electric Ry. Co., 18 App. Div. (N. Y.) 67; O'Connor v. Union Ry. Co., 67 App. Div. (N. Y.) 99.

223 Hennessy v. Brooklyn Heights R. Co., 57 App. Div. (N. Y.) 27.

224 Owens v. Peoples' Passenger Ry., 155 Pa. 334.

225 Lewis v. Binghamton R. Co., 35 App. Div. (N. Y.) 12.

226 D'Oro v. Atlantic Ave. R. Co., 13 N. Y. Supp. 789.

ceeded at a walk, struck the pipe, and injured a workman, there was held to be no evidence of negligence.[227] Where a motorman sees that a workman on the track is not aware of the approach of a car, he must use every precaution to avoid an accident, and a mere sounding of the gong is not enough to relieve the company from liability.[228]

Where a workman relied on the direction of his foreman, and was injured, there was held to be no negligence on the part of the company.[229] Where a man in search of work slipped on the track of an elevated railroad, it was held that he was a licensee, and was owed the duty of reasonable care.[230]

Where the rules of an elevated railroad required its trains to slow up on seeing a green flag, evidence of an employe that the signal was not heeded as a rule was held not to show such a general violation of the rule as to charge the company with constructive notice thereof.[231] Where a company assumed the duty of giving warning, and then omitted it, negligence is for the jury.[232]

## § 97. Same—Miscellaneous.

It has been held that a city cannot make a street railway company liable to a citizen by means of an ordinance, without proof of an acceptance of the ordinance by the company;[233] but see the late cases of Gebhardt v. St. Louis Trans-

227 Schmidt v. Steinway & H. P. Ry. Co., 132 N. Y. 566.

228 Houston City St. Ry. Co. v. Woodlock (Tex. Civ. App.) 29 S. W. 817.

229 Floettl v. Third Ave. R. Co., 10 App. Div. (N. Y.) 308.

230 Wells v. Brooklyn Heights R. Co., 34 Misc. Rep. (N. Y.) 44.

231 Clark v. Manhattan Ry. Co., 77 App. Div. (N. Y.) 284.

232 Daum v. North Jersey St. Ry. Co. (N. J. Law) 54 Atl. 221.

233 Murphy v. Lindell Ry. Co., 153 Mo. 252; Holwerson v. St. Louis & S. Ry. Co., 157 Mo. 216.

it Co.,[234] and McLain v. St. Louis & S. Ry. Co.[235] In Johnson's Adm'r v. Louisville City Ry. Co.[236] it was held that a street railway was liable for an injury in a statute imposing liability on "the proprietors of any railroad."

Where a traveler was kicked by a street car horse, it was held that the mischievous propensity of the horse, and the defendant's knowledge of it, must be proved.[237] Where a traveler was injured by a blast, due care and negligence were left to the jury.[238] Where an electric car broke through a safety gate, and injured a brakeman on a steam railroad, the case was held to be for the jury.[239]

Where a street railway company owned a park and used it for picnic purposes, a boy who came to the park on a school picnic party, and was drowned in a pond, was held unable to recover;[240] and where a street railway company owned a pleasure resort, and allowed a man to operate a roller coaster there, it was held that the company did not thereby become liable for his carelessness.[241] Where a street railway company advertised a balloon ascension at its park, it was held liable for the negligence of an independent contractor to a boy, no matter whether the boy came by car or not, since the advertisment constituted an invitation to the public.[242]

234 (Mo. App.) 71 S. W. 448.

235 (Mo. App.) 73 S. W. 909.

236 10 Bush (Ky.) 231.

237 West Chicago St. R. Co. v. Walsh, 78 Ill. App. 59ō.

238 Mills v. Wilmington City Ry. Co., 1 Marvel (Del.) 269.

239 Todd v. Second Ave. Traction Co., 192 Pa. 587.

240 Le Grand v. Wilkes-Barre & W. V. Traction Co., 10 Pa. Super. Ct. 12.

241 Knottnerus v. North Park St. Ry. Co., 93 Mich. 348.

242 Richmond & M. Ry. Co. v. Moore's Adm'r, 94 Va. 493.

In Thompson v. Lowell, L. & H. St. Ry. Co.[243] it was held that, if a street railway corporation maintains a pleasure resort under St. 1895, c. 316, on the line of its railway, containing a stage for exhibitions, and enters into a contract with a manager, under which the latter furnishes and manages, among other entertainments there, an exhibition of marksmanship by a man born without hands, a butt being provided to receive the bullets, and the corporation pays for advertising these exhibitions, and carries posters on its cars, all the appliances being furnished by the manager or the performer, and nobody in the corporation's employ exercising any superintendence or control over the performance, a spectator who comes to the exhibition on the corporation's car, and who, immediately after a shot had been fired, is struck in the eye by something which probably was a small fragment of a bullet or other metallic substance that flew from the impact when the bullet hit the butt, is entitled, in an action against the corporation for his injury, to have the case submitted to the jury, and cannot be held tc have assumed the risk of the accident.

## II. Children.

**There is a conflict of authority as to the capacity of a child for using due care. Some jurisdictions hold that the due care of a child is always a question of fact for the jury; others that, up to a certain age, a child is incapable of using due care. Children have been held to be sui juris from the age of sixteen to the age of four years and ten months; non sui juris from the age of sixteen months to the age of nearly seven; and the question has been held for the jury from the age of five years and four months to the age of ten.**

243 170 Mass. 577.

It is almost universally held that the standard of care for a child who is sui juris is that degree of care which might reasonably be expected from a child of his age and capacity.

There is a conflict of authority as to whether the lack of due care of a parent or person in charge of a child who is not sui juris may be imputed to the child.

In general, it is held that allowing a child to play in the street alone, or leaving a child alone or in the company of other children in or near the house, does not show lack of due care on the part of parents as a matter of law, although lack of due care in some cases is so obvious as to bar a recovery.

While a street car has a superior right of way except at street crossings, those in charge of the car must use more care towards children than towards adults; and a child may recover, although he is guilty of lack of due care, if those in charge of the car could have prevented the accident by the exercise of due care.

All the circumstances surrounding each particular case must be taken into consideration in determining the questions of due care and negligence. The lookout, both of the child and of the man in charge of the car, the speed of the car, and its distance from the child, whether or not a warning was given, the obstruction of the view or of the track, are all important considerations.

## § 98. Capacity of child.

There are two views as to the doctrine of contributory negligence in the case of young children,—one that children must use the degree of care usually exercised by children of the same age and capacity, and that the due care of a child, however young, is always a question of fact for the jury; the other that, up to a certain age, not precisely defined, a child is incapable of contributory negligence, and that the court may so declare as a matter of law.[244] Even where the sec-

[244] Chicago City Ry. Co. v. Wilcox, 138 Ill. 370.

ond of these views is adopted, the law has realized the impossibility of fixing the exact age at which a child becomes *sui juris*,[245] but the following rulings, although absolutely irreconcilable in many cases, show pretty clearly the tendency of the courts in passing on these questions.

Children in the following cases have been held to be *sui juris:* A girl of sixteen,[246] a boy of fourteen years and ten months,[247] a girl of ten,[248] a boy of nine years and nine months,[249] a girl of nine,[250] a boy of eight years and nine months,[251] a boy of eight,[252] a boy of seven,[253] a boy of six and a half,[253a] a boy of six,[254] and a boy of four years and ten months.[255]

In the following cases a child has been held *non sui juris:* A girl of sixteen months,[256] a boy of sixteen months,[257] a child of twenty-one months,[258] a child under two,[259] a girl

245 Mangam v. Brooklyn R. Co., 38 N. Y. 455.

246 Street Ry. Co. v. Eadie, 43 Ohio St. 91.

247 Zlotovsky v. Twenty-Third St. Ry. Co., 8 Misc. Rep. (N. Y.) 463.

248 Sheets v. Connolly St. Ry., &c., Co., 54 N. J. Law, 518.

249 George v. Los Angeles Ry. Co., 126 Cal. 357.

250 Fitzhenry v. Consolidated Traction Co., 64 N. J. Law, 674.

251 Ryan v. La Crosse City Ry. Co., 108 Wis. 122.

252 Henderson v. Detroit Citizens' St. Ry. Co., 116 Mich. 368.

253 Springfield Consol. Ry. Co. v. Welsch, 56 Ill. App. 196.

253a McDermott v. Boston El. Ry. Co. (Mass.) 68 N. E. 34.

254 Allen v. Ames College Ry. Co., 106 Iowa, 602.

255 Mason v. Minneapolis St. Ry. Co., 54 Minn. 216.

256 Passamaneck's Adm'r v. Louisville Ry. Co., 98 Ky. 195; Fisselmayer v. Third Ave. R. Co., 2 N. Y. State Rep. 75.

257 Chicago West Div. Ry. Co. v. Ryan, 131 Ill. 474.

258 Budd v. Meriden Electric R. Co., 69 Conn. 272.

259 Farris v. Cass Ave. & F. G. Ry. Co., 80 Mo. 325.

of two,[260] a boy of two,[261] a child of two years and three months,[262] a girl of two and a half,[263] a girl of two years and eight months,[264] a boy of three,[265] a girl of three,[266] a boy of three years and two months,[267] a girl of three years and four months,[268] a girl of three and a half,[269] a boy of three and a half, in company with a brother of five and a half,[270] a boy of three years and seven months,[271] a girl of three years and ten months,[272] a girl of four,[273] a boy of four and a half,[274] a girl of four years and nine months,[275] a boy of five,[276] a boy of five and a half,[277] a boy of nearly six,[278] a boy of six and a half,[279] and a boy not quite seven.[280]

260 Newman v. Phillipsburg Horse Car R. Co., 52 N. J. Law, 446.

261 Wright v. Malden & M. R. Co., 4 Allen (Mass.) 283.

262 Bergen County Traction Co. v. Heitman's Adm'r, 61 N. J. Law, 682; Adams v. Metropolitan St. Ry. Co., 60 App. Div. (N. Y.) 188.

263 Martineau v. Rochester Ry. Co., 81 Hun (N. Y.) 263.

264 O'Flaherty v. Union Ry. Co., 45 Mo. 70.

265 Barnes v. Shreveport City R. Co., 47 La. Ann. 1218; Bamberger v. Citizens' St. Ry. Co., 95 Tenn. 18.

266 Mascheck v. St. Louis R. Co., 3 Mo. App. 600.

267 Ihl v. Forty-Second St. & G. St. Ferry R. Co., 47 N. Y. 317.

268 North Kankakee St. Ry. Co. v. Blatchford, 81 Ill. App. 609.

269 Rice v. Crescent City R. Co., 51 La. Ann. 108.

270 Government St. R. Co. v. Hanlon, 53 Ala. 70.

271 Mangam v. Brooklyn R. Co., 38 N. Y. 455.

272 Woeckner v. Erie Electric Motor Co., 176 Pa. 451.

273 Erie City Passenger Ry. Co. v. Schuster, 113 Pa. 412.

274 Evers v. Philadelphia Traction Co., 176 Pa. 376.

275 Elwood Electric St. Ry. Co. v. Ross, 26 Ind. App. 258.

276 Citizens' St. R. Co. v. Stoddard, 10 Ind. App. 278.

277 Chilton v. Central Traction Co., 152 Pa. 425.

278 Schnur v. Citizens' Traction Co., 153 Pa. 29.

279 Hoon v. Beaver Valley Traction Co., 204 Pa. 369; Lombard & S. Sts. Passenger Ry. Co. v. Steinhart, 2 Penny. (Pa.) 358.

280 Smith v. Hestonville, M. & F. P. Ry. Co., 92 Pa. 450.

In the following cases the question as to whether or not the child was *sui juris* was held to be a question for the jury: A boy of five years and four months,[281] a boy between five and six,[282] a boy of six,[283] a boy of seven,[284] a girl of seven,[285] a boy of seven years and two months,[286] a girl of seven years and three months,[287] a girl of eight,[288] a boy between eight and nine,[289] a girl of nine years and two months,[290] and a boy of ten.[291] In Trumbo's Adm'r v. City St. Car Co.[292] it was held that, between the ages of seven and fourteen, the presumption is that the child is *non sui juris,* but that evidence is admissible to show the contrary.

When the vexed question as to whether or not a child is capable of exercising care is once settled, it is almost universally held that the standard of care for a child who is *sui*

281 Paducah St. Ry. Co. v. Adkins' Adm'r, 14 Ky. Law Rep. 425.

282 Muller v. Brooklyn Heights R. Co., 18 App. Div. (N. Y.) 177.

283 Chicago City Ry. Co. v. Robinson, 127 Ill. 9; Mason v. Atlantic Ave. R. Co., 4 Misc. Rep. (N. Y.) 291; Lhowe v. Third Ave. R. Co., 14 Misc. Rep. (N. Y.) 612; Lafferty v. Third Ave. R. Co., 85 App. Div. (N. Y.) 592.

284 Vogel v. North Jersey St. Ry. Co. (N. J. Law) 54 Atl. 563; Block v. Harlem Bridge, H. & F. Ry. Co., 9 N. Y. Supp. 164.

285 Kitchell v. Brooklyn Heights R. Co., 6 App. Div. (N. Y.) 99.

286 Penny v. Rochester Ry. Co., 7 App. Div. (N. Y.) 595.

287 Stone v. Dry Dock, E. B. & B. R. Co., 115 N. Y. 104.

288 Bennett v. Brooklyn Heights R. Co., 1 App. Div. (N. Y.) 205; Goldstein v. Dry Dock, E. B. & B. R. Co., 35 Misc. Rep. (N. Y.) 200.

289 East St. Louis Electric St. Ry. Co. v. Burns, 77 Ill. App. 529.

290 Wihnyk v. Second Ave. R. Co., 14 App. Div. (N. Y.) 515.

291 Consolidated City & C. P. Ry. Co. v. Carlson, 58 Kan. 62.

292 89 Va. 780.

*juris* is that degree of care which might reasonably be expected from a child of his age and capacity.[293]

In Charlton v. Forty-Second St., M. & St. N. Ave. R. Co.[294] and in McDonald v. Metropolitan St. Ry. Co.[295] it was held that a child of twelve or over must be held to the standard of care required of an adult, unless it is shown as a fact that the child does not possess such capacity.

293 Washington & G. Ry. Co. v. Gladmon, 15 Wall. (U. S.) 401; Moore v. Metropolitan R. Co., 2 Mackey (D. C.) 437; Quincy Horse Ry. & Carrying Co. v. Gruse, 26 Ill. App. 397; Springfield Consol. Ry. Co. v. Welsch, 56 Ill. App. 196; West Chicago St. R. Co. v. Stoltenberg, 62 Ill. App. 420; West Chicago St. R. Co. v. Sullivan, 64 Ill. App. 628; Pfeiffer v. Chicago City Ry. Co., 96 Ill. App. 10; Citizens' St. R. Co. v. Stoddard, 10 Ind. App. 278; Allen v. Ames College Ry. Co., 106 Iowa, 602; Paducah St. Ry. Co. v. Adkins' Adm'r, 14 Ky. Law Rep. 425; Louisville Ry. Co. v. Phillips, 22 Ky. Law Rep. 842; Baltimore City Passenger Ry. Co. v. McDonnell, 43 Md. 534; Mason v. Minneapolis St. Ry. Co., 54 Minn. 216; Holmgren v. Twin City Rapid Transit Co., 61 Minn. 85; Boland v. Missouri R. Co., 36 Mo. 484; O'Flaherty v. Union Ry. Co., 45 Mo. 70; McCarthy v. Cass Ave. & F. G. Ry. Co., 92 Mo. 536; Lynch v. Metropolitan St. Ry. Co., 112 Mo. 420; Van Natta v. People's St. Ry., E. L. & P. Co., 133 Mo. 13; Schmidt v. St. Louis R. Co., 149 Mo. 269; Fitzhenry v. Consolidated Traction Co., 64 N. J. Law, 674; Thurber v. Harlem Bridge, M. & F. R. Co., 60 N. Y. 326; Stone v. Dry Dock, E. B. & B. R. Co., 115 N. Y. 104; Thompson v. Buffalo Ry. Co., 145 N. Y. 196; Costello v. Third Ave. R. Co., 161 N. Y. 317; Penny v. Rochester Ry. Co., 7 App. Div. (N. Y.) 595; Ellick v. Metropolitan St. Ry. Co., 15 App. Div. (N. Y.) 556; Weiss v. Metropolitan St. Ry. Co., 33 App. Div. (N. Y) 221; Lafferty v. Third Ave. R. Co., 85 App. Div. (N. Y.) 592; Wallace v. Suburban Ry. Co., 26 Or. 174; Riley v. Salt Lake Rapid Transit Co., 10 Utah, 428; Mitchell v. Tacoma Ry. & Motor Co., 9 Wash. 120.

294 79 App. Div. (N. Y.) 546.

295 80 App. Div. (N. Y.) 233.

An absolute difference of opinion exists on the question of whether the lack of due care of a parent or person in charge of a child *non sui juris* may be imputed to the child. Some courts affirm this doctrine,[296] and others deny it most emphatically.[297]

In the jurisdictions which refuse to sanction this doctrine it is held that while, where an action is brought by an administrator, or by a next friend for the benefit of the child, contributory negligence on the part of those in charge of the child is no defense, on the other hand, when an action is brought by the parents or for their benefit, contributory negligence is a defense.[298] In Murphy v. Derby St. Ry. Co.[299]

[296] Citizens' St. R. Co. v. Stoddard, 10 Ind. App. 278; Wright v. Malden & M. R. Co., 4 Allen (Mass.) 283; Reed v. Minneapolis St. Ry. Co., 34 Minn. 557; Strutzel v. St. Paul City Ry. Co., 47 Minn. 543; Mangam v. Brooklyn R. Co., 38 N. Y. 455; Ihl v. Forty-Second St. & G. St. Ferry R. Co., 47 N. Y. 317; Juskowitz v. Dry Dock, E. B. & B. R. Co., 25 Misc. Rep. (N. Y.) 64; Lafferty v. Third Ave. R. Co., 85 App. Div. (N. Y.) 592.

[297] Government St. R. Co. v. Hanlon, 53 Ala. 70; Murphy v. Derby St. Ry. Co., 73 Conn. 249; Moore v. Metropolitan R. Co., 2 Mackey (D. C.) 437; Chicago City Ry. Co. v. Wilcox, 138 Ill. 370; Metropolitan West Side El. R. Co. v. Kersey, 80 Ill. App. 301; Chicago City Ry. Co. v. Tuohy, 196 Ill. 410; Boland v. Missouri R. Co., 36 Mo. 484; Winters v. Kansas City Cable Ry. Co., 99 Mo 509; Newman v. Phillipsburg Horse Car R. Co., 52 N. J. Law, 446; Bergen County Traction Co. v. Heitman's Adm'r, 61 N. J. Law 682; Erie City Passenger Ry. Co. v. Schuster, 113 Pa. 412; Bamberger v. Citizens' St. Ry. Co., 95 Tenn. 18; Ploof v. Burlington Traction Co., 70 Vt. 509; Trumbo's Adm'r v. City St. Car Co., 89 Va. 780.

[298] Moore v. Metropolitan R. Co., 2 Mackey (D. C.) 437; Chicago City Ry. Co. v. Wilcox, 138 Ill. 370; Consolidated Traction Co v. Hone, 59 N. J. Law, 275; Glassey v. Hestonville, M. & F. P Ry. Co., 57 Pa. 172; Smith v. Hestonville, M. & F. Passenger Ry Co., 92 Pa. 450; Ploof v. Burlington Traction Co., 70 Vt. 509.

the court held that the benefit to the parents must be affirmatively shown.

A curious question arises where the father, while suing as administrator, is at the same time the sole beneficiary. In Consolidated Traction Co. v. Hone,[300] the court was equally divided on the question of whether the father's contributory negligence would be a bar; but in Bamberger v. Citizens' St. Ry. Co.[301] the court held squarely that a father in such a case could not recover.

Even where the doctrine of imputed negligence prevails, it is held that, if those in charge of a child are guilty of lack of due care, to bar a recovery it must be shown that the conduct of the child was such as would have amounted to contributory negligence in the case of a person *sui juris*;[302] and a child may recover for injuries,[303] or those in charge of him may recover for his injury[304] or death,[305] even though they are guilty of lack of due care in permitting him to be in the street, where the street railway company could have prevented the accident by the exercise of ordinary care. Some cases,

299 73 Conn. 249.

300 60 N. J. Law, 444.

301 95 Tenn. 18.

302 Chicago City Ry. Co. v. Robinson, 127 Ill. 9; Ihl v. Forty-Second St. & G. St. Ferry R. Co., 47 N. Y. 317; Cumming v. Brooklyn City R. Co., 104 N. Y. 669.

303 Cunningham v. Los Angeles Ry. Co., 115 Cal. 561; Chicago West Div. Ry. Co. v. Ryan, 131 Ill. 474; Barnes v. Shreveport City R. Co., 47 La. Ann. 1218.

304 Baltimore City Passenger Ry. Co. v. McDonnell, 43 Md. 534.

305 Fox v. Oakland Consol. St. Ry., 118 Cal. 55; Passamaneck's Adm'r v. Louisville Ry. Co., 98 Ky. 195; O'Flaherty v. Union Ry. Co., 45 Mo. 70; Dan v. Street R. Co., 99 Tenn. 88.

however, hold that there must be something more than ordinary negligence on the part of the company under these circumstances.[306]

## § 99. Due care of child, for jury.

In many cases where children are run over, the general ruling is made that, under all the circumstances of the case, due care is for the jury, and no special fact or group of facts is singled out as forming a basis for these decisions.[307]

The question as to whether a child looked for a car or not is a very important one. It has been held that it is not lack of due care, as a matter of law, for a boy of eight to fail to look up or down before crossing a street railway track, or to fail to see or hear an approaching car.[308] It is not lack of due care for a child to cross a street railway track without stopping and looking for a car,[309] or to be playing in the street,[310] and the care required in crossing a steam railroad is not the test to be applied in crossing a street railway.[311]

306 West Chicago St. R. Co. v. Egan, 74 Ill. App. 442.

307 Quincy Horse Ry. & Carrying Co. v. Gnuse, 38 Ill. App. 212; West Chicago St. R. Co. v. Sullivan, 64 Ill. App. 628; Calumet Electric St. Ry. Co. v. Van Pelt, 68 Ill. App. 582; Aiken v. Holyoke St. Ry. Co., 180 Mass. 8; Holmgren v. Twin City Rapid Transit Co., 61 Minn. 85; Dunn v. Cass Ave. & F. G. Ry. Co., 21 Mo. App. 188; Oldfield v. New York & H. R. Co., 14 N. Y. 310; Thurber v. Harlem Bridge, M. & F. R. Co., 60 N. Y. 326; Iaquinta v. Citizens' Traction Co., 166 Pa. 63; Mitchell v. Tacoma Ry. & Motor Co., 9 Wash. 120; Holdridge v. Mendenhall, 108 Wis. 1.

308 Mentz v. Second Ave. R. Co., 2 Rob. (N. Y.) 356. And see McDermott v. Boston El. Ry. Co. (Mass.) 68 N. E. 34

309 Chicago City Ry. Co. v. Robinson, 127 Ill. 9.

310 Mitchell v. Tacoma Ry. & Motor Co., 13 Wash. 560.

311 Holmgren v. Twin City Rapid Transit Co., 61 Minn. 85; Consolidated Traction Co. v. Scott, 58 N. J. Law, 682.

Where a boy of fourteen was thrown off a car, fell on his back, and walked slowly, owing to his dazed condition, in front of another car, a nonsuit was held proper on the ground that there was insufficient evidence of any excuse for not looking and listening.[312] A girl of nine who sees a car one hundred and twenty-seven feet away, rapidly approaching a crossing, and who proceeds to cross without looking again, is not guilty of lack of due care as a matter of law.[313] It has been held that a boy of fourteen, who is deaf and dumb, is the more bound to use his eyesight, and that the question of his due care under all the circumstances of the case was for the jury.[314] A boy of ten has no right to presume that a street car company has complied with the law that it should have bells on its mules.[315] Where a boy of twelve looked for a car, and then walked along the track beside an ice cart, and was struck by a car coming at high speed, due care was held to be for the jury;[316] and the same ruling was made where a boy of fifteen, walking on the track, was struck by a car coming from the rear.[317]

A number of cases have arisen where a child fell while crossing a street car track. In Block v. Harlem Bridge, H. & F. Ry. Co.,[318] the due care of a child of seven was held, under these circumstances, to be for the jury; and the same ruling was made in the cases of a boy of six[319] and one of eight,[320]

312 Pinder v. Brooklyn Heights R. Co., 173 N. Y. 519.

313 Hicks v. Nassau Electric R. Co., 47 App. Div. (N. Y.) 479.

314 Thompson v. Salt Lake Rapid Transit Co., 16 Utah, 281.

315 Lynch v. Metropolitan St. Ry. Co., 112 Mo. 420.

316 Howland v. Union St. Ry. Co., 150 Mass. 86.

317 Quirk v. Rapid Ry. (Mich.) 90 N. W. 673.

318 9 N. Y. Supp. 164.

319 Aaron v. Second Ave. R. Co., 2 Daly (N. Y.) 127.

320 Silberstein v. Houston, W. St. & P. F. R. Co., 4 N. Y. Supp. 843.

where it appeared that each could have crossed the track in safety if he had not fallen. In Lhowe v. Third Ave. R. Co.,[321] where it appeared that a boy of six would have had plenty of time to cross in front of a car if he had not fallen, an instruction that the boy was not guilty of lack of due care was held correct.

The speed at which a car was coming, and its distance from the child at the time it attempted to cross the track, are also important considerations. Where a child of five was run over, and there was evidence that the car was running at twice the speed allowed by law, and that the driver saw the child thirty-five feet away, but did not slacken speed, due care was held to be for the jury.[322] Similarly, due care is for the jury where a boy of ten,[323] a girl of nine,[324] and one of eight[325] were struck by a car coming at high speed without warning; where the plaintiff was struck by a car at a crossing, and carried a distance of sixty-three feet, while the motorman testified that he could have stopped the car within a distance of twenty-five feet;[326] and where a child was carried one hundred and two feet after he was struck.[327] That the driver suddenly increased the speed of the car is a still stronger circumstance in favor of the plaintiff, and due care under these circumstances has been held to be for the jury

321 14 Misc. Rep. (N. Y.) 612.

322 Huerzeler v. Central Crosstown R. Co., 1 Misc. Rep. (N. Y.) 136.

323 Consolidated City & C. P. Ry. Co. v. Carlson, 58 Kan. 62.

324 Rosenberg v. West End St. Ry. Co., 168 Mass. 561.

325 Goldstein v. Dry Dock, E. B. & B. R. Co., 35 Misc. Rep. (N. Y.) 200.

326 Cohen v. Metropolitan St. Ry. Co., 63 App. Div. (N. Y.) 165.

327 Young v. Atlantic Ave. R. Co., 10 Misc. Rep. (N. Y.) 541.

in a number of cases.[328] Due care is also for the jury where it appeared that a driver, traveling at a very rapid rate of speed, was urging his horses to a still faster rate.[329]

It is not lack of due care, as a matter of law, to attempt to cross a street railway track when an electric car is at such a distance that the motorman, in the exercise of due care, could prevent an accident;[330] and due care has been held to be for the jury where a boy of eight attempted to cross a street car track when an electric car was fifty feet away;[331] and where a boy of five was run over by a car coming at high speed, which was half a block away when the child first started to cross the track.[332] In several cases where there were double tracks, and a boy was run over by a car coming on a parallel track, due care has been held to be a question for the jury.[333]

Where a boy between seven and eight years of age stood on a street railway track waiting for a car on the other track to pass, and was struck by a car which gave no warning,[334] and where a girl between nine and ten years old stood close to a track,[335] due care in each case was held to be for the

328 Stone v. Dry Dock, E. B. & B. R. Co., 115 N. Y. 104; Costello v. Third Ave. R. Co., 161 N. Y. 317; Ellick v. Metropolitan St. Ry. Co., 15 App. Div. (N. Y.) 556.

329 Pendril v. Second Ave. R. Co., 34 N. Y. Super. Ct. 481.

330 Legare v. Union Ry. Co., 61 App. Div. (N. Y.) 202.

331 Dowd v. Brooklyn Heights R. Co., 9 Misc. Rep. (N. Y.) 279.

332 Timony v. Brooklyn City & N. R. Co., 10 Misc. Rep. (N. Y.) 261.

333 Chicago City Ry. Co. v. Robinson, 127 Ill. 9; Chicago City Ry. Co. v. Wilcox, 138 Ill. 370; Consolidated Traction Co. v. Scott, 58 N. J. Law, 682.

334 Griffiths v. Metropolitan St. Ry. Co., 63 App. Div. (N. Y.) 86.

335 Mallard v. Ninth Ave. R. Co., 15 Daly (N. Y.) 376.

jury. Where a boy went on the track to pick up his hat, and was struck by a car coming at high speed without warning, due care was held to be for the jury;[336] and the same ruling was made where a boy chased other boys, who had his cap.[337]

## § 100. Lack of due care of child.

As noted in the preceding section, whether or not a child looked before crossing a street car track is a very important consideration, and it is generally held that, where a child walks directly in front of a street car, either without looking or having a clear view and an opportunity of looking, there is no evidence of due care. This ruling has been made in the case of a boy of sixteen,[338] a boy of fourteen,[339] a boy of thirteen,[340] a boy of eleven,[341] a girl of ten,[342] a boy of nine and a half,[343] a girl of nine,[344] a boy of eight years and nine months,[345] a girl of eight years and four months,[346] and a boy of eight.[347] Where a girl of fourteen crossed in the rear

336 Davidson v. Metropolitan St. Ry. Co., 75 App. Div. (N. Y.) 426.

337 Sullivan v. Union Ry. Co., 81 App. Div. (N. Y.) 596.

338 Downs v. St. Paul City Ry. Co., 75 Minn. 41.

339 Wills v. Ashland L. P. & St. Ry. Co., 108 Wis. 255.

340 Kaiser v. New Orleans & C. R. Co., 107 La. 539; Funk v. Electric Traction Co., 175 Pa. 559.

341 Ledman v. Dry Dock, E. B. & B. R. Co., 28 App. Div. (N. Y.) 197.

342 Sheets v. Connolly St. Ry., etc., Co., 54 N. J. Law, 518.

343 Brady v. Consolidated Traction Co., 63 N. J. Law, 25, 64 N. J. Law, 373.

344 Fitzhenry v. Consolidated Traction Co., 64 N. J. Law, 674.

345 Ryan v. La Crosse City Ry. Co., 108 Wis. 122.

346 Weiss v. Metropolitan St. Ry. Co., 33 App. Div. (N. Y.) 221.

347 Morey v. Gloucester St. Ry. Co., 171 Mass. 164; Henderson v. Detroit Citizens' St. Ry. Co., 116 Mich. 368.

of a car without looking, where there were double tracks, she was held not to be in the exercise of due care.[348] Where a girl of thirteen, with her head wrapped up in a large shawl, crossed leisurely in front of a street car, and it appeared that her view was unobstructed, she was held to be guilty of lack of due care;[349] and a boy of nine who ran from behind some wagons in front of a street car was likewise held not to be entitled to recover.[350]

Where a boy of fifteen stood between the rails of a street car track without looking for a car, when he might have reached a place of safety by stepping back two feet, he was held not to be in the exercise of due care;[351] and a similar holding was made where a boy of eleven stood on a car track with his back towards the direction from which the car approached.[352] Where a boy of eight saw a car coming, and tried to cross ahead of it, it was held that he voluntarily assumed the risk of the accident.[353] Where a boy of seventeen jumped on and off of a car, and was run over, he was held guilty of lack of due care.[354] Where a boy of nine jumped from a wagon directly in front of a car, he was held not to be in the exercise of due care.[355]

348 Thompson v. Buffalo Ry. Co., 145 N. Y. 196.

349 Biederman v. Dry Dock, E. B. & B. R. Co., 54 App. Div. (N. Y.) 291.

350 Bello v. Metropolitan St. Ry. Co., 2 App. Div. (N. Y.) 313.

351 Zlotovsky v. Twenty-Third St. Ry. Co., 8 Misc. Rep. (N. Y.) 463.

352 Baltimore City Passenger Ry. Co. v. Cooney, 87 Md. 261.

353 Motel v. Sixth Ave. R. Co., 2 How. Pr. (N. S.; N. Y.) 30.

354 Taylor's Adm'r v. South Covington & C. St. R. Co., 14 Ky. Law Rep. 355.

355 Mullen v. Springfield St. Ry. Co., 164 Mass. 450.

## § 101. Due care of parent or person in charge of child—Allowing child in street.

Numerous rulings, not entirely in harmony, have been made on the question of the due care of parents in allowing children to be in the street alone. It has been held, on the one hand, that it is not lack of due care, as a matter of law, for the parents of a boy seven years and eight months old,[356] a boy seven years and two months old,[357] a boy of seven,[358] a boy a little less than seven,[359] and a girl of five[360] to be in the street alone, but that their due care is a question for the jury. Where a mother sued for the death of her son, a boy of ten, and there was evidence that he had been taken out of school because of a defect in his speech, the due care of the mother in allowing him to be in the street unattended was held to be for the jury;[361] and where a sick mother sent a bright boy of five on a necessary errand, and he was run over by a horse car, it was held that it could not be said, as a matter of law, that the mother was guilty of contributory negligence.[362] It is not lack of due care, as matter of law, for a father to allow a bright boy of five and a half to be in the street alone.[363] In Ploof v. Burlington Traction Co.,[364]

356 Sullivan v. Union Ry. Co., 81 App. Div. (N. Y.) 596.

357 Penny v. Rochester Ry. Co., 7 App. Div. (N. Y.) 595.

358 Schierhold v. North Beach & M. R. Co., 40 Cal. 447; Riley v. Salt Lake Rapid Transit Co., 10 Utah, 428.

359 Holdridge v. Mendenhall, 108 Wis. 1.

360 Huerzeler v. Central Cross Town R. Co., 139 N. Y. 490.

361 Lynch v. Metropolitan St. Ry. Co., 112 Mo. 420.

362 Citizens' St. R. Co. v. Stoddard, 10 Ind. App. 278.

363 Barksdull v. New Orleans & C. R. Co., 23 La. Ann. 180.

364 70 Vt. 509.

where a boy of ten was run over, it was held that, even if his parents were negligent in allowing him to be in the street, such negligence was the remote cause of the injury, and therefore could not be a bar to recovery.

On the other hand, it has been held that, where the parents of a girl of three and a half allowed her to play alone on a dark night where there were street car tracks, the negligence of the parents would prevent a recovery by the child.[365] In Glassey v. Hestonville, M. & F. P. Ry. Co.,[366] the case of a boy of four, in Wright v. Malden & M. R. Co.,[367] the case of a boy of two, and in Boland v. Missouri R. Co.,[368] the case of a girl of two, it was held that the fact that the child was found alone in the street where there were street railway tracks was in itself *prima facie* evidence of negligence. Where a mother allowed a boy of seven to sell water to the drivers and conductors of a street car line, this was held to be lack of due care as a matter of law.[369]

Where a child is allowed to go in the street in charge of another, older child, the due care of the parents or persons in charge of the child is almost invariably held to be for the jury. Such a ruling has been made in the case of a child one year and four months old, in charge of a brother of fifteen,[370] a girl of two years and one month, in charge of a girl of sixteen,[371] a girl two years and three months old, in

365 Juskowitz v. Dry Dock, E. B. & B. R. Co., 25 Misc. Rep. (N. Y.) 64.

366 57 Pa. 172.

367 4 Allen (Mass.) 283.

368 36 Mo. 484.

369 Smith v. Hestonville, M. & F. P. Ry. Co., 92 Pa. 450.

370 Chicago West Div. Ry. Co. v. Ryan, 131 Ill. 474.

371 Commonwealth v. Metropolitan R. Co., 107 Mass. 236.

charge of a brother of seven,[372] a child of two and a half, in charge of a sister of five,[373] a girl of two years and eight months, in charge of a sister of eight,[374] a girl of two years and ten months, in charge of an older sister,[375] a boy of two years and eleven months, in charge of an uncle of fourteen,[376] a boy of three years and two months, in charge of a sister of nine and a half,[377] a girl of three years and nine months, in charge of a brother of nine,[378] a girl of three years and eleven months, in charge of a sister of ten,[379] a boy of four, in charge of a sister of eleven,[380] a girl of four, in charge of a sister of twelve,[381] a boy of four and a half, in charge of a brother of eight,[382] a girl of five, in charge of a brother of fifteen,[383] and a girl of five, in charge of a sister of twenty-four.[384] Where the mother of a boy of four stood at an open window twenty-five feet away, and the child's nurse was standing not far from the child, who was seated in a chair on the sidewalk, the due care of the mother was held to be for the jury.[385] Where a father stood on the sidewalk with a girl of

372 Adams v. Metropolitan St. Ry. Co., 60 App. Div. (N. Y.) 188.

373 Martineau v. Rochester Ry. Co., 81 Hun (N. Y.) 263.

374 O'Flaherty v. Union Ry. Co., 45 Mo. 70.

375 Woeckner v. Erie Electric Motor Co., 182 Pa. 182.

376 Harkins v. Pittsburg, A. & M. Traction Co., 173 Pa. 146.

377 Ihl v. Forty-Second St. & G. St. Ferry R. Co., 47 N. Y. 317.

378 Hedin v. Suburban Ry. Co., 26 Or. 155.

379 West Chicago St. R. Co. v. Scanlan, 68 Ill. App. 626.

380 Collins v. South Boston R. Co., 142 Mass. 301.

381 Jones v. Brooklyn Heights R. Co., 10 Misc. Rep. (N. Y.) 543.

382 Evers v. Philadelphia Traction Co., 176 Pa. 376.

383 Ehrmann v. Nassau Electric R. Co., 23 App. Div. (N. Y.) 21.

384 Weitzman v. Nassau Electric R. Co., 33 App. Div. (N. Y.) 585.

385 Kroesen v. New Castle Electric St. Ry. Co., 198 Pa. 30.

four, and she got onto the track and was run over, and there was evidence that a boy of five was with her, the due care of the father was held to be for the jury;[386] and the same ruling was made where a father, after alighting, was looking after his wife, and a girl of seven was run over by a car which approached at high speed without warning.[387] Where the grandmother of a girl of eight left a horse car with the child, and went onto a parallel track without taking hold of the child, the grandmother was held to be guilty of lack of due care.[388] Where a boy of five, in charge of a boy of eleven, was injured, the due care of the boy of eleven was held to be for the jury;[389] and where a boy of six and a half, in charge of a boy of twelve, was injured, the due care of the parents and of the boy of twelve was a question for the jury.[390]

### § 102. Same—Leaving child alone in or near the house.

The reports are filled with a painfully large number of cases where the small children of parents who are in moderate circumstances have escaped from the care of their parents or others in charge of them, and have got onto the street railway tracks and been run over. The question as to whether the moderate circumstances of the parents, and their consequent inability to exercise the very highest degree of watchfulness over their children by the employment of a nurse or by other means, is a proper fact to be considered by the jury in passing upon the question of their due care, has arisen in

386 Levy v. Dry Dock, E. B. & B. R. Co., 12 N. Y. Supp. 485.
387 Kitchell v. Brooklyn Heights R. Co., 6 App. Div. (N. Y.) 99.
388 Reed v. Minneapolis St. Ry. Co., 34 Minn. 557.
389 Gumby v. Metropolitan St. Ry. Co., 65 App. Div. (N. Y.) 38.
390 Levine v. Metropolitan St. Ry. Co., 78 App. Div. (N. Y.) 426.

a number of cases. In Fox v. Oakland Consol. St. Ry.[391] it was held that the fact that a man was too poor to keep servants to look after his child was not a matter to be considered by the jury; and in Cunningham v. Los Angeles Ry. Co.[392] it was held that, although it is true, as an abstract proposition, that the law does not require parents to keep an attendant with their young children, or to shut them up, it is error to give such instruction to the jury, since the question as to whether such precautions are necessary in any particular state of facts is for them to decide. It seems from the case of Cumming v. Brooklyn City R. Co.[393] that evidence is inadmissible to show that a mother was unable to hire anybody to aid her in looking after her child, but, on the other hand, it has been squarely held in a number of cases that the financial condition and station in life of parents may be considered in determining the question of their due care in caring for their children.[394]

The courts are very unwilling to declare parents negligent in these cases as a matter of law, and whether they are negligent, in any given case, in allowing a child to play in or near the house or store, alone, or in charge of other children or some older person, is almost invariably held to be a ques-

391 118 Cal. 55.

392 115 Cal. 561.

393 104 N. Y. 669.

394 Cotter v. Lynn & B. R. Co., 180 Mass. 145; O'Flaherty v. Union Ry. Co., 45 Mo. 70; Rosenkranz v. Lindell Ry. Co., 108 Mo. 9; Czezewzka v. Benton-Bellefontaine Ry. Co., 121 Mo. 201; Levin v. Metropolitan St. Ry. Co., 140 Mo. 624; Fullerton v. Metropolitan St. Ry. Co., 63 App. Div. (N. Y.) 1; Hedin v. Suburban Ry. Co., 26 Or. 155; Pittsburg, A. & M. Ry. Co. v. Pearson, 72 Pa. 169; Evers v. Philadelphia Traction Co., 176 Pa. 376.

tion for the jury under all the circumstances of each particular action. This ruling has been made where a child was left alone in the case of a child of fourteen months,[395] a child of seventeen months,[396] a child of eighteen months,[397] a boy of nineteen months,[398] a child under two,[399] a girl of two,[400] a child of two years and three months,[401] a boy of two and a half,[402] a girl of two and a half,[403] a boy of two years and seven months,[404] a boy of two years and eight months,[405] a boy of two years and ten months,[406] a boy of three years and eight months,[407] a boy of four,[408] a boy of four and a half,[409] a boy of five,[410] a girl of five,[411] and a boy of nearly six years old;[412] and where a child was left in the care of

395 San Antonio St. Ry. Co. v. Cailloutte, 79 Tex. 341.

396 Weissner v. St. Paul City Ry. Co., 47 Minn. 468.

397 Pittsburg, A. & M. Ry. Co. v. Pearson, 72 Pa. 169.

398 Reinike v. Philadelphia Traction Co., 31 Wkly. Notes Cas. (Pa.) 471.

399 Czezewzka v. Benton-Bellefontaine Ry. Co., 121 Mo. 201.

400 Weil v. Dry Dock, E. B. & B. R. Co., 119 N. Y. 147.

401 Henne v. Peoples' St. Ry. Co., 1 Pa. Super. Ct. 311.

402 Karahuta v. Schuylkill Traction Co., 6 Pa. Super. Ct. 319.

403 Hyland v. Yonkers R. Co., 4 N. Y. Supp. 305; Houston City St. Ry. Co. v. Dillon, 3 Tex. Civ. App. 303.

404 Slensby v. Milwaukee St. Ry. Co., 95 Wis. 179.

405 Powers v. Quincy & B. St. Ry. Co., 163 Mass. 5.

406 Levin v. Metropolitan St. Ry. Co., 140 Mo. 624.

407 Hewitt v. Taunton St. Ry. Co., 167 Mass. 483.

408 Rosenkranz v. Lindell Ry. Co., 108 Mo. 9; Mangam v. Brooklyn R. Co., 38 N. Y. 455; Barry v. Second Ave. R. Co., 16 N. Y. Supp. 518.

409 Fox v. Oakland Consol. St. Ry., 118 Cal. 55.

410 Fallon v. Central Park, N. & E. R. R. Co., 64 N. Y. 13; Dunseath v. Pittsburg, A. & M. Traction Co., 161 Pa. 124.

411 Ames v. Broadway & S. A. R. Co., 56 N. Y. Super. Ct. 3.

412 Strutzel v. St. Paul City Ry. Co., 47 Minn. 543.

someone else, in the case of a child of sixteen months, in charge of a sister of eleven,[413] a child of sixteen months, in charge of a sister twenty years old,[414] a child of two, in charge of its grandmother,[415] a child of two, in charge of a sister of fifteen,[416] a child of three, with other children,[417] and a girl of four years and four months old, in charge of a brother of thirteen.[418]

The circumstances may be such, however, as to justify the court in holding that the parents have been guilty of lack of due care as a matter of law. Thus, where the mother of a boy twenty months old left her child in the kitchen, to accompany some callers to the front door, and the child passed its mother at the door, went onto a street railway track, and was killed, it was held that the mother was guilty of contributory negligence, and that neither she nor her husband could recover for the loss of the child.[419] In Cotter v. Lynn & B. R. Co.,[420] where a girl of four was allowed to play, in a yard opening onto a busy city street, with a boy of five, and the boy was sent on an errand, there was held to be no evidence of due care on the part of the parents. There are also cases where the court could rule, as matter of law, that there is no evidence of lack of due care, and that it is not proper to submit this question to the jury. Thus, where some children

413 Passamaneck's Adm'r v. Louisville Ry. Co., 98 Ky. 195.

414 Fisselmayer v. Third Ave. R. Co., 2 N. Y. State Rep. 75.

415 Roller v. Sutter St. R. Co., 66 Cal. 230.

416 Jones v. United Traction Co., 201 Pa. 346.

417 Buente v. Pittsburg, A. & M. Traction Co., 2 Pa. Super. Ct. 185.

418 Dahl v. Milwaukee City Ry. Co., 62 Wis. 652.

419 Johnson v. Reading City Passenger Ry., 160 Pa. 647.

420 180 Mass. 145.

unlatched the gate in a yard, and a child under two years of age escaped, there was held to be no evidence of contributory negligence, since it appeared that the father was a laboring man, and the mother could not afford to keep a servant.[421] In Becker v. Cincinnati St. Ry. Co.,[422] where a mother allowed a girl of three and a boy of five to play in a yard, and the children escaped, and the younger one was run over by an electric car, whether the act of the mother was the proximate cause of the injury was held to be for the jury.

## § 103. Negligence of company—Right of way.

While it is clear that the right of a street railway to that part of the street on which its tracks are laid is not an exclusive one,[423] it is generally held that its rights are superior to those of the general public,[424] except at street crossings, where the rights of both are equal.[425] It has been held that a street railway company is bound to know that men, women, and children have a right to use the track,[426] and that children have a right to use the city streets, not merely as a

421 Farris v. Cass Ave. & F. G. Ry. Co., 80 Mo. 325.

422 2 Ohio Dec. 137.

423 Evers v. Philadelphia Traction Co., 176 Pa. 376; Memphis City Ry. Co. v. Logue, 13 Lea (Tenn.) 32; Galveston City R. Co. v. Hewitt, 67 Tex. 473; San Antonio St. Ry. Co. v. Mechler, 87 Tex. 628; Thompson v. Salt Lake Rapid Transit Co., 16 Utah, 281.

424 Fenton v. Second Ave. R. Co., 126 N. Y. 625; Thompson v. Buffalo Ry. Co., 145 N. Y. 196; Baker v. Eighth Ave. R. Co., 62 Hun (N. Y.) 39; Evers v. Philadelphia Traction Co., 176 Pa. 376; Thompson v. Salt Lake Rapid Transit Co., 16 Utah, 281.

425 Consolidated Traction Co. v. Scott, 58 N. J. Law, 682; Cohen v. Metropolitan St. Ry. Co., 63 App. Div. (N. Y.) 165.

426 Winters v. Kansas City Cable Ry. Co., 99 Mo. 509.

means of going to school, but to play upon.[427] In Government St. R. Co. v. Hanlon[428] the court went so far as to declare that the easement of a street railway company is enjoyed subordinate to the paramount right of citizens to the absolute and unqualified use of the street.

## § 104. Same—General considerations.

While, as we have seen, the degree of care which a street railway company is bound to use towards travelers is only ordinary care under the circumstances,[429] it is universally held that more care must be used towards children than towards adults.[430] While greater care is required in running

427 Quincy Horse Ry. & Carrying Co. v. Gnuse, 38 Ill. App. 212.

428 53 Ala. 70.

429 Cunningham v. Los Angeles Ry. Co., 115 Cal. 561; West Chicago St. R. Co. v. Binder, 51 Ill. App. 420; Pfeiffer v. Chicago City Ry. Co., 96 Ill. App. 10; Gorman's Adm'r v. Louisville Ry. Co. (Ky.) 72 S. W. 760; Stanley v. Union Depot R. Co., 114 Mo. 606; Cumming v. Brooklyn City R. Co., 104 N. Y. 669; Memphis City Ry. Co. v. Logue, 13 Lea (Tenn.) 32; Dallas Rapid Transit Ry. Co. v. Dunlap, 7 Tex. Civ. App. 471.

430 Government St. R. Co. v. Hanlon, 53 Ala. 70; Schierhold v. North Beach & M. R. Co., 40 Cal. 447; West Chicago St. R. Co. v. Schwartz, 93 Ill. App. 387; Passamaneck's Adm'r v. Louisville Ry. Co., 98 Ky. 195; Gorman's Adm'r v. Louisville Ry. Co. (Ky.) 72 S. W. 760; Barnes v. Shreveport City R. Co., 47 La. Ann. 1218; Gannon v. New Orleans, C. & L. R. Co., 48 La. Ann. 1002; Boland v. Missouri R. Co., 36 Mo. 484; O'Flaherty v. Union Ry. Co., 45 Mo. 70; Elwood Electric St. Ry. Co. v. Ross, 26 Ind. App. 258; Murray v. Paterson Ry. Co., 61 N. J. Law, 301; Bergen County Traction Co. v. Heitman's Adm'r, 61 N. J. Law, 682; Pendril v. Second Ave. R. Co., 34 N. Y. Super. Ct. 481; Hedin v. Suburban Ry. Co., 26 Or. 155; Galveston City R. Co. v. Hewitt, 67 Tex. 473; San Antonio St. Ry. Co. v. Mechler, 87 Tex. 628; San Antonio Traction Co. v. Court (Tex. Civ. App.) 71 S. W. 777; Sample v. Consolidated Light & Ry. Co., 50 W. Va. 472.

electric cars than in running horse cars,[431] the driver of a street car is not required to use more care than the drivers of other vehicles in the streets.[432]

It is well settled that, even if a child is guilty of lack of due care, he may nevertheless recover if those in charge of the car could have prevented the accident by the use of ordinary care;[433] and it is not enough that the man in charge of the car uses due care after he once sees the child. If, in the exercise of due care, he should have seen the child, and did not, the company is liable.[434] *A fortiori*, a child, though guilty of lack of due care, may recover if a motorman acts wantonly or recklessly.[434a] Conversely, if those in charge of the car do all that they can when they see or should have seen the child's danger, the company must be held not liable.[435] In Goodman v. Metropolitan St. Ry. Co.[436] it was held error to charge that, even if the plaintiff was negligent, if the defendant could have avoided the accident by the use of ordinary care, it should be held liable. In some cases, while the general rule is admitted, it is held not applicable

431 Thompson v. Salt Lake Rapid Transit Co., 16 Utah, 281.

432 Falotio v. Broadway & S. A. R. Co., 9 Daly (N. Y.) 243.

433 Baltimore City Passenger Ry. Co. v. McDonnell, 43 Md. 534; Baltimore City Passenger Ry. Co. v. Cooney, 87 Md. 261; Pearson v. Union Ry. Co., 14 Mo. App. 579; Hays v. Gainesville St. Ry. Co., 70 Tex. 602; Thompson v. Salt Lake Rapid Transit Co., 16 Utah, 281.

434 Welsh v. Jackson County Horse R. Co., 81 Mo. 466.

434a Aiken v. Holyoke St. Ry. Co. (Mass.) 68 N. E. 238.

435 West Chicago St. R. Co. v. Camp, 46 Ill. App. 503; Ackerman v. Union Traction Co., 205 Pa. 477.

436 63 App. Div. (N. Y.) 84.

where there is no intervening cause between the plaintiff's lack of due care and the accident.[437]

Too great a degree of care cannot be required of the company. Thus, the simple fact that an accident occurred raises no presumption of negligence,[438] and an injured person cannot rely upon the provisions of an ordinance which requires a higher degree of care than that prescribed by the common law.[439]

## § 105. Same—Negligence in operation.

Numerous rulings have been made as to the degree of care required from a driver, motorman, or gripman when children are standing near the track, or are approaching the track. It has been held that a gripman need not slacken the usual speed of his car because he sees children standing in the street near the track;[440] and a motorman who sees a boy of eleven standing near the track has a right to assume that he will not attempt to cross the track just ahead of the car.[441] While a motorman may reasonably expect that an adult on the track will get off of it, he cannot expect a child nineteen months old to do so.[442] As to the degree of care

437 Csatlos v. Metropolitan St. Ry. Co., 70 App. Div. (N. Y.) 606; Sciurba v. Metropolitan St. R. Co., 73 App. Div. (N. Y.) 170; Bortz v. Dry Dock, E. B. & B. R. Co., 78 App. Div. (N. Y.) 386; Delkowsky v. Dry Dock, E. B. & B. R. Co., 79 N. Y. Supp. 1104.

438 Mascheck v. St. Louis R. Co., 3 Mo. App. 600.

439 Fath v. Tower Grove & L. Ry. Co., 39 Mo. App. 447.

440 Rack v. Chicago City Ry. Co., 173 Ill. 289; Citizens' St. Ry. Co. v. Carey, 56 Ind. 396; Paducah St. Ry. Co. v. Adkins' Adm'r, 14 Ky. Law Rep. 425; Gannon v. New Orleans, C. & L. R. Co., 48 La. Ann. 1002.

441 O'Rourke v. New Orleans, C. & L. R. Co., 51 La. Ann. 755.

442 Galveston City R. Co. v. Hewitt, 67 Tex. 473.

required when children are seen approaching the tracks, the decisions do not seem to be in entire harmony. A city ordinance has been held valid which requires conductors and drivers to keep a vigilant watch for all vehicles and persons on foot, especially children, and to stop the car on the first appearance of danger,[443] and violation of such an ordinance has been held negligence;[444] and it has been held that drivers of street cars in a large city must not only see that the track is clear, but must exercise a constant watchfulness over persons who may be approaching the track.[445] It has further been held that the driver of a street car must be on the watch for boys coasting down a hill crossing a street car track, although this is unlawful;[446] and that, where the driver of a horse car saw two women and seven small children endeavoring to cross a street at a crossing, it was his duty to have his horses and car well under control.[447] Where a motorman saw a child six and a half years old approaching the track, it was held to be his duty to slacken speed and keep his car under control;[448] and the same ruling was made in the case of a girl of four.[449] On the other hand, it has been held that the street is not a playground for children, that a gripman is not bound to anticipate that a child on the sidewalk will

443 Fath v. Tower Grove & L. Ry., 105 Mo. 537.

444 Hays v. Gainesville St. Ry. Co., 70 Tex. 602.

445 North Chicago St. R. Co. v. Johnson (Ill.) 68 N. E. 463; Baltimore City Passenger Ry. Co. v. McDonnell, 43 Md. 534; San Antonio Traction Co. v. Court (Tex. Civ. App.) 71 S. W. 777; Forrestal v. Milwaukee Elec. Ry. & Light Co. (Wis.) 97 N. W. 182.

446 Strutzel v. St. Paul City Ry. Co., 47 Minn. 543.

447 Wihnyk v. Second Ave. R. Co., 14 App. Div. (N. Y.) 515.

448 Tholen v. Brooklyn City R. Co., 10 Misc. Rep. (N. Y.) 283.

449 Jones v. Brooklyn Heights R. Co., 10 Misc. Rep. (N. Y.) 543.

run suddenly upon the track, and, even if he does see a child running toward the track, it is not absolutely his duty to stop the car at once.[450] In Philadelphia City Passenger Ry. Co. v. Henrice[451] it was held that a driver is not bound, as a matter of law, to stop his car when he sees a child approaching a track; and in West Chicago St. R. Co. v. Schwartz[452] it was held that a motorman who sees persons approaching the track has a right to assume that they will stop before reaching it, and need not stop his car or slacken speed. Great care must be exercised at street crossings,[453] or at a place near a street intersection.[454]

In Budd v. Meriden Electric R. Co.[455] it was held that an ordinance providing that no person should play in the street so as to interfere with their safe, free, and convenient use by travelers cannot lessen the duty of a motorman to use due care towards a child twenty-one months old alone in the street.

It has been held that the cab of a car is for the motorman alone, and that, while running his car, he should attend strictly to business.[456] No man should have charge of an electric car running through city streets who has not the full use of both eyes.[457] It is not the duty of those in charge

450 Mt. Adams & E. P. R. Co. v. Cavagna, 6 Ohio Cir. Ct. R. 606.

451 92 Pa. 431.

452 93 Ill. App. 387.

453 Chicago City Ry. Co. v. Tuohy, 196 Ill. 410; Fenton v. Second Ave. R. Co., 126 N. Y. 625; Ellick v. Metropolitan St. Ry. Co., 15 App. Div. (N. Y.) 556; Hedin v. Suburban Ry. Co., 26 Or. 155.

454 Louisville Ry. Co. v. French (Ky.) 71 S. W. 486.

455 69 Conn. 272.

456 Schnur v. Citizens' Traction Co., 153 Pa. 29; Henne v. Peoples' St. Ry. Co., 1 Pa. Super. Ct. 311.

457 Rice v. Crescent City R. Co., 51 La. Ann. 108.

of street cars to be at all times so stationed that children cannot jump on them in sport.[458] While it is not negligence not to have the conductor on a street car in addition to a driver,[459] the fact that a driver performs the duty of a conductor in addition to his own will not excuse him for running over a child if he could have avoided the accident if his attention had not been so taken up, since the duty of a car driver to the public is paramount to that which he owes to his employer.[460] A driver is not necessarily guilty of negligence in turning his head for a moment to see if a person on the sidewalk desires to take passage.[461]

On the question of keeping a proper lookout, it has been held to be evidence of negligence that the driver or motorman was not looking ahead,[462] that he was facing at right angles to the course of his car,[463] and that he was looking to-

458 Chicago West Div. Ry. Co. v. Hair, 57 Ill. App. 587.

459 Dunn v. Cass Ave. & F. G. Ry. Co., 21 Mo. App. 188.

460 Anderson v. Minneapolis St. Ry. Co., 42 Minn. 490; Dahl v. Milwaukee City Ry. Co., 65 Wis. 371.

461 Johnson v. Reading City Passenger Ry., 160 Pa. 647.

462 Commonwealth v. Metropolitan R. Co., 107 Mass. 236; Rosenkranz v. Lindell Ry. Co., 108 Mo. 9; Humbird v. Union St. Ry. Co., 110 Mo. 76; Mangam v. Brooklyn R. Co., 38 N. Y. 455; Nugent v. Metropolitan St. Ry. Co., 17 App. Div. (N. Y.) 582; Dowd v. Brooklyn Heights R. Co., 9 Misc. Rep. (N. Y.) 279; Jones v. Brooklyn Heights R. Co., 10 Misc. Rep. (N. Y.) 543; Sciurba v. Metropolitan St. R. Co., 73 App. Div. (N. Y.) 170; Harkins v. Pittsburg, A. & M. Traction Co., 173 Pa. 149; Reilley v. Philadelphia Traction Co., 176 Pa. 335; Evers v. Philadelphia Traction Co., 176 Pa. 376; Kroesen v. New Castle Electric St. Ry. Co., 198 Pa. 26; San Antonio Traction Co. v. Court (Tex. Civ. App.) 71 S. W. 777.

463 Washington & G. Ry. Co. v. Gladmon, 15 Wall. (U. S.) 401; Reiners v. Washington & G. R. Co., 9 App. D. C. 19; Senn v. Southern Ry. Co., 108 Mo. 143; Adams v. Metropolitan St. Ry. Co., 60 App. Div. (N. Y.) 188.

wards the rear platform.[464] A charge that a driver must keep a strict lookout forward was held to be erroneous, since his due care, in the absence of such lookout, was a question for the jury.[465] Where the driver of a car ran over a girl two and a half years old, and it appeared that he was making change for a passenger at the time, this was held to be negligence;[466] and when it appeared tl the driver of a car ran over a child, and that he had his back turned to the horses and was giving change to a passenger when the accident occurred, this was held to be evidence of negligence for the jury.[467] Negligence is for the jury where a driver could have seen a boy from fifty to one hundred feet away,[468] or ninety feet away,[469] and where a boy fell on the track eighty feet ahead of a street car, and the motorman did not see him in time to avoid running over him.[470] Negligence was held to be for the jury in a number of cases, in all of which there was more or less evidence that an insufficient watch was kept.[471]

464 Collins v. South Boston R. Co., 142 Mass. 301; Weissner v. St. Paul City Ry. Co., 47 Minn. 468; Levy v. Dry Dock, E. B. & B. R. Co., 12 N. Y. Supp. 485; Dallas Rapid Transit Ry. Co. v. Elliott, 7 Tex. Civ. App. 216.

465 Wright v. Third Ave. Ry. Co., 5 N. Y. Supp. 707.

466 Hyland v. Yonkers R. Co., 4 N. Y. Supp. 305.

467 Pascoshell v. Twenty-Third St. R. Co., 23 N. Y. Wkly. Dig. 200.

468 Muller v. Brooklyn Heights R. Co., 18 App. Div. (N. Y.) 177.

469 Shenners v. West Side St. Ry. Co., 78 Wis. 383.

470 Kitay v. Brooklyn, Q. C. & S. R. Co., 23 App. Div. (N. Y.) 228.

471 Duncan v. Rome St. R. Co., 99 Ga. 98; Quincy Horse Ry. & Carrying Co. v. Gnuse, 38 Ill. App. 212; Elwood Electric St. Ry. Co. v. Ross, 26 Ind. App. 258; Nelson v. Crescent City R. Co., 49 La. Ann. 491; Rice v. Crescent City R. Co., 51 La. Ann. 108; Gray

Where the driver of a car saw a girl standing close to the track, with her back to the car, fifty feet away, and did not check the speed of his car;[472] where a driver saw a child under two years of age playing in the street within six feet of the track, and kept his horses on a fast trot until within seven feet of the child;[473] where a motorman saw a boy of five running towards the car with his hands outstretched, but did not stop his car as quickly as possible;[474] and where there was evidence that a driver was blind in one eye, was not looking, and did not stop his car as soon as he could,[475]—negligence in all of these cases is for the jury. Negligence was also for the jury in a number of cases where children were run over.[476]

v. St. Paul City Ry. Co., 87 Minn. 280; Winters v. Kansas City Cable Ry. Co., 99 Mo. 509; Baird v. Citizens' Ry. Co., 146 Mo. 265; Hogan v. Citizens' Ry. Co., 150 Mo. 36; Burnstein v. Cass Ave & F. G. Ry. Co., 56 Mo. App. 45; Aaron v. Second Ave. R. Co., 2 Daly (N. Y.) 127; Giraldo v. Coney Island & B. R. Co., 16 N. Y Supp. 774; Citizens' Passenger Ry. Co. v. Foxley, 107 Pa. 537, Woeckner v. Erie Electric Motor Co., 176 Pa. 451; McCullough v Pittsburg, A. & M. Traction Co., 183 Pa. 241; Jones v. United Traction Co., 201 Pa. 344; San Antonio St. Ry. Co. v. Cailloutte, 79 Tex. 341; Mitchell v. Tacoma Ry. & Motor Co., 9 Wash. 120, Slensby v. Milwaukee St. Ry. Co., 95 Wis. 179; Dahl v. Milwaukee City Ry. Co., 62 Wis. 652.

472 Mallard v. Ninth Ave. R. Co., 15 Daly (N. Y.) 376.

473 Farris v. Cass Ave. & F. G. Ry. Co., 80 Mo. 325.

474 Mason v. Minneapolis St. Ry. Co., 54 Minn. 216.

475 Silberstein v. Houston, W. St. & P. F. R. Co., 4 N. Y. Supp. 843

476 West Chicago St. R. Co. v. Stoltenberg, 62 Ill. App. 420; West Chicago St. R. Co. v. Sullivan, 64 Ill. App. 628; Calumet Electric St. Ry. Co. v. Van Pelt, 68 Ill. App. 582; Calumet Electric Ry Co. v. Lewis, 68 Ill. App. 598; West Chicago St. R. Co. v. Whittaker, 72 Ill. App. 48; North Chicago St. R. Co. v. Hoffart, 82 Ill App. 539.

In many cases where children have been run over, the court has held, as a matter of law, that there was not sufficient evidence of negligence on the part of the company to justify a verdict for the plaintiff.[477] Such a ruling has been made in the case of a child eighteen months old,[478] a child of two,[479] a child of three years and eight months,[480] a boy of four,[481] a boy of six years and four months,[482] a boy of six and a half,[483] a girl of seven and a half,[484] a boy of seven and a half,[485] a boy of eight,[486] and a boy of ten.[487]

A very common case where there is held to be no negligence on the part of the company is where a child runs unexpectedly in front of a street car.[488] The case is still stronger for the company where a child runs in front of a car in an unusual place, as in the middle of a block.[489]

477 Kline v. Electric Traction Co., 181 Pa. 276; Cords v. Third Ave. R. Co., 56 N. Y. Super. Ct. 319.

478 Sciortino v. Crescent City R. Co., 49 La. Ann. 7.

479 Boland v. Missouri R. Co., 36 Mo. 484; Citizens' Passenger Ry. Co. v. Costigan (Pa.) 7 Atl. 91.

480 Moss v. Philadelphia Traction Co., 180 Pa. 389.

481 Jaquinto v. Broadway & S. Ave. R. Co., 2 Misc. Rep. (N. Y.) 174.

482 Cominskey v. Connellsville, N. H. & L. St. Ry. Co., 4 Pa Super. Ct. 631.

483 Lombard & S. Sts. Passenger Ry. Co. v. Steinhart, 2 Penny (Pa.) 358.

484 Flanagan v. People's Passenger Ry. Co., 163 Pa. 102.

485 Finley v. West Chicago St. R. Co., 90 Ill. App. 368.

486 Squire v. Central Park, N. & E. R. R. Co., 36 N. Y. Super. Ct 436.

487 Foy v. Toledo Consol. St. Ry. Co., 3 Ohio Dec. 22.

488 White v. Albany Ry., 35 App. Div. (N. Y.) 23; Chilton v Central Traction Co., 152 Pa. 425.

489 Reich v. Union Ry. Co., 78 Hun (N. Y.) 417; Greenberg v Third Ave. R. Co., 35 App. Div. (N. Y.) 619.

A ruling of no negligence on the part of the company where a child goes suddenly in front of a car has been made in the case of a child of three,[490] a boy of four,[491] a boy of five years and four months,[492] a child of five years and nine months,[493] a boy of five years and eleven months,[494] a child between five and six,[495] a boy of six,[496] a boy of six and a half,[497] a boy nearly seven,[498] a boy of seven,[499] a child of eight,[500] a boy of nine,[501] a girl of ten,[502] a boy of ten,[503] a boy of eleven,[504] a boy of twelve,[505] and one of sixteen.[506]

Where a child comes directly from in front of some obstruction, the case is stronger in favor of the company; and

490 Maschek v. St. Louis R. Co., 71 Mo. 276; Gallaher v. Crescent City R. Co., 37 La. Ann. 288; Kierzenkowski v. Philadelphia Traction Co., 184 Pa. 459.

491 Schneidau v. New Orleans & C. R. Co., 48 La. Ann. 866.

492 Sciurba v. Metropolitan St. Ry. Co., 84 N. Y. Supp. 85; Tishacek v. Milwaukee Electric Ry. & Light Co., 110 Wis. 417.

493 Trumbo's Adm'r v. City St. Car Co., 89 Va. 780.

494 Adams v. Nassau Electric R. Co., 41 App. Div. (N. Y.) 334.

495 Campbell v. New Orleans City R. Co., 104 La. 183.

496 Fleishman v. Neversink Mountain R. Co., 174 Pa. 510; Callary v. Easton Transit Co., 185 Pa. 176; Hunter v. Consolidated Traction Co., 193 Pa. 557.

497 Klein v. Crescent City R. Co., 23 La. Ann. 729.

498 Culbertson v. Crescent City R. Co., 48 La. Ann. 1376; Holdridge v. Mendenhall, 108 Wis. 1.

499 Stanley v. Union Depot R. Co., 114 Mo. 606.

500 Baker v. Eighth Ave. R. Co., 62 Hun (N. Y.) 39.

501 Dunn v. Cass Ave. & F. G. Ry. Co., 98 Mo. 652; North Hudson County Ry. Co. v. Flanagan, 57 N. J. Law, 696.

502 Kennedy v. St. Louis R. Co., 43 Mo. App. 1.

503 Winterfeld v. Second Ave. R. Co., 20 N. Y. Supp. 801.

504 McLaughlin v. New Orleans & C. R. Co., 48 La. Ann. 23 Miller v. Union Traction Co., 198 Pa. 639.

505 Pletcher v. Scranton Traction Co., 185 Pa. 147.

506 Mulcahy v. Electric Traction Co., 185 Pa. 427.

it has been held that, where a boy of five years and three months,[507] and where a boy of seven,[508] rushed suddenly from behind a team directly in front of a car, there was no negligence on the part of the company. In like manner, where a boy of six darted from a pile of lumber in front of a street car, there was held to be no evidence of negligence on the part of the motorman, even though he did not sound his gong.[509]

There have been numerous rulings on the question of negligence where a child attempts to cross in front of a street car, and falls on the track. In a number of cases there was held to be no negligence;[510] and in Stabenau v. Atlantic Ave. R. Co.,[511] where a child would have crossed the track in safety if she had not fallen, it was held not to be negligence on the part of the motorman not to try to stop the car until the child fell. Where the horses and the front part of the car passed a child less than two years of age in safety, and the child then ran against or fell near the car, there was held to be no evidence of negligence.[512]

Where a child two and a half years old was standing at a street crossing, and moved suddenly in front of a street car,[513] where a child of two placed itself in front of the mule drawing a car, where the driver could not see it,[514] and where

507 Ogier v. Albany Ry., 88 Hun (N. Y.) 486.

508 Flynn v. Metropolitan St. Ry. Co., 10 App. Div. (N. Y.) 258.

509 Perry v. Macon Consol. St. R. Co., 101 Ga. 400.

510 Fenton v. Second Ave. R. Co., 126 N. Y. 625; Lavin v. Second Ave. R. Co., 12 App. Div. (N. Y.) 381; De Ioia v. Metropolitan St. Ry. Co., 37 App. Div. (N. Y.) 455.

511 155 N. Y. 511.

512 Bulger v. Albany Ry., 42 N. Y. 459.

513 Citizens' St. Ry. Co. v. Carey, 56 Ind. 396.

514 Hearn v. St. Charles St. R. Co., 34 La. Ann. 160.

a boy of six stepped on the track to look for a penny which he had lost, and was run over,[515] there was held in each case to be no evidence of negligence. Similarly, there was held to be no negligence where a boy of twelve was run over while trying to board a moving car when the driver had not seen his signal,[516] and where a boy of four years and five months was compelled to leave the car on which he was a trespasser, and ran in front of another car.[517]

In an emergency it is not negligence for a motorman to apply the brake instead of ringing the gong, or to use the brake instead of the apparatus used to control the electric power.[518]

In an action for willfully injuring a deaf mute of thirteen, a verdict for the defendant is justified when there is evidence that the street was dark, and that the motorman rang his gong and reversed.[519] Where an employe in charge of a car catches a boy and lectures him for stealing a ride, the company is not liable when the boy, on being released, rushes blindly in front of another car.[520] When a boy jumps from the rear of a wagon directly in front of a car, there is no negligence on the part of the motorman.[521]

A number of cases have been decided on the question of what is proper speed for a car. Permission by ordinance to

515 Frank v. Metropolitan St. Ry. Co., 44 App. Div. (N. Y.) 243.

516 West Chicago St. R. Co. v. Binder, 51 Ill. App. 420.

517 Mack v. Lombard & S. Sts. Passenger Ry. Co., 20 Phila. (Pa.) 207.

518 Stabenau v. Atlantic Ave. R. Co., 155 N. Y. 511.

519 Bonham v. Citizens' St. R. Co., 158 Ind. 106.

520 Palmisano v. New Orleans City R. Co., 108 La. 243.

521 Baier v. Camden & S. Ry. Co. (N. J. Law) 52 Atl. 215.

run a car at a certain rate of speed is not an authority to run the car up to that limit, regardless of circumstances.[522] All persons in a street have a right to expect that an ordinance as to speed will be observed;[523] and if the speed is greater than an ordinance allows, and an accident happens which would not have occurred if the car had been traveling at ordinary speed, this is negligence.[524] In Riley v. Salt Lake Rapid Transit Co.[525] it was held that running a car faster than a city ordinance allows is presumptive evidence of negligence, but it is not conclusive.[526]

In the absence of an ordinance it has been held that cars may be run at any convenient rate of speed which is not dangerous to travelers;[527] and it has been held more specifically that running twelve miles an hour[528] or twelve to fifteen miles an hour[529] is not negligence as a matter of law. It is error to instruct the jury that a motorman should run a car so that it could be stopped readily and quickly if the occasion requires it, without explanation or qualification.[530]

On the question of speed, negligence has been held to be for the jury where a car was traveling at "rapid speed,"[531]

522 Quincy Horse Ry. & Carrying Co. v. Gnuse, 38 Ill. App. 212; Schmidt v. St. Louis R. Co., 149 Mo. 269.

523 Wright v. Malden & M. R. Co., 4 Allen (Mass.) 283.

524 Baltimore City Passenger Ry. Co. v. McDonnell, 43 Md. 534

525 10 Utah, 428.

526 Hanlon v. South Boston Horse R. Co., 129 Mass. 310.

527 Citizens' St. Ry. v. Steen, 42 Ark. 321.

528 Rack v. Chicago City Ry. Co., 69 Ill. App. 656.

529 Bittner v. Crosstown St. Ry. Co., 153 N. Y. 76.

530 Day v. Citizens' Ry. Co., 81 Mo. App. 471.

531 Gumby v. Metropolitan St. Ry. Co., 29 App. Div. (N. Y.) 335; Timony v. Brooklyn City & N. R. Co., 10 Misc. Rep. (N. Y.) 261; Thompson v. United Traction Co., 193 Pa. 555; Beard v. Reading City Passenger Ry. Co., 3 Pa. Super. Ct. 171.

"a very rapid speed,"[532] "unusual speed,"[533] and "twice the speed allowed by law."[534]

Negligence is for the jury where a motorman ran an electric car down a grade in a crowded city street, so that he could not stop it within forty feet;[535] where a motorman slackened his speed while two boys were crossing the track, and then suddenly increased it when fifteen feet away;[536] and where a driver was traveling at the rate of ten to twelve miles an hour, and was urging his horses to still greater speed.[537] Negligence is also for the jury where a car was being driven fourteen or fifteen miles an hour,[538] and where a motorman increased his speed as he approached a crossing.[539] A number of cases have arisen where children were run over while near the track after getting out of school; and where there is evidence that children were crowding around the track, negligence is for the jury when it appears that a motorman did not keep his car under control,[540] that he put on the power when near the children,[541] that he ran his car twelve miles an hour without warning,[542] and that he ran his car at a speed of eight or ten miles an hour.[543]

532 Pendril v. Second Ave. R. Co., 34 N. Y. Super. Ct. 481.

533 Dunseath v. Pittsburg, A. & M. Traction Co., 161 Pa. 124.

534 Huerzeler v. Central Crosstown R. Co., 1 Misc. Rep. (N. Y.) 136.

535 Fullerton v. Metropolitan St. Ry. Co., 37 App. Div. (N. Y.) 386.

536 Legare v. Union Ry. Co., 61 App. Div. (N. Y.) 202

537 Gumby v. Metropolitan St. Ry. Co., 65 App. Div. (N. Y.) 38.

538 Adams v. Nassau Electric R. Co., 51 App. Div. (N. Y.) 241.

539 Ellick v. Metropolitan St. Ry. Co., 15 App. Div. (N. Y.) 556.

540 Oster v. Schuylkill Traction Co., 195 Pa. 320.

541 Howell v. Rochester Ry. Co., 24 App. Div. (N. Y.) 502.

542 Consolidated City & C. P. Ry. Co. v. Carlson, 58 Kan. 62.

543 Buente v. Pittsburg, A. & M. Traction Co., 2 Pa. Super. Ct. 185.

Where a boy between seven and eight years old stood on a street railway track waiting for cars to pass on the other track, and was struck by a car which approached without any signal, negligence was held to be for the jury.[544] Where a car is running twelve miles an hour at a place where it is permitted to do so by a city ordinance, it is not running at excessive speed, so that the jury can impute negligence to the company on account of the speed alone.[545]

The varying facts as to the speed, lack of warning, and failure to keep a proper lookout may be combined in the same cases. Thus, there was held to be evidence of negligence for the jury where the motorman gave no signal, and had his face turned away from the track,[546] where the car was traveling at high speed, and the driver was looking away from the track,[547] and where there was evidence that a car was traveling at a high rate of speed without giving any warning.[548]

Where a plaintiff was struck by a car and carried a distance of sixty-three feet, and the motorman testified that he could

544 Griffiths v. Metropolitan St. Ry. Co., 63 App. Div. (N. Y.) 86.

545 White v. Albany Ry., 35 App. Div. (N. Y.) 23.

546 Finkelstein v. Brooklyn Heights R. Co., 51 App. Div. (N. Y.) 287; Karahuta v. Schuylkill Traction Co., 6 Pa. Super. Ct. 319.

547 Mason v. Atlantic Ave. R. Co., 4 Misc. Rep. (N. Y.) 291; Goldstein v. Dry Dock, E. B. & B. R. Co., 35 Misc. Rep. (N. Y.) 200.

548 Chicago City Ry. Co. v. Robinson, 27 Ill. App. 26; Chicago City Ry. Co. v. Robinson, 127 Ill. 9; Chicago City Ry. Co. v. Tuohy, 196 Ill. 410; Consolidated Traction Co. v. Scott, 58 N. J. Law, 682; Davidson v. Metropolitan St. Ry. Co., 75 App. Div. (N. Y.) 426; Lafferty v. Third Ave. R. Co., 85 App. Div. (N. Y.) 592; Iaquinta v. Citizens' Traction Co., 166 Pa. 63; Maher v. Philadelphia Traction Co., 181 Pa. 391; Walbridge v. Schuylkill Electric Ry. Co., 190 Pa. 274; Hoon v. Beaver Valley Traction Co., 204 Pa. 369.

have stopped within twenty-five feet;[549] where the body of a child was on the fender, and remained there for a distance of seventy feet, while the car could have been stopped within twenty-five or thirty feet;[550] where the body of a child remained on the fender for one hundred feet, and was finally run over, and it appeared that the car could have been stopped within twenty-five or fifty feet;[551] and where the body of a child was carried along for some distance, and finally run over,[552]—it was held in all of these cases that there was evidence of negligence for the jury. Where a driver paid no attention to a warning, and did not have his hand on the brake,[553] where the driver detached his horses and swung them into a team, so that they ran away and injured a boy,[554] and where a boy who fell on the track was run over, and it appeared that the car could have been stopped in from two to four feet,[555] there was held to be evidence of negligence. The company was held not to be liable where it appeared that a motorman used his best judgment in reversing his car after running over a child,[556] and where the driver of a car used his best judgment when his horses ran away.[557] Where the company had notice of a defective brake, but did not remedy

549 Cohen v. Metropolitan St. Ry. Co., 63 App. Div. (N. Y.) 165.

550 Green v. Metropolitan St. Ry. Co., 42 App. Div. (N. Y.) 160

551 Green v. Metropolitan St. Ry. Co., 65 App. Div. (N. Y.) 54.

552 Weitzman v. Nassau Electric R. Co., 33 App. Div. (N. Y.) 585.

553 Block v. Harlem Bridge, H. & F. Ry. Co., 9 N. Y. Supp. 164.

554 Sutter v. Omnibus Cable Co., 107 Cal. 369.

555 Totarella v. New York & Q. C. Ry. Co., 53 App. Div. (N. Y.) 413.

556 Bittner v. Crosstown St. Ry. Co., 153 N. Y. 76.

557 Benoit v. Troy & L. R. Co., 154 N. Y. 223.

it, this was held to be a clear case of negligence;[558] and where boys had a habit of meddling with the brakes of a car, and the company knew this, and usually tied down their brakes, evidence that the brake was not tied down, and that the accident would not have happened but for this, is sufficient to show negligence.[559]

It is not negligence to leave a small flatcar unsecured, so that children, while playing with it, ran over one of their number, a girl of seven;[560] and it has been held that a car standing on a track when not in use, and secured by ordinary brakes, is not a dangerous machine, within the meaning of the turntable cases.[561]

Ordinances restricting the speed of horse cars are not applicable to a succeeding company operating its cars by electricity.[562] Evidence that there were no lights on the car, and no bell was rung, is sufficient on the question of negligence.[563] A street railway company is required to use the best precautions against danger, in general use, the value of which has been proved by experience,[564] but an instruction that a street railway company must use such lights as will enable it to avoid accidents requires too great a degree of care.[565]

558 Thompson v. Salt Lake Rapid Transit Co., 16 Utah, 281.

559 Dintruff v. Rochester City & B. R. Co., 10 N. Y. Supp. 402.

560 Kaumeier v. City Electric Ry. Co., 116 Mich. 306.

561 George v. Los Angeles Ry. Co., 126 Cal. 357.

562 Bonham v. Citizens' St. R. Co., 158 Ind. 106.

563 Welsh v. United Traction Co., 202 Pa. 530.

564 Mock v. Los Angeles Traction Co. (Cal.) 73 Pac. 455; Zimmerman v. Denver Consol. Tramway Co. (Colo. App.) 72 Pac. 607; Buente v. Pittsburg, A. & M. Traction Co., 2 Pa. Super. Ct. 185.

565 Memphis City Ry. Co. v. Logue, 13 Lea (Tenn.) 32.

An instruction that a company is negligent, as a matter of law, in not having fenders, is erroneous,[566] even when they are required by law,[566a] and in Platt v. Albany Ry.,[567] where an ordinance required the use of fenders, and the company used due diligence in procuring them, there was held to be no negligence.

The fact that a pair of ordinarily gentle horses ran away through fright caused by a third party does not show vicious propensity, and it is not negligence to continue using them after they have so run away.[568]

The words "any railroad" in a statute include street railways.[569]

566 Hogan v. Citizens' Ry. Co., 150 Mo. 36.

566a Henderson v. Durham Traction Co., 132 N. C. 779.

567 170 N. Y. 115.

568 Benoit v. Troy & L. R. Co., 154 N. Y. 223.

569 Bammel v. Kirby, 19 Tex. Civ. App. 198.

## CHAPTER VII.

### ACCIDENTS TO DRIVERS OF WAGONS.

I. COLLISIONS BETWEEN CAR AND WAGON.

§ 106. Due Care—Crossing Tracks—Stopping, Looking, and Listening.
107. Same—Driving on or near Tracks.
108. Same—Imputed Negligence.
109. Same—Age and Occupation.
110. Right of Way.
111. Negligence of Company—General Considerations.
112. Negligence in Operation—Lookout, Speed, Warning, etc.

II. FRIGHTENING HORSES.

§ 113. Due Care of Driver of Horse.
114. Negligence of Company.

### I. COLLISION BETWEEN CAR AND WAGON.

**A street car has a superior right of way over a wagon, since it cannot leave its tracks, and since it is run for the benefit of the public, but at street crossings the rights of the car and of the wagon are equal.**

**Both the driver of the wagon and the man in charge of the car must use reasonable care to avoid collisions, and a plaintiff, although guilty of lack of due care, may recover if the defendant could have prevented the accident by the exercise of due care.**

**Whether a case is left to the jury, or whether a ruling is made on the questions of due care and negligence as a matter of law, must depend upon all the circumstances of each indi-**

**vidual case. Chief among these circumstances to be considered are the lookout, both of the driver and of the man in charge of car, the speed of the car and its distance from the wagon, whether a signal was given, the obstruction of the view and of the track, and the character of the locality.**

## § 106. Due care—Crossing tracks—Stopping, looking, and listening.

The most important circumstance bearing on a driver's due care is whether or not he looked for an approaching car before crossing a street railway track. It has been held that a man is not in the exercise of due care when he drives onto a street railway track without looking,[1] without stopping or looking,[2] or without looking and listening,[3] even although,

[1] Central Passenger Ry. Co. v. Chatterson, 14 Ky. Law Rep. 663; Cowden v. Shreveport Belt Ry. Co., 106 La. 236; Hurley v. West End St. Ry. Co., 180 Mass. 370; Wood v. Detroit City St. Ry. Co., 52 Mich. 402; Fritz v. Detroit Citizens' St. Ry. Co., 105 Mich. 50; Wosika v. St. Paul City Ry. Co., 80 Minn. 364; Smith v. Citizens' Ry. Co., 52 Mo. App. 36; Reynolds v. Third Ave. R. Co., 8 Misc. Rep. (N. Y.) 313; Campbell v. Union Ry. Co., 9 Misc. Rep. (N. Y.) 484; Devine v. Metropolitan St. Ry. Co., 29 Misc. Rep. (N. Y.) 301; Vonelling v. Metropolitan St. Ry. Co., 35 Misc. Rep. (N. Y.) 301; Ward v. Rochester Electric Ry. Co., 17 N. Y. Supp. 427; Schmidt v. Interurban St. Ry. Co., 81 N. Y. Supp. 832; Schausten v. Toledo Consol. St. Ry. Co., 7 Ohio Cir. Dec. 389; Carson v. Federal St. & P. V. Ry. Co., 147 Pa. 219; Darwood v. Union Traction Co., 189 Pa. 592; Bornscheuer v. Consolidated Traction Co., 198 Pa. 332; Beerman v. Union R. Co. (R. I.) 52 Atl. 1090.

[2] Trout v. Altoona & L. V. Electric Ry. Co., 13 Pa. Super. Ct. 17.

[3] Highland Ave. & B. R. Co. v. Sampson, 91 Ala. 560, 112 Ala. 425; Burns v. Metropolitan St. Ry. Co. (Kan.) 71 Pac. 244; Van Patten v. Schenectady St. Ry. Co., 80 Hun (N. Y.) 494; Lockwood v. Belle City St. Ry. Co., 92 Wis. 97; Dummer v. Milwaukee Electric Ry. & Light Co., 108 Wis. 589; Tesch v. Milwaukee Electric Ry. & Light Co., 108 Wis. 593.

in the latter case, the car was being run at an unlawful rate of speed.[4] Where a driver's view is obstructed on account of the construction of his wagon or of the load he may be carrying, the case is still stronger against him.[5] In Omslaer v. Pittsburg & B. Traction Co.,[6] where a driver's view at a crossing was very much obstructed, and a wagon loaded with iron was making noise enough to drown that made by an approaching car, it was held lack of due care to drive upon the track without stopping to listen; and in Kelly v. Wakefield & S. St. Ry. Co.,[7] where the view was obstructed, and the driver did not listen, this was held to be contributory negligence.

It is not enough for a driver to look when he is some distance away from the track, and then to drive on the track without making any further effort to look for a car; and in a number of cases, where the driver of a team, when some distance from the track, either saw a car or looked for a car and saw none, and then drove upon the track without taking further precautions, he was held not to be in the exercise of due care.[8] The fact that an electric road is in the

4 Highland Ave. & B. R. Co. v. Sampson, 91 Ala. 560, 112 Ala. 425; Citizens' St. Ry. Co. v. Helvie, 22 Ind. App. 515.

5 Solatinow v. Jersey City, H. & P. St. Ry. Co. (N. J. Sup.) 56 Atl. 235; Roth v. Metropolitan St. Ry. Co., 13 Misc. Rep. (N. Y.) 213; Lang v. Metropolitan St. Ry. Co., 26 Misc. Rep. (N. Y.) 754; Thomas v. Citizens' Passenger Ry. Co., 132 Pa. 504; Wheelahan v. Philadelphia Traction Co., 150 Pa. 187; Helber v. Spokane St. Ry. Co., 22 Wash. 319; Boerth v. West Side R. Co., 87 Wis. 288.

6 168 Pa. 519.

7 175 Mass. 331.

8 State v. United Rys. & Electric Co. (Md.) 54 Atl. 612; Rohe v. Third Ave. R. Co., 10 Misc. Rep. (N. Y.) 740; Winch v. Third Ave. R. Co., 12 Misc. Rep. (N. Y.) 403; Carvanío v. Union Ry.

country does not relieve a driver of the duty of continuing to look until he reaches the track.[9] If a car is within a driver's range of vision, he is chargeable with knowledge of its approach, even if he claims he did not see it.[10]

Besides being careless in not keeping a proper lookout for a car, a driver may be equally at fault when he sees a car, but makes a reckless attempt to cross in front of it, and takes his chances as to the success of the attempt, although attempting to cross in front of a car seen to be approaching is not of itself contributory negligence.[11] Under this state of facts, the driver of a wagon has been held not to be in the exercise of due care;[12] and in De Lon v. Kokomo City St.

Co., 84 N. Y. Supp. 246; Ehrisman v. East Harrisburg City Passenger Ry. Co., 150 Pa. 180; Kern v. Second Ave. Traction Co., 194 Pa. 75; Burke v. Union Traction Co., 198 Pa. 497; Cupps v. Traction Co., 13 Pa. Super. Ct. 630; Brown v. Traction Co., 14 Pa. Super. Ct. 594; Pieper v. Union Traction Co., 202 Pa. 100; Keenan v. Union Traction Co., 202 Pa. 107; Moser v. Union Traction Co., 205 Pa. 481.

9 Keenan v. Union Traction Co., 202 Pa. 107.

10 Metropolitan St. Ry. Co. v. Agnew, 65 Kan. 478; Barrie v. St. Louis Transit Co. (Mo. App.) 76 S. W. 706; Stafford v. Chippewa Valley Electric R. Co., 110 Wis. 331.

11 Campbell v. Los Angeles Traction Co., 137 Cal. 565.

12 West Chicago St. R. Co. v. Boeker, 70 Ill. App. 67; South Covington & C. St. Ry. Co. v. Enslen, 18 Ky. Law Rep. 921; Mercier v. New Orleans & C. R. Co., 23 La. Ann. 264; McNab v. United Rys. & Electric Co., 94 Md. 719; Graff v. Detroit Citizens' St. Ry. Co., 109 Mich. 77; O'Connell v. St. Paul City Ry. Co., 64 Minn. 466; Ledwidge v. St. Louis Transit Co. (Mo. App.) 73 S. W. 1008; Schwanewede v. North Hudson County Ry. Co., 67 N. J. Law, 449; Rider v. Syracuse Rapid Transit Ry. Co., 171 N. Y. 139; Clancy v. Troy & L. R. Co., 88 Hun (N. Y.) 496; Hamilton v. Third Ave. R. Co., 6 Misc. Rep. (N. Y.) 382; Reiss v. Metropolitan St. Ry. Co., 28 Misc. Rep. (N. Y.) 198; Petri v. Third Ave. R. Co., 30 Misc.

Ry. Co.[13] a similar ruling was made in the case of a street sprinkler. Similarly, a driver has been held guilty of lack of due care when he knew that he could not cross ahead of a car unless the motorman slackened speed;[14] where he made a reckless attempt to cross in front of an electric car running at a high rate of speed;[15] where he could have passed a car in safety, but took the risk of speeding his horses through a narrow space, where there was no room for his buggy to pass;[16] and where he could have gone another way in safety, but chose to drive between an elevated post and a rapidly approaching car.[17]

There is another class of cases where the driver of a team goes directly in front of a street car; and in a number of cases there has been held to be lack of due care, irrespective of the question as to whether or not he looked for a car.[18]

Rep. (N. Y.) 254; Seggerman v. Metropolitan St. Ry. Co., 38 Misc. Rep. (N. Y.) 374; Steinman v. Interurban St. Ry. Co., 84 N. Y. Supp. 231; Smith v. Electric Traction Co., 187 Pa. 110; Tyson v. Union Traction Co., 199 Pa. 264; Brown v. Traction Co., 14 Pa. Super. Ct. 594; Haas v. Chester St. Ry. Co., 202 Pa. 145; Christensen v. Union Trunk Line, 6 Wash. 75; Watermolen v. Fox River Electric Ry. & Power Co., 110 Wis. 153.

13 22 Ind. App. 377.

14 Smith v. Chicago General Ry. Co., 86 Ill. App. 647; Williamson v. Metropolitan St. Ry. Co., 29 Misc. Rep. (N. Y.) 324.

15 Borschall v. Detroit Ry., 115 Mich. 473.

16 Culbertson v. Metropolitan St. Ry. Co., 140 Mo. 35.

17 May v. Metropolitan St. Ry. Co., 26 Misc. Rep. (N. Y.) 748.

18 McGrath v. City & Suburban Ry. Co., 93 Ga. 312; Fritz v. Detroit Citizens' St. Ry. Co., 105 Mich. 50; Weaver v. Benton-Bellefontaine Ry. Co., 60 Mo. App. 207; Meyer v. Brooklyn Heights R. Co., 9 App. Div. (N. Y.) 79; Schlitz v. Nassau Electric R. Co., 44 App. Div. (N. Y.) 542; Boston & P. Dispatch Exp. Co. v. Metropolitan St. Ry. Co., 14 Misc. Rep. (N. Y.) 25; Mason v. Metro-

The rules as to stopping, looking, and listening which are in force in the case of steam railroads are not applied in all their strictness to street railways,[19] so that it is held that the driver of a wagon about to cross a street railway track need not stop, look, and listen as a matter of law.[20] Whether or not he must look and listen is a disputed point. Some cases hold that failure to do so is lack of due care, as a matter of law,[21] and others that it is merely one circumstance for the consideration of the jury.[22]

politan St. Ry. Co., 30 Misc. Rep. (N. Y.) 108; Morrow v. Delaware County & P. Electric Ry. Co., 199 Pa. 156; Cawley v. La Crosse City Ry. Co., 101 Wis. 145.

19 Orr v. Cedar Rapids & M. C. Ry. Co., 94 Iowa, 423; Citizens' St. Ry. Co. v. Abright, 14 Ind. App. 433; Cooke v. Baltimore Traction Co., 80 Md. 551; Garrity v. Detroit Citizens' St. Ry. Co., 112 Mich. 369; Shea v. St. Paul City Ry. Co., 50 Minn. 395; Hicks v. Citizens' Ry. Co., 124 Mo. 115; Smith v. Citizens' Ry. Co., 52 Mo. App. 36; Smith v. Metropolitan St. Ry. Co., 7 App. Div. (N. Y) 253; Brozek v. Steinway Ry. Co., 10 App. Div. (N. Y.) 360; Read v. Brooklyn Heights R. Co., 32 App. Div. (N. Y.) 503.

20 Cincinnati St. Ry. Co. v. Whitcomb, 66 Fed. 915; Tacoma Ry. & Power Co. v. Hays, 110 Fed. 496; Davidson v. Denver Tramway Co., 4 Colo. App. 283; Lawler v. Hartford St. Ry. Co., 72 Conn. 74; Frank v. St. Louis Transit Co. (Mo. App.) 73 S. W. 239; Dennis v. North Jersey St. Ry. Co., 64 N. J. Law, 439; Weiser v. Broadway & N. St. R. Co., 2 Ohio Dec. 463; Lewis v. Cincinnati St. Ry. Co., 10 Ohio S. & C. P. Dec. 53.

21 Highland Ave. & B. R. Co. v. Sampson, 91 Ala. 560; Citizens' St. Ry. Co. v. Helvie, 22 Ind. App. 515; Burns v. Metropolitan St. Ry. Co. (Kan.) 71 Pac. 244; Honick v. Metropolitan St. Ry. Co. (Kan.) 71 Pac. 265; Dieck v. New Orleans, C. & L. R. Co., 51 La. Ann. 262; Sanitary Dairy Co. v. St. Louis Transit Co. (Mo. App.) 71 S. W. 726; Murray v. St. Louis Transit Co. (Mo.) 75 S. W. 611; Cawley v. La Crosse City Ry. Co., 101 Wis. 145; Dummer v. Milwaukee Electric Ry. & Light Co., 108 Wis. 589; Tesch v. Milwaukee Electric Ry. & Light Co., 108 Wis. 593.

22 Robbins v. Springfield St. Ry. Co., 165 Mass. 30; Riley v. Min-

Failure to listen before crossing a street railway track is not lack of due care as a matter of law,[23] and though a failure to look usually bars recovery, it is generally held that the duty of looking is not an absolute one.[24] In Pennsylvania it is held that the duty to look is an absolute one, and continues until the track is reached.[25]

Cable and electric cars are regarded as more dangerous than horse cars;[26] and in Pennsylvania the rule has been declared to be that a person is bound to look and listen before crossing cable or electric street railway tracks, and that, while he need not stop, as a matter of law, there are many cases where it is his duty to do so.[27] This rule has been incorrectly quoted in subsequent cases as holding that a person must always look, and in some instances, if his view is obstructed, listen, and perhaps stop.[28] Other Pennsylvania

neapolis St. Ry. Co., 80 Minn. 424; Consolidated Traction Co. v. Haight, 59 N. J. Law, 577; Read v. Brooklyn Heights R. Co., 32 App. Div. (N. Y.) 503; Wilson v. Citizens' St. Ry. Co., 105 Tenn. 74; Memphis St. Ry. Co. v. Riddick (Tenn.) 75 S. W. 924.

23 Citizens' St. Ry. Co. v. Abright, 14 Ind. App. 433.

24 Dennis v. North Jersey St. Ry. Co., 64 N. J. Law, 439; Curry v. Union Electric Ry. Co., 86 Hun (N. Y.) 559; Campbell v. Union Ry. Co., 9 Misc. Rep. (N. Y.) 484; Vonelling v. Metropolitan St. Ry. Co., 35 Misc. Rep. (N. Y.) 301; Westerman v. Metropolitan St. Ry. Co., 84 N. Y. Supp. 501; Carson v. Federal St. & P. V. Ry. Co., 147 Pa. 219.

25 Burke v. Union Traction Co., 198 Pa. 497. And see Wilman v. People's Ry. Co. (Del.) 55 Atl. 332.

26 Garrity v. Detroit Citizens' St. Ry. Co., 112 Mich. 369; Winter v. Federal St. & P. V. Passenger Ry. Co., 153 Pa. 26.

27 Omslaer v. Pittsburg & B. Traction Co., 168 Pa. 519.

28 Jones Bros. v. Greensburg, J. & P. St. Ry. Co., 9 Pa. Super. Ct. 65; Trout v. Altoona & L. V. Electric Ry. Co., 13 Pa. Super. Ct. 17.

cases hold that a person must look in both directions just before crossing the track, and, if there is any obstruction, must listen.[29] In Smith v. Citizens' Ry. Co.[30] the rule is held to be that a driver need not stop, but must listen, and look unless his view is obstructed. Other cases refuse to lay down any specific rule as to stopping, looking, and listening, but hold the person crossing the tracks to the exercise of ordinary care.[31]

A person coming from a private road onto a highway is not bound to look and listen for an approaching car.[32] Whether a car is being driven in a crowded street or a thinly settled surburban district is a circumstance bearing on the plaintiff's due care, and not looking, under the latter conditions, is lack of due care.[33]

In the many cases where the due care of the driver of a team has been left to the jury, certain special circumstances need to be considered. The speed of the car, its distance from the driver of the team, whether warning was given, the obstruction of the view, and whether the accident occurred at a crossing are important considerations. Where it appeared that the driver looked before crossing a track, but

29 Ehrisman v. East Harrisburg City Passenger Ry. Co., 150 Pa. 180; Wheelahan v. Philadelphia Traction Co., 150 Pa. 187.

30 52 Mo. App. 36.

31 Davidson v. Denver Tramway Co., 4 Colo. App. 283; Brown v. Wilmington City Ry. Co., 1 Pennewill (Del.) 332; Price v. Charles Warner Co., 1 Pennewill (Del.) 462; Cox v. Wilmington City Ry. Co. (Del.) 53 Atl. 569; Snyder v. People's Ry. Co. (Del.) 53 Atl. 433; Fritz v. Detroit Citizens' St. Ry. Co., 105 Mich. 50.

32 Dunican v. Union Ry. Co., 39 App. Div. (N. Y.) 497.

33 Wosika v. St. Paul City Ry. Co., 80 Minn. 364.

was struck by a car coming at a high rate of speed, due care was held to be for the jury.[34]

It is not lack of due care, as a matter of law, to pass in front of a cable car which is standing still, although the car is but a short distance away,[35] or one hundred feet away,[36] but where a driver saw a car standing still thirty feet away, and drove slowly on, without looking again, this was held lack of due care.[36a] Whether it is lack of due care to attempt to cross a street railway track about thirty feet in front of a slowly moving car is a question for the jury;[37] and it is not lack of due care, as a matter of law, to attempt to cross a street car track when a car is about one hundred feet away,[38] half a block away,[39] from

[34] Hays v. Tacoma Ry. & Power Co., 106 Fed. 48; Tacoma Ry. & Power Co. v. Hays, 110 Fed. 496; Lawler v. Hartford St. Ry. Co., 72 Conn. 74; Metropolitan St. Ry. Co. v. Slayman, 64 Kan. 722; Galbraith v. West End St. Ry. Co., 165 Mass. 572; Creavin v. Newton St. Ry. Co., 176 Mass. 529; Coleman v. Lowell, L. & H. St. R. Co., 181 Mass. 591; Ryan v. Detroit Citizens' St. Ry. Co., 123 Mich. 597; Moran v. Detroit, Y. & A. A. Ry., 124 Mich. 582; Blate v. Third Ave. R. Co., 44 App. Div. (N. Y.) 163; Vitelli v. Nassau Electric R. Co., 53 App. Div. (N. Y.) 639; Morris v. Metropolitan St. Ry. Co., 63 App. Div. (N. Y.) 78; Kilbane v. Westchester Electric R. Co., 19 Misc. Rep. (N. Y.) 184; Lane v. Brooklyn Heights R. Co., 82 N. Y. Supp. 1057; Moore v. Charlotte Electric St. Ry. Co., 128 N. C. 455; Conyngham v. Erie Electric Motor Co., 15 Pa. Super. Ct. 573; Hamilton v. Consolidated Traction Co., 201 Pa. 351.

[35] Riegelman v. Third Ave. R. Co., 9 Misc. Rep. (N. Y.) 51.

[36] Lowy v. Metropolitan St. Ry. Co., 30 Misc. Rep. (N. Y.) 775.

[36a] Cosgrove v. Interurban St. Ry. Co., 84 N. Y. Supp. 885.

[37] Thoresen v. La Crosse City Ry. Co., 87 Wis. 597.

[38] San Antonio Traction Co. v. Upson (Tex. Civ. App.) 71 S. W. 565.

[39] Chicago City Ry. Co. v. Sandusky, 198 Ill. 400.

two hundred and fifty to three hundred feet away,[40] four hundred feet away,[41] or to attempt to cross a street car track twenty-eight feet away, when a car is five hundred feet distant.[42] Where the driver of an ice wagon started to turn onto the track when a car was being started about one hundred and thirty feet away, due care was held to be for the jury;[43] and while, as a general rule, it is lack of due care to cross a street railway track a short distance in front of an approaching car, where a street is so crowded that a driver would have to wait a long time before crossing at all, he cannot be held to the same degree of care as he would be in a locality where cars pass only at intervals.[44]

Due care is for the jury when a driver attempts to cross at a street crossing when a street car is distant seventy feet,[45] seventy-five feet,[46] eighty feet,[47] one hundred feet,[48] two hundred and fifty feet,[49] one hundred yards,[50] or half a block;[51] or where two cars are approaching, in opposite directions, one a block away and one three-fourths of a block

40 West Chicago St. R. Co. v. Dedloff, 92 Ill. App. 547.

41 Driscoll v. West End St. Ry. Co., 159 Mass. 142.

42 Mackie v. Brooklyn City R. Co., 10 Misc. Rep. (N. Y.) 4.

43 McCormack v. Nassau Electric R. Co., 16 App. Div. (N. Y.) 24.

44 Kelly v. Brooklyn Heights R. Co., 12 Misc. Rep. (N. Y.) 568; Prince v. Third Ave. R. Co., 84 N. Y. Supp. 542.

45 Bruss v. Metropolitan St. Ry. Co., 66 App. Div. (N. Y.) 554.

46 Schoener v. Metropolitan St. Ry. Co., 72 App. Div. (N. Y.) 23.

47 Reilly v. Third Ave. R. Co., 16 Misc. Rep. (N. Y.) 11.

48 Kerr v. Atlantic Ave. R. Co., 10 Misc. Rep. (N. Y.) 264; Moore v. Metropolitan St. Ry. Co., 84 App. Div. (N. Y.) 613.

49 Woodland v. North Jersey St. Ry. Co., 66 N. J. Law, 455.

50 Richmond Traction Co. v. Clarke (Va.) 43 S. E. 618.

51 Reilly v. Metropolitan St. Ry. Co., 26 Misc. Rep. (N. Y.) 814. And see Carter v. Interurban St. Ry. Co., 84 N. Y. Supp. 134.

away,[52] or one a block away and one half a block away,[53] or one a block away and one one hundred and fifty feet away,[54] or one a block away, and one two blocks away.[54a] There is no evidence of lack of due care where a driver could have got across in safety at a crossing if the motorman had exercised ordinary care, and had reasonable control of the car;[55] and even where a driver at a street crossing saw a car approaching at high speed, it was held that he had a right to assume that the motorman would use proper care, and that he was not guilty of lack of due care as a matter of law.[56] Where the driver of a team reached a crossing ahead of a car, and proceeded to cross the track at a walk, due care was held to be for the jury.[57]

The circumstances of the speed of a car, its failure to give warning, and its distance from the driver may be combined in the same case. Thus, where a driver looked before crossing a track, and a car came around a corner sixty-five feet away at high speed;[58] where the driver of a team saw a car moving slowly about one hundred feet away, and, as he started to cross the track, the car increased its speed;[59] and where the driver of a team attempted to cross when a street car was coming at high speed about three hundred

52 McDonald v. Third Ave. R. Co., 16 Misc. Rep. (N. Y.) 52.

53 Hunter v. Third Ave. R. Co., 21 Misc. Rep. (N. Y.) 1.

54 Dise v. Metropolitan St. Ry. Co., 22 Misc. Rep. (N. Y.) 97.

54a Chauvin v. Detroit United Ry. (Mich.) 97 N. W. 160.

55 Citizens' Rapid Transit Co. v. Seigrist, 96 Tenn. 119; Saunders v. City & Suburban R. Co., 99 Tenn. 130.

56 Buhrens v. Dry Dock, E. B. & B. R. Co., 53 Hun (N. Y.) 571.

57 Zimmerman v. Union Ry. Co., 3 App. Div. (N. Y.) 219.

58 Walsh v. Atlantic Ave. R. Co., 23 App. Div. (N. Y.) 19.

59 Burgess v. Sixth Ave. R. Co., 13 N. Y. Wkly. Dig. 499.

feet away,—due care in each case was held to be for the jury.[60] Where a driver looked for a car, but was struck by a car coming at high speed without warning, due care was held to be for the jury;[61] and the same ruling was made where a driver attempted to cross a street car track at a crossing with his horse at a walk, when a car was three hundred and thirty feet away, and there was evidence that the motorman gave no warning.[62]

Where a driver was injured where there were double tracks, and there was evidence that one car approached without warning, due care was held to be for the jury.[63]

In a number of cases, where a driver's view was somewhat obstructed, due care was held to be for the jury, where the additional circumstances were that he looked in both directions before crossing,[64] that he looked and listened before crossing,[65] that he stopped, looked, and listened before crossing,[66] that it was dusk when he made the attempt,[67] that the car which struck him came at high speed without

60 Consolidated Traction Co. v. Lambertson, 59 N. J. Law, 297.

61 O'Callaghan v. Metropolitan St. Ry. Co., 69 App. Div. (N. Y.) 574; Greenfield v. East Harrisburg Passenger Ry. Co., 178 Pa. 194; Frame v. Electric Traction Co., 180 Pa. 49; Hall v. Ogden City St. Ry. Co., 13 Utah, 243; Tesch v. Milwaukee Electric Ry. & Light Co., 108 Wis. 593.

62 Raulston v. Traction Co., 13 Pa. Super. Ct. 412.

63 Plant v. Heraty (Mich.) 92 N. W. 284.

64 Curry v. Union Electric Ry. Co., 86 Hun (N. Y.) 559.

65 Lahti v. Fitchburg & L. St. Ry. Co., 172 Mass. 147; Kelly v. Wakefield & S. St. Ry. Co., 179 Mass. 542; Gebhardt v. St. Louis Transit Co. (Mo. App.) 71 S. W. 448; Manayunk & R. Boarding & Livery Stable Co. v. Union Traction Co., 7 Pa. Super. Ct. 104.

66 Marchal v. Indianapolis St. Ry. Co., 28 Ind. App. 133.

67 Thoresen v. La Crosse City Ry. Co., 94 Wis. 129.

warning,[68] or was coming eight or ten miles an hour.[69] In a number of cases, where there were wagons and other cars on the track, due care was held to be a question for the jury.[70]

Certain unusual circumstances bearing on the question of due care remain to be considered. Where the driver of a team was signaled to cross by the company's watchman, and was struck by a car;[71] where a driver involuntarily pulled up his horses while crossing a street railway track on account of a sudden lurch of his carriage;[72] where a car came on the wrong track without a headlight and without warning on a dark winter's morning;[73] and where the driver of a patrol wagon tried to pass in front of a street car,—due care in each case was held to be for the jury.[74] Where the driver started to cross in the rear of a car, and the car suddenly backed, while there was evidence that no signal was given, and that there was no one on the rear end of the car, due care was held to be for the jury.[75] Where a driver stopped, looked, and listened, but was struck by a car coming without

68 Hart v. Cedar Rapids & M. C. Ry. Co., 109 Iowa, 631.

69 Brozek v. Steinway Ry. Co., 10 App. Div. (N. Y.) 360.

70 Kerrigan v. West End St. Ry. Co., 158 Mass. 305; Flannagan v. St. Paul City Ry. Co., 68 Minn. 300; Schron v. Staten Island Electric R. Co., 16 App. Div. (N. Y.) 111; Murphy v. Nassau Electric R. Co., 19 App. Div. (N. Y.) 583; Seagriff v. Brooklyn Heights R. Co., 31 App. Div. (N. Y.) 595; Lenkner v. Citizens' Traction Co., 179 Pa. 486.

71 Fay v. Brooklyn Heights R. Co., 69 App. Div. (N. Y.) 563; Haney v. Pittsburgh, A. & M. Traction Co., 159 Pa. 395.

72 Sheehan v. Citizens' Ry. Co., 72 Mo. App. 524.

73 R. F. Stevens Co. v. Brooklyn Heights R. Co., 59 App. Div. (N. Y.) 23.

74 Decker v. Brooklyn Heights R. Co., 64 App. Div. (N. Y.) 430.

75 Central Ry. Co. v. Knowles, 191 Ill. 241.

warning, due care was held to be for the jury when it appeared that a car could not be seen one thousand five hundred feet east of the crossing, owing to a hill, that the driver crossed at a slow walk, and that the wheels of the wagon made a grinding noise in the gravel.[76] Where a plaintiff's violation of an ordinance as to speed caused the accident, he was held unable to recover.[77]

## § 107. Same—Driving on or near tracks.

Numerous rulings have been made as to the duty of a man driving on the track to look behind him for approaching cars. While it has been held that it is the duty of a man driving on a street railway track to use his senses and to look back occasionally,[78] it is not lack of due care, as a matter of law, for a man not to look behind him in the distance of a single block after he looked once when he first went on the track, and there was no evidence of any warning;[79] and where the wife of the driver of a wagon looked back twice in a single block, and was struck with great force by a car coming from the rear, due care was held to be for the jury.[80] It has been held that, while it is not lack of due care, as a matter of law, for a person driving upon a street railway track at night not to look backwards for an approaching car,[81] at the same time he cannot rely wholly

76 Howard v. Indianapolis St. Ry. Co., 29 Ind. App. 514.

77 McGrath v. City & Suburban Ry. Co., 93 Ga. 312.

78 Adolph v. Central Park, N. & E. R. R. Co., 76 N. Y. 530; Quinn v. Atlantic Ave. R. Co., 12 N. Y. Supp. 223.

79 Schilling v. Metropolitan St. Ry. Co., 47 App. Div. (N. Y.) 500.

80 Seifter v. Brooklyn Heights R. Co., 55 App. Div. (N. Y.) 10.

81 Bossert v. Nassau Electric R. Co., 40 App. Div. (N. Y.) 144; Quinn v. Brooklyn City R. Co., 40 App. Div. (N. Y.) 608.

upon the supposition that those in charge of the car will see him in time, but he must be on the alert to discover the approach of the car.[82] On the other hand, it is equally clear that the duty to keep a lookout does not rest wholly upon the driver of the wagon; and in most cases where a car approaching from behind ran into a wagon, the due care of the driver of the wagon is held to be a question for the jury,[83] especially where there are other circumstances, such as the fact that the wagon was a covered one,[84] or that the driver's view was obstructed by the load of his wagon, or that the car was not lighted, and was running at high speed.[85] Where a driver

[82] Kupferschmid v. Southern Electric R. Co., 70 Mo. App. 438; Devine v. Brooklyn Heights R. Co., 34 App. Div. (N. Y.) 248; Belford v. Brooklyn Heights R. Co., 86 App. Div. (N. Y.) 388.

[83] Chicago General Ry. Co. v. Kriz, 94 Ill. App. 277; Indianapolis St. Ry. Co. v. Darnell (Ind. App.) 68 N. E. 609; Wilkins v. Omaha & C. B. Ry. & Bridge Co., 96 Iowa, 668; Metropolitan St. Ry. Co. v. Rouch (Kan.) 71 Pac. 257; Lynam v. Union Ry. Co., 114 Mass. 83; Le Blanc v. Lowell, L. & H. St. Ry. Co., 170 Mass. 564; Tashjian v. Worcester Consol. St. Ry. Co., 177 Mass. 75; Vincent v. Norton & T. St. Ry. Co., 180 Mass. 104; Manor v. Bay Cities Consol. Ry. Co., 118 Mich. 1; Klockenbrink v. St. Louis & M. R. R. Co. (Mo.) 72 S. W. 900; Noll v. St. Louis Transit Co. (Mo. App.) 73 S. W. 907; Schafstette v. St. Louis & M. R. R. Co. (Mo.) 74 S. W. 826; Twelkemeyer v. St. Louis Transit Co. (Mo. App.) 76 S. W. 682; Fishbach v. Steinway Ry. Co., 11 App. Div. (N. Y.) 152; Warren v. Union Ry. Co., 46 App. Div. (N. Y.) 517; Brachfeld v. Third Ave. R. Co., 29 Misc. Rep. (N. Y.) 586; Cohen v. Metropolitan St. Ry. Co., 34 Misc. Rep. (N. Y.) 186; Connor v. Metropolitan St. Ry. Co., 77 App. Div. (N. Y.) 384; Blum v. Metropolitan St. Ry. Co., 80 N. Y. Supp. 157.

[84] Blakeslee v. Consolidated St. Ry. Co., 112 Mich. 63.

[85] Rascher v. East Detroit & G. P. Ry. Co., 90 Mich. 413.

is injured while endeavoring to turn from one track onto another, due care is held to be for the jury.[86]

Various circumstances tend to make the question of the driver's due care more likely to be left to the jury, as, for instance, where the condition of the street[87] or the nature of the driver's load[88] made it necessary for him to drive on the tracks, or where there was snow between the tracks and the sidewalk,[89] or where the space between the track and the sidewalk was a narrow one,[90] or where a man driving under a viaduct was struck by a car coming at high speed.[91] Where the driver of a heavily loaded wagon tried to turn off the tracks, but was prevented by the slippery rails,[92] where a car came suddenly over the crest of a hill at high speed,[93] and where the chain on a wagon broke, and the driver continued to zigzag down the hill between the sidewalk and the track,[94] due care in each case was held to be

86 Hughes v. Camden & S. Ry. Co., 65 N. J. Law, 203; Adams v. Camden & S. Ry. Co. (N. J. Err. & App.) 55 Atl. 254; Meyer v. Brooklyn, Q. C. & S. R. Co., 47 App. Div. (N. Y.) 286; McConnell v. Atlantic Ave. R. Co., 11 Misc. Rep. (N. Y.) 177; Jackson v. Pittsburgh, A. & M. Traction Co., 159 Pa. 399; Harper v. Philadelphia Traction Co., 175 Pa. 129.

87 Delaney v. Yonkers R. Co., 13 App. Div. (N. Y.) 114; Gaughan v. Second Ave. Traction Co., 189 Pa. 408.

88 Heffran v. Brooklyn Heights R. Co., 8 Misc. Rep. (N. Y.) 41; Calumet Electric St. Ry. Co. v. Christenson, 70 Ill. App. 84.

89 Harper v. Philadelphia Traction Co., 175 Pa. 129.

90 Geipel v. Steinway Ry. Co., 14 App. Div. (N. Y.) 551; Gibbons v. Wilkes-Barre, &c., St. Ry. Co., 155 Pa. 279.

91 Tait v. Buffalo Ry. Co., 55 App. Div. (N. Y.) 507.

92 Lynam v. Union Ry. Co., 114 Mass. 83; Will v. West Side R. Co., 84 Wis. 42.

93 Cannon v. Pittsburg & B. Traction Co., 194 Pa. 159.

94 Cross v. California St. Cable Ry. Co., 102 Cal. 313.

for the jury. A mistake in judgment in turning off a street car track in the wrong direction to avoid a collision with an approaching car is not lack of due care as a matter of law.[95]

While many cases of this character are thus left to the jury with regard to the question of the driver's due care, there are cases where the necessary standard of care is held not to have been complied with, and the driver held guilty of lack of due care as a matter of law. Thus, a driver was held unable to recover when he drove on a street railway track for three hundred feet without once looking back;[96] where one saw a car two hundred and fifty feet away, and did not look again;[97] where one drove upon the track for half a block without trying to find out if a car was following;[98] where one drove upon the track for an eighth of a mile,[98a] or for half a mile, but did not look behind him or pay attention enough to hear the bell of an approaching car;[99] where a woman drove on the track with her ears muffled up in a fur coat and cap, without looking back more than one hundred and twenty feet;[100] and where the driver of a milk wagon drove on the track in a suburban district for a mile or more without once looking behind him.[101]

95 Kane v. Worcester Consol. St. Ry. Co., 182 Mass. 201.

96 Hill v. Metropolitan St. Ry. Co., 30 Misc. Rep. (N. Y.) 440.

97 Pechesky v. Metropolitan St. Ry. Co., 30 Misc. Rep. (N. Y.) 432.

98 Bryant v. Metropolitan St. Ry. Co., 28 Misc. Rep. (N. Y.) 532.

98a Reynolds v. Larchmont Horse Ry. Co., 83 App. Div. (N. Y.) 189.

99 Winter v. Crosstown St. Ry. Co., 8 Misc. Rep. (N. Y.) 362; Geleta v. Buffalo & N. F. Elec. Ry., 84 N. Y. Supp. 629.

100 Cawley v. La Crosse City Ry. Co., 106 Wis. 239.

101 Johnson v. Brooklyn Heights R. Co., 34 App. Div. (N. Y.) 271.

Where the plaintiff deliberately turned upon the track when there was plenty of room on either side, and he knew that a car was about due, he was held guilty of lack of due care;[102] and where there are double tracks, and the driver of a team turns from one track to another directly in front of a car, he cannot recover.[103] A driver must be prompt in getting out of the way; and where the plaintiff saw a car coming about one hundred and twenty-five feet away, but took a slanting course to get off the track, he was held not to be in the exercise of due care.[104] In like manner, where the driver of a truck did not turn off the tracks, but, instead, shouted to the driver of a street car to stop, he was held to be barred from recovery.[105] Where a man drove on the track in a closed wagon for half a mile without looking behind but once, he was held unable to recover.[106]

As in the case of driving upon the track, the question of due care in bringing a team to a halt near the track or on the track itself is in some cases held to be for the jury, and in others held to be lack of due care as a matter of law. Leaving a horse unattended in a city street has been held to be negligence.[107] Whether leaving a horse with the reins tied to the dasher in such a manner that the horse cannot move without pulling the wagon by his mouth is lack of

102 Donnelly v. Brooklyn City R. Co., 109 N. Y. 16.

103 Baumann v. Metropolitan St. Ry. Co., 21 Misc. Rep. (N. Y.) 658; Reichenberg v. Interurban St. Ry. Co., 84 N. Y. Supp. 523; Boehmer v. Pittsburgh, A. & M. Traction Co., 194 Pa. 313.

104 Morrissey v. Bridgeport Traction Co., 68 Conn. 215.

105 Barker v. Hudson River R. Co., 4 Daly (N. Y.) 274.

106 U. P. Steam Baking Co. v. Omaha St. Ry. Co. (Neb.) 94 N. W. 533.

107 Higgins v. Wilmington City Ry. Co., 1 Marv. (Del.) 352.

due care is for the jury;[108] and it has been held that the violation of an ordinance requiring the driver of a team not to leave his horse unfastened in the street is not lack of due care.[109] It is not lack of due care as a matter of law, for an expressman to leave his horse standing untied near a street railway track, in the absence of any evidence as to the bad disposition of the horse.[110] Stopping a team on or near the tracks has been held in a number of cases not to be lack of due care, as a matter of law, as where a doctor stopped his carriage in a narrow space between the car track and the sidewalk,[111] where a man stopped his wagon near the track to converse with a friend,[112] and where there were snowbanks on each side of the street, and the driver of a cab stopped on a street car track to receive orders.[113] It has been held that an expressman has a right to a reasonable time to unload his wagon, although a portion of it is on the street car track;[114] and due care is for the jury where the driver of a brewery wagon was waiting for the gate to be opened on a dark night in such a position that the rear of the wagon was necessarily upon the tracks.[115] Where a street was obstructed, and a boy backed a delivery wagon

108 Johnson v. Stewart, 62 Ark. 164.

109 McCambley v. Staten Island Midland R. Co., 32 App. Div. (N. Y.) 346.

110 Albert v. Bleecker St., &c., R. Co., 2 Daly (N. Y.) 389.

111 Tarler v. Metropolitan St. Ry. Co., 21 Misc. Rep. (N. Y.) 684.

112 Redford v. Spokane St. Ry. Co., 15 Wash. 419.

113 Mullen v. Central Park & E. R. R. Co., 1 Misc. Rep. (N. Y.) 216.

114 Holzman v. Metropolitan St. Ry. Co., 31 Misc. Rep. (N. Y.) 644.

115 McGrane v. Flushing & C. P. Electric Ry. Co., 13 App. Div. (N. Y.) 177.

so that the horse stood across the track, this was held not to be lack of due care as a matter of law;[116] and the same ruling was made where the street was so narrow that a delivery wagon necessarily obstructed the track.[117] An instruction that, if a hack stood near a track and backed into a car as it approached, the plaintiff cannot recover, should not be given.[118]

A driver has been held not to be in the exercise of due care when he stopped his team at what he thought was a safe distance from the track, but was mistaken;[119] and where the driver of a wagon and the driver of a car both thought that the wagon was a safe distance from the track, but miscalculated, there was held to be either no negligence on the part of the company, or joint negligence, and therefore no recovery.[120] In Gray v. Second Ave. R. Co.,[121] where the driver of a carriage stopped near the track, and was reading a newspaper, so that he did not notice the approach of a snow plow, he was held not to be in the exercise of due care. One who leaves a horse and wagon unguarded upon an electric railway track in a narrow, unlighted alley on a dark night is not in the exercise of due care;[122] and one who places his

[116] Fenner v. Wilkes-Barre & W. V. Traction Co., 202 Pa. 365.

[117] Black v. Staten Island Electric R. Co., 40 App. Div. (N. Y.) 238.

[118] El Paso Electric St. Ry. Co. v. Ballinger & Longwell (Tex. Civ. App.) 72 S. W. 612. And see Montgomery St. Ry. v. Hastings (Ala.) 35 So. 412.

[119] Spaulding v. Jarvis, 32 Hun (N. Y.) 621.

[120] Patton v. Philadelphia Traction Co., 132 Pa. 76.

[121] 65 N. Y. 561.

[122] Watson v. Interurban St. Ry. Co., 84 N. Y. Supp. 556; Gilmore v. Federal St. & P. V. Passenger Ry. Co., 153 Pa. 31.

horses across a street railway track on a dark night while unloading his wagon, when it appears that there is no necessity for placing them in such a position, is likewise barred from recovery,—the court holding that greater care must be used by travelers since the introduction of electric and cable cars.[123] The driver of a delivery wagon, who left his horse untied, in violation of an ordinance, on a stormy night, in the narrow space between the gutter and the track, was held guilty of lack of due care.[124] The driver of a wagon who dismounts, when his wagon is stopped near the track, with his back to a car approaching at full speed in plain view, is not in the exercise of due care.[125]

### § 108. Same—Imputed negligence.

Where a person is injured while riding in company with the driver of a team, the interesting question arises as to whether or not the driver's lack of due care can be imputed to the plaintiff. It is certain that the lack of due care of a driver cannot, of necessity, be imputed to a fellow passenger,[126] and the general rule seems to be that the opportunity of controlling the movements of the team is the test. Thus, the lack of due care of a father cannot be imputed to a daughter of nineteen asleep in the team,[127] or to a girl of twenty-one months sitting in her mother's lap,[128] or to a

[123] Winter v. Federal St. & P. V. Passenger Ry., 153 Pa. 26

[124] Hoffman v. Syracuse Rapid Transit Ry. Co., 50 App. Div. (N. Y.) 83.

[125] Crowley v. Metropolitan St. Ry. Co., 24 App. Div. (N. Y.) 101.

[126] West Chicago St. R. Co. v. Dedloff, 92 Ill. App. 547; Chicago City Ry. Co. v. Wall, 93 Ill. App. 411.

[127] Consolidated Traction Co. v. Behr, 59 N. J. Law, 477.

[128] Hennessy v. Brooklyn City R. Co., 6 App. Div. (N. Y.) 206.

daughter of sixteen driving with him,[129] or to a son riding on the front seat, but exercising no control.[130] In Metcalf v. Rochester Ry. Co.[131] it was held that the lack of due care of the driver of a team could be imputed to a child of four and a half. In Central Passenger Ry. Co. v. Chatterson[132] it was held that the negligence of a servant employed to drive by a husband was imputable to a wife driving with the husband, as well as to the husband; but it has been held that the lack of due care of a husband is not imputable to a wife.[133] The lack of due care of the driver cannot be imputed to a mere gratuitous passenger, who is invited to ride, and who has no management or control;[134] but if a gratuitous passenger is giving directions, not merely as to finding the way, but as to managing the horse, such negligence is imputable to him.[135] The contributory negligence of the driver of a hose cart cannot be imputed to another fireman driving with him.[136]

129 Street Ry. Co. v. Eadie, 43 Ohio St. 91.

130 Morris v. Metropolitan St. Ry. Co., 63 App. Div. (N. Y.) 78.

131 12 App. Div. (N. Y.) 147.

132 14 Ky. Law Rep. 663.

133 Hennessy v. Brooklyn City R. Co., 73 Hun (N. Y.) 569; Ulrich v. Toledo Consol. St. Ry. Co., 10 Ohio Cir. Ct. R. 635.

134 Farley v. Wilmington & N. Electric Ry. Co. (Del.) 52 Atl. 543; Wosika v. St. Paul City Ry. Co., 80 Minn. 364; Consolidated Traction Co. v. Hoimark, 60 N. J. Law, 456; Noonan v. Consolidated Traction Co., 64 N. J. Law, 579; Weldon v. Third Ave. R. Co., 3 App. Div. (N. Y.) 370; Kessler v. Brooklyn Heights R. Co., 3 App. Div. (N. Y.) 426; Strauss v. Newburgh Electric Ry. Co., 6 App. Div. (N. Y.) 264; Zimmermann v. Union Ry. Co., 28 App. Div. (N. Y.) 445; Westerman v. Metropolitan St. Ry. Co., 84 N. Y. Supp. 501.

135 Zimmermann v. Union Ry. Co., 28 App. Div. (N. Y.) 445.

136 Elyton Land Co. v. Mingea, 89 Ala. 521; Geary v. Metropolitan St. R. Co., 84 App. Div. (N. Y.) 514.

The lack of due care of a fellow servant who is driving a team is not imputable to a boy of seventeen,[137] or that of the driver of an omnibus to a passenger,[138] or that of the driver of an ice wagon to a helper, who has no control over the horse,[139] or that of a driver to a boy of fourteen, who is stealing a ride.[140] Where a woman was invited to drive, and told the driver to "ride slow," it was held that the words must be understood as words of caution, and not of command, so that she was not chargeable with his lack of due care.[141] It is obvious, however, that a person riding with another is not thereby wholly relieved from responsibility, but is still bound to use due care under all the circumstances.[142] Where a school teacher hired a wagon to take small children to school, and directed the driver when and where to go, she was held chargeable with his lack of due care;[143] and where two men were engaged in moving goods, they were held to be engaged in a common enterprise, so that the negligence of the driver was imputable to the plaintiff.[144] The mere fact that a driver of an ice team and his

137 Brennan v. Metropolitan St. Ry. Co., 60 App. Div. (N. Y.) 264.

138 West Chicago St. R. Co. v. Piper, 64 Ill. App. 605.

139 Anderson v. Metropolitan St. Ry. Co., 30 Misc. Rep. (N. Y.) 104.

140 Cincinnati St. Ry. Co. v. Wright, 54 Ohio St. 181.

141 Bergold v. Nassau Elec. R. Co., 30 App. Div. (N. Y.) 438.

142 Farley v. Wilmington & N. Elec. Ry. Co., 3 Pen. (Del.) 581; Johnson v. St. Paul City Ry. Co., 67 Minn. 260; Wosika v. St. Paul City Ry. Co., 80 Minn. 364; Ulrich v. Toledo Consol. St. Ry. Co., 10 Ohio Cir. Ct. R. 635; Johnson v. Superior Rapid Transit Ry. Co., 91 Wis. 233.

143 Reed v. Metropolitan St. Ry. Co., 58 App. Div. (N. Y.) 87.

144 Schron v. Staten Island Elec. R. Co., 16 App. Div. (N. Y.) 111; Cass v. Third Ave. R. Co., 20 App. Div. (N. Y.) 591.

helper are fellow servants does not make the negligence of the driver attributable to the helper,[145] but the negligence of a driver has been imputed to a fellow servant.[145a]

**§ 109. Same—Age and occupation.**

A boy of fourteen is held to the degree of care common to a boy of that age,[146] as is one of fifteen,[146a] and one of sixteen;[146b] and aged people, like children, have a right to rely upon those stronger mentally than themselves.[147] A man of seventy-nine, partially blind and deaf, must use a degree of care commensurate with the danger when driving alone in a city street.[148] A person placed in sudden peril is not held to the usual standard of care;[149] and in Geary v. Metropolitan St. Ry. Co.,[150] where a fireman saw that a collision would take place, and jumped from the truck, the jury were warranted in finding that there was no lack of due care.

While it is held, on the one hand, that the driver of a hook and ladder has duties of a public character, and must take chances that an ordinary citizen would not think of taking,[151] it is also held that he must use his faculties and

145 McCormack v. Nassau Elec. R. Co., 18 App. Div. (N. Y.) 333.

145a Krintzman v. Interurban St. Ry. Co., 84 N. Y. Supp. 243.

146 Cincinnati St. Ry. Co. v. Wright, 54 Ohio St. 181.

146a Dubiver v. City & S. Ry. Co. (Or.) 74 Pac. 915.

146b Campbell v. St. Louis & S. Ry. Co. (Mo.) 75 S. W. 86.

147 Johnson v. St. Paul City Ry. Co., 67 Minn. 260.

148 Robbins v. Springfield St. Ry. Co., 165 Mass. 30.

149 Edgerton v. O'Neil, 4 Kan. App. 73; Bush v. St. Joseph & B. H. St. Ry. Co., 113 Mich. 513; Nicholsburg v. Second Ave. R. Co., 11 Misc. Rep. (N. Y.) 432.

150 73 App. Div. (N. Y.) 441.

151 Warren v. Mendenhall, 77 Minn. 145; Cameron v. Mendenhall, 80 Minn. 150; Geary v. Metropolitan St. Ry. Co., 84 App. Div. (N.

use ordinary care in crossing a street railway track;[152] and that, although the driver of a fire truck is given the right of way by charter when going to a fire, he is bound to have his horses under control while approaching a street car line.[153] In Magee v. West End St. Ry. Co.,[154] a fireman, who was unable to dress himself completely before starting for a fire, proceeded to do so while riding upon a rapidly driven ladder truck, and, in so doing, threw one leg over the side piece, and between the rounds of the ladder, but only for the purpose of holding on while adjusting his belt. While he was in that position the truck came into collision with a street car, and the ladder was pushed back upon the truck, and injured him. It was held that it could not be said, as matter of law, that he was not in the exercise of due care. The court said: "He could not be expected to use the same degree of care as might properly be required of one who had no such duty to perform as he had." In case of a collision between a patrol wagon and a car, the jury have a right to consider that it is a public emergency which called out the patrol wagon,[155] although, in Swain v. Fourteenth St. R. Co.,[156] the court seemed to regard a patrol wagon as on the same footing as any other vehicle; but a repair wagon has no superior right of way.[157] It has been held that the fact that one is driving in a funeral procession, which is readily seen, and not usually interrupted by those in charge of street

Y.) 514; Hanlon v. Milwaukee Elec. Ry. & Light Co. (Wis.) 95 N. W. 100.

152 Guiney v. Southern Elec. R. Co., 167 Mo. 595.

153 Garrity v. Detroit Citizens' St. Ry. Co., 112 Mich. 369.

154 151 Mass. 240.

155 Decker v. Brooklyn Heights R. Co., 64 App. Div. (N. Y.) 430.

156 93 Cal. 179.

157 Northridge v. Atlantic Ave. R. Co., 15 Misc. Rep. (N. Y.) 66.

cars, is calculated to inspire a feeling of safety.[158] The driver of a hose carriage cannot drive recklessly over a track which projects above the street if he is familiar with the track. The driver of a fire wagon has the right of way in the streets, and it is not lack of due care to drive ten or fifteen miles an hour.[159] In Quinn v. Dubuque St. Ry. Co., the due care of a fireman injured in a collision was held to be for the jury.[160] An ordinance giving an ambulance the right of way is admissible in evidence.[161]

## § 110. Right of way.

There have been a number of decisions on the question of the relative rights of street cars and teams in the street, but the general principles are well settled. Between street crossings, the right of the street car, while not exclusive, is held to be superior,[162] since the car cannot leave its tracks,[163] and

158 Johnson v. St. Paul City Ry. Co., 67 Minn. 260.

159 Flynn v. Louisville Ry. Co., 23 Ky. Law Rep. 57, 62 S. W. 490.

160 (Iowa) 94 N. W. 476.

161 Buys v. Third Ave. R. Co., 45 App. Div. (N. Y.) 11.

162 Cincinnati St. Ry. Co. v. Whitcomb, 66 Fed. 915; Robinson v. Louisville Ry. Co., 112 Fed. 484; Mahoney v. San Francisco & S. M. Ry. Co., 110 Cal. 471; Davidson v. Denver Tramway Co., 4 Colo. App. 283; Laufer v. Bridgeport Traction Co., 68 Conn. 475; Brown v. Wilmington City Ry. Co., 1 Pen. (Del.) 332; Price v. Charles Warner Co., 1 Pen. (Del.) 462; Maxwell v. Wilmington City Ry. Co., 1 Marvel (Del.) 199; Higgins v. Wilmington City Ry. Co., 1 Marvel (Del.) 352; Adams v. Wilmington & N. Elec. Ry. Co., 3 Pen. (Del.) 512; Farley v. Wilmington & N. Elec. Ry. Co., 3 Pen. (Del.) 581; Snyder v. People's Ry. Co. (Del.) 53 Atl. 433; Cox v. Wilmington City Ry. Co. (Del.) 53 Atl. 569; Wilman v. People's Ry. Co. (Del.) 55 Atl. 332; Chicago West Div. Ry. Co. v. Bert, 69 Ill. 388; North Chicago St. R. Co. v. Smadraff, 189 Ill. 155; North Chicago Elec. Ry. Co. v. Peuser, 190 Ill. 67; West Chicago St. R.

since the convenience of the public demands that the cars

Co. v. Dougherty, 89 Ill. App. 362; Joliet R. Co. v. Eich, 96 Ill. App. 240; Joliet R. Co. v. Barty, 96 Ill. App. 351; De Lon v. Kokomo City St. Ry. Co., 22 Ind. App. 377; Patterson v. Townsend, 91 Iowa, 725; Metropolitan St. Ry. Co. v. Rouch (Kan.) 71 Pac. 257; Edgerton v. O'Neil, 4 Kan. App. 73; Central Passenger Ry. Co. v. Chatterson, 14 Ky. Law Rep. 663; Atwood v. Bangor, O. & O. T. Ry. Co., 91 Me. 399; Driscoll v. West End St. Ry. Co., 159 Mass. 142; White v. Worcester Consol. St. Ry. Co., 167 Mass. 43; Rascher v. East Detroit & G. P. Ry. Co., 90 Mich. 413; Blakeslee v. Consolidated St. Ry. Co., 105 Mich. 462; Manor v. Bay Cities Consol. Ry. Co., 118 Mich. 1; Shea v. St. Paul City Ry. Co., 50 Minn. 395; Hicks v. Citizens' Ry. Co., 124 Mo. 115; Moore v. Kansas City & I. Rapid Transit Ry. Co., 126 Mo. 265; Camden, G. & W. Ry. Co. v. Preston, 59 N. J. Law, 264; Consolidated Traction Co. v. Lambertson, 59 N. J. Law, 297; Adolph v. Central Park, N. & E. R. R. Co., 76 N. Y. 530; Fleckenstein v. Dry Dock, E. B. & B. R. Co., 105 N. Y. 655; Buhrens v. Dry Dock, E. B. & B. R. Co., 53 Hun (N. Y.) 571; Bernhard v. Rochester Ry. Co., 68 Hun (N. Y.) 369; Hennessy v. Brooklyn City R. Co., 73 Hun (N. Y.) 569; Kessler v. Brooklyn Heights R. Co., 3 App. Div. (N. Y.) 426; Brozek v. Steinway Ry. Co., 10 App. Div. (N. Y.) 360; Rosenblatt v. Brooklyn Heights R. Co., 26 App. Div. (N. Y.) 600; Johnson v. Brooklyn Heights R. Co., 34 App. Div. (N. Y.) 271; Black

[163] Robinson v. Louisville Ry. Co., 112 Fed. 484; Mahoney v. San Francisco & S. M. Ry. Co., 110 Cal. 471; Laufer v. Bridgeport Traction Co., 68 Conn. 475; Brown v. Wilmington City Ry. Co., 1 Pen. (Del.) 332; Price v. Charles Warner Co., 1 Pen. (Del.) 462; Maxwell v. Wilmington City Ry. Co., 1 Marvel (Del.) 199; Higgins v. Wilmington City Ry. Co., 1 Marvel (Del.) 352; Adams v. Wilmington & N. Elec. Ry. Co., 3 Pen. (Del.) 512; Farley v. Wilmington & N. Elec. Ry. Co., 3 Pen. (Del.) 581; Cox v. Wilmington City Ry. Co. (Del.) 53 Atl. 569; Chicago West Div. Ry. Co. v. Bert, 69 Ill. 388; North Chicago St. R. Co. v. Smadraff, 189 Ill. 155; North Chicago Elec. Ry. Co. v. Peuser, 190 Ill. 67; West Chicago St. R. Co. v. Dougherty, 89 Ill. App. 362; Joliet R. Co. v. Eich, 96 Ill. App. 240; Joliet R. Co. v. Barty, 96 Ill. App. 351; Patterson v. Townsend, 91 Iowa, 725; Metropolitan St. Ry. Co. v. Rouch (Kan.) 71 Pac. 257;

be run without unnecessary delay.[164] Hence an instruction that a street railway company has an absolute right of way

v. Staten Island Elec. R. Co., 40 App. Div. (N. Y.) 238; Lawson v. Metropolitan St. Ry. Co., 40 App. Div. (N. Y.) 307; Cambeis v. Third Ave. R. Co., 1 Misc. Rep. (N. Y.) 158; O'Neill v. Third Ave. R. Co., 3 Misc. Rep. (N. Y.) 521; Heffran v. Brooklyn Heights R. Co., 8 Misc. Rep. (N. Y.) 41; Arnesen v. Brooklyn City R. Co., 9 Misc. Rep. (N. Y.) 270; Kennedy v. Metropolitan St. Ry. Co., 11 Misc. Rep. (N. Y.) 320; Northridge v. Atlantic Ave. R. Co., 15 Misc. Rep. (N. Y.) 66; Hunter v. Third Ave. R. Co., 21 Misc. Rep. (N. Y.) 1; McFarland v. Third Ave. R. Co., 29 Misc. Rep. (N. Y.) 121; Cohen v. Metropolitan St. Ry. Co., 34 Misc. Rep. (N. Y.) 186; Barker v. Hudson River R. Co., 4 Daly (N. Y.) 274; Moore v. Charlotte Elec. St. Ry. Co., 128 N. C. 455; Thomas v. Citizens' Passenger Ry. Co., 132 Pa. 504; Ehrisman v. East Harrisburg City Passenger Ry. Co.,

---

Central Passenger Ry. Co. v. Chatterson, 14 Ky. Law Rep. 663; Atwood v. Bangor, O. & O. T. Ry. Co., 91 Me. 399; Driscoll v. West End St. Ry. Co., 159 Mass. 142; White v. Worcester Consol. St. Ry. Co., 167 Mass. 43; Manor v. Bay Cities Consol. Ry. Co., 118 Mich. 1; Shea v. St. Paul City Ry. Co., 50 Minn. 395; Hicks v. Citizens' Ry. Co., 124 Mo. 115; Moore v. Kansas City & I. Rapid Transit Ry. Co., 126 Mo. 265; Camden, G. & W. Ry. Co. v. Preston, 59 N. J. Law, 264; Consolidated Traction Co. v. Lambertson, 59 N. J. Law, 297; Adolph v. Central Park, N. & E. R. R. Co., 76 N. Y. 530; Buhrens v. Dry Dock, E. B. & B. R. Co., 53 Hun (N. Y.) 571; Bernhard v. Rochester Ry. Co., 68 Hun (N. Y.) 369; Brozek v. Steinway Ry. Co., 10 App. Div. (N. Y.) 360; Rosenblatt v. Brooklyn Heights R. Co., 26 App. Div. (N. Y.) 600; Lawson v. Metropolitan St. Ry. Co., 40 App. Div. (N. Y.) 307; O'Neill v. Third Ave. R. Co., 3 Misc. Rep. (N. Y.) 521; Northridge v. Atlantic Ave. R. Co., 15 Misc. Rep. (N. Y.) 66; Moore v. Charlotte Elec. St. Ry. Co., 128 N. C. 455; Thomas v. Citizens' Passenger Ry. Co., 132 Pa. 504; Ehrisman v. East Harrisburg City Passenger Ry. Co., 150 Pa. 180; Breary v. Traction Co., 5 Pa. Dist. Ct. 95; Goldrick v. Union R. Co., 20 R. I. 128; Hall v. Ogden City St. Ry. Co., 13 Utah, 243; Helber v. Spokane St. Ry. Co., 22 Wash. 319.

164 Brown v. Wilmington City Ry. Co., 1 Pen. (Del.) 332; Price v.

is erroneous.[165] A few cases apparently hold that the street railway company has no superior right of way, but it is probable, from the cases referred to to support this doctrine, that no deviation from the regular rule is intended.[166] The public, therefore, have a perfect right to use any part of the street on which a street railway runs, including the tracks themselves, so long as they use reasonable care not to unnecessarily impede the progress of the cars, and to avoid the risk

150 Pa. 180; Gilmore v. Federal St. & P. V. Passenger Ry. Co., 153 Pa. 31; Gibbons v. Wilkes-Barre, &c., Ry. Co., 155 Pa. 279; Smith v. Electric Traction Co., 187 Pa. 110; Burke v. Union Traction Co., 198 Pa. 497; Smith v. Philadelphia Traction Co., 3 Pa. Super. Ct. 129; Davidson v. Schuylkill Traction Co., 4 Pa. Super. Ct. 86; Jones Bros. v. Greensburg, J. & P. St. Ry. Co., 9 Pa. Super. Ct. 65; Trout v. Altoona & L. V. Elec. Ry. Co., 13 Pa. Super. Ct. 17; Cupps v. Traction Co., 13 Pa. Super. Ct. 630; Breary v. Traction Co., 5 Pa. Dist. Ct. 95; Goldrick v. Union R. Co., 20 R. I. 128; Hall v. Ogden City St. Ry. Co., 13 Utah, 243; Helber v. Spokane St. Ry. Co., 22 Wash. 319; Tesch v. Milwaukee Elec. Ry. & Light Co., 108 Wis. 593.

---

Charles Warner Co., 1 Pen. (Del.) 462; Maxwell v. Wilmington City Ry. Co., 1 Marvel (Del.) 199; Higgins v. Wilmington City Ry. Co., 1 Marvel (Del.) 352; North Chicago Elec. Ry. Co. v. Peuser, 190 Ill. 67; West Chicago St. R. Co. v. Dougherty, 89 Ill. App. 362; Central Passenger Ry. Co. v. Chatterson, 14 Ky. Law Rep. 663; Blakeslee v. Consolidated St. Ry. Co., 105 Mich. 462; Hicks v. Citizens' Ry. Co., 124 Mo. 115; Moore v. Kansas City & I. Rapid Transit Ry. Co., 126 Mo. 265; Rosenblatt v. Brooklyn Heights R. Co., 26 App. Div. (N. Y.) 600; Lawson v. Metropolitan St. Ry. Co., 40 App. Div. (N. Y.) 307; Moore v. Charlotte Elec. St. Ry. Co., 128 N. C. 455; Ehrisman v. East Harrisburg City Passenger Ry. Co., 150 Pa. 180; Tesch v. Milwaukee Elec. Ry. & Light Co., 108 Wis. 593.

165 Chicago West Div. Ry. Co. v. Ingraham, 33 Ill. App. 351.

166 Cooke v. Baltimore Traction Co., 80 Md. 551; Lake Roland El. Ry. Co. v. McKewen, 80 Md. 593; Ludecke v. Metropolitan St. Ry. Co., 32 Misc. Rep. (N. Y.) 635.

of collisions.[167] The fact that a street car has the right of way does not give it the right to disregard the presence of wagons in the street.[168]

In Laufer v. Bridgeport Traction Co.[169] the court apparently considered that the law of the road applies to a team meeting a street car, but this doctrine has been expressly

167 Citizens' St. Ry. v. Steen, 42 Ark. 321; Swain v. Fourteenth St. R. Co., 93 Cal. 179; Snyder v. People's Ry. Co. (Del.) 53 Atl. 433; Wilman v. People's Ry. Co. (Del.) 55 Atl. 332; Louisville Ry. Co. v. Stammers, 20 Ky. Law Rep. 688; North Chicago Elec. Ry. Co. v. Peuser, 190 Ill. 67; West Chicago St. R. Co. v. Levy, 82 Ill. App. 202; North Chicago St. R. Co. v. Zeiger, 78 Ill. App. 463; Driscoll v. West End St. Ry. Co., 159 Mass. 142; White v. Worcester Consol. St. Ry. Co., 167 Mass. 43; Scannell v. Boston El. Ry. Co., 176 Mass. 170; Rascher v. East Detroit & G. P. Ry. Co., 90 Mich. 413; Moore v. Kansas City & I. Rapid Transit Ry. Co., 126 Mo. 265; Camden, G. & W. Ry. Co. v. Preston, 59 N. J. Law, 264; Adolph v. Central Park, N. & E. R. R. Co., 76 N. Y. 530; Fleckenstein v. Dry Dock, E. B. & B. R. Co., 105 N. Y. 655; Bernhard v. Rochester Ry. Co., 68 Hun (N. Y.) 369; Hennessy v. Brooklyn City R. Co., 73 Hun (N. Y.) 569; Kessler v. Brooklyn Heights R. Co., 3 App. Div. (N. Y.) 426; Johnson v. Brooklyn Heights R. Co., 34 App. Div. (N. Y.) 271; Lawson v. Metropolitan St. Ry. Co., 40 App. Div. (N. Y.) 307; Cambeis v. Third Ave. R. Co., 1 Misc. Rep. (N. Y.) 158, Arnesen v. Brooklyn City R. Co., 9 Misc. Rep. (N. Y.) 270; Cohen v. Metropolitan St. Ry. Co., 34 Misc. Rep. (N. Y.) 186; Wilbrand v. Eighth Ave. R. Co., 3 Bosw. (N. Y.) 314; Moore v. Charlotte Elec. St. Ry. Co., 128 N. C. 455; Gilmore v. Federal St. & P. V. Passenger Ry. Co., 153 Pa. 31; Gibbons v. Wilkes-Barre, etc., Ry. Co., 155 Pa. 279; Smith v. Philadelphia Traction Co., 3 Pa. Super. Ct. 129; Goldrick v. Union R. Co., 20 R. I. 128; Hall v. Ogden City St. Ry. Co., 13 Utah, 243.

168 Higgius v. Wilmington City Ry. Co., 1 Marvel (Del.) 352; Laethem v. Ft. Wayne & B. I. Ry. Co., 100 Mich. 297; Klockenbrink v. St. Louis & M. R. R. Co., 172 Mo. 678; Black v. Staten Island Elec. R. Co., 40 App. Div. (N. Y.) 238; Thoresen v. La Crosse City Ry. Co., 87 Wis. 597.

169 68 Conn. 475.

disapproved in numerous other cases.[170] Running a car on the left-hand track is not of itself negligence.[171]

Even if the driver of a team reaches a crossing first, if he sees that a motorman is not going to respect his rights, he must wait;[172] and it is error to instruct that the driver of a team has a right of way at a crossing, if he could get upon the track before the car, traveling at reasonable speed, would reach that point, since this ignores the fact that the driver's rate of speed must be reasonable.[173] The driver of a street car approaching a private road, when he has reason to believe that persons are likely to come from the private road onto the highway, must use the same care that he would use at a public crossing,[174] and this is merely ordinary care.[175]

Although the driver of a fire truck is given the right of way, by charter, when going to a fire, he is bound to have his horses under control while approaching a street car line.[176] Where a wagon and a car are traveling side by side, and a collision ensues, the presumption is against the driver of the wagon, since the car cannot leave its tracks.[177] It is error to charge that the driver of a team must use the same precaution in crossing a street railway track as is required

170 Shea v. St. Paul City Ry. Co., 50 Minn. 395; Hegan v. Eighth Ave. R. Co., 15 N. Y. 380; Whitaker v. Eighth Ave. R. Co., 51 N. Y. 295; Spurrier v. Front St. Cable Ry. Co., 3 Wash. 659.

171 Altreuter v. Hudson River R. Co., 2 E. D. Smith (N. Y.) 151.

172 Earle v. Consolidated Traction Co., 64 N. J. Law, 573.

173 New Jersey Elec. Ry. Co. v. Miller, 59 N. J. Law, 423.

174 Dunican v. Union Ry. Co., 39 App. Div. (N. Y.) 497.

175 Reardon v. Third Ave. R. Co., 24 App. Div. (N. Y.) 163.

176 Garrity v. Detroit Citizens' St. Ry. Co., 112 Mich. 369.

177 Suydam v. Grand St. & N. R. Co., 41 Barb. (N. Y.) 375.

of pedestrians.[178] The repair wagon of a street railway company has no superior right of way.[179]

A wagon has no right to unnecessarily obstruct the tracks,[180] but those in charge of the car cannot take the law into their own hands.[181] At street crossings however, the rights of the car and the team are equal, and neither has a right of way superior to that of the other.[182] This rule ap-

178 Consolidated Traction Co. v. Behr, 59 N. J. Law, 477.

179 Northridge v. Atlantic Ave. R. Co., 15 Misc. Rep. (N. Y.) 66.

180 State v. Foley, 31 Iowa, 527; Commonwealth v. Temple, 14 Gray (Mass.) 69; Commonwealth v. Hicks, 7 Allen (Mass.) 573; Wood v. Detroit City St. Ry. Co., 52 Mich. 402.

181 Camden, G. & W. Ry. Co. v. Preston, 59 N. J. Law, 264; Consolidated Traction Co. v. Haight, 59 N. J. Law, 577.

182 Eckington & S. H. R. Co. v. Hunter, 6 App. D. C. 287; Chicago General Ry. Co. v. Carroll, 91 Ill. App. 356; Marchal v. Indianapolis St. Ry. Co., 28 Ind. App. 133; Edgerton v. O'Neil, 4 Kan. App. 73; Watson v. Minneapolis St. Ry. Co., 53 Minn. 551; Moore v. Kansas City & I. Rapid Transit Ry. Co., 126 Mo. 265; Woodland v. North Jersey St. Ry. Co., 66 N. J. Law, 455; O'Neil v. Dry Dock, E. B. & B. R. Co., 129 N. Y. 125; Buhrens v. Dry Dock, E. B. & B. R. Co., 53 Hun (N. Y.) 571; Bernhard v. Rochester Ry. Co., 68 Hun (N. Y.) 369; Zimmerman v. Union Ry. Co., 3 App. Div. (N. Y.) 219; Brozek v. Steinway Ry. Co., 10 App. Div. (N. Y.) 360; Bresky v. Third Ave. R. Co., 16 App. Div. (N. Y.) 83; Huber v. Nassau Elec. R. Co., 22 App. Div. (N. Y.) 426; Reardon v. Third Ave. R. Co., 24 App. Div. (N. Y.) 163; Hergert v. Union Ry. Co., 25 App. Div. (N. Y.) 218; Kennedy v. Third Ave. R. Co., 31 App. Div. (N. Y.) 30; O'Rourke v. Yonkers R. Co., 32 App. Div. (N. Y.) 8; Read v. Brooklyn Heights R. Co., 32 App. Div. (N. Y.) 503; Weidinger v. Third Ave. R. Co., 40 App. Div. (N. Y.) 197; Lawson v. Metropolitan St. Ry. Co., 40 App. Div. (N. Y.) 307; Johnson v. Rochester Ry. Co., 61 App. Div. (N. Y.) 12; Hewlett v. Brooklyn Heights R. Co., 63 App. Div. (N. Y.) 423; Reilly v. Brooklyn Heights R. Co., 65 App. Div. (N. Y.) 453; Bruss v. Metropolitan St. Ry. Co., 66 App. Div. (N. Y.) 554; Chapman v. Atlantic Ave. R. Co., 14 Misc. Rep. (N. Y.) 384; Degnan v. Brooklyn City R. Co., 14 Misc. Rep. (N. Y.) 388;

plies to a practical continuation of an intersecting street,[183] but not to a street which bisects, but does not intersect.[184] The rule does not apply where a wagon and car come along the same street, and the wagon crosses the track at the crossing.[184a] While the doctrine of equal rights at a street crossing is true as a general rule, an instruction ignoring the construction, motive power, mode of operation, and speed of the car is erroneous.[185]

## § 111. Negligence of company—General considerations.

A street railway company must use ordinary care towards travelers, and must use reasonable care in operating its cars, and must provide competent employes.[186] It must provide its cars with suitable machinery, but it is not required to

Shanley v. Union R. Co., 14 Misc. Rep. (N. Y.) 442; Reilly v. Third Ave. R. Co., 16 Misc. Rep. (N. Y.) 11; Hunter v. Third Ave. R. Co., 21 Misc. Rep. (N. Y.) 1; Dise v. Metropolitan St. Ry. Co., 22 Misc. Rep. (N. Y.) 97; Reilly v. Metropolitan St. Ry. Co., 26 Misc. Rep. (N. Y.) 814; Reilly v. Metropolitan St. Ry. Co., 30 Misc. Rep. (N. Y.) 110; Petri v. Third Ave. R. Co., 30 Misc. Rep. (N. Y.) 254; Piercy v. Metropolitan St. Ry. Co., 30 Misc. Rep. (N. Y.) 612; Omaha St. Ry. Co. v. Cameron, 43 Neb. 297; Atlantic Coast Elec. R. Co. v. Rennard, 62 N. J. Law, 773; Earle v. Consolidated Traction Co., 64 N. J. Law, 573; Citizens' Rapid Transit Co. v. Seigrist, 96 Tenn. 119; Saunders v. City & Suburban R. Co., 99 Tenn. 130; Nashville Ry. Co. v. Norman, 108 Tenn. 324; Memphis St. Ry. Co. v. Wilson, 108 Tenn. 618.

183 Reilly v. Brooklyn Heights R. Co., 65 App. Div. (N. Y.) 453; Freeman v. Brooklyn Heights R. Co., 87 App. Div. (N. Y.) 127.

184 Hewlett v. Brooklyn Heights R. Co., 63 App. Div. (N. Y.) 423.

184a Schmedding v. New York & Q. C. Ry. Co., 82 N. Y. Supp. 1034.

185 Wilson v. Minneapolis St. Ry. Co., 74 Minn. 436.

186 West Chicago St. R. Co. v. Wizemann, 83 Ill. App. 402; Pendleton St. R. Co. v. Stallmann, 22 Ohio St. 1.

use the very latest improvements.[187] It has been held that more care is necessary in running a street car than in running a wagon or omnibus,[188] and that a higher degree of care is necessary in operating an electric car than in operating a wagon or horse car.[189]

It is generally held that, even if a plaintiff is guilty of lack of due care, he may nevertheless recover if the defendant could have prevented the accident by the exercise of due care,[190] although it is held in a few isolated cases that the

187 Maxwell v. Wilmington City Ry. Co., 1 Marvel (Del.) 199; Brown v. Wilmington City Ry. Co., 1 Pen. (Del.) 332.

188 Richmond Ry. & Elec. Co. v. Garthright, 92 Va. 627.

189 Cincinnati St. Ry. Co. v. Whitcomb, 66 Fed. 915; Winter v. Federal St. & P. V. Passenger Ry., 153 Pa. 26.

190 Cincinnati St. Ry. Co. v. Whitcomb, 66 Fed. 915; Highland Ave. & B. R. Co. v. Sampson, 91 Ala. 560; Citizens' St. Ry. Co. v. Steen, 42 Ark. 321; Cox v. Wilmington City Ry. Co. (Del.) 53 Atl. 569; Central Passenger Ry. Co. v. Chatterson, 14 Ky. Law Rep. 663, 17 Ky. Law Rep. 5; Orr v. Cedar Rapids & M. C. Ry. Co., 94 Iowa, 423; McDivitt v. Des Moines St. Ry. Co., 99 Iowa, 141; Atwood v. Bangor, O. & O. T. Ry. Co., 91 Me. 399; Lake Roland El. Ry. Co. v. McKowon, 80 Md. 593; Baltimore Traction Co. v. Appel, 80 Md. 603; Pope v. Kansas City Cable Ry. Co., 99 Mo. 400; Bindbeutal v. Street Ry. Co., 43 Mo. App. 463; Smith v. Citizens' Ry. Co., 52 Mo. App. 36; Sheehan v. Citizens' Ry. Co., 72 Mo. App. 524; McAndrews v. St. Louis & S. Ry. Co., 83 Mo. App. 233, 88 Mo. App. 97; Meyers v. St. Louis Transit Co. (Mo. App.) 73 S. W. 379; Degel v. St. Louis Transit Co. (Mo. App.) 74 S. W. 156; Septowsky v. St. Louis Transit Co. (Mo. App.) 76 S. W. 693; Barrie v. St. Louis Transit Co. (Mo. App.) 76 S. W. 706; Omaha St. Ry. Co. v. Larson (Neb.) 97 N. W. 824; Wagner v. Metropolitan St. Ry. Co., 79 App. Div. (N. Y.) 591; Ward v. Lakeside Ry. Co., 20 Pa. Co. Ct. R. 494; Hall v. Ogden City St. Ry. Co., 13 Utah, 243; Shaw v. Salt Lake City R. Co., 21 Utah, 76.

due care of the company is in question only if they actually discover the dangerous position of the plaintiff, and are not liable for a negligent failure to see him in time.[191]

A party may be guilty of wanton or willful misconduct, without actually intending to do the thing which caused the injury;[192] and where it appeared that the motorman was doing all in his power to prevent the accident, it was held that he could not be considered guilty of a wanton injury.[193] The owners of a private street railroad must use extraordinary care to avoid injury.[194]

It is held that the mere happening of a collision does not raise a presumption of negligence.[195] Where a car stopped suddenly in the middle of a street, in violation of an ordinance, this was held to be sufficient proof of negligence.[196]

Where a car, which was being negligently driven, struck a team, so that the horse ran away, and his driver was injured while trying to stop him, the company was held liable;[197] and where the driver of a sleigh turned rapidly from the track to avoid a collision, the fact that the car did not strike the sleigh does not necessarily relieve the company from the charge of negligence.[198]

191 Johnson v. Stewart, 62 Ark. 164; Austin Dam & S. Ry. Co. v. Goldstein, 18 Tex. Civ. App. 704.

192 Birmingham Ry. & Elec. Co. v. Pinckard, 124 Ala. 372.

193 Birmingham Ry. & Elec. Co. v. Franscomb, 124 Ala. 621.

194 Wilson v. Cunningham, 3 Cal. 241.

195 Kissock v. Traction Co., 15 Pa. Super. Ct. 103; Goldrick v. Union R. Co., 20 R. I. 128; North Side St. Ry. Co. v. Want, 4 Willson, Civ. Cas. Ct. App. (Tex.) § 168.

196 Mueller v. Milwaukee St. Ry. Co., 86 Wis. 340.

197 Duffy v. Street Ry. Co., 3 Ohio Dec. 678.

198 Countryman v. Fonda, J. & G. R. Co., 166 N. Y. 201.

### § 112. Negligence in operation—Lookout, speed, warning, etc.

Numerous rulings have been made as to the rights and duties of the driver, motorman, or gripman in charge of a street car. It has been held that a motorman has a right to expect that the driver of a wagon, who is turning towards the track, will stop at the warning of the gong;[199] that the driver of a wagon, who sees a car one hundred and twenty-five feet away while he is driving on the track, will turn off the track before the car reaches him;[200] and that, when a horse and wagon are standing at a safe distance from the track, the horse will not back upon the track.[201] A motorman has a right to assume that a driver on the track, who is apparently capable of taking care of himself, will leave it before the car reaches him,[202] and there is no absolute duty to ring the gong.[203] There is some difference of opinion as to the direction in which a motorman should look to avoid danger. On the one hand it is held that the motorman's eyes should be kept constantly on the track before him;[204] on the other, that a motorman must not only look ahead to see that the track is clear, but on each side, to see that no one is about to cross the track.[205] A motorman must use greater care than usual when he sees a vehicle ahead of

199 Cawley v. La Crosse City Ry. Co., 106 Wis. 239.

200 Morrissey v. Bridgeport Traction Co., 68 Conn. 215.

201 Higgins v. Wilmington City Ry. Co., 1 Marvel (Del.) 352.

202 Glazebrook v. West End St. Ry. Co., 160 Mass. 239; Citizens' St. R. Co. v. Shepherd, 107 Tenn. 444.

203 Citizens' Ry. Co. v. Holmes, 19 Tex. Civ. App. 266.

204 Smith v. Philadelphia Traction Co., 3 Pa. Super. Ct. 129.

205 City Ry. Co. v. Thompson, 20 Tex. Civ. App. 16.

him on the track,[206] and must have his car well under control at a street crossing.[207]

More care should be used by those in charge of street cars at street crossings and in crowded streets;[208] but a street railway company is under no duty to stop its cars before reaching a crossing, and to look or listen when there is no apparent reason for doing so.[209]

Evidence that a driver was looking behind him at a car to which he expected to change,[210] that a motorman omitted to look ahead to see that the track was clear,[211] and that a motorman was not at his post[212] has been held evidence of negligence; and the negligence of a motorman approaching a crossing cannot be limited to the moment when he notices a person trying to cross the track.[213] Where a car is suddenly stopped and backed, there should be some one on the rear platform to look out for travelers.[214] Where the driver of a team was aware of the approach of a car, it was held not to be negligence on the part of the motorman not to warn

206 North Chicago St. R. Co. v. Allen, 82 Ill. App. 128.

207 Memphis St. Ry. Co. v. Wilson, 108 Tenn. 618; West Chicago St. R. Co. v. Petters, 196 Ill. 298; Schoener v. Metropolitan St. Ry. Co., 72 App. Div. (N. Y.) 23; Wilson v. Citizens' St. Ry. Co., 105 Tenn. 74.

208 Price v. Charles Warner Co., 1 Pen. (Del.) 462; Chicago City Ry. Co. v. Jennings, 157 Ill. 274; West Chicago St. R. Co. v. McCallum, 169 Ill. 240; Jacksonville Ry. Co. v. Lamb, 86 Ill. App. 487; Thoresen v. La Crosse City Ry. Co., 87 Wis. 597.

209 Savannah, T. & I. of H. Ry. v. Beasley, 94 Ga. 142.

210 Thoresen v. La Crosse City Ry. Co., 87 Wis. 597.

211 Swain v. Fourteenth St. R. Co., 93 Cal. 179.

212 Montgomery v. Johnson, 22 Ky. Law Rep. 596.

213 Chicago City Ry. Co. v. Anderson, 193 Ill. 9.

214 Central Ry. Co. v. Knowles, 93 Ill. App. 581, affirmed 191 Ill. 241.

him by ringing the bell.[215] In Kestner v. Pittsburgh & B. Traction Co.[216] it was held that a motorman's duty is to use reasonable care under the circumstances, and, where a motorman's attention was momentarily diverted by a duty connected with the safe carriage of his passengers, it was held that this duty was paramount to his duty to keep a constant lookout for travelers.[217]

The high speed of a car is evidence of negligence,[218] and when, in addition, no warning was given, this makes a still stronger case.[219]

215 Murray v. St. Louis Transit Co. (Mo.) 75 S. W. 611; Huber v. Nassau Elec. R. Co., 22 App. Div. (N. Y.) 426; Coyle v. Third Ave. R. Co., 18 Misc. Rep. (N. Y.) 9; Williamson v. Metropolitan St. Ry. Co., 29 Misc. Rep. (N. Y.) 324; Anderson v. Metropolitan St. Ry. Co., 30 Misc. Rep. (N. Y.) 104.

216 158 Pa. 422.

217 Culbertson v. Metropolitan St. Ry. Co., 140 Mo. 35.

218 Chicago City Ry. Co. v. Sandusky, 198 Ill. 400; North Chicago St. R. Co. v. Rodert (Ill.) 67 N. E. 812; Marchal v. Indianapolis St. Ry. Co., 28 Ind. App. 133; Galbraith v. West End St. Ry. Co., 165 Mass. 572; Ryan v. Detroit Citizens' St. Ry. Co., 123 Mich. 597; Westphal v. St. Joseph & B. H. St. Ry. Co. (Mich.) 96 N. W. 19; Hughes v. Camden & Suburban Ry. Co., 65 N. J. Law, 203; Brozek v. Steinway Ry. Co., 10 App. Div. (N. Y.) 360; Blate v. Third Ave. R. Co., 44 App. Div. (N. Y.) 163; Knoll v. Third Ave. R. Co., 46 App. Div. (N. Y.) 527; Morris v. Metropolitan St. Ry. Co., 63 App. Div. (N. Y.) 78; Kilbane v. Westchester Elec. R. Co., 19 Misc. Rep. (N. Y.) 184; Street Ry. Co. v. Rohner, 3 Ohio Dec. 570; Gress v. Railway Co., 14 Pa. Super. Ct. 87; Hamilton v. Consolidated Traction Co., 201 Pa. 351; San Antonio Traction Co. v. Upson (Tex. Civ. App.) 71 S. W. 565.

219 Howard v. Indianapolis St. Ry. Co., 29 Ind. App. 514; Driscoll v. West End St. Ry. Co., 159 Mass. 142; Shea v. St. Paul City Ry. Co., 50 Minn. 395; Campbell v. St. Louis & S. Ry. Co. (Mo.) 75 S. W. 86; Dennis v. North Jersey St. Ry. Co., 64 N. J. Law, 439; Brennan v. Metropolitan St. Ry. Co., 60 App. Div. (N. Y.) 264;

In some cases the circumstances are such that the courts have no hesitation in declaring a street railway company to be guilty of negligence as a matter of law. Thus, there was held to be negligence where a dummy train was driven at high speed on a dark night without giving any warning;[220] where a car with no headlight came around a corner at full speed, without ringing any bell, in the nighttime;[221] where a car came at a prohibited rate of speed without giving any signal;[222] where the driver of a car started his car, and ran into a wagon which was in the act of turning around forty feet away;[223] and where the driver of a wagon turned into a side street, and the repair wagon of a street railway company, which was being driven rapidly behind him, collided with his team.[224] When a heavy sprinkling cart was on the track, it was held that the motorman was not justified in giving a signal when he was seven hundred feet away, and then increasing his speed on the assumption that the cart would get out of the way;[225] and when a collision occurred at about 5 o'clock on a November morning, and the motorman

O'Callaghan v. Metropolitan St. Ry. Co., 69 App. Div. (N. Y.) 574; Andres v. Brooklyn Heights R. Co., 84 App. Div. (N. Y.) 596; Strauss v. Brooklyn Heights R. Co., 82 N. Y. Supp. 767; Sophian v. Metropolitan St. Ry. Co., 38 Misc. Rep. (N. Y.) 787; Greenfield v. East Harrisburg Passenger Ry. Co., 178 Pa. 194; Frame v. Electric Traction Co., 180 Pa. 49; Kaechele v. Traction Co., 15 Pa. Super. Ct. 73; Fenner v. Wilkes-Barre & W. V. Traction Co., 202 Pa. 365; Dederichs v. Salt Lake City R. Co., 13 Utah, 34; Hanlon v. Milwaukee Elec. Ry. & Light Co. (Wis.) 95 N. W. 100.

220 Hennessy v. Brooklyn City R. Co., 73 Hun (N. Y.) 569.

221 Cooke v. Baltimore Traction Co., 80 Md. 551.

222 Savannah St. R. Co. v. Jackson, 95 Ga. 366.

223 Riegelman v. Third Ave. R. Co., 9 Misc. Rep. (N. Y.) 51.

224 Northridge v. Atlantic Ave. R. Co., 15 Misc. Rep. (N. Y.) 66.

225 Abrahams v. Los Angeles Traction Co., 124 Cal. 411.

testified that the car was going twenty-five miles an hour, and that he was asleep, this was held to be such an utter want of care as not to be excused even by the plaintiff's negligence.[226] It is negligence to overcrowd a car so that it cannot be readily stopped at a street crossing.[227] It is negligence not to have a car under control in a crowded street.[228]

Where there were double tracks, and a driver, turning from one track to another, was struck by a car coming at high speed, negligence is for the jury;[229] and also where a car came from the rear of a wagon at high speed.[230] Where a wagon was standing very near the tracks,[231] and where one was of necessity actually upon the tracks after dark,[232] negligence in both cases was held to be for the jury.

226 Mapes v. Union Ry. Co., 56 App. Div. (N. Y.) 508.

227 Richmond Ry. & Elec. Co. v. Garthright, 92 Va. 627.

228 Dallas Consol. Elec. St. Ry. Co. v. Illo (Tex. Civ. App.) 73 S. W. 1076.

229 Jackson v. Pittsburgh, A. & M. Traction Co., 159 Pa. 399; Thatcher v. Central Traction Co., 166 Pa. 66; Harper v. Philadelphia Traction Co., 175 Pa. 129; Julius v. Pittsburg, A. & M. Traction Co., 184 Pa. 19.

230 Wilkins v. Omaha & C. B. Ry. & Bridge Co., 96 Iowa, 668; Hart v. Cedar Rapids & M. C. Ry. Co., 109 Iowa, 631; Vincent v. Norton & T. St. Ry. Co., 180 Mass. 104; Rascher v. East Detroit & G. P. Ry. Co., 90 Mich. 413; Blakeslee v. Consolidated St. Ry. Co., 112 Mich. 63; Tunison v. Weadock (Mich.) 89 N. W. 703; Boettcher v. Detroit Citizens' St. Ry. Co. (Mich.) 91 N. W. 125; White v. Vicksburg R. Power & Mfg. Co. (Miss.) 31 So. 709; Klockenbrink v. St. Louis & M. R. R. Co., 172 Mo. 678; Noll v. St. Louis Transit Co. (Mo. App.) 73 S. W. 907; Fishbach v. Steinway Ry. Co., 11 App. Div. (N. Y.) 152; Blum v. Metropolitan St. R. Co., 79 App. Div. (N. Y.) 611.

231 Koch v. St. Paul City Ry. Co., 45 Minn. 407.

232 McGrane v. Flushing & C. P. Elec. Ry. Co., 13 App. Div. (N. Y.) 177.

It has been held in a number of cases that, where the driver of a wagon turns suddenly in front of an approaching car, there is no evidence of negligence on the part of the company;[233] and where a wagon and a street car are proceeding side by side, and the wagon was turned so that it struck the car, there was held to be no evidence of negligence.[234] Where the driver of a wagon and the driver of a car both thought a wagon was stopped at a safe distance from the track, but both miscalculated the distance, there was held to be either no negligence on the part of the company or joint negligence, and therefore no recovery.[235] It is error to leave to the jury the question as to whether a street railway company should have a flagman at a crossing.[236] Where a train on a dummy line backed suddenly, owing to some unauthorized person meddling with the brake, there was held to be no negligence on the part of the company.[237]

Proof of violation of a city ordinance regulating the speed of a car is not negligence as a matter of law,[238] although the contrary has been held;[239] and the mere fact of a collision

233 Kessler v. Citizens' St. R. Co., 20 Ind. App. 427; Hemingway v. New Orleans City & Lake R. Co., 50 La. Ann. 1087; Cowden v. Shreveport Belt Ry. Co., 106 La. 236; Mathieson v. Omaha St. Ry. Co. (Neb.) 92 N. W. 639; Thomas v. Citizens' Passenger Ry. Co., 132 Pa. 504; Kane v. People's Passenger Ry. Co., 181 Pa. 53; McManigal v. South Side Passenger Ry. Co., 181 Pa. 358; Nashville Ry. Co. v. Norman, 108 Tenn. 324.

234 Rombach v. Crescent City R. Co., 50 La. Ann. 473.

235 Patton v. Philadelphia Traction Co., 132 Pa. 76.

236 Eckington & S. H. R. Co. v. Hunter, 6 App. D. C. 287.

237 Rome St. R. Co. v. McGinnis, 94 Ga. 229.

238 Davidson v. Schuylkill Traction Co., 4 Pa. Super. Ct. 86; Hall v. Ogden City St. Ry. Co., 13 Utah, 243.

239 Meyers v. St. Louis Transit Co. (Mo. App.) 73 S. W. 379.

between an electric car and a wagon is not enough to show that the car was running at an improper rate of speed.[240] The schedule of a company is no excuse if it requires its cars to run at excessive speed.[241] In the absence of an ordinance, a car may be run at any rate of speed which is not dangerous.[242]

The distance of the team from the track is another circumstance to be considered. Negligence is for the jury where a truck is caught in the track when an electric car was three hundred feet away;[243] and where a car was nearly a block away;[244] where a man in charge of a car saw a team three hundred and thirty feet away,[245] two hundred and fifty feet away,[246] one hundred and fifty feet away,[247] one hundred and thirty-three feet away;[248] and where there was evidence that a motorman could have seen a team ahead of him on the track in time to avoid a collision.[249] Where there was a collision at a crossing, and the wagon was visible one hundred feet away, negligence was held to be for the jury.[250] Where a motorman does all in his power, there is no negligence,[250a] and the company has the right to show that the collision was a pure accident.[250b]

240 Guilloz v. Ft. Wayne & B. I. Ry. Co., 108 Mich. 41.

241 Central Ry. Co. v. Allmon, 147 Ill. 471.

242 Citizens' St. Ry. v. Steen, 42 Ark. 321.

243 Saffer v. Westchester Elec. Ry. Co., 22 Misc. Rep. (N. Y.) 555.

244 Ludecke v. Metropolitan St. Ry. Co., 32 Misc. Rep. (N. Y.) 635.

245 Raulston v. Traction Co., 13 Pa. Super. Ct. 412.

246 Watkins v. Atlantic Ave. R. Co., 20 Hun (N. Y.) 237.

247 Strauss v. Newburgh Elec. Ry. Co., 6 App. Div. (N. Y.) 264.

248 McCormack v. Nassau Elec. R. Co., 16 App. Div. (N. Y.) 24.

249 Woelfel v. Federal St. & P. V. P. Ry. Co., 183 Pa. 213.

250 Cass v. Third Ave. R. Co., 20 App. Div. (N. Y.) 591; Kerr v. Atlantic Ave. R. Co., 10 Misc. Rep. (N. Y.) 264.

250a Ellermann v. St. Louis Transit Co. (Mo. App.) 76 S. W. 661.

250b Atlanta Ry. & Power Co. v. Gaston (Ga.) 45 S. E. 508.

The condition of the street is another factor. Negligence is a question for the jury where the place of a collision was a narrow space between the track and the sidewalk,[251] the track and a hedge,[252] and the track and a wall;[253] and the same ruling has been made where there were snowbanks on each side of the street, and the driver of a cab stopped on the track to receive orders,[254] and where a wagon was driven under a viaduct, and was struck by a car coming fifteen or twenty miles an hour.[255]

When it was the motorman's duty to have his car under control, it was held that a slippery track was no excuse.[256]

Numerous miscellaneous rulings have been made on the question of negligence where the facts are somewhat out of the ordinary. For instance, negligence is for the jury where there was a block of wagons and other cars on the track;[257] where a brake on a street car was in good order, but could not be depended upon to check the car on a wet track;[258] where the driver of a team was signaled to cross by the company's watchman, and was struck by a car coming at high speed;[259] and where a car came over the crest of a hill at a high rate of speed.[260] Where there was a space of eight

251 Tarler v. Metropolitan St. Ry. Co., 21 Misc. Rep. (N. Y.) 684.

252 Geipel v. Steinway Ry. Co., 14 App. Div. (N. Y.) 551.

253 Gibbons v. Wilkes-Barre, etc., St. Ry. Co., 155 Pa. 279.

254 Mullen v. Central Park & E. R. R. Co., 1 Misc. Rep. (N. Y.) 216.

255 Tait v. Buffalo Ry. Co., 55 App. Div. (N. Y.) 507.

256 Sickler v. North Jersey St. Ry. Co. (N. J. Law) 46 Atl. 779.

257 Kerrigan v. West End St. Ry. Co., 158 Mass. 305; Lenkner v. Citizens' Traction Co., 179 Pa. 486.

258 Chicago City Ry. Co. v. Mager, 185 Ill. 336.

259 Haney v. Pittsburgh, A. & M. Traction Co., 159 Pa. 395.

260 Cannon v. Pittsburg & B. Traction Co., 194 Pa. 159.

fect between the side of a bridge and the track, and a collision took place at this point, negligence was held to be for the jury.[261] Where a car followed close behind a buggy, and a collision ensued, negligence was held to be for the jury.[262] Where a truck is near the track, the conductor must look out, as well as the motorman.[262a]

Where a street car stopped suddenly in front of the first carriage in a funeral procession, causing it to stop so suddenly that it collided with the second carriage, the sudden stopping of the car was held to be the proximate cause of the injury;[263] and where a car struck a wagon, which in turn struck the wagon of the plaintiff, it was held that, if the company and the driver of the wagon were jointly negligent, the plaintiff could recover.[264] In Wilson v. Duluth St. Ry. Co.,[265] "stations at each end of the lines" in a statute was construed to mean stations at each end of the tracks, and not at each end of the run of particular cars. An ordinance requiring a vigilant watch in the case of all street railways governs a cable road.[266]

Where a car slipped back while ascending a grade from a ferry, and struck a team,[267] and where a motorman tried to pass a carriage standing near the tracks,[268] negligence in each case was held to be for the jury.

261 Reilly v. Troy City Ry. Co., 32 App. Div. (N. Y.) 131.

262 Hicks v. Citizens' Ry. Co., 124 Mo. 115; Connor v. Metropolitan St. Ry. Co., 77 App. Div. (N. Y.) 384.

262a Martin v. Interurban St. Ry. Co., 84 N. Y. Supp. 921.

263 Mueller v. Milwaukee St. Ry. Co., 86 Wis. 340.

264 Comey v. Philadelphia Traction Co., 175 Pa. 133.

265 64 Minn. 363.

266 Lamb v. St. Louis Cable & W. Ry. Co., 33 Mo. App. 489.

267 Cook v. Metropolitan R. Co., 98 Mass. 361.

268 O'Leary v. Brockton St. Ry. Co., 177 Mass. 187.

Any one of several tort feasors may be held responsible for the entire tort,[269] but the law will not enforce contribution between tort feasors.[270] An ordinance requiring the conductor and driver of each car to keep a vigilant watch, and to stop the car in the shortest possible time on the first appearance of danger, does not apply to a cable car.[271] It has been held that an ordinance will not bind a street railway company unless there is evidence that it agreed to it;[272] but see the late cases of Gebhardt v. St. Louis Transit Co.,[273] and McLain v. St. Louis & S. Ry. Co.[274]

A street car should be lighted at night, and between twilight and dark, if not lighted, should be run slowly enough to avoid collisions, or else should give warning of its approach;[275] and in Calumet Elec. St. Ry. Co. v. Lynholm[276] it was held that a street car company should have such a headlight on the car as to enable a motorman to see a wagon on a track on a dark night in time to prevent a collision. Not having a headlight is not negligence as matter of law.[277]

## II. FRIGHTENING HORSES.

**The driver of a horse must use reasonable care to avoid an accident from the horse taking fright at a street car, and if he needlessly exposes himself to danger he cannot recover.**

[269] West Chicago St. R. Co. v. Feldstein, 69 Ill. App. 36; Comey v. Philadelphia Traction Co., 175 Pa. 133.

[270] Rend v. Chicago West Div. Ry. Co., 8 Ill. App. 517.

[271] Glenville v. St. Louis R. Co., 51 Mo. App. 629.

[272] Sanders v. Southern Elec. Ry. Co., 147 Mo. 411; McAndrews v. St. Louis & S. Ry. Co., 83 Mo. App. 233.

[273] (Mo. App.) 71 S. W. 448.

[274] (Mo. App.) 73 S. W. 909.

[275] Rascher v. East Detroit & G. P. Ry. Co., 90 Mich. 413.

[276] 70 Ill. App. 371.

[277] Frank v. St. Louis Transit Co. (Mo. App.) 73 S. W. 239.

**A street railway company cannot be made liable by the mere fact that a horse took fright, and the man in charge of the car is not required to stop or check his speed, or to omit the customary signals merely because a horse shows signs of fright. He must do what he reasonably can, however, in every case to avoid an injury.**

### § 113. Due care of driver of horse.

The driver of a horse, especially an unbroken or uncertain horse, should exercise very great care to pass the cars in safety, but he must be allowed a reasonable opportunity to accustom his horse to the sight and sound of the car.[278] It is not lack of due care, as matter of law, to take horses along a street without knowledge as to what will be their probable conduct on the approach of a car.[279] A person who drives a young horse alongside of an electric street railway for the express purpose of testing the horse is guilty of contributory negligence, and cannot recover for injuries sustained through the fright of the horse.[280] Similarly where the plaintiff voluntarily exposed himself to the risk of an accident, which was caused by his mule's taking fright at the usual noise made by an electric car, he was held unable to recover;[281] and a man who drives along a street railway track when he knows that a train is likely to pass, and knows that his horses are afraid of cars, cannot recover unless the defendant, in the exercise of due care, could have prevented the accident.[282]

[278] Flewelling v. Lewiston & A. Horse R. Co., 89 Me. 585.

[279] Doran v. Cedar Rapids & M. C. Ry. Co., 117 Iowa, 442. And see Montgomery St. Ry. v. Hastings (Ala.) 35 So. 412.

[280] Cornell v. Detroit Elec. Ry. Co., 82 Mich. 495.

[281] Doster v. Charlotte St. Ry. Co., 117 N. C. 651.

[282] Moore v. Kansas City & I. R. Transit Ry. Co., 126 Mo. 265.

Where the driver of a hack stood by the door of the carriage reading a paper, and a snow plow operated on the track frightened his horses, it was held that a nonsuit would have been proper, and that the plaintiff could not complain of a verdict for six cents.[283]

Where the plaintiff drove his team in a narrow space between the track and a wall, due care was held to be for the jury.[284]

Whether a woman was wanting in due care because a horse was an improper one for her to manage, and because she failed to look for a car before entering upon a street, has been held to be for the jury;[285] and even although the plaintiff's evidence tends to show that his horse was unsuitable, and that he knew it, or should have known it, if the court cannot say that such were the facts, as a matter of law, a verdict for the plaintiff will not be disturbed.[286]

The lack of due care of the owner of a horse cannot be imputed to a person driving with him, who is not the owner of the horse, and has no part in the management of the wagon.[287] A person placed in sudden peril is not held to the usual standard of care.[288]

## § 114. Negligence of company.

A street railway company cannot be made liable from the mere fact that a horse took fright at an electric car,[289] since

283 Gray v. Second Ave. R. Co., 65 N. Y. 561.

284 Gibbons v. Wilkes-Barre, etc., St. Ry. Co., 155 Pa. 279; Adsit v. Catskill Elec. Ry. Co., 84 N. Y. Supp. 393.

285 Benjamin v. Holyoke St. Ry. Co., 160 Mass. 3.

286 Thompson v. Holyoke St. Ry. Co., 170 Mass. 365.

287 Metropolitan St. R. Co. v. Powell, 89 Ga. 601.

288 Richmond Ry. & Elec. Co. v. Hudgins (Va.) 41 S. E. 736.

289 Kankakee Elec. Ry. Co. v. Lade, 56 Ill. App. 454; Galesburg

an electric car running in the ordinary way is not a defect in the highway, or an object naturally calculated to frighten horses of ordinary gentleness.[290]

Mere fright on the part of horses does not show that the driver is in peril, for the presumption is that he will be able to control them.[291] A motorman is not required to slow up or stop his car every time a horse shows signs of uneasiness, and is not bound to stop his car simply because a horse on the same street is frightened,[292] but, on the contrary, may proceed at the usual speed, and with the usual noise, so long as he does not show a wanton disregard for the safety of the driver.[293] A driver must take the risk of the ordinary signals which a street car is bound to give;[294] and it has been held that it is the duty of a gripman to ring his bell as he approaches a street crossing, and that he is not liable where horses took fright at the noise.[295] Similarly

Elec. Motor & Power Co. v. Manville, 61 Ill. App. 490; Terre Haute Elec. Ry. Co. v. Yant, 21 Ind. App. 486; Marion City Ry. Co. v. Dubois, 23 Ind. App. 342; Lincoln Traction Co. v. Moore (Neb.) 97 N. W. 605; Hazel v. People's Passenger Ry. Co., 132 Pa. 96; Yingst v. Lebanon & A. St. Ry. Co., 167 Pa. 438; Smith v. Holmesburg, T. & F. Elec. Ry. Co., 187 Pa. 451; Davison v. Wilkes-Barre & W. V. Traction Co., 10 Pa. Super. Ct. 442; Bishop v. Belle City St. Ry. Co., 92 Wis. 139; Flaherty v. Harrison, 98 Wis. 559.

290 Bishop v. Belle City St. Ry. Co., 92 Wis. 139.

291 East St. Louis & St. L. Elec. St. Ry. Co. v. Wachtel, 63 Ill. App. 181.

292 Eastwood v. La Crosse City Ry. Co., 94 Wis. 163.

293 Molyneux v. Southwest Missouri Elec. Ry. Co., 81 Mo. App. 25; Chapman v. Zanesville St. Ry. Co., 27 Wkly. Law Bul. (Ohio) 70; Myers v. Brantford St. Ry., 27 Ont. App. 513.

294 East St. Louis & St. L. Elec. St. Ry. Co. v. Wachtel, 63 Ill. App. 181.

295 Philadelphia Traction Co. v. Bernheimer, 125 Pa. 615; Steiner v. Philadelphia Traction Co., 134 Pa. 199.

it has been held that ringing the gong is a necessary warning, and that mere fright at such noise does not show negligence.[296] Where a driver allowed his horses to remain near the track until they became unmanageable, there was held to be no evidence of negligence on the part of the company.[297]

Where the man in charge of the car does notice the fright of a horse near the track, his duty is to do what he reasonably can to avoid injury;[298] and it has been further held that it is not enough for a motorman to do what he reasonably can after he discovers a horse's fright, but that he must also do what he reasonably can to discover the plaintiff's peril.[299] It has been held that, if danger is apparent, he must cease ringing his gong and stop the car;[300] that he must slacken speed, and, if necessary to avoid injury, stop the car altogether;[301] and the negligence of a motorman in not checking speed has been held to be for the jury.[302] To ring a gong and not to slacken speed after seeing the fright

[296] North Side St. Ry. Co. v. Tippens, 4 Willson, Civ. Cas. Ct. App. § 160.

[297] Coughtry v. Willamette St. Ry. Co., 21 Or. 245.

[298] East St. Louis & St. L. Elec. St. Ry. Co. v. Wachtel, 63 Ill. App. 181; Doran v. Cedar Rapids & M. C. Ry. Co., 117 Iowa, 442; Ellis v. Lynn & B. R. Co., 160 Mass. 341; Danville Ry. & Elec. Co. v. Hodnett (Va.) 43 S. E. 606.

[299] Doran v. Cedar Rapids & M. C. Ry. Co., 117 Iowa, 442.

[300] Galesburg Elec. Motor & Power Co. v. Manville, 61 Ill. App. 490.

[301] Muncie St. Ry. Co. v. Maynard, 5 Ind. App. 372; Citizens' St. Ry. Co. v. Lowe, 12 Ind. App. 47.

[302] Adsit v. Catskill Elec. Ry. Co., 84 N. Y. Supp. 393; Kelly v. Pittsburg & B. Traction Co., 10 Pa. Super. Ct. 644; Lines v. Winnipeg Elec. St. Ry. Co., 11 Manitoba, 77.

of a horse has been held to be negligence;[303] and where there was evidence that the motorman might have seen the danerous position of the plaintiff, but went by at a speed of eight or ten miles an hour, it was held that a verdict for the plaintiff would not be disturbed.[304] Negligence in ringing a gong near a frightened horse has been held to be for the jury.[305]

Where a horse was frightened by noise and sparks, but there was not shown to be any defect in construction or negligence in operation, a verdict for the defendant was held to be rightly ordered.[306] The rule that a steam railroad company is not liable for fright of horses from escaping steam or the blowing of whistles in the usual operation of the road applies with all its force to street car companies;[307] but where the engineer on a dummy engine sounded his whistle in an unusual manner as he approached the plaintiff's wagon,[308] and where he blew off steam after seeing that the plaintiff's horses were frightened,[309] negligence in

303 Richter v. Cicero & P. St. Ry. Co., 70 Ill. App. 196; Springfield Consol. Ry. Co. v. Ankrom, 93 Ill. App. 655; Owensboro City R. Co. v. Lyddane, 19 Ky. Law Rep. 698; Benjamin v. Holyoke St. Ry. Co., 160 Mass. 3; Ellis v. Lynn & B. R. Co., 160 Mass. 341; Oates v. Metropolitan St. Ry. Co., 168 Mo. 535; Citizens' Ry. Co. v. Hair (Tex. Civ. App.) 32 S. W. 1050.

304 Marion St. R. Co. v. Carr, 10 Ind. App. 200.

305 Lightcap v. Philadelphia Traction Co., 60 Fed. 212; Philadelphia Traction Co. v. Lightcap, 61 Fed. 762.

306 Henderson v. Greenfield & T. F. St. Ry. Co., 172 Mass. 542.

307 Wachtel v. East St. Louis & St. L. Elec. Ry. Co., 77 Ill. App. 465.

308 Lott v. Frankford & S. Passenger R. Co., 159 Pa. 471.

309 Hanlon v. Philadelphia & W. C. Turnpike Road Co., 182 Pa. 115.

each case was held to be for the jury; and to discharge a sudden jet of steam as a horse was passing has been held to establish a *prima facie* case.[310] In the case last cited, where it appeared that the horse was accustomed to the dummy engine, and the driver drove him between the track and the curb by the side of a passing train, the due care of the driver was held to be for the jury. Where an electric car ran through a pool of water, making a loud and unusual noise,[311] and where black coats were allowed to hang on an electric sprinkler,[312] negligence in each case was held to be for the jury. Where a car ran at great speed at a place where the ground near the track was obstructed, and a frightened horse was injured while trying to get over an embankment, negligence was held to be for the jury;[313] and also where a man drove in a narrow space between the track and a wall.[314] It is not enough that the noise made by an electric car is unusual. It must be unnecessary as well;[315] but a loud and unusual noise, and a volume of smoke issuing from the car, raises a presumption of negligence.[316]

Where a horse suddenly reared and fell over dead, it was held that whether he took fright at a street car or not was absolute conjecture, and that the company was not liable.[317]

310 Stamm v. Southern R. Co., 1 Abb. N. C. (N. Y.) 438.

311 Ayars v. Camden & Suburban Ry. Co., 63 N. J. Law, 416.

312 McCann v. Consolidated Traction Co., 59 N. J. Law, 481.

313 Geipel v. Steinway Ry. Co., 14 App. Div. (N. Y.) 551; Greeley v. Federal St. & P. V. Passenger Ry., 153 Pa. 218.

314 Gibbons v. Wilkes-Barre, etc., St. Ry. Co., 155 Pa. 279.

315 Hill v. Rome St. R. Co., 101 Ga. 66.

316 Richmond Ry. & Elec. Co. v. Hudgins (Va.) 41 S. E. 736.

317 Hazel v. People's Passenger Ry. Co., 132 Pa. 96.

Where the cause of a horse's fright is uncertain, the company is not liable.[318] Where a horse was frightened by an unusual noise of passengers on a car, the company was held not liable;[319] and although an ordinance forbade rails projecting above the street, this was held not to be the proximate cause of the fright of a horse when the wagon scraped along the rails.[320] It is not negligence to start an electric car in the ordinary manner while horses which show no signs of fright are being driven past.[321] Where a horse took fright at the repair wagon of a street railway company, it was held that the repair wagon had a right to repair overhead wires for a reasonable time, and that its right was superior to that of the drivers of teams.[322] Where a motorman had to choose one of two courses, and chose the least successful in good faith, he was held not to be negligent.[323]

Where a trolley wire broke, and there was noise and flashing of electricity, so that the plaintiff's horse was frightened, this was held to raise a presumption of negligence.[324] In City & Suburban Ry. Co. v. Moores[325] it was held that, although work is done by an independent contractor, the persons hiring him may nevertheless be liable if they should have anticipated the injury, or if the work must result in

318 North Chicago St. R. Co. v. Harms, 59 Ill. App. 374.

319 Boatwright v. Chester & M. Elec. Ry. Co., 4 Pa. Super. Ct. 279.

320 Mayor of Macon v. Dykes, 103 Ga. 847.

321 McDonald v. Toledo Consol. St. Ry. Co., 74 Fed. 104.

322 Potter v. Scranton Traction Co., 38 Wkly. Notes Cas. (Pa.) 453.

323 Bishop v. Belle City St. Ry. Co., 92 Wis. 139.

324 Kepner v. Harrisburg Traction Co., 183 Pa. 24.

325 80 Md. 348.

a nuisance, or if they owe a duty to a third person or the public in the execution of the work. It was held in the same case that a steam engine is not a nuisance *per se.* Where a horse was frightened at something falling from a window, and ran into a pile of iron rails used in rebuilding a railway track, the proximate cause of the accident was held to be for the jury.[326]

[326] Bleil v. Detroit St. Ry. Co., 98 Mich. 228.

# CHAPTER VIII.

## BICYCLE RIDERS; HORSEBACK RIDERS; ANIMALS RUN OVER.

I. Bicycle Riders.

§ 115. Due Care.
116. Negligence.

II. Horseback Riders.

§ 117. In General.

III. Animals Run Over.

§ 118. In General.

### I. Bicycle Riders.

### § 115. Due care.

A bicycle rider was held not to be in the exercise of due care when he attempted to cross in front of a car coming at high speed, and in plain sight seventy-five feet away;[1] and where two men on a tandem tried to cross directly in front of a car, and were injured, they were likewise held not to be in the exercise of due care.[2] A man cannot recover when he looks to the east before crossing a track, and is struck by a car coming from the west, and it appears that, if he had looked when he was twenty-eight feet from the track, he could have seen the car.[3] If a bicycle rider

1 Chicago North Shore St. Ry. Co. v. McCarthy, 66 Ill. App. 667.

2 Lurie v. Metropolitan St. Ry. Co., 18 Misc. Rep. (N. Y.) 81.

3 Bennett v. Detroit Citizens' St. Ry. Co., 123 Mich. 692.

suddenly swerves against the car when he is riding parallel with the track, he cannot recover.[4] Although a person on a bicycle has a right to use the slot of a cable road, and need not look back as a matter of law, he must nevertheless use a degree of care commensurate with the danger of the place where he chooses to ride;[5] and where a bicycle rider rode between the tracks in front of a rapidly moving electric train without looking back, and without hearing the gong and other warnings, he was held not to be in the exercise of due care.[6] One who rides dangerously near the track and fails to look behind him for three hundred feet is not in the exercise of due care.[7]

Where a man rode in the narrow space between two tracks, and suddenly turned in front of an electric car,[8] and where a man turned from one track, and ran into a car coming in the opposite direction on a parallel track,[9] there was held to be lack of due care in both cases; but where, under the latter state of facts, a boy of ten was injured, and there was evidence that the car could have been stopped if it had not been for defective appliances, due care and negligence were held to be for the jury.[10] A bicycle rider who went on a street railway track at night in a state of intoxication, and was run over, was held not to be in the exercise of due care.[11]

4 South Chicago City Ry. Co. v. Kinnare, 96 Ill. App. 210.

5 Rooks v. Houston, W. S. & P. Ferry R. Co., 10 App. Div. (N. Y.) 98.

6 Everett v. Los Angeles Consol. Elec. Ry. Co., 115 Cal. 105.

7 Robards v. Indianapolis St. Ry. Co. (Ind. App.) 66 N. E. 66.

8 Gagne v. Minneapolis St. Ry. Co., 77 Minn. 171.

9 Medcalf v. St. Paul City Ry. Co., 82 Minn. 18.

10 Roberts v. Spokane St. Ry. Co., 23 Wash. 325.

11 Chicago North Shore Ry. Co. v. Green, 93 Ill. App. 105.

If a bicycle rider stops on the track, it is not lack of due care not to look for a car, when no gong is sounded.[11a]

Where a deaf man rode in the space between the parallel tracks of a street railway, and was struck by a car approaching from behind, it was held that, since he was deaf, he was bound to use more care in looking, and was guilty of gross negligence.[12] Where a bicycle rider was riding in a bent position, and was injured by a hose reaching from a hydrant to a street railway company's tank car, due care was held to be for the jury.[13]

A bicycle rider riding between the tracks of a street railway in the same direction as the cars must turn out for a wagon belonging to a street railway company which is approaching in the opposite direction, in spite of an act putting bicycles on the same footing with vehicles, and an ordinance giving vehicles going in the same direction as the car the right on the track over those going in the opposite direction.[14]

In two cases where a boy on a velocipede was run over, a verdict for the plaintiff was held to be justified.[15]

Where a man on a bicycle was run over by a car going north on the south-bound track at midnight, due care and negligence were held to be for the jury.[16]

11a Zolpher v. Camden & S. Ry. Co. (N. J. Err. & App.) 55 Atl. 249.

12 Nein v. La Crosse City Ry. Co., 92 Fed. 85.

13 Morhart v. North Jersey St. Ry. Co., 64 N. J. Law, 236.

14 Taylor v. Union Traction Co., 184 Pa. 465.

15 City & Suburban Ry. Co. v. Waldhaur, 84 Ga. 706; Phillips v. Duquesne Traction Co., 183 Pa. 255.

16 North Chicago St. R. Co. v. Irwin, 202 Ill. 345.

## § 116. Negligence.

There was held to be no evidence of negligence where a bicycle rider suddenly turned in front of a car;[17] and where a boy was crossing a street on a bicycle, and ran into a car which he did not see until it was almost on him.[18] Where a man on a bicycle rode behind a car, and then turned suddenly in front of a car coming in the opposite direction, there was held to be no negligence on the part of the company;[19] and where a man was riding a bicycle on a dry asphalt pavement, and it appeared that both rubber and dry asphalt were nonconductors of electricity, the plaintiff was held unable to recover, under the circumstances.[20]

Where a boy of nine, riding a bicycle, was run over on a crowded street, and there was evidence that the car was run at high speed without warning,[21] and where a bicycle rider was injured by a hose reaching from a hydrant to a street railway company's tank car,[22] negligence in each case was held to be for the jury. Where a girl unused to bicycle riding was caught on a street railway track, and there was evidence that the company could have avoided the injury, a verdict for the plaintiff was held to be justified.[23]

Where an electric wire falls in a city street, injuring a

17 Zolpher v. Camden & S. Ry. Co. (N. J. Err. & App.) 55 Atl. 249; Schroder v. Metropolitan St. Ry. Co., 84 N. Y. Supp. 371; Sauers v. Union Traction Co., 193 Pa. 602.

18 Gould v. Union Traction Co., 190 Pa. 198.

19 Cardonner v. Metropolitan St. Ry. Co., 26 App. Div. (N. Y.) 8, 38 App. Div. 597.

20 Walters v. Syracuse Rapid Transit Ry. Co., 64 App. Div. (N. Y.) 150.

21 Phillips v. Duquesne Traction Co., 183 Pa. 255.

22 Morhart v. North Jersey St. Ry. Co., 64 N. J. Law, 236.

23 Louisville Ry. Co. v. Blaydes, 21 Ky. Law Rep. 480, 668.

bicycle rider, this raises a presumption of negligence.[24] Where the rider of a bicycle was injured while using the slot of a cable road, because it was unusually wide, a verdict that this was a nuisance was held to be justified.[25] Where a deaf bicycle rider did not understand the signals of his companions that a car was approaching, and there was evidence that the motorman saw these signals were unheeded, the case was held to be rightly left to the jury.[26]

Where a bicycle rider is injured by the negligence of a contractor, and the contractor is exercising some charter privilege of the street car company with its consent, which he could not exercise independently of its charter, he will be regarded as the servant of the corporation.[27] Even if the plaintiff was not in the exercise of due care, he may recover if the defendant, in the exercise of ordinary care, could have prevented the accident,[27a] but this rule does not apply where the plaintiff's lack of due care was a contributing cause.[27b]

## II. Horseback Riders.

### § 117. In general.

A car has the right of way over travelers on horseback, and they should allow a car coming from the opposite direction to pass without impediment.[28] Although a car has the right of way, the motorman must use due care, and, although

24 Chattanooga Elec. Ry. Co. v. Mingle, 103 Tenn. 667.

25 Brown v. Metropolitan St. Ry. Co., 60 App. Div. (N. Y.) 184.

26 Bedell v. Detroit, Y. & A. A. Ry. (Mich.) 92 N. W. 349.

27 Suburban R. Co. v. Balkwill, 94 Ill. App. 454.

27a Harrington v. Los Angeles Ry. (Cal.) 74 Pac. 15; Metropolitan St. Ry. Co. v. Arnold (Kan.) 72 Pac. 857.

27b Robards v. Indianapolis St. Ry. Co. (Ind. App.) 67 N. E. 953.

28 Jatho v. Green & C. St. Passenger Ry. Co., 4 Phila. (Pa.) 24.

he is not required to stop when he sees a horse is frightened, he must have his car under control.[29] When a motorman is suddenly confronted by a runaway horse on which a person is riding, he cannot be held to the usual standard of care;[30] and where a newsboy on horseback went directly in front of a car, there was held to be no negligence;[31] while in Omaha St. Ry. Co. v. Duvall,[32] where a man on horseback went in front of a car, the question whether the motorman could have prevented the accident was held to be for the jury. It is not lack of due care, as a matter of law, to ride alongside of the track.[33] Where the plaintiff was riding one horse and leading another, and was struck by a car, a verdict in his favor was held to be justified;[34] but in Harman v. Pennsylvania Traction Co.,[35] where a boy was riding one of a pair of mules, which suddenly became unmanageable, and went directly in front of a car, there was held to be no negligence. Where a horseback rider was run over in a city street, it was held negligence to have the car in charge of a boy of eighteen, with only three weeks' experience.[35a]

## III. Animals Run Over.

### § 118. In general.

In Smith v. St. Paul City Ry. Co.,[36] where an electric car ran over a dog, it was held that a verdict in favor of the

29 Danville Ry. & Elec. Co. v. Hodnett (Va.) 43 S. E. 606.

30 Phillips v. People's Passenger Ry. Co., 190 Pa. 222.

31 Schutt v. Shreveport Belt R. Co., 109 La. 500.

32 40 Neb. [illegible]

33 Brooks v. Lincoln St. Ry. Co., 22 Neb. 816.

34 Berke v. Twenty-Third St. Ry. Co., 4 N. Y. Supp. 905.

35 200 Pa. 311.

35a Crisman v. Shreveport Belt Ry. Co. (La.) 34 So. 718.

36 79 Minn. 254.

owner of the dog would not be disturbed; and in Citizens' Rapid Transit Co. v. Dew[37] it was held that an owner could maintain an action for the wrongful killing of his dog, and that a motorman could not rely upon the quickness of the dog so as to excuse himself from all duty to avoid running over him. A dog may be rightfully upon the track of a street car company, and, if the motorman could have avoided the accident by the exercise of due care, he is negligent.[38] Where a dog was running on the tracks, and there were banks of snow on each side, it was held that the motorman would not be justified in running him down, and that whether he was negligent in not discovering the danger in time is a question for the jury. The due care of the owner of the dog is also for the jury.[39] Where a dog was caught by an electric car in the middle of a block, while the car was running at unusual speed, this was held insufficient to show negligence.[40] In Fullerton v. Cedar Rapids & M. C. Ry. Co.,[41] where a cow was run over, it was held error to instruct that, if the car was going so fast that it could not be stopped in time to avoid an accident, this was negligence, since the cow might have come suddenly in front of the car. Where a cow was run over, the question of a sufficient headlight was held to be for the jury;[41a] and in a similar case it was held that it must be shown that the car could have been stopped or checked after the danger was known, or should have been known.[41b]

37 100 Tenn. 317.

38 West Chicago St. R. Co. v. Klecka, 94 Ill. App. 346.

39 Meisch v. Rochester Elec. Ry. Co., 72 Hun (N. Y.) 604.

40 Dettmers v. Brooklyn Heights R. Co., 22 App. Div. (N. Y.) 488.

41 101 Iowa, 156.

41a Ensley v. Detroit United Ry. (Mich.) 96 N. W. 34.

41b Kotila v. Houghton County St. Ry. Co. (Mich.) 96 N. W. 437.

# CHAPTER IX.

## ACCIDENTS FROM DEFECTS IN CONSTRUCTION AND OPERATION.

I. Electric Shock.

§ 119. Care of Company.
120. Presumption of Negligence.
121. Negligence in Operation.

II. Obstructions—Defects in Track—Defects in Operation.

§ 122. Liability of Company—City, Contractor, Lessee, etc.
123. Excavations between or near Tracks.
124. Obstruction near Track.
125. Defects in Tracks.
126. Wire.
127. Obstructing Tracks by Snow, Dirt, etc.
128. Miscellaneous.

## I. Electric Shock.

**It is generally held that the company must use a high degree of care where electricity is used, and in many cases the mere happening of the accident is enough to raise a presumption of negligence. This is by no means the invariable rule, however, as the conduct of the plaintiff may show such a lack of due care as to absolve the company from liability.**

### § 119. Care of company.

While a street railway company is not an insurer of safety in the use of electric wires,[1] according to most of the cases

[1] City Elec. St. Ry. Co. v. Conery, 61 Ark. 381.

it is held to the exercise of a high degree of care. This duty is differently expressed in different cases. It is held that the company must use the highest degree of care,[2] and that, where a highly dangerous force is used, correspondingly great care must be used.[3] In other cases the degree of care necessary has been held to be reasonable care under all the circumstances;[4] and in Calumet Elec. St. Ry. Co. v. Grosse[5] it was held that, where an electric wire is so arranged that it will not injure anybody in the exercise of his rights upon the highway, the company is under no duty to have absolutely protected the insulation, so that no person, however extraordinary his duties may be, will be injured by it.

An electric street railway must adopt all usual methods to prevent contact between its wires and the wires of a telephone company on the same highway;[6] and the fact that a street car company has authority to erect wires, and the fact that it erects them in a proper manner, will not excuse the company when it knowingly permits a telephone wire to be suspended over its own in such a manner that it is

2 Thomas' Adm'r v. Maysville Gas Co., 21 Ky. Law Rep. 1690; Macon v. Paducah St. Ry. Co., 23 Ky. Law Rep. 46; Lexington R. Co. v. Fain's Adm'r, 24 Ky. Law Rep. 1443; Memphis St. Ry. Co. v. Kartright (Tenn.) 75 S. W. 719.

3 Neal v. Wilmington & N. C. Elec. Ry. Co., 3 Pen. (Del.) 467; Godfrey v. Streator Ry. Co., 56 Ill. App. 378.

4 Atlanta Consol. St. Ry. Co. v. Owings, 97 Ga. 663; Kennealy v. Westchester Elec. Ry. Co., 86 App. Div. (N. Y.) 293; Central Pennsylvania Tel. Co. v. Wilkes-Barre & W. S. Ry. Co., 1 Pa. Dist. Ct. 628; Citizens' Ry. Co. v. Gifford, 19 Tex. Civ. App. 631.

5 70 Ill. App. 381.

6 Central Pennsylvania Tel. Co. v. Wilkes-Barre & W. S. Ry. Co., 1 Pa. Dist. Ct. 628.

likely to cause injury, or when it allows the wire to remain crossed on the ground, whereby two horses are injured.[7] In Block v. Milwaukee St. Ry. Co.[8] it was held that negligence in not having a guard wire over the trolley wires to prevent contact with falling telephone wires was a question for the jury; and where a horse was killed, and it appeared that a telephone company negligently allowed its wires to fall upon the trolley wire of an electric street railway company, and the latter company had no guard wire, and failed to notice the condition of the broken telephone wire, although a prudent man in the business of either company would have noticed it, both companies were held liable.[9] In a case of defective insulation, it has been held that frequent inspection is not enough, but that the company must know of the defect.[9a]

## § 120. Presumption of negligence.

In many cases the mere happening of the accident is held sufficient to raise a presumption of negligence, as where a horse was injured by an electric shock while crossing a street railway track,[10] and where a horse was killed from a shock from a broken electric wire hanging loose in the street.[11] Similarly there was held to be a presumption of negligence where a pedestrian was injured by an electric shock from

[7] McKay v. Southern Bell Tel. Co., 111 Ala. 337.

[8] 89 Wis. 371.

[9] Electric Ry. Co. v. Shelton, 89 Tenn. 423.

[9a] Potts v. Shreveport Belt Ry. Co. (La.) 34 So. 103.

[10] Trenton Passenger Ry. Co. v. Cooper, 60 N. J. Law, 219; Clarke v. Nassau Elec. R. Co., 9 App. Div. (N. Y.) 51.

[11] Larson v. Central Ry. Co., 56 Ill. App. 263; Smith v. Brooklyn Heights R. Co., 81 N. Y. Supp. 838.

stepping on the rail of a street railway track,[12] and where a broken wire struck a traveler.[13] In O'Flaherty v. Nassau Elec. R. Co.,[14] where a broken trolley wire injured a traveler, this was held to raise a presumption of negligence which the defendant did not rebut by evidence of its system of inspection; and where a boy was injured by a shock from a broken telephone wire, a finding that the current came from a trolley wire running below it will be sustained without positive proof as to the contact, where there is no other reasonable theory to explain how the telephone wire became charged.[15] In Chattanooga Elec. Ry. Co. v. Mingle[16] it was held that, where a wire charged with electricity falls in a city street, this raises a presumption of negligence; and where an unused telephone wire broke, and was allowed to hang for two weeks over a trolley wire, and to become charged with electricity, so that a child in the street received a shock, this was held to raise a presumption of negligence.[17]

## § 121. Negligence in operation.

Although electricity is thus held to be such a dangerous agency, the company is not held liable in every case. Where an employe engaged in taking down electric wires was warned of his danger, and he disregarded the warning, and was injured, he was held not to be in the exercise of due

12 Ludwig v. Metropolitan St. Ry. Co., 71 App. Div. (N. Y.) 210; Braham v. Nassau Elec. R. Co., 72 App. Div. (N. Y.) 456.

13 Jones v. Union Ry. Co., 18 App. Div. (N. Y.) 267; Clancy v. New York & Q. C. Ry. Co., 81 N. Y. Supp. 875; Memphis St. Ry. Co. v. Kartright (Tenn.) 75 S. W. 719.

14 34 App. Div. (N. Y.) 74.

15 City Elec. St. Ry. Co. v. Conery, 61 Ark. 381.

16 103 Tenn. 667.

17 Western Union Tel. Co. v. State, 82 Md. 293.

care.[18] Where an employe of a telephone company received a shock from the wire of a street railway company, and it did not appear that the plaintiff had any permission, or was anything more than a trespasser, it was held that no action could be maintained;[19] and where a man was riding a bicycle on dry asphalt, and it appeared that both rubber and dry asphalt were nonconductors of electricity, the plaintiff was held, under all the circumstances of the case, to be unable to recover.[20] Where an experienced lineman of an electric light company touched a wire of a street car company in a dangerous place, and at the same time touched an iron post with his naked hand, and completed the circuit, it was held that these facts did not show negligence on the part of the company;[21] and where the lineman of a telephone company climbed the pole of a street railway company, when he could have gone up the telephone pole, and received a shock, it was held that he must use active diligence, and had no right to assume that the wires were in a safe condition.[22] In like manner, where an experienced lineman of a telephone company allowed the contact of two wires, which he could have prevented, he was held not to be in the exercise of due care.[23] Where a boy climbed over the girder of a bridge, and was burned by a guard wire which had somehow become charged with electricity, there was held

18 Tri-City Ry. Co. v. Killeen, 92 Ill. App. 57.

19 Augusta Ry. Co. v. Andrews, 89 Ga. 653; Sias v. Lowell, L. & H. St. Ry. Co., 179 Mass. 343.

20 Walters v. Syracuse Rapid Transit Ry. Co., 64 App. Div. (N. Y.) 150.

21 Huber v. La Crosse City Ry. Co., 92 Wis. 636.

22 Jackson & S. St. R. R. & Tel. Cos. v. Simmons, 107 Tenn. 392.

23 Bergin v. Southern New England Tel. Co., 70 Conn. 54.

not to be sufficient evidence of negligence.[24] Where an employe of a contractor employed to paint poles was injured, due care and negligence were held to be for the jury.[24a]

Where the trolley pole of a car knocked down a telephone wire, and a horse was killed by the shock, a verdict for the plaintiff was held to be justified;[25] and where a charged wire hung down for two or three weeks, and finally injured a boy, and there was evidence that the company had notice of its condition, this was held to be evidence of gross negligence.[26] Where a charged wire was allowed to hang down in a city street, and a boy of fourteen touched it, there was held to be sufficient evidence of negligence, and due care was held to be for the jury.[27]

## II. Obstructions—Defects in Track—Defects in Operation.

**In general, a street railway company must construct its tracks in a reasonably careful manner, and must keep them in a reasonably safe condition, so that they will not render the street unsafe for ordinary travel. This principle applies to excavations between or near the tracks, obstructions near the track, obstructing the track with snow, defects in the track itself, and the care of wires and other appliances used in the general operation of the road.**

**A traveler, on the other hand, must use reasonable care to avoid danger, and in many cases the existence of the defect is held to be sufficient warning.**

24 Freeman v. Brooklyn Heights R. Co., 54 App. Div. (N. Y.) 596.

24a Kennealy v. Westchester Elec. Ry. Co., 86 App. Div. (N. Y.) 293.

25 Kankakee Elec. Ry. Co. v. Whittemore, 45 Ill. App. 484.

26 Macon v. Paducah St. Ry. Co., 23 Ky. Law Rep. 46.

27 Lexington R. Co. v. Fain's Adm'r, 24 Ky. Law Rep. 1443.

**In some cases of negligence the street railway company is not held liable, but a city, contractor, or a lessee is compelled to assume the responsibility for the accident.**

### § 122. Liability of company—City, contractor, lessee, etc.

In many cases where negligence on the part of some one is undisputed, the question has arisen whether a street railway company itself is liable, or whether it is able to place the responsibility upon some other party.

It is clear that two street car companies are jointly and severally liable for their concurrent negligence;[28] but where a street railway company was allowed to lay a track by a connecting road, which assumed the duty of keeping it in repair, the defendant was held not to be liable for the sinking of the adjoining cross walk.[29]

A street railway company which takes possession of and operates a road under a lease from another company assumes all the duties imposed upon the lessors in their original incorporation;[30] and, on the other hand, if the lessor leases a street railway with knowledge of its defective condition, he cannot give as an excuse that it is in the hands of the lessee.[31] It is the duty of a street railway company as to third persons to keep in repair that portion of a switch which is a part of its own track, and forms a connection with the track of a railway of another corporation, although, as between the corporations, the duty of repairing may rest upon the latter.[32]

28 Rahenkamp v. Traction Co., 14 Pa. Super. Ct. 635; Shelton v. Northern Texas Traction Co. (Tex. Civ. App.) 75 S. W. 338.

29 Lowery v. Brooklyn City & N. R. Co., 76 N. Y. 28.

30 Mullen v. Philadelphia Traction Co., 19 Phila. (Pa.) 441.

31 Schaefer v. City of Fond Du Lac, 99 Wis. 333.

32 McKenna v. Metropolitan R. Co., 112 Mass. 55.

Where an injury was caused because of an excavation between the tracks, and the company had agreed with the city to keep the streets in and about the tracks in repair, an action was held maintainable against the company.[33] It is no excuse that a pole was erected according to the company's charter and the city ordinance,[34] or that a street railway track is approved by the city;[35] and a street railway company is not excused for a defective rail because of permission from the city to operate its road.[36]

Where a street railway company allows a defect in its tracks, and a city suffers the defect to continue, both are liable;[37] and if a street railway company agrees to keep its crossing in good repair, it is liable for a defective culvert at a crossing, although a city itself may not be liable for injuries from defective streets,[38] since a street car company which has contracted, as consideration for its franchises, to keep the street between its rails in repair, is held to a stricter performance of its duty than a municipal corporation.[39] A street railway company must repair a known defect, irrespective of a statute or notice from the proper authorities.[40]

A street railway company, however, is not liable for the condition of a drain between its tracks, when the drain is constructed by the city, and the company is not at liberty

33 City of Brooklyn v. Brooklyn City R. Co., 47 N. Y. 475; McMahon v. Second Ave. R. Co., 75 N. Y. 231.

34 Cleveland v. Bangor St. Ry., 86 Me. 232.

35 Houston City St. Ry. Co. v. Delesdernier, 84 Tex. 82.

36 Dominguez v. Orleans R. Co., 35 La. Ann. 751.

37 Union St. Ry. Co. v. Stone, 54 Kan. 83; Doyle v. City of New York, 58 App. Div. (N. Y.) 588.

38 Houston City St. Ry. Co. v. Dawson, 2 Tex. Unrep. Cas. 223.

39 Mahnke v. New Orleans City & Lake R. Co., 104 La. 411.

40 Simon v. Metropolitan St. Ry. Co., 29 Misc. Rep. (N. Y.) 126.

to make alterations;[41] and, similarly, the company is not liable for the condition of a drain maintained by order of the city,[42] or for a hole between the rails of its tracks caused by the negligence of a city plumber.[43] Where a child was run over, and a street railway company had laid its tracks according to the directions of the road supervisors, and there was no evidence that the accident occurred by reason of the way in which they laid their track, there was held to be no evidence of negligence.[44]

As a general rule, a street railway company is not liable for the negligence of an independent contractor, since the company has no control over the work,[45] but this is not an invariable rule. The company is liable where it contracts with the state to see that the work is properly done,[46] and is liable where work is done by a contractor under the supervision of the superintendent of the railroad company, subject to his approval.[47] Where repairs were being made under the charge of officers of the street railway company, it was held that they were bound to give warning to the public of the dangerous condition of the road.[48] The dangerous character of the work which is being done may be consid-

41 Snell v. Rochester Ry. Co., 64 Hun (N. Y.) 476.

42 Campbell v. Frankford & S. C. Ry. Co., 139 Pa. 522.

43 Citizens' Passenger Ry. Co. v. Ketcham, 122 Pa. 228.

44 Miller v. Lebanon & A. St. Ry. Co., 186 Pa. 190.

45 Fulton County St. R. Co. v. McConnell, 87 Ga. 756; Hauser v. Metropolitan St. Ry. Co., 27 Misc. Rep. (N. Y.) 538; Thomas v. Altoona & L. V. Elec. Ry. Co., 191 Pa. 361; Sanford v. Pawtucket St. Ry. Co., 19 R. I. 537.

46 Weber v. Buffalo Ry. Co., 20 App. Div. (N. Y.) 292.

47 Donovan v. Oakland & B. Rapid Transit Co., 102 Cal. 245.

48 Wagner v. Pittsburgh & W. E. Passenger Ry., 158 Pa. 419.

ered; and in Woodman v. Metropolitan R. Co.[49] it was held that the mere fact that work was being done under an independent contractor would not exonerate the company from liability. If work is being done by a contractor, but no evidence of the relation of the contractor to the company is introduced, the responsibility of the company is properly submitted to the jury.[50]

### § 123. Excavation between or near tracks.

One who drives upon a street railway track assumes the ordinary risks, such as the risk arising from a deep rut outside the rail.[51] Where a plaintiff sued for an injury from an unguarded trench, it was held that the visible condition of the highway may of itself be a warning to one driving over it;[52] and where it was perfectly safe to alight on one side of the car, and a woman chose to alight on the other, and fell into a ditch which could have been easily seen, she was held not to be in the exercise of due care.[53] Where a woman fell into an open manhole without looking where she was going, in broad daylight, she was held not to be in the exercise of due care;[54] and where a woman was driving with her husband, and they fell into a ditch, the contributory negligence of the husband was held to be imputable to the wife.[55] Although a driver knows that wires are negligently exposed, he is not guilty of lack of due care, as a

49 149 Mass. 335.

50 Slayton v. West End St. Ry. Co., 174 Mass. 55.

51 Kornetzski v. City of Detroit, 94 Mich. 341.

52 Rowell v. Stamford St. R. Co., 64 Conn. 376.

53 Bland v. Roxborough, C. H. & N. Ry. Co., 13 Pa. Super. Ct. 93.

54 Lumis v. Philadelphia Traction Co., 181 Pa. 268.

55 McFadden v. Santa Ana, O. & T. St. Ry. Co., 87 Cal. 464.

matter of law, if he drives upon them because his horses are partially beyond control.[56] A number of cases of accidents arising from excavations in the street have been held properly left to the jury.[57]

Where a horse stepped into a hole between the rails of a horse car track, and it did not appear that it was the duty of the company to keep this space in repair, there was held to be no negligence;[58] and where a horse stepped into a hole a foot square and four feet deep, and the cause and the company's knowledge of the hole were both uncertain, it was held that a nonsuit was properly entered;[59] but where an employe testified that a dangerous hole had existed for three or four weeks, the company was held clearly negligent.[60]

## § 124. Obstruction near track.

In a number of cases where a traveler has tripped over rails or bars left in the street, the case has been held to be one for the jury,[61] but one who attempts to pass over pav-

56 Farmer v. Findlay St. Ry. Co., 60 Ohio St. 36.

57 Citizens' St. R. Co. v. Marvil (Ind.) 67 N. E. 921; Kearns v. South Middlesex St. R. Co., 181 Mass. 587; Oakland Ry. Co. v. Fielding, 48 Pa. 320; Kraut v. Frankford & S. P. City Passenger Ry., 160 Pa. 327; McLaughlin v. Philadelphia Traction Co., 175 Pa. 565; Leary v. Electric Traction Co., 180 Pa. 136; Fielders v. North Jersey St. Ry. Co., 67 N. J. Law, 76.

58 Egan v. Forty-Second St., M. & St. N. A. R. Co., 4 N. Y. Supp. 530.

59 Sanford v. Union Passenger Ry. Co., 16 Pa. Super. Ct. 393.

60 Conroy v. Twenty-Third St. R. Co., 52 How. Pr. (N. Y.) 49.

61 Slayton v. West End St. Ry. Co., 174 Mass. 55; Thomas v. Consolidated Traction Co., 62 N. J. Law, 36; Wells v. Steinway Ry. Co., 18 App. Div. (N. Y.) 180; Higgins v. Brooklyn, Q. C. & S. R. Co., 54 App. Div. (N. Y.) 69; Parkes v. Metropolitan St. Ry. Co., 76 N. Y. Supp. 983; Southside Passenger Ry. Co. v. Cox, 2 Mona. (Pa.) 140.

ing stones scattered across the sidewalk in the daytime assumes the risk of the injury;[62] and where repairs were being made, and some granite blocks were lying in the street, the driver of a team was held guilty of lack of due care when his horse stepped on a block.[63] Where a plaintiff knew that a rail was on the sidewalk, and had seen others fall over it, but forgot it was there, it was held that she was not in the exercise of due care, and the company's failure to keep a lantern there, as required by an ordinance, was held no excuse for the plaintiff for not using ordinary care.[64] Where a street railway company tore up the street to lay its tracks, and replaced the paving, a pedestrian has the right to presume that the street is safe.[65] Where a horse became frightened at something falling from a window, and ran into a pile of iron rails used in rebuilding a street railway track, the frightening of the horse was held to be the proximate cause of the injury.[66]

### § 125. Defects in tracks.

A traveler on a public street is bound to use reasonable care to avoid danger;[67] and a defective track is no excuse if a driver could have avoided a collision by the exercise of due care.[68] If the driver of a team sees a defect in the tracks, and chooses to drive over it, he is not in the exercise of due care;[69] and where there was evidence that a track

62 Grandorf v. Detroit Citizens' St. Ry. Co., 113 Mich. 496.
63 Watson v. Brooklyn City R. Co., 14 Misc. Rep. (N. Y.) 405.
64 Davis v. California St. Cable R. Co., 105 Cal. 131.
65 Union Traction Co. v. Barnett (Ind. App.) 67 N. E. 205.
66 Bleil v. Detroit St. Ry. Co., 98 Mich. 228.
67 Indianapolis St. Ry. Co. v. Walton, 29 Ind. App. 368.
68 Joslin v. Grand Rapids Ice & Coal Co., 53 Mich. 322.
69 Calumet Elec. St. Ry. Co. v. Nolan, 69 Ill. App. 104.

projected three or four inches above the street, and that the driver of a hose carriage knew this, it was held that, if he drove recklessly over the track in the nighttime he could not recover.[70] Where a pedestrian stumbled over a plank two inches above the level of a bridge of a street railway company, she was held not to be in the exercise of due care.[71] In a number of cases, where the driver of a team was injured while driving over a defective track, due care was held to be a question for the jury.[72] Where the driver of a hose cart knew that a street railway company had been notified of a defect, and had promised to repair it, it was held that this was one circumstance to be considered on the question of due care, and that reliance on such a promise could not defeat the defense of contributory negligence.[73] Where a switch extended higher than was reasonable above the pavement, and was concealed by snow, which the company had melted by the use of salt, the due care of the driver of a team was held to be for the jury;[74] and if a driver waives his right to the rule of the road, and, turning to the left, is injured by a defective track, this will not excuse the railroad company.[75] Where a boy stepped with his bare feet on a rail heated by electricity, and there was nothing to warn the plaintiff of his danger, due care was held to be for

70 Smith v. Union Ry. Co., 61 Mo. 588.

71 Peetz v. St. Charles St. R. Co., 42 La. Ann. 541.

72 Hawks v. Inhabitants of Northampton, 121 Mass. 10; Cook v. Union Ry. Co., 125 Mass. 57; Bradwell v. Pittsburgh & W. E. Passenger Ry. Co., 153 Pa. 105.

73 Houston City St. Ry. Co. v. Reichart, 87 Tex. 539.

74 Wooley v. Grand St. & N. R. Co., 83 N. Y. 121.

75 Atlanta St. R. Co. v. Walker, 93 Ga. 462.

the jury.[76] Where a woman caught her foot under a rail, a verdict for the plaintiff was not disturbed.[77]

In general it is held that a street railway company must construct its tracks in a reasonably careful manner, and must maintain them in a reasonably safe condition, so that they will not render the street unsafe for ordinary travel.[78] There is evidence of negligence for the jury where it appeared that a rail had been loose for a week,[79] where there was a defective gutter,[80] in cases of loose rails and projecting spikes,[81] in the case of a loose plank in a bridge,[82] and where a horse was caught in the slot of a cable road.[83] Where a traveler was injured by a projecting rail, but not at a regular crossing, it was held error to instruct that the company was guilty of negligence unless they might have anticipated that people were liable to cross at that point.[84]

76 Kane v. West End St. Ry. Co., 169 Mass. 64.

77 Williams v. Minneapolis St. Ry. Co. (Minn.) 92 N. W. 479.

78 Citizens' St. R. Co. v. Ballard, 22 Ind. App. 151; Groves v. Louisville Ry. Co., 22 Ky. Law Rep. 599; Cline v. Crescent City R. Co., 41 La Ann. 1031; Bangs v. Lewiston & A. Horse R. Co., 89 Me. 104; Baumgartner v. City of Mankato, 60 Minn. 244; Worster v. Forty-Second St. & G. St. Ferry R. Co., 50 N. Y. 203; Mazetti v. New York & H. R. Co., 3 E. D. Smith (N. Y.) 98; Gray v. Washington Water Power Co., 27 Wash. 713, 30 Wash. 665.

79 Schnell v. Metropolitan St. Ry. Co., 50 App. Div. (N. Y.) 616.

80 Mayberry v. Second & Third Sts. Ry. Co., 15 Phila. (Pa.) 253.

81 Cline v. Crescent City R. Co., 43 La. Ann. 327; Cook v. Union Ry. Co., 125 Mass. 57; Schild v. Central Park, N. & E. R. R. Co., 16 N. Y. Supp. 701; Fash v. Third Ave. R. Co., 1 Daly (N. Y.) 148; Carpenter v. Central Park, N. & E. R. R. Co., 11 Abb. Pr. (N. S.; N. Y.) 416.

82 Murphy v. Suburban Rapid Transit Co., 60 N. Y. Super. Ct. 9.

83 Humbert v. Brooklyn Cable Co., 12 N. Y. State Rep. 172.

84 Wiley v. Smith, 25 App. Div. (N. Y.) 351.

Where a wheel caught in the slot of a cable line, it was held that the company was liable for defects in original construction or for defects likely to occur from the action of the elements, or from traffic upon the streets;[85] and where a rail became worn and split so that the defect was apparent, it was held error to enter a nonsuit, for a street railway company is bound to know that the action of the elements will produce defects in rails, and must make continuous inspections to discover apparent defects.[86]

If a rail complained of as a defect is necessary to the operation of a street railway, and the railway is constructed in the proper manner, although the rail may be an obstacle to travel, it will not, on that account, be a defect in the way.[87] Omission to know of a patent defect is *prima facie* negligence.[88]

Where a wheel caught in the slot of a cable line, it was held that the plaintiff need not show knowledge on the part of the company, since its duty was to exercise continuous inspection;[89] but in two cases of injury from a defective rail, where there was evidence of proper inspection, there was held to be no negligence on the part of the company.[90] Where a company lays its tracks in accordance with the grade planned, but not yet finished, it is liable if the street

85 Griveaud v. St. Louis Cable & W. Ry. Co., 33 Mo. App. 458.

86 Gilton v. Hestonville, M. & F. Passenger Ry., 166 Pa. 460.

87 Fowler v. Inhabitants of Gardner, 169 Mass. 505.

88 Worster v. Forty-Second St. & G. St. Ferry R. Co., 50 N. Y. 203.

89 Keitel v. St. Louis Cable & W. Ry. Co., 28 Mo. App. 657.

90 Casper v. Dry Dock, E. B. & B. R. Co., 23 App. Div. (N. Y.) 451, 56 App. Div. 372; Kelly v. Metropolitan St. Ry. Co., 25 Misc. Rep. (N. Y.) 194.

is unsafe until the change is made,[91] but the level of the roadbed need not conform to irregularities in the street.[92] Where a horse was injured by a nail used by a street railway company in constructing or repairing its tracks, it was held that this alone was not sufficient to show negligence.[93] Where a driver was thrown from his wagon while turning off the tracks, but merely from the jolt caused by so doing, the company was held not liable.[94]

In Robbins v. Omnibus R. Co.[95] it was held, on the construction of a statute, a street railway company was not required to keep the part of the street between a double track in repair.

## § 126. Wire.

A brakeman passing from the top of one car to another without necessity therefor, and striking a wire of an electric street car company, with the position of which he is familiar, is not in the exercise of due care;[96] and where an employe of a steam railroad was standing on the roof of a freight car, and was injured by a wire of an electric street railway, it was held negligence not to give the steam railroad sufficient space to pass without danger to its employes, but it was further held that, if the employe knew or should have known of the danger, he must be held to have assumed the risk.[97]

91 McKillop v. Duluth St. Ry. Co., 53 Minn. 532.

92 Galveston City Ry. Co. v. Nolan, 53 Tex. 139.

93 Houston City St. Ry. Co. v. Autrey, 4 Tex. Civ. App. 635.

94 Nivette v. New Orleans & L. S. R. Co., 42 La. Ann. 1153.

95 32 Cal. 472.

96 Danville St. Car Co. v. Watkins, 97 Va. 713.

97 Erslew v. New Orleans & N. R. Co., 49 La. Ann. 86.

In Banks v. Highland St. Ry. Co.,[98] where the employe of a telegraph company was climbing a telegraph pole without permission from the city, and was injured by a street car running against the wire attached to his person, it was held that he was doing an illegal act, which contributed to his injury, and precluded his maintaining an action, unless the driver of the car acted recklessly or wantonly. Where two men on a team were injured by a wire which was allowed to hang so low that it grazed the horse and struck the men in the face, due care was held to be for the jury.[99]

Where a traveler was injured by a falling trolley wire, it was held that the jury might find negligence without knowing just why the wire broke at that particular time and place.[100] In Read v. City & Suburban Ry. Co.[101] it was held that, if a wire sags, and a traveler is injured before the company had a reasonable time to make repairs, the company is not liable if the sagging is caused by the falling of the wire of another company, and this could not ordinarily have been expected. It was further held that notice to the motorman and conductor of the car would not be notice to the company, and that the negligence of a servant while driving his master is imputable to the master. Where the wire of a street railway company was hanging at such a height that ordinary cars of a steam railroad could pass in safety with persons standing on the top of them, an employe of a steam railroad standing on an unusually high car was held unable to recover on the ground that there was no

98 136 Mass. 485.

99 Lloyd v. City & Suburban Ry. Co., 110 Ga. 165.

100 Citizens' St. R. Co. v. Batley, 159 Ind. 368.

101 115 Ga. 366.

negligence.[102] A street railway company is not liable for the negligence of an independent contractor in placing a wire across a highway, where it has no control over the contractor.[103] Where a wagon was struck by a wire broken by a trolley of a car, and there was evidence that the custom was to tie down the trolley pole, and the conductor, though told to do so by another conductor, refused, the case is for the jury.[104]

### § 127. Obstructing tracks by snow, dirt, etc.

In removing snow from its tracks, a street railway company must have due regard for the rights of the public, and must not create dangerous obstructions in the street.[105] In case of an extraordinary storm, the company must make extraordinary efforts.[106] The company is not negligent, however, if they allow snow taken from between the rails to remain standing in the street near the track for a few hours in the daytime;[107] and the same ruling was made where the obstruction was a pile of dirt.[108] There is no negligence

102 Gross v. South Chicago City Ry. Co., 73 Ill. App. 217.

103 Sanford v. Pawtucket St. Ry. Co., 19 R. I. 537.

104 Schenkel v. Pittsburg & B. Traction Co., 194 Pa. 182.

105 McDonald v. Toledo Consol. St. Ry. Co., 74 Fed. 104; Ovington v. Lowell & S. St. R. Co., 163 Mass. 440; Bowen v. Detroit City Ry. Co., 54 Mich. 496; Wallace v. Detroit City Ry. Co., 58 Mich. 231; Laughlin v. Street Ry. Co., 62 Mich. 220; Smith v. Nashua St. Ry., 69 N. H. 504; Dixon v. Brooklyn City & N. R. Co., 100 N. Y. 170; Schrank v. Rochester Ry. Co., 83 Hun (N. Y.) 290; Markowitz v. Dry Dock, E. B. & B. R. Co., 12 Misc. Rep. (N. Y.) 412; Friedman v. Dry Dock, E. B. & B. R. Co., 11 N. Y. Supp. 429; Somerville v. City R. Co., 17 N. Y. Supp. 719; Gerrard v. La Crosse City R. Co., 113 Wis. 258.

106 Bowen v. Detroit City Ry. Co., 54 Mich. 496.

107 Zanger v. Detroit City Ry. Co., 87 Mich. 646.

108 Cowan v. Muskegon Ry. Co., 84 Mich. 583.

where the company is clearing away snow, and a horse is struck by a piece of snow, but there is no proof that it came from the sweeper.[109] Where a switch was higher than necessary, aud it was hidden by snow partly melted by means of salt, negligence was held to be for the jury.[110] If a street railway company obstructs the street with snow, and with a repair wagon, it must use more care in the portion of the street left unobstructed.[111] Where a street car company ran an electric car at great speed at a place where dirt was piled near the track, and frightened a horse, who was injured in trying to get over the embankment, negligence was held to be for the jury.[112] Where a bicycle rider was riding in a bent position, and was injured by a hose reaching from a hydrant to a street railway company's tank car, due care and negligence were held to be for the jury.[113] Where a man is excavating a street, and interferes temporarily with the running of street cars, a finding of no willful obstruction is justified;[114] but where an ordinance protects street railway cars from willful obstruction, a man who moves a dwelling house onto the track is liable.[115]

The fact that a driver realizes that an obstruction is dangerous is not conclusive on the question of his lack of due care; and the same ruling has been made in the case of a pedestrian.[116]

109 Connor v. Metropolitan St. Ry. Co., 48 App. Div. (N. Y.) 580.

110 Wooley v. Grand St. & N. R. Co., 83 N. Y. 121.

111 West Chicago St. R. Co. v. O'Connor, 85 Ill. App. 278.

112 Greeley v. Federal St. & P. V. Passenger Ry., 153 Pa. 218.

113 Morhart v. North Jersey St. Ry. Co., 64 N. J. Law, 236.

114 Kolzem v. Broadway & S. Ave. R. Co., 1 Misc. Rep. (N. Y.) 148.

115 State v. Pratt, 52 Minn. 131

116 Mahoney v. Metropolitan R. Co., 104 Mass. 73; Gerrard v. La

### § 128. Miscellaneous.

An electric car running in the usual way is not a defect in the highway;[117] and the use of an electric car with the rear fender projecting does not constitute an obstruction of the highway.[118] Where the driver of a team was injured by a defect in a turntable, negligence was held to be for the jury;[119] and where a street railway company built a narrow bridge for its own convenience, and a horse fell through it, the negligence of the company in leaving the bridge without rails was held to be for the jury.[120] If a piece of iron which forms part of the overhead apparatus of an electric street railway breaks and falls upon a traveler, this raises a presumption of negligence;[121] and where a traveler was injured by a switch stick, which flew from the hands of a conductor on top of an electric car, it was held that there was evidence of negligence, and that a person was not bound to take special precautions against being struck in this manner.[122] Where a cable in the street was suddenly raised, tossing a boy into the air,[123] and where a man was injured by the breaking of a wire cable, and there was evidence that it had been broken before, and hastily repaired,[124] negligence in both cases was held to be for the jury. In like manner

Crosse City R. Co., 113 Wis. 258; Stanton v. Scranton Traction Co., 11 Pa. Super. Ct. 180.

117 Bishop v. Belle City St. Ry. Co., 92 Wis. 139.

118 Gargan v. West End St. Ry. Co., 176 Mass. 106.

119 Fitts v. Cream City R. Co., 59 Wis. 323.

120 Little Rock Traction & Elec. Co. v. Dunlap, 68 Ark. 291.

121 Uggla v. West End St. Ry. Co., 160 Mass. 351.

122 Manning v. West End St. Ry. Co., 166 Mass. 230.

123 Devine v. Brooklyn Heights R. Co., 1 App. Div. (N. Y.) 237.

124 Musser v. Lancaster City St. Ry. Co., 176 Pa. 621.

there is evidence of negligence for the jury where the company left small holes in the covers of its manholes, and a man on crutches was injured;[125] and where a street railway company ordered coal to be put in through a manhole, and the coal company failed to replace the cover properly. Whether notice can be imputed to the company so as to render it liable for an accident which occurred fifteen minutes later was held to be a question for the jury.[126] To fasten a horse to the car by a ring and a hook is a reasonably safe method, and not a defect.[127] Where a boy of ten was injured while playing on an unguarded car, it was held that he was a trespasser, and that no action could be maintained.[128]

Where a passenger, alighting after dark, caught her foot in a rope attached to the car by a trespasser, there was held to be no negligence on the part of the company;[129] and where a traveler tripped over the fender of a stationary car, there was held to be no negligence.[130] In Ekman v. Minneapolis St. Ry. Co.,[131] a complaint alleging injury to a child from a defective turntable was held to state a cause of action. Where a trolley pole fell and injured a traveler on foot, this was held to raise no presumption of negligence, and the case was held to be properly submitted to the jury.[132] Where

125 Wood v. Third Ave. R. Co., 91 Hun (N. Y.) 276.

126 Benjamin v. Metropolitan St. Ry. Co., 133 Mo. 274.

127 Black v. Forty-Second St. & G. St. Ferry R. Co., 19 N. Y. Wkly. Dig. 24.

128 Gay v. Essex Elec. St. Ry. Co., 159 Mass. 238, 242.

129 La Fond v. Detroit Citizens' St. Ry. Co. (Mich.) 92 N. W. 99.

130 Adams v. Metropolitan St. Ry. Co., 81 N. Y. Supp. 553.

131 34 Minn. 24.

132 Bamford v. Pittsburg & B. Traction Co., 194 Pa. 17.

a street railway company contracted to keep its road in thorough order, and was allowed to construct it on the grounds of a university, it was held liable for a defect injuring the servant of one of the university professors.[133] Where a company hired a contractor to build a cable road, and the contractor exercised the entire control, the company was held not to be liable to a child injured while playing around one of the contractor's machines.[134] Where a traveler tripped over a coil of wire dragging behind a car, there was held to be no negligence.[135]

133 Bolster v. Ithaca St. R. Co., 79 App. Div. (N. Y.) 239.

134 Chicago City Ry. Co. v. Hennessy, 16 Ill. App. 153.

135 McCaffrey v. Twenty-Third St. R. Co., 47 Hun (N. Y.) 404.

# PART III.

## ACCIDENTS TO EMPLOYES.

---

### CHAPTER X.

#### ACCIDENTS TO EMPLOYES.

An employe assumes all the risks naturally incident to his employment, and those arising from obvious defects, and may operate his car in such a manner as to be held guilty of lack of due care as matter of law; but in some cases, where the danger could not reasonably be foreseen, due care is held to be a question for the jury. When an employe discovers a defect, he may continue working for a reasonable time without making complaint, unless the danger is so apparent that no man of ordinary prudence would do so.

A watchman and a gripman, a track repairer and a motorman, a track foreman and a motorman, an inspector of electrical appliances and a conductor, and a man hauling coal and one in charge of a steam boiler have been held to be fellow servants. On the other hand, a foreman and a gripman, a member of a wrecking crew and a gripman, a track foreman and one of the gang working under him, a track master and a workman, an agent in charge of machinery and a conductor, and a passenger helping to put a car upon the track and the motorman of another car, which injured him, have been held not to be fellow servants. Whether a starter and a gripman and a conductor and a motorman are fellow servants has been left to the jury.

A street railway company must furnish reasonably safe machinery and appliances, and a reasonably safe place for its employes to work in, and must use reasonable care in selecting

**its servants. The company is not liable for injuries caused by the negligence of an independent contractor, but it will not be excused if the contractor was exercising a privilege which he could not have exercised without the consent of the company.**

I. ACCIDENTS TO CONDUCTORS.

§ 129. Assumption of Risk and Lack of Due Care.
130. Due Care for Jury.
131. Who are Fellow Servants.
132. Negligence of Company.

II. ACCIDENTS TO MOTORMEN, GRIPMEN AND DRIVERS.

§ 133. Assumption of Risk and Lack of Due Care.
134. Due Care for Jury.
135. Who are Fellow Servants.
136. Negligence of Company.

III. ACCIDENTS TO MISCELLANEOUS EMPLOYES.

§ 137. Assumption of Risk and Lack of Due Care.
138. Due Care for Jury.
139 Who are Fellow Servants.
140. Negligence of Company.

## I. ACCIDENTS TO CONDUCTORS.

### § 129. Assumption of risk and lack of due care.

An employe assumes all the risks naturally incident to his employment and those arising from obvious defects.[1] Where a conductor strained himself in turning a defective turntable, and it appeared that he knew of the defect, he was held to have assumed the risk of the accident which ensued.[2] In like manner, where a conductor was collecting

1 Denver Tramway Co. v. Nesbit, 22 Colo. 408; Houston Elec. Co. v. Robinson (Tex. Civ. App.) 76 S. W. 209.

2 Roberts v. Indianapolis St. R. Co., 158 Ind. 634.

fares on the running board of an open electric car, and, in stepping around a superintendent of the defendant, who was standing on the running board, struck a tree near the track, it was held that the plaintiff assumed the risk of the accident, and that no action was maintainable.[3] And in Ladd v. Brockton St. Ry. Co., where a conductor of previous experience was learning his duties, and, stepping on the running board, was struck by a trolley post, he was held to have assumed the risk of the accident.[4] Where a conductor was injured by a turntable, with the operation of which he was familiar;[5] where a conductor was pushing a car from a stable, and was caught between the car and the wall;[6] where a conductor, in coming out of a barn, chose a door where a car was standing, and it was obvious that the space was so narrow that he would be crushed if the car started;[7] and where a conductor stood on the bumper of a car to connect the trolley, and was thrown off by a jolt,—in all these cases the doctrine of assumption of risk was held to bar a recovery.[8] Where a conductor was familiar with his route, and was killed by striking a tree near the track, he was held to have assumed the risk.[9]

If an employe discovers a defect, it is not lack of due care, as a matter of law, to continue in the service of his

3 Hall v. Wakefield & S. St. Ry. Co., 178 Mass. 98.

4 180 Mass. 454.

5 Whelton v. West End St. Ry. Co., 172 Mass. 555.

6 Jennings v. Tacoma Ry. & Motor Co., 7 Wash. 275.

7 Collins v. Second Ave. Traction Co., 7 Pa. Super. Ct. 318.

8 McCauley v. Springfield St. Ry. Co., 169 Mass. 301.

9 Drake v. Auburn City R. Co., 173 N. Y. 466. And see Govan v. New Orleans & C. R. Co. (La.) 35 So. 484.

employer.[10] In Murdock v. Oakland, S. L. & H. Elec. Ry.[11] it was held that a servant has a right to work for a reasonable time after he has made complaint, in expectation that the defect will be remedied, and that what is a reasonable time is a question for the jury.

In Highland Ave. & B. R. Co. v. Walters[12] it was held that, if an employe gives reasonable notice, continuing to work will not amount to contributory negligence unless the danger is so apparent that a man of ordinary prudence would not have done so. Where a conductor knew of a defect, and continued to work for a year before the injury, he was held to have assumed the risk of the accident;[13] and where an employe continues in the service of his employer, with means of knowledge of any defects equal to that of his employer, and without objection, or promises on the part of the employer to remedy the defect, he cannot recover.[14]

If a conductor is injured through the negligence of his gripman, but it appears that the gripman ran his car according to the directions of the conductor, the lack of due care of the gripman is imputed to the conductor, so that he cannot recover,[15] but the lack of due care of the driver is not imputable to the conductor in an action against the driver of a truck.[16] Where a conductor had been working for over nine

10 Highland Ave. & B. R. Co. v. Walters, 91 Ala. 435.

11 128 Cal. 22.

12 91 Ala. 435.

13 Birmingham Ry. & Elec. Co. v. Allen, 99 Ala. 359.

14 Denver Tramway Co. v. Nesbit, 22 Colo. 408.

15 Minster v. Citizens' Ry. Co., 53 Mo. App. 276; Bailey v. Citizens' Ry. Co., 152 Mo. 449.

16 Hobson v. New York Condensed Milk Co., 25 App. Div. (N. Y.) 111.

years, but was not familiar with open cars, and was killed by a collision with another car while collecting fares on the running board, he was held unable to recover;[17] and where a conductor, while on the running board, was struck by a timber which he had passed every day for six weeks, and it appeared that he was familiar with a rule requiring him to warn passengers at this point, he was held not to be in the exercise of due care.[18] Where a steam railroad had the right of way at a crossing, and the conductor, if he had looked, could have seen the train eight hundred and eighty feet away, but attempted to cross in front of it,[19] and where a conductor stood between two tracks while switching his car from one to the other,[20] there was held to be lack of due care in both cases.

### § 130. Due care for jury.

Where the company operated a defective car, and the conductor had used the car only once before, a week before the accident, and had been on it only one hour on the second trip, and there was no evidence that he knew the car was the same one, or that he knew that it had not been repaired, due care is a question of fact for the jury;[21] and the same ruling was made where an extra conductor had run his car only one day over the place where the accident happened, and was killed by striking his head against a pole only six and a half inches from the platform step.[22] Where a con-

17 Fletcher v. Philadelphia Traction Co., 190 Pa. 117.
18 District of Columbia v. Ashton, 14 App. D. C. 571.
19 Highland Ave. & B. R. Co. v. Fennell, 111 Ala. 356.
20 Gier v. Los Angeles Consol. Elec. Ry. Co., 108 Cal. 129.
21 Murdock v. Oakland, S. L. & H. Elec. Ry., 128 Cal. 22.
22 Pierce v. Camden, G. & W. Ry. Co., 58 N. J. Law, 400.

ductor of four years' experience was collecting fares on the running board of a crowded car, and was struck by a trolley pole which slanted inwards, and was only nineteen inches from the car, and much nearer than any other pole, due care was held to be for the jury.[22a] Where a conductor was collecting fares on the running board, and came in contact with a barrier guarding an excavation in the street, due care was held to be for the jury;[23] and where two cars passed so close together at one point on the line that the conductor, standing on the running board, was struck by the other car, it was held that this was not lack of due care as a matter of law.[24] Where a conductor was thrown from a car by its rocking motion,[25] and where a conductor was injured by a collision with another car, both cases were held to be for the jury.[26]

## § 131. Who are fellow servants.

A conductor injured in a collision is a fellow servant of the motorman of the car which ran into his;[27] and a conductor on a street car is a fellow servant of a gripman and another conductor who are in charge of another car on the same train.[28] An inspector of electrical appliances is a fellow servant of a conductor killed by the unexpected starting of a car.[29] Where a conductor was injured through the

22a Withee v. Somerset Traction Co. (Me.) 56 Atl. 204.

23 Powers v. City of Boston, 154 Mass. 60.

24 True v. Niagara Gorge R. Co., 70 App. Div. (N. Y.) 383.

25 Coughlin v. Brooklyn Heights R. Co., 59 App. Div. (N. Y.) 126.

26 Wetzel v. Philadelphia Traction Co., 184 Pa. 407.

27 Hoover v. Carbon County Elec. Ry. Co., 191 Pa. 146.

28 North Chicago St. R. Co. v. Dudgeon, 69 Ill. App. 57.

29 Shugard v. Union Traction Co., 201 Pa. 562.

negligence of a gripman of another car, a verdict that the conductor and the gripman were not fellow servants was sustained.[30] An agent charged with the duty of procuring safe machinery, or with the duty of keeping it in repair, is not to be regarded as a fellow servant,[31] and the duty to furnish proper appliances cannot be delegated, so as to make the fellow-servant rule a defense.[32]

## § 132. Negligence of company.

A street railway company must furnish reasonably safe machinery.[33] Where a conductor was injured by a defective brake, there was held to be sufficient evidence to justify a verdict in his favor.[34] There is no negligence in not using a resistance coil, when, at the time of the accident, such an appliance was not recognized as a useful device.[35] Where a conductor was thrown from a car by its rocking motion, and there was evidence that the tracks were in a dangerous condition,[36] where a conductor was injured by a collision with another car,[37] and where a conductor was collecting fares on the running board, and was struck by a pole unusually near the tracks,[38] evidence of negligence was

30 Chicago City Ry. Co. v. Leach, 80 Ill. App. 354.

31 Denver Tramway Co. v. Crumhaugh, 23 Colo. 363.

32 McNamara v. Brooklyn City R. Co., 11 Misc. Rep. (N. Y.) 667.

33 Denver Tramway Co. v. Nesbit, 22 Colo. 408; Denver Tramway Co. v. Crumhaugh, 23 Colo. 363.

34 Newhart v. St. Paul City Ry. Co., 51 Minn. 42.

35 Lorimer v. St. Paul City Ry. Co., 48 Minn. 391.

36 Coughlin v. Brooklyn Heights R. Co., 59 App. Div. (N. Y.) 126.

37 Stucke v. Orleans R. Co., 50 La. Ann. 172; Wetzel v. Philadelphia Traction Co., 184 Pa. 407.

38 Pikesville, R. & E. G. R. Co. v. State, 88 Md. 563.

held to be justified. A finding of negligence is also justified where two cars ran so close together as to injure a conductor on the running board.[39] Where an accident would not have happened in the ordinary course of things if a person used due care, this raises a presumption of negligence.[40]

Where an employe sues for an injury resulting from the negligence of the company in keeping an incompetent motorman, it is enough to show that the company actually knew, or, in the exercise of due care, might have known, of the incompetency;[41] and where a conductor was killed, and the motorman testified that the accident was due to his defective eyesight, of which he had told the company, the verdict of negligence was held to be justified.[42] It has been held that, if a former employer says that an employe is competent, it is not lack of due care to omit to question the employe himself, and that a bad reputation is not enough to reqnire a discharge.[43]

The company is not liable for injuries caused by the negligence of a contractor who was engaged in repairing the pavement in the street;[44] but because the work is given to a contractor, this will not excuse the company if he was exercising a privilege, with the consent of the company, which he could not have exereised without their charter.[45] Where a conductor was injured by a defective bridge built by one

39 True v. Niagara Gorge R. Co., 70 App. Div. (N. Y.) 383.
40 Minster v. Citizens' Ry. Co., 53 Mo. App. 276.
41 Calumet Elec. St. Ry. Co. v. Peters, 88 Ill. App. 112.
42 Irwin v. Brooklyn Heights R. Co., 59 App. Div. (N. Y.) 95.
43 Gier v. Los Angeles Consol. Elec. Ry. Co., 108 Cal. 129.
44 North Chicago St. R. Co. v. Dudgeon, 69 Ill. App. 57.
45 North Chicago St. R. Co. v. Dudgeon, 83 Ill. App. 528.

company, across which a street railway company had laid its tracks, the companies were held jointly liable.[46]

## II. Accidents to Motormen, Gripmen, and Drivers.

### § 133. Assumption of risk and lack of due care.

A driver who is injured by the defective floor of his platform assumes the risk;[1] and if a motorman knows that a brake is not in good order, but continues working, he assumes the risk of the accident.[2] A motorman does not assume the risk arising from the company's failure to employ a sandman;[3] and a motorman cannot be charged with lack of due care for remaining at work after the company allows a contractor to run construction cars on its tracks.[4] Where a servant knows of a defect, and notifies the master, who promises to remedy it, but neglects to do so, and the servant is injured within a reasonable time, the employer is liable unless to continue working would be so dangerous that a man of ordinary prudence would not do it.[5] Where a motorman was injured by a car in front backing into his, he was held to have assumed the risk.[5a]

Where a motorman was injured in a head-on collision, and it appeared that he was running his car at such speed, upon a foggy morning, that he could not stop it in time to avoid a collision, he was held not to be in the exercise of

[46] Toledo Consol. St. R. Co. v. Sweeney, 8 Ohio Cir. Ct. R. 298.

[1] Rogers v. Galveston City Ry. Co., 76 Tex. 502.

[2] Windover v. Troy City Ry. Co., 4 App. Div. (N. Y.) 203.

[3] Windover v. Troy City Ry. Co., 4 App. Div. (N. Y.) 203.

[4] Ortlip v. Philadelphia & W. C. Traction Co., 198 Pa. 586.

[5] Harris v. Hewitt, 64 Minn. 54.

[5a] Seccombe v. Detroit Elec. Ry. (Mich.) 94 N. W. 747.

due care;[6] and where a motorman was injured in a head-on collision, and the inference was that he was running at high speed, when he had reason to expect the coming of the other car, he was held not to be in the exercise of due care.[7] A motorman who runs an electric car, on a foggy morning, at such speed that he cannot stop in time to avoid a collision, is not in the exercise of due care.[8] A motorman who runs his car twelve miles an hour, and does not slacken speed at a steam railroad crossing, although he sees a train standing near the crossing, cannot recover;[9] and where a motorman was directed by the company to run his car across a steam railroad track without stopping, and was assured that no accident would happen, he was held guilty of contributory negligence in crossing without looking or listening, although he did not know that the track was frequently used.[10] Where a driver's view was obstructed, and he collided at a crossing with a steam railroad train, he was held not to be in the exercise of due care.[11]

## § 134. Due care for jury.

Where a borough negligently allowed a tree to blow down and injure a motorman of a car, he is not prevented from recovering because he was running his car at greater speed than that permitted by an ordinance of the borough.[12] Where a motorman was injured by a collision with a wagon, it was

6 Savage v. Nassau Elec. R. Co., 42 App. Div. (N. Y.) 241.
7 Hudson v. Peoples' St. Ry. Co., 175 Mass. 23.
8 La Pontney v. Shedden Cartage Co., 116 Mich. 514.
9 Einsfeld v. Niagara Junction Ry. Co., 49 App. Div. (N. Y.) 470.
10 Goodrich v. Chippewa Valley Elec. R. Co., 108 Wis. 329.
11 Mantel v. Chicago, M. & St. P. Ry. Co., 33 Minn. 62.
12 Berry v. Borough of Sugar Notch, 191 Pa. 345.

held that both the motorman and the driver of the wagon were bound to use reasonable care to avoid a collision.[13] Where a car stopped so that the plaintiff's car projected over the track of another company and was run into, he was held not to be guilty of lack of due care as a matter of law.[14] Where a motorman was ordered to haul a gravel car behind his passenger car, and the motorman knew that there were no brakes on the gravel car, due care was held to be for the jury;[15] and where a driver was killed through a defect in a harness, his lack of due care in not knowing of the defect was likewise held to be for the jury.[16] Where there was an ordinance requiring electric cars to come to a full stop twenty feet from the crossing of another line, a motorman who had made this stop, and saw a car from one hundred and fifty to two hundred feet away on the other line, is not guilty of lack of due care, as matter of law, in going ahead.[17] Where the gates at a railroad crossing were open, and the gateman was not at his post, the driver of a street car going upon the track is entitled to have his case submitted to the jury.[18] Where a flagman at a crossing was not at his post, and a street car driver was killed by a collision with some freight cars, and, after leaving a railroad crossing about one hundred and eighty-five feet away, the driver could not see the cars until within twenty feet of the crossing, it was

13 Price v. Charles Warner Co., 1 Pen. (Del.) 462.

14 Tyler v. Third Ave. R. Co., 18 Misc. Rep. (N. Y.) 165.

15 Griffin v. Ithaca St. Ry. Co., 62 App. Div. (N. Y.) 551.

16 McKnight v. Brooklyn Heights R. Co., 23 Misc. Rep. (N. Y.) 527.

17 Becker v. Detroit Citizens' St. Ry. Co., 121 Mich. 580.

18 Evans v. Lake Shore & M. S. R. Co., 88 Mich. 442.

held that due care was for the jury.[19] Where there was evidence that the driver of a car put his car in motion first, and that another car then started to cross at an intersection of streets, the case was held to be rightly submitted to the jury.[20]

## § 135. Who are fellow servants.

A gripman and a wrecking crew in the employ of a street car company are not fellow servants;[21] and a foreman and a gripman injured while passing from one car to another are not fellow servants.[22] Whether a starter is a fellow servant of the gripman of a car is a question for the jury.[23] Where a street railway company allows a contractor to operate construction cars on its lines, it is liable to one of its own motormen for the negligence of a gripman of the contractor.[24] A motorman and a track foreman have been held to be fellow servants.[25]

## § 136. Negligence of company.

It has been held that a street railway company must furnish its servants with suitable appliances, which may be used with safety,[26] that it must use ordinary care to furnish reasonably safe machinery and a reasonably safe place to work in,[27] and that it need not furnish the very best appli-

19 Richmond v. Chicago & W. M. Ry. Co., 87 Mich. 374.
20 Metropolitan St. Ry. Co. v. Kennedy, 82 Fed. 158.
21 West Chicago St. R. Co. v. Dwyer, 57 Ill. App. 440.
22 Keown v. St. Louis R. Co., 141 Mo. 87.
23 West Chicago St. R. Co. v. Dwyer, 162 Ill. 482.
24 Ortlip v. Philadelphia & W. C. Traction Co., 198 Pa. 586.
25 Rittenhouse v. Wilmington St. Ry. Co., 120 N. C. 544.
26 Leigh v. Omaha St. Ry. Co., 36 Neb. 131.
27 West Chicago St. R. Co. v. Dwyer, 57 Ill. App. 440.

ances, but must use reasonable care to see that the appliances are reasonably safe.[28] The duty of the company not to furnish a defective harness is not one which can be delegated.[29]

Where a motorman stooped down and was injured by the starting of the car, but the cause of the starting was wholly uncertain, there was held to be no evidence of negligence.[30] Where a foreman started some cars and injured a gripman who was passing from one car to another, there was held to be no negligence on the part of the company;[31] and a superintendent is under no obligation to warn the engineer on a dummy line of the proximity of posts, when it is reasonable to suppose that the engineer saw them, and that the possibility of injury is very remote.[32]

Where a driver was injured because the conductor did not know how to manage the brake, the failure of the company to instruct the conductor, who had been recently hired, was held to be negligence;[33] and where a horse was fastened to a car by a straight pin, instead of a safety pin, it was held that the negligence of the company was for the jury.[34] To charge the company with having an incompetent employe, it must be shown that they knew or should have known of the incompetency.[34a] Where two cars collide at a crossing,

28 Sappenfield v. Main St. & A. P. R. Co., 91 Cal. 48; Friel v. Citizens' Ry., 115 Mo. 503.

29 McKnight v. Brooklyn Heights R. Co., 23 Misc. Rep. (N. Y.) 527.

30 Kenneson v. West End St. Ry. Co., 168 Mass. 1.

31 Keown v. St. Louis R. Co., 141 Mo. 87.

32 North Birmingham St. Ry. Co. v. Wright, 130 Ala. 419.

33 Sullivan v. Metropolitan St. Ry. Co., 53 App. Div. (N. Y.) 89.

34 Sappenfield v. Main St. & A. P. R. Co., 91 Cal. 48.

34a Seccombe v. Detroit Elec. Ry. (Mich.) 94 N. W. 747.

the fact that the hind end of one car is struck by the front end of the other while passing over the crossing raises a presumption that the second car was carelessly managed;[35] and where a driver was killed by a horse which would kick when struck, and the master knew this, while the driver did not, it was held that the case must be submitted to the jury.[36] Where a superintendent ordered a motorman to take a dangerous position, and then ordered another car to come ahead, the jury were held justified in finding negligence.[37]

A law providing for the use of screens for the motormen of electric cars is constitutional;[38] and an ordinance to equip cars with air or electric brakes.[38a]

Where a driver was killed, the fact that a motorman disobeyed an ordinance as to right of way was held not to be negligence per se;[39] and the same ruling was made where a motorman was injured.[40]

### III. Accidents to Miscellaneous Employes.

### § 137. Assumption of risk and lack of due care.

The doctrine that an employe assumes the ordinary risks of his employment operates to bar a recovery in a large number of cases. Thus, an employe has been held unable to recover where he jumped off a ladder to avoid a snowdrift, and fell through a skylight covered with snow;[1] where he

[35] Chicago City Ry. Co. v. McLaughlin, 40 Ill. App. 496.

[36] Leigh v. Omaha St. Ry. Co., 36 Neb. 131.

[37] O'Brien v. West End St. Ry. Co., 173 Mass. 105.

[38] State v. Smith, 58 Minn. 35; State v. Whitaker, 160 Mo. 59.

[38a] People v. Detroit United Ry. (Mich.) 97 N. W. 36.

[39] Connor v. Electric Traction Co., 173 Pa. 602.

[40] McLain v. St. Louis & S. Ry. Co. (Mo. App.) 73 S. W. 909.

[1] Reinig v. Broadway R. Co., 49 Hun (N. Y.) 269.

fell off an iron bridge[2] or a ladder[3] in a boiler room; where he was attempting to repair a pump which had become clogged;[4] and where his horses took fright at escaping steam, but he knew that the engine and boilers of the company blew off steam from time to time.[5] An employe cannot recover while repairing an old wooden pole,[6] when run down by a car which had no fender or guard,[7] when injured while cleaning a commutator of an electric car,[8] when injured by stepping backwards in front of a car to avoid being run over,[9] when injured by a falling bank of earth,[10] when injured while lifting a heavy log,[10a] when injured by a hay-cutting machine,[11] when injured by a windlass in lowering a car,[12] and when injured by being caught between the running boards of two open cars near the car house.[13] A contract limiting liability of the company while an employe is riding to and from work is not against public policy, as the employe need not enter the company's service, or remain there.[14]

2 Rohan v. Metropolitan St. Ry. Co., 59 App. Div. (N. Y.) 250.

3 Nealand v. Lynn & B. R. Co., 173 Mass. 42.

4 Kelley v. Forty-Second St., M. & St. N. Ave. Ry. Co., 58 Hun (N. Y.) 93.

5 Denver Tramway Co. v. O'Brien, 8 Colo. App. 74.

6 Kellogg v. Denver City Tramway Co. (Colo. App.) 72 Pac. 609; Broderick v. St. Paul City Ry. Co., 74 Minn. 163.

7 Chandler v. Atlantic Coast Elec. Ry. Co., 61 N. J. Law, 380.

8 Burnell v. West Side R. Co., 87 Wis. 387.

9 Thompson v. Citizens' St. Ry. Co., 152 Ind. 461.

10 Brown v. Electric Ry. Co., 101 Tenn. 252.

10a San Antonio Traction Co. v. De Rodriguez (Tex. Civ. App.) 77 S. W. 420.

11 Stuart v. West End St. Ry. Co., 163 Mass. 391.

12 Cunningham v. Lynn & B. St. Ry. Co., 170 Mass. 298.

13 Goldthwait v. Haverhill & G. St. Ry. Co., 160 Mass. 554.

14 Peterson v. Seattle Traction Co., 23 Wash. 615.

Where an oiler was set to work coupling cars, it was held that, while engaged temporarily on work more dangerous than that for which he was employed, a servant assumes all risks of danger equally open to the observation of himself and his employer.[15] If an employe knows of a defect, and makes no complaint, he assumes the risk;[16] and where a hostler was killed by a vicious horse, and it appeared that he knew the horse was vicious, but made no complaint, it was held that no action was maintainable.[17]

Where an employe stepped into an uncovered manhole, he was held not to be in the exercise of due care;[18] and the same ruling was made where a motorman sent out as a relief man was struck by a pole some twelve or eighteen inches from the car, and it appeared that he stood on the platform steps, looking outwards and backwards, without any necessity for doing so.[19]

## § 138. Due care, for jury.

An employe is not always prevented from recovering on the ground of assumption of risk, and the cases where his due care is held to be a question for the jury are usually those where the danger is one which could not reasonably be foreseen. Thus, due care has been held to be for the jury where an employe was ordered to go onto a pile of lumber, the dangerous condition of which was not appar-

15 North Chicago St. R. Co. v. Conway, 76 Ill. App. 621.
16 Van Sickle v. Atlantic Ave. R. Co., 12 Misc. Rep. (N. Y.) 217.
17 Green & C. St. Passenger Ry. Co. v. Bresmer, 97 Pa. 103.
18 Brennan v. Front St. Cable Ry. Co., 8 Wash. 363.
19 Sundy v. Savannah St. R., 96 Ga. 819.

ent;[20] where an employe tripped over a misplaced rail;[21] where an inexperienced lineman was told that the vise given him was a suitable tool, and it slipped and injured him;[22] where a blacksmith's helper was taken from his employment and set to work on the dangerous task of repairing lines, without warning or direction as to the danger;[23] where an employe was injured while coupling cars;[24] where a lineman was injured by a defective pole;[25] where an employe was injured by an explosion from the pipe of a steam boiler;[26] and where an employe received a shock while cleaning a car.[26a] An employe riding from work, and injured by a defective switch, was held not to have assumed the risk of the accident.[26b] A man placed in sudden peril is not held to the usual standard of care.[27]

## § 139. Who are fellow servants.

No action can be maintained when an employe is injured by one who is acting as a fellow servant;[28] and the fellow-servant rule has been held to be a bar where a watchman at a curve was injured by the gripman of a car,[29] where an

20 Millard v. West End St. Ry. Co., 173 Mass. 512.

21 Duggan v. Third Ave. R. Co., 9 Misc. Rep. (N. Y.) 158.

22 Shadford v. Ann Arbor St. Ry. Co., 121 Mich. 224.

23 Stapleton v. Citizens' Traction Co., 5 Pa. Super. Ct. 253.

24 Delude v. St. Paul City Ry. Co., 55 Minn. 63.

25 Bland v. Shreveport Belt Ry. Co., 48 La. Ann. 1057.

26 Sullivan v. Union Ry. Co., 7 App. Div. (N. Y.) 238.

26a Karczewski v. Wilmington City Ry. Co. (Del.) 54 Atl. 746

26b Noe v. Rapid Ry. Co. (Mich.) 94 N. W. 743.

27 Denver & B. P. Rapid Transit Co. v. Dwyer, 20 Colo. 132.

28 Brittain v. West End St. Ry. Co., 168 Mass. 10; Norman v. Middlesex & S. Traction Co., 68 N. J. Law, 728.

29 Murray v. St. Louis Cable & W. Ry. Co., 98 Mo. 573.

employe engaged in repairing a brake was injured by a motorman,[30] and where a man employed to haul coal had his horses frightened by escaping steam.[31] Where a conductor got a boy of eleven to help him in operating a car, it was held that, assuming the boy to be an emergency employe, the conductor was his fellow servant.[32]

If a track foreman has the power to hire and discharge employes, he is not a fellow servant to one of the gang working under him;[33] and it has likewise been held that a track foreman is a vice principal and not a fellow servant of a sectionman working under him.[34] A master is liable for the willful acts of his servant within the scope of his employment;[35] but the mere fact that a man is a foreman over a servant who is injured will not make the company liable, but the act must be in the line of his services as foreman.[36] A passenger who is helping to put a car back upon the track is not a fellow servant of a motorman of another car, which injured him.[37]

Where an employe in a machine shop was injured while trying to put a belt over some pulleys, it was held that an employe charged with the duty of working machinery with another employe is not a fellow servant in such a sense as to relieve the employer from responsibility for an injury to one of them, which happened through a defect in the ma-

30 Lundquist v. Duluth St. Ry. Co., 65 Minn. 387.
31 Denver Tramway Co. v. O'Brien, 8 Colo. App. 74.
32 Marks v. Rochester Ry. Co., 41 App. Div. (N. Y.) 66.
33 Austin Rapid Transit Ry. Co. v. Grothe, 88 Tex. 262.
34 Electric Ry. Co. v. Lawson, 101 Tenn. 406.
35 Baltimore Consol. Ry. Co. v. Pierce, 89 Md. 495.
36 Metropolitan West Side El. R. Co. v. Skola, 83 Ill. App. 659.
37 Street Ry. Co. v. Bolton, 43 Ohio St. 224.

chinery, although that defect may have been brought about by the negligence of the other employe, and that the whole case was properly left to the jury.[38] An employe injured by a switch opened by a third person is not precluded from recovering because the car is run by a fellow servant, since the negligence is not that of the fellow servant.[38a]

A street railway company is responsible for overloading a floor, regardless of the rank of the agent who represents it, since this is an act which it performs as a master;[39] and a track master represents the company when he tells a workman to go down into a hole, and, if he promises to tell the engineer not to start the cable, but fails to do so, the company is liable.[40]

## § 140. Negligence of company.

It has been held that it is the duty of a street railway company to furnish reasonably safe machinery and premises,[41] and that it is not bound to furnish the safest known appliances, but it is enough if it furnishes appliances which are in general use throughout the country.[42]

Where a lineman was injured by a defective wire, it was held that, in the use of an agency like electricity, the com-

38 McDade v. Washington & G. R. Co., 5 Mackey (D. C.) 144.

38a Noe v. Rapid Ry. Co. (Mich.) 94 N. W. 743.

39 Dillon v. Sixth Ave. R. Co., 48 N. Y. Super. Ct. 283.

40 Mullane v. Houston, W. St. & P. Ferry R. Co., 21 Misc. Rep. (N. Y.) 10.

41 Denver Tramway Co. v. O'Brien, 8 Colo. App. 74; Karczewski v. Wilmington City Ry. Co. (Del.) 54 Atl. 746; Lincoln St. Ry. Co. v. Cox, 48 Neb. 807; Green & C. St. Passenger Ry. Co. v. Bresmer, 97 Pa. 103; Gustafson v. Seattle Traction Co., 28 Wash. 227.

42 Shadford v. Ann Arbor St. Ry. Co., 111 Mich. 390.

pany was bound to use a very high degree of care.[43] A master must use reasonable care in the selection of fellow servants, and is responsible for knowingly keeping an incompetent workman.[44]

"Railroads" in a statute does not mean a street railway,[45] and an act applying to "any railway corporation" does not include a street railway company.[46]

Where a workman in a barn was made to move some iron frogs, but no danger was shown, there was held to be no evidence of negligence;[47] and, similarly, there was held to be no negligence where a workman was injured while tearing down a building.[48]

Where a defect in a brake was discovered at noon, and the car was used through the afternoon and evening, negligence of the company was held to be for the jury;[49] and the same ruling was made where an employe was injured by an explosion from the pipe of a steam boiler.[50]

Even if a plaintiff is guilty of lack of due care, he may recover if the defendant could have prevented the injury by the exercise of due care on its part.[51]

Where an employe was injured through the negligence of another employe, and both were working under an independent contractor, a street railway company was held lia-

43 McAdam v. Central Ry. & Elec. Co., 67 Conn. 445.

44 Metropolitan West Side El. Ry. Co. v. Fortin, 203 Ill. 454; Chandler v. Atlantic Coast Elec. Ry. Co., 61 N. J. Law, 380.

45 Riley v. Galveston City Ry. Co., 13 Tex. Civ. App. 247.

46 Funk v. St. Paul City Ry. Co., 61 Minn. 435.

47 Citizens' St. R. Co. v. Brown, 29 Ind. App. 185.

48 Weideman v. Tacoma Ry. & Motor Co., 7 Wash. 517.

49 Kingan v. Pittsburg Traction Co., 5 Pa. Super. Ct. 436.

50 Sullivan v. Union Ry. Co., 7 App. Div. (N. Y.) 238.

51 Denver & B. P. Rapid Transit Co. v. Dwyer, 20 Colo. 132.

ble;[52] and where a street railway company leased part of its building to a compressed-air company, and allowed it to use tracks, cars, and employes to conduct its experiment, an employe of the street railway company was allowed to recover for an injury, on the ground that those in charge of the car were employes of the compressed-air company.[53]

A rule forbidding an employe in uniform off duty to sit on the front seat of a car has been held to be a reasonable one.[54]

A head-on collision raises a presumption of negligence.[55]

Where an employe relied upon the viciousness of a horse and on a defective brake, it was held that the accident was not due to either cause;[56] and where an employe could have taken a place of safety, but stayed near an obstruction, and was crushed by a car, there was held to be no evidence of negligence.[57] Where an employe was repairing a car, and was run over by another car because a switch was not blocked, there was held to be no negligence.[58]

Negligence has been held to be a question for the jury under the following circumstances: Where a lineman was injured by a defective insulator, and it appeared that the company made no inspections or tests;[59] where a foreman ordered an employe to go upon the flooring, which was

52 Jones v. Philadelphia Traction Co., 185 Pa. 75.

53 Goetz v. Metropolitan St. Ry. Co., 54 App. Div. (N. Y.) 365.

54 Rowe v. Brooklyn Heights R. Co., 71 App. Div. (N. Y.) 474.

55 Peterson v. Seattle Traction Co., 23 Wash. 615.

56 Devlin v. Metropolitan St. Ry. Co., 17 App. Div. (N. Y.) 491.

57 Sullivan v. Third Ave. R. Co., 19 App. Div. (N. Y.) 195.

58 Van Sickle v. Atlantic Ave. R. Co., 12 Misc. Rep. (N. Y.) 217.

59 Murphy v. Coney Island & B. R. Co., 65 App. Div. (N. Y.) 546.

made partly of glass concealed by dirt;[60] where an employe fell through a defective floor in the nighttime;[61] where an employe was ordered by his superintendent to dig away the earth around a pole, and the pole fell on him;[62] and where the foreman of a gang of workmen sent a train down the track without warning a man who was working underneath the car.[63] It is not enough for a fireman to show that a dummy engine ran into a coal car, but he must show, further, that the engineer could have seen it in time.[64] Where an employe repairing trolley wires on a tower wagon was struck by a car, the question of the necessity of having a sand box was held to be for the jury.[65]

Where an employe was injured by the breaking of a platform elevator used for hoisting cars, negligence was held to be for the jury.[66] Where an employe on a construction car fell off, whether the company should have had stakes or uprights on the car was held to be for the jury.[67] A street railroad company comes within an act making railroads liable to a servant injured by a fellow servant.[68]

60 Raftery v. Central Park, N. & E. R. R. Co., 14 Misc. Rep. (N. Y.) 560.

61 Chicago General Ry. Co. v. McNamara, 94 Ill. App. 188.

62 East St. Louis Connecting Ry. Co. v. Enright, 47 Ill. App. 494.

63 Metropolitan West Side El. R. Co. v. Skola, 83 Ill. App. 659.

64 Telle v. Leavenworth Rapid Transit Ry. Co., 50 Kan. 455.

65 Van Dyke v. Atlantic Ave. R. Co., 67 Fed. 296; Atlantic Ave. R. Co. v. Van Dyke, 72 Fed. 458.

66 Swenson v. Metropolitan St. Ry. Co., 78 App. Div. (N. Y.) 379.

67 Kerrigan v. Market St. Ry. Co., 138 Cal. 506.

68 Savannah, T. & G. of H. Ry. v. Williams (Ga.) 43 S. E. 751.

# PART IV.

## EVIDENCE AND DAMAGES.

---

### CHAPTER XI.

#### THE VALUE OF EVIDENCE.

§ 141. Credibility of Witnesses in General.
142. Credibility as Affected by Interest or Bias.
143. Credibility as Affected by Corroboration.
144. Credibility as Affected by Contradictory Statements.

#### § 141. Credibility of witnesses in general.

The value of the testimony of witnesses is for the jury,[1] and they may find negligence from the physical facts, although all the witnesses testified that there was no negligence.[2] It is error to instruct the jury to consider the character of the witnesses as they know them,[3] and a judgment will be reversed where it is clear that the plaintiff's

[1] Brown v. Washington & G. R. Co., 11 App. D. C. 37; Washington & G. R. Co. v. Adams, 11 App. D. C. 396; Kean v. West Chicago St. R. Co., 75 Ill. App. 38; Fox v. Oakland Consol. St. Ry., 118 Cal. 55; Maxwell v. Wilmington City Ry. Co., 1 Marvel (Del.) 199; Higgins v. Wilmington City Ry. Co., 1 Marvel (Del.) 352; Chicago City Ry. Co. v. Young, 62 Ill. 238; West Chicago St. R. Co. v. Mueller, 64 Ill. App. 601; Kornazsewska v. West Chicago St. R. Co., 76 Ill. App. 366; Olfermann v. Union Depot R. Co., 125 Mo. 408.

[2] Hunt v. Missouri R. Co., 14 Mo. App. 160.

[3] Johnson v. Superior Rapid Transit Ry. Co., 91 Wis. 233.

story is a mere fabrication.[4] Where it is clear, by a mathematical test, that a witness is wrong, the jury cannot consider his testimony.[5] The mere number of witnesses does not determine the weight of the evidence,[6] nor is intelligence the test of credibility.[7] Affirmative testimony is of more weight than negative;[8] but where the attention of witnesses was called to a fact, and their intelligence and opportunities for observation were equal, testimony that an event did not happen cannot be regarded as negative testimony, and is entitled to as much weight as testimony that it did happen.[9]

§ **142. Credibility as affected by interest or bias.**

The jury have a right to consider the interest of any witness in a suit.[10] They may consider that the plaintiff is an

4 Kummer v. Christopher & T. St. R. Co., 2 Misc. Rep. (N. Y.) 298.

5 Bornscheuer v. Consolidated Traction Co., 198 Pa. 332.

6 Denver Tramway Co. v. Owens, 20 Colo. 107; North Chicago St. R. Co. v. Anderson, 176 Ill. 635; North Chicago St. R. Co. v. Fitzgibbons, 180 Ill. 466; North Chicago City Ry. Co. v. Gastka, 27 Ill. App. 518; North Chicago St. R. Co. v. Fitzgibbons, 79 Ill. App. 632; Schick v. Brooklyn City R. Co., 10 N. Y. Supp. 528; Scholl v. Broadway R. Co., 63 Hun (N. Y.) 629, 17 N. Y. Supp. 755; Hardy v. Milwaukee St. Ry. Co., 89 Wis. 183; Schmitt v. Milwaukee St. Ry. Co., 89 Wis. 195; Bading v. Milwaukee Elec. Ry. & Light Co., 105 Wis. 480.

7 Chicago West Div. Ry. Co. v. Bert, 69 Ill. 388; Eastman v. West Chicago St. R. Co., 79 Ill. App. 585; Hope v. West Chicago St. R. Co., 82 Ill. App. 311; Chicago City Ry. Co. v. Keenan, 85 Ill. App. 367; Gilmore v. Seattle & R. Ry. Co., 29 Wash. 150.

8 Chicago General St. Ry. Co. v. Capek, 68 Ill. App. 500; Ryan v. La Crosse City Ry. Co., 108 Wis. 122; Street Ry. Co. v. Rohner, 3 Ohio Dec. 570; Hinton v. Cream City R. Co., 65 Wis. 323.

9 West Chicago St. R. Co. v. Mueller, 165 Ill. 499.

10 North Chicago St. R. Co. v. Anderson, 176 Ill. 635; Chicago City Ry. Co. v. Mager, 85 Ill. App. 524; Cicero & P. St. Ry. Co. v. Rollins, 95 Ill. App. 497.

interested party,[11] and may consider the interest of an employe of the defendant,[12] but the interest of the latter is not considered as great as that of the plaintiff.[13] "Interest" has been defined as a legal interest, and not a mere prejudice or bias,[14] and it has been held that a motorman has no legal interest in a suit.[15] It is not error to exclude evidence that the officers of the defendant corporation were members of another corporation, by which the witness was employed.[16] The interest of a witness is sufficiently shown where it appeared that he tried to obtain a settlement for the plaintiff.[17] Where there are a number of interested witnesses, it is error to single out one and call attention to his interest;[18] but where all reasonable probabilities are on one side, the testimony of one interested witness does not constitute a conflict of evidence requiring the submission of the case to the jury.[19]

Statements against a plaintiff's interest must be taken as true;[20] and similarly, where an employe testifies as to the

11 Metropolitan R. Co. v. Jones, 1 App. D. C. 200; West Chicago St. R. Co. v. Estep, 162 Ill. 130; West Chicago St. R. Co. v. Nash, 166 Ill. 528; Irwin v. Metropolitan St. Ry. Co., 25 Misc. Rep. (N. Y.) 187.

12 West Chicago St. R. Co. v. Raftery, 85 Ill. App. 319; Hoes v. Third Ave. R. Co., 5 App. Div. (N. Y.) 151.

13 Uransky v. Dry Dock, E. B. & B. R. Co., 59 Hun (N. Y.) 626, 13 N. Y. Supp. 670.

14 Chicago City Ry. Co. v. Mager, 185 Ill. 336.

15 Callary v. Easton Transit Co., 185 Pa. 176.

16 Wallace v. Taunton St. Ry. Co., 119 Mass. 91.

17 Pomaski v. Grant, 119 Mich. 675.

18 North Chicago St. R. Co. v. Dudgeon, 83 Ill. App. 528.

19 McCoy v. Milwaukee St. Ry. Co., 82 Wis. 215; Flaherty v. Harrison, 98 Wis. 559.

20 Feary v. Metropolitan St. Ry. Co., 162 Mo. 75.

cause of a collision, the jury are justified in accepting his statements as true, without knowing whether his reason is a good one.[21]

The absence of a witness, where the usual means are employed to reach him, is not a proper subject of comment;[22] and the mere failure to examine employes does not raise a presumption of negligence;[23] but it has been held that, where a motorman is not called, the jury are at liberty to presume that his testimony would not have been favorable to the defendant.[24] In Harriman v. Reading & L. St. Ry. Co.[25] it was held that the fair inference to be drawn from not calling a witness is for the jury under all the circumstances of the case. The fact that a witness is not compelled to incriminate himself is a personal privilege,[26] and, where a witness takes advantage of this privilege to exclude material testimony, this is a proper subject of comment.[27]

The fact that a witness receives money in excess of his legal fees may be considered on the question of his credibility;[28] but it has been held that a moderate sum in excess of the legal witness' fee does not impeach the credibility of a witness.[29] An expert witness may be asked on cross-

21 North Chicago St. R. Co. v. Boyd, 57 Ill. App. 535.

22 Mitchell v. Tacoma Ry. & Motor Co., 9 Wash. 120.

23 Peetz v. St. Charles St. R. Co., 42 La. Ann. 541.

24 Fonda v. St. Paul City Ry. Co., 71 Minn. 438.

25 173 Mass. 28.

26 Chicago City Ry. Co. v. Canevin, 72 Ill. App. 81; San Antonio St. Ry. Co. v. Muth, 7 Tex. Civ. App. 443.

27 McCooe v. Dighton, S. & S. St. Ry. Co., 173 Mass. 117.

28 Green v. Metropolitan St. Ry. Co., 60 App. Div. (N. Y.) 317.

29 Chicago West Div. Ry. Co. v. Conley, 43 Ill. App. 347.

examination what fees he is to receive for testifying,[30] but an expert witness cannot refuse to testify because only the ordinary witness' fee has been paid or promised him.[31]

## § 143. Credibility as affected by corroboration.

If a witness has intentionally given false testimony on a material point, the jury may disregard his testimony altogether,[32] but such parts of his testimony as are corroborated may be believed;[33] and it is error to instruct that, if the plaintiff has knowingly misrepresented the extent of her injuries, the jury may disregard her testimony as to how the accident happened, especially where such testimony is fully corroborated.[34] It is error to charge that the jury cannot disbelieve the plaintiff if he is corroborated;[35] and where all reasonable probabilities are on one side, the testimony of one interested witness does not constitute a conflict of evidence requiring the submission of the case to the jury.[36] Where contradictory testimony of a witness stands alone, the court

30 Zimmer v. Third Ave. R. Co., 36 App. Div. (N. Y.) 273.

31 North Chicago St. R. Co. v. Zeiger, 182 Ill. 9.

32 Chicago City Ry. Co. v. Allen, 169 Ill. 287; North Chicago St. R. Co. v. Fitzgibbons, 180 Ill. 466; Kornazsewska v. West Chicago St. R. Co., 76 Ill. App. 366; Chicago City Ry. Co. v. Olis, 94 Ill. App. 323; Peyser v. Coney Island & B. R. Co., 81 Hun (N. Y.) 70; Little v. Superior Rapid Transit Ry. Co., 88 Wis. 402; Schmitt v. Milwaukee St. Ry. Co., 89 Wis. 195.

33 North Chicago St. R. Co. v. Fitzgibbons, 79 Ill. App. 632; Lieserowitz v. West Chicago St. R. Co., 80 Ill. App. 248.

34 Heddle v. City Elec. Ry. Co., 112 Mich. 547.

35 Duygan v. Third Ave. R. Co., 6 Misc. Rep. (N. Y.) 66.

36 McCoy v. Milwaukee St. Ry. Co., 82 Wis. 215; Flaherty v. Harrison, 98 Wis. 559.

must call attention to this,[37] and it has been held that such testimony will not justify a verdict for the plaintiff.[38]

### § 144. Credibility as affected by contradictory statements.

To affect the credibility of a witness it may be shown that he gave different testimony at a former trial,[39] and statements made out of court,[40] a letter,[41] a written statement,[42] entries in a time book,[43] and evidence given at an inquest,[44] all contradictory to his testimony at the trial, may properly be admitted. A previous expression of opinion cannot be used to contradict a witness,[45] and a copy of a stenographer's notes of testimony at a former trial is not properly admissible for the purpose of impeachment.[46]

Where a witness is impeached, he may properly be given an opportunity to explain an affidavit[47] or a different statement[48] made by him.

37 Fineburg v. Second & T. Sts. Passenger Ry. Co., 182 Pa. 97.

38 Cole v. Detroit Elec. Ry. Co. (Mich.) 92 N. W. 935.

39 Bageard v. Consolidated Traction Co., 64 N. J. Law, 316.

40 Paducah St. Ry. Co. v. Adkins' Adm'r, 14 Ky. Law Rep. 425; Nussbaum v. Louisville Ry. Co., 22 Ky. Law Rep. 271, 57 S. W. 249; Chicago West Div. Ry. Co. v. Ingraham, 131 Ill. 659; Central Ry. Co. v. Allmon, 45 Ill. App. 389; McClellan v. Ft. Wayne & B. I. Ry. Co., 105 Mich. 101; Leahey v. Cass Ave. & F. G. Ry. Co., 97 Mo. 165; Shaw v. Salt Lake City R. Co., 21 Utah, 76.

41 Brace v. St. Paul City Ry. Co., 87 Minn. 292.

42 Smith v. Metropolitan R. Co., 137 Mass. 61; Rittenhouse v. Wilmington St. Ry. Co., 120 N. C. 544.

43 Healey v. Wellesley & B. St. Ry. Co., 176 Mass. 440.

44 West Chicago St. R. Co. v. Dooley, 76 Ill. App. 424.

45 Sweeney v. Kansas City Cable Ry. Co., 150 Mo. 385.

46 Redford v. Spokane St. Ry. Co., 15 Wash. 419.

47 Chicago City Ry. Co. v. Hastings, 136 Ill. 251; Sullivan v. Jefferson Ave. Ry. Co., 133 Mo. 1.

48 Marsullo v. Metropolitan St. Ry. Co., 30 App. Div. (N. Y.) 505; Baber v. Broadway & S. A. R. Co., 9 Misc. Rep. (N. Y.) 20.

# CHAPTER XII.

## ADMISSIBILITY OF EVIDENCE.

I. Evidence Bearing upon Plaintiff's Injuries.

§ 145. The Plaintiff Himself as Evidence.
146. Physical Examination of Plaintiff.
147. Exclamations and Statements of Plaintiff.
148. Medical Testimony.
149. Evidence of Other Witnesses.

II. Evidence Bearing on the Question of the Defendant's Negligence.

§ 150. Competency of Employes.
151. Starting and Stopping Cars.
152. Condition of Car.
153. Condition of Track.
154. Speed of Car.
155. General Negligence in Operation of Road.

### I. Evidence Bearing upon Plaintiff's Injuries.

### § 145. The plaintiff himself as evidence.

It is proper for a physician to exhibit the plaintiff himself to the jury, and to plaee him in different positions;[1] and it is proper to permit the plaintiff to write his name and to drink a glass of water in the presence of the jury to show the extent of his injuries.[2] Similarly, it has been held proper for a plaintiff to exhibit his mutilated limbs to the jury,[3] but, on the other hand, the exhibition of a ehild's

1 Citizens' St. R. Co. v. Willoeby, 134 Ind. 563.

2 Clark v. Brooklyn Heights R. Co., 78 App. Div. (N. Y.) 478.

3 West Chicago St. R. Co. v. Grenell, 90 Ill. App. 30.

injured foot has been held to prejudice the jury to such an extent as to require a new trial,[4] and it is not proper to exhibit a child's amputated leg to the jury.[5] The clothing of a person who is run over by a street car,[6] and a boot worn at the time of the accident,[7] are properly admitted in evidence, but evidence that the jacket of a companion was torn while alighting from a crowded car is rightly excluded.[8]

A photograph of the plaintiff, taken a few days before the trial, is admissible when the plaintiff could not be present;[9] but the admission of a photograph taken the summer before the accident, as a proof of physical condition prior to the accident, is rightly refused.[10]

### § 146. Physical examination of plaintiff.

Numerous decisions have been made on the question of the power of the court to compel a physical examination of the plaintiff. In Joliet St. Ry. Co. v. Call[11] it was held that it was discretionary with the trial court to order the plaintiff to be examined by doctors out of court, but on appeal it was held that the court had no power to compel the plaintiff to submit to such an examination before the giving of any testimony.[12] It has been held that the plaintiff cannot be made to submit to a physical examination, or to exhibit the

4 Butez v. Fonda, J. & G. R. Co., 20 Misc. Rep. (N. Y.) 123.
5 Rost v. Brooklyn Heights R. Co., 10 App. Div. (N. Y.) 477.
6 Senn v. Southern Ry. Co., 108 Mo. 142.
7 Hays v. Gainesville St. Ry. Co., 70 Tex. 602.
8 Jacobs v. West End St. Ry. Co., 178 Mass. 116.
9 Cooper v. St. Paul City Ry. Co., 54 Minn. 379.
10 Gilbert v. West End St. Ry. Co., 160 Mass. 403.
11 42 Ill. App. 41.
12 143 Ill. 177.

injured parts of his body to the jury;[13] that an examination of the plaintiff by a doctor while the trial is in progress is not proper;[14] and that, where a father sued for the loss of his daughter's services, the case will not be dismissed because the daughter refuses to submit to a physical examination.[15] It has been held, however, that the court may compel a physical examination,[16] especially if the defendant makes an affidavit that it is in ignorance of the plaintiff's injury.[17] A concealment of injuries upon an examination by the company's doctor is ground for a new trial.[18]

### § 147. Exclamations and statements of plaintiff.

Exclamations of pain at the time of the accident are admissible,[19] and also statements of the plaintiff made at the time of the accident, or shortly after.[20] In like manner it has been held that the fact that no complaint was made by the plaintiff at the time of the injury may properly be considered in evidence.[21] On the other hand, it has been held in a number of cases that expressions and declarations of pain subsequent to the injury should not be admitted in evidence, on

[13] Mills v. Wilmington City Ry. Co., 1 Marvel (Del.) 269.

[14] Archer v. Sixth Ave. R. Co., 52 N. Y. Super. Ct. 373.

[15] Bagwell v. Atlanta Consol. St. Ry. Co., 109 Ga. 611.

[16] Camden & S. Ry. Co. v. Stetson, 177 U. S. 172; Harvey v. Philadelphia Traction Co., 26 Wkly. Notes Cas. (Pa.) 231; White v. Milwaukee City Ry. Co., 61 Wis. 536.

[17] Moses v. Newburgh Elec. Ry. Co., 91 Hun (N. Y.) 278.

[18] Dixon v. Brooklyn Heights R. Co., 35 Misc. Rep. (N. Y.) 422.

[19] Harris v. Detroit City Ry. Co., 76 Mich. 227; Hagenlocher v. Coney Island & B. R. Co., 99 N. Y. 136.

[20] Springfield Consol. Ry. Co. v. Hoeffner, 175 Ill. 634.

[21] Fuller v. Jamestown St. Ry. Co., 75 Hun (N. Y.) 273.

the familiar ground that they are not part of the *res gestae*,[22] while entirely apart from this rule, exclamations and complaints of pain at varying times after the occurrence of the accident have been held properly admissible to show the nature and extent of the plaintiff's injuries.[23] A plaintiff may testify as to internal injuries,[24] and may testify as to the length of time he was confined to his bed, and to the pain suffered in consequence of his injury,[25] and to present suffering.[26] On the other hand, it has been held that it is not proper to receive the testimony of the plaintiff as to the pain and inconvenience he has suffered as a result of the injuries,[27] or his opinion as to his future condition.[28]

### § 148. Medical testimony.

The testimony of a physician as to the cause of the injury is admissible,[29] and also his testimony as to the present and

22 Laughlin v. Street Ry. Co., 80 Mich. 154; Weber v. St. Paul City Ry. Co., 67 Minn. 155; Roche v. Brooklyn City & N. R. Co., 105 N. Y. 294; Donohue v. Brooklyn, Q. C. & S. R. Co., 53 App. Div. (N. Y.) 348.

23 West Chicago St. R. Co. v. Kennelly, 170 Ill. 508; Death v. Rapid Ry. Co., 119 Mich. 512; Omaha St. Ry. Co. v. Emminger, 57 Neb. 240; Nichols v. Brooklyn City R. Co., 30 Hun (N. Y.) 437; Lewke v. Dry Dock, E. B. & B. R. Co., 46 Hun (N. Y.) 283; Farrell v. Metropolitan St. Ry. Co., 51 App. Div. (N. Y.) 456.

24 Spurrier v. Front St. Cable Ry. Co., 3 Wash. St. 659.

25 North Chicago St. R. Co. v. Cook, 145 Ill. 551.

26 Lacas v. Detroit City Ry. Co., 92 Mich. 412.

27 North Chicago St. R. Co. v. Cook, 43 Ill. App. 634.

28 Price v. Charles Warner Co., 1 Pen. (Del.) 462; Atlanta St. R. Co. v. Walker, 93 Ga. 462.

29 Hammond, W. & E. C. Elec. Ry. Co. v. Spyzchalski, 17 Ind. App. 7; Baltimore City Passenger Ry. Co. v. Tanner, 90 Md. 315; Benja-

future condition of the plaintiff.[30] It is proper to show that the physical examination of the plaintiff was made while he was under the influence of chloroform;[31] and it is also proper to show that a boy who made an admission was not given a drug.[32] Exclamations of pain made when a doctor is examining the plaintiff with a view to treating him are properly admitted in evidence,[33] and a doctor may testify to the complaints of pain made to him by the plaintiff.[34]

The testimony of a physician in regard to the plaintiff's condition has been held inadmissible where the basis for the doctor's opinion appeared to be insufficient;[35] and statements

min v. Holyoke St. Ry. Co., 160 Mass. 3; Lacas v. Detroit City Ry. Co., 92 Mich. 412; Bush v. St. Joseph & B. H. St. Ry. Co., 113 Mich. 513; Donnelly v. St. Paul City Ry. Co., 70 Minn. 278; Joyce v. St. Paul City Ry. Co., 70 Minn. 339; Tracey v. Metropolitan St. Ry. Co., 49 App. Div. (N. Y.) 197; Hunter v. Third Ave. R. Co., 20 Misc. Rep. (N. Y.) 432.

30 Denver Tramway Co. v. Reid, 4 Colo. App. 53; Laughlin v. Street Ry. Co., 62 Mich. 220; Consolidated Traction Co. v. Lambertson, 59 N. J. Law, 297; Dale v. Brooklyn City, H. P. & P. P. R. Co., 1 Hun (N. Y.) 146; Clegg v. Metropolitan St. Ry. Co., 1 App. Div. (N. Y.) 207; Duggan v. Third Ave. R. Co., 8 Misc. Rep. (N. Y.) 89; O'Neil v. Dry Dock, E. B. & B. R. Co., 59 N. Y. Super. Ct. 123; Johnson v. Broadway & S. A. Ry. Co., 6 N. Y. Supp. 113; King v. Second Ave. R. Co., 75 Hun (N. Y.) 17; Mitchell v. Tacoma Ry. & Motor Co., 13 Wash. 560; Block v. Milwaukee St. Ry. Co., 89 Wis. 371.

31 Pueblo Elec. St. Ry. Co. v. Sherman, 25 Colo. 114.

32 Holman v. Union St. Ry. Co., 114 Mich. 208.

33 Heddle v. City Elec. Ry. Co., 112 Mich. 547.

34 Birmingham Union Ry. Co. v. Hale, 90 Ala. 8; Ashton v. Detroit City Ry. Co., 78 Mich. 587; Lammiman v. Detroit Citizens' St. Ry. Co., 112 Mich. 602; Brusch v. St. Paul City Ry. Co., 52 Minn. 512; Edlund v. St. Paul City Ry. Co., 78 Minn. 434.

35 Miller v. St. Paul City Ry. Co., 62 Minn. 216; Sullivan v. Metropolitan St. Ry. Co., 63 App. Div. (N. Y.) 46; Swenson v. Brooklyn Heights R. Co., 15 Misc. Rep. (N. Y.) 69; McCabe v. Third Ave. R.

of the plaintiff to a physician are not admissible when they were made to enable the doctor to be a witness.[36]

### § 149. Evidence of other witnesses.

The testimony of nonexperts as to the physical and mental condition of the plaintiff after the accident is admissible,[37] and it is proper to show the physical condition of the plaintiff prior to the accident.[38]

Mere opinion evidence, such as that of a daughter that her father was to blame,[39] or the opinion of a daughter as to the extent of her mother's sufferings,[40] is properly rejected.

## II. Evidence Bearing on the Question of the Defendant's Negligence.

### § 150. Competency of employes.

The care used in selecting a driver cannot be shown;[41]

Co., 22 Misc. Rep. (N. Y.) 707; Kummer v. Christopher & T. S. R. Co., 20 N. Y. Supp. 116.

36 West Chicago St. R. Co. v. Carr, 170 Ill. 479; West Chicago St. R. Co. v. Kennelly, 170 Ill. 508; Heddle v. City Elec. Ry. Co., 112 Mich. 547; Consolidated Traction Co. v. Lambertson, 60 N. J. Law, 452.

37 Chicago City Ry. Co. v. Van Vleck, 143 Ill. 480; West Chicago St. Ry. v. Fishman, 169 Ill. 196; Cicero & P. St. Ry. Co. v. Priest, 190 Ill. 592; Baltimore City Passenger Ry. Co. v. Nugent, 86 Md. 349; Harris v. Detroit City Ry. Co., 76 Mich. 227; Sharp v. Kansas City Cable Ry. Co., 114 Mo. 94; Bigelow v. Metropolitan St. Ry. Co., 48 Mo. App. 367; Webb v. Yonkers R. Co., 51 App. Div. (N. Y.) 194; Hamel v. Brooklyn Heights R. Co., 59 App. Div. (N. Y.) 135; King v. Second Ave. Ry. Co., 75 Hun (N. Y.) 17; Lombard & S. St. P. Ry. Co. v. Christian, 124 Pa. 114.

38 West Chicago St. R. Co. v. Cahill, 165 Ill. 496; North Chicago St. R. Co. v. Gillow, 166 Ill. 444; Gardner v. Detroit St. Ry. Co., 99 Mich. 182.

39 Saunders v. City & S. R. Co., 99 Tenn. 130.

40 Lombard & S. St. P. Ry. Co. v. Christian, 124 Pa. 114.

41 Augusta & S. R. Co. v. Randall, 85 Ga. 297.

and, in general, it is not competent to prove similar conduct of employes on other occasions, or their custom in operating a car, to show general competency or incompetency.[42] The discharge of a driver after an accident cannot be shown,[43] although in one case the contrary has been held.[44]

The acts of a driver on the same trip,[45] or of a motorman on the same day,[46] are admissible on the question of intoxication.

## § 151. Starting and stopping cars.

A city ordinance regulating the stopping of cars is admissible in evidence.[47] It has been held proper to show the custom of passengers in boarding[48] and in alighting,[49] and in giving the signals for starting and stopping cars;[50] but, on the

42 Railway Co. v. Harrell, 58 Ark. 454; Denver Tramway Co. v. Owens, 20 Colo. 107; Price v. Charles Warner Co., 1 Pen. (Del.) 462; Fitzpatrick v. Bloomington City Ry. Co., 73 Ill. App. 516; Hanson v. Urbana & C. El. St. Ry. Co., 75 Ill. App. 474; Maguire v. Middlesex R. Co., 115 Mass. 239; Blanchette v. Holyoke St. Ry. Co., 175 Mass. 51; Fonda v. St. Paul City Ry. Co., 71 Minn. 438; McBride v. St. Paul City Ry. Co., 72 Minn. 291; Hayes v. St. Louis R. Co., 15 Mo. App. 583; Wooster v. Broadway & S. A. R. Co., 72 Hun (N. Y.) 197; Hinton v. Cream City Ry. Co., 65 Wis. 323.

43 Hewitt v. Taunton St. Ry. Co., 167 Mass. 483; Schmitt v. Dry Dock, E. B. & B. R. Co., 3 N. Y. St. Rep. 257; Christensen v. Union Trunk Line, 6 Wash. 75.

44 Morrow v. St. Paul City Ry. Co., 74 Minn. 480.

45 Sears v. Seattle Consol. St. Ry. Co., 6 Wash. 227.

46 Pyne v. Broadway & S. A. R. Co., 19 N. Y. Supp. 217.

47 Harrison v. Sutter St. Ry. Co., 116 Cal. 156; Macon Consol. St. R. Co. v. Barnes, 113 Ga. 212; Jackson v. Grand Ave. R. Co., 118 Mo. 199.

48 Houston v. Gate City St. R. Co., 89 Ga. 272; North Chicago St. R. Co. v. Kaspers, 186 Ill. 246.

49 McDonald v. Montgomery St. Ry., 110 Ala. 161.

50 Nichols v. Lynn & B. R. Co., 168 Mass. 528.

contrary, it has been held that the custom of passengers in boarding[51] or leaving cars[52] should not be admitted. Expert evidence has been received on the question of the possibility of stopping a car,[53] and nonexpert evidence has been received on the question of what constitutes proper time for a passenger to alight.[54]

It has been held that nonexpert evidence as to the distance within which a car could be stopped should be rejected,[55] and that the opinion of a motorman as to stopping a car on the reverse power could not be received.[56] It is not proper to show that a car was stopped at the same place, on the same day, without accident,[57] or to show the construction of the car, where the accident was for an injury while alighting,[58] but it has been held proper to show experience in stopping cars on the day of the accident.[59]

## § 152. Condition of car.

Evidence is admissible to show the condition of a car,[60] and expert testimony has been admitted on the question of the

51 Citizens' St. R. Co. v. Spahr, 7 Ind. App. 23.

52 Atlanta Consol. St. Ry. Co. v. Bates, 103 Ga. 333; Louisville Ry. Co. v. Rammaker, 21 Ky. Law Rep. 250, 51 S. W. 175.

53 Watson v. Minneapolis St. Ry. Co., 53 Minn. 551; O'Neil v. Dry Dock, E. B. & B. R. Co., 59 N. Y. Super. Ct. 123.

54 Ward v. Charleston City Ry. Co., 19 S. C. 521.

55 Haggerty v. Brooklyn City & N. R. Co., 61 N. Y. 624; Barry v. Second Ave. R. Co., 1 Misc. Rep. (N. Y.) 502; Dominick v. Toledo Consol. St. Ry. Co., 3 Ohio Dec. 22.

56 Bliss v. United Traction Co., 75 App. Div. (N. Y.) 235.

57 Joliet St. Ry. Co. v. Call, 42 Ill. App. 41.

58 Lombard & S. St. P. Ry. Co. v. Christensen, 4 Pa. Super. Ct. Dig. 139.

59 Cunningham v. Fair Haven & W. R. Co., 72 Conn. 244.

60 North Chicago St. Ry. Co. v. Cotton, 140 Ill. 486; South Chicago

condition of electrical appliances.[61] It has been held that the defective condition of a car on the day before an accident may properly be shown,[62] and, in like manner, the prior condition of the brake, unchanged at the time of the accident.[63]

Opinion evidence of a driver as to the safety of a pin is not admissible,[64] and it cannot be shown that a safer appliance was substituted after the accident.[65] A rumor that a car had been on the line ever since it was built is inadmissible.[66] A photograph of another car has been held inadmissible.[67]

## § 153. Condition of track.

A city ordinance regulating the repair of tracks is admissible in evidence,[68] and evidence is admissible to show the dangerous character of the place[69] and of the track[70] where

City Ry. Co. v. Purvis, 193 Ill. 454; Chicago General Ry. Co. v. Capek 82 Ill. App. 168.

61 Beardsley v. Minneapolis St. Ry. Co., 54 Minn. 504.

62 Dougherty v. Missouri R. Co., 97 Mo. 647.

63 Denver Tramway Co. v. Crumbaugh, 23 Colo. 363.

64 Sappenfield v. Main St. & A. P. R. Co., 91 Cal. 48.

65 Sappenfield v. Main St. & A. P. R. Co., 91 Cal. 48.

66 Wormsdorf v. Detroit City Ry. Co., 75 Mich. 472.

67 People's Passenger Ry. Co. v. Green, 56 Md. 84.

68 Birmingham Union Ry. Co. v. Alexander, 93 Ala. 133.

69 Rowell v. Stamford St. R. Co., 64 Conn. 376; Burnstein v. Cass Ave. & F. G. Ry. Co., 56 Mo. App. 45; Cumming v. Brooklyn City R Co., 1 Silv. (N. Y.) 327; Toledo Consol. St. Ry. Co. v. Mammet, [illegible] Ohio Dec. 532; Dimmey v. Wheeling & E. G. R. Co., 27 W. Va. 32.

70 Fitch v. Mason City & C. L. Traction Co., 116 Iowa, 716.

the accident occurred. Nonexpert evidence has been received on the question of the safety of a crossing[71] or of the track.[72]

The previous condition of the track in an action for a defect in the track has been held admissible;[73] and the unchanged condition of the track from one to five months after the accident,[74] and the occurrence of a similar accident about the same time and place,[75] may be shown. In a derailment case it may be shown that other cars left the track at the same point;[76] and evidence of alterations in a curve since the accident has been admitted.[77]

In direct contrast to these rulings it has been held that repairs made on the floor of a car house after an accident cannot be shown in evidence;[78] and in cases of derailment, evidence of previous similar accidents has been held inadmissible.[79] The condition of the track at other times and places cannot be shown,[80] nor the fact that other accidents happened at the same place.[81] In general, conditions or customs

71 Laughlin v. Street Ry. Co., 62 Mich. 220; Kraut v. Frankford & S. P. City Passenger Ry., 160 Pa. 327.

72 Houston City St. Ry. Co. v. Medlenka, 17 Tex. Civ. App. 621.

73 Richmond Ry. & Elec. Co. v. Bowles, 92 Va. 738.

74 Joliet St. Ry. Co. v. Call, 42 Ill. App. 41.

75 Birmingham Union Ry. Co. v. Alexander, 93 Ala. 133.

76 Wooley v. Grand St. & N. R. Co., 83 N. Y. 121; Brooklyn St. R. Co. v. Kelley, 6 Ohio Cir. Ct. R. 155.

77 Augusta & S. R. Co. v. Renz, 55 Ga. 126.

78 Whelton v. West End St. Ry. Co., 172 Mass. 555.

79 Morrow v. Westchester Elec. Ry. Co., 54 App. Div. (N. Y.) 592; Reading City Passenger Ry. Co. v. Eckert, 1 Pa. Sup. Ct. Dig. 55

80 Cunningham v. Fair Haven & W. R. Co., 72 Conn. 244; Miller v St. Louis R. Co., 5 Mo. App. 471.

81 North Chicago St. Ry. Co. v. Hudson, 44 Ill. App. 60.

on other roads are inadmissible,[82] and it cannot be shown that the street was in the same condition as any other street.[83] The removal of a snowbank on the day after the accident cannot be shown.[84]

## § 154. Speed of car.

A city ordinance regulating the speed of a car is properly admitted in evidence,[85] although the contrary has been held;[86] and a schedule of the company showing the average speed of its cars is rightly admitted.[87] Expert testimony has been held proper on the subject of speed;[88] and nonexpert testimony has been received on the same question in a number of instances,[89] while in other cases such testimony has

82 Bosqui v. Sutro R. Co., 131 Cal. 390; Laufer v. Bridgeport Traction Co., 68 Conn. 475; Wilkins v. Omaha & C. B. Ry. & Bridge Co., 96 Iowa, 668; Moldenhauer v. Minneapolis St. Ry. Co., 80 Minn. 426.

83 McLaughlin v. Philadelphia Traction Co., 175 Pa. 565.

84 Markowitz v. Dry Dock, E. B. & B. R. Co., 12 Misc. Rep. (N. Y.) 412.

85 Highland Ave. & B. R. Co. v. Sampson, 112 Ala. 425; Atlanta Consol. St. Ry. Co. v. Foster, 108 Ga. 223; Baltimore City Passenger Ry. Co. v. McDonnell, 43 Md. 534; Wright v. Malden & M. R. Co., 4 Allen (Mass.) 283; Kelly v. Union Ry. & Transit Co., 95 Mo. 279; Wade v. City Ry. Co., 36 Or. 311; Hall v. Ogden City St. Ry. Co., 13 Utah, 243.

86 Rockford City Ry. Co. v. Blake, 173 Ill. 354; East Cleveland R. Co. v. Rosecrans, 24 Wkly. Law Bul. (Ohio) 220.

87 Central Ry. Co. v. Allmon, 147 Ill. 471.

88 Garduhn v. Union Ry. Co., 50 App. Div. (N. Y.) 602.

89 Robinson v. Louisville Ry. Co. (C. C. A.) 112 Fed. 484; Highland Ave. & B. R. Co. v. Sampson, 112 Ala. 425; Johnsen v. Oakland, S. L. & H. Elec. Ry., 127 Cal. 608; Eckington & S. H. R. Co. v. Hunter, 6 App. D. C. 287; West Chicago St. R. Co. v. Dedloff, 92 Ill. App. 547; Owensboro City R. Co. v. Lyddane, 19 Ky. Law Rep. 698, 41 S. W. 578.

been classed as mere opinion evidence, and, as such, inadmissible.[90]

An ordinance regulating the speed of steam cars is inadmissible to show what is reasonable speed for an electric car;[91] and an ordinance regulating the speed of a car while crossing a bridge is inadmissible to show negligence before crossing.[92] The rate of speed of other cars of the company[93] or of another company[94] is not material; and neither is the fact that the car was running at high speed on other occasions.[95] When the issue is whether a car was running thirty miles an hour, evidence that the company contracted for the cars to run twenty miles an hour is not admissible;[96] and evidence of a witness that he had seen races of a similar kind between horse cars on other occasions is rightly rejected.[97]

## § 155. General negligence in operation of road.

In many cases the admission or rejection of evidence connected with the operation of the road depends on whether it was connected with the accident to a sufficient extent to bring it within the familiar rule of forming a part of the

90 Chicago City Ry. Co. v. Wall, 93 Ill. App. 411; Pfeiffer v. Chicago City Ry. Co., 96 Ill. App. 10.

91 Maxwell v. Wilmington City Ry. Co., 1 Marvel (Del.) 199.

92 Ulrich v. Toledo Consol. St. Ry. Co., 5 Ohio Circ. Dec. 111.

93 West Chicago St. R. Co. v. Torpe, 187 Ill. 610; Hewlett v. Brooklyn Heights R. Co., 63 App. Div. (N. Y.) 423; Wade v. City Ry. Co., 36 Or. 311.

94 Schierhold v. North Beach & M. R. Co., 40 Cal. 447.

95 Christensen v. Union Trunk Line, 6 Wash. 75.

96 Orr v. Cedar Rapids & M. C. Ry. Co., 94 Iowa, 423.

97 Whitbeck v. Atlantic Ave. R. Co., 4 N. Y. Supp. 100.

*res gestae.* On the question of negligence, exclamations of plaintiff at the time of the accident,[98] and statements made at the time of the accident, or shortly afterwards, have been held admissible.[99] In like manner, the fact that no complaint was made by the plaintiff at the time of the accident has been admitted.[100] Conduct of passengers at the time of the collision,[101] the crying of the plaintiff's children during their ejection,[102] and the cries of bystanders to explain the conduct of persons hearing them[103] are all admissible in evidence; and it is proper to show that no bell was rung,[104] and that the driver was whipping his horses when the accident occurred.[105] On the same principle, declarations made immediately before the accident,[106] and declarations of the defendant's servants while the car was still on top of the plaintiff, have been admitted.[107]

98 Anderson v. Citizens' St. R. Co., 12 Ind. App. 194; Trenton Passenger Ry. Co. v. Cooper, 60 N. J. Law, 219.

99 Washington & G. R. Co. v. McLane, 11 App. D. C. 220; Brown v. Louisville Ry. Co., 21 Ky. Law Rep. 995, 53 S. W. 1041; Chicago West Div. Ry. Co. v. Becker, 30 Ill. App. 200; Leahey v. Cass Ave. & F. G. Ry. Co., 97 Mo. 165; Stein v. Railway Co., 10 Phila. (Pa.) 440.

100 Kummer v. Christopher & T. S. R. Co., 20 N. Y. Supp. 116.

101 Holman v. Union St. Ry. Co., 114 Mich. 208; Kleiber v. People's Ry. Co., 107 Mo. 240.

102 O'Rourke v. Street Ry. Co., 103 Tenn. 124.

103 Atlanta Consol. St. Ry. Co. v. Bagwell, 107 Ga. 157; Kleiber v. People's Ry. Co., 107 Mo. 240.

104 East St. Louis Elec. St. Ry. Co. v. Burns, 77 Ill. App. 529; Chicago General Ry. Co. v. Kriz, 94 Ill. App. 277.

105 Atlanta St. R. Co. v. Walker, 93 Ga. 462.

106 Denver & B. P. Rapid Transit Co. v. Dwyer, 20 Colo. 132; Witsell v. West Asheville & S. S. Ry. Co., 120 N. C. 557.

107 Quincy Horse Ry. & Carrying Co. v. Gnuse, 137 Ill. 264; Springfield Consol. Ry. Co. v. Welsch, 56 Ill. App. 196.

On the other hand, declarations of the plaintiff made after the accident,[108] as, for instance, after having walked to the house of a relative,[109] or while in an ambulance on the way to the hospital,[110] have been held inadmissible; and declarations of the defendant's servants[111] and other parties,[112] made after the accident, have been held inadmissible.

Evidence is admissible to show the number of passengers on a car,[113] and the custom of passengers in using the running board;[114] and a rule forbidding intoxicated persons to

108 Washington & G. R. Co. v. McLane, 11 App. D. C. 220; Augusta & S. R. Co. v. Randall, 79 Ga. 304; Chicago West Div. Ry. Co. v. Becker, 128 Ill. 545; Citizens' St. R. Co. v. Stoddard, 10 Ind. App. 278; Leahey v. Cass Ave. & F. G. Ry. Co., 97 Mo. 165; McCabe v. Dry Dock, E. B. & B. R. Co., 15 Daly (N. Y.) 504.

109 Augusta & S. R. Co. v. Randall, 79 Ga. 304.

110 Washington & G. R. Co. v. McLane, 11 App. D. C. 220; Citizens' St. R. Co. v. Stoddard, 10 Ind. App. 278.

111 Wilcox v. Wilmington City Ry. Co., 2 Pen. (Del.) 157; Metropolitan R. Co. v. Collins, 1 App. D. C. 383; Electric Ry. Co. v. Carson, 98 Ga. 652; Dietrich v. Baltimore & H. S. Ry. Co., 58 Md. 347; Williamson v. Cambridge R. Co., 144 Mass. 148; Wormsdorf v. Detroit City Ry. Co., 75 Mich. 472; Gardner v. Detroit St. Ry. Co., 99 Mich. 182; Reem v. St. Paul City Ry. Co., 77 Minn. 503; North Hudson County Ry. Co. v. May, 48 N. J. Law, 401; Blackman v. West Jersey & S. R. Co., 68 N. J. Law, 1; Luby v. Hudson River R. Co., 17 N. Y. 131; Whitaker v. Eighth Ave. R. Co., 51 N. Y. 295; Furst v. Second Ave. R. Co., 72 N. Y. 542; Seipp v. Dry Dock, E. B. & B. R. Co., 45 App. Div. (N. Y.) 489; Wilson v. Nassau Elec. R. Co., 56 App. Div. (N. Y.) 570; Street R. Co. v. Howard, 102 Tenn. 474.

112 Budd v. Meriden Elec. R. Co., 69 Conn. 272; Baltimore City Passenger Ry. Co. v. McDonnell, 43 Md. 534; Senn v. Southern Ry. Co., 108 Mo. 142; Murray v. Salt Lake City R. Co., 16 Utah, 356.

114 Citizens' St. R. Co. v. Hoffbauer, 23 Ind. App. 614.

114 Citizens St. R. Co. v. Hoffbauer, 23 Ind. App. 614.

ride on the front platform, and a notice forbidding persons from riding on the front platform, are both admissible.[115]

Evidence of the noise made by a cable is properly admitted;[116] and it is proper to introduce evidence that the attention of one of the directors of the company was called to a defective cable,[117] and to show the failure of an engineer, in a collision case, to throw sand upon the tracks.[118]

The rules of a company as to operating its cars are admissible;[119] but the records of the company, to show that the cars were not crowded,[120] and the trip sheet of a conductor,[121] have both been held inadmissible. It is proper to show that a trolley wire had broken frequently before;[122] but the negligence of a telephone company in placing a wire cannot be shown, where the action was for the negligence of the street railway in knocking it down.[123]

Opinion evidence of witnesses has been held inadmissible on questions of the general operation of the road.[124]

115 O'Neill v. Lynn & B. R. Co., 155 Mass. 371.

116 Mitchell v. Tacoma Ry. & Motor Co., 13 Wash. 560.

117 Musser v. Lancaster City St. Ry. Co., 176 Pa. 621.

118 Highland Ave. & B. R. Co. v. Swope, 115 Ala. 287.

119 Percy v. Metropolitan St. Ry. Co., 58 Mo. App. 75; Cincinnati St. Ry. Co. v. Altemeier, 60 Ohio St. 10; Pittsburg, A. & M. P. Ry. Co. v. Caldwell, 74 Pa. 421.

120 Dickson v. Ridge Ave. Passenger Ry. Co., 19 Phila. (Pa.) 430.

121 West Chicago St. R. Co. v. Kromshinsky, 185 Ill. 92.

122 Rockford City Ry. Co. v. Blake, 173 Ill. 354.

123 Kankakee El. Ry. Co. v. Whittemore, 45 Ill. App. 484.

124 Orr v. Cedar Rapids & M. C. Ry. Co., 94 Iowa, 423; Bergen County Traction Co. v. Bliss, 62 N. J. Law, 410; Musser v. Lancaster City St. Ry. Co., 176 Pa. 621; Woeckner v. Erie Elec. Motor Co., 187 Pa. 206.

## CHAPTER XIII.

DAMAGES.

§ 156. Excessive and Inadequate Damages.
157. Damages for Mental Suffering.
158. Special Damages.
159. Vindictive Damages.
160. Aggravation of Injuries.
161. Damages for Death.

### § 156. Excessive and inadequate damages.

It is well settled that a verdict will not be set aside on the ground of excessive damages unless it is so large as to indicate passion or prejudice on the part of the jury.[1] Where

[1] Wheaton v. North Beach & Mission R. Co., 36 Cal. 590; Swain v. Fourteenth St. R. Co., 93 Cal. 179; Redfield v. Oakland Consol. St. Ry. Co., 110 Cal. 277; Howland v. Oakland Consol. St. Ry. Co., 110 Cal. 513; City & Suburban Ry. v. Brauss, 70 Ga. 368; North Chicago St. R. Co. v. Zeiger, 182 Ill. 9; North Chicago St. R. Co. v. Eldridge, 51 Ill. App. 430; West Chicago St. Ry. Co. v. Craig, 57 Ill. App. 411; North Chicago St. Ry. Co. v. Brodie, 57 Ill. App. 564; North Chicago St. R. Co. v. Anderson, 70 Ill. App. 336; North Chicago St. R. Co. v. Hoffart, 82 Ill. App. 539; West Chicago St. R. Co. v. Luleich, 85 Ill. App. 643; West Chicago St. R. Co. v. Shiplett, 85 Ill. App. 683; Cicero & P. St. Ry. Co. v. Boyd, 95 Ill. App. 510; Henderson St. Ry. Co. v. Wood, 21 Ky. Law Rep. 808, 53 S. W. 1116; Lowe v. Minneapolis St. Ry. Co., 37 Minn. 283; McKenna v. North Hudson County Ry. Co., 64 N. J. Law, 106; Pollak v. Metropolitan St. Ry. Co., 28 Misc. Rep. (N. Y.) 791; Mitchell v. Broadway & S. A. R. Co., 70 Hun (N. Y.) 387; Cincinnati St. Ry. Co. v. Kelsey, 2 Ohio Dec. 440; Whipple v. West Phila. Passenger Ry. Co., 2 Wkly. Notes Cas. (Pa.) 559; McGowan v. Interstate Consol. St. Ry. Co., 20 R. I. 264; Richmond Ry. & Elec. Co. v. Garthright, 92 Va. 627.

a verdict is excessive, but not sufficiently so to show passion or prejudice, it is proper for the court to require a remittitur of part of the amount.[2] Where a verdict is so excessive, however, as to show passion or prejudice, it is not a case for a remittitur, and the whole verdict must be set aside.[3] The court has power to allow a remittitur of one-half the amount of the verdict, entered on the plaintiff's own motion;[4] and where a woman consented to take $750, a verdict for $1,000 was reduced to that sum.[5] A charge that the jury may award fair compensation to any amount not exceeding $30,000 amounts to an intimation that the jury may render a verdict for that sum, and is error, where such a verdict would clearly be excessive.[6] An appellate court may reduce still further a verdict where a remittitur was ordered.[7]

A verdict will be reversed where the damages are too small, as well as where they are too large,[8] and, on this principle, verdicts have been set aside in the following cases:

[2] Doolin v. Omnibus Cable Co., 125 Cal. 141; Sinclair v. Washington & G. R. Co., MacArthur & M. (D. C.) 13; West Chicago St. R. Co. v. Fishman, 68 Ill. App. 445; North Chicago St. R. Co. v. Shreve, 70 Ill. App. 666; Cicero & P. St. Ry. Co. v. Brown, 89 Ill. App. 318; South Chicago City Ry. Co. v. McDonald, 94 Ill. App. 612; Pendleton St. R. Co. v. Rahmann, 22 Ohio St. 446.

[3] West Chicago St. R. Co. v. Johnson, 69 Ill. App. 147; West Chicago St. R. Co. v. Wheeler, 73 Ill. App. 368; Chicago City Ry. Co. v. Fennimore, 78 Ill. App. 478; North Chicago St. R. Co. v. Hoffart, 82 Ill. App. 539.

[4] North Chicago St. R. Co. v. Wrixon, 150 Ill. 532.

[5] Flournoy v. Shreveport Belt Ry. Co., 50 La. Ann. 635.

[6] Gilbertson v. Forty-Second St., M. & St. N. Ave. Ry. Co., 14 App Div. (N. Y.) 294.

[7] Stemmerman v. Nassau Elec. R. Co., 36 App. Div. (N. Y.) 218.

[8] Boggess v. Metropolitan St. Ry. Co., 118 Mo. 328; Landneier v Cincinnati St. Ry. Co., 4 Ohio S. & C. P. Dec. 265.

Where the plaintiff lost a leg, was idle for a year, and his earning capacity was greatly diminished, $1,000 was held to be insufficient.[9] $500 is inadequate where a plaintiff was severely injured, and spent $400 as a result of the accident.[10] Where the plaintiff was in bed six weeks, and spent $88 for medicine, a verdict for $55 was held to be insufficient.[11] A verdict for 85 cents in an assault case is inadequate;[12] and a verdict for 6 cents is not enough where there was clear evidence of $100 damages,[13] where a plaintiff was considerably injured, and had a doctor's bill for $150,[14] and where a healthy boy of 16 was killed.[15] Where the plaintiff suffered considerably, and was put to expense, it was held that a verdict for 1 cent could not stand.[16] A verdict for doctors' bills, without any allowance for the injury, is insufficient.[17]

Where there was clear evidence of substantial damages, and the jury rendered a verdict for 6¼ cents, an order for a new trial unless the plaintiff paid $400 is error, since the plaintiff is entitled to have his damages assessed by a jury.[18]

9 Eberhardt v. Metropolitan St. Ry. Co., 69 App. Div. (N. Y.) 560.

10 Morrissey v. Westchester Elec. Ry. Co., 30 App. Div. (N. Y.) 424.

11 Saperstone v. Rochester Ry. Co., 25 App. Div. (N. Y.) 285.

12 Hanson v. Urbana & C. Elec. St. Ry. Co., 75 Ill. App. 474.

13 Kerr v. Union Ry. Co., 20 Misc. Rep. (N. Y.) 171.

14 De La Torre v. Metropolitan St. Ry. Co., 48 App. Div. (N. Y.) 126.

15 Morris v. Metropolitan St. Ry. Co., 51 App. Div. (N. Y.) 512.

16 Chouquette v. Southern Elec. R. Co., 152 Mo. 257.

17 Katz v. Brooklyn Heights R. Co., 35 Misc. Rep. (N. Y.) 302.

18 Bradwell v. Pittsburgh & W. E. Passenger Ry. Co., 139 Pa. 404.

—— **Verdict held not excessive.**

$25,000 is not excessive for the death of an active and successful business man.[19] $22,500 was held not to be excessive where a boy of 11 lost a leg.[20] $20,000 was held not to be excessive where a plaintiff lost both legs.[21] $16,500 is not excessive where a man 45 years old, in good health, and with prospects of the average American man who has to make his own career, is injured so severely that his ability to get ahead in life is almost ended.[22] $15,000 is not excessive where a child of 6 had his leg cut off.[23] $15,000 was held not excessive where a strong, healthy woman was rendered an invalid.[24] $15,000 was held not to be excessive where a plaintiff was in an incurable paralytic condition.[25] $15,000 is not excessive where a person is physically disabled from all active exercise for the rest of his life, and can walk only with crutches, and, at the end of 4 years, is suffering great pain.[26] $15,000 is not excessive for a severe and permanent injury to a leg.[27] $15,000 is held not excessive where a woman became partially crazy from her injuries.[28] $15,000 is not excessive where a child lost a leg below the knee.[29]

19 Sternfels v. Metropolitan St. Ry. Co., 73 App. Div. (N. Y.) 494.

20 Williamson v. Brooklyn Heights R. Co., 53 App. Div. (N. Y.) 399.

21 Fonda v. St. Paul City Ry. Co., 77 Minn. 336.

22 Orbann v. Philadelphia Traction Co., 19 Phila. (Pa.) 413.

23 Chicago City Ry. Co. v. Leach, 80 Ill. App. 354.

24 Chicago City Ry. Co. v. Wilcox, 33 Ill. App. 450.

25 Sears v. Seattle Consol. St. Ry. Co., 6 Wash. 227.

26 Bishop v. St. Paul City Ry. Co., 48 Minn. 26.

27 Chicago City Ry. Co. v. Taylor, 68 Ill. App. 613.

28 Mitchell v. Broadway & S. A. R. Co., 70 Hun (N. Y.) 387.

29 Texarkana St. Ry. Co. v. Hart (Tex. Civ. App.) 26 S. W. 435.

$15,000 was held proper where a child lost a leg.[30] $14,000 is not an excessive verdict in an action by a husband and minor children for the death of a wife and mother, the statutory restrictions in other states not being in force in California.[31] $12,500 was not excessive where a man over 60 years of age received injuries which rendered him an invalid and incapable of performing manual or mental labor in the future.[32] $12,500 was held not to be excessive where a woman suffered serious and incurable internal injuries.[33] $12,000 was held not to be excessive where a plaintiff, who was an expert telegraph operator, had to have his left arm amputated, and suffered very much.[34] $12,000 is not excessive for loss of a child's leg.[35] $12,000 was not excessive where a traveler was permanently injured and rendered almost helpless.[36] $10,000 is not excessive where a healthy woman was rendered a complete wreck.[37] $10,000 was not excessive where a woman suffered a miscarriage, and was left in pain and bad health.[38] $10,000 is not excessive where a woman was earning $75 a month as a stenographer, and was injured so that she was unable to do anything in her business.[39] $10,000 was held not to be excessive for injury to a previously

30 Kalfur v. Broadway Ferry & M. Ave. R. Co., 34 App. Div. (N. Y.) 267.

31 Redfield v. Oakland Consol. St. Ry. Co., 110 Cal. 277.

32 West Chicago St. R. Co. v. Bode, 51 Ill. App. 440.

33 Cannon v. Brooklyn City R. Co., 9 Misc. Rep. (N. Y.) 282.

34 Dougherty v. Missouri R. Co., 97 Mo. 647.

35 Akersloot v. Second Ave. R. Co., 59 N. Y. Super. Ct. 555.

36 North Chicago St. R. Co. v. Dudgeon, 83 Ill. App. 528.

37 Mattis v. Philadelphia Traction Co., 6 Pa. Dist. Ct. R. 94.

38 Howland v. Oakland Consol. St. Ry. Co., 110 Cal. 513.

39 North Chicago St. R. Co. v. Eldridge, 51 Ill. App. 430.

healthy and active woman and mother leading a useful life.[40] $10,000 was not excessive where a woman fractured her hip, which was permanently injured, and, seven years after the accident, was obliged to walk with the aid of a cane.[41] $10,000 is not excessive where a strong, healthy woman of 38 became a confirmed invalid.[42] $10,000 was held not to be excessive where a man who was earning $3,000 a year suffered terribly, and recovery was doubtful.[43] $10,000 is not excessive where two ribs were broken, and a severe, incurable disease developed.[44] $9,000 is not excessive for unusually severe and permanent injuries.[45] $9,000 was held not excessive where a conductor 56 years old was so injured in his leg that he was practically deprived of the power of earning a living, and the injury was likely to be permanent, and it appeared that he acted as conductor only in the winter, and earned $1,200 a year as a dealer in vegetables.[46] $8,800 was held not to be excessive where a plaintiff suffered greatly, and it appeared that his disease was incurable.[47] $8,400 is not excessive where a man 40 years old lost one foot, the hearing of one ear, his sense of smell, and suffered great pain for many months, and lost his business.[48] $8,000 was held not to be excessive where a man of 25 lost his right

40 North Chicago St. R. Co. v. Anderson, 70 Ill. App. 336.
41 North Chicago St. R. Co. v. Fitzgibbons, 79 Ill. App. 632.
42 Cannon v. Brooklyn City R. Co., 14 Misc. Rep. (N. Y.) 400.
43 Macon Consol. St. R. Co. v. Barnes, 113 Ga. 212.
44 Clark v. Brooklyn Heights R. Co., 78 App. Div. (N. Y.) 478.
45 Houston City Ry. Co. v. Medlenka, 17 Tex. Civ. App. 621.
46 Furman v. Brooklyn Heights R. Co., 25 App. Div. (N. Y.) 133.
47 Cooper v. St. Paul City Ry. Co., 54 Minn. 379.
48 Central Ry. Co. v. Bannister, 96 Ill. App. 332.

arm.[49] $8,000 was held not to be excessive for the death of a husband who made a good living for his widow, who was an invalid, and was left with a daughter of 23.[50] $7,500 is not excessive for permanent injury to a man earning $300 a month.[51] $7,500 is not excessive where an injury to the plaintiff results in an incurable disease.[52] $7,500 was held not to be excessive where a police officer was thrown from a patrol wagon and seriously injured.[53] $7,500 was held to be proper where an accident to a woman caused a marked deformity, and she was permanently crippled.[54] $7,500 was held to be proper where a healthy man of 40 earned $12 a week, and, after the accident, suffered severely, lost forty pounds, and was unable to work.[55] $7,500 is not excessive for great suffering and permanent disability of a man who had been earning $300 a month.[56] $7,250 is not an excessive verdict where a husband sues for the loss of his wife's services, and she is so injured that she can contribute nothing to his aid, comfort, or society.[57] $7,000 was held not excessive where a child was rendered a cripple for life.[58] $7,000 is proper where plaintiff lost a leg, was idle a year, and his earning capacity was diminished.[59] $7,000 was held to be

49 O'Keefe v. Eighth Ave. R. Co., 33 App. Div. (N. Y.) 324.

50 Cook v. Clay St. Hill R. Co., 60 Cal. 604.

51 Lowry v. Mt. Adams & E. P. I. P. Ry. Co., 68 Fed. 827.

52 Galveston City R. Co. v. Hewitt, 67 Tex. 473.

53 Swain v. Fourteenth St. R. Co., 93 Cal. 179.

54 West Chicago St. R. Co. v. Tuerk, 90 Ill. App. 105.

55 Chicago City Ry. Co. v. Anderson, 93 Ill. App. 419.

56 Lowry v. Mt. Adams & E. P. I. P. Ry. Co., 68 Fed. 827.

57 Zingrebe v. Union Ry. Co., 56 App. Div. (N. Y.) 555.

58 Ft. Worth St. R. Co. v. Witten, 74 Tex. 202.

59 Eberhardt v. Metropolitan St. Ry. Co., 69 App. Div. (N. Y.) 560.

a proper verdict where a child suffered much pain, actual disfigurement, and loss of earning capacity.[60] $6,950 was held proper where the plaintiff lost part of his right foot, and was permanently disabled from standing any length of time.[61] $6,750 is not excessive where a strong man became a wreck.[62] $6,000 was held not excessive where a girl had her face permanently disfigured, and her collar bone and four ribs broken.[63] $6,000 was held not to be excessive where injuries were severe, lasting, and liable to end fatally.[64] $5,500 was held not to be excessive where a woman fractured her knee, causing a permanent injury.[65] $5,500 was held not to be an excessive verdict where a woman suffered in her eyesight, lost flesh, and was apparently permanently disabled.[66] $5,000 was held not to be an excessive verdict where a healthy, active woman of 70 had the use of one of her limbs permanently destroyed.[67] $5,000 is not excessive for the death of a bright boy of 7.[68] $5,000 is not excessive for the death of a woman 63 years old, who did all the work in her husband's household, and was in good health.[69] $5,000 was held not to be excessive where a strong, healthy woman was in bed six months, suffered much pain, and there was evidence tending to show that an injury to her hip might be

60 Allen v. Ames College Ry. Co., 106 Iowa, 602.

61 Elliott v. Newport St. Ry. Co., 18 R. I. 707.

62 Gidionsen v. Union Depot R. Co., 129 Mo. 392.

63 Bennett v. Brooklyn Heights R. Co., 1 App. Div. (N. Y.) 205.

64 Watson v. Minneapolis St. Ry. Co., 53 Minn. 551.

65 Whipple v. West Phila. Passenger Ry. Co., 2 Wkly. Notes Cas. (Pa.) 559.

66 Chicago City Ry. Co. v. Lace, 62 Ill. App. 535.

67 Hinton v. Cream City R. Co., 65 Wis. 323.

68 Cicero & P. St. Ry. Co. v. Boyd, 95 Ill. App. 510.

69 Lyons v. Second Ave. R. Co., 89 Hun (N. Y.) 374.

permanent.[70] $5,000 was held not to be excessive where a plaintiff suffered a fracture of the thigh bone, followed by pain, permanent after effects, etc.[71] $5,000 was held not to be excessive where a boy suffered terribly, and his legs were permanently deformed.[72] $5,000 was held not to be an excessive verdict where a woman was pregnant at the time of the accident, and gave birth prematurely to twins, who died when they were 2 years old, and the mother suffered severely, and was unable to work.[73] $5,000 is not excessive for the death of a healthy young man who has been supporting his family.[74] $5,000 was held not to be excessive for serious injuries.[75] $5,000 was held to be a proper verdict where a healthy woman was killed, and she left two small children.[76] $5,000 in an action by a mother is not excessive, although the child had recovered $10,000.[77] $4,950 was held not to be excessive where a woman fractured two ribs.[78] $4,500 is not excessive where a man was killed by an electric shock.[79] $4,000 was held not to be an excessive verdict where a boy of 17 suffered a permanent and almost total loss of the use of his left arm.[80] $4,000 was held not to be excessive where a woman earned $75 a month, and suffered for seventeen

70 North Chicago St. R. Co. v. Brown, 76 Ill. App. 654.

71 O'Connell v. St. Louis Cable & W. Ry. Co., 106 Mo. 482.

72 Metropolitan St. R. Co. v. Moore, 83 Ga. 453.

73 North Chicago St. R. Co. v. Smadraff, 89 Ill. App. 411.

74 San Antonio St. Ry. Co. v. Renken, 15 Tex. Civ. App. 229.

75 Lowe v. Minneapolis St. Ry. Co., 37 Minn. 283.

76 Dimmey v. Wheeling & E. G. R. Co., 27 W. Va. 32.

77 Cummings v. Brooklyn City R. Co., 52 Hun, 613, 5 N. Y. Supp. 476.

78 Omaha Horse Ry. Co. v. Doolittle, 7 Neb. 481.

79 Atlanta Consol. St. Ry. Co. v. Owings, 97 Ga. 663.

80 McCoy v. Milwaukee St. Ry. Co., 88 Wis. 56.

months without being able to do any work, and it seemed that her injuries were likely to be permanent.[81] $4,000 is not excessive where there is evidence that injury to a woman is permanent.[82] $4,000 was held to be a proper verdict where a plaintiff suffered severe pain for months, and had not entirely recovered three years after the accident, and the doctors were not sure that she would ever entirely recover.[83] $3,750 is not an excessive verdict where a woman suffered severe internal injury, probably permanent.[84] $3,600 was held not to be excessive where a man of 64 broke a rib, and suffered severe injuries in consequence.[85] $3,500 was held not to be excessive where a child of 7 had two bones broken, and recovery was uncertain.[86] $3,500 is not excessive for a person injured internally and externally.[87] $3,500 was held not to be excessive in an action by a widow for the death of her husband, who was 69 years old, but in good health.[88] $3,500 was not excessive where a man of 65 was rendered unable to work, and suffered a great deal.[89] $3,500 was held not to be excessive where a man of 50, permanently injured, was growing steadily worse, and had spent $600 in doctor's bills.[90] $3,500, where a man had his leg very badly injured,

81 Bryant v. Omaha & C. B. Ry. & Bridge Co., 98 Iowa, 483.

82 Fitton v. Brooklyn City R. Co., 5 N. Y. Supp. 641.

83 Heucke v. Milwaukee City Ry. Co., 69 Wis. 401.

84 Rippe v. Metropolitan St. Ry. Co., 35 App. Div. (N. Y.) 321.

85 Eifinger v. Brooklyn Heights R. Co., 13 Misc. Rep. (N. Y.) 389.

86 Hutchinson v. Atlantic Ave. R. Co., 33 App. Div. (N. Y.) 569.

87 Willis v. Second Ave. Traction Co., 189 Pa. 430.

88 Gross v. Electric Traction Co., 18 Pa. Co. Ct. R. 29.

89 McCready v. Staten Island Elec. R. Co., 51 App. Div. (N. Y.) 338.

90 Mowbray v. Brooklyn Heights R. Co., 59 App. Div. (N. Y.) 239.

and there was evidence tending to show that his injuries were permanent, was held proper.[91] $3,500 was held proper where plaintiff had a rib broken, and was a nervous wreck.[92] $3,250 is not excessive where permanent nervous injury causes a loss of muscular power in the plaintiff's hand, and $175 is spent in doctor's bills.[93] $3,000 was held not to be excessive where a plaintiff's arm was crushed.[94] $3,000 is not an excessive verdict where the plaintiff's general health was greatly impaired, and she suffered great bodily pain.[95] $3,000 was held not excessive where an employe ruptured the ligaments of his back, broke a rib, and became entirely deaf in one ear.[96] $3,000 was held not to be excessive where a boy suffered a permanent injury to his leg.[97] $3,000 was held not excessive where a plaintiff's leg was severely injured, and she had not recovered two years and a half after the accident.[98] $3,000 was held not an excessive verdict where a muscle in a man's leg was cut so that he suffered considerably, and the leg was permanently weakened.[99] $3,000 is not excessive for killing a boy 5 years old.[100] $2,950 is not excessive where a man 56 years old is suddenly deprived of following his trade.[101] $2,750 was held not to be excessive where a woman suffered severe injuries to her

91 Joliet R. Co. v. McPherson, 96 Ill. App. 286.
92 Bertram v. People's Ry. Co., 154 Mo. 639.
93 Wilson v. Broadway & S. A. R. Co., 8 Misc. Rep. (N. Y.) 450.
94 Chicago West Div. Ry. Co. v. Hughes, 69 Ill. 170.
95 Louisville Ry. Co. v. Park, 96 Ky. 580.
96 Chicago General Ry. Co. v. McNamara, 94 Ill. App. 188.
97 Buck v. People's St. Ry. & E. L. & P. Co., 108 Mo. 179.
98 Demond v. Brooklyn City R. Co., 8 Misc. Rep. (N. Y.) 610.
99 West Chicago St. R. Co. v. Johnson, 77 Ill. App. 142.
100 West Chicago St. R. Co. v. Waniata, 68 Ill. App. 481.
101 Street Ry. Co. v. Rohner, 3 Ohio Dec. 570.

side and recovery was doubtful.[102] $2,750 was held not to be excessive where plaintiff's leg was injured.[103] $2,500 is not excessive in an assault case.[104] $2,500 is not excessive where a person, who was two months in the hospital, walked on crutches for four years, and recovery was a matter of doubt.[105] $2,500 is not excessive where a plaintiff fractured three ribs, and was permanently injured.[106] $2,500 is not excessive for an unwarrantable ejection in a rude and violent manner, although the injuries are not very serious.[107] $2,500 was held not to be an excessive verdict where a plaintiff had to have part of his ear removed, and suffered pain and general ill health.[108] $2,500 was held not to be excessive where a woman injured her collar bone so that she could not fully perform her household duties, and there was some evidence tending to show that it was a permanent injury.[109] $2,500 was held not to be excessive where a boy broke his leg in two places, and suffered greatly.[110] $2,500 was held not to be excessive where a plaintiff contracted blood poisoning.[111] $2,500 was held not to be excessive where a man was much injured, and complete recovery was doubtful.[112] $2,500 for the loss of services of a wife is not excessive.[113] $2,500 for a

102 Fulmore v. St. Paul City Ry. Co., 72 Minn. 448.
103 Delude v. St. Paul City Ry. Co., 55 Minn. 63.
104 Birmingham Ry. & Elec. Co. v. Baird, 130 Ala. 334.
105 Chicago City Ry. Co. v. Cooney, 95 Ill. App. 471.
106 Keiffert v. Nassau Elec. R. Co., 51 App. Div. (N. Y.) 301.
107 Nashville St. Ry. v. Griffin, 104 Tenn. 81.
108 West Chicago St. R. Co. v. Lups, 74 Ill. App. 420.
109 Calumet El. St. Ry. Co. v. Jennings, 83 Ill. App. 612.
110 City & Suburban Ry. Co. v. Waldhaur, 84 Ga. 706.
111 Miller v. St. Paul City Ry. Co., 66 Minn. 192.
112 Wilkins v. Omaha & C. B. Ry. & Bridge Co., 96 Iowa, 668.
113 Cregin v. Brooklyn Crosstown R. Co., 18 Hun (N. Y.) 368.

broken leg is not excessive.[114] $2,500 is not excessive where a passenger was assaulted by a conductor.[115] $2,500 was held not to be excessive where a healthy woman suffered hemorrhages, and an injury to her lung.[116] $2,500 is proper for injuries to general health and nervous suffering.[117] $2,300 is not excessive for the death of a child of 6.[118] $2,000 is not excessive for a broken arm.[119] $2,000 was held not to be excessive where a passenger was beaten, kicked, cut with a knife, and his arm broken.[120] $2,000 was held not to be an excessive verdict where a woman suffered a serious and painful injury to her wrist.[121] $2,000 is not excessive in an action by a father for injury to his child, who lost a leg.[122] $2,000 is not excessive for the death of a child 18 months old.[123] $2,000 is not excessive where a child of 5 fractured her thigh, and the limb was permanently shortened to a slight extent, and after two years was still weak and painful.[124] $2,000 is not excessive for a broken leg and a confinement for five months.[125] $1,500 was held proper in an ejection case.[126] $1,500 is not

114 Newport News & O. P. Ry. & Elec. Co. v. Bradford (Va.) 40 S. E. 900.

115 Birmingham Ry. & Elec. Co. v. Baird, 130 Ala. 334.

116 Donnelly v. St. Paul City Ry. Co., 70 Minn. 278.

117 Choquette v. Southern Elec. R. Co., 80 Mo. App. 515.

118 Strutzel v. St. Paul City Ry. Co., 47 Minn. 543.

119 New Orleans & C. R. Co. v. Schneider (C. C. A.) 60 Fed. 210.

120 Savannah St., &c., R. Co. v. Bryan, 86 Ga. 312.

121 Wheaton v. North Beach & M. R. Co., 36 Cal. 590.

122 Akersloot v. Second Ave. Ry. Co., 56 Hun (N. Y.) 640, 8 N. Y. Supp. 926.

123 Houston City St. Ry. Co. v. Sciacca, 80 Tex. 350.

124 Metropolitan West Side El. R. Co. v. Kersey, 80 Ill. App. 301.

125 South Covington & C. St. Ry. Co. v. Pelzer, 19 Ky. Law Rep. 88, 39 S. W. 496.

126 Foley v. Metropolitan St. Ry. Co., 80 App. Div. (N. Y.) 262.

excessive where plaintiff's arm was injured.[127] $1,500 is not excessive in a case of severe personal injury.[128] $1,500 was held not excessive where a person was severely injured.[129] $1,500 is not excessive where a working girl of 19 suffered considerably, and could not work for two years.[130] $1,500 is not an excessive verdict where an accident produced lameness likely to be permanent, and other injuries impairing the plaintiff's capacity for work.[131] $1,350 is not excessive where a married woman, 69 years old, suffered severe injuries to her arm and wrist, where there is much suffering, and the injuries are probably permanent.[132] $1,325 was held not to be excessive as vindictive damages where a passenger was wantonly expelled.[133] $1,240 was held not to be an excessive verdict where a woman's arm was very much injured.[134] $1,054 was held not to be excessive where a man was severely injured in the head.[135] $1,000 is not excessive for a badly sprained ankle.[136] $1,000 was held to be not so excessive that the court could set it aside, where a man was injured in a collision.[137] $1,000 was held to be not excessive where

127 Wagner v. Metropolitan St. Ry. Co., 79 App. Div. (N. Y.) 591.

128 Deuster v. Milwaukee St. Ry. Co., 89 Wis. 191.

129 Henderson St. Ry. Co. v. Wood, 21 Ky. Law Rep. 808, 53 S. W. 1116.

130 Fowler v. Broadway & S. A. R. Co., 59 Hun (N. Y.) 623, 13 N. Y. Supp. 453.

131 West Chicago St. R. Co. v. Williams, 87 Ill. App. 548.

132 Bading v. Milwaukee Elec. Ry. & Light Co., 105 Wis. 480.

133 Louisville City Ry. Co. v. Mercer, 11 Ky. Law Rep. 810.

134 Coast Line R. Co. v. Boston, 83 Ga. 387.

135 Smith v. Nassau Elec. R. Co., 57 App. Div. (N. Y.) 152.

136 Louisville Ry. Co. v. Casey, 24 Ky. Law Rep. 1527, 71 S. W 876.

137 Koch v. St. Paul City Ry. Co., 45 Minn. 407.

an injury was serious, and recovery was uncertain.[138] $1,000 was held not to be an excessive verdict where a man was much bruised and injured.[139] $1,000 was held not to be excessive where a man broke two ribs, and suffered considerably.[140] $1,000 was held not to be excessive where a plaintiff was badly bruised, and suffered considerably for some time.[141] $1,000 was held not to be excessive where a woman hurt her side severely.[142] $1,000 was held not excessive where the plaintiff, her wagon, horse, and goods were all injured.[143] $1,000 was held not excessive where a woman broke her wrist, and it was still weak a year after the accident.[144] $800 is not excessive for the death of a woman 68 years old, supported by her children.[145] $800 was held not excessive in an action for false imprisonment.[146] $750 was held not excessive where a milliner could not pursue her occupation.[147] $750 was held not excessive where a boy suffered concussion of the brain, and his complete recovery was doubtful.[148] $500 was held proper where a person was thrown from a team.[149] $500 is not excessive where the plaintiff was struck by a street car, and thrown underneath the feet of the horses.[150] $400

138 Brusch v. St. Paul City Ry. Co., 52 Minn. 512.

139 Richmond Ry. & Elec. Co. v. Garthright, 92 Va. 627.

140 Sinclair v. Washington & G. R. Co., MacArthur & M. (D. C.) 13.

141 Joyce v. St. Paul City Ry. Co., 70 Minn. 339.

142 Collins Park & Belt R. Co. v. Ware, 112 Ga. 663.

143 Spurrier v. Front St. Cable Ry. Co., 3 Wash. 659.

144 Wahlgren v. Market St. Ry. Co., 132 Cal. 656.

145 Phalen v. Rochester Ry. Co., 31 App. Div. (N. Y.) 448.

146 West Chicago St. R. Co. v. Luleich, 85 Ill. App. 643.

147 Robinson v. Metropolitan St. Ry. Co., 31 Misc. Rep. (N. Y.) 171.

148 Jackson v. St. Paul City Ry. Co., 74 Minn. 48.

149 Houston City St. Ry. Co. v. Delesdernier, 84 Tex. 82.

150 Nashville St. Ry. Co. v. O'Bryan, 104 Tenn. 28.

was held not to be excessive where a man of 70 injured his side so that he was unable to work, and he suffered pain three months after the accident.[151] $400 was held to be a proper verdict where a plaintiff was disabled for several weeks, and suffered much pain.[152] $375 was held proper where a father sued as administrator of his daughter of 3½.[153] $350 is not excessive in ejection case.[154] $350 is not excessive for a broken leg.[155] $300 is not excessive for injury to an eye.[156] $250 was held not to be excessive where a man was injured in a collision.[157] $220 was held very moderate where a traveler, his horse, and buggy were all injured in a collision case.[158] $50 is not an excessive verdict where a passenger was made to get off in the mud before a number of people.[159] $1 is a proper verdict where a passenger was thrown from a car or a wagon.[160]

**——Verdicts held excessive.**

$30,000 was held excessive, and $12,000 proper, although a child suffered severe injuries.[161] $25,000 was held excessive, and $15,000 and medical expenses proper, where plaintiff's left arm was permanently injured, and he had to

151 French v. Brooklyn Heights R. Co., 57 App. Div. (N. Y.) 204.

152 Knowlton v. Milwaukee City Ry. Co., 59 Wis. 278.

153 Reger v. Rochester Ry. Co., 2 App. Div. (N. Y.) 5.

154 Hamilton v. Third Ave. R. Co., 40 N. Y. Super. Ct. 376.

155 Schapierer v. Third Ave. R. Co., 14 N. Y. Supp. 921.

156 Schuler v. Third Ave. R. Co., 17 N. Y. Supp. 834.

157 Montgomery v. Johnson, 22 Ky. Law Rep. 596, 58 S. W. 476.

158 Jacksonville Ry. Co. v. Lamb, 86 Ill. App. 487.

159 City & Suburban Ry. v. Brauss, 70 Ga. 368.

160 Weinberg v. Metropolitan St. Ry. Co., 139 Mo. 286; Brown v. Union Ry. Co., 51 Mo. App. 192.

161 Mitchell v. Tacoma Ry. & Motor Co., 13 Wash. 560.

undergo a serious and expensive surgical operation.[162] $20,000 was held to be excessive, and $7,500 proper, where a woman was injured internally, but was probably not permanently injured.[163] $18,000 for the loss of a right arm is excessive.[164] $15,000 should be reduced to $7,000 and expenses, where it appeared that a plaintiff would always suffer more or less, and would always have some difficulty in walking.[165] $12,500 was reduced to $4,000 where a child of 3½ was killed.[166] $12,000 was held to be grossly excessive where there was no evidence of any serious injury.[167] $10,000 was held to be an excessive verdict where a plaintiff was run over.[168] $10,000 was held excessive, and $5,000 proper, where a school teacher suffered to some extent from concussion of the brain, and could not attend to her school work for four months.[169] $10,000 is excessive, and $4,000 proper, in case of nervousness and other injuries to a woman over 40.[170] $9,000 was held to be excessive, and $5,000 proper, where a laborer who earned $2 a day when he was at work lost a leg.[171] $8,000 was held excessive, and $6,000 proper, where a man fractured his skull and suffered a great deal.[172] $8,000 as excessive would not be disturbed upon

162 De Wardener v. Metropolitan St. Ry. Co., 1 App. Div. (N. Y.) 240.

163 Hamilton v. Great Falls St. Ry. Co., 17 Mont. 334.

164 Musser v. Lancaster City St. Ry. Co., 15 Pa. Co. Ct. R. 430.

165 Kraemer v. Metropolitan St. Ry. Co., 51 App. Div. (N. Y.) 475.

166 Rice v. Crescent City R. Co., 51 La. Ann. 108.

167 Chicago City Ry. Co. v. Henry, 62 Ill. 142.

168 Chicago West Div. Ry. Co. v. Haviland, 12 Ill. App. 561.

169 Smith v. Third Ave. R. Co., 10 App. Div. (N. Y.) 409.

170 Lockwood v. Twenty-Third St. Ry. Co., 15 Daly (N. Y.) 374.

171 Morris v. Eighth Ave. R. Co., 68 Hun (N. Y.) 39.

172 McKenna v. North Hudson County Ry. Co., 64 N. J. Law, 106.

appeal for the death of a man of 69, who earned $1,300 a year, and had a wife and a little daughter depending upon him.[173] $7,500 is excessive where the plaintiff received very severe and dangerous injuries.[174] $7,000 was held excessive, and $5,000 proper, where a woman's earnings were very small.[175] $7,000 is so excessive as to demand reversal, unless a remittitur of one-half the verdict is filed, where a woman 59 years old worked about half the time at from $12 to $15 a week, and spent the rest of the time in taking care of her home, her youngest child was 17, and her eldest 36 years of age, and her injuries, except temporarily, were wholly subjective.[176] $7,000 was held excessive, and $5,000 ample, where a carpenter injured his right knee, and it was not clear whether the injury would be permanent or not.[177] $6,500 was held excessive, and $4,000 proper, where a fireman was considerably injured, but was able to go back to work in less than two months.[178] $6,000 for a broken knee is excessive.[179] $6,000 is excessive for the death of a child 4½ years old.[180] $5,000 was held to be an excessive verdict where a boy of 10 was killed.[181] $5,000 was held to be excessive in an action for death, where the damages could be figured on a mathematical basis.[182] $5,000 was held to be

173 Harrison v. Sutter St. Ry. Co., 116 Cal. 156.
174 Jacques v. Bridgeport Horse R. Co., 41 Conn. 61.
175 Downer v. Metropolitan St. Ry. Co., 54 App. Div. (N. Y.) 315.
176 Chicago City Ry. Co. v. Anderson, 80 Ill. App. 71.
177 Cogswell v. West St. & N. E. Elec. Ry. Co., 5 Wash. 46.
178 Mullady v. Brooklyn Heights R. Co., 65 App. Div. (N. Y.) 549.
179 Langley v. Sixth Ave. R. Co., 48 N. Y. Super. Ct. 542.
180 Fox v. Oakland Consol. St. Ry. Co., 118 Cal. 55.
181 North Chicago St. R. Co. v. Wrixon, 51 Ill. App. 307.
182 Jackson v. Consolidated Traction Co., 59 N. J. Law, 25.

excessive where a man 67 years old broke his leg.[183] $5,000 is grossly excessive for the death of a child between 4 and 5 years old, and will be set aside, regardless of the number of times it has been awarded.[184] $5,000 is excessive, and $2,500 proper, where no loss of earning capacity is shown.[185] $5,000 is excessive to the amount of $2,000 for the death of a 7 year old boy.[186] $4,500 was held excessive, and $2,000 proper, where a man was confined to his house for seven weeks, but no bones were broken.[187] $4,500 was held an excessive verdict where the plaintiff fractured his arm, and the only proof of the permanence of the injury was that of the plaintiff and a fellow laborer, from which it was claimed that he could not do the work of an able-bodied man.[188] $4,300, it was held, should be reduced to $3,510.97, where an infant was able to earn half wages, and it appeared that he would recover entirely in three or four years.[189] $4,000 is excessive, owing to the age of a woman of 75, who suffered great pain and would never be able to walk without crutches.[190] $4,000 was held to be flagrantly excessive where a man injured his ankle, but not very severely.[191] Anything over $3,600 is excessive for the death of a man of 50 who earned $10 a week, and left a wife and one self-supporting child and three small children.[192]

183 North Chicago St. R. Co. v. Wiswell, 68 Ill. App. 443.

184 Graham v. Consolidated Traction Co., 62 N. J. Law, 90, 64 N. J. Law, 10.

185 Kaplan v. Metropolitan St. Ry. Co., 52 App. Div. (N. Y.) 296.

186 Riley v. Salt Lake Rapid Transit Co., 10 Utah, 428.

187 Meade v. Brooklyn Heights R. Co., 3 App. Div. (N. Y.) 432.

188 Chicago West Div. Ry. Co. v. Hughes, 87 Ill. 94.

189 Levitt v. Nassau Elec. R. Co., 14 App. Div. (N. Y.) 83.

190 Johnson v. St. Paul City Ry. Co., 67 Minn. 260.

191 South Covington & C. St. Ry. Co. v. Ware, 84 Ky. 267.

192 Garbaccio v. Jersey City, H. & P. St. Ry. Co. (N. J. Law) 53 Atl. 707.

$3,500 is excessive for the death of a 4 year old girl.[193] $3,-500 is excessive where a tailor lost the tip of his thumb, so that he was unable to earn the same wages, and suffered generally in health.[194] $3,100 was held excessive, and a reduction to $2,100 proper, where a plaintiff's foot was badly bruised, and his ankle perhaps permanently weakened.[195] $2,500 is excessive, and a remittitur of $500 is necessary where a person is able to earn the same wages shoveling coal after an accident as he earned before as a scavenger.[196] $1,-500 is excessive, while only $25 is clear, for the actual ejection, where a passenger is ejected from a street car.[197] $1,454 is excessive in an assault and battery case.[198] $750 was held excessive where a conductor wrongly refused to take a colored woman on the car.[199] $500 was held excessive where a conductor wrongly refused to take a colored woman on the car, but there was no evidence of willfulness or wantonness.[200] $350 was held to be excessive, and $200 proper, where a plaintiff was merely bruised, and lost no time from business.[201] $250 is excessive in an action for injury to a woman.[202] $250 is excessive, and $100 proper, in an ejection case where no force was used.[203] $200 was held excessive where a plaintiff had his lip cut, and lost one day's work.[204]

193 West Chicago St. R. Co. v. Scanlan, 68 Ill. App. 626.

194 North Chicago St. R. Co. v. Broms, 62 Ill. App. 127.

195 Kennedy v. St. Paul City Ry. Co., 59 Minn. 45.

196 West Chicago St. R. Co. v. Musa, 80 Ill. App. 223.

197 Cunningham v. Seattle Elec. Ry. & Power Co., 3 Wash. St. 471.

198 Birmingham Ry. & Elec. Co. v. Ward, 124 Ala. 409.

199 Turner v. North Beach & M. R. Co., 34 Cal. 594.

200 Pleasants v. North Beach & M. R. Co., 34 Cal. 586.

201 Weiner v. Minneapolis St. Ry. Co., 80 Minn. 312.

202 Cady v. Third Ave. R. Co., 29 Misc. Rep. (N. Y.) 741.

203 Conlon v. Metropolitan St. Ry. Co., 34 Misc. Rep. (N. Y.) 394.

204 Texas & P. Ry. Co. v. Doherty, 4 Willson, Civ. Cas. Ct. App. § 164.

## § 157. Damages for mental suffering.

It is well settled that a plaintiff may recover for mental suffering or fright connected with or resulting from a physical injury.[205] It has even been held in cases of ejection that a passenger may recover for humiliation to his feelings;[206] but it has been held in such a case that disgrace or impairment of social standing are not proper elements of damages.[207] Shame arising from having to use crutches is a proper element for damages,[208] but it has been held, on the contrary,

205 Birmingham Ry. & Elec. Co. v. Ward, 124 Ala. 409; Washington & G. R. Co. v. Dashiell, 7 App. D. C. 507; Central Ry. Co. v. Serfass, 153 Ill. 379; Chicago City Ry. Co. v. Taylor, 170 Ill. 49; West Chicago St. R. Co. v. Foster, 175 Ill. 396; Chicago City Ry. Co. v. Canevin, 72 Ill. App. 81; West Chicago St. R. Co. v. Lups, 74 Ill. App. 420; West Chicago St. R. Co. v. Dooley, 76 Ill. App. 424; Chicago City Ry. Co. v. Anderson, 80 Ill. App. 71, affirmed 182 Ill. 298; North Chicago St. R. Co. v. Lehman, 82 Ill. App. 238; Cicero & P. St. Ry. Co. v. Brown, 193 Ill. 274; Baltimore Traction Co. v. Wallace, 77 Md. 435; Baltimore City Passenger Ry. Co. v. Baer, 90 Md. 97; Chartrand v. Southern Ry. Co., 57 Mo. App. 425; Omaha St. Ry. Co. v. Emminger, 57 Neb. 240; Consolidated Traction Co. v. Lambertson, 59 N. J. Law, 297; Consolidated Traction Co. v. Lambertson, 60 N. J. Law, 457; Jones v. Brooklyn Heights R. Co., 23 App. Div. (N. Y.) 141; Pittsburg, A. & M. Passenger Ry. Co. v. Donahue, 70 Pa. 119; Bamford v. Pittsburg & B. Traction Co., 194 Pa. 17; Schenkel v. Pittsburg & B. Traction Co., 194 Pa. 182; Machen v. Railway Co., 13 Pa. Super. Ct. 642; Ft. Worth St. Ry. Co. v. Ferguson, 9 Tex. Civ. App. 610.

206 Mabry v. City Elec. Ry. Co. (Ga.) 42 S. E. 1025; Curtis v. Sioux City & H. P. Ry. Co., 87 Iowa, 622; Conlon v. Metropolitan St. Ry. Co., 34 Misc. Rep. (N. Y.) 394; Perry v. Pittsburgh Union Passenger Ry., 153 Pa. 236.

207 Schmitt v. Milwaukee St. Ry. Co., 89 Wis. 195.

208 Beath v. Rapid Ry. Co., 119 Mich. 512.

that the humiliation of going through life a cripple is too remote to consider as an element of damage.[209]

On the other hand, the plaintiff cannot recover for fright, mental suffering, or mental shock, unaccompanied by any physical injury,[210] or for bodily injury resulting from fright.[211] Damages cannot be recovered for mental suffering when a widow sues for the death of her husband,[212] when parents sue for the injury[213] or death[214] of a child, or when the next of kin sue for the death of a deceased person.[215]

Where there is a battery, and a jar of the nervous system, the plaintiff may recover for a shock resulting from the jar, without proving that the shock was in consequence of the battery.[216]

## § 158. Special damages.

The general principle is clear that special damages are such as do not necessarily result from an injurious act of the

209 Chicago City Ry. Co. v. Anderson, 80 Ill. App. 71.

210 Terre Haute Elec. Ry. Co. v. Lauer, 21 Ind. App. 466; Chicago City Ry. Co. v. Taylor, 170 Ill. 49; Chicago City Ry. Co. v. Canevin, 72 Ill. App. 81; West Chicago St. R. Co. v. Liebig, 79 Ill. App. 567; North Chicago St. R. Co. v. Duebner, 85 Ill. App. 602; Mitchell v Rochester Ry. Co., 151 N. Y. 107; Lehman v. Brooklyn City R. Co., 47 Hun (N. Y.) 355.

211 Spade v. Lynn & B. R. Co., 168 Mass. 285.

212 Chicago City Ry. Co. v. Gillam, 27 Ill. App. 386.

213 Woeckner v. Erie Elec. Motor Co., 182 Pa. 182.

214 Fox v. Oakland Consol. St. Ry., 118 Cal. 55; Bunyea v. Metropolitan R. Co., 19 D. C. 76; Covington St. Ry. Co. v. Packer, 9 Bush (Ky.) 455.

215 North Chicago St. R. Co. v. Wrixon, 51 Ill. App. 307; Willis v. Second Ave. Traction Co., 189 Pa. 430.

216 Homans v. Boston El. Ry. Co., 180 Mass. 456

defendant, and must be specially pleaded.[217] On this theory it has been held that loss of time,[218] of business,[219] and of profits[220] must be specially pleaded; and, similarly, employing a substitute to work in the plaintiff's place must be specially pleaded.[221] In cases of personal injuries to the plaintiff it has been held that mental pain,[222] loss of an eye,[223] epilepsy,[224] heart disease,[225] and mental suffering on account of postponement of the plaintiff's marriage[226] must be specially pleaded.

As a corollary to the main proposition, damages which are the necessary and proximate result of the injury need not be specially pleaded,[227] and, on this principle, special pleading has been held unnecessary in case of injury to particular parts of the body,[228] injuries to eyesight,[229] mental suffering caused

[217] Chicago West Div. Ry. Co. v. Klauber, 9 Ill. App. 613; North Chicago St. Ry. Co. v. Cotton, 41 Ill. App. 311; North Chicago St. R. Co. v. Barber, 77 Ill. App. 257; West Chicago St. R. Co. v. Levy, 82 Ill. App. 202.

[218] Slaughter v. Metropolitan St. Ry. Co., 116 Mo. 269.

[219] South Covington & C. St. Ry. Co. v. Ware, 84 Ky. 267; Citizens' St. Ry. Co. v. Burke, 98 Tenn. 650.

[220] Lombardi v. California St. Ry. Co., 124 Cal. 311; Chicago City Ry. Co. v. Anderson, 80 Ill. App. 71.

[221] Gumb v. Twenty-Third St. Ry. Co., 114 N. Y. 411; Brachfeld v. Third Ave. R. Co., 30 Misc. Rep. (N. Y.) 425.

[222] North Chicago St. R. Co. v. Lehman, 82 Ill. App. 238.

[223] Geoghegan v. Third Ave. R. Co., 51 App. Div. (N. Y.) 369.

[224] Ackman v. Third Ave. R. Co., 52 App. Div. (N. Y.) 483.

[225] Kleiner v. Third Ave. R. Co., 162 N. Y. 193.

[226] Beath v. Rapid Ry. Co., 119 Mich. 512.

[227] Edgerton v. O'Neil, 4 Kan. App. 73; Montgomery v. Lansing City Elec. Ry. Co., 103 Mich. 46.

[228] West Chicago St. R. Co. v. Levy, 182 Ill. 525.

[229] Brooklyn Heights R. Co. v. MacLaury (C. C. A.) 107 Fed. 644; West Chicago St. R. Co. v. Levy, 182 Ill. 525; Baltimore City Passenger Ry. Co. v. Baer, 90 Md. 97.

by serious bodily injury,[230] loss of time as the result of a broken thigh,[231] rheumatism, and impaired hearing[232] and pleurisy.[233]

## § 159. Vindictive damages.

In some jurisdictions, where an act is done willfully or wantonly, damages in excess of mere compensation are allowed. There must be something more than negligence to warrant the granting of vindictive damages,[234] and mere ejection,[235] or the fact that the passenger was injured by the jerk[236] or by the derailment[237] of a car, does not furnish sufficient ground for awarding them.

In some jurisdictions, corporations are held liable for vindictive damages without any inquiry as to whether they were to blame for the act of their servants.[238] In fact it has been

230 McCoy v. Milwaukee St. Ry. Co., 88 Wis. 56.

231 Chicago City Ry. Co. v. Hastings, 35 Ill. App. 434.

232 Chicago General Ry. Co. v. Kriz, 94 Ill. App. 277.

233 Hunter v. Third Ave. R. Co., 20 Misc. Rep. (N. Y.) 432.

234 McKeon v. Citizens' Ry. Co., 42 Mo. 79.

235 Denver Tramway Co. v. Cloud, 6 Colo. App. 445; Pine v. St. Paul City Ry. Co., 50 Minn. 144.

236 Wigton v. Metropolitan St. Ry. Co., 38 App. Div. (N. Y.) 207.

237 Louisville & P. R. Co. v. Smith, 2 Duv. (Ky.) 556.

238 Citizens' St. Ry. v. Steen, 42 Ark. 321; City & Suburban Ry. v. Brauss, 70 Ga. 368; Augusta & S. R. Co. v. Randall, 79 Ga. 304; Atlanta Consol. St. Ry. Co. v. Keeny, 99 Ga. 266; Citizens' St. Ry. Co. v. Willoeby, 134 Ind. 563; Kiley v. Chicago City Ry. Co., 90 Ill. App. 275; Kirton v. North Chicago St. R. Co., 91 Ill. App. 554; Louisville City Ry. Co. v. Mercer, 11 Ky. Law Rep. 810; Central Passenger Ry. Co. v. Chatterson, 17 Ky. Law Rep. 5, 29 S. W. 18; Baltimore & Y. Turnpike Road v. Boone, 45 Md. 344; Malecek v. Tower Grove & L. Ry. Co., 57 Mo. 17; Philadelphia Traction Co. v. Orbann, 119 Pa. 37; Wade v. Columbia Elec. St. Ry. L. & P. Co., 51 S

held that prompt repudiation of the act of a servant is no excuse.[239] On the other hand, some jurisdictions hold that, to render the company liable in such a case, there must be evidence of authorization or ratification of the act complained of.[240] Evidence of the wealth of the defendant has been held admissible in such a case.[241]

## § 160. Aggravation of injuries.

A person who is injured cannot recover damages for aggravation of his injuries caused by failure to use ordinary care in securing medical aid.[242] The degree of care required to avoid aggravation of injuries, however, is only reasonable care;[243] and aggravation of injuries caused by improper medical treatment through no fault of the injured party will not prevent a recovery.[244] The defendant may show that the plaintiff increased his injuries by using liquor.[245] If a

C. 296; Nashville St. Ry. v. Griffin, 104 Tenn. 81; Vassau v. Madison Elec. Ry. Co., 106 Wis. 301.

239 Knoxville Traction Co. v. Lane, 103 Tenn. 376.

240 Redwood v. Metropolitan R. Co., 6 D. C. 302; Rouse v. Metropolitan St. Ry. Co., 41 Mo. App. 298; Fohrmann v. Consolidated Traction Co., 63 N. J. Law, 391; Muckle v. Rochester Ry. Co., 79 Hun (N. Y.) 32; Wright v. Glens Falls, S. H. & F. E. St. R. Co., 24 App. Div. (N. Y.) 617; Eddy v. Syracuse Rapid Transit Ry. Co., 50 App. Div. (N. Y.) 109; Murphy v. Central Park, N. & E. R. R. Co., 48 N. Y. Super. Ct. 96; Donivan v. Manhattan Ry. Co., 49 N. Y. State Rep. 722.

241 Nashville St. Ry. Co. v. O'Bryan, 104 Tenn. 28; Hayes v. St. Louis R. Co., 15 Mo. App. 584.

242 Citizens' St. R. Co. v. Hobbs, 15 Ind. App. 610.

243 Webb v. Metropolitan St. Ry. Co., 89 Mo. App. 604.

244 Chicago City Ry. Co. v. Cooney, 95 Ill. App. 471.

245 Boggess v. Metropolitan St. Ry. Co., 118 Mo. 328.

plaintiff is injured, and later is injured again, he may recover for aggravation of the first injury.[246]

A plaintiff is not bound to undergo a serious operation as a matter of law;[247] and while he ought to submit to a surgical operation when a person of ordinary prudence would do so, he need not submit to a comparatively new surgical operation, even though the danger is regarded, by the weight of authority, as slight.[248]

## § 161. Damages for death.

It is generally held that damages for death are limited to pecuniary damages, and that nothing can be recovered for sorrow and mental suffering.[249] In Cleary v. City Ry. Co. it was held, however, that a father could recover damages for mental anguish on the death of a child, under the California statute.[250]

In the following cases, verdicts for death were held not to be excessive: $14,000 for the death of a wife.[251] $8,000

246 Brooks v. Rochester Ry. Co., 156 N. Y. 244.

247 Kehoe v. Allentown & L. V. Traction Co., 187 Pa. 474.

248 Mattis v. Philadelphia Traction Co., 6 Pa. Dist. Ct. R. 94.

249 Fox v. Oakland Consol. St. Ry., 118 Cal. 55; Bunyea v. Metropolitan R. Co., 19 D. C. 76; Covington St. Ry. Co. v. Packer, 9 Bush (Ky.) 455; Chicago City Ry. Co. v. Gillam, 27 Ill. App. 386; North Chicago St. R. Co. v. Wrixon, 51 Ill. App. 307; West Chicago St. R. Co. v. Dooley, 76 Ill. App. 424; Hurst v. Detroit City Ry., 84 Mich. 539; Richmond v. Chicago & W. M. Ry. Co., 87 Mich. 374; Cincinnati St. Ry. Co. v. Altemeier, 60 Ohio St. 10; Waechter v. Second Ave. Traction Co., 198 Pa. 129; San Antonio St. Ry. Co. v. Renken, 15 Tex. Civ. App. 229.

250 Cleary v. City R. Co., 76 Cal. 240.

251 Redfield v. Oakland Consol. St. Ry. Co., 110 Cal. 277.

where a widow was an invalid, and was left with one daughter, 23 years old.[252] $5,000 for the death of a bright boy of 7.[253] $5,000 for the death of a woman of 63, who did all the work in the household, and was in good health.[254] $5,000 for the death of a healthy young man, who had been supporting his family.[255] $5,000 for the death of a healthy woman, who left two small children.[256] $4,500 for the death of a man killed by an electric shock.[257] $3,000 for the death of a boy 5 years old.[258] $2,300 for the death of a child of 6.[259] $2,000 for the death of a child 18 months old.[260] $800 for the death of a woman of 68, supported by her children.[261] $375 for the death of a child of 3½.[262]

In the following cases, verdicts were held excessive: $12,500 was reduced to $4,000 where a child of 3½ was killed.[263] $8,000 was held excessive where a man of 69 earned $1,300 a year, and had a wife and child dependent upon him.[264] $5,000 for the death of a child of 4 was held grossly excessive, regardless of the number of times it had been awarded.[265]

252 Cook v. Clay St. Hill Ry. Co., 60 Cal. 604.

253 Cicero & P. St. Ry. Co. v. Boyd, 95 Ill. App. 510.

254 Lyons v. Second Ave. R. Co., 89 Hun (N. Y.) 374.

255 San Antonio St. Ry. Co. v. Renken, 15 Tex. Civ. App. 229.

256 Dimmey v. Wheeling & E. G. R. Co., 27 W. Va. 32.

257 Atlanta Consol. St. Ry. Co. v. Owings, 97 Ga. 663.

258 West Chicago St. R. Co. v. Waniata, 68 Ill. App. 481.

259 Strutzel v. St. Paul City Ry. Co., 47 Minn. 543.

260 Houston City St. Ry. Co. v. Sciacca, 80 Tex. 350.

261 Phalen v. Rochester Ry. Co., 31 App. Div. (N. Y.) 448.

262 Reger v. Rochester Ry. Co., 2 App. Div. (N. Y.) 5.

263 Rice v. Crescent City R. Co., 51 La. Ann. 108.

264 Harrison v. Sutter St. Ry. Co., 116 Cal. 156.

265 Graham v. Consolidated Traction Co., 62 N. J. Law, 90, 64 N. J. Law, 10.

$5,000 for the death of a boy of 10.[266] $5,000 for the death of a boy of 7.[267] $3,500 for the death of a girl of 4.[268]

Where a healthy boy of 16 was killed, a verdict for 6 cents was held to be inadequate.[269]

In an action for death, damages are left to the discretion of the jury within the limit of the statutes.[270] Only nominal damages should be recovered for the death of a brother incapable of supporting himself by reason of habitual drunkenness.[271] Where there is a standard for calculating damages, a verdict in excess of any possible calculation will not be allowed to stand.[272] Where a father 72 years old furnished the board and lodging to his boy of 18, and the boy paid his earnings—$7 a week—to the father, the question of pecuniary damages to the father from the death of the son was held to be a question for the jury.[273] Age, health, and habits may be shown in estimating earning capacity.[274]

A provision in the constitution that damages in an action for death shall not be limited by statute does not do away with the power of the supreme court to supervise and reduce verdicts.[275] Where a person is injured in October, 1894, and

266 North Chicago St. R. Co. v. Wrixon, 51 Ill. App. 307.

267 Riley v. Salt Lake Rapid Transit Co., 10 Utah, 428.

268 West Chicago St. R. Co. v. Scanlan, 68 Ill. App. 626.

269 Morris v. Metropolitan St. Ry. Co., 51 App. Div. (N. Y.) 512.

270 North Chicago St. Ry. Co. v. Brodie, 57 Ill. App. 564; Cicero & P. St. Ry. Co. v. Boyd, 95 Ill. App. 510.

271 North Chicago St. R. Co. v. Brodie, 156 Ill. 317.

272 Jackson v. Consolidated Traction Co., 59 N. J. Law, 25.

273 Morhart v. North Jersey St. Ry. Co., 64 N. J. Law, 236.

274 Maxwell v. Wilmington City Ry. Co., 1 Marvel (Del.) 199; Wilcox v. Wilmington City Ry. Co., 2 Pen. (Del.) 157.

275 Medinger v. Brooklyn Heights R. Co., 6 App. Div. (N. Y.) 42.

died in June, 1895, the right of action for death is governed by the statute which took effect January 1, 1895;[276] and the same ruling was made where the plaintiff was injured on December 30, 1894, and died January 2, 1895.[277]

Funeral expenses have been held not recoverable by the next of kin.[278]

[276] Weber v. Third Ave. R. Co., 12 App. Div. (N. Y.) 512.

[277] Smith v. Metropolitan St. Ry. Co., 15 Misc. Rep. (N. Y.) 158.

[278] Consolidated Traction Co. v. Hone, 60 N. J. Law, 444.

# TABLE OF CASES.

[REFERENCES ARE TO PAGES.]

## A.

Aaron v. Second Ave. R. Co. (2 Daly [N. Y.] 127) 257, 277.
Abrahams v. Los Angeles Traction Co. (124 Cal. 411) 326.
Abright, Citizens' St. Ry. Co. v. (14 Ind. App. 433) 293, 294.
Ackerman v. Union Traction Co. (205 Pa. 477) 271.
Ackerstadt v. Chicago City Ry. Co. (194 Ill. 616) 163.
Ackman v. Third Ave. R. Co. (52 App. Div. [N. Y.] 483) 435.
Adams v. Camden & S. Ry. Co. (55 Atl. [N. J. Err. & App.] 254) 303.
v. Metropolitan St. Ry. Co. (60 App. Div. [N. Y.] 188) 251, 264, 275.
v. Metropolitan St. Ry. Co. (81 N. Y. Supp. 553) 368.
v. Nassau Electric R. Co. (41 App. Div. [N. Y.] 334) 279.
v. Nassau Electric R. Co. (51 App. Div. [N. Y.] 241) 283.
v. Union Ry. Co. (80 App. Div. [N. Y.] 136) 117.
v. Washington & G. R. Co. (9 App. D. C. 26) 65, 68, 72, 75, 112, 129.
Washington & G. R. Co. v. (11 App. D. C. 396) 392.
v. Wilmington & N. Electric Ry. Co. (3 Pen. [Del.] 512) 313, 314.
Adkins' Adm'r, Paducah St. Ry. Co. v. (14 Ky. L. R. 425) 252, 253, 272, 397.
Adolph v. Central Park, N. & E. R. R. Co. (76 N. Y. 530) 301, 314, 315, 317.
Adsit v. Catskill Electric Ry. Co. (84 N. Y. Supp. 393) 334, 336.
Agnew, Metropolitan St. Ry. Co. v. (65 Kan. 478) 291.
Aiken v. Holyoke St. Ry. Co. (180 Mass. 8) 256.
v. Holyoke St. Ry. Co. (68 N. E. [Mass.] 238) 271.
Aikin v. Frankford & S. P. C. P. R. Co. (142 Pa. 47) 81.
Akersloot v. Second Ave. R. Co. (131 N. Y. 599) 53.
v. Second Ave. R. Co. (59 N. Y. Super. Ct. 555) 417.
v. Second Ave. Ry. Co. (56 Hun, 640, 8 N. Y. Supp. 926) 425.
Akron St. R. Co., Dussel v. (10 Ohio S. & C. P. Dec. 631) 103, 143.
Albany Ry., Bulger v. (42 N. Y. 459) 280.
Conley v. (22 App. Div. [N. Y.] 321) 215.
Dowd v. (47 App. Div. [N. Y.] 202) 33, 180, 183.
Ogier v. (88 Hun [N. Y.] 486) 280.
Platt v. (170 N. Y. 115) 287.
White v. (35 App. Div. [N. Y.] 23) 278, 284.

[REFERENCES ARE TO PAGES.]

Albert v. Bleeker St., etc., R. Co. (2 Daly [N. Y.] 389) 306.
Aldrich v. St. Louis Transit Co. (74 S. W. [Mo. App.] 141) 210, 214, 235, 239.
Alexander, Birmingham Union Ry. Co. v. (93 Ala. 133) 406, 407.
v. Rochester City & B. R. Co. (128 N. Y. 13) 124.
Allegheny Traction Co., Goorin v. (179 Pa. 327) 122.
Allen v. Ames College Ry. Co. (106 Iowa, 602) 250, 253, 420.
Birmingham Ry. & Electric Co. v. (99 Ala. 359) 373.
Chicago City Ry. Co. v. (169 Ill. 287) 396.
v. Dry Dock, E. B. & B. R. Co. (2 N. Y. Supp. 738) 111.
v. Galveston City Ry. Co. (79 Tex. 631) 133.
North Chicago St. R. Co. v. (82 Ill. App. 128) 324.
v. United Traction Co. (67 App. Div. [N. Y.] 363) 112.
Allentown & L. V. Traction Co., Kehoe v. (187 Pa. 474) 122, 438.
Allmon, Central Ry. Co. v. (147 Ill. 471) 329, 408.
Central Ry. Co. v. (45 Ill. App. 389) 397.
Altemeier, Cincinnati St. Ry. Co. v. (60 Ohio St. 10) 412, 438.
Altoona & L. V. Elec. Ry. Co., Thomas v. (191 Pa. 361) 356.
Trout v. (13 Pa. Super. Ct. 17) 289, 294, 315.
Altreuter v. Hudson River R. Co. (2 E. D. Smith [N. Y.] 151) 318.
Amato v. Sixth Ave. R. Co. (9 Misc. Rep. [N. Y.] 4) 29, 171, 183.
Ames v. Broadway & S. A. R. Co. (56 N. Y. Super. Ct. 3) 267.
v. Waterloo & C. F. Rapid Transit Co. (95 N. W. [Iowa] 161) 219.
Ames College Ry. Co., Allen v. (106 Iowa, 602) 250, 253, 420.
Anacostia & P. R. Co. v. Klein (8 App. D. C. 75) 53.
Anderson v. Brooklyn Heights R. Co. (32 App. Div. [N. Y.] 266) 119.
Chicago City Ry. Co. v. (193 Ill. 9) 324.
Chicago City Ry. Co. v. (80 Ill. App. 71; affirmed 182 Ill. 298) 124, 430, 433, 435.
Chicago City Ry. Co. v. (93 Ill. App. 419) 419.
v. Citizens' St. R. Co. (12 Ind. App. 194) 144, 153, 410.
v. City & Suburban Ry. Co. (71 Pac. [Or.] 659) 83, 84, 89, 106, 108.
v. Des Moines St. Ry. Co. (97 Iowa, 739) 137.
v. Metropolitan St. Ry. Co. (30 Misc. Rep. [N. Y.] 104) 310, 325.
v. Minneapolis St. Ry. Co. (42 Minn. 490) 275.
North Chicago St. R. Co. v. (176 Ill. 635) 393.
North Chicago St. R. Co. v. (70 Ill. App. 336) 413, 418.
North Hudson County Ry. Co. v. (61 N. J. Law, 248) 175.
v. Union Traction Co. (7 Pa. Dist. R. 41) 196, 197.
Andres v. Brooklyn Heights R. Co. (84 App. Div. [N. Y.] 596) 326.
Andrews, Augusta Ry. Co. v. (89 Ga. 653) 352.
v. Capitol, N. O. St. & S. W. R. Co. (2 Mackey [D. C.] 137) 79.
Ankrom, Springfield Consol. Ry. Co. v. (93 Ill. App. 655) 337.
Ann Arbor St. Ry. Co., Shadford v. (111 Mich. 390) 388.
Shadford v. (121 Mich. 224) 386.
Annis, West Chicago St. Ry. Co. v. (62 Ill. App. 180) 243.

[REFERENCES ARE TO PAGES.]

Ansteth v. Buffalo Ry. Co. (9 Misc. [N. Y.] 419; affirmed 145 N. Y. 210) 171, 182, 185.
Appel, Baltimore Traction Co. v. (80 Md. 603) 321.
Appleby v. St. Paul City Ry. Co. (54 Minn. 169) 205.
Archer v. Ft. Wayne & E. Ry. Co. (87 Mich. 101) 64, 68, 74, 108, 112.
v. Sixth Ave. R. Co. (52 N. Y. Super. Ct. 373) 400.
Armstrong, Baltimore Consol. Ry. Co. v. (92 Md. 554) 225.
v. Metropolitan St. Ry. Co. (23 App. Div. [N. Y.] 137) 93, 160.
v. Metropolitan St. Ry. Co. (36 App. Div. [N. Y.] 525) 161.
v. Montgomery St. Ry. Co. (123 Ala. 233) 92, 159.
Arnesen v. Brooklyn City R. Co. (9 Misc. [N. Y.] 270) 315, 317.
Arnold, Metropolitan St. Ry. Co. v. (72 Pac. [Kan.] 857) 345.
Arnreich, North Baltimore Passenger Ry. Co. v. (78 Md. 589) 210, 235.
Asbury v. Charlotte Electric Ry. & Power Co. [125 N. C. 568] 144.
Ashbrook v. Frederick Ave. Ry. Co. (18 Mo. App. 290) 80, 82.
Asheville St. Ry. Co., Cawfield v. (111 N. C. 597) 156.
Ashland L. P. & St. Ry. Co., Wills v. (108 Wis. 255) 260.
Ashtabula Rapid Transit Co. v. Holmes (67 Ohio St. 153) 143, 163.
Ashton v. Detroit City Ry. Co. (78 Mich. 587) 167, 402.
District of Columbia v. (14 App. D. C. 571) 374.
Atlanta Consol. St. Ry. Co. v. Bagwell (107 Ga. 157) 410.
v. Bagwell (109 Ga. 611) 400.
v. Bates (103 Ga. 33) 13, 15, 165, 405.
v. Foster (108 Ga. 223) 408.
v. Keeny (99 Ga. 266) 174, 192, 436.
v. Owings (97 Ga. 663) 349, 421, 430.
White v. (92 Ga. 494) 47.
Atlanta Ry. Co. v. Randall (43 S. E. [Ga.] 412) 141, 142.
Atlanta Ry. & Power Co. v. Gaston (45 S. E. [Ga.] 508) 329.
v. Walker (112 Ga. 725) 210, 235.
Atlanta St. R. Co., Holly v. (61 Ga. 215) 101, 113.
Tucker v. (77 Ga. 61) 6.
v. Walker (93 Ga. 462) 360, 401, 410.
Atlantic Ave. R. Co., Cassidy v. (9 Misc. [N. Y.] 275) 64, 73.
Chapman v. (14 Misc. [N. Y.] 384) 319.
Devlin v. (57 Hun [N. Y.] 591) 124.
D'Oro v. (13 N. Y. Supp. 789) 230, 245.
Ewing v. (11 N. Y. Supp. 626) 239.
Hutchinson v. (33 App. Div. [N. Y.] 569) 422.
Kerr v. (10 Misc. [N. Y.] 264) 297, 329.
v. Kinkade (9 Misc. [N. Y.] 273; affirmed 149 N. Y. 615) 53, 55, 82, 108.
McConnell v. (11 Misc. [N. Y.] 177) 303.
Mason v. (4 Misc. [N. Y.] 291) 252, 284.
Medler v. (12 N. Y. Supp. 930) 92, 131, 159.
Morris v. (116 N. Y. 552) 180.

[REFERENCES ARE TO PAGES.]

Atlantic Ave. R. Co., Northridge v. (15 Misc. [N. Y.] 66) 312, 315, 319, 326.
Quinn v. (12 N. Y. Supp. 223) 301.
Stabenau v. (155 N. Y. 511) 280, 281.
Van Dyke v. (67 Fed. 296) 391.
v. Van Dyke (72 Fed. 458) 391.
Van Sickle v. (12 Misc. [N. Y.] 217) 385, 390.
Walsh v. (23 App. Div. [N. Y.] 19) 220, 298.
Watkins v. (20 Hun [N. Y.] 237) 124, 329.
Whitbeck v. (4 N. Y. Supp. 100) 409.
Wynne v. (14 Misc. [N. Y.] 394) 120.
Young v. (10 Misc. [N. Y.] 541) 258.
Atlantic Coast Elec. R. Co. v. Rennard (62 N. J. Law, 773) 320.
Chandler v. (61 N. J. Law, 380) 384, 389.
Atwood v. Bangor, O. & O. T. Ry. Co. (91 Me. 399) 314, 315, 321.
v. Metropolitan St. R. Co. (25 Misc. [N. Y.] 758) 96.
Auburn City R. Co., Drake v. (173 N. Y. 466) 372.
Augusta Ry. Co. v. Andrews (89 Ga. 653) 352.
Augusta & S. R. Co. v. Randall (79 Ga. 304) 411, 436.
v. Randall (85 Ga. 297) 403.
v. Renz (55 Ga. 126) 64, 68, 104, 407.
Austin Dam & S. Ry. Co. v. Goldstein (18 Tex. Civ. App. 704) 322.
Austin Rapid Transit Ry. Co. v. Grothe (88 Tex. 262) 387.
Autrey, Houston City St. Ry. Co. v. (4 Tex. Civ. App. 635) 363.
Ayars v. Camden & Suburban Ry. Co. (63 N. J. Law, 416) 338.
Ayers v. Rochester Ry. Co. (156 N. Y. 104) 130.

## B.

Babcock v. Los Angeles Traction Co. (128 Cal. 173) 93, 160.
Baber v. Broadway & S. A. R. Co. (9 Misc. [N. Y.] 20) 397.
v. Broadway & S. A. R. Co. (10 Misc. [N. Y.] 109) 185.
v. Broadway & S. A. R. Co. (13 Misc. [N. Y.] 169) 191.
Bachrach v. Nassau Electric R. Co. (54 N. Y. Supp. 958) 49.
Bading v. Milwaukee Elec. Ry. & Light Co. (105 Wis. 480) 393, 426.
Baer, Baltimore City Passenger Ry. Co. v. (90 Md. 97) 53, 433, 435.
Bageard v. Consolidated Traction Co. (64 N. J. Law, 316) 211, 244, 397.
Bagwell, Atlanta Consol. St. Ry. Co. v. (107 Ga. 157) 410.
Atlanta Consol. St. Ry. Co. v. (109 Ga. 611) 400.
Baier v. Camden & S. Ry. Co. (52 Atl. [N. J. Law] 215) 281.
Bailey v. Citizens' Ry. Co. (152 Mo. 449) 373.
v. Market St. Cable Ry. Co. (110 Cal. 320) 217, 227, 233, 234.
Smith v. (14 App. Div. [N. Y.] 283) 230.
v. Tacoma Traction Co. (16 Wash. 48) 65, 67, 68, 73.
Bainbridge v. Union Traction Co. (55 Atl. [Pa.] 836) 84.
Baird, Birmingham Ry. & Elec. Co. v. (130 Ala. 334) 424, 425.
v. Citizens' Ry. Co. (146 Mo. 265) 277.

[REFERENCES ARE TO PAGES.]

Baker v. Eighth Ave. R. Co. (62 Hun [N. Y.] 39) 269, 279.
Omaha St. Ry. Co. v. (44 Neb. 511) 58.
Baldwin v. Fair Haven & W. R. Co. (68 Conn. 567) 166.
Balkwill, Suburban R. Co. v. (94 Ill. App. 454) 345.
Ballard, Citizens' St. R. Co. v. (22 Ind. App. 151) 361.
Ballinger & Longwell, El Paso Electric St. Ry. Co. v. (72 S. W. [Tex. Civ. App.] 612) 307.
Baltimore City Passenger Ry. Co. v. Baer (90 Md. 97) 53, 433, 435.
v. Cooney (87 Md. 261) 261, 271.
v. McDonnell (43 Md. 534) 253, 255, 271, 273, 282, 408, 411.
v. Nugent (86 Md. 349) 101, 102, 110, 403.
v. Tanner (90 Md. 315) 401.
v. Wilkinson (30 Md. 224) 50.
Baltimore Consol. Ry. Co. v. Armstrong (92 Md. 554) 225.
v. Pierce (89 Md. 495) 387.
v. Rifcowitz (89 Md. 338) 209, 210, 216, 217, 235.
v. State (91 Md. 506) 134.
Baltimore Traction Co. v. Appel (80 Md. 603) 321.
Cooke v. (80 Md. 551) 293, 316, 326.
v. Helms (84 Md. 515) 216, 224, 234, 236.
v. State (78 Md. 409) 2, 7, 46, 47, 60.
v. Wallace (77 Md. 435) 210, 235, 236, 238, 433.
Baltimore & H. S. Ry. Co., Dietrich v. (58 Md. 347) 48, 411.
Baltimore & P. R. Co., Woodiey v. (19 D. C. 542) 125.
Baltimore & Y. Turnpike Road v. Boone (45 Md. 344) 192, 436.
v. Cason (72 Md. 377) 71, 72, 74.
v. Leonhardt (66 Md. 70) 95, 101, 102.
Baly v. St. Paul City Ry. Co. (95 N. W. [Minn.] 757) 213.
Bamberger v. Citizens' St. Ry. Co. (95 Tenn. 18) 251, 254, 255.
Bamford v. Pittsburg & B. Traction Co. (194 Pa. 17) 368, 433.
Bammel v. Kirby (19 Tex. Civ. App. 198) 287.
Bangor, O. & O. T. Ry. Co., Atwood v. (91 Me. 399) 314, 315, 321.
Bangor St. Ry. Co., Cleveland v. (86 Me. 232) 355.
Bangs v. Lewiston & A. Horse R. Co. (89 Me. 104) 361.
Banks v. Highland St. Ry. Co. (136 Mass. 485) 364.
Bannister, Central Ry. Co. v. (96 Ill. App. 332) 418.
Barber, North Chicago St. R. Co. v. (77 Ill. App. 257) 435.
Barbour, Jensen v. (15 Mont. 582) 77.
Bard v. Pennsylvania Traction Co. (176 Pa. 97) 91.
Barger v. North Chicago St. R. Co. (54 Ill. App. 284) 20.
Barker v. Central Park N. & E. R. R. Co. (151 N. Y. 237) 175, 176.
v. Hudson River R. Co. (4 Daly [N. Y.] 274) 305, 315.
Barksdull v. New Orleans & C. R. Co. (23 La. Ann. 180) 262.
Barlow v. Jersey City H. & P. Ry. Co. (67 N. J. Law, 364) 32.
Barnes, Macon Consol. St. R. Co. v. (113 Ga. 212) 101, 404, 418.
v. Shreveport City R. Co. (47 La. Ann. 1218) 251, 255, 270.
Barnett, Union Traction Co. v. (67 N. E. [Ind. App.] 205) 359.
Barre v. Reading City Pass. Ry. Co. (155 Pa. 170) 28, 185.

[REFERENCES ARE TO PAGES.]

Barrett v. Market St. Ry. Co. (81 Cal. 296) 175.
v. Third Ave. R. Co. (45 N. Y. 628) 120, 122.
Barrie v. St. Louis Transit Co. (76 S. W. [Mo. App.] 706) 291, 321
Barry v. Second Ave. R. Co. (1 Misc. [N. Y.] 502) 405.
v. Second Ave. R. Co. (16 N. Y. Supp. 518) 267.
v. Third Ave. R. Co. (51 App. Div. [N. Y.] 385) 191.
v. Union Traction Co. (194 Pa. 576) 107.
Barth v. Kansas City El. Ry. Co. (142 Mo. 535) 4, 6, 53, 55.
Bartle v. Houghton County St. Ry. Co. (93 N. W. [Mich.] 620) 145.
Bartley v. Metropolitan St. Ry. Co. (148 Mo. 124) 129.
Barton, Third Ave. R. Co. v. (107 Fed. 215) 89, 96.
Barty, Joliet R. Co. v. (96 Ill. App. 351) 314.
Basch v. North Chicago St. Ry. Co. (40 Ill. App. 583) 10, 49.
Bass v. Concord St. Ry. Co. (70 N. H. 170) 158.
Bassett v. Los Angeles Traction Co. (133 Cal. xix., 65 Pac. 470) 115.
Bates, Atlanta Consol. St. Ry. Co. v. (103 Ga. 333) 13, 15, 165, 405.
Batley, Citizens' St. R. Co. v. (159 Ind. 368) 364.
Baumann v. Metropolitan St. Ry. Co. (21 Misc. [N. Y.] 658) 305.
Baumgartner v. City of Mankato (60 Minn. 244) 361.
Baur, North Chicago St. R. Co. v. (179 Ill. 126) 79.
North Chicago St. R. Co. v. (79 Ill. App. 121) 92, 159.
Baxter v. Second Ave. R. Co. (3 Rob. [N. Y.] 510) 221.
Bay Cities Consol. Ry. Co., Lyons v. (115 Mich. 114) 230.
Manor v. (118 Mich. 1) 302, 314, 315.
Bay Shore R. Co. v. Harris (67 Ala. 6) 182.
Beal v. Lowell & D. St. Ry. Co. (157 Mass. 444) 64.
Beard v. Reading City Pass. Ry. Co. (3 Pa. Super. Ct. 171) 282.
Beardsley v. Minneapolis St. Ry. Co. (54 Minn. 504) 406.
Beasley, Savannah T. & I. of H. Ry. v. (94 Ga. 142) 324.
Beath v. Rapid Ry. Co. (119 Mich. 512) 401, 433, 435.
Beatty, South Covington & C. St. Ry. Co. v. (20 Ky. L. R. 1845) 19.
Beaver Valley Traction Co., Hoon v. (204 Pa. 369) 251, 284.
Becker, Chicago West Div. Ry. Co. v. (128 Ill. 545) 411.
Chicago West Div. Ry. Co. v. (30 Ill. App. 200) 410.
v. Cincinnati St. Ry. Co. (2 Ohio Dec. 137) 269.
v. Detroit Citizens' St. Ry. Co. (121 Mich. 580) 380.
Bedell v. Detroit, Y. & A. A. Ry. (92 N. W. [Mich.] 349) 345.
Beem v. Tama & T. Electric Ry. & Light Co. (104 Iowa, 563) 212, 214, 237.
Beerman v. Union Ry. Co. (52 Atl. [R. I.] 1090) 289.
Beers v. Metropolitan St. Ry. Co. (84 N. Y. Supp. 785) 225.
Behr, Consolidated Traction Co. v. (59 N. J. Law, 477) 308, 319.
Belford v. Brooklyn Heights R. Co. (86 App. Div. [N. Y.] 388) 302.
Belle City St. Ry. Co., Bishop v. (92 Wis. 139) 335, 339, 367.
Lockwood v. (92 Wis. 97) 289.
Bellefontaine Ry. Co., Burns v. (50 Mo. 139) 64, 68.
Bello v. Metropolitan St. Ry. Co. (2 App. Div. [N. Y.] 313) 261.
Belt Electric Line Co. v. Tomlin (19 Ky. L. R. 433) 142.

[REFERENCES ARE TO PAGES.]

Bemiss v. New Orleans City & L. R. Co. (47 La. Ann. 1671) 94.
Bengivenga v. Brooklyn Heights R. Co. (48 App. Div. [N. Y.] 515) 229.
Benjamin v. Holyoke St. Ry. Co. (160 Mass. 3) 334, 337, 402.
v. Metropolitan St. Ry. Co. (133 Mo. 274) 368.
Bennett v. Brooklyn Heights R. Co. (1 App. Div. [N. Y.] 205) 252, 420.
v. Detroit Citizens' St. Ry. Co. (123 Mich. 692) 341.
v. New Jersey R. & T. Co. (36 N. J. Law, 225) 125.
Benoit v. Troy & L. R. Co. (154 N. Y. 223) 285, 287.
Bensing v. People's Electric St. Ry. Co. (9 Pa. Super. Ct. 142) 162.
Benson v. Manhattan Ry. Co. (31 Misc. [N. Y.] 723) 61.
Benton-Bellefontaine Ry. Co., Czezewzka v. (121 Mo. 201) 266, 267.
Weaver v. (60 Mo. App. 207) 292.
Bergen County Traction Co. v. Bliss (62 N. J. Law, 410) 412.
v. Demarest (62 N. J. Law, 755) 115.
v. Heitman's Adm'r (61 N. J. Law, 682) 251, 254, 270.
Scott v. (63 N. J. Law, 407) 92, 151, 159.
Bergin v. Southern New England Tel. Co. (70 Conn. 54) 352.
Bergold v. Nassau Elec. R. Co. (30 App. Div. [N. Y.] 438) 310.
Beringer v. Dubuque St. Ry. Co. (91 N. W. [Iowa] 931) 143.
Berke v. Twenty-Third St. Ry. Co. (4 N. Y. Supp. 905) 346.
Bernhard v. Rochester Ry. Co. (68 Hun [N. Y.] 369) 314, 315, 317, 319.
Bernheimer, Philadelphia Traction Co. v. (125 Pa. 615) 335.
Berry v. Borough of Sugar Notch (191 Pa. 345) 379.
South Covington & C. St. Ry. Co. v. (93 Ky. 43) 133.
v. Utica & Belt Line St. R. Co. (76 App. Div. [N. Y.] 490) 39.
Bert, Chicago West Div. Ry. Co. v. (69 Ill. 388) 313, 314, 393.
Bertram v. People's Ry. Co. (154 Mo. 639) 54, 423.
Bessenger v. Metropolitan St. Ry. Co. (79 App. Div. [N. Y.] 32) 145.
Bethel v. Cincinnati St. Ry. Co. (8 Ohio Circ. Dec. 310) 226, 242.
Betts v. Wilmington City Ry. Co. (53 Atl. [Del.] 358) 139, 143.
Biddle v. Hestonville, M. & F. P. Ry. Co. (112 Pa. 551) 26, 27, 185.
Biedermann v. Dry Dock, E. B. & B. R. Co. (54 App. Div. [N. Y.] 291) 261.
Bigelow v. Metropolitan St. Ry. Co. (48 Mo. App. 367) 403.
v. West End St. Ry. Co. (161 Mass. 393) 14, 158.
Bindbeutal v. Street Ry. Co. (43 Mo. App. 463) 321.
Binder, West Chicago St. R. Co. v. (51 Ill. App. 420) 9, 233, 235, 239, 270, 281.
Binghamton R. Co., Lewis v. (35 App. Div. [N. Y.] 12) 229, 245.
Birmingham v. Rochester City & B. R. Co. (137 N. Y. 13) 137.
Birmingham Electric Ry. Co. v. Clay (108 Ala. 233) 38, 47.
Birmingham R. & E. Co. v. Brannon (132 Ala. 431) 46, 47, 51.
v. Butler (135 Ala. 388) 121.
v. James (121 Ala. 120) 92, 140, 159.
Jefferson v. (116 Ala. 294) 58.
Watkins v. (120 Ala. 147) 92, 140, 159.

[REFERENCES ARE TO PAGES.]

gham R. & E. Co. v. Wildman (119 Ala. 547) 144.
Allen (99 Ala. 359) 373.
Baird (130 Ala. 334) 424, 425.
Franscomb (124 Ala. 621) 322.
Jackson (136 Ala. 279) 238.
Mason (34 So. [Ala.] 207) 191.
Pinckard (124 Ala. 372) 322.
Ward (124 Ala. 409) 432, 433.
gham Ry., L. & P. Co., Kennedy v. (35 So. [Ala.] 108) 174.
gham St. Ry. Co., Ricketts v. (85 Ala. 600) 156.
gham Union Ry. Co. v. Alexander (93 Ala. 133) 406, 407.
Hale (90 Ala. 8) 128, 402.
ll v. (100 Ala. 447) 94.
Smith (90 Ala. 60) 143.
f v. People's Ry. Co. (121 Mo. 216) 125.
v. Belle City St. Ry. Co. (92 Wis. 139) 335, 339, 367.
ntral Passenger Ry. Co. v. (8 Ky. L. R. 781) 102.
ntral Passenger Ry. Co. v. (9 Ky. L. R. 348) 126.
St. Paul City Ry. Co. (48 Minn. 26) 115, 416.
Union R. Co. (14 R. I. 314) 27, 97.
v. Crosstown St. Ry. Co. (153 N. Y. 76) 282, 285.
v. Brooklyn City R. Co. (108 N. Y. 640) 53, 244.
Forty-Second St. & G. St. Ferry R. Co. (19 N. Y. Wkly. Dig. 24) 368.
Staten Island Electric R. Co. (40 App. Div. [N. Y.] 238) 307, 314, 317.
an v. West Jersey & S. R. Co. (68 N. J. Law, 1) 411.
ore v. Toronto St. Ry. Co. (38 U. C. Q. B. 172) 28.
Rockford City Ry. Co. v. (173 Ill. 354) 408, 412.
ee v. Consolidated St. Ry. Co. (105 Mich. 462) 314, 316.
Consolidated St. Ry. Co. (112 Mich. 63) 302, 327.
y v. Seattle Electric Co. (28 Wash. 607) 163.
ette v. Holyoke St. Ry. Co. (175 Mass. 51) 121, 404.
v. Roxborough, C. H. & N. Ry. Co. (13 Pa. Super. Ct. 93) 357.
Shreveport Belt Ry. Co. (48 La. Ann. 1057) 386.
v. Electric Traction Co. (184 Pa. 524) 226.
ord, North Kankakee St. Ry. Co. v. (81 Ill. App. 609) 251.
. Third Ave. R. Co. (44 App. Div. [N. Y.] 163) 296, 325.
s, Louisville Ry. Co. v. (21 Ky. L. R. 480, 668) 344.
St. & F. Ferry R. Co., Albert v. (2 Daly [N. Y.] 389) 306.
rnett v. (49 N. Y. Super. Ct. 185) 213.
Detroit St. Ry. Co. (98 Mich. 228) 340, 359.
ergen County Traction Co. v. (62 N. J. Law, 410) 412.
United Traction Co. (75 App. Div. [N. Y.] 235) 405.
. Harlem Bridge H. & F. Ry. Co. (9 N. Y. Supp. 164) 252, 257, 285.
Milwaukee St. Ry. Co. (89 Wis. 371) 350, 402.

Block, Newark Pass. Ry. Co. v. (56 N. J. Law, 605) 209, 217, 219, 220, 234.
Blondel v. St. Paul City Ry. Co. (66 Minn. 284) 92, 159.
Bloomington City Ry. Co., Fitzpatrick v. (73 Ill. App. 516) 404.
Blum v. Metropolitan St. R. Co. (79 App. Div. [N. Y.] 611) 327.
v. Metropolitan St. Ry. Co. (80 N. Y. Supp. 157) 302.
Boatwright v. Chester & M. Elec. Ry. Co. (4 Pa. Super. Ct. 279) 339
Boddy, Street R. Co. v. (105 Tenn. 666) 14, 16.
Bode, West Chicago R. Co. v. (51 Ill. App. 440) 417.
Boehmer v. Pittsburg, A. & M. Traction Co. (194 Pa. 313) 305.
Boehncke v. Brooklyn City R. Co. (3 Misc. [N. Y.] 49) 59.
Boeker, West Chicago St. R. Co. v. (70 Ill. App. 67) 291.
Boerth v. West Side R. Co. (87 Wis. 288) 290.
Boettcher v. Detroit Citizens' St. Ry. Co. (91 N. W. [Mich.] 125) 327.
Boggess v. Metropolitan St. Ry. Co. (118 Mo. 328) 414, 437.
Bohn, East Saginaw City Ry. v. (27 Mich. 503) 75, 77.
Boland v. Missouri R. Co. (36 Mo. 484) 253, 254, 263, 270, 278.
Bolster v. Ithaca St. R. Co. (79 App. Div. [N. Y.] 239) 369.
Bolton, Street Ry. Co. v. (43 Ohio St. 224) 35, 387.
Bonce v. Dubuque St. Ry. Co. (53 Iowa, 278) 104.
Bonham v. Citizens' St. R. Co. (158 Ind. 106) 281, 286.
Bonne, Baltimore & Y. Turnpike Road v. (45 Md. 344) 192, 436.
Bornscheuer v. Consolidated Traction Co. (198 Pa. 332) 289, 393.
Borough of Sugar Notch, Berry v. (191 Pa. 345) 379.
Borschall v. Detroit Ry. (115 Mich. 473) 292.
Bortz v. Dry Dock, E. B. & B. R. Co. (78 App. Div. [N. Y.] 386) 272.
Bosqui v. Sutro R. Co. (131 Cal. 390) 101, 115, 408.
Bossert v. Nassau Electric R. Co. (40 App. Div. [N. Y.] 144) 301.
Boston, Coast Line R. Co. v. (83 Ga. 387) 426.
Boston El. Ry. Co., Burns v. (66 N. E. [Mass.] 418) 70-72, 106.
Cobb v. (179 Mass. 212) 178, 179.
Hannon v. (182 Mass. 425) 94, 161.
Homans v. (180 Mass. 456) 434.
Lee v. (182 Mass. 454) 158.
v. McDermott (68 N. E. [Mass.] 34) 250, 256.
Scannell v. (176 Mass. 170) 317.
Boston & M. R. R., Little v. (55 Atl. [N. H.] 190) 237.
Boston & P. Dispatch Exp. Co. v. Metropolitan St. Ry. Co. (14 Misc. [N. Y.] 25) 292.
Bosworth v. Union R. Co. (55 Atl. [R. I.] 490) 103.
Boudrou, Thirteenth & F. St. Pass. Ry. Co. v. (92 Pa. 475) 121.
Bowdle v. Detroit St. Ry. Co. (103 Mich. 272) 166.
Bowen v. Detroit City Ry. Co. (54 Mich. 496) 365.
Bowie v. Greenville St. Ry. Co. (69 Miss. 196) 92, 159.
Bowles, Richmond R. & E. Co. v. (92 Va. 738) 109, 407.
Boyd, Cicero & P. St. Ry. Co. v. (95 Ill. App. 510) 413, 420, 439, 440.
North Chicago St. R. Co. v. (57 Ill. App. 535) 119, 395.
Boyer, Philadelphia & R. R. Co. v. (97 Pa. 91) 103, 126.

[REFERENCES ARE TO PAGES.]

Boyer v. St. Paul City Ry. Co. (54 Minn. 127) 125.
Brace v. St. Paul City Ry. Co. (87 Minn. 292) 397.
Brachfeld v. Third Ave. R. Co. (29 Misc. [N. Y.] 586) 302.
v. Third Ave. R. Co. (30 Misc. [N. Y.] 425) 435.
Bradford, Newport News & O. P. Ry. Co. v. (40 S. E. [Va.] 900) 425.
Bradley v. Ft. Wayne & E. Ry. Co. (94 Mich. 35) 92, 159, 167.
v. Second Ave. R. Co. (34 App. Div. [N. Y.] 284) 64, 70, 131.
v. Second Ave. R. Co. (8 Daly [N. Y.] 289) 211.
Bradshaw v. South Boston R. Co. (135 Mass. 407) 196, 197.
Bradwell v. Pittsburgh & W. E. Pass. Ry. Co. (139 Pa. 404) 415.
v. Pittsburgh & W. E. Pass. Ry. Co. (153 Pa. 105) 360.
Brady v. Consolidated Traction Co. (63 N. J. Law, 25; 64 N. J. Law, 373) 260.
v. Metropolitan St. Ry. Co. (33 Misc. [N. Y.] 793) 143.
Braham v. Nassau Elec. R. Co. (72 App. Div. [N. Y.] 456) 351.
Brainard v. Nassau Electric R. Co. (44 App. Div. [N. Y.] 613) 83, 84.
Brannon v. Birmingham R. & E. Co. (132 Ala. 431) 46, 47, 51.
Brantford St. Ry., Myers v. (27 Ont. App. 513) 335.
Braslin v. Somerville Horse R. Co. (145 Mass. 64) 137.
Brauss, City & Suburban Ry. v. (70 Ga. 368) 192, 205, 413, 428, 436.
Brazis v. St. Louis Transit Co. (76 S. W. [Mo. App.] 708) 150.
Breary v. Traction Co. (5 Pa. Dist. Ct. 95) 315, 316.
Brennan v. Brooklyn Heights R. Co. (12 Misc. [N. Y.] 570) 130.
v. Fair Haven & W. R. Co. (45 Conn. 284) 23, 72, 139, 152.
v. Front St. Cable Ry. Co. (8 Wash. 363) 385.
v. Metropolitan St. Ry. Co. (60 App. Div. [N. Y.] 264) 310, 325.
Bresky v. Third Ave. R. Co. (16 App. Div. [N. Y.] 83) 319.
Bresmer, Green & C. St. Passenger Ry. Co. v. (97 Pa. 385) 388.
Brewer, Central Ry. Co. v. (78 Md. 394) 190.
Bridgeport Horse R. Co., Jacques v. (41 Conn. 61) 430.
Bridgeport Traction Co., Laufer v. (68 Conn. 475) 313, 314, 317, 408.
Morrissey v. (68 Conn. 215) 305, 323.
Briggs v. Minneapolis St. Ry. Co. (52 Minn. 36) 179.
v. Union St. Ry. Co. (148 Mass. 72) 38-40.
Brightman v. Union St. Ry. Co. (167 Mass. 113) 147, 153.
Brightwood Ry. Co. v. Carter (12 App. D. C. 155) 84.
Brittain v. West End St. Ry. Co. (168 Mass. 10) 386.
Britton v. Street Ry. Co. (90 Mich. 159) 142.
Broadhurst, Dallas Consol. Electric St. Ry. Co. v. (68 S. W. [Tex. Civ. App.] 315) 61.
Broadway Ferry & M. Ave. Co., Kalfur v. (34 App. Div. [N. Y.] 267) 417.
Broadway R. Co., Reinig v. (49 Hun [N. Y.] 269) 383.
Scholl v. (63 Hun [N. Y.] 629, 17 N. Y. Supp. 755) 393.
Vail v. (147 N. Y. 377) 64, 66, 67, 70.
Broadway & N. St. R. Co., Weiser v. (2 Ohio Dec. 463) 293.

[REFERENCES ARE TO PAGES.]

Broadway & S. A. R. Co., Ames v. (56 N. Y. Super. Ct. 3) 267.
Baber v. (9 Misc. [N. Y.] 20) 397.
Baber v. (10 Misc. [N. Y.] 109) 185.
Baber v. (13 Misc. [N. Y.] 169) 191.
Dickson v. (33 N. Y. Super. Ct. 330) 163.
Falotio v. (9 Daly [N. Y.] 243) 271.
Fowler v. (59 Hun [N. Y.] 623, 13 N. Y. Supp. 453) 426.
Jaquinto v. (2 Misc. [N. Y.] 174) 278.
Johnson v. (6 N. Y. Supp. 113) 402.
Kolzem v. (1 Misc. [N. Y.] 148) 366.
Lyons v. (10 N. Y. Supp. 237) 188, 189.
McSwyny v. (7 N. Y. Supp. 456) 39, 50.
Mitchell v. (70 Hun [N. Y.) 387) 413, 416.
Morrison v. (130 N. Y. 166) 38, 40, 46.
Poulin v. (61 N. Y. 621) 142.
Poulin v. (34 N. Y. Super. Ct. 296) 155.
Putnam v. (55 N. Y. 108) 33, 113, 114, 178, 179.
Pyne v. (19 N. Y. Supp. 217) 404.
Valentine v. (14 Daly [N. Y.] 540) 39.
Wilson v. (8 Misc. [N. Y.] 450) 423.
Wooster v. (72 Hun [N. Y.] 197) 404.
Brockton St. Ry. Co., Commonwealth v. (143 Mass. 501) 136.
Ladd v. (180 Mass. 454) 372.
O'Leary v. (177 Mass. 187) 331.
Broderick v. St. Paul City Ry. Co. (74 Minn. 163) 384.
Brodie, North Chicago St. Ry. Co. v. (156 Ill. 317) 440.
North Chicago St. Ry. Co. v. (57 Ill. App. 564) 413, 440.
Broms, North Chicago St. R. Co. v. (62 Ill. App. 127) 432.
Brooklyn Cable Co., Humbert v. (12 N. Y. State Rep. 172) 361.
Brooklyn City, H. P. & P. P. R. Co., Dale v. (1 Hun [N. Y.] 146) 48, 402.
Brooklyn City R. Co., Arnesen v. (9 Misc. [N. Y.] 270) 315, 317.
Black v. (108 N. Y. 640) 53, 244.
Boebncke v. (3 Misc. [N. Y.] 49) 59.
Bruno v. (5 Misc. [N. Y.] 327) 83, 84.
Cannon v. (9 Misc. [N. Y.] 282) 417.
Cannon v. (14 Misc. [N. Y.] 400) 418.
City of Brooklyn v. (47 N. Y. 475) 355.
Craighead v. (123 N. Y. 391) 86.
Cumming v. (104 N. Y. 669) 255, 266, 270.
Cumming v. (104 N. Y. 669) 255, 266, 270.
Cummings v. (52 Hun, 613, 5 N. Y. Supp. 476) 421.
Davenport v. (100 N. Y. 632) 48.
Degnan v. (14 Misc. [N. Y.] 388) 319.
Demond v. (8 Misc. [N. Y.] 610) 423.
Donnelly v. (109 N. Y. 16) 305.
Fitton v. (5 N. Y. Supp. 641) 422.
Fleming v. (1 Abb. N. C. 433; affirmed 74 N. Y. 618) 28, 29.

[REFERENCES ARE TO PAGES.]

Brooklyn City R. Co., Fox v. (7 Misc. [N. Y.] 285) 124.
Hennessey v. (6 App. Div. [N. Y.] 206) 308.
Hennessy v. (73 Hun [N. Y.] 569) 309, 314, 317, 326.
Hitchcock v. (3 N. Y. Supp. 218) 136, 165.
Hourney v. (7 N. Y. Supp. 602) 64, 122.
Lehman v. (47 Hun [N. Y.] 355) 434.
Lynch v. (1 Silv. [N. Y.] 361) 135.
McClain v. (116 N. Y. 459) 226, 242.
McCormick v. (10 Misc. [N. Y.] 8) 227.
McNamara v. (11 Misc. [N. Y.] 667) 376.
Mackie v. (10 Misc. [N. Y.] 4) 297.
Maloney v. (18 N. Y. Wkly. Dig. 152) 225.
Mills v. (10 Misc. [N. Y.] 1) 218, 241.
Mulhado v. (30 N. Y. 370) 142, 150.
Murray v. (7 N. Y. Supp. 900) 111, 131.
Nichols v. (30 Hun [N. Y.] 437) 401.
Norris v. (4 Misc. [N. Y.] 294) 79.
Paulson v. (13 Misc. [N. Y.] 387) 40, 47.
Quinn v. (40 App. Div. [N. Y.] 608) 301.
Saltzman v. (73 Hun [N. Y.] 567) 80, 81.
Schick v. (10 N. Y. Supp. 528) 393.
Seidlinger v. (28 Hun [N. Y.] 503) 124.
Spooner v. (54 N. Y. 230) 83.
Tholen v. (10 Misc. [N. Y.] 283) 273.
Van Winkle v. (46 Hun [N. Y.] 564) 98.
Watson v. (14 Misc. [N. Y.] 405) 359.
Wells v. (58 Hun [N. Y.] 389) 218, 219, 236.
Brooklyn City & N. R. Co., Dixon v. (100 N. Y. 170) 365.
Eppendorf v. (69 N. Y. 195) 38, 39, 41, 42.
Faris v. (46 App. Div. [N. Y.] 231) 85.
Haggerty v. (61 N. Y. 624) 405.
Lowery v. (76 N. Y. 28) 354.
Nolan v. (87 N. Y. 63) 64, 68, 70, 131.
Roche v. (105 N. Y. 294) 401.
Sheridan v. (36 N. Y. 39) 76, 77, 104, 114.
Timony v. (10 Misc. [N. Y.] 261) 259, 282.
Brooklyn Crosstown R. Co., Coddington v. (102 N. Y. 66) 102.
Cregin v. (18 Hun [N. Y.] 368) 424.
McGlynn v. (6 N. Y. St. Rep. 51) 133.
Brooklyn Heights R. Co., Anderson v. (32 App. Div. [N. Y.] 266) 119.
Andres v. (84 App. Div. [N. Y.] 596) 326.
Belford v. (86 App. Div. [N. Y.] 388) 302.
Bengivenga v. (48 App. Div. [N. Y.] 515) 229.
Bennett v. (1 App. Div. [N. Y.] 205) 252, 420.
Brennan v. (12 Misc. [N. Y.] 570) 130.
Bruce v. (68 App. Div. [N. Y.] 242) 129.
Clark v. (78 App. Div. [N. Y.] 478) 398, 418.
Conway v. (81 N. Y. Supp. 878) 104.

[REFERENCES ARE TO PAGES.]

Brooklyn Heights R. Co., Coughlin v. (59 App. Div. [N. Y.] 126) 375, 376.
Decker v. (64 App. Div. [N. Y.] 430) 300, 312.
Denton v. (78 N. Y. Supp. 157) 241.
Dettmers v. (22 App. Div. [N. Y.] 488) 347.
Devine v. (34 App. Div. [N. Y.] 248) 302.
Devine v. (61 App. Div. [N. Y.] 237) 367.
Dixon v. (35 Misc. [N. Y.] 422) 400.
Dochtermann v. (32 App. Div. [N. Y.] 13; affirmed 164 N. Y. 586) 132.
Dowd v. (9 Misc. [N. Y.] 279) 259, 275.
Eifinger v. (13 Misc. [N. Y.] 389) 422.
Ericius v. (63 App. Div. [N. Y.] 353) 60.
Fahner v. (86 App. Div. [N. Y.] 488) 62.
Faurot v. (14 Misc. [N. Y.] 398) 219, 241.
Fay v. (69 App. Div. [N. Y.] 563) 300.
Finkelstein v. (51 App. Div. [N. Y.] 287) 284.
Freeman v. (54 App. Div. [N. Y.] 596) 353.
Freeman v. (87 App. Div. [N. Y.] 127) 320.
Freeman v. (81 N. Y. Supp. 828) 220.
French v. (57 App. Div. [N. Y.] 204) 428.
Furman v. (25 App. Div. [N. Y.] 133) 418.
Gilmore v. (6 App. Div. [N. Y.] 117) 110.
Halliday v. (59 App. Div. [N. Y.] 57) 219, 243.
Hamel v. (59 App. Div. [N. Y.] 135) 403.
Heffran v. (8 Misc. [N. Y.] 41) 303, 315.
Hennessy v. (57 App. Div. [N. Y.] 27) 229, 245.
Hewlett v. (63 App. Div. [N. Y.] 423) 319, 320, 409.
Irwin v. (59 App. Div. [N. Y.] 95) 377.
Jenkins v. (29 App. Div. [N. Y.] 8) 195.
Johnson v. (34 App. Div. [N. Y.] 271) 304, 314, 317.
Johnson v. (63 App. Div. [N. Y.] 374) 88.
Jones v. (23 App. Div. [N. Y.] 141) 433.
Jones v. (10 Misc. [N. Y.] 543) 264, 273, 275.
Katz v. (35 Misc. [N. Y.] 302) 415.
Kelly v. (12 Misc. [N. Y.] 568) 297.
Kessler v. (3 App. Div. [N. Y.] 426) 309, 314, 317.
Killen v. (48 App. Div. [N. Y.] 557) 218, 241.
Killen v. (31 Misc. [N. Y.] 290) 218.
Kitchell v. (6 App. Div. [N. Y.] 99) 252, 265.
Landrigan v. (23 App. Div. [N. Y.] 43) 224.
Lane v. (82 N. Y. Supp. 1057) 296.
Leonard v. (57 App. Div. [N. Y.] 125) 109.
Luhrs v. (11 App. Div. [N. Y.] 173) 188, 189.
v. MacLaury (107 Fed. 644) 435.
Mauer v. (87 App. Div. [N. Y.] 119) 218.
McKnight v. (23 Misc. [N. Y.] 527) 380, 382.
Meade v. (3 App. Div. [N. Y.] 432) 431.

[REFERENCES ARE TO PAGES.]

Brooklyn Heights R. Co., Medinger v. (6 App. Div. [N. Y.] 42) 440.
Meyer v. (9 App. Div. [N. Y.] 79) 292.
Mowbray v. (59 App. Div. [N. Y.] 239) 422.
Mullady v. (65 App. Div. [N. Y.] 549) 430.
Muller v. (18 App. Div. [N. Y.] 177) 252, 276.
Myers v. (10 App. Div. [N. Y.] 335) 21.
Nies v. (68 App. Div. [N. Y.] 259) 84, 130.
Pinder v. (173 N. Y. 519) 257.
O'Reilly v. (81 N. Y. Supp. 572) 215.
R. F. Steavens Co. v. (59 App. Div. [N. Y.] 23) 300.
Read v. (32 App. Div. [N. Y.] 503) 293, 294, 319.
Reilly v. (65 App. Div. [N. Y.] 453) 319, 320.
Rosenblatt v. (26 App. Div. [N. Y.] 600) 314, 316.
Rost v. (10 App. Div. [N. Y.] 477) 399.
Rowe v. (71 App. Div. [N. Y.] 474) 390.
Seagriff v. (31 App. Div. [N. Y.] 595) 300.
Seifter v. (55 App. Div. [N. Y.] 10) 301.
Smith v. (81 N. Y. Supp. 838) 350.
Strauss v. (82 N. Y. Supp. 767) 326.
Swenson v. (15 Misc. [N. Y.] 69) 402.
Taft v. (14 Misc. [N. Y.] 390) 65.
Tullis v. (71 App. Div. [N. Y.] 494) 206.
Wells v. (34 Misc. [N. Y.] 44) 246.
Williamson v. (53 App. Div. [N. Y.] 399) 416.
Wise v. (46 App. Div. [N. Y.] 246) 225.
Brooklyn, Q. C. & S. R. Co., Donohue v. (53 App. Div. [N. Y.] 348) 401.
Higgins v. (54 App. Div. [N. Y.] 69) 358.
Kitay v. (23 App. Div. [N. Y.] 228) 276.
McGrath v. (87 Hun [N. Y.] 310) 83, 84.
Meyer v. (47 App. Div. [N. Y.] 286) 303.
Weber v. (47 App. Div. [N. Y.] 306) 32, 33, 183.
Brooklyn R. Co., Mangam v. (38 N. Y. 455) 250, 251, 254, 267, 275.
Brooklyn St. R. Co. v. Kelley (6 Ohio Cir. Ct. R. 155) 103, 115, 407.
Brooklyn & C. T. R. Co., Pollock v. (15 N. Y. Supp. 189) 115.
Brooklyn & C. R. Co., Stewart v. (90 N. Y. 588) 188, 189.
Brooklyn & R. B. Co., Strutt v. (18 App. Div. [N. Y.] 134) 99.
Brooks v. Lincoln St. Ry. Co. (22 Neb. 816) 222, 236, 346.
v. Mt. Auburn Cable Co. (29 Wkly. Law Bul. [Ohio] 50) 10, 45.
v. Rochester Ry. Co. (156 N. Y. 244) 438.
Brophy, Germantown Pass. Ry. Co. v. (105 Pa. 38) 99.
Brown, Cicero & P. St. Ry. Co. v. (193 Ill. 274) 433.
Cicero & P. St. Ry. Co. v. (89 Ill. App. 318) 414.
Citizens' St. R. Co. v. (29 Ind. App. 185) 389.
v. Congress & B. St. Ry. Co. (49 Mich. 153) 145.
v. Electric Ry. Co. (101 Tenn. 252) 384.
v. Elizabeth, P. & C. J. R. Co. (68 N. J. Law, 618) 220.

Brown v. Louisville Ry. Co. (21 Ky. L. R. 995, 53 S. W. 1041) 410.
v. Manhattan Ry. Co. (81 N. Y. Supp. 755) 56.
v. Metropolitan St. Ry. Co. (60 App. Div. [N. Y.] 184) 345.
North Chicago St. R. Co. v. (178 Ill. 187) 93, 160.
North Chicago St. R. Co. v. (76 Ill. App. 654) 421.
v. Seattle City Ry. Co. (16 Wash. 465) 140, 142.
v. Traction Co. (14 Pa. Super. Ct. 594) 291, 292.
v. Twenty-Third St. R. Co. (56 N. Y. Super. Ct. 356) 215, 217, 241.
v. Union Ry. Co. (51 Mo. App. 192) 428.
v. Washington & G. R. Co. (11 App. D. C. 37) 38, 39, 392.
v. Wilmington City Ry. Co. (1 Pen. [Del.] 332) 295, 313, 314, 315, 321.
Brozek v. Steinway Ry. Co. (10 App. Div. [N. Y.] 360) 293, 300, 314, 315, 319, 325.
Bruce v. Brooklyn Heights R. Co. (68 App. Div. [N. Y.] 242) 129.
Bruno v. Brooklyn City R. Co. (5 Misc. [N. Y.] 327) 83, 84.
Brunswick Traction Co., Foley v. (66 N. J. Law, 637) 157.
Hayter v. (66 N. J. Law, 575) 196, 202.
Brusch v. St. Paul City Ry. Co. (52 Minn. 512) 106, 402, 427.
Bruss v. Metropolitan St. Ry. Co. (66 App. Div. [N. Y.] 554) 297, 319.
Bryan, Savannah St., etc., R. Co. v. (86 Ga. 312) 187, 189, 425.
Bryant v. Metropolitan St. Ry. Co. (28 Misc. [N. Y.] 532) 304.
v. Omaha & C. B. Ry. & Bridge Co. (98 Iowa, 483) 422.
Buck v. Manhattan Ry. Co. (15 Daly [N. Y.] 550) 167.
v. People's St. Ry., E. L. & P. Co. (46 Mo. App. 555) 23, 25, 77.
v. People's St. Ry. & E. L. & P. Co. (108 Mo. 179) 23, 25, 153, 423.
Buckbee v. Third Ave. R. Co. (64 App. Div. [N. Y.] 360) 109.
Budd v. Meriden Electric R. Co. (69 Conn. 272) 250, 274, 411.
Buehler v. Union Traction Co. (200 Pa. 177) 134.
Buente v. Pittsburg, A. & N. Traction Co. (2 Pa. Super. Ct. 185) 268, 283, 286.
Buffalo Ry. Co., Ansteth v. (9 Misc. [N. Y.] 419; affirmed 145 N. Y. 210) 171, 182, 185.
Montgomery v. (165 N. Y. 139) 33, 180.
Pfeffer v. (4 Misc. [N. Y.] 465) 43, 51, 53.
Tait v. (55 App. Div. [N. Y.] 507) 303, 330.
Thompson v. (145 N. Y. 196) 253, 261, 269.
Tucker v. (53 App. Div. [N. Y.] 571) 99.
Weber v. (20 App. Div. [N. Y.] 292) 356.
Buffalo & N. F. Elec. Ry., Geleta v. (84 N. Y. Supp. 629) 304.
Buhrens v. Dry Dock, E. B. & B. R. Co. (53 Hun [N. Y.] 571) 298, 314, 315, 319.
Bulger v. Albany Ry. Co. (42 N. Y. 459) 280.
Bumbear v. United Traction Co. (198 Pa. 198) 83, 84, 86.
Bunyan v. Citizens' Ry. Co. (127 Mo. 12) 209, 210, 213, 217, 235-237.
Bunyea v. Metropolitan R. Co. (19 D. C. 76) 434, 438.
Burbridge v. Kansas City Cable R. Co. (36 Mo. App. 669) 17.

[REFERENCES ARE TO PAGES.]

Burgess, Lake St. El. R. Co. v. (200 Ill. 628) 4, 62.
v. Salt Lake City R. Co. (17 Utah, 406) 224.
v. Sixth Ave. R. Co. (13 N. Y. Wkly. Dig. 499) 298.
Burke, Citizens' St. Ry. Co. v. (98 Tenn. 650) 435.
v. Union Traction Co. (198 Pa. 497) 291, 294, 316.
Burlington Traction Co., Ploof v. (70 Vt. 509) 254, 262.
Burnell v. West Side R. Co. (87 Wis. 387) 384.
Burns v. Bellefontaine Ry. Co. (50 Mo. 139) 64, 68.
v. Boston El. Ry. Co. (66 N. E. [Mass.] 418) 70-72, 106.
East St. Louis Electric St. Ry. Co. v. (77 Ill. App. 529) 252, 410
v. Glens Falls, S. H. & F. E. St. R. Co. (4 App. Div. [N. Y.] 426) 188-190.
v. Metropolitan St. Ry. Co. (71 Pac. [Kan.] 244) 289, 293.
v. Second Ave. R. Co. (21 App. Div. [N. Y.] 521) 228, 245.
Burnstein v. Cass Ave. & F. G. Ry. Co. (56 Mo. App. 45) 277, 406.
Burrell, Chicago City Ry. Co. v. (70 Ill. App. 60) 97.
Burt v. Douglas County St. Ry. Co. (83 Wis. 229) 95, 109.
Burt, Highland Ave. & B. R. Co. v. (92 Ala. 291) 143.
Bush v. St. Joseph & B. H. St. Ry. Co. (113 Mich. 513) 311, 402.
Buttelli v. Jersey City, H. & R. Electric Ry. Co. (59 N. J. Law, 302) 212, 222, 233, 234, 238.
Butez v. Fonda, J. & G. R. Co. (20 Misc. [N. Y.] 123) 399.
Butler, Birmingham R. & E. Co. v. (135 Ala. 388) 121.
v. Pittsburgh & B. P. Ry. Co. (139 Pa. 195) 73, 76.
v. Steinway Ry. Co. (87 Hun [N. Y.] 10) 33, 180, 183.
Buys v. Third Ave. R. Co. (45 App. Div. [N. Y.] 11) 313.
Buzby v. Philadelphia Traction Co. (126 Pa. 559) 14, 17, 224.
Byington v. St. Louis R. Co. (147 Mo. 673) 136.
Byrd v. New Orleans City & L. R. Co. (43 La. Ann. 822) 47.
Byron v. Lynn & B. R. Co. (177 Mass. 303) 79, 129.

## C.

Cady v. Third Ave. R. Co. (29 Misc. [N. Y.] 741) 432.
Cahill, West Chicago St. R. Co. v. (165 Ill. 496) 403.
West Chicago St. Ry. Co. v. (64 Ill. App. 539) 157.
Cailloutte, San Antonio St. Ry. Co. v. (79 Tex. 341) 267, 277.
Cain v. Macon Consol. St. R. Co. (97 Ga. 298) 213.
Calderwood v. North Birmingham St. Ry. Co. (89 Ala. 247) 158, 163, 169.
v. North Birmingham St. Ry. Co. (96 Ala. 318) 146.
Caldwell v. Central Park, N. & E. R. Co. (7 Misc. Rep. [N. Y.] 67) 183.
Pittsburgh, A. & M. P. Ry. Co. v. (74 Pa. 421) 26, 76, 77, 412.
California St. Cable Ry. Co., Cross v. (102 Cal. 313) 303.
Davis v. (105 Cal. 131) 359.
Samuels v. (124 Cal. 294) 131.
California St. Ry. Co., Lombardi v. (124 Cal. 311) 435.

[REFERENCES ARE TO PAGES.]

Call, Joliet St. Ry. Co. v. (143 Ill. 177) 399.
Joliet St. Ry. Co. v. (42 Ill. App. 41) 399, 405, 407.
v. Portsmouth, K. & Y. St. Ry. (69 N. H. 562) 56.
Callary v. Easton Transit Co. (185 Pa. 176) 279, 394.
Calumet Elec. St. Ry. Co. v. Christenson (70 Ill. App. 84) 303.
v. Grosse (70 Ill. App. 381) 349.
v. Jennings (83 Ill. App. 612) 115, 424.
v. Lewis (68 Ill. App. 598) 277.
v. Lynholm (70 Ill. App. 371) 332.
v. Nolan (69 Ill. App. 104) 359.
v. Peters (88 Ill. App. 112) 377.
v. Van Pelt (68 Ill. App. 582) 256, 277.
Cambeis v. Third Ave. Ry. Co. (1 Misc. [N. Y.] 158) 315, 317.
Cambridge R. Co., Williamson v. (144 Mass. 148) 411.
Camden, G. & W. Ry. Co., Pierce v. (58 N. J. Law, 400) 374.
v. Preston (59 N. J. Law, 264) 314, 315, 317, 319.
v. Young (60 N. J. Law, 193) 232, 238, 244.
Camden & S. Ry. Co., Adams v. (55 Atl. [N. J. Err. & App.] 254) 303.
Ayars v. (63 N. J. Law, 416) 338.
Baier v. (52 Atl. [N. J. Law] 215) 281.
Corkhill v. (54 Atl. [N. J. Law] 522) 127.
Hughes v. (65 N. J. Law, 203) 303, 325.
v. Stetson (177 U. S. 172) 400.
Zolpher v. (55 Atl. [N. J. Err. & App.] 249) 342, 344.
Cameron v. Mendenhall (80 Minn. 150) 311.
Omaha St. Ry. Co. v. (43 Neb. 297) 320.
v. Union Trunk Line (10 Wash. 507) 221, 243.
Camp, West Chicago St. R. Co. v. (46 Ill. App. 503) 271.
v. Frankford & S. C. Ry. Co. (139 Pa. 522) 356.
v. Los Angeles Ry. Co. (135 Cal. 137) 164.
v. Los Angeles Traction Co. (137 Cal. 565) 291.
v. New Orleans City R. Co. (104 La. 183) 279.
v. St. Louis & S. Ry. Co. (75 S. W. [Mo.] 86) 311, 325.
v. Union Ry. Co. (9 Misc. [N. Y.] 484) 289, 294.
Canal & C. R. Co., Johnson v. (27 La. Ann. 53) 222.
Jones v. (109 La. 214) 147.
Knoker v. (52 La. Ann. 806) 215.
Canedo v. New Orleans & C. R. Co. (52 La. Ann. 2149) 216.
Canevin, Chicago City Ry. Co. v. (72 Ill. App. 81) 395, 433, 434.
Cannon v. Brooklyn City R. Co. (9 Misc. [N. Y.] 282) 417.
v. Brooklyn City R. Co. (14 Misc. [N. Y.] 400) 418.
v. Pittsburgh & B. Traction Co. (194 Pa. 159) 303, 330.
Capek, Chicago General Ry. Co. v. (82 Ill. App. 168) 406.
Chicago General St. Ry. Co. v. (68 Ill. App. 500) 393.
Capital Traction Co. v. Lusby (12 App. D. C. 295) 19, 215, 242.
Capitol, N. O. St. & S. W. R. Co., Andrews v. (2 Mackey [D. C.] 137) 79.
Carbon County Elec. Ry. Co., Hoover v. (191 Pa. 146) 375.

[REFERENCES ARE TO PAGES.]

Cardonner v. Metropolitan St. Ry. Co. (26 App. Div. [N. Y.] 8) 344.
v. Metropolitan St. Ry. Co. (38 App. Div. [N. Y.] 597) 344.
Carey, Citizens' St. Ry. Co. v. (56 Ind. 396) 272, 280.
Carlson, Consolidated City & C. P. Ry. Co. v. (58 Kan. 62) 252, 258, 283.
v. Lynn & B. R. Co. (172 Mass. 388) 222.
Carney v. Cincinnati St. Ry. Co. (8 Ohio S. & C. P. Dec. 587) 10.
Carpenter v. Central Park, N. & E. R. R. Co. (11 Abb. Pr. [N. S.; N. Y.] 416) 361.
v. Washington & G. R. Co. (121 U. S. 474) 196, 203.
Carr, Marion St. R. Co. v. (10 Ind. App. 200) 337.
West Chicago St. R. Co. v. (170 Ill. 478) 124, 403.
Carroll, Chicago City Ry. v. (68 N. E. [Ill.] 1086) 12.
Chicago General Ry. Co. v. (91 Ill. App. 356) 319.
Carson, Electric Ry. Co. v. (98 Ga. 652) 115, 411.
v. Federal St. & P. V. Ry. Co. (147 Pa. 219) 289, 294.
Carter, Brightwood Ry. Co. v. (12 App. D. C. 155) 84.
v. Interurban St. Ry. Co. (84 N. Y. Supp. 134) 297.
v. Kansas City Cable Ry. Co. (42 Fed. 37) 119, 122.
Carvanio v. Union Ry. Co. (84 N. Y. Supp. 246) 290.
Casey, Louisville Ry. Co. v. (24 Ky. L. R. 1527, 71 S. W. 876) 426.
Cason, Baltimore & Y. Turnpike Road v. (72 Md. 377) 71, 72, 74.
Casper v. Dry Dock, E. B. & B. R. Co. (23 App. Div. [N. Y.] 451; 56 App. Div. [N. Y.] 372) 362.
v. Metropolitan St. Ry. Co. (84 App. Div. [N. Y.] 639) 224.
Caspers v. Dry Dock, E. B. & B. R. Co. (22 App. Div. [N. Y.] 156) 85.
Cass v. Third Ave. R. Co. (20 App. Div. [N. Y.] 591) 310, 329.
Cass Ave. & F. G. Ry. Co., Burnstein v. (56 Mo. App. 45) 277, 406.
Dunn v. (98 Mo. 652) 279.
Dunn v. (21 Mo. App. 188) 256, 275.
Farris v. (80 Mo. 325) 250, 269, 277.
Leahey v. (97 Mo. 165) 397, 410, 411.
McCarthy v. (92 Mo. 536) 253.
Cassady v. Old Colony St. Ry. Co. (68 N. E. [Mass.] 10) 108.
Cassidy v. Atlantic Ave. R. Co. (9 Misc. [N. Y.] 275) 64, 73.
Catlin, Chicago City Ry. Co. v. (70 Ill. App. 97) 167.
Catskill Elec. Ry. Co., Adsit v. (84 N. Y. Supp. 393) 334, 336.
Cattano v. Metropolitan St. Ry. Co. (173 N. Y. 565) 64, 106.
Causler, Gadsden & A. U. Ry. Co. v. (97 Ala. 235) 168.
Cavagna, Mt. Adams & E. P. R. Co. v. (6 Ohio Cir. Ct. R. 606) 274
Cawfield v. Asheville St. Ry. Co. (111 N. C. 597) 156.
Cawley v. La Crosse City Ry. Co. (101 Wis. 145) 293.
v. La Crosse City Ry. Co. (106 Wis. 239) 304, 323.
Cedar Rapids & M. C. Ry. Co., Doran v. (117 Iowa, 442) 333, 336.
Eddy v. (98 Iowa, 626) 231.
Fullerton v. (101 Iowa, 156) 347.
Hart v. (109 Iowa, 631) 300, 327.
Orr v. (94 Iowa, 423) 293, 321, 409, 412.

[REFERENCES ARE TO PAGES.]

Central Crosstown R. Co., Hastings v. (7 App. Div. [N. Y.] 312) 64, 71, 72, 116.
Huerzeler v. (139 N. Y. 490) 262.
Huerzeler v. (1 Misc. [N. Y.] 136) 258, 283.
McGill v. (84 N. Y. Supp. 477) 54.
Schaefer v. (30 Misc. [N. Y.] 114) 143, 151, 156, 162.
Central Park, etc., R. Co., Flynn v. (49 N. Y. Super. Ct. 81) 33, 176, 178, 186, 190.
Lahey v. (2 Misc. [N. Y.] 537) 228, 233, 245.
Central Park, N. & E. R. R. Co., Adolph v. (76 N. Y. 530) 301, 314, 317.
Barker v. (151 N. Y. 237) 175, 176.
Caldwell v. (7 Misc. [N. Y.] 67) 183.
Carpenter v. (11 Abb. Pr. [N. S.; N. Y.] 416) 361.
Fallon v. (64 N. Y. 13) 267.
Hogan v. (124 N. Y. 647) 163.
Maher v. (67 N. Y. 52) 38, 40.
Maher v. (39 N. Y. Super. Ct. 155) 51.
Mullen v. (1 Misc. [N. Y.] 216) 306, 330.
Murphy v. (48 N. Y. Super. Ct. 96) 192, 437.
O'Toole v. (12 N. Y. Supp. 347) 223.
Raftery v. (14 Misc. [N. Y.] 560) 391.
Schild v. (16 N. Y. Supp. 701) 361.
Scott v. (53 Hun [N. Y.] 414) 183.
Solomon v. (31 N. Y. Super. Ct. 298) 76.
Squire v. (36 N. Y. Super. Ct. 436) 278.
Twomleyn v. (69 N. Y. 158) 125.
Ward v. (38 N. Y. Super. Ct. 392) 64, 72.
Wynn v. (133 N. Y. 575) 110, 111.
Central Passenger Ry. Co. v. Bishop (8 Ky. L. R. 781) 102.
v. Bishop (9 Ky. L. R. 348) 126.
v. Chatterson (14 Ky. L. R. 663) 289, 309, 314, 315, 321.
v. Chatterson (17 Ky. L. R. 5, 29 S. W. 18) 436.
v. Kuhn (86 Ky. 578) 126.
v. Rose (15 Ky. L. R. 209) 38, 39, 60.
Winnegar's Adm'r v. (85 Ky. 547) 187, 189, 190.
Central Penn. Tel. Co. v. Wilkes-Barre & W. S. Ry. Co. (1 Pa. Dist. Ct. 628) 349.
Central Ry. Co. v. Allmon (147 Ill. 471) 329, 408.
v. Allmon (45 Ill. App. 389) 397.
v. Bannister (96 Ill. App. 332) 418.
v. Brewer (78 Md. 394) 190.
v. Knowles (191 Ill. 241) 300, 324.
v. Knowles (93 Ill. App. 581) 324.
v. Larson v. (56 Ill. App. 263) 350.
v. Peacock (69 Md. 257) 14.
v. Serfass (153 Ill. 379) 433.
Central Ry. & Elec. Co., McAdam v. (67 Conn. 445) 389.

[REFERENCES ARE TO PAGES.]

Central Traction Co., Chilton v. (152 Pa. 425) 251, 278.
Thatcher v. (166 Pa. 66) 327.
Chandler v. Atlantic Coast Elec. Ry. Co. (61 N. J. Law, 380) 384, 389.
Chapman v. Atlantic Ave. R. Co. (14 Misc. [N. Y.] 384) 319.
v. Zanesville St. Ry. Co. (27 Wkly. Law Bul. [Ohio] 70) 335.
Chappell, Jacksonville St. Ry. Co. v. (21 Fla. 175) 104, 129.
Charles Warner Co., Price v. (1 Pen. [Del.] 462) 295, 313, 314, 316, 324, 380, 401, 404.
Charleston City Ry. Co., Ward v. (19 S. C. 521) 405.
Charlotte Electric R. & P. Co., Asbury v. (125 N. C. 568) 144.
Charlotte Electric St. Ry. Co., Moore v. (128 N. C. 455) 296, 315, 317.
Charlotte St. Ry. Co., Doster v. (117 N. C. 651) 333.
Charlton v. Forty-Second St., M. & St. N. Ave. R. Co. (79 App. Div. [N. Y.] 546) 253.
Chartrand v. Southern Ry. Co. (57 Mo. App. 425) 96, 155, 433.
Chase v. Jamestown St. Ry. Co. (15 N. Y. Supp. 35) 142, 151.
Chattanooga Elec. Ry. Co. v. Mingle (103 Tenn. 667) 345, 351.
Chatterson, Central Pass. Ry. Co. v. (14 Ky. L. R. 663) 289, 309, 314, 316, 321.
Central Passenger Ry. Co. v. (17 Ky. L. R. 5, 29 S. W. 18) 436.
Chauvin v. Detroit United Ry. Co. (97 N. W. [Mich.] 160) 298.
Chenowith, Consol. Traction Co. v. (58 N. J. Law, 416) 209, 217.
Chester St. Ry. Co., Haas v. (202 Pa. 145) 292.
Chester & M. Elec. Ry. Co., Boatwright v. (4 Pa. Super. Ct. 279) 339.
Chicago City Ry. Co., Ackerstadt v. (194 Ill. 616) 163.
v. Allen (169 Ill. 287) 396.
v. Anderson (193 Ill. 9) 324.
v. Anderson (80 Ill. App. 71; affirmed 182 Ill. 298) 124, 430, 433, 435.
v. Anderson (93 Ill. App. 419) 419.
v. Burrell (70 Ill. App. 60) 97.
v. Canevin (72 Ill. App. 81) 395, 433, 434.
Carroll v. (68 N. E. [Ill.] 1086) 12.
v. Catlin (70 Ill. App. 97) 167.
v. Considine (50 Ill. App. 471) 107.
v. Cooney (95 Ill. App. 471) 424, 437.
v. Delcourt (33 Ill. App. 430) 45.
v. Dinsmore (162 Ill. 658) 144.
v. Engel (35 Ill. App. 490) 102, 126.
v. Fennimore (199 Ill. 1) 219, 243.
v. Fennimore (78 Ill. App. 478) 414.
v. Gillam (27 Ill. App. 386) 434, 438.
v. Gregg (69 Ill. App. 77) 163.
v. Hastings (136 Ill. 251) 397.
v. Hastings (35 Ill. App. 434) 45, 436.
v. Hennessy (16 Ill. App. 153) 369.
v. Henry (62 Ill. 142) 429.
v. Jennings (157 Ill. 274) 324.

[REFERENCES ARE TO PAGES.]

Chicago City Ry. Co. v. Keenan (85 Ill. App. 367) 393.
Kiley v. (189 Ill. 384) 186, 196, 198.
Kiley v. (90 Ill. App. 275) 192, 436.
v. Lace (62 Ill. App. 535) 420.
v. Leach (80 Ill. App. 354) 376, 416.
v. Lewis (5 Ill. App. 242) 211, 223, 240, 244.
v. Loomis (201 Ill. 118) 242.
v. Mager (185 Ill. 336) 330, 394.
v. Mager (85 Ill. App. 524) 393.
v. McLaughlin (40 Ill. App. 496) 383.
v. Meehan (77 Ill. App. 215) 140, 148, 154.
v. Mogk (80 Ill. App. 411) 190.
v. Mumford (97 Ill. 560) 139, 140, 143.
v. Olis (94 Ill. App. 323) 396.
v. Pelletier (134 Ill. 120) 32, 171, 177, 182, 184.
v. Pelletier (33 Ill. App. 455) 32, 176.
Pfeiffer v. (96 Ill. App. 10) 253, 270, 409.
Potts v. (33 Fed. 610) 124.
Rack v. (173 Ill. 289) 272.
Rack v. (69 Ill. App. 656) 282.
v. Roach (76 Ill. App. 496) 241.
v. Robinson (127 Ill. 9) 252, 255, 256, 259, 284.
v. Robinson (27 Ill. App. 26) 284.
v. Rood (163 Ill. 477) 123.
v. Rood (62 Ill. App. 550) 123.
v. Sandusky (198 Ill. 400) 296, 325.
v. Sullivan (76 Ill. App. 505) 45.
v. Taylor (170 Ill. 49) 433, 434.
v. Taylor (68 Ill. App. 613) 416.
Thorsell v. (82 Ill. App. 375) 224.
v. Tuohy (196 Ill. 410) 254, 274, 284.
Van de Venter v. (26 Fed. 32) 52, 53.
v. Van Vleck (143 Ill. 480) 403.
v. Wall (93 Ill. App. 411) 308, 409.
Webb v. (83 Ill. App. 565) 223.
v. Wilcox (138 Ill. 370) 249, 254, 259.
v. Wilcox (33 Ill. App. 450) 416.
v. Young (62 Ill. 238) 106, 392.
Chicago General Ry. Co. v. Capek (82 Ill. App. 168) 406.
v. Carroll (91 Ill. App. 356) 319.
v. Kriz (94 Ill. App. 277) 302, 410, 436.
v. McNamara (94 Ill. App. 188) 391, 423.
Smith v. (86 Ill. App. 647) 292.
Chicago General St. Ry. Co. v. Capek (68 Ill. App. 500) 393.
Chicago, M. & St. P. Ry. Co., Mantel v. (33 Minn. 62) 379.
Chicago North Shore St. Ry. Co., Eickhof v. (77 Ill. App. 196) 94.
v. Green (93 Ill. App. 105) 342.
v. McCarthy (66 Ill. App. 667) 341.

[REFERENCES ARE TO PAGES.]

Chicago Ry. Co. v. Volk (45 Ill. 175) 127.
Chicago West Div. Ry. Co. v. Becker (128 Ill. 545) 411.
v. Becker (30 Ill. App. 200) 410.
v. Bert (69 Ill. 388) 313, 314, 393.
v. Conley (43 Ill. App. 347) 395.
v. Hair (57 Ill. App. 587) 275.
v. Haviland (12 Ill. App. 561) 210, 212, 429.
v. Hughes (69 Ill. 170) 97, 135, 423.
v. Hughes (87 Ill. 94) 431.
v. Ingraham (131 Ill. 659) 397.
v. Ingraham (33 Ill. App. 351) 234, 316.
v. Klauber (9 Ill. App. 613) 65, 70, 435.
v. Mills (91 Ill. 39) 163.
v. Mills (105 Ill. 63) 142, 143, 162.
Rend v. (8 Ill. App. 517) 122, 332.
v. Ryan (131 Ill. 474) 250, 255, 263.
Chicago & W. M. Ry. Co., Richmond v. (87 Mich. 374) 381, 438.
Childs v. New Orleans City R. Co. (33 La. Ann. 154) 227.
Chilton v. Central Traction Co. (152 Pa. 425) 251, 278.
Chippewa Valley Elec. Ry. Co., Goodrich v. (108 Wis. 329) 379.
Stafford v. (110 Wis. 331) 291.
Wanzer v. (108 Wis. 319) 123, 124.
Chouquette v. Southern Elec. R. Co. (152 Mo. 257) 415.
v. Southern Elec. R. Co. (80 Mo. App. 515) 425.
Christensen v. Lombard & St. Ry. Co. v. (4 Pa. Super. Ct. Dig. § 139) 405.
v. Union Trunk Line (6 Wash. 75) 292, 404, 409.
Christenson v. Calumet Electric St. Ry. Co. (70 Ill. App. 84) 303.
Christian, Lombard & S. St. P. Ry. Co. v. (124 Pa. 114) 403.
Christie v. Galveston City R. Co. (39 S. W. [Tex. Civ. App.] 638) 60.
Christopher v. T. St. R. Co., Kummer v. (2 Misc. [N. Y.] 298) 393.
Kummer v. (20 N. Y. Supp. 116) 403, 410.
Rown v. (34 Hun [N. Y.] 471) 188, 189.
Cicero & P. St. Ry. Co. v. Boyd (95 Ill. App. 510) 413, 420, 439, 440.
v. Brown (89 Ill. App. 318) 414.
v. Brown (193 Ill. 274) 433.
v. Meixner (160 Ill. 320) 6, 38-43, 57.
v. Priest (190 Ill. 592) 403.
Richter v. (70 Ill. App. 196) 337.
v. Rollins (95 Ill. App. 497) 393.
Cincinnati Inclined Plane Ry. Co., Vail v. (7 Ohio Cir. Dec. 28) 117.
Cincinnati, L. & A. Electric St. R. Co. v. Lohe (67 N. E. [Ohio] 161) 78.
Cincinnati Omnibus Co. v. Kuhnell (11 Wkly. Law Bul. [Ohio] 189) 78.
Cincinnati St. Ry. Co. v. Altemeier (60 Ohio St. 10) 412, 438.
Becker v. (2 Ohio Dec. 137) 269.
Bethel v. (8 Ohio Circ. Dec. 310) 226, 242.

[REFERENCES ARE TO PAGES.]

Cincinnati St. Ry. Co., Carney v. (8 Ohio S. & C. P. Dec. 587) 10.
Hawthorne v. (2 Ohio Dec. 548) 210.
v. Kelsey (2 Ohio Dec. 440) 115, 413.
Landneier v. (4 Ohio S. & C. P. Dec. 265) 414.
Lewis v. (10 Ohio S. & C. P. Dec. 53) 293.
v. Murray (53 Ohio St. 570) 126.
Schwartz v. (1 Ohio Dec. 197) 80, 82.
v. Snell (54 Ohio St. 197) 19, 224, 242.
v. Whitcomb (66 Fed. 915) 293, 313, 321.
v. Wright (54 Ohio St. 181) 310, 311.
Citizens' Passenger Ry. Co. v. Costigan (7 Atl. [Pa.] 91) 278.
v. Foxley (107 Pa. 537) 277.
Ketcham v. (122 Pa. 228) 356.
Thomas v. (132 Pa. 504) 315, 316, 328.
Citizens' Ry. Co., Bailey v. (152 Mo. 449) 373.
Baird v. (146 Mo. 265) 277.
Bunyan v. (127 Mo. 12) 209, 210, 213, 217, 235-237.
v. Craig (69 S. W. [Tex. Civ. App.] 239) 103.
Day v. (81 Mo. App. 471) 136, 282.
Friel v. (115 Mo. 503) 382.
v. Gifford (19 Tex. Civ. App. 631) 349.
v. Hair (32 S. W. [Tex. Civ. App.] 1050) 337.
Hicks v. (124 Mo. 115) 293, 314-316, 331.
Hogan v. (150 Mo. 36) 277, 287.
v. Holmes (19 Tex. Civ. App. 266) 323.
Huelsenkamp v. (34 Mo. 45) 81.
Huelsenkamp v. (37 Mo. 537) 80, 101, 102.
McKeon v. (42 Mo. 79) 150, 436.
Minster v. (53 Mo. App. 276) 373, 377.
Olsen v. (152 Mo. 426) 123.
Seymour v. (114 Mo. 266) 80, 82.
Sheehan v. (72 Mo. App. 524) 300, 321.
Smith v. (52 Mo. App. 36) 289, 293, 295, 321.
Werner v. (81 Mo. App. 368) 210, 235, 240.
Wyatt v. (55 Mo. 485) 139, 152.
Citizens' Rapid Transit Co. v. Dew (100 Tenn. 317) 347.
v. Seigrist (96 Tenn. 119) 298, 320.
Citizens' St. R. Co., Anderson v. (12 Ind. App. 194) 144, 153, 410.
v. Ballard (22 Ind. App. 151) 361.
v. Batley (159 Ind. 368) 364.
Bonham v. (158 Ind. 106) 281, 286.
v. Brown (29 Ind. App. 185) 389.
Conner v. (146 Ind. 430) 141, 144.
Dresslar v. (19 Ind. App. 383) 93, 146, 160, 167.
v. Hobbs (15 Ind. App. 610) 437.
v. Hoffbauer (23 Ind. App. 614) 84, 87, 411.
v. Jolly (67 N. E. [Ind.] 935) 5, 6, 52.
Kessler v. (20 Ind. App. 427) 328.

Citizens' St. R. Co. v. Marvil (67 N. E. [Ind.] 921) 358.
v. Shepherd (29 Ind. App. 412) 155.
v. Shepherd (107 Tenn. 444) 323.
v. Spahr (7 Ind. App. 23) 6, 38, 39, 42, 43, 45, 55, 57, 405.
v. Stoddard (10 Ind. App. 278) 251, 253, 254, 262, 411.
Udell v. (152 Ind. 507) 31, 89.
v. Willoeby (134 Ind. 563) 187, 189, 192, 398, 436.
Young v. (148 Ind. 54) 216, 222, 232.
Citizens' St. Ry. Co. v. Abright (14 Ind. App. 433) 293, 294.
Bamberger v. (95 Tenn. 18) 251, 254, 255.
v. Burke (98 Tenn. 650) 435.
v. Carey (56 Ind. 396) 272, 280.
Conner v. (105 Ind. 62) 6, 38-40, 42, 55, 57.
v. Furgason (16 Ind. App. 171) 153, 166.
v. Helvie (22 Ind. App. 515) 290, 293.
v. Huffer (26 Ind. App. 575) 144.
v. Lowe (12 Ind. App 47) 336.
v. Merl (26 Ind. App. 284) 6, 38, 39, 41, 55, 57, 89.
Prothero v. (134 Ind. 431) 98, 102.
v. Steen (42 Ark. 321) 282, 317, 321, 339, 436.
Stowers v. (21 Ind. App. 434) 224.
Thompson v. (152 Ind. 461) 384.
v. Twiname (111 Ind. 587) 102, 134.
Wilson v. (105 Tenn. 74) 294, 324.
Citizens' Traction Co., Iaquinta v. (166 Pa. 63) 256, 284.
Lenkner v. (179 Pa. 486) 300, 330.
Schnur v. (153 Pa. 29) 251, 274.
Stapleton v. (5 Pa. Super. Ct. 253) 386.
Wrasse v. (146 Pa. 417) 149.
City Elec. Ry. Co., Heddle v. (112 Mich. 547) 396, 402, 403.
v. Jones (61 Ill. App. 183) 218, 237.
Kaumeier v. (116 Mich. 306) 286.
Mabry v. (42 S. E. [Ga.] 1025) 433.
v. Shropshire (101 Ga. 33) 183.
City Elec. St. Ry. Co. v. Conery (61 Ark. 381) 348, 351.
City of Boston, Powers v. (154 Mass. 70) 375.
City of Brooklyn v. Brooklyn City R. Co. (47 N. Y. 47) 355.
City of Detroit, Kornetzski v. (94 Mich. 341) 357.
City of Fond du Lac, Schaefer v. (99 Wis. 333) 354.
City of Mankato, Baumgartner v. (60 Minn. 244) 361.
City of New York, Doyle v. (58 App. Div. [N. Y.] 588) 355.
City Passenger R. Co., Healey v. (28 Ohio St. 23) 186.
City R. Co., Cleary v. (76 Cal. 240) 438.
Somerville v. (17 N. Y. Supp. 719) 365.
City Ry. Co. v. Lee (50 N. J. Law, 435) 83, 101, 102.
Smith v. (29 Or. 539) 14, 213, 217.
v. Thompson (20 Tex. Civ. App. 16) 323.
Wade v. (36 Or. 311) 408, 409.

[REFERENCES ARE TO PAGES.]

City St. Car Co., Trumbo's Adm'r v. (89 Va. 780) 252, 254, 279.
City & Suburban Ry. Co., Anderson v. (71 Pac. [Or.] 659) 83, 84, 89, 106, 108.
v. Brauss (70 Ga. 368) 192, 205, 413, 428, 436.
Dubiver v. (74 Pac. [Or.] 915) 311.
v. Findley (76 Ga. 311) 141, 167, 168.
Lloyd v. (110 Ga. 165) 364.
McGrath v. (93 Ga. 312) 292, 301.
v. Moores (80 Md. 348) 339.
Read v. (115 Ga. 366) 364.
Saunders v. (99 Tenn. 130) 298, 320, 403.
v. Waldhaur (84 Ga. 706) 343, 424.
Wolf v. (72 Pac. [Or.] 329) 213, 216, 237.
Wynn v. (91 Ga. 344) 21, 31, 75-77, 411.
Clair, Omaha St. Ry. Co. v. (39 Neb. 454) 244.
Clancy v. New York & Q. C. Ry. Co. (81 N. Y. Supp. 875) 351.
v. Troy & L. R. Co. (88 Hun [N. Y.] 496), 291.
Clark v. Brooklyn Heights R. Co. (78 App. Div. [N. Y.] 478) 398, 418.
v. Eighth Ave. R. Co. (36 N. Y. 135) 80.
v. Manhattan Ry. Co. (77 App. Div. [N. Y.] 284) 246.
Clarke v. Nassau Elec. R. Co. (9 App. Div. [N. Y.] 51) 350.
Richmond Traction Co. v. (43 S. E. [Va.] 618) 297.
Clay, Birmingham Electric Ry. Co. v. (108 Ala. 233) 38, 47.
Clay St. Hill R. Co., Cook v. (60 Cal. 604) 124, 419, 439.
Clay St. R. Co., Tompkins v. (66 Cal. 163) 119, 122.
Cleary v. City R. Co. (76 Cal. 240) 438.
v. Pittsburgh A. & M. Traction Co. (179 Pa. 526) 219.
Clegg v. Metropolitan St. Ry. Co. (1 App. Div. [N. Y.] 207) 402.
Cleveland v. Bangor St. Ry. Co. (86 Me. 232) 355.
Cleveland City Ry. Co. v. Osborn (66 Ohio St. 45) 125.
Cline v. Crescent City R. Co. (41 La. Ann. 1031) 361.
v. Crescent City R. Co. (43 La. Ann. 327) 361.
Cloud, Denver Tramway Co. v. (6 Colo. App. 445) 192, 436.
Clow v. Pittsburgh Traction Co. (158 Pa. 410) 128.
Clutzbeher v. Union Pass. Ry. Co. (1 Atl. [Pa.] 597) 163.
Coast Line R. Co. v. Boston (83 Ga. 387) 426.
Cobb v. Boston El. Ry. Co. (179 Mass. 212) 178, 179.
v. Lindell Ry. Co. (149 Mo. 135) 142, 143.
Coddington v. Brooklyn Crosstown R. Co. (102 N. Y. 66) 102.
Cogswell v. West St. & N. E. Elec. Ry. Co. (5 Wash. 46) 21, 83, 84, 430.
Cohen v. Metropolitan St. Ry. Co. (63 App. Div. [N. Y.] 165) 258, 269, 285.
v. Metropolitan St. Ry. Co. (34 Misc. [N. Y.] 186) 302, 315, 317.
v. West Chicago St. Ry. Co. (60 Fed. 698) 53, 54.
Coit, West Chicago St. R. Co. v. (50 Ill. App. 640) 233, 235, 237.
Cole v. Detroit Elec. Ry. Co. (92 N. W. [Mich.] 935) 397.

[REFERENCES ARE TO PAGES.]

Coleman v. Lowell, L. & H. St. Ry. Co. (181 Mass. 591) 296.
v. Metropolitan St. Ry. Co. (81 N. Y. Supp. 836) 148.
v. Second Ave. R. Co. (114 N. Y. 609) 87, 95.
Colgan v. West Philadelphia Pass. Ry. Co. (4 Wkly. Notes Cas. [Pa.] 400) 149.
Coll v. Easton Transit Co. (180 Pa. 618) 239.
v. Toronto Ry. Co. (25 Ont. App. 55) 191.
Coller v. Frankford & S. Ry. Co. (9 Wkly. Notes Cas. [Pa.] 477) 58.
Collins, Metropolitan R. Co. v. (1 App. D. C. 383) 411.
v. Second Ave. Traction Co. (7 Pa. Super. Ct. 318) 372.
v. South Boston R. Co. (142 Mass. 301) 264, 276.
Collins Park & Belt R. Co. v. Ware (112 Ga. 663) 427.
Colt v. Sixth Ave. R. Co. (33 N. Y. Super. Ct. 189) 142, 153, 155.
Columbia Electric St. Ry., L. & P. Co., Wade v. (51 S. C. 296) 121, 436.
Comey v. Philadelphia Traction Co. (175 Pa. 133) 331, 332.
Cominskey v. Connellsville, N. H. & L. St. Ry. Co. (4 Super. Ct. 631) 278.
Commonwealth v. Brockton St. Ry. Co. (143 Mass. 501) 136.
v. Hicks (7 Allen [Mass.] 573) 319.
v. Metropolitan R. Co. (107 Mass. 236) 263, 275.
v. Temple (14 Gray [Mass.] 69) 319.
Concord St. Ry. Co., Bass v. (70 N. H. 170) 158.
Parkinson v. (71 N. H. 28) 210, 236.
Conery, City Elec. St. Ry. Co. v. (61 Ark. 381) 348, 351.
Coney Island & B. R. Co., Giraldo v. (16 N. Y. Supp. 774) 277.
Hagenlocher v. (99 N. Y. 136) 400.
Jager v. (84 Hun [N. Y.] 307) 214.
Lansing v. (16 App. Div. [N. Y.] 146) 102, 131.
Murphy v. (36 Hun [N. Y.] 199) 128.
Murphy v. (65 App. Div. [N. Y.] 546) 390.
Peyser v. (81 Hun [N. Y.] 70) 396.
Schmidt v. (26 App. Div. [N. Y.] 391) 91.
Sheeron v. (78 App. Div. [N. Y.] 476) 83, 84, 132.
Congress & B. St. Ry. Co., Brown v. (49 Mich. 153) 145.
Conley v. Albany Ry. (22 App. Div. [N. Y.] 321) 215.
Chicago West Div. Ry. Co. v. (43 Ill. App. 347) 395.
Conlon v. Metropolitan St. Ry. Co. (34 Misc. [N. Y.] 394) 432, 433.
Connell, Hestonville Pass. Ry. Co. v. (88 Pa. 520) 58, 61, 112.
Connelly v. Metropolitan St. Ry. Co. (84 N. Y. Supp. 305) 233.
v. Trenton Passenger Ry. Co. (56 N. J. Law, 700) 209, 217, 219.
Connelsville, N. H. & L. St. Ry. Co., Cominskey v. (4 Pa. Super. Ct. 631) 278.
Conner v. Citizens' St. R. Co. (146 Ind. 430) 141, 144.
v. Citizens' St. Ry. Co. (105 Ind. 62) 6, 38-40, 42, 55, 57.
Connolly v. Knickerbocker Ice Co. (114 N. Y. 104) 75, 76.
Connolly St. Ry., etc., Co., Sheets v. (54 N. J. Law, 518) 250, 260.

[REFERENCES ARE TO PAGES.]

Connor v. Electric Traction Co. (173 Pa. 602) 383.
v. Metropolitan St. Ry. Co. (48 App. Div. [N. Y.] 580) 366.
v. Metropolitan St. Ry. Co. (77 App. Div. [N. Y.] 384) 302, 331.
Conolly v. Crescent City R. Co. (41 La. Ann. 57) 179, 184.
Conroy v. Twenty-Third St. R. Co. (52 How. Pr. [N. Y.] 49) 358.
Considine, Chicago City R. Co. v. (50 Ill. App. 471) 107.
Consolidated City & C. P. Ry. Co. v. Carlson (58 Kan. 62) 252, 258, 283.
Consolidated Light & Ry. Co., Sample v. (50 W. Va. 472) 270.
Consolidated St. Ry. Co., Blakeslee v. (105 Mich. 462) 314, 316.
Blakeslee v. (112 Mich. 63) 302, 327.
McGee v. (102 Mich. 107) 212, 216, 218.
Poole v. (100 Mich. 379) 158, 165.
Consolidated Traction Co., Bageard v. (64 N. J. Law, 316) 211, 244, 397.
v. Behr (59 N. J. Law, 477) 308, 319.
Bornscheuer v. (198 Pa. 332) 289, 393.
Brady v. (63 N. J. Law, 25; 64 N. J. Law, 373) 260.
v. Chenowith (58 N. J. Law, 416) 209, 217.
Earle v. (64 N. J. Law, 573) 318, 320.
Fitzhenry v. (64 N. J. Law, 674) 250, 253, 260.
Flynn v. (64 N. J. Law, 375) 84, 85.
Fohrmann v. (63 N. J. Law, 391) 437.
v. Glynn (59 N. J. Law, 432) 209, 217-219, 234.
Graham v. (62 N. J. Law, 90; 64 N. J. Law, 10) 431, 439.
v. Haight (59 N. J. Law, 577) 294, 319.
Hamilton v. (201 Pa. 351) 296, 325.
v. Hoimark (60 N. J. Law, 456) 309.
v. Hone (59 N. J. Law, 275) 254, 255.
v. Hone (60 N. J. Law, 444) 441.
Hunter v. (193 Pa. 557) 279.
Jackson v. (59 N. J. Law, 25) 430, 440.
v. Lambertson (59 N. J. Law, 297) 299, 314, 315, 402, 433.
v. Lambertson (60 N. J. Law, 452) 403.
v. Lambertson (60 N. J. Law, 457) 433.
McCann v. (59 N. J. Law, 481) 338.
Noonan v. (64 N. J. Law, 579) 309.
v. Randolph (8 Tex. Civ. App. 213) 102.
v. Scott (58 N. J. Law, 682) 256, 259, 269, 284.
Sowash v. (188 Pa. 618) 134.
Sullivan v. (198 Pa. 187) 213.
v. Taborn (58 N. J. Law, 1) 182, 193, 206.
v. Thalheimer (59 N. J. Law, 474) 92, 102, 128, 159.
Thomas v. (62 N. J. Law, 36) 358.
Whalen v. (61 N. J. Law, 606) 84, 89, 102.
Constans, South Covington & C. St. Ry. Co. v. (74 S. W. [Ky.] 705) 118.
Continental Passenger Ry. Co. v. Swain (13 Wkly. Notes Cas. [Pa.] 41) 91, 131.

[REFERENCES ARE TO PAGES.]

Converse v. Washington & G. R. Co. (2 MacArthur [D. C.] 504) 179, 182, 187.
Conway v. Brooklyn Heights R. Co. (81 N. Y. Supp. 878) 104.
v. Lewiston & A. H. R. Co. (87 Me. 283) 14, 157.
v. Lewiston & A. H. R. Co. (90 Me. 199) 14, 157.
v. New Orleans, C. & L. R. Co. (51 La. Ann. 146) 243.
v. New Orleans & C. R. Co. (46 La. Ann. 1429) 142.
North Chicago St. R. Co. v. (76 Ill. App. 621) 385.
Conyngham v. Erie Electric Motor Co. (15 Pa. Super. Ct. 573) 296.
Cook v. Clay St. Hill R. Co. (60 Cal. 604) 124, 419, 439.
v. Metropolitan R. Co. (98 Mass. 361) 331.
North Chicago St. R. Co. v. (145 Ill. 551) 52, 54, 60, 401.
North Chicago St. R. Co. v. (43 Ill. App. 634) 5, 6, 54, 401.
v. Union Ry. Co. (125 Mass. 57) 360, 361.
Cooke v. Baltimore Traction Co. (80 Md. 551) 293, 316, 326.
Cooney, Baltimore City Passenger Ry. Co. v. (37 Md. 261) 261, 271.
Chicago City Ry. Co. v. (95 Ill. App. 471) 424, 437.
Cooper v. St. Paul City Ry. Co. (54 Minn. 379) 399, 418.
Trenton Pass. Ry. Co. v. (60 N. J. Law, 219) 350, 410.
Copeland v. Metropolitan St. Ry. Co. (67 App. Div. [N. Y.] 483) 243.
v. Metropolitan St. Ry. Co. (78 App. Div. [N. Y.] 418) 218.
Corbett v. Twenty-Third St. Ry. Co. (42 Hun [N. Y.] 587) 172.
Cords v. Third Ave. R. Co. (56 N. Y. Super. Ct. 319) 278.
Corkhill v. Camden & S. Ry. Co. (54 Atl. [N. J. Law] 522) 127.
Corletto, Norfolk Ry. & Light Co. v. (41 S. E. [Va.] 740) 235.
Corlin v. West End St. Ry. Co. (154 Mass. 197) 38-40, 44.
Cornell v. Detroit Elec. Ry. Co. (82 Mich. 495) 333.
Cornish v. Toronto St. Ry. Co. (23 U. C. C. P. 355) 72.
Corrigan Consol. St. Ry. Co., Wilkerson v. (26 Mo. App. 144) 102, 115.
Willmott v. (106 Mo. 535) 82, 102.
Cortland & H. Traction Co., Ray v. (19 App. Div. [N. Y.] 530) 182, 197, 202.
Cosgrove v. Interurban St. Ry. Co. (84 N. Y. Supp. 885) 296.
v. Metropolitan St. Ry. Co. (74 App. Div. [N. Y.] 166) 243.
Costello v. Third Ave. R. Co. (161 N. Y. 317) 253, 259.
Costigan, Citizens' Pass. Ry. Co. v. (7 Atl. [Pa.] 91) 278.
Cotter v. Lynn & B. R. Co. (180 Mass. 145) 266, 268.
Cotton, North Chicago St. Ry. Co. v. (140 Ill. 486) 119, 405.
North Chicago St. Ry. Co. v. (41 Ill. App. 311) 119, 435.
Coughlin v. Brooklyn Heights R. Co. (59 App. Div. [N. Y.] 126) 375, 376.
Coughtry v. Willamette St. Ry. Co. (21 Or. 245) 336.
Coulahan v. Metropolitan St. R. Co. (28 App. Div. [N. Y.] 394) 124.
Countryman v. Fonda, J. & G. R. Co. (166 N. Y. 201) 322.
Court, San Antonio Traction Co. v. (71 S. W. [Tex. Civ. App.] 777) 270, 273, 275.

[REFERENCES ARE TO PAGES.]

Covington St. Ry. Co. v. Packer (9 Bush [Ky.] 455) 434, 438.
Cowan v. Muskegon Ry. Co. (84 Mich. 583) 365.
v. Third Ave. R. Co. (1 N. Y. Supp. 612) 213.
v. Third Ave. R. Co. (9 N. Y. Supp. 610) 218.
Cowden v. Shreveport Belt Ry. Co. (106 La. 236) 289, 328.
Cox, Lincoln St. Ry. Co. v. (48 Neb. 807) 388.
v. South Shore & B. St. Ry. Co. (182 Mass. 497) 223.
Southside Pass. Ry. Co. v. (2 Mona. [Pa.] 140) 358.
v. Wilmington City Ry. Co. (53 Atl. [Del.] 569) 295, 313, 314, 321.
Coyle v. Third Ave. R. Co. (18 Misc. [N. Y.] 9) 325.
Cozine, Lexington Ry. Co. v. (23 Ky. L. R. 1137, 64 S. W. 848) 192.
Craig, Citizens' Ry. Co. v. (69 S. W. [Tex. Civ. App.] 239) 103.
Omaha St. Ry. Co. v. (39 Neb. 601) 92, 151, 159.
West Chicago St. Ry. Co. v. (57 Ill. App. 411) 101, 102, 413.
Craighead v. Brooklyn City R. Co. (123 N. Y. 391) 86.
Cram v. Metropolitan R. Co. (112 Mass. 38) 147, 152.
Crawford, San Antonio Traction Co. v. (71 S. W. [Tex. Civ. App.] 306) 191.
Cream City R. Co., Fitts v. (59 Wis. 323) 367.
Hinton v. (65 Wis. 323) 393, 404, 420.
Creamer v. West End St. Ry. Co. (156 Mass. 320) 14, 15, 17, 139, 140, 225.
Creavin v. Newton St. Ry. Co. (176 Mass. 529) 296.
Cregin v. Brooklyn Crosstown R. Co. (18 Hun [N. Y.] 368) 424.
Crescent City R. Co., Cline v. (41 La. Ann. 1031) 361.
Cline v. (43 La. Ann. 327) 361.
Conolly v. (41 La. Ann. 57) 179, 184.
Cronan v. (49 La. Ann. 65) 97, 152, 153.
Culbertson v. (48 La. Ann. 1376) 279.
Gallaghor v. (37 La. Ann. 288) 279.
Hoelzel v. (49 La. Ann. 1302) 215, 216.
Klein v. (23 La. Ann. 729) 279.
Nelson v. (49 La. Ann. 491) 276.
Ober v. (44 La. Ann. 1059) 139, 148, 158.
Rice v. (51 La. Ann. 108) 251, 274, 276, 429, 439.
Rombach v. (50 La. Ann. 473) 328.
Schwartz v. (30 La. Ann. 15) 212.
Sciortino v. (49 La. Ann. 7) 278.
Smith v. (47 La. Ann. 833) 222.
Summers v. (34 La. Ann. 139) 99.
Crisman v. Shreveport Belt Ry. Co. (34 So. [La.] 718) 346.
Crissey v. Hestonville, M. & F. P. Ry. Co. (75 Pa. 83) 75-77, 139, 140, 152, 163.
Cronan v. Crescent City R. Co. (49 La. Ann. 65) 97, 152, 153.
Cronin v. Highland St. Ry. Co. (144 Mass. 249) 207.
Cross v. California St. Cable Ry. Co. (102 Cal. 313) 303.
v. Detroit Citizens' St. Ry. Co. (120 Mich. 137) 113.

[REFERENCES ARE TO PAGES.]

Crosstown St. Ry. Co., Bittner v. (153 N. Y. 76) 282, 285.
Winter v. (8 Misc. [N. Y.] 362) 304.
Crowley v. Metropolitan St. Ry. Co. (24 App. Div. [N. Y.] 101) 308.
Crumbaugh, Denver Tramway Co. v. (23 Colo. 363) 376, 406.
Csatlos v. Metropolitan St. Ry. Co. (70 App. Div. [N. Y.] 606) 272.
Culbertson v. Crescent City R. Co. (48 La. Ann. 1376) 279.
v. Metropolitan St. Ry. Co. (140 Mo. 35) 292, 325.
Cumming v. Brooklyn City R. Co. (104 N. Y. 669) 255, 266, 270.
v. Brooklyn City R. Co. (1 Silv. [N. Y.] 327) 406.
Cummings v. Brooklyn City R. Co. (52 Hun, 613, 5 N. Y. Supp. 476) 421
v. Worcester, L. & S. St. Ry. Co. (166 Mass. 220) 82.
Cunningham v. Dry Dock, E. B. & B. R. Co. (29 Misc. [N. Y.] 772) 139.
v. Fairhaven & W. R. Co. (72 Conn. 244) 405, 407.
v. Los Angeles Ry. Co. (115 Cal. 561) 255, 266, 270.
v. Lynn & B. St. Ry. Co. (170 Mass. 298) 384.
v. Seattle Elec. Ry. & Power Co. (3 Wash. 471) 190, 432.
Wilson v. (3 Cal. 241) 322.
Cupps v. Traction Co. (13 Pa. Super. Ct. 680) 291, 315.
Currie v. Mendenhall (77 Minn. 179) 92, 143, 159.
Curtin v. Metropolitan St. Ry. Co. (22 Misc. [N. Y.] 83) 218, 219.
Curtis v. Louisville City Ry. Co. (94 Ky. 573) 33, 171, 172.
v. Sioux City & H. P. Ry. Co. (87 Iowa, 622) 182, 433.
Curry v. Rochester Ry. Co. (90 Hun [N. Y.] 230) 213.
v. Union Electric Ry. Co. (86 Hun (N. Y.] 559) 294, 299.
Cusick, Leavenworth Electric R. Co. v. (60 Kan. 590) 142, 144, 166.
Czezewzka v. Benton-Bellefontaine Ry. Co. (121 Mo. 201) 266, 267.

## D.

Dahl v. Milwaukee City Ry. Co. (62 Wis. 652) 268, 277.
v. Milwaukee City Ry. Co. (65 Wis. 371) 275.
Dahlberg v. Minneapolis St. Ry. Co. (32 Minn. 404) 99.
Dale v. Brooklyn City, H. P. & P. P. R. Co. (1 Hun [N. Y.] 146) 48, 402.
Dallas Consol. Electric St. Ry. Co. v. Broadhurst (68 S. W. [Tex. Civ. App.] 315) 61.
v. Illo (73 S. W. [Tex. Civ. App.] 1076) 327.
Dallas Consol. Traction Ry. Co. v. Hurley (10 Tex. Civ. App. 246) 211, 221, 240.
Dallas Rapid Transit Ry. Co. v. Dunlap (7 Tex. Civ. App. 471) 270.
v. Elliott (7 Tex. Civ. App. 216) 211, 220, 276.
Daly v. Detroit Citizens' St. Ry. Co. (105 Mich. 193) 230, 237.
Dan v. Street R. Co. (99 Tenn. 88) 255.
Danbeck v. New Jersey Traction Co. (57 N. J. Law, 463) 23, 24, 26, 77.
Daniel v. North Jersey St. Ry. Co. (64 N. J. Law, 603) 180.

[REFERENCES ARE TO PAGES.]

Danville Ry. & Elec. Co. v. Hodnett (43 S. E. [Va.] 606) 336, 346.
Danville St. Car Co. v. Payne (24 S. E. [Va.] 904) 133.
v. Watkins (97 Va. 713) 363.
D'Arcy v. Westchester Electric Ry. Co. (81 N. Y. Supp. 952) 109.
Darnell, Indianapolis St. Ry. Co. v. (68 N. E. [Ind. App.] 609) 302.
Darwood v. Union Traction Co. (189 Pa. 592) 289.
Dashiell, Washington & G. R. Co. v. (7 App. D. C. 507) 433.
Daub v. Yonkers R. Co. (69 Hun [N. Y.] 138) 134.
Daum v. North Jersey St. Ry. Co. (54 Atl. [N. J. Law] 221) 229, 246.
Davenport v. Brooklyn City R. Co. (100 N. Y. 632) 48.
Davey v. Greenfield & T. F. St. Ry. Co. (177 Mass. 106) 5, 6, 38, 39, 41.
Davidson v. Denver Tramway Co. (4 Colo. App. 283) 293, 295, 313.
v. Metropolitan St. Ry. Co. (75 App. Div. [N. Y.] 426) 260, 284.
v. Schuylkill Traction Co. (4 Pa. Super. Ct. 86) 315, 328.
Davies v. People's Ry. Co. (159 Mo. 1) 231.
v. People's Ry. Co. (67 Mo. App. 598) 210, 235.
Davis v. California St. Cable R. Co. (105 Cal. 131) 359.
v. Ottawa Electric Ry. Co. (28 Ont. 654) 180.
Davison v. Wilkes-Barre & W. V. Traction Co. (10 Pa. Super. Ct. 442) 335.
Dawson, Houston City St. Ry. Co. v. (2 Tex. Unrep. Cas. 223) 355.
v. St. Louis Transit Co. (76 S. W. [Mo. App.] 689) 152.
Day v. Citizens' Ry. Co. (81 Mo. App. 471) 136, 282.
Dean v. Third Ave. R. Co. (34 App. Div. [N. Y.] 220) 55.
Decker v. Brooklyn Heights R. Co. (64 App. Div. [N. Y.] 430) 300, 312.
Dederichs v. Salt Lake City R. Co. (13 Utah, 34) 326.
Dedloff, West Chicago St. R. Co. v. (92 Ill. App. 547) 297, 308, 408.
De Foe v. St. Paul City Ry. Co. (65 Minn. 319) 148.
Degel v. St. Louis Transit Co. (74 S. W. [Mo. App.] 156) 321.
Degnan v. Brooklyn City R. Co. (14 Misc. [N. Y.] 388) 319.
De Ioia v. Metropolitan St. Ry. Co. (37 App. Div. [N. Y.] 455) 280.
Delaney v. Yonkers R. Co. (13 App. Div. [N. Y.] 114) 303.
De la Torre v. Metropolitan St. Ry. Co. (48 App. Div. [N. Y.] 126) 415.
Delaware County & P. Electric Ry. Co., Morrow v. (199 Pa. 156) 293.
Delaware, L. & W. Ry. Co., Matthews v. (56 N. J. Law, 34) 127.
Delcourt, Chicago City Ry. Co. v. (33 Ill. App. 430) 45.
Delesdernier, Houston City St. Ry. Co. v. (84 Tex. 82) 355, 427.
Delkowsky v. Dry Dock, E. B. & B. R. Co. (79 N. Y. Supp. 1104) 272.
De Lon v. Kokomo City St. Ry. Co. (22 Ind. App. 377) 291, 314.
De Lucas v. New Orleans & C. R. Co. (38 La. Ann. 930) 195.
Delude v. St. Paul City Ry. Co. (55 Minn. 63) 386, 424.
Demann v. Eighth Ave. R. Co. (10 Misc. [N. Y.] 191) 92. 159.
Demarest, Bergen County Traction Co. v. (65 N. J. Law. 755) 115.
Demond v. Brooklyn City R. Co. (8 Misc. [N. Y.] 610) 423.

[REFERENCES ARE TO PAGES.]

Denison & S. Ry. Co. v. Randell (69 S. W. [Tex. Civ. App.] 1013) 193.
Dennis v. North Jersey St. Ry. Co. (64 N. J. Law, 439) 293, 294, 325.
Denton v. Brooklyn Heights R. Co. (78 N. Y. Supp. 157) 241.
Denver & B. P. Rapid Transit Co. v. Dwyer (20 Colo. 132) 35, 65, 89, 386, 389, 410.
Denver City Tramway Co., Kellogg v. (72 Pac. [Colo. App.] 609) 384.
Denver Consol. Tramway Co., Griffith v. (14 Colo. App. 504) 220.
Posten v. (11 Colo. App. 187) 139, 141, 168.
v. Rush (73 Pac. [Colo. App.] 664) 142.
Zimmerman v. (72 Pac. [Colo. App.] 607) 286.
Denver Tramway Co. v. Cloud (6 Colo. App. 445) 192, 436.
v. Crumbaugh (23 Colo. 363) 376, 406.
Davidson v. (4 Colo. App. 283) 293, 295, 313.
v. Nesbit (22 Colo. 408) 371, 373, 376.
v. O'Brien (8 Colo. App. 74) 384, 387, 388.
Oliver v. (13 Colo. App. 543) 210, 235.
v. Owens (20 Colo. 107) 146, 393, 404.
v. Reed (4 Colo. App. 500) 187.
v. Reid (4 Colo. App. 53) 109, 402.
v. Reid (22 Colo. 349) 139, 140, 148, 152.
Derby St. Ry. Co., Murphy v. (73 Conn. 249) 254.
Derry v. Lowry (6 Phila. [Pa.] 30) 181.
De Rodriguez, San Antonio Traction Co. v. (77 S. W. [Tex. Civ. App.] 420) 384.
De Rozas v. Metropolitan St. Ry. Co. (13 App. Div. [N. Y.] 296) 53.
Des Moines City Ry. Co., Root v. (113 Iowa, 675) 139, 140, 142, 143.
Des Moines St. Ry. Co., Anderson v. (97 Iowa, 739) 137.
McDivitt v. (99 Iowa, 141) 321.
Detroit Citizens' St. Ry. Co., Becker v. (121 Mich. 580) 380.
Bennett v. (123 Mich. 692) 341.
Boettcher v. (91 N. W. [Mich.] 125) 327.
Cross v. (120 Mich. 137) 113.
Dalyn v. (105 Mich. 193) 230, 237.
Doherty v. (118 Mich. 209) 219.
Fritz v. (105 Mich. 50) 289, 292, 295.
Garrity v. (112 Mich. 369) 293, 294, 312, 318.
Graff v. (109 Mich. 77) 291.
Grandorf v. (113 Mich. 496) 359.
Henderson v. (116 Mich. 368) 250, 260.
La Fond v. (92 N. W. [Mich.] 99) 368.
Lammiman v. (112 Mich. 602) 402.
McCarthy v. (120 Mich. 400) 226.
Ryan v. (123 Mich. 597) 296, 325.
Detroit City Ry. Co., Ashton v. (78 Mich. 587) 167, 402.
Bowen v. (54 Mich. 496) 365.
Harris v. (76 Mich. 227) 400, 403.
Heffron v. (92 Mich. 406) 195.

Detroit City Ry. Co., Hurst v. (84 Mich. 539) 438.
Kirchner v. (91 Mich. 400) 156.
Lacas v. (92 Mich. 412) 93, 160, 401, 402.
McCahill v. (96 Mich. 156) 153.
Upham v. (85 Mich. 12) 64, 66, 68.
Wallace v. (58 Mich. 231) 365.
Wormsdorf v. (75 Mich. 472) 111, 406, 411.
Zanger v. (87 Mich. 646) 365.
Detroit City St. Ry. Co., Wood v. (52 Mich. 402) 289, 319.
Detroit Elec. Ry. Co., Cole v. (92 N. W. [Mich.] 935) 397.
Cornell v. (82 Mich. 495) 333.
Keen v. (123 Mich. 247) 196, 199.
Nieboer v. (128 Mich. 486) 91.
Seccombe v. (94 N. W. [Mich.] 747) 378, 382.
Detroit, R. R. & L. O. Ry., Richard v. (89 N. W. [Mich.] 52) 137.
Detroit Ry. Co., Borschall v. (115 Mich. 473) 292.
Selby v. (122 Mich. 311) 142, 153.
Detroit St. Ry. Co., Bleil v. (98 Mich. 228) 340, 359.
Bowdle v. (103 Mich. 272) 166.
Gardner v. (99 Mich. 182) 144, 403, 411.
Mahoney v. (93 Mich. 612) 204.
Detroit United Ry. Co., Chauvin v. (97 N. W. [Mich.] 160) 298.
Ensley v. (96 N. W. [Mich.] 34) 347.
People v. (97 N. W. [Mich.] 36) 383.
Detroit, Y. & A. A. Ry. Co., Bedell v. (92 N. W. [Mich.] 249) 345.
Kissane v. (121 Mich. 175) 206.
Moran v. (124 Mich. 582) 296.
Rice v. (122 Mich. 677) 206.
Dettmers v. Brooklyn Heights R. Co. (22 App. Div. [N. Y.] 488) 347.
Deuster v. Milwaukee St. Ry. Co. (89 Wis. 191) 232, 244, 426.
Devine v. Brooklyn Heights R. Co. (1 App. Div. [N. Y.] 237) 367.
v. Brooklyn Heights R. Co. (34 App. Div. [N. Y.] 248) 302.
v. Metropolitan St. Ry. Co. (29 Misc. [N. Y.] 301) 289.
Devlin v. Atlantic Ave. R. Co. (57 Hun [N. Y.] 591) 124.
v. Metropolitan St. Ry. Co. (17 App. Div. [N. Y.] 491) 390.
Dew, Citizens' Rapid Transit Co. v. (100 Tenn. 317) 347.
DeWardener v. Metropolitan St. Ry. Co. (1 App. Div. [N. Y.] 240) 429.
Dickinson v. West End St. Ry. Co. (177 Mass. 365) 22, 34.
Dickert v. Salt Lake City R. Co. (20 Utah, 394) 131.
Dickson v. Broadway & S. A. R. Co. (33 N. Y. Super. Ct. 330) 163
v. Ridge Ave. Pass. Ry. Co. (19 Phila. [Pa.] 430) 77, 412.
Dieck v. New Orleans, C. & L. R. Co. (51 La. Ann. 262) 293.
Dietrich v. Baltimore & H. S. Ry. Co. (58 Md. 347) 48, 411.
Dighton, S. & S. St. Ry. Co., McCooe v. (173 Mass. 117) 395.
Dillon v. Forty-Second St., M. & St. N. Ave. Ry. Co. (28 App. Div. [N. Y.] 404) 132.

[REFERENCES ARE TO PAGES.]

Dillon, Houston City St. Ry. Co. v. (3 Tex. Civ. App. 303) 267.
v. Sixth Ave. R. Co. (48 N. Y. Super. Ct. 283) 388.
Dimmey v. Wheeling & E. G. R. Co. (27 W. Va. 32) 135, 406, 421, 439.
Dinsmore, Chicago City Ry. Co. v. (162 Ill. 658) 144.
Dintruff v. Rochester City & B. R. Co. (10 N. Y. Supp. 402) 286.
Dipaolo v. Third Ave. R. Co. (55 App. Div. [N. Y.] 566) 230.
Dise v. Metropolitan St. Ry. Co. (22 Misc. [N. Y.] 97) 298, 320.
District of Columbia v. Ashton (14 App. D. C. 571) 374.
Dix v. Railway Co. (15 Pa. Super. Ct. 350) 222.
Dixey v. Philadelphia Traction Co. (180 Pa. 401) 128.
Dixon v. Brooklyn City & N. R. Co. (100 N. Y. 170) 365.
v. Brooklyn Heights R. Co. (35 Misc. [N. Y.] 422) 400.
Diabola v. Manhattan Ry. Co. (8 N. Y. Supp. 334) 103.
Dobert v. Troy City Ry. Co. (91 Hun [N. Y.] 28) 225, 242.
Dochtermann v. Brooklyn Heights R. Co. (32 App. Div. [N. Y.] 13; affirmed 164 N. Y. 586) 132.
Doherty v. Detroit Citizens' St. Ry. Co. (118 Mich. 209) 219.
Mt. Adams & E. P. Inclined Ry. Co. v. (8 Ohio Circ. Ct. R. 349) 182, 185.
Texas & P. Ry. Co. v. (4 Willson, Civ. Cas. Ct. App. § 164) 137, 432.
Doller v. Union Ry. Co. (7 App. Div. [N. Y.] 283) 213.
Dominguez v. Orleans R. Co. (35 La. Ann. 751) 355.
Dominick v. Toledo Consol. St. Ry. Co. (3 Ohio Dec. 22) 405.
Donahue, Pittsburg, A. & M. P. Ry. Co. v. (70 Pa. 119) 188, 433.
Donivan v. Manhattan Ry. Co. (49 N. Y. State Rep. 732) 192, 193, 437.
Donnelly v. Brooklyn City R. Co. (109 N. Y. 16) 305.
v. St. Paul City Ry. Co. (70 Minn. 278) 402, 425.
Donoho v. Metropolitan St. Ry. Co. (30 Misc. [N. Y.] 433) 80.
Donohue v. Brooklyn Q. C. & S. R. Co. (53 App. Div. [N. Y.] 348) 401.
Donovan v. Hartford St. Ry. Co. (65 Conn. 201) 3, 9.
Highland Ave. & B. R. Co. v. (94 Atl. 299) 65, 67, 68.
v. Oakland & B. Rapid Transit Co. (102 Cal. 245) 356.
Dooley v. Greenfield & T. F. St. Ry. Co. (68 N. E. [Mass.] 203) 212.
West Chicago St. R. Co. v. (76 Ill. App. 424) 397, 433, 438.
Doolin v. Omnibus Cable Co. (125 Cal. 141) 414.
v. Omnibus Cable Co. (73 Pac. [Cal.] 1060) 118.
Doolittle, Omaha Horse Ry. Co. v. (7 Neb. 481) 421.
Doran v. Cedar Rapids & M. C. Ry. Co. (117 Iowa, 442) 333, 336.
D'Oro v. Atlantic Ave. R. Co. (13 N. Y. Supp. 789) 230, 245.
Doster v. Charlotte St. Ry. Co. (117 N. C. 651) 333.
Dougherty v. Frankford & S. Pass. Ry. Co. (5 Wkly. Notes Cas. [Pa.] 14) 239.
v. Missouri R. Co. (81 Mo. 325) 128.
v. Missouri R. Co. (97 Mo. 647) 406, 417.
v. Missouri Pac. R. Co. (9 Mo. App. 478) 128.

[REFERENCES ARE TO PAGES.]

Dougherty, West Chicago St. R. Co. v. (89 Ill. App. 362) 313, 314, 316.
Douglas County St. Ry. Co., Burt v. (83 Wis. 229) 95, 109.
Douglass v. Sioux City Ry. Co. (91 Iowa, 94) 102, 137.
Dowd v. Albany Ry. (47 App. Div. [N. Y.] 202) 33, 180, 183.
v. Brooklyn Heights R. Co. (9 Misc. [N. Y.] 279) 259, 275.
Downer v. Metropolitan St. Ry. Co. (54 App. Div. [N. Y.] 315) 430.
Downey v. Hendrie (46 Mich. 498) 73.
v. Philadelphia Traction Co. (14 Pa. Co. Ct. R. 251) 125, 127.
Downs v. St. Paul City Ry. Co. (75 Minn. 41) 260.
Doyle v. City of New York (58 App. Div. [N. Y.] 588) 355.
v. Lynn & B. Ry. Co. (118 Mass. 195) 105.
v. Metropolitan St. Ry. Co. (29 Misc. [N. Y.] 331) 155.
Drake v. Auburn City R. Co. (173 N. Y. 466) 372.
Dresslar v. Citizens' St. R. Co. (19 Ind. App. 383) 93, 146, 160, 167.
Drew v. Sixth Ave. R. Co. (26 N. Y. 49) 59.
Driscoll v. Market St. Cable Ry. Co. (97 Cal. 553) 209, 214, 215, 233, 235, 237, 238.
v. West End St. Ry. Co. (159 Mass. 142) 297, 314, 315, 317, 325.
Dry Dock, E. B. & B. R. Co., Allen v. (2 N. Y. Supp. 738) 111.
Biedermann v. (54 App. Div. [N. Y.] 291) 261.
Bortz v. (78 App. Div. [N. Y.] 386) 272.
Buhrens v. (53 Hun [N. Y.] 571) 298, 314, 315, 319.
Casper v. (23 App. Div. [N. Y.] 451) 362.
Casper v. (56 App. Div. [N. Y.] 372) 362.
Caspers v. (22 App. Div. [N. Y.] 156) 85.
Cunningham v. (29 Misc. [N. Y.] 772) 139.
Delkowsky v. (79 N. Y. Supp. 1104) 272.
Fleckenstein v. (105 N. Y. 655) 314, 317.
Friedman v. (11 N. Y. Supp. 429) 221, 365.
Goldstein v. (35 Misc. [N. Y.] 200) 252, 258, [illegible].
Healey v. (46 N. Y. Super. Ct. 473) 210, 236.
Juskowitz v. (25 Misc. [N. Y.] 64) 254, 263.
Ledman v. (28 App. Div. [N. Y.] 197) 260.
Levy v. (12 N. Y. Supp. 485) 265, 276.
Lewke v. (46 Hun [N. Y.] 283) 401.
Littman v. (6 Misc. [N. Y.] 34) 85.
Maisels v. (16 App. Div. [N. Y.] 391) 139, 140, 147.
Markowitz v. (12 Misc. [N. Y.] 412) 365, 408.
McCabe v. (15 Daly [N. Y.] 504) 411.
O'Neil v. (59 N. Y. Super. Ct. 123) 402, 405.
O'Neil v. (129 N. Y. 125) 319.
Saffer v. (5 N. Y. Supp. 700) 147.
Schiller v. (26 Misc. [N. Y.] 392) 153.
Seipp v. (45 App. Div. [N. Y.] 489) 411.
Seitz v. (16 Daly [N. Y.] 264) 39.
Stone v. (115 N. Y. 104) 252, 253, 259.
Tregear v. (14 Abb. Pr. [N. S.; N. Y.] 49) 74, 107.

[REFERENCES ARE TO PAGES.]

Dry Dock, E. B. & B. R. Co., Uransky v. (59 Hun [N. Y.] 626, 13 N. Y. Supp. 670) 394.
Walker v. (33 How. Pr. [N. Y.] 327) 193.
Weil v. (119 N. Y. 147) 267.
Dubiver v. City & S. Ry. Co. (74 Pac. [Or.] 915) 311.
Dubois, Marion City Ry. Co. v. (23 Ind. App. 342) 335.
Duhuque St. Ry. Co., Beringer v. (91 N. W. [Iowa] 931) 143.
Bonce v. (53 Iowa, 278) 104.
Quinn v. (94 N. W. [Iowa] 476) 313.
Dudgeon, North Chicago St. R. Co. v. (69 Ill. App. 57) 375, 377.
North Chicago St. R. Co. v. (83 Ill. App. 528) 377, 394, 417.
Dudley v. Front St. Cable Ry. Co. (73 Fed. 128) 53, 54.
Dudzik, West Chicago St. R. Co. v. (67 Ill. App. 681) 38, 40.
Duebner, North Chicago St. R. Co. v. (85 Ill. App. 602) 434.
Duffy v. Street Ry. Co. (3 Ohio Dec. 678) 322.
Du Frane v. Metropolitan St. Ry. Co. (83 App. Div. [N. Y.] 298) 213.
Dufresne, South Chicago City R. Co. v. (200 Ill. 456) 38-40.
Duggan, Joliet St. Ry. Co. v. (45 Ill. App. 450) 5.
v. Third Ave. R. Co. (8 Misc. [N. Y.] 89) 402.
v. Third Ave. R. Co. (9 Misc. [N. Y.] 158) 386.
Duluth St. Ry. Co., Isackson v. (75 Minn. 27) 233, 235, 236.
Jarmy v. (55 Minn. 271) 166.
Lundquist v. (65 Minn. 387) 387.
McKillop v. (53 Minn. 532) 363.
Wilson v. (64 Minn. 363) 331.
Dummer v. Milwaukee Electric Ry. & Light Co. (108 Wis. 589) 289, 293.
Duncan v. Rome St. R. Co. (99 Ga. 98) 276.
v. Wyatt Park Ry. Co. (48 Mo. App. 659) 139, 140, 146, 164.
Dunican v. Union Ry. Co. (39 App. Div. [N. Y.] 497) 295, 318.
Dunlap, Dallas Rapid Transit Ry. Co. v. (7 Tex. Civ. App. 471) 270.
Little Rock Traction & Elec. Co. v. (68 Ark. 291) 367.
Dunlay v. United Traction Co. (18 Pa. Super. Ct. 206) 109.
Dunn v. Cass Ave. & F. G. Ry. Co. (98 Mo. 652) 279.
v. Cass Ave. & F. G. Ry. Co. (21 Mo. App. 198) 256, 275.
Dunseath v. Pittsburgh, A. & M. Traction Co. (161 Pa. 124) 267, 283.
Duquesne Traction Co., Phillips v. (183 Pa. 255) 343, 344.
Durham Traction Co., Henderson v. (132 N. C. 779) 287.
Dusenbury v. North Hudson County Ry. Co. (66 N. J. Law, 44) 115, 118.
Dussel v. Akron St. R. Co. (10 Ohio S. & C. P. Dec. 631) 103, 143.
Duvall, Omaha St. Ry. Co. v. (40 Neb. 29) 346.
Duygan v. Third Ave. R. Co. (6 Misc. [N. Y.] 66) 396.
Dwyer, Denver & B. P. Rapid Transit Co. v. (20 Colo. 132) 35, 65, 89, 386, 389, 410.
West Chicago St. R. Co. v. (162 Ill. 482; 57 Ill. App. 440) 381.
Dykes, Mayor of Macon v. (103 Ga. 847) 339.

[REFERENCES ARE TO PAGES.]

## E.

Eadie, Street Ry. Co. v. (43 Ohio St. 91) 250, 309.
Eads v. Metropolitan Ry. Co. (43 Mo. App. 536) 32, 176, 182, 188.
Earle v. Consolidated Traction Co. (64 N. J. Law, 573) 318, 320.
East Cleveland R. Co. v. Rosecrans (24 Wkly. Law Bul. [Ohio] 220) 408.
East Detroit & G. P. Ry. Co., Rascher v. (90 Mich. 413) 302, 314, 317, 327, 332.
East Harrisburg City Pass. Ry. Co., Ehrisman v. (150 Pa. 180) 291, 295, 315, 316.
Greenfield v. (178 Pa. 194) 299, 226.
East Omaha St. Ry. Co. v. Godola (50 Neb. 906) 65, 68, 102, 106, 132.
East Saginaw City Ry. Co. v. Bohn (27 Mich. 503) 75, 77.
East St. Louis Connecting Ry. Co. v. Enright (47 Ill. App. 494) 391.
East St. Louis Electric St. Ry. Co. v. Burns (77 Ill. App. 529) 252, 410.
East St. Louis & St. L. Elec. St. Ry. Co. v. Wachtel (63 Ill. App. 181) 335, 336.
Wachtel v. (77 Ill. App. 465) 337.
Eastman v. West Chicago St. R. Co. (79 Ill. App. 585) 393.
Easton Transit Co., Callery v. (185 Pa. 176) 279, 394.
Coll v. (180 Pa. 618) 239.
Eastwood v. La Crosse City Ry. Co. (94 Wis. 163) 335.
Ebaugh, Ft. Clark St. R. Co. v. (49 Ill. App. 582) 33, 78, 179, 182.
Eberhardt v. Metropolitan St. Ry. Co. (69 App. Div. [N. Y.] 560) 131, 415, 419.
Eckert, Reading City Pass. Ry. Co. v. (1 Pa. Sup. Ct. Dig. 55) 115, 407.
Eckington & S. H. R. Co. v. Hunter (6 App. D. C. 287) 319, 328, 408.
Eddy v. Cedar Rapids & M. C. Ry. Co. (98 Iowa, 626) 231.
v. Syracuse Rapid Transit Ry. Co. (50 App. Div. [N. Y.] 109) 182, 192, 197, 201, 437.
Edgerly v. Union St. R. Co. (67 N. H. 312) 33, 178, 184.
Edgerton v. O'Neil (4 Kan. App. 73) 311, 314, 319, 435.
Edlund v. St. Paul City Ry. Co. (78 Minn. 434) 133, 402.
Egan v. Forty-Second St., M. & St. N. A. R. Co. (4 N. Y. Supp. 530) 358.
West Chicago St. R. Co. v. (74 Ill. App. 442) 256.
Ehrisman v. East Harrisburg City Pass. Ry. Co. (150 Pa. 180) 291, 295, 315, 316.
Ehrmann v. Nassau Elec. R. Co. (23 App. Div. [N. Y.] 21) 264.
Eich, Joliet R. Co. v. (96 Ill. App. 240) 314.
Eickhof v. Chicago North Shore St. Ry. Co. (77 Ill. App. 196) 94.
Eifinger v. Brooklyn Heights R. Co. (13 Misc. [N. Y.] 389) 422.
Eighth Ave. R. Co., Baker v. (62 Hun [N. Y.] 39) 269, 279.
Clark v. (36 N. Y. 135) 80.

[REFERENCES ARE TO PAGES.]

Eighth Ave. R. Co., Demann v. (10 Misc. [N. Y.] 191) 92, 159.
Hegan v. (15 N. Y. 380) 318.
Loudoun v. (16 App. Div. [N. Y.] 152) 120.
Maverick v. (36 N. Y. 378) 79, 102.
Morris v. (68 Hun [N. Y.] 39) 61, 429.
O'Keefe v. (33 App. Div. [N. Y.] 324) 419.
Sanford v. (23 N. Y. 343) 22, 32, 171, 184, 187.
Whitaker v. (51 N. Y. 295) 318, 411.
Wilbrand v. (3 Bosw. [N. Y.] 314) 317.
Einsfeld v. Niagara Junction Ry. Co. (49 App. Div. [N. Y.] 470) 379.
Eisen, Seigel v. (41 Cal. 109) 77, 99, 121.
Ekman v. Minneapolis St. Ry. Co. (34 Minn. 24) 368.
Eldridge, North Chicago St. R. Co. v. (151 Ill. 542) 96.
North Chicago St. R. Co. v. (51 Ill. App. 430) 413, 417.
Electric Ry. Co., Brown v. (101 Tenn. 252) 384.
v. Carson (98 Ga. 652) 115, 411.
v. Lawson (101 Tenn. 406) 387.
v. Shelton (89 Tenn. 423) 350.
Electric Traction Co., Blaney v. (184 Pa. 524) 226.
Connor v. (173 Pa. 602) 383.
Cross v. (18 Pa. Co. Ct. R. 29) 422.
Frame v. (180 Pa. 49) 299, 326.
Funk v. (175 Pa. 559) 260.
Kline v. (181 Pa. 276) 278.
Leary v. (180 Pa. 136) 358.
Mitchell v. (12 Pa. Super. Ct. 472) 92, 159.
Mulcahy v. (185 Pa. 427) 279.
Smith v. (187 Pa. 110) 292, 315.
Elgin City Ry. Co. v. Wilson (56 Ill. App. 364) 115, 132.
Elizabeth, P. C. & J. Ry. Co., Brown v. (68 N. J. Law, 618) 220.
Lee v. (55 Atl. [N. J. Sup.] 106) 163.
Elkins, Judge v. (66 N. E. [Mass.] 708) 222.
Ellerman v. St. Louis Transit Co. (76 S. W. [Mo. App.] 661) 329.
Ellick v. Metropolitan St. Ry. Co. (15 App. Div. [N. Y.] 556) 253, 259, 274, 283.
Elliott, Dallas Rapid Transit Ry. Co. v. (7 Tex. Civ. App. 216) 211, 220, 276.
v. Newport St. Ry. Co. (18 R. I. 707) 83, 84, 87, 103, 420.
Ellis v. Lynn & B. R. Co. (160 Mass. 341) 336, 337.
v. Milwaukee City Ry. Co. (67 Wis. 135) 194.
El Paso Elec. St. Ry. Co. v. Ballinger & Longwell (72 S. W. [Tex. Civ. App.] 612) 307.
Elwood Elec. St. Ry. Co. v. Ross (26 Ind. App. 258) 251, 270, 276.
Elyton Land Co. v. Mingee (89 Ala. 521) 309.
Emminger, Omaha St. Ry. Co. v. (57 Neb. 240) 401, 433.
Engel, Chicago City Ry. Co. v. (35 Ill. App. 490) 102, 126.
Enright, East St. Louis Connecting Ry. Co. v. (47 Ill. App. 494) 391.

[REFERENCES ARE TO PAGES.]

Enslen, South Covington & C. St. Ry. Co. v. (18 Ky. Law Rep. 921) 291.
Ensley v. Detroit United Ry. Co. (96 N. W. [Mich.] 34) 347.
Eppendorf v. Brooklyn City & N. R. Co. (69 N. Y. 195) 38, 39, 41, 42.
Ericius v. Brooklyn Heights R. Co. (63 App. Div. [N. Y.] 353) 60.
Erie City Pass. Ry. Co. v. Schuster (113 Pa. 412) 251, 254.
Erie Electric Motor Co., Conyngham v. (15 Pa. Super. Ct. 573) 296.
Woeckner v. (176 Pa. 451) 251, 277.
Woeckner v. (182 Pa. 182) 264, 434.
v., Woeckner (187 Pa. 206) 412.
Erslew v. New Orleans & N. R. Co. (49 La. Ann. 86) 363.
Essex Elec. St. Ry. Co., Gay v. (159 Mass. 238, 242) 368.
Estep, West Chicago St. R. Co. v. (162 Ill. 130) 394.
Etson v. Ft. Wayne & B. I. Ry. Co. (110 Mich. 494) 92, 159, 167.
v. Ft. Wayne & B. I. Ry. Co. (114 Mich. 605) 110, 131.
Evans v. Lake Shore & M. S. R. Co. (88 Mich. 442) 380.
Evansville St. R. Co. v. Gentry (147 Ind. 408) 19, 216, 242.
v. Meadows (13 Ind. App. 155) 23, 25, 76.
Everett v. Los Angeles Consol. Elec. Ry. Co. (115 Cal. 105) 342.
Evers v. Philadelphia Traction Co. (176 Pa. 376) 251, 264, 266, 269, 275.
Ewing v. Atlantic Ave. R. Co. (11 N. Y. Supp. 626) 239.

## F.

Fahner v. Brooklyn Heights R. Co. (86 App. Div. [N. Y.] 488) 62.
Fain's Adm'r, Lexington R. Co. v. (24 Ky. L. R. 1443) 349, 353.
Fair Haven & W. R. Co., Baldwin v. (68 Conn. 567) 166.
Brennan v. (45 Conn. 284) 23, 26, 72, 139, 152.
Cunningham v. (72 Conn. 244) 405, 407.
Fairmount & A. S. P. Ry. Co. v. Stutler (54 Pa. 375) 143.
Falke v. Third Ave. R. Co. (38 App. Div. [N. Y.] 49) 119.
Fallon v. Central Park, N. & E. R. R. Co. (64 N. Y. 13) 267.
Falotio v. Broadway & S. A. R. Co. (9 Daly [N. Y.] 243) 271.
Falvey, Metropolitan R. Co. v. (5 App. D. C. 176) 97, 101.
Fandel v. Third Ave. R. Co. (15 App. Div. [N. Y.] 426) 234, 243.
Faris v. Brooklyn City & N. R. Co. (46 App. Div. [N. Y.] 231) 85.
Farley v. Philadelphia Traction Co. (6 Pa. Co. Ct. R. 347) 98.
v. Wilmington & N. Elec. Ry. Co. (52 Atl. [Del.] 543) 309.
v. Wilmington & N. Elec. Ry. Co. (3 Pen. [Del.] 581) 310, 313, 314.
Farmer v. Findlay St. Ry. Co. (60 Ohio St. 36) 358.
Farrar v. New Orleans & C. R. Co. (52 La. Ann. 417) 216, 237.
Farrell v. Houston, W. St. & P. Ferry R. Co. (4 N. Y. Supp. 597) 90.
v. Metropolitan St. Ry. Co. (51 App. Div. [N. Y.] 456) 401.
v. Waterbury Horse R. Co. (60 Conn. 239) 228.
Farris v. Cass Ave. & F. G. Ry. Co. (80 Mo. 325) 250, 269, 277.
Fash v. Third Ave. R. Co. (1 Daly [N. Y.] 148) 361.

[REFERENCES ARE TO PAGES.]

Fath v. Tower Grove & L. Ry. Co. (105 Mo. 537) 136, 273.
v. Tower Grove & L. Ry. Co. (39 Mo. App. 447) 272.
Faurot v. Brooklyn Heights R. Co. (14 Misc. [N. Y.] 398) 219, 241.
Fay v. Brooklyn Heights Ry. Co. (69 App. Div. [N. Y.] 563) 300.
v. Metropolitan St. Ry. Co. (62 App. Div. [N. Y.] 51) 53.
Feary v. Metropolitan St. Ry. Co. (162 Mo. 75) 110, 394.
Federal St. & P. V. Ry. Co., Carson v. (147 Pa. 219) 289.
v. Gibson (96 Pa. 83) 123.
Gilmore v. (153 Pa. 31) 307, 315, 317.
Greeley v. (153 Pa. 218) 338, 366.
McMillan v. (172 Pa. 523) 33, 71, 179.
Winter v. (153 Pa. 26) 294, 308, 321.
Woelfel v. (183 Pa. 213) 329.
Feingold v. Philadelphia Traction Co. (21 Pa. Co. Ct. R. 183) 152.
Feital v. Middlesex R. Co. (109 Mass. 398) 105, 115, 137.
Feldstein, West Chicago St. R. Co. v. (69 Ill. App. 36) 332.
Fenig v. North Jersey St. Ry. Co. (64 N. J. Law, 715) 142.
Fennell, Highland Ave. & B. R. Co. v. (111 Ala. 356) 374.
Fenner v. Wilkes-Barre & W. V. Traction Co. (202 Pa. 365) 307, 326.
Fennimore. Chicago City Ry. Co. v. (78 Ill. App. 478) 414.
Chicago City Ry. Co. v. (199 Ill. 1) 219, 243.
Fenton v. Second Ave. R. Co. (126 N. Y. 625) 269, 274, 280.
Ferguson, Ft. Worth St. Ry. Co. v. (9 Tex. Civ. App. 610) 433.
Fernandes v. Sacramento City Ry. Co. (52 Cal. 45) 228.
Fewings v. Mendenhall (93 N. W. [Minn.] 127) 114.
Fielders v. North Jersey St. Ry. Co. (67 N. J. Law, 76) 358.
Fielding, Oakland Ry. Co. v. (48 Pa. 320) 358.
Fillingham v. St. Louis Transit Co. (77 S. W. [Mo. App.] 314) 14.
Findlay St. Ry. Co., Farmer v. (60 Ohio St. 36) 358.
Findley, City & Suburban Ry. Co. v. (76 Ga. 311) 141, 167, 168.
Fineburg v. Second & Third Sts. Pass. Ry. Co. (182 Pa. 97) 397.
Finkeldey v. Omnibus Cable Co. (114 Cal. 28) 6, 38-40, 42, 57, 60.
Finkelstein v. Brooklyn Heights R. Co. (51 App. Div. [N. Y.] 287) 284.
Finley v. Hudson Elec. Ry. Co. (64 Hun [N. Y.] 373) 26.
v. West Chicago St. R. Co. (90 Ill. App. 368) 278.
Finn v. Valley City St. & Cable Ry. Co. (86 Mich. 74) 14, 142.
Finseth v. Suburban Ry. Co. (32 Or. 1) 14, 19.
Fishback v. Steinway Ry. Co. (11 App. Div. [N. Y.] 152) 302, 327.
Fisher v. Union Ry. Co. (86 App. Div. [N. Y.] 365) 133.
Fishman, West Chicago St. R. Co. v. (68 Ill. App. 445) 414.
West Chicago St. Ry. Co. v. (169 Ill. 196) 403.
Fisselmayer v. Third Ave. R. Co. (2 N. Y. State Rep. 75) 250, 268.
Fitch v. Mason City & C. L. Traction Co. (116 Iowa, 716) 406.
Fitchburg & L. St. Ry. Co., Lahti v. (172 Mass. 147) 299.
Fitton v. Brooklyn City R. Co. (5 N. Y. Supp. 641) 422.
Fitts v. Cream City R. Co. (59 Wis. 323) 367.
Fitzgibbons, North Chicago St. R. Co. v. (180 Ill. 466) 393.

[REFERENCES ARE TO PAGES.]

Fitzgibbons, North Chicago St. R. Co. v. (79 Ill. App. 632) 393, 418.
Fitzhenry v. Consolidated Traction Co. (64 N. J. Law, 674) 250, 253, 260.
Fitzpatrick v. Bloomington City Ry. Co. (73 Ill. App. 516) 404.
Flack v. Nassau Electric R. Co. (41 App. Div. [N. Y.] 399) 157.
Flaherty v. Harrison (98 Wis. 559) 335, 394, 396.
Flanagan v. Metropolitan St. Ry. Co. (31 Misc. [N. Y.] 820) 143.
North Hudson County Ry. Co. v. (57 N. J. Law, 696) 279.
v. People's Pass. Ry. Co. (163 Pa. 102) 278.
Flannagan v. St. Paul City Ry. Co. (68 Minn. 300) 300.
Fleishman v. Neversink Mountain R. Co. (174 Pa. 510) 279.
Fleck v. Union Ry. Co. (134 Mass. 480) 77, 79, 92.
Fleckenstein v. Dry Dock, E. B. & B. R. Co. (105 N. Y. 655) 314, 317.
Fleming v. Brooklyn City R. Co. (1 Abb. N. C. 433; affirmed 74 N. Y. 618) 28, 29.
v. St. Louis & S. Ry. Co. (74 S. W. [Mo. App.] 382) 169.
Fletcher v. Philadelphia Traction Co. (190 Pa. 117) 374.
Flewelling v. Lewiston & A. Horse R. Co. (89 Me. 585) 333.
Floettl v. Third Ave. R. Co. (10 App. Div. [N. Y.] 308) 246.
Flournoy v. Shreveport Belt Ry. Co. (50 La. Ann. 635) 127, 414.
Floyd v. Paducah Ry. & Light Co. (73 S. W. [Ky.] 1122) 210, 235.
Flushing & C. P. Elec. Ry. Co., McGrane v. (13 App. Div. [N. Y.] 177) 306, 327.
Flynn v. Central Park, etc., R. Co. (49 N. Y. Super. Ct. 81) 33, 176, 178, 186, 190.
v. Consolidated Traction Co. (64 N. J. Law, 375) 84, 85.
v. Louisville Ry. Co. (23 Ky. L. R. 57, 62 S. W. 490) 313.
v. Metropolitan St. Ry. Co. (10 App. Div. [N. Y.] 258) 280.
Springfield Consol. Ry. Co. v. (55 Ill. App. 600) 191.
Fuhrman v. Consolidated Traction Co. (63 N. J. Law, 391) 437.
Foley v. Brunswick Traction Co. (66 N. J. Law, 637) 157.
v. Metropolitan St. R. Co. (80 App. Div. [N. Y.] 262) 425.
State v. (31 Iowa, 527) 319.
Fonda, J. & G. R. Co., Butez v. (20 Misc. [N. Y.] 123) 399.
Countryman v. (166 N. Y. 201) 322.
Fonda v. St. Paul City Ry. Co. (71 Minn. 438) 226, 395, 404.
v. St. Paul City Ry. Co. (77 Minn. 336) 233, 416.
Forman v. New Orleans & C. R. Co. (40 La. Ann. 446) 172.
Forrestal v. Milwaukee Elec. Ry. & Light Co. (97 N. W. [Wis.] 182) 273.
Ft. Clark St. R. Co. v. Ebaugh (49 Ill. App. 582) 33, 78, 179, 182.
Ft. Pitt Traction Co., Gray v. (198 Pa. 184) 224.
Ft. Wayne & B. I. Ry. Co., Etson v. (110 Mich. 494) 92, 159, 167.
Etson v. (114 Mich. 605) 110, 131.
Guilloz v. (108 Mich. 41) 329.
Laethem v. (100 Mich. 297) 317.
McClellan v. (105 Mich. 101) 397.

[REFERENCES ARE TO PAGES.]

Ft. Wayne & E. Ry. Co., Archer v. (87 Mich. 101) 64, 68, 74, 108, 112.
Bradley v. (94 Mich. 35) 92, 159, 167.
Kingston v. (112 Mich. 40) 88.
Werbowlsky v. (86 Mich. 236) 142, 147, 164.
Ft. Wayne Traction Co. v. Morvilius (68 N. E. [Ind. App.] 304) 13, 141, 157.
Ft. Worth St. Ry. Co. v. Ferguson (9 Tex. Civ. App. 610) 433.
v. Witten (74 Tex. 202) 419.
Fortin, Metropolitan West Side El. Ry. Co. v. (203 Ill. 454) 389.
Fortune v. Missouri R. Co. (10 Mo. App. 252) 139, 140, 168.
Forty-Second St. & G. St. Ferry R. Co., Black v. (19 N. Y. Wkly. Dig. 24) 368.
Hayes v. (97 N. Y. 259) 129.
Ihl v. (47 N. Y. 317) 251, 254, 255, 264.
Lax v. (46 N. Y. Super. Ct. 448) 67, 73, 144.
McCooey v. (79 Hun [N. Y.] 255) 228, 245.
Payne v. (40 N. Y. Super. Ct. 8) 98.
Platt v. (2 Hun [N. Y.] 124) 14, 236.
Rott v. (56 N. Y. Super. Ct. 151) 59.
Unger v. (51 N. Y. 497) 239.
Worster v. (50 N. Y. 203) 361, 362.
Forty-Second St., M. & St. N. Ave. R. Co., Charlton v. (79 App. Div. [N. Y.] 546) 253.
Dillon v. (28 App. Div. [N. Y.] 404) 132.
Egan v. (4 N. Y. Supp. 530) 358.
Gilbertson v. (14 App. Div. [N. Y.] 294) 414.
Hennessey v. (84 N. Y. Supp. 158) 229.
Kellegher v. (171 N. Y. 309) 53.
Kelley v. (58 Hun [N. Y.] 93) 384.
Kreuzen v. (13 N. Y. Supp. 588) 124.
Murray v. (9 App. Div. [N. Y.] 610) 240.
Phelan v. (79 App. Div. [N. Y.] 548) 211, 236.
Riddle v. (173 N. Y. 327) 231.
Foster, Atlanta Consol. St. Ry. Co. v. (108 Ga. 223) 408.
v. Old Colony St. Ry. Co. (182 Mass. 378) 165.
v. Union Traction Co. (199 Pa. 498) 92, 159.
West Chicago St. R. Co. v. (175 Ill. 396) 433.
Fourteenth St. R. Co., Swain v. (93 Cal. 179) 312, 317, 324, 413, 419.
Fowler v. Broadway & S. A. R. Co. (59 Hun [N. Y.] 623, 13 N. Y. Supp. 453) 426.
v. Inhabitants of Gardner (169 Mass. 505) 362.
Fox v. Brooklyn City R. Co. (7 Misc. [N. Y.] 285) 124.
v. Oakland Consol. St. Ry. (118 Cal. 55) 255, 266, 267, 392, 430, 434, 438.
Fox River Electric Ry. & Power Co., Watermolen v. (110 Wis. 153) 292.
Fox River Valley Elec. Ry. Co., Zimmer v. (95 N. W. [Wis.] 957) 74, 130.

[REFERENCES ARE TO PAGES.]

Foxley, Citizens' Passenger Ry. Co. v. (107 Pa. 537) 277.
Foy v. Toledo Consol. St. Ry. Co. (3 Ohio Dec. 22) 278.
Frame v. Electric Traction Co. (180 Pa. 49) 299, 326.
Francisco v. Troy & L. R. Co. (78 Hun [N. Y.] 13) 133.
v. Troy & L. R. Co. (88 Hun [N. Y.] 464) 65, 71, 72, 131.
Francis v. New York Steam Co. (114 N. Y. 380) 99.
Frank v. Metropolitan St. Ry. Co. (44 App. Div. [N. Y.] 243) 281.
v. Metropolitan St. Ry. Co. (58 App. Div. [N. Y.] 100) 211, 220, 221.
v. St. Louis Transit Co. (73 S. W. [Mo. App.] 239) 293, 332.
Frankford, S. & P. C. P. R. Co., Randall v. (139 Pa. 464) 113, 114.
Frankford & S. C. Ry. Co., Campbell v. (139 Pa. 522) 356.
Frankford & S. P. C. R. Co., Aikin v. (143 Pa. 47) 81.
Kraut v. (160 Pa. 327) 358, 407.
Frankford & S. P. Ry. Co., Dougherty v. (5 Wkly. Notes Cas. [Pa.] 14) 239.
Lott v. (159 Pa. 471) 337.
Randall v. (8 Pa. Co. Ct. R. 277) 107.
Frankford & S. Ry. Co., Coller v. (9 Wkly. Notes Cas. [Pa.] 477) 58.
Franklin v. Third Ave. R. Co. (52 App. Div. [N. Y.] 512) 188, 189.
Franscomb, Birmingham Ry. & Elec. Co. v. (124 Ala. 621) 322.
Frederick Ave. Ry. Co., Ashbrook v. (18 Mo. App. 290) 80, 82.
Freeman v. Brooklyn Heights R. Co. (54 App. Div. [N. Y.] 596) 353.
v. Brooklyn Heights R. Co. (87 App. Div. [N. Y.] 127) 320.
v. Brooklyn Heights R. Co. (81 N. Y. Supp. 828) 220.
v. Metropolitan St. Ry. Co. (95 Mo. App. 94) 102.
Fremont v. Metropolitan St. Ry. Co. (82 N. Y. Supp. 307) 49.
French v. Brooklyn Heights R. Co. (57 App. Div. [N. Y.] 204) 428.
Louisville Ry. Co. v. (71 S. W. [Ky.] 486) 274.
Friedman v. Dry Dock, E. B. & B. R. Co. (11 N. Y. Supp. 429) 221, 365.
Friel v. Citizens' Ry. Co. (115 Mo. 503) 382.
Fritz v. Detroit Citizens' St. Ry. Co. (105 Mich. 50) 289, 292, 295.
Front St. Cable Ry. Co., Brennan v. (8 Wash. 363) 385.
Dudley v. (73 Fed. 128) 53, 54.
Hawkins v. (3 Wash. 592) 65.
Spurrier v. (3 Wash. 659) 318, 401, 427.
Fry v. People's Pass. Ry. Co. (17 Phila. [Pa.] 61) 150.
Fuller v. Jamestown St. R. Co. (75 Hun [N. Y.] 273) 400.
Toledo Consol. St. R. Co. v. (17 Ohio Cir. Ct. R. 562) 22.
Fullerton v. Cedar Rapids & M. C. Ry. Co. (101 Iowa, 156) 347.
v. Metropolitan St. Ry. Co. (37 App. Div. [N. Y.] 386) 283.
v. Metropolitan St. Ry. Co. (63 App. Div. [N. Y.] 1) 266.
Fulmore v. St. Paul City Ry. Co. (72 Minn. 448) 424.
Fulton County St. R. Co. v. McConnell (87 Ga. 756) 356.
Funk v. Electric Traction Co. (175 Pa. 559) 260.
v. St. Paul City Ry. Co. (61 Minn. 435) 389.
Furgason v. Citizens' St. Ry. Co. (16 Ind. App. 171) 153, 166.

[REFERENCES ARE TO PAGES.]

Furgason v. Philadelphia Traction Co. (20 Phila. [Pa.] 249) 231.
Furman v. Brooklyn Heights R. Co. (25 App. Div. [N. Y.] 133) 418.
Furst v. Second Ave. R. Co. (72 N. Y. 542) 411.

## G.

Gadsden & A. U. Ry. Co. v. Causler (97 Ala. 235) 168.
Gaffney v. St. Paul City Ry. Co. (81 Minn. 459) 5, 6.
Gagne v. Minneapolis St. Ry. Co. (77 Minn. 171) 342.
Gainesville St. Ry. Co., Hays v. (70 Tex. 602) 271, 273, 399.
Galbraith v. West End St. Ry. Co. (165 Mass. 572) 296, 325.
Galesburg Elec. Motor & Power Co. v. Manville (61 Ill. App. 490) 334, 336.
Gallagher v. Crescent City R. Co. (37 La. Ann. 288) 279.
v. West End St. Ry. Co. (156 Mass. 157) 50.
West Phila. Pass. Ry. Co. v. (108 Pa. 524) 80, 81, 112.
Galveston City Ry. Co., Allen v. (79 Tex. 631) 133.
Christie v. (39 S. W. [Tex. Civ. App.] 638) 60.
Hewitt (67 Tex. 473) 269, 270, 272, 419.
v. Nolan (53 Tex. 139) 363.
Riley v. (13 Tex. Civ. App. 247) 389.
Rogers v. (76 Tex. 502) 378.
Ganiard v. Rochester City & B. R. Co. (50 Hun, 22; affirmed 121 N. Y. 661) 6, 51-53, 61.
Gannon v. New Orleans, C. & L. R. Co. (48 La. Ann. 1002) 270, 272.
Garbaccio v. Jersey City, H. & P. St. Ry. Co. (53 Atl. [N. J. Law] 707) 431.
Gardner v. Detroit St. Ry. Co. (99 Mich. 182) 144, 403, 411.
New Jersey Traction Co. v. (58 N. J. Law, 176) 141.
New Jersey Traction Co. v. (60 N. J. Law, 571) 139, 140.
Garduhn v. Union Ry. Co. (50 App. Div. [N. Y.] 602) 408.
Gargan v. West End St. Ry. Co. (176 Mass. 106) 14, 367.
Garrison v. United Rys. & Elec. Co. (55 Atl. [Md.] 371) 173, 195.
Garrity v. Detroit Citizens' St. Ry. Co. (112 Mich. 369) 293, 294, 312, 318.
Garthwright, Richmond Ry. & Elec. Co. v. (92 Va. 627) 321, 327, 413, 427.
Gastka, North Chicago City Ry. Co. v. (128 Ill. 613) 171, 183, 187, 189, 190.
North Chicago City Ry. Co. v. (27 Ill. App. 518) 393.
Gaston, Atlanta Ry. & Power Co. v. (45 S. E. [Ga.] 508) 329.
Gate City St. R. Co., Houston v. (89 Ga. 272) 60, 404.
Gaughan v. Second Ave. Traction Co. (189 Pa. 408) 303.
Gay v. Essex Elec. St. Ry. Co. (159 Mass. 238) 242, 368.
Geary v. Metropolitan St. Ry. Co. (73 App. Div. [N. Y.] 441) 311.
v. Metropolitan St. Ry. Co. (84 App. Div. [N. Y.] 514) 309, 311.
Gebhardt v. St. Louis Transit Co. (71 S. W. [Mo. App.] 448) 136, 246, 299, 332.
Geddes v. Metropolitan R. Co. (103 Mass. 391) 91, 108.

[REFERENCES ARE TO PAGES.]

Geipel v. Steinway Ry. Co. (14 App. Div. [N. Y.] 551) 303, 330, 338.
Geitz v. Milwaukee City Ry. Co. (72 Wis. 307) 83, 84, 87.
Geleta v. Buffalo & N. F. Elec. Ry. (84 N. Y. Supp. 629) 304.
Gentry, Evansville St. R. Co. v. (147 Ind. 408) 19, 216, 242.
Geoghegan v. Third Ave. R. Co. (51 App. Div. [N. Y.] 369) 435.
George v. Los Angeles Ry. Co. (126 Cal. 357) 250, 286.
Georgia Pac. Ry. Co. v. Hughes (87 Ala. 610) 125.
Germantown Pass. Ry. Co. v. Brophy (105 Pa. 38) 99.
v. Walling (97 Pa. 55) 80, 81.
Gerrard v. La Crosse City R. Co. (113 Wis. 258) 365, 366.
Gibbons v. Wilkes-Barre, etc., St. Ry. Co. (155 Pa. 279) 303, 306, 317, 330, 334, 338.
Gibson, Federal St. & P. V. Ry. Co. v. (96 Pa. 83) 123.
Gidionsen v. Union Depot R. Co. (129 Mo. 392) 131, 132, 420.
Gier v. Los Angeles Consol. Elec. Ry. Co. (108 Cal. 129) 374, 377.
Gifford, Citizens' Ry. Co. v. (19 Tex. Civ. App. 631) 349.
Gilbert v. Third Ave. Ry. Co. (54 N. Y. Super. Ct. 270) 39.
v. West End St. Ry. Co. (160 Mass. 403) 141, 142, 163, 399.
Gilbertson v. Forty-Second St., M. & St. N. Ave. Ry. Co. (14 App. Div. [N. Y.] 294) 414.
Gildea v. Metropolitan St. Ry. Co. (58 App. Div. [N. Y.] 528) 219, 240.
Gillam, Chicago City Ry. Co. v. (27 Ill. App. 386) 434, 438.
Gillespie v. Yonkers R. Co. (83 N. Y. Supp. 1043) 163.
Gilliland v. Middlesex & S. Traction Co (67 N. J. Law, 542) 220.
Gillow, North Chicago St. R. Co. v. (166 Ill. 444) 403.
Gilmore v. Brooklyn Heights R. Co. (6 App. Div. [N. Y.] 117) 110.
v. Federal St. & P. V. Pass. Ry. Co. (153 Pa. 31) 307, 316, 317.
v. Seattle & R. Ry. Co. (29 Wash. 150) 393.
Gilson v. Jackson County Horse Ry. Co. (76 Mo. 282) 101, 102.
Gilton v. Hestonville, M. & F. Pass. Ry. Co. (166 Pa. 460) 362.
Ginna v. Second Ave. R. Co. (67 N. Y. 596) 64, 67, 72.
Giraldo v. Coney Island & B. R. Co. (16 N. Y. Supp. 774) 277.
Gladmon, Washington & G. Ry. Co. v. (15 Wall. [U. S.] 401) 253, 275.
Glassey v. Hestonville, M. & F. P. Ry. Co. (57 Pa. 172) 254, 263.
Glazebrook v. West End St. Ry. Co. (160 Mass. 239) 323.
Gleason v. Worcester Consol. St. Ry. Co. (68 N. E. [Mass.] 223) 231.
Glens Falls, S. H. & F. E. St. R. Co., Burns v. (4 App. Div. [N. Y.] 426) 188-190.
Regner v. (74 Hun [N. Y.] 202) 179.
Wright v. (24 App. Div. [N. Y.] 617) 173, 192, 437.
Glenville v. St. Louis R. Co. (51 Mo. App. 629) 332.
Gloucester St. Ry. Co., Morey v. (171 Mass. 164) 260.
Glynn, Consolidated Traction Co. v. (59 N. J. Law, 432) 209, 217-219, 234
Gnuse, Quincy Horse Ry. & Carrying Co. v. (137 Ill. 264) 410.
Quincy Horse Ry. & Carrying Co. v. (38 Ill. App. 212) 256, 270, 276. 282.

[REFERENCES ARE TO PAGES.]

Godfrey v. Streator Ry. Co. (56 Ill. App. 378) 349.
Godola, East Omaha St. Ry. Co. v. (50 Neb. 906) 65, 68, 102, 106, 132.
Goetz v. Metropolitan St. Ry. Co. (54 App. Div. [N. Y.] 365) 390.
Goldrick v. Union R. Co. (20 R. I. 128) 315-317, 322.
Goldstein, Austin Dam & S. Ry. Co. v. (18 Tex. Civ. App. 704) 322.
v. Dry Dock, E. B. & B. R. Co. (35 Misc. [N. Y.] 200) 252, 258, 284.
Goldthwait v. Haverhill & G. St. Ry. Co. (160 Mass. 554) 384.
Goldwasser v. Metropolitan St. Ry. Co. (32 Misc. [N. Y.] 682) 59, 85.
Goodman v. Metropolitan St. Ry. Co. (63 App. Div. [N. Y.] 84) 271.
Goodrich v. Chippewa Valley Elec. R. Co. (108 Wis. 329) 379.
Goodspeed v. Ithaca St. Ry. Co. (84 N. Y. Supp. 383) 206.
Goorin v. Allegheny Traction Co. (179 Pa. 327) 122.
Gordon v. Grand St. & N. R. Co. (40 Barb. [N. Y.] 546) 3, 20.
v. West End St. Ry. Co. (175 Mass. 181) 6, 38, 39, 41.
Gorman's Adm'r v. Louisville Ry. Co. (72 S. W. [Ky.] 760) 270.
Gould v. Union Traction Co. (190 Pa. 198) 344.
Govan v. New Orleans & C. R. Co. (35 So. [La.] 484) 372.
Government St. R. Co. v. Hanlon (53 Ala. 70) 251, 254, 270.
Grabenstein v. Metropolitan St. Ry. Co. (84 N. Y. Supp. 261) 163.
Grace v. St. Louis R. Co. (156 Mo. 295) 142.
Graff v. Detroit Citizens' St. Ry. Co. (109 Mich. 77) 291.
Graham v. Consolidated Traction Co. (62 N. J. Law, 90) 431, 439
v. Consolidated Traction Co. (64 N. J. Law, 10) 431, 439.
v. Manhattan Ry. Co. (149 N. Y. 336) 15, 65, 67, 74, 106.
Grand Ave. Cable Co., Jacquin v. (57 Mo. App. 320) 102, 127.
Grand Ave. Ry. Co., Henry v. (113 Mo. 525) 211, 234.
Jackson v. (118 Mo. 199) 102, 143, 164, 404.
Taylor v. (137 Mo. 363) 120, 121, 137.
Grand Rapids Ice & Coal Co., Joslin v. (53 Mich. 322) 359.
Grand St. & N. R. Co., Gordon v. (40 Barb. [N. Y.] 546) 320.
Suydam v. (41 Barb. [N. Y.] 375) 318.
Wooley v. (83 N. Y. 121) 360, 366, 407.
Grandorf v. Detroit Citizens' St. Ry. Co. (113 Mich. 496) 359.
Grant, Pomaski v. (119 Mich. 675) 83, 394.
Washington & G. R. Co. v. (11 App. D. C. 107) 143, 162.
Grant St. Electric Ry. Co., Henry v. (24 Wash. 246) 157.
Vasele v. (16 Wash. 602) 49, 57.
Graven, Macleod v. (73 Fed. 627) 215.
Graves, Memphis St. Ry. Co. v. (75 S. W. [Tenn.] 729) 200.
Gray v. Ft. Pitt Traction Co. (198 Pa. 184) 224.
Hestonville, M. & F. P. R. Co. v. (3 Wkly. Notes Cas. [Pa.] 421) 185.
v. Rochester City & B. R. Co. (61 Hun [N. Y.] 212) 86.
v. Second Ave. R. Co. (65 N. Y. 561) 307, 334.
v. St. Paul City Ry. Co. (87 Minn. 280) 276.
v. Washington Water Power Co. (27 Wash. 713, 30 Wash. 665) 361.

[REFERENCES ARE TO PAGES.]

Great Falls St. Ry. Co., Hamilton v. (17 Mont. 334) 102, 119, 429.
Greeley v. Federal St. & P. V. Pass. Ry. Co. (153 Pa. 218) 338, 366.
Green, Chicago North Shore Ry. Co. v. (93 Ill. App. 105) 342.
v. Metropolitan St. Ry. Co. (42 App. Div. [N. Y.] 160) 285.
v. Metropolitan St. Ry. Co. (60 App. Div. [N. Y.] 317) 395.
v. Metropolitan St. Ry. Co. (65 App. Div. [N. Y.] 54) 285.
People's Pass. Ry. Co. v. (56 Md. 84) 53, 406.
Green & C. St. Passenger Ry. Co. v. Bresmer (97 Pa. 103) 385, 388.
Jatho v. (4 Phila. [Pa.] 24) 345.
Reilly v. (4 Wkly. Notes Cas. [Pa.] 273) 151.
Greenbaum v. Interurban St. Ry. Co. (84 N. Y. Supp. 588) 231.
Greenberg v. Third Ave. R. Co. (35 App. Div. [N. Y.] 619) 278.
Greenfield v. East Harrisburg Pass. Ry. Co. (178 Pa. 194) 299, 326.
Greenfield & T. F. St. Ry. Co., Davey v. (177 Mass. 106) 5, 6, 38, 39, 41.
Dooley v. (68 N. E. [Mass.] 203) 212.
Henderson v. (172 Mass. 542) 337.
Greengard v. St. Paul City Ry. Co. (72 Minn. 181) 226.
Greensburg, J. & P. St. Ry. Co., Jones Bros. v. (9 Pa. Super. Ct. 65) 294, 315.
Greenville St. Ry. Co., Bowie v. (69 Miss. 196) 92, 159.
Gregg, Chicago City Ry. Co. v. (69 Ill. App. 77) 163.
Grenell, West Chicago St. R. Co. v. (90 Ill. App. 30) 398.
Gress v. Railway Co. (14 Pa. Super. Ct. 87) 325.
Gretzner v. New Orleans & C. R. Co. (105 La. 266) 150.
Grieve v. North Jersey St. R. Co. (65 N. J. Law, 409) 91.
Griffin v. Ithaca St. Ry. Co. (62 App. Div. [N. Y.] 551) 380.
Nashville St. Ry. v. (104 Tenn. 81) 192, 194, 424, 437.
Griffith v. Denver Consol. Tramway Co. (14 Colo. App. 504) 220.
v. Utica & M. R. Co. (17 N. Y. Supp. 692) 89.
Griffiths v. Metropolitan St. Ry. Co (63 App. Div. [N. Y.] 86) 238, 259, 284.
Griveaud v. St. Louis Cable & W. Ry. Co. (33 Mo. App. 458) 362.
Gross v. Electric Traction Co. (18 Pa. Co. Ct. R. 29) 422.
Gross v. South Chicago City Ry. Co. (73 Ill. App. 217) 365.
Grosse, Calumet Elec. St. Ry. Co. v (70 Ill. App. 381) 349.
Grothe, Austin Rapid Transit Co. v. (88 Tex. 262) 387.
Grotsch v. Steinway Ry. Co. (19 App. Div. [N. Y.] 130) 113, 131.
Groves v. Louisville Ry. Co. (22 Ky. L. R. 599) 361.
Gruse, Quincy Horse Ry. & Carrying Co. v. (26 Ill. App. 397) 253.
G'Sell v. Metropolitan St. Ry. Co. (35 Misc. [N. Y.] 387) 224, 243.
Guilloz v. Ft. Wayne & B. I. Ry. Co. (108 Mich. 41) 329.
Gumney v. Southern Elec. R. Co. (167 Mo. 595) 312.
Gumb v. Twenty-Third St. Ry. Co. (114 N. Y. 411) 435.
Gumby v. Metropolitan St. Ry. Co. (29 App. Div. [N. Y.] 335) 282.
v. Metropolitan St. Ry. Co. (65 App. Div. [N. Y.] 38) 265, 283.
Guntzer v. Yonkers R. Co. (51 App. Div. [N. Y.] 222) 144.
Gustafson v. Seattle Traction Co. (28 Wash. 227) 388.

[REFERENCES ARE TO PAGES.]

## H.

Haas v. Chester St. Ry. Co. (202 Pa. 145) 292.
Hadencamp v. Second Ave. R. Co. (31 N. Y. Super. Ct. 490) 64, 68, 103.
Haderlein v. St. Louis R. Co. (3 Mo. App. 601) 102, 115.
Hafner v. St. Paul City Ry. Co. (73 Minn. 252) 231.
Hagan v. Philadelphia & G. Ferry Ry. Co. (10 Wkly. Notes Cas. [Pa.] 360) 147.
Hagenlocher v. Coney Island & B. R. Co. (99 N. Y. 136) 400.
Hagestrom v. West Chicago St. Ry. Co. (78 Ill. App. 574) 27, 30.
Haggerty v. Brooklyn City & N. R. Co. (61 N. Y. 624) 405.
Haight, Consolidated Traction Co. v. (59 N. J. Law, 577) 294, 319.
Hair, Chicago West Div. Ry. Co. v. (57 Ill. App. 587) 275.
Citizens' Ry. Co. v. (32 S. W. [Tex. Civ. App.] 1050) 337.
Hale, Birmingham Union Ry. Co. v. (90 Ala. 8) 128, 402.
Hall v. Ogden City St. Ry. Co. (13 Utah, 243) 299, 315-317, 321, 328, 408.
v. Second & Third Sts. Pass. Ry. Co. (14 Wkly. Notes Cas. [Pa.] 242) 173.
v. Wakefield & S. St. Ry. Co. (178 Mass. 98) 372.
v. West End St. Ry. Co. (168 Mass. 461) 212, 214.
Halliday v. Brooklyn Heights R. Co. (59 App. Div. [N. Y.] 57) 219, 243.
Halpin v. Third Ave. R. Co. (40 N. Y. Super. Ct. 175) 48, 227.
Haman v. Omaha Horse Ry. Co. (35 Neb. 74) 182, 183.
Hamel v. Brooklyn Heights R. Co. (59 App. Div. [N. Y.] 135) 403.
Hamilton v. Consolidated Traction Co. (201 Pa. 351) 296, 325.
v. Great Falls St. Ry. Co. (17 Mont. 334) 102, 119, 429.
v. Third Ave. R. Co. (53 N. Y. 25) 192, 205.
v. Third Ave. R. Co. (40 N. Y. Super. Ct. 376) 428.
v. Third Ave. R. Co. (6 Misc. [N. Y.] 382) 291.
v. West End St. Ry. Co. (163 Mass. 199) 135, 136.
Hammett, Metropolitan R. Co. v. (13 App. D. C. 370) 120.
Hammond, W. & E. C. Electric Ry. Co. v. Spyzchalski (17 Ind. App. 7) 102, 127, 401.
Haney v. Pittsburgh, A. & M. Traction Co. (159 Pa. 395) 300, 330.
Hanlon, Government St. R. Co. v. (53 Ala. 70) 251, 254, 270.
v. Milwaukee Elec. Ry. & Light Co. (95 N. W. [Wis.] 100) 311, 326.
v. Philadelphia & W. C. Turnpike Road Co. (182 Pa. 115) 337.
v. South Boston Horse R. Co. (129 Mass. 316) 282.
Hanna v. Nassau Electric R. Co. (18 App. Div. [N. Y.] 137) 22, 68, 180, 196.
Hannon v. Boston El. Ry. Co. (182 Mass. 425) 94, 161.
Hansberger v. Sedalia Elec. Ry. Co. (82 Mo. App. 566) 38-40, 45.
Hansen v. North Jersey St. Ry. Co. (64 N. J. Law, 686) 102.
Hanson, Metropolitan St. Ry. Co. v. (72 Pac. [Kan.] 773) 142.

[REFERENCES ARE TO PAGES.]

Hanson v. Urbana & C. Elec. St. Ry. Co. (75 Ill. App. 474) 14, 183, 404, 415.
Harbison v. Metropolitan R. Co. (9 App. D. C. 60) 83, 84, 86, 95.
Hardy v. Milwaukee St. Ry. Co. (89 Wis. 183) 393.
Harkins v. Pittsburgh, A. & M. Traction Co. (173 Pa. 149) 264, 275.
Harlem Bridge H. & F. R. Co., Block v. (9 N. Y. Supp. 164) 252, 257, 285.
Thurber v. (60 N. Y. 326) 253, 256.
Harman v. Pennsylvania Traction Co. (200 Pa. 311) 346.
Harmon's Adm'r, Washington & G. R. Co. v. (147 U. S. 571) 92, 141, 159.
Harmon v. Washington & G. R. Co. (6 Mackey [D. C.] 571) 147.
Harms, North Chicago St. R. Co. v. (59 Ill. App. 374) 339.
Harnett v. Bleeker St. & F. Ferry R. Co. (49 N. Y. Super. Ct. 185) 213.
Harper v. Philadelphia Traction Co. (175 Pa. 129) 303, 327.
Harrell, Railway Co. v. (58 Ark. 454) 125, 126, 404.
Harriman v. Reading & L. St. Ry. Co. (173 Mass. 28) 115, 395.
Harrington v. Los Angeles Traction Co. (74 Pac. [Cal.] 15) 345.
Harris, Bay Shore R. Co. v. (67 Ala. 6) 182.
v. Detroit City Ry. Co. (76 Mich. 227) 400, 403.
v. Hewitt (64 Minn. 54) 378.
v. Union Ry. Co. (69 App. Div. [N. Y.] 385) 139, 161.
Harrisburg Traction Co., Kepner v. (183 Pa. 24) 339.
Neff v. (192 Pa. 501) 146.
Harrisburg & M. Elec. Ry. Co., Light v. (4 Pa. Super. Ct. 427) 182, 184.
Harrison, Flaherty v. (98 Wis. 559) 335, 394, 396.
v. Sutter St. Ry. Co. (116 Cal. 156) 404, 430, 439.
Hart v. Cedar Rapids & M. C. Ry. Co. (109 Iowa, 631) 300, 327.
Texarkana St. Ry. Co. v. (26 S. W. [Tex. Civ. App.] 435) 135, 416.
v. West Side R. Co. (86 Wis. 483) 23, 26, 36, 185.
Hartford St. Ry. Co., Donovan v. (65 Conn. 201) 3, 9.
Lawler v. (72 Conn. 74) 293, 296.
Post v. (72 Conn. 362) 53, 54.
Harvey v. Nassau Electric R. Co. (35 App. Div. [N. Y.] 307) 236, 237.
v. Philadelphia Traction Co. (26 Wkly. Notes Cas. [Pa.] 231) 400.
Hassard, Philadelphia City Pass. Ry. Co. v. (75 Pa. 367) 77, 112, 154.
Hassen v. Nassau Electric R. Co. (34 App. Div. [N. Y.] 71) 83, 84, 132.
Hastings v. Central Crosstown R. Co. (7 App. Div. [N. Y.] 312) 64, 71, 72, 116.
Chicago City Ry. Co. v. (136 Ill. 251) 397.
Chicago City Ry. Co. v. (35 Ill. App. 434) 45, 436.
Montgomery St. Ry. Co. v. (35 So. [Ala.] 412) 307, 333.

[REFERENCES ARE TO PAGES.]

Hauser v. Metropolitan St. Ry. Co. (27 Misc. [N. Y.] 538) 356.
Haverhill & G. St. Ry. Co., Goldthwait v. (160 Mass. 554) 384.
Haviland, Chicago West Div. Ry. Co. v. (12 Ill. App. 561) 210, 212, 429.
Hawkins v. Front St. Cable Ry. Co. (3 Wash. 592) 65.
Hawks v. Inhabitants of Northampton (121 Mass. 10) 360.
Hawthorne v. Cincinnati St. Ry. Co. (2 Ohio Dec. 548) 210.
Hayes v. Forty-Second St. & G. St. Ferry R. Co. (97 N. Y. 259) 129.
v. St. Louis R. Co. (15 Mo. App. 584) 186, 404, 437.
Hays v. Gainesville St. Ry. Co. (70 Tex. 602) 271, 273, 399.
v. Tacoma Ry. & Power Co. (106 Fed. 48) 296.
Tacoma Ry. & Power Co. v. (110 Fed. 496) 293, 296.
Hayter v. Brunswick Traction Co. (66 N. J. Law, 575) 196, 202.
Hazel v. People's Pass. Ry. Co. (132 Pa. 96) 335, 338.
Healey v. City Pass. R. Co. (28 Ohio St. 23) 186.
v. Dry Dock, E. B. & B. R. Co. (46 N. Y. Super. Ct. 473) 210, 236.
v. Wellesley & B. St. Ry. Co. (176 Mass. 440) 397.
Hearn v. St. Charles St. R. Co. (34 La. Ann. 160) 280.
Heddle v. City El. Ry. Co. (112 Mich. 547) 396, 402, 403.
Hedin v. Suburban Ry. Co. (26 Or. 155) 264, 266, 270, 274.
Heffran v. Brooklyn Heights R. Co. (8 Misc. [N. Y.] 41) 303, 315.
Heffron v. Detroit City Ry. Co. (92 Mich. 406) 195.
Hegan v. Eighth Ave. R. Co. (15 N. Y. 380) 318.
Heitman's Adm'r, Bergen County Traction Co. v. (61 N. J. Law, 682) 251, 254, 270.
Helber v. Spokane St. Ry. Co. (22 Wash. 319) 290, 315, 316.
Helena St. Ry. Co., Wall v. (12 Mont. 44) 242.
Helms, Baltimore Traction Co. v. (84 Md. 515) 216, 224, 234, 236.
Helvie, Citizens' St. Ry. Co. v. (22 Ind. App. 515) 290, 293.
Hemingway v. New Orleans City & Lake R. Co. (50 La. Ann. 1087) 328.
Henderson v. Detroit Citizens' St. Ry. Co. (116 Mich. 368) 250, 260.
v. Durham Traction Co. (132 N. C. 779) 287.
v. Greenfield & T. F. St. Ry. Co. (172 Mass. 542) 337.
v. Nassau Electric R. Co. (46 App. Div. [N. Y.] 280) 83, 85.
v. United Traction Co. (202 Pa. 527) 219, 243.
Henderson St. Ry. Co. v. Wood (21 Ky. L. R. 808, 53 S. W. 1116) 413, 426.
Hendricks v. Sixth Ave. R. Co. (44 N. Y. Super. Ct. 8) 113.
Hendrie, Downey v. (46 Mich. 498) 73.
Kelly v. (26 Mich. 255) 212.
Henne v. People's St. Ry. Co. (1 Pa. Super. Ct. 311) 267, 274.
Hennessey v. Brooklyn City R. Co. (6 App. Div. [N. Y.] 206) 308.
v. Forty-Second St., M. & St. N. Ave. Ry. Co. (84 N. Y. Supp. 158) 229.
Hennessy v. Brooklyn City R. Co. (73 Hun [N. Y.] 569) 309, 314, 317, 326.

[REFERENCES ARE TO PAGES.]

Hennessy v. Brooklyn Heights R. Co. (57 App. Div. [N. Y.] 27) 229, 245.
Chicago City Ry. Co. v. (16 Ill. App. 153) 369.
Henning v. Louisville Ry. Co. (74 S. W. [Ky.] 209) 142.
Henrice, Philadelphia City Pass. Ry. Co. v. (92 Pa. 431) 274.
Henry, Chicago City Ry. Co. v. (62 Ill. 142) 429.
v. Grand Ave. Ry. Co. (113 Mo. 525) 211, 234.
v. Grant St. Elec. Ry. Co. (24 Wash. 246) 157.
Heraty, Plant v. (92 N. W. [Mich.] 284) 299.
Herbert v. St. Paul City Ry. Co. (85 Minn. 341) 164.
Herdt v. Rochester City & B. R. Co. (20 N. Y. Supp. 346) 83, 84, 86.
Hergert v. Union Ry. Co. (25 App. Div. [N. Y.] 218) 319.
Hertel, United Rys. & Elec. Co. v. (55 Atl. [Md.] 428) 143.
Hesse v. Meriden, S. & C. P. Tramway Co. (54 Atl. [Conn.] 299) 83, 87.
Hestonville, M. & F. P. Ry. Co., Biddle v. (112 Pa. 551) 26, 27, 185.
Crissey v. (75 Pa. 83) 75-77, 139, 140, 152, 163.
Gilton v. (166 Pa. 460) 362.
Glassey v. (57 Pa. 172) 254, 263.
v. Gray (3 Wkly. Notes Cas. [Pa.] 421) 185.
Keller v. (149 Pa. 65) 48.
Malpass v. (189 Pa. 599) 227.
Sandford v. (136 Pa. 84) 64, 74, 75, 108.
Smedley v. (184 Pa. 620) 103, 128, 134.
Smith v. (92 Pa. 450) 251, 254, 263.
Smith v. (17 Phila. [Pa.] 184) 188, 189.
Hestonville Passenger Ry. Co. v. Connell (88 Pa. 520) 58, 61, 112.
Heucke v. Milwaukee City Ry. Co. (69 Wis. 401) 103, 124, 422.
Hewitt, Galveston City R. Co. v. (67 Tex. 473) 269, 270, 272, 419.
Harris v. (64 Minn. 54) 378.
v. Taunton St. Ry. Co. (167 Mass. 483) 267, 404.
Hewlett v. Brooklyn Heights R. Co. (63 App. Div. [N. Y.] 423) 319, 320, 409.
Hickey v. St. Paul City Ry. Co. (60 Minn. 119) 212.
Washington & G. R. Co. v. (12 App. D. C. 269) 127.
Washington & G. R. Co. v. (166 U. S. 521) 126.
Hickman v. Nassau Electric R. Co. (36 App. Div. [N. Y.] 376) 214, 238.
v. Nassau Electric R. Co. (41 App. Div. [N. Y.] 629) 218.
Hicks v. Citizens' Ry. Co. (124 Mo. 115) 293, 314-316, 331.
Commonwealth v. (7 Allen [Mass.] 573) 319.
v. Nassau Electric R. Co. (47 App. Div. [N. Y.] 479) 257.
Higgins v. Brooklyn, Q. C. & S. R. Co. (54 App. Div. [N. Y.] 69) 358.
v. Watervliet Turnpike & R. Co. (46 N. Y. 23) 33, 178, 188.
v. Wilmington City Ry. Co. (1 Marvel [Del.] 352) 305, 313, 314, 316, 317, 323, 392.
Higgs, Topeka City Ry. Co. v. (38 Kan. 375) 83, 87, 102, 107.

[REFERENCES ARE TO PAGES.]

Highland Ave. & B. R. Co v. Burt (92 Ala. 291) 143.
v. Donovan (94 Ala. 299) 65, 67, 68.
v. Fennell (111 Ala. 356) 374.
McDaniel v. (90 Ala. 64) 35, 94.
v. Sampson (91 Ala. 560) 289, 290, 293, 321.
v. Sampson (112 Ala. 425) 289, 408.
v. Swope (115 Ala. 287) 412.
v. Walters (91 Ala. 425) 373.
v. Winn (93 Ala. 306) 182.
Highland St. Ry. Co., Banks v. (136 Mass. 485) 364.
Cronin v. (144 Mass. 249) 207.
Hildebrand, Richmond Traction Co. v. (98 Va. 22) 213.
Hill v. Birmingham Union Ry. Co. (100 Ala. 447) 94.
v. Metropolitan St. Ry. Co. (30 Misc. [N. Y.] 440) 304.
v. Ninth Ave. R. Co. (109 N. Y. 239) 123.
Owensboro City R. Co. v. (21 Ky. L. R. 1638) 236, 237.
v. Rome St. R. Co. (101 Ga. 66) 338.
Hinton v. Cream City Ry. Co. (65 Wis. 323) 393, 404, 420.
Hitchcock v. Brooklyn City R. Co. (3 N. Y. Supp. 218) 136, 165.
Hite v. Metropolitan St. Ry. Co. (130 Mo. 132) 101, 102, 130.
Hobbs, Citizens' St. R. Co. v. (15 Ind. App. 610) 437.
Hobson v. New York Condensed Milk Co. (25 App. Div. [N. Y.] 111) 373.
Hockett, Indianapolis St. Ry. Co. v. (64 N. E. [Ind. App.] 633) 30.
Indianapolis St. Ry. Co. v. (159 Ind. 677) 139, 160.
Indianapolis St. Ry. Co. v. (67 N. E. [Ind.] 106) 30, 182, 186.
Hodnett, Danville Ry. & Elec. Co. v. (43 S. E. [Va.] 606), 336, 346.
Hoeffner, Springfield Consol. Ry. Co. v. (175 Ill. 634) 139, 143, 400.
Springfield Consol. Ry. Co. v. (71 Ill. App. 162) 92, 159.
Hoelzel v. Crescent City R. Co. (49 La. Ann. 1302) 215, 216.
Hoes v. Third Ave. R. Co. (5 App. Div. [N. Y.] 151) 394.
Hoffart, North Chicago St. R. Co. v. (82 Ill. App. 539) 277, 413, 414.
Hoffbauer, Citizens' St. R. Co. v. (23 Ind. App. 614) 84, 87, 411.
Hoffman v. Syracuse Rapid Transit Ry. Co. (50 App. Div. [N. Y.] 83) 308.
v. Third Ave. R. Co. (45 App. Div. [N. Y.] 586) 130.
Hogan v. Central Park, N. & E. R. R. Co. (124 N. Y. 647) 163.
v. Citizens' Ry. Co. (15 Mo. 36) 277, 287.
Hoimark, Consolidated Traction Co. v. (60 N. J. Law, 456) 309.
Holdridge v. Mendenhall (108 Wis. 1) 256, 262, 279.
Hollahan v. Metropolitan St. Ry. Co. (73 App. Div. [N. Y.] 164) 117.
Holland v. West End St. Ry. Co (155 Mass. 387) 75.
Holloway v. Pasadena & P. Ry. Co. (130 Cal. 177) 65, 68, 106, 131.
Holly v. Atlanta St. R. Co. (61 Ga. 215) 101, 113.
Holman v. Union St. Ry. Co. (114 Mich. 208) 402, 410.
Holmes, Ashtabula Rapid Transit Co. v. (67 Ohio St. 153) 143, 163.
Citizens' Ry. Co. v. (19 Tex. Civ. App. 266) 323.
Macon & I. S. St. Ry. Co. v. (103 Ga. 655) 210, 237.

[REFERENCES ARE TO PAGES.]

Holmes v. Union Traction Co. (199 Pa. 229) 214, 237.
Holmesburg, T. & F. Elec. Ry. Co., Smith v. (187 Pa. 451) 335.
Holmgren v. Twin City Rapid Transit Co. (61 Minn. 85) 253, 256.
Holohan v. Washington & G. R. Co. (19 D. C. 316) 46, 57.
Hole v. Southwest Electric Ry. Co. (84 Mo. App. 443) 61.
Holwerson v. St. Louis & S. Ry. Co. (157 Mo. 216) 210, 235, 246.
Holyoke St. Ry. Co., Aiken v. (180 Mass. 8) 256.
Aiken v. (68 N. E. [Mass.] 238) 271.
Benjamin v. (160 Mass. 3) 334, 337, 402.
Blanchette v. (175 Mass. 51) 121, 404.
McGarry v. (182 Mass. 123) 174.
Thompson v. (170 Mass. 365) 334.
Holzab v. New Orleans & C. R. Co. (38 La. Ann. 185) 125.
Holzman v. Metropolitan St. Ry. Co. (31 Misc. [N. Y.] 644) 306.
Homans v. Boston El. R. Co. (180 Mass. 456) 434.
Hone, Consolidated Traction Co. v. (59 N. J. Law, 275) 254, 255.
Consolidated Traction Co. v. (60 N. J. Law, 444) 441.
Honick v. Metropolitan St. Ry. Co. (71 S. W. [Kan.] 265) 293.
Hoon v. Beaver Valley Traction Co. (204 Pa. 369) 251, 284.
Hoover v. Carbon County Elec. Ry. Co. (191 Pa. 146) 375.
Hope v. West Chicago St. R. Co. (82 Ill. App. 311) 150, 393.
Horgan v. Jones (131 Cal. 521) 242.
Horton v. Norwalk Tramway Co. (66 Conn. 272) 104.
Hot Springs St. Ry. Co. v. Johnson (64 Ark. 420) 233, 234.
Houghton County St. Ry. Co., Bartle v. (93 N. W. [Mich.] 620) 145.
Kotila v. (96 N. W. [Mich.] 437) 347.
Hourney v. Brooklyn City R. Co. (7 N. Y. Supp. 602) 64, 122.
Houston v. Gate City St. R. Co. (89 Ga. 272) 60, 404.
Houston City St. Ry. Co. v. Autrey (4 Tex. Civ. App. 635) 363.
v. Dawson (2 Tex. Unrep. Cas. 223) 355.
v. Delesdernier (84 Tex. 82) 355, 427.
v. Dillon (3 Tex. Civ. App. 303) 267.
v. Medlenka (17 Tex. Civ. App. 621) 407, 418.
v. Reichart (87 Tex. 539) 360.
v. Sciacca (80 Tex. 350) 425, 439.
v. Woodlock (29 S. W. [Tex. Civ. App.] 817) 230, 245.
Houston Elec. Co. v. Robinson (76 S. W. [Tex. Civ. App.] 209) 371.
Houston, W. S. & P. Ferry R. Co., Darrel v. (4 N. Y. Supp. 597) 90.
Lamline v. (14 Daly [N. Y.] 144) 53, 61.
Lang v. (75 Hun [N. Y.] 151) 211, 220.
Mullane v. (21 Misc. [N. Y.] 10) 388.
Rooks v. (10 App. Div. [N. Y.] 98) 342.
Schulman v. (15 Misc. [N. Y.] 30) 233, 235, 244.
Silberstein v. (4 N. Y. Supp. 843) 257, 277.
Vroman v. (7 Misc. [N. Y.] 234) 88, 95.
Howard v. Indianapolis St. Ry. Co. (29 Ind. App. 514) 301, 325.
Street R. Co. v. (102 Tenn. 474) 233-235, 411.
v. Union Traction Co. (195 Pa. 391) 137.

[REFERENCES ARE TO PAGES.]

Howell v. Rochester Ry. Co. (24 App. Div. [N. Y.] 502) 283.
v. Union Traction Co. (202 Pa. 338) 164.
Howland v. Oakland Consol. St. Ry. Co. (110 Cal. 513) 413, 417.
v. Union St. Ry. Co. (150 Mass. 86) 257.
Hoyt v. Metropolitan St. R. Co. (73 App. Div. [N. Y.] 249) 241.
v. Sixth Ave. R. Co. (1 Daly [N. Y.] 528) 172.
Huber v. La Crosse City Ry. Co. (92 Wis. 636) 352.
v. Nassau Electric R. Co. (22 App. Div. [N. Y.] 426) 319, 325.
Hudgins, Richmond Ry. & Elec. Co. v. (41 S. E. [Va.] 736) 334, 338.
Hudson v. Lynn & B. R. Co. (178 Mass. 64) 32, 33, 171, 178, 184.
North Chicago St. Ry. Co. v. (44 Ill. App. 60) 407.
v. People's St. Ry. Co. (175 Mass. 23) 379.
Hudson Electric Ry. Co., Finley v. (64 Hun [N. Y.] 373) 26.
Hudson River R. Co., Altreuter v. (2 E. D. Smith [N. Y.] 151) 318.
Barker v. (4 Daly [N. Y.] 274) 305, 315.
Luby v. (17 N. Y. 131) 411.
Hudson Valley Ry. Co., Powell v. (84 N. Y. Supp. 337) 109.
Huelsenkamp v. Citizens' Ry. Co. (37 Mo. 537 [N. Y.] 136) 34, 45, 80, 81, 101, 102.
Huerzeler v. Central Crosstown R. Co. (1 Misc. [N. Y.] 136) 258, 283.
v. Central Crosstown R. Co. (139 N. Y. 490) 262.
Huffer, Citizens' St. Ry. Co. v. (26 Ind. App. 575) 144.
Hughes v. Camden & S. Ry. Co. (65 N. J. Law, 203) 303, 325.
Chicago West Div. Ry. Co. v. (69 Ill. 170) 97, 135, 423.
Chicago West Div. Ry. Co. v. (87 Ill. 94) 431.
Georgia Pac. Ry. Co. v. (87 Ala. 610) 125.
Humbert v. Brooklyn Cable Co. (12 N. Y. St. Rep. 172) 361.
Humbird v. Union St. Ry. Co. (110 Mo. 76) 275.
Hunt v. Missouri R. Co. (14 Mo. App. 160) 77, 79, 392.
Hunter v. Consolidated Traction Co. (193 Pa. 557) 279.
Eckington & S. H. R. Co. v. (6 App. D. C. 287) 319, 328, 408.
v. Third Ave. R. Co. (20 Misc. [N. Y.] 432) 402, 436.
v. Third Ave. R. Co. (21 Misc. [N. Y.] 1) 298, 315, 320.
Hunterson v. Union Traction Co. (55 Atl. [Pa.] 543) 8, 43, 55, 58.
Hurdle v. Washington & G. R. Co. (8 App. D. C. 120) 227.
Hurley, Dallas Consol. Traction Ry. Co. v. (10 Tex. Civ. App. 246) 211, 221, 240.
v. New York & B. Brew. Co. (13 App. Div. [N. Y.] 167) 124.
v. West End St. Ry. Co. (180 Mass. 370) 289.
Hurst v. Detroit City Ry. Co. (84 Mich. 539) 438.
Hutchins v. Macomber (68 N. H. 473) 145.
Hutchinson v. Atlantic Ave. R. Co. (33 App. Div. [N. Y.] 569) 422.
Hyland v. Yonkers R. Co. (4 N. Y. Supp. 305) 267, 276.

## I.

Iaquinta v. Citizens' Traction Co. (166 Pa. 63) 256, 284.
Ihl v. Forty-Second St. & G. St. Ferry R. Co. (47 N. Y. 317) 251, 254, 255, 264.

[REFERENCES ARE TO PAGES.]

Illo, Dallas Consol. Elec. St. Ry. Co. v. (73 S. W. [Tex. Civ. App.] 1076) 327.
Inclined Plane Ry. Co., Paterson v. (5 Ohio S. & C. P. Dec. 665) 155.
Indiana Ry. Co. v. Maurer (66 N. E. [Ind. Sup.] 156) 150.
Indianapolis St. Ry. Co., Darnell v. (68 N. E. [Ind. App.] 609) 302.
v. Hockett (64 N. E. [Ind. App.] 633) 30.
v. Hockett (67 N. E. [Ind. Sup.] 106) 30, 182, 186.
v. Hockett (159 Ind. 677) 139, 160.
Howard v. (29 Ind. App. 514) 301, 325.
v. Lawn (66 N. E. [Ind. App.] 508) 161.
Marchal v. (28 Ind. App. 133) 299, 319, 325.
Robards v. (66 N. E. [Ind. App.] 66) 342.
Robards v. (67 N. E. [Ind. App.] 953) 345.
Roberts v. (158 Ind. 634) 371.
v. Tenner (67 N. E. [Ind. App.] 1044) 14, 224.
v. Walton (29 Ind. App. 368) 359.
v. Wilson (66 N. E. [Ind. Sup.] 950) 196, 203.
Ingraham, Chicago West Div. Ry. Co. v. (33 Ill. App. 351) 234, 316.
Chicago West Div. Ry. Co. v. (131 Ill. 659) 397.
Inhabitants of Gardener, Fowler v. (169 Mass. 505) 362.
Inhabitants of Northampton, Hawks v. (121 Mass. 10) 360.
Interstate Consol. St. Ry. Co., McGowan v. (20 R. I. 264) 413.
Interurban St. Ry. Co., Carter v. (84 N. Y. Supp. 134) 297.
Cosgrove v. (84 N. Y. Supp. 885) 296.
Greenbaum v. (84 N. Y. Supp. 588) 231.
Krintzman v. (84 N. Y. Supp. 243) 311.
Martin v. (84 N. Y. Supp. 921) 331.
Moritz v. (84 N. Y. Supp. 162) 188.
Reichenberg v. (84 N. Y. Supp. 523) 305.
Schmidt v. (81 N. Y. Supp. 832) 289.
Stelnman v. (84 N. Y. Supp. 231) 232.
Watson v. (84 N. Y. Supp. 556) 307.
Irwin v. Brooklyn Heights R. Co. (59 App. Div. [N. Y.] 95) 377.
v. Metropolitan St. Ry. Co. (25 Misc. [N. Y.] 187) 394.
North Chicago St. R. Co. v. (202 Ill. 345) 343.
Isaacs v. Third Ave. R. Co. (47 N. Y. 122) 188-190.
Isackson v. Duluth St. Ry. Co. (75 Minn. 27) 233, 235, 236.
Ithaca St. R. Co., Bolster v. (79 App. Div. [N. Y.] 239) 369.
Goodspeed (84 N. Y. Supp. 383) 206.
Griffin v. (62 App. Div. [N. Y.] 551) 380.

## J.

Jackson, Birmingham Ry. & Elec. Co. v. (136 Ala. 279) 238.
v. Consolidated Traction Co. (59 N. J. Law, 25) 430, 440.
v. Grand Ave. Ry. Co. (118 Mo. 199) 102, 143, 164, 404.
v. Philadelphia Traction Co. (182 Pa. 104) 91.
v. Pittsburgh, A. & M. Traction Co. (159 Pa. 399) 303, 327.

[REFERENCES ARE TO PAGES.]

Jackson, Savannah St. R. Co. v. (95 Ga. 366) 326.
v. Second Ave. R. Co. (47 N. Y. 274) 182, 188.
v. St. Paul City Ry. Co. (74 Minn. 48) 27, 28, 80, 97, 427.
v. Union Ry. Co. (77 App. Div. [N. Y.] 161) 226, 239.
Jackson County Horse Ry. Co., Gilson v. (76 Mo. 282) 101, 102.
Welsch v. (81 Mo. 466) 271.
Jackson Electric Ry., L. & P. Co. v. Lowry (79 Miss. 431) 56.
Jackson & S. St. R. R. & Tel. Cos. v. Simmons (107 Tenn. 392) 352.
Jacksonville Ry. Co. v. Lamb (86 Ill. App. 487) 324, 428.
Jacksonville St. Ry. Co. v. Chappell (21 Fla. 175) 104, 129.
Jacobs v. Third Ave. R. Co. (71 App. Div. [N. Y.] 199) 197, 202.
v. West End St. Ry. Co. (178 Mass. 116) 14, 163, 399.
Jacques v. Bridgeport Horse R. Co. (41 Conn. 61) 430.
Jacquin v. Grand Ave. Cable Co. (57 Mo. App. 320) 102, 127.
Jager v. Coney Island, etc., R. Co. (84 Hun [N. Y.] 30) 214.
Jagger v. People's St. Ry. Co. (180 Pa. 436) 143, 146, 157.
James, Birmingham R. & E. Co. v. (121 Ala. 120) 92, 140, 159.
v. Metropolitan St. Ry. Co. (80 N. Y. Supp. 710) 184.
West Chicago St. R. Co. v. (69 Ill. App. 609) 5, 6.
Jamestown St. Ry. Co., Chase v. (15 N. Y. Supp. 35) 142, 151.
Fuller v. (75 Hun [N. Y.] 273) 400.
Jamison v. San Jose & S. C. R. Co. (55 Cal. 593) 13, 100.
Jaquinto v. Broadway & S. Ave. R. Co. (2 Misc. [N. Y.] 174) 278.
Jarmy v. Duluth St. Ry. Co. (55 Minn. 271) 166.
Jarvis, Spaulding v. (32 Hun [N. Y.] 621) 307.
Jatho v. Green & C. St. Pass. Ry. Co. (4 Phila. [Pa.] 24) 345.
Jefferson Ave. Ry. Co., Sullivan v. (133 Mo. 1) 114, 397.
Jefferson v. Birmingham R. & E. Co. (116 Ala. 294) 58.
Jenkins v. Brooklyn Heights R. Co. (29 App. Div. [N. Y.] 8) 195.
Jennings, Calumet Elec. St. Ry. Co. v. (83 Ill. App. 612) 115, 424.
Chicago City Ry. Co. v. (157 Ill. 274) 324.
v. Tacoma Ry. & Motor Co. (7 Wash. 275) 372.
v. Union Traction Co. (55 Atl. [Pa.] 765) 93.
Jensen v. Barbour (15 Mont. 582) 77.
Jersey City, H. & P. Ry. Co., Barlow v. (67 N. J. Law, 364) 32.
Garbaccio v. (53 Atl. [N. J. Law] 707) 431.
Solatinow v. (56 Atl. [N. J. Sup.] 235) 290.
Jersey City, H. & R. Electric Ry. Co., Buttelli v. (59 N. J. Law, 302) 212, 222, 233, 234, 238.
Jersey City & B. R. Co. v. Morgan (52 N. J. Law, 60) 174.
Johnsen v. Oakland, S. L. & H. Electric Ry. Co. (127 Cal. 608) 117, 133, 408.
Johnson v. Broadway & S. A. Ry. Co. (6 N. Y. Supp. 113) 402.
v. Brooklyn Heights R. Co. (34 App. Div. [N. Y.] 271) 304, 314, 317.
v. Brooklyn Heights R. Co. (63 App. Div. [N. Y.] 374) 88.
v. Canal & R. Co. (27 La. Ann. 53) 222.
Hot Springs St. Ry. Co. v. (64 Ark. 420) 233, 234.

Johnson, Montgomery v. (22 Ky. L. R. 596, 58 S. W. 476) 324, 428.
Newport St. R. Co. v. (2 Ky. L. R. 225) 121.
North Chicago St. Ry. Co. v. (68 N. E. [Ill.] 463) 273.
v. Reading City Pass. Ry. (160 Pa. 647) 268, 275.
v. Rochester Ry. Co. (61 App. Div. [N. Y.] 12) 319.
v. St. Paul City Ry. Co. (67 Minn. 260) 310, 311, 313, 431.
v. Stewart (62 Ark. 164) 306, 322.
v. Superior Rapid Transit Ry. Co. (91 Wis. 233) 310, 392.
West Chicago St. R. Co. v. (180 Ill. 285) 90, 101, 107.
West Chicago St. R. Co. v. (69 Ill. App. 147) 414.
West Chicago St. R. Co. v. (77 Ill. App. 142) 90, 107, 423.
Johnson's Adm'r v. Louisville City Ry. Co. (9 Bush [Ky.] 231) 247.
Joliet R. Co. v. Barty (96 Ill. App. 351) 314.
v. Eich (96 Ill. App. 351) 314.
v. McPherson (96 Ill. App. 286) 423.
Joliet St. Ry. v. Call (143 Ill. 177) 399.
v. Call (42 Ill. App. 41) 399, 405, 407.
v. Duggan (45 Ill. App. 450) 5.
v. McCarthy (42 Ill. App. 49) 135.
Jolly, Citizens' St. R. Co. v. (67 N. E. [Ind. Sup.] 935) 5, 6, 52.
Jones v. Brooklyn Heights R. Co. (23 App. Div. [N. Y.] 141) 433.
v. Brooklyn Heights R. Co. (10 Misc. [N. Y.] 543) 264, 273, 275.
v. Canal & C. R. Co. (109 La. 214) 147.
City Electric Ry. Co. v. (61 Ill. App. 183) 218, 237.
Horgan v. (131 Cal. 521) 242.
Metropolitan R. Co. v. (1 App. D. C. 200) 143, 394.
v. Philadelphia Traction Co. (185 Pa. 75) 390.
v. Union Ry. Co. (18 App. Div. [N. Y.] 267) 351.
v. United Traction Co. (201 Pa. 346) 268, 277.
Jones Bros. v. Greensburg, J. & P. St. Ry. Co. (9 Pa. Super. Ct. 65) 294, 316.
Joslin v. Grand Rapids Ice & Coal Co. (53 Mich. 322) 359.
Joslyn v. Milford H. & E. St. Ry. Co. (67 N. E. [Mass.] 866) 157.
Joyce v. St. Paul City Ry. Co. (70 Minn. 339) 402, 427.
Judge v. Elkins (66 N. E. [Mass.] 708) 222.
Julius v. Pittsburgh, A. & M. Traction Co. (184 Pa. 19) 327.
Juskowitz v. Dry Dock, E. B. & B. R. Co. (25 Misc. [N. Y.] 64) 254, 263.

## K.

Kaechele v. Traction Co. (15 Pa. Super. Ct. 73) 326.
Kaiser v. New Orleans & C. R. Co. (107 La. 539) 260.
Kalfur v. Broadway Ferry & M. Ave. R. Co. (34 App. Div. [N. Y.] 267) 417.
Kane v. People's Pass. Ry. Co. (181 Pa. 53) 328.
v. West End St. Ry. Co. (169 Mass. 64) 361.
v. Worcester Consol. St. Ry. Co. (182 Mass. 201) 304.

[REFERENCES ARE TO PAGES.]

Kankakee Elec. Ry. Co. v. Lade (56 Ill. App. 454) 334.
v. Whittemore (45 Ill. App. 484) 353, 412.
Kansas City Cable R. Co., Burbridge v. (36 Mo. App. 669) 17.
Carter v. (42 Fed. 37) 119, 122.
McDonald v. (32 Mo. App. 70) 161.
Meriwether v. (45 Mo. App. 528) 53, 54.
Pope v. (99 Mo. 400) 321.
Ridenhour v. (102 Mo. 270) 142, 152, 153.
Sharp v. (114 Mo. 94) 110, 403.
Sweeney v. (150 Mo. 385) 86, 92, 159, 397.
Weber v. (100 Mo. 194) 133, 140, 142.
Winters v. (99 Mo. 509) 254, 269, 277.
Kansas City El. Ry. Co., Barth v. (142 Mo. 535) 4, 6, 53, 55.
Kansas City & I. Rapid Transit Ry. Co., McDonald v. (127 Mo. 38) 158.
Moore v. (126 Mo. 265) 314-317, 319, 333.
Kantrowitz v. Metropolitan St. Ry. Co. (63 App. Div. [N. Y.] 65) 125.
Kaplan v. Metropolitan St. Ry. Co. (52 App. Div. [N. Y.] 296) 431.
Kappus v. Metropolitan St. Ry. Co. (82 App. Div. [N. Y.] 13) 213.
Karahuta v. Schuylkill Traction Co. (6 Pa. Super. Ct. 319) 267, 284.
Kareczewski v. Wilmington City Ry. Co. (54 Atl. [Del.] 746) 386, 388.
Kartwright, Memphis St. Ry. Co. v. (75 S. W. [Tenn.] 719) 349, 351.
Kaspers, North Chicago St. R. Co. v. (85 Ill. App. 316; affirmed 176 Ill. 246) 12, 38, 40.
North Chicago St. R. Co. v. (186 Ill. 246) 404.
Katz v. Brooklyn Heights R. Co. (35 Misc. [N. Y.] 302) 415.
Kaumeier v. City Electric R. Co. (116 Mich. 306) 286.
Kay v. Metropolitan St. Ry. Co. (29 App. Div. [N. Y.] 466) 119.
Kean v. West Chicago St. R. Co. (75 Ill. App. 38) 72, 392.
Kearns v. South Middlesex St. R. Co. (181 Mass. 587) 358.
Keator v. Scranton Traction Co. (191 Pa. 102) 12.
Keegan v. Third Ave. R. Co. (34 App. Div. [N. Y.] 297; affirmed 165 N. Y. 622) 102, 124.
Keen v. Detroit Elec. Ry. Co. (123 Mich. 247) 196, 199.
Keenan, Chicago City Ry. Co. v. (85 Ill. App. 367) 393.
v. Union Traction Co. (202 Pa. 107) 291.
Keeny, Atlanta Consol. St. Ry. Co. v. (99 Ga. 266) 174, 192, 436.
Kehoe v. Allentown & L. V. Traction Co. (187 Pa. 474) 122, 438.
Keiffert v. Nassau Electric R. Co. (51 App. Div. [N. Y.] 301) 424.
Keitel v. St. Louis Cable & W. Ry. Co. (28 Mo. App. 657) 362.
Kellegher v. Forty-Second St., M. & St. N. Ave. R. Co. (171 N. Y. 309) 53.
Keller v. Hestonville, M. & F. P. Ry. Co. (149 Pa. 65) 48.
Kelley, Brooklyn St. R. Co. v. (6 Ohio Cir. Ct. R. 155) 103, 115, 407.
v. Forty-Second St., M. & St. N. Ave. Ry. Co. (58 Hun [N. Y.] 93) 384.

[REFERENCES ARE TO PAGES.]

Kellogg v. Denver City Tramway Co. (72 Pac. [Colo. App.] 609) 384.
Kelly v. Brooklyn Heights R. Co. (12 Misc. [N. Y.] 568) 297.
v. Hendrie (26 Mich. 255) 212.
v. Metropolitan St. Ry. Co. (25 Misc. [N. Y.] 194) 362.
v. New York & S. B. Ry. Co. (109 N. Y. 44) 96, 112, 165.
v. Pittsburg & B. Traction Co. (10 Pa. Super. Ct. 644) 336.
Pittsburgh Elec. Ry. Co. v. (57 Kan. 514) 228, 245.
v. Third Ave. R. Co. (25 App. Div. [N. Y.] 603) 139, 148.
Transfer Co. v. (36 Ohio St. 86) 123.
v. Union Ry. & Transit Co. (95 Mo. 279) 408.
v. Wakefield & S. St. Ry. Co. (175 Mass. 331) 290.
v. Wakefield & S. St. Ry. Co. (179 Mass. 542) 299.
Kelsey, Cincinnati St. Ry. Co. v. (2 Ohio Dec. 440) 115, 413.
Kennealy v. Westchester Elec. Ry. Co. (86 App. Div. [N. Y.] 293) 349, 353.
Kennedy v. Birmingham Ry., L. & P. Co. (35 So. [Ala.] 108) 174.
v. Metropolitan St. Ry. Co. (11 Misc. [N. Y.] 320) 315.
Metropolitan St. Ry. Co. v. (82 Fed. 158) 381.
v. St. Louis R. Co. (43 Mo. App. 1) 279.
v. St. Paul City Ry. Co. (59 Minn. 45) 432.
v. Third Ave. R. Co. (31 App. Div. [N. Y.] 30) 319.
Kennelly, West Chicago St. R. Co. v. (170 Ill. 508) 401, 403.
West Chicago St. R. Co. v. (66 Ill. App. 244) 128.
Kenneson v. West End St. Ry. Co. (168 Mass. 1) 382.
Keown v. St. Louis R. Co. (141 Mo. 87) 381, 382.
Kepner v. Harrisburgh Traction Co. (183 Pa. 24) 339.
Kern v. Second Ave. Traction Co. (194 Pa. 75) 291.
Kernan v. Market St. Ry. Co. (137 Cal. 326) 209, 217.
Kerr v. Atlantic Ave. R. Co. (10 Misc. [N. Y.] 264) 297, 329.
v. Union Ry. Co. (20 Misc. [N. Y.] 171) 415.
Kerrigan v. Market St. Ry. Co. (138 Cal. 506) 391.
v. West End St. Ry. Co. (158 Mass. 305) 300, 330.
Kersey, Metropolitan West Side El. R. Co. v. (80 Ill. App. 301) 254, 425.
Kessler v. Brooklyn Heights R. Co. (3 App. Div. [N. Y.] 426) 309, 314. 317.
v. Citizens' St. R. Co. (20 Ind. App. 427) 328.
Kestner v. Pittsburgh & B. Traction Co. (158 Pa. 422) 325.
Ketcham, Citizens' Pass. Ry. Co. v. (122 Pa. 228) 356.
Kierzenkowski v. Philadelphia Traction Co. (184 Pa. 459) 279.
Kilbane v. Westchester Elec. R. Co. (19 Misc. [N. Y.] 184) 296, 325.
Kiley v. Chicago City Ry. Co. (189 Ill. 384) 186, 196, 198.
v. Chicago City Ry. Co. (90 Ill. App. 275) 192, 436.
Killeen, Tri-City Ry. Co. v. (92 Ill. App. 57) 352.
Killen v. Brooklyn Heights R. Co. (31 Misc. [N. Y.] 290) 218.
v. Brooklyn Heights R. Co. (48 App. Div. [N. Y.] 557) 218, 241.
Kimber v. Metropolitan St. Ry. Co. (69 App. Div. [N. Y.] 353) 39, 40.

[REFERENCES ARE TO PAGES.]

King v. Second Ave. R. Co. (75 Hun [N. Y.] 17) 402, 403.
Kingan v. Pittsburgh Traction Co. (5 Pa. Super. Ct. 436) 389.
Kingman v. Lynn & B. R. Co. (181 Mass. 387) 112.
Kingston v. Ft. Wayne & E. Ry. Co. (112 Mich. 40) 88.
Kingston City R. Co., Smith v. (55 App. Div. [N. Y.] 143) 142, 154, 155.
Kinkade v. Atlantic Ave. R. Co. (9 Misc. [N. Y.] 273; affirmed 149 N. Y. 615) 53, 55, 82, 108.
Kinnare, South Chicago City Ry. Co. v. (96 Ill. App. 210) 342.
Kirby, Bammel v. (19 Tex. Civ. App. 198) 287.
Kirchner v. Detroit City Ry. (91 Mich. 400) 156.
Kirton v. North Chicago St. R. Co. (91 Ill. App. 554) 184, 436.
Kissane v. Detroit, Y. & A. A. Ry. (121 Mich. 175) 206.
Kissock v. Traction Co. (15 Pa. Super. Ct. 103) 322.
Kitay v. Brooklyn, Q. C. & S. R. Co. (23 App. Div. [N. Y.] 228) 276.
Kitchell v. Brooklyn Heights R. Co. (6 App. Div. [N. Y.] 99) 252, 265.
Klauber, Chicago West Div. Ry. Co. v. (9 Ill. App. 613) 65, 70, 435.
Klecka, West Chicago St. R. Co. v. (94 Ill. App. 346) 347.
Kleiber v. People's Ry. Co. (107 Mo. 240) 125, 410.
Klein, Anacostia & P. R. R. Co. v. (8 App. D. C. 75) 53.
v. Crescent City R. Co. (23 La. Ann. 729) 279.
Kleiner v. Third Ave. R. Co. (162 N. Y. 193) 435.
Kline v. Electric Traction Co. (181 Pa. 276) 278.
Klockenbrink v. St. Louis & M. R. R. Co. (72 S. W. [Mo.] 900) 302.
v. St. Louis & M. R. R. Co. (172 Mo. 678) 317, 327.
Knickerbocker Ice Co., Connolly v. (114 N. Y. 104) 75, 76.
Knoker v. Canal & C. R. Co. (52 La. Ann. 806) 215.
Knoll v. Third Ave. R. Co. (46 App. Div. [N. Y.] 527) 325.
Knottnerus v. North Park St. Ry. Co. (93 Mich. 348) 247.
Knowles, Central Ry. Co. v. (93 Ill. App. 581) 324.
Central Ry. Co. v. (191 Ill. 241) 300, 324.
Knowlton v. Milwaukee City Ry. Co. (59 Wis. 278) 104, 150, 428.
Knoxville Traction Co. v. Lane (103 Tenn. 376) 136, 437.
Koch v. St. Paul City Ry. Co. (45 Minn. 407) 327, 426.
Koehl v. New York & Q. C. Ry. Co. (32 App. Div. [N. Y.] 419; affirmed 165 N. Y. 603) 102.
Kokomo City St. Ry. Co., De Lon v. (22 Ind. App. 377) 291, 314.
Kolzem v. Broadway & S. Ave. R. Co. (1 Misc. [N. Y.] 148) 366.
Kornazsewska v. West Chicago St. R. Co. (76 Ill. App. 366) 392, 396.
Kornetzski v. City of Detroit (94 Mich. 341) 357.
Kotila v. Houghton County St. Ry. Co. (96 N. W. [Mich.] 437) 347.
Koues v. Metropolitan St. Ry. Co. (83 N. Y. Supp. 380) 143.
Kraemer v. Metropolitan St. Ry. Co. (51 App. Div. [N. Y.] 475) 429.
Kramer v. New Orleans, C. & L. R. Co. (51 La. Ann. 689) 223, 240.
Krausz, Third Ave. R. Co. v. (112 Fed. 379) 228, 233, 235.
Kraut v. Frankford & S. P. City Pass. Ry. (160 Pa. 327) 358, 407.
Kreuzen v. Forty-Second St. M. & St. N. Ave. R. Co. (13 N. Y. Supp. 588) 124.

[REFERENCES ARE TO PAGES.]

Krintzman v. Interurban St. Ry. Co. (84 N. Y. Supp. 243) 311.
Kriz, Chicago General Ry. Co. v. (94 Ill. App. 277) 302, 410, 436.
Kroesen v. New Castle Electric St. Ry. Co. (198 Pa. 30) 264.
v. New Castle Electric St. Ry. Co. (198 Pa. 26) 275.
Kromshinsky, West Chicago St. R. Co. v. (185 Ill. 92) 102, 412.
Krone v. Southwest Missouri Electric Ry. Co. (71 S. W. [Mo. App.] 712) 166.
Kuhlman v. Metropolitan St. Ry. Co. (30 Misc. [N. Y.] 417) 139, 148.
Kuhn, Central Pass. Ry. Co. v. (86 Ky. 578) 126.
Kuhnell, Cincinnati Omnibus Co. v. (11 Wkly. Law Bul. [Ohio] 189) 78.
Kuhnen v. Union Ry. Co. (10 App. Div. [N. Y.] 195) 242.
Kummer v. Christopher & T. S. R. Co. (2 Misc. [N. Y.] 298) 393.
v. Christopher & T. S. R. Co. (20 N. Y. Supp. 116) 403, 410.
Kupferschmid v. Southern Electric R. Co. (70 Mo. App. 438) 302.
Kuttner v. Lindell Ry. Co. (29 Mo. App. 502) 121, 122.

## L.

Lacas v. Detroit City Ry. Co. (92 Mich. 412) 93, 160, 401, 402.
Lace, Chicago City Ry. Co. v. (62 Ill. App. 535) 420.
La Crosse City Ry. Co., Cawley v. (101 Wis. 145) 293.
Cawley v. (106 Wis. 239) 304, 323.
Eastwood v. (94 Wis. 163) 335.
Gerrard v. (113 Wis. 258) 365, 366.
Huber v. (92 Wis. 636) 352.
Nein v. (92 Fed. 85) 343.
Ryan v. (108 Wis. 122) 250, 260, 393.
Thoresen v. (94 Wis. 129) 299.
Thoresen v. (87 Wis. 597) 296, 317, 324.
Ladd v. Brockton St. Ry. Co. (180 Mass. 454) 372.
Lade, Kankakee Elec. Ry. Co. v. (56 Ill. App. 454) 334.
Laethem v. Ft. Wayne & B. I. Ry. Co. (100 Mich. 297) 317.
Lafferty v. Third Ave. R. Co. (85 App. Div. [N. Y.] 592) 252-254, 284.
Lafitte v. New Orleans, C. & L. R. Co. (43 La. Ann. 34) 190.
La Fond v. Detroit Citizens' St. Ry. Co. (92 N. W. [Mich.] 99) 368.
Lahey v. Central Park, etc., R. Co. (2 Misc. [N. Y.] 537) 228, 233, 245.
Lahti v. Fitchburg & L. St. Ry. Co. (172 Mass. 147) 299.
Laird v. Pittsburgh Traction Co. (166 Pa. 4) 182, 197, 200.
Lake Roland El. Ry. Co. v. McKewen (80 Md. 593) 316, 321.
State v. (84 Md. 163) 87, 88, 95.
Lake Shore & M. S. R. Co., Evans v. (88 Mich. 442) 380.
Lake St. El. R. Co. v. Burgess (200 Ill. 628) 4, 62.
Lakeside Ry. Co., Ward v. (20 Pa. Co. Ct. R. 494) 321.
Lamb, Jacksonville Ry. Co. v. (86 Ill. App. 487) 324, 428.
v. St. Louis Cable & W. Ry. Co. (33 Mo. App. 489) 331.

[REFERENCES ARE TO PAGES.]

Lambertson, Consolidated Traction Co. v. (59 N. J. Law, 297) 299, 314, 315, 402, 433.
Consolidated Traction Co. v. (60 N. J. Law, 452) 403.
Consolidated Traction Co. v. (60 N. J. Law, 457) 433.
Lamline v. Houston, W. St. & P. Ferry R. Co. (14 Daly [N. Y.] 144) 53, 61.
Lammiman v. Detroit Citizens' St. Ry. Co. (112 Mich. 602) 402.
Lancaster City St. Ry. Co., Musser v. (176 Pa. 621) 367, 412.
Musser v. (15 Pa. Co. Ct. R. 430) 429.
Landneier v. Cincinnati St. Ry. Co. (4 Ohio S. & C. P. Dec. 265) 414.
Landrigan v. Brooklyn Heights R. Co. (23 App. Div. [N. Y.] 43) 224.
Lane v. Brooklyn Heights R. Co. (82 N. Y. Supp. 1057) 296.
Knoxville Traction Co. v. (103 Tenn. 376) 136, 437.
Lang v. Houston, W. S. & P. Ferry R. Co. (75 Hun [N. Y.] 151) 211, 220.
v. Metropolitan St. Ry. Co. (26 Misc. [N. Y.] 754) 290.
Langley v. Sixth Ave. R. Co. (48 N. Y. Super. Ct. 542) 430.
Lansing v. Coney Island & B. R. Co. (16 App. Div. [N. Y.] 146) 102, 131.
Lansing City Elec. Ry. Co., Montgomery v. (103 Mich. 46) 435.
Lapointe v. Middlesex R. Co. (144 Mass. 18) 90.
La Pontney v. Shedden Cartage Co. (116 Mich. 514) 379.
Larchmont Horse Ry. Co., Reynolds v. (83 App. Div. [N. Y.] 189) 304.
Larson v. Central Ry. Co. (56 Ill. App. 263) 350.
Omaha St. Ry. Co. v. (97 N. W. [Neb.] 824) 321.
Laschinger v. St. Paul City Ry. Co. (84 Minn. 333) 229.
Lasker v. Third Ave. R. Co. (27 Misc. [N. Y.] 824) 173.
Lauderbach, People's Pass. Ry. Co. v. (4 Pennyp. [Pa.] 406) 99.
Lauer, Terre Haute Elec. Ry. Co. v. (21 Ind. App. 466) 77, 79, 434.
Laufer v. Bridgeport Traction Co. (68 Conn. 475) 313, 314, 317, 408.
Laughlin v. Street Ry. Co. (62 Mich. 220) 365, 402, 407.
v. Street Ry. Co. (80 Mich. 154) 401.
Lavin v. Second Ave. R. Co. (12 App. Div. [N. Y.] 381) 280.
Lawler v. Hartford St. Ry. Co. (72 Conn. 74) 293, 296.
Lawn, Indianapolis St. Ry. Co. v. (68 N. E. [Ind. App.] 508) 161.
Lawshe v. Tacoma Ry. & Power Co. (29 Wash. 681) 197, 200.
Lawson, Electric Ry. Co. v. (101 Tenn. 406) 387.
v. Metropolitan St. Ry. Co. (40 App. Div. [N. Y.] 307) 315-317, 319.
Lax v. Forty-Second & G. St. Ferry R. Co. (46 N. Y. Super. Ct. 448) 67, 73, 144.
Leach, Chicago City Ry. Co. v. (80 Ill. App. 354) 376, 416.
Leahey v. Cass Ave. & F. G. Ry. Co. (97 Mo. 165) 397, 410, 411.
Leary v. Electric Traction Co. (180 Pa. 136) 358.
Leavenworth Electric R. Co. v. Cusick (60 Kan. 590) 142, 144, 166.
Leavenworth Rapid Transit Ry. Co., Telle v. (50 Kan. 455) 391.
Lebanon & A. St. Ry. Co., Miller v. (186 Pa. 190) 356.
Yingst v. (167 Pa. 438) 335.

Le Blanc v. Lowell, L. & H. St. Ry. Co. (170 Mass. 564) 302.
Ledman v. Dry Dock, E. B. & B. R. Co. (28 App. Div. [N. Y.] 197) 260.
Ledwidge v. St. Louis Transit Co. (73 S. W. [Mo. App.] 1008) 291.
Lee v. Boston El. Ry. Co. (182 Mass. 454) 158.
City Ry. Co. v. (50 N. J. Law, 435) 83, 101, 102.
v. Elizabeth, P. & C. J. Ry. Co. (55 Atl. [N. J. Sup.] 106) 163.
Legare v. Union Ry. Co. (61 App. Div. [N. Y.] 202) 259, 283.
Le Grand v. Wilkes-Barre & W. V. Traction Co. (10 Pa. Super. Ct. 12) 247.
Lehman v. Brooklyn City R. Co. (47 Hun [N. Y.] 355) 434.
Lehman, North Chicago St. R. Co. v. (82 Ill. App. 238) 433, 435.
Lehr v. Steinway & H. P. R. Co. (118 N. Y. 556) 80, 81, 106.
Leigh v. Omaha St. Ry. Co. (36 Neb. 131) 381, 383.
Lemont v. Washington & G. R. Co. (1 Mackey [D. C.] 180) 33, 178.
Lenkner v. Citizens' Traction Co. (179 Pa. 486) 300, 330.
Leonard v. Brooklyn Heights R. Co. (57 App. Div. [N. Y.] 125) 109.
Leonhardt, Baltimore & Y. Turnpike Road v. (66 Md. 70) 95, 101, 102.
Lesser v. St. Louis & S. Ry. Co. (85 Mo. App. 326) 171, 180, 182.
Leveret v. Shreveport Belt Ry. Co. (34 So. [La.] 579) 62.
Levin v. Metropolitan St. Ry. Co. (140 Mo. 624) 266, 267.
v. Second Ave. Traction Co. (194 Pa. 156) 28, 76, 77.
v. Second Ave. Traction Co. (201 Pa. 58) 28, 77.
Levine v. Metropolitan St. Ry. Co. (78 App. Div. [N. Y.] 426) 265.
Levinston, Omaha & C. B. R. & B. Co. v. (49 Neb. 17) 144.
Levitt v. Nassau Elec. R. Co. (14 App. Div. [N. Y.] 83) 431.
Levy v. Dry Dock, E. B. & B. R. Co. (12 N. Y. Supp. 485) 265, 276.
West Chicago St. R. Co. v. (182 Ill. 525) 435.
West Chicago St. R. Co. v. (82 Ill. App. 202) 317, 435.
Lewis v. Binghamton R. Co. (35 App. Div. [N. Y.] 12) 229, 245.
Calumet Electric Ry. Co. v. (68 Ill. App. 598) 277.
Chicago City Ry. Co. v. (5 Ill. App. 242) 211, 223, 240, 244.
v. Cincinnati St. Ry. Co. (10 Ohio S. & C. P. Dec. 53) 293.
Lewiston & A. H. R. Co., Bangs v. (89 Me. 104) 361.
Conway v. (87 Me. 283) 14, 157.
Conway v. (90 Me. 199) 14, 157.
Flewelling v. (89 Me. 585) 333.
Lewke v. Dry Dock, E. B. & B. R. Co. (46 Hun [N. Y.] 283) 401.
Lexington Ry. Co. v. Cozine (23 Ky. L. R. 1137, 64 S. W. 848) 192.
v. Fain's Adm'r (24 Ky. L. R. 1443) 349, 353.
Leyh v. Newburgh Electric Ry. Co. (41 App. Div. [N. Y.] 218) 112.
Lezinsky v. Metropolitan St. Ry. Co. (88 Fed. 437) 190.
Lhowe v. Third Ave. R. Co. (14 Misc. [N. Y.] 612) 252, 258.
Liddicoat, North Birmingham Ry. Co. v. (99 Ala. 545) 2, 3, 27, 38, 40, 42.
Liderman, West Chicago St. R. Co. v. (187 Ill. 463) 232.
West Chicago St. R. Co. v. (87 Ill. App. 638) 232.

[REFERENCES ARE TO PAGES.]

Liddy v. St. Louis R. Co. (40 Mo. 506) 234, 242, 638.
Liebig, West Chicago St. R. Co. v. (79 Ill. App. 567) 434.
Lieserowitz v. West Chicago St. R. Co. (80 Ill. App. 248) 396.
Light v. Harrisburg & M. Electric Ry. Co. (4 Pa. Super. Ct. 427) 182, 184.
Lightcap v. Philadelphia Traction Co. (60 Fed. 212) 337.
Philadelphia Traction Co. v. (61 Fed. 762) 337.
Lima R. Co. v. Little (67 Ohio St. 91) 62.
Linch v. Pittsburg Traction Co. (153 Pa. 102) 92, 159.
Lincoln Rapid Transit Co., Spellman v. (36 Neb. 890) 115.
Lincoln St. Ry. Co., Brooks v. (22 Neb. 816) 222, 236, 346.
v. Cox (48 Neb. 807) 388.
v. McClellan (54 Neb. 672) 102.
Lincoln Traction Co. v. Moore (97 N. W. [Neb.] 605) 335.
Lindell Ry. Co., Cobb v. (149 Mo. 135) 142, 143.
Kuttner v. (29 Mo. App. 502) 121, 122.
Meyer v. (6 Mo. App. 27) 210, 235, 238.
Moore v. (75 S. W. [Mo.] 672) 213.
Murphy v. (153 Mo. 252) 246.
O'Rourke v. (142 Mo. 342) 119.
Rosenkranz v. (108 Mo. 9) 266, 267, 275.
Worthington v. (72 Mo. App. 162) 49.
Lines v. Winnipeg Elec. St. Ry. Co. (11 Manitoba, 77) 336.
Little v. Boston & M. R. R. (55 Atl. [N. H.] 190) 237.
Lima Ry. Co. v. (67 Ohio St. 91) 62.
v. Street Ry. Co. (78 Mich. 205) 228.
v. Superior Rapid Transit Ry. Co. (88 Wis. 402) 396.
v. Third Ave. Ry. Co. (83 App. Div. [N. Y.] 330) 226.
Little Rock Traction & Electric Co. v. Dunlap (68 Ark. 291) 367.
v. Nelson (66 Ark. 494) 23, 25, 27, 58.
v. Trainer (68 Ark. 106) 206.
v. Walker (65 Ark. 144) 191.
Littman v. Dry Dock, E. B. & B. R. Co. (6 Misc. [N. Y.] 34) 85.
v. City & Suburban Ry. Co. (110 Ga. 165) 364.
Lobsenz v. Metropolitan St. Ry. Co. (72 App. Div. [N. Y.] 181) 39, 40.
Lockwood v. Belle City St. Ry. Co. (92 Wis. 97) 289.
v. Twenty-Third St. Ry. Co. (15 Daly [N. Y.] 374) 429.
Loder v. Metropolitan St. Ry. Co. (84 App. Div. [N. Y.] 591) 224.
Loehneisen v. Omaha St. Ry. Co. (40 Neb. 37) 225, 233, 235.
Logue, Memphis City Ry. Co. v. (13 Lea [Tenn.] 32) 269, 270, 286.
Lohe, Cincinnati, L. & A. Electric St. R. Co. v. (67 N. E. [Ohio] 161) 78.
Lombard & S. Sts. Pass. Ry. Co. v. Christensen (4 Pa. Super. Ct. Dig. 139) 405.
v. Christian (124 Pa. 114) 403.
Mack v. (20 Phila. 207) 281.
v. Steinhart (2 Pennyp. [Pa.] 358) 251, 278.

[REFERENCES ARE TO PAGES.]

Lombardi v. California St. Ry. Co. (124 Cal. 311) 435.
Loomis, Chicago City R. Co. v. (201 Ill. 118) 242.
Lorimer v. St. Paul City Ry. Co. (48 Minn. 391) 376.
Los Angeles Consol. Elec. Ry. Co., Everett v. (115 Cal. 105) 432.
Gier v. (108 Cal. 129) 374, 377.
Los Angeles Ry. Co., Campbell v. (135 Cal. 137) 164.
Cunningham v. (115 Cal. 561) 255, 266, 270.
George v. (126 Cal. 357) 250, 286.
Los Angeles Traction Co., Abrahams v. (124 Cal. 411) 326.
Babcock v. (128 Cal. 173) 93, 160.
Bassett v. (65 Pac. 470, 133 Cal. xix.) 115.
Campbell v. (137 Cal. 565) 291.
Harrington v. (74 Pac. [Cal.] 15) 345.
Mock v. (73 Pac. [Cal.] 455) 286.
Osgood v. (137 Cal. 280) 119.
Losee v. Watervliet Turnpike & R. Co. (63 Hun [N. Y.] 404) 143, 163.
Lott v. Frankford & S. Pass. Ry. Co. (159 Pa. 471) 337.
v. New Orleans City & L. R. Co. (37 La. Ann. 337) 114.
Loudoun v. Eight Ave. R. Co. (16 App. Div. [N. Y.] 152) 120.
Louis, North Chicago St. R. Co. v. (35 Ill. App. 477) 211, 244.
Louisville City Ry. Co., Curtis v. (94 Ky. 573) 33, 171, 172.
Johnson's Adm'r v. (10 Bush [Ky.] 231) 247.
v. Mercer (11 Ky. L. R. 810) 187, 192, 426, 436.
v. Weams (80 Ky. 420) 102, 142.
v. Wood (2 Ky. L. R. 387) 238.
Louisville Ry. Co. v. Blaydes (21 Ky. L. R. 480, 668) 344.
Brown v. (21 Ky. L. R. 995, 53 S. W. 1041) 410.
v. Casey (24 Ky. L. R. 1527, 71 S. W. 876) 426.
Flynn v. (23 Ky. L. R. 51, 62 S. W. 490) 313.
v. French (71 S. W. [Ky.] 486) 274.
Gorman's Adm'r v. (72 S. W. [Ky.] 760) 270.
Groves v. (22 Ky. L. R. 599) 361.
Henning v. (74 S. W. [Ky.] 209) 142.
Lutz v. (20 Ky. L. R. 1163) 142.
Nussbaum v. (22 Ky. L. R. 271, 57 S. W. 249) 182, 397.
v. Park (96 Ky. 580) 14, 142, 165, 423.
Passamaneck's Adm'r v. (98 Ky. 195) 250, 255, 268, 270.
v. Phillips (22 Ky. L. R. 842) 253.
v. Poe (24 Ky. L. R. 1700, 72 S. W. 6) 217.
v. Rammaker (21 Ky. L. R. 250, 51 S. W. 175) 162, 405.
Robinson v. (112 Fed. 484) 313, 314, 408.
v. Russell's Adm'r (20 Ky. L. R. 1246) 110.
v. Stammers (20 Ky. L. R. 688) 317.
v. Will's Adm'x (66 S. W. [Ky.] 628) 243.
Louisville & P. R. Co. v. Smith (2 Duv. [Ky.] 556) 101, 102, 115, 436.
Lovett v. Salem & S. D. R. Co. (9 Allen [Mass.] 557) 185.
Lowe, Citizens' St Ry. Co. v. (12 Ind. App. 47) 336.
v. Minneapolis St. Ry. Co. (37 Minn. 283) 413, 421.

[REFERENCES ARE TO PAGES.]

Lowell, L. & H. St. Ry. Co., Coleman v. (181 Mass. 591) 296.
Le Blanc v. (170 Mass. 564) 302.
Mathes v. (177 Mass. 416) 212.
Sias v. (179 Mass. 343) 352.
Thompson v. (170 Mass. 577) 248.
Lowell & D. St. Ry. Co., Beal v. (157 Mass. 444) 64.
Lowell & S. St. R. Co., Ovington v. (163 Mass. 440) 365.
Lowery v. Brooklyn City & N. R. Co. (76 N. Y. 28) 354.
Mt. Adams & E. P. I. Ry. Co. v. (74 Fed. 463) 124.
Mt. Adams & E. P. I. Ry. Co. v. (68 Fed. 827) 419.
Derry v. (6 Phila. [Pa.] 30) 181.
Jackson Electric Ry., L. & P. Co. v. (79 Miss. 431) 56.
Lowy v. Metropolitan St. Ry. Co. (30 Misc. [N. Y.] 775) 296.
Luby v. Hudson River R. Co. (17 N. Y. 131) 411.
Lucas v. Metropolitan St. Ry. Co. (56 App. Div. [N. Y.] 405) 74.
Ludecke v. Metropolitan St. Ry. Co. (32 Misc. [N. Y.] 635) 316, 329.
Ludwig v. Metropolitan St. Ry. Co. (71 App. Div. [N. Y.] 210) 351.
Luhrs v. Brooklyn Heights R. Co. (11 App. Div. [N. Y.] 173) 188, 189.
Luka, West Chicago St. R. Co. v. (72 Ill. App. 60) 141-143.
Luleich, West Chicago St. R. Co. v. (85 Ill. App. 643) 32, 33, 171, 178, 189, 413, 427.
Lumis v. Philadelphia Traction Co. (181 Pa. 268) 357
Lundquist v. Duluth St. Ry. Co. (65 Minn. 387) 387.
Lundy v. Second Ave. R. Co. (1 Misc. [N. Y.] 100) 243.
Lups, West Chicago St. R. Co. v. (74 Ill. App. 420) 38, 40, 424, 433.
Lurie v. Metropolitan St. Ry. Co. (18 Misc. [N. Y.] 81) 341.
Lusby, Capital Traction Co. v. (12 App. D. C. 295) 19, 215, 242.
Lusk, Rapid Transit Ry. Co. v. (66 S. W. [Tex. Civ. App.] 799) 143.
Lutterbeck, Toledo Consol. St. Ry. Co. v. (11 Ohio Cir. Ct. R. 279) 224.
Lutz v. Louisville Ry. Co. (20 Ky. L. R. 1163) 142.
Lyddane, Owensboro City R. Co. v. (19 Ky. L. R. 698, 41 S. W. 578) 337, 408.
Lynam v. Union Ry. Co. (114 Mass. 83) 302, 303.
Lynch v. Brooklyn City R. Co. (1 Silv. [N. Y.] 361) 135.
v. Metropolitan El. Ry. Co. (90 N. Y. 77) 171, 182, 184, 189.
v. Metropolitan St. Ry. Co. (112 Mo. 420) 253, 257, 262.
Lynholm, Calumet Elec. St. Ry. Co. v. (70 Ill. App. 371) 332.
Lynn & B. R. Co., Byron v. (177 Mass. 303) 79, 129.
Carlson v. (172 Mass. 388) 222.
Cotter v. (180 Mass. 145) 266, 268.
Doyle v. (118 Mass. 195) 105.
Ellis v. (160 Mass. 341) 336, 337.
Hudson v. (178 Mass. 64) 32, 33, 171, 178, 184.
Kingman v. (181 Mass. 387) 112.
Meesel v. (8 Allen [Mass.] 234) 64, 65, 71, 106.
Nealand v. (173 Mass. 42) 384.
Nichols v. (168 Mass. 528) 404.
O'Neil v. (180 Mass. 576) 166.

[REFERENCES ARE TO PAGES.]

Lynn & B. R. Co., O'Neill v. (155 Mass. 371) 71, 412.
Spade v. (168 Mass. 285) 434.
Sweetland v. (177 Mass. 574) 65, 70, 131, 132.
Wilde v. (163 Mass. 533) 80, 81.
Wills v. (129 Mass. 351) 71.
Witherington v. (182 Mass. 596) 98.
Lynn & B. St. Ry. Co., Cunningham v. (170 Mass. 298) 384.
Lyon, West Chicago St. R. Co. v. (57 Ill. App. 536) 141.
Lyons v. Bay Cities Consol. Ry. Co. (115 Mich. 114) 230.
v. Broadway & S. A. R. Co. (10 N. Y. Supp. 237) 188, 189.
v. Second Ave. R. Co. (89 Hun [N. Y.] 374) 420, 439.

M.

McAdam v. Central Ry. & Elec. Co. (67 Conn. 445) 389.
McAllister v. People's Ry. Co. (54 Atl. [Del.] 743) 111.
McAndrews v. St. Louis & S. Ry. Co. (83 Mo. App. 233) 321, 332.
McBride v. St. Paul City Ry. Co. (72 Minn. 291) 404.
McCabe v. Dry Dock, E. B. & B. R. Co. (15 Daly [N. Y.] 504) 411.
v. Third Ave. R. Co. (22 Misc. [N. Y.] 707) 403.
McCaffrey v. Twenty-Third St. R. Co. (47 Hun [N. Y.] 404) 369.
McCahill v. Detroit City Ry. Co. (96 Mich. 156) 153.
McCallum, West Chicago St. R. Co. v. (169 Ill. 240) 241, 324.
McCambley v. Staten Island Midland R. Co. (32 App. Div. [N. Y.] 346) 306.
McCann v. Consolidated Traction Co. (59 N. J. Law, 481) 338.
Newark & S. O. R. Co. v. (58 N. J. Law, 642) 104, 136.
McCarthy v. Cass Ave. & F. G. Ry. Co. (92 Mo. 536) 253.
Chicago North Shore St. Ry. Co. v. (66 Ill. App. 667) 341.
v. Detroit Citizens' St. Ry. Co. (120 Mich. 400) 226.
Joliet St. Ry. Co. v. (42 Ill. App. 49) 135.
McCauley v. Philadelphia Traction Co. (13 Pa. Super. Ct. 354) 213, 215, 216.
v. Springfield St. Ry. Co. (169 Mass. 301) 372.
McCaw v. Union Traction Co. (54 Atl. [Pa.] 893) 68, 108.
McClain v. Brooklyn City R. Co. (116 N. Y. 459) 226, 242.
McCleave, South Covington & C. St. Ry. Co. v. (18 Ky. L. R. 1036) 100.
McClellan v. Ft. Wayne & B. I. Ry. Co. (105 Mich. 101) 397.
Lincoln St. Ry. Co. v. (54 Neb. 672) 102.
McConnell v. Atlantic Ave. R. Co. (11 Misc. [N. Y.] 177) 303.
Fulton County St. R. Co. v. (87 Ga. 756) 356.
McCooe v. Dighton. S. & S. St. Ry. Co. (173 Mass. 117) 395.
McCooey v. Forty-Second St. & G. St. Ferry R. Co. (79 Hun [N. Y.] 255) 228, 245.
McCormack v. Nassau Elec. R. Co. (16 App. Div. [N. Y.] 24) 297, 329.
v. Nassau Elec. R. Co. (18 App. Div. [N. Y.] 333) 311.

[REFERENCES ARE TO PAGES.]

McCormick v. Brooklyn City R. Co. (10 Misc. [N. Y.] 8) 227.
McCoy v. Milwaukee St. Ry. Co. (82 Wis. 215) 394, 396.
  v. Milwaukee St. Ry. Co. (88 Wis. 56) 421, 436.
McCready v. Staten Island Elec. R. Co. (51 App. Div. [N. Y.] 338) 422.
McCullough v. Pittsburgh, A. & M. Traction Co. (183 Pa. 241) 277.
McCurdy v. Traction Co. (15 Pa. Super. Ct. 29) 53, 60.
McDade v. Washington & G. R. Co. (5 Mackey, D. C. 144) 388.
McDaniel v. Highland Ave. & B. R. Co. (90 Ala. 64) 35, 94.
McDermott v. Boston El. Ry. Co. (68 N. E. [Mass.] 34) 250, 256.
  v. Third Ave. R. Co. (44 Hun [N. Y.] 107) 223.
McDivitt v. Des Moines St. Ry. Co. (99 Iowa, 141) 321.
McDonald v. Kansas City & I. Rapid Transit Co. (127 Mo. 38) 158.
  v. Kansas City Cable Ry. Co. (32 Mo. App. 70) 161.
  v. Metropolitan St. Ry. Co. (80 App. Div. [N. Y.] 233) 253.
  v. Montgomery St. Ry. Co. (110 Ala. 161) 147, 404.
  South Chicago City Ry. Co. v. (94 Ill. App. 612) 414.
  State v. (7 Mo. App. 510) 192.
  v. Third Ave. R. Co. (16 Misc. [N. Y.] 52) 298.
  v. Toledo Consol. St. Ry. Co. (74 Fed. 104) 339, 365.
McDonnell, Baltimore City Pass. Ry. Co. v. (43 Md. 534) 253, 255, 271, 273, 282, 408, 411.
McDonnell, Baltimore City Pass. Ry. Co. v. (43 Md. 534) 253, 355, 271, 273, 282, 408, 411.
McDonough v. Metropolitan R. Co. (137 Mass. 210) 6, 7, 38-40, 42, 59.
McFadden v. Santa Ana, O. & T. St. Ry. Co. (87 Cal. 464) 357.
McFarland v. Third Ave. R. Co. (29 Misc. [N. Y.] 121) 315.
McGarry v. Holyoke St. Ry. Co. (182 Mass. 123) 174.
McCary v. West Chicago St. R. Co. (85 Ill. App. 610) 137.
McGee v. Consolidated St. Ry. Co. (102 Mich. 107) 212, 216, 218.
McGill v. Central Crosstown R. Co. (84 N. Y. Supp. 477) 54.
McGinnis, Rome St. R. Co. v. (94 Ga. 229) 328.
McGlynn v. Brooklyn Crosstown R. Co. (6 N. Y. St. Rep. 51) 133.
McGovern v. Union Traction Co. (192 Pa. 344) 218.
McGowan v. Interstate Consol. St. Ry. Co. (20 R. I. 264) 413.
McGrane v. Flushing & C. P. Elec. Ry. Co. (13 App. Div. [N. Y.] 177) 306, 327.
McGrath v. Brooklyn, Q. C. & S. R. Co. (87 Hun [N. Y.] 310) 83, 84.
  v. City & Suburban Ry. Co. (93 Ga. 312) 292, 301.
  v. North Jersey St. Ry. Co. (66 N. J. Law, 312) 209, 213, 217.
McKay v. Southern Bell Tel. Co. (111 Ala. 337) 350.
McKelvey v. Twenty-Third St. Ry. Co. (5 Misc. [N. Y.] 424) 231, 233, 234.
McKenna v. Metropolitan R. Co. (112 Mass. 55) 354.
  v. North Hudson County Ry. Co. (64 N. J. Law, 106) 413, 429.
McKeon v. Citizens' Ry. Co. (42 Mo. 79) 150, 436.
  v. Steinway Ry. Co. (20 App. Div. [N. Y.] 601) 210, 236.
McKewen, Lake Roland El. Ry. Co. v. (80 Md. 593) 316, 321.

[REFERENCES ARE TO PAGES.]

McKillop v. Duluth St. Ry. Co. (53 Minn. 532) 363.
McKinley v. Metropolitan St. Ry. Co. (77 App. Div. [N. Y.] 256) 213.
McKnight v. Brooklyn Heights R. Co. (23 Misc. [N. Y.] 527) 380, 382.
McLain v. St. Louis & S. Ry. Co. (73 S. W. [Mo. App.] 909) 136, 247, 332, 383.
McLane, Washington & G. R. Co. v. (11 App. D. C. 220) 410, 411.
McLaughlin, Chicago City Ry. Co. v. (40 Ill. App. 496) 383.
v. New Orleans & C. R. Co. (48 La. Ann. 23) 279.
v. Philadelphia Traction Co. (175 Pa. 565) 358, 408.
McMahon v. Second Ave. R. Co. (75 N. Y. 231) 355.
v. Third Ave. R. Co. (47 N. Y. Super. Ct. 282) 197, 203.
McManigal v. South Side Pass. Ry. Co. (181 Pa. 358) 328.
McMillan v. Federal St. & P. V. Pass. Ry. Co. (172 Pa. 523) 33, 71, 179.
McNab v. United Ry. & Electric Co. (94 Md. 719) 291.
McNamara v. Brooklyn City R. Co. (11 Misc. [N. Y.] 667) 376.
Chicago, General Ry. Co. v. (94 Ill. App. 188) 391, 423.
McNulta, Stelk v. (99 Fed. 138) 241.
McNulty, West Chicago St. R. Co. v. (166 Ill. 203) 123.
West Chicago St. R. Co. v. (64 Ill. App. 549) 83, 86.
McPherson, Joliet R. Co. v. (96 Ill. App. 286) 423.
McQuade v. Manhattan Ry. Co. (53 N. Y. Super. Ct. 91) 53.
v. Metropolitan St. Ry. Co. (17 Misc. [N. Y.] 154) 210, 214, 237.
McSwyny v. Broadway & S. A. R. Co. (7 N. Y. Supp. 456) 39, 50.
Mabry v. City Elec. Ry. Co. (42 S. E. [Ga.] 1025) 433.
Macer v. Third Ave. R. Co. (47 N. Y. Super. Ct. 461) 168.
Machen v. Railway Co. (13 Pa. Super. Ct. 642) 156, 433.
Mack v. Lombard & S. Sts. Pass. Ry. Co. (20 Phila. [Pa.] 207) 281.
Mackie v. Brooklyn City R. Co. (10 Misc. [N. Y.] 4) 297.
Mackin v. People's St. Ry. & E. L. & P. Co. (45 Mo. App. 82) 133.
MacLaury, Brooklyn Heights R. Co. v. (107 Fed. 644) 435.
MacLeod v. Graven (73 Fed. 627) 215.
Macomber, Hutchins v. (63 N. H. 473) 145.
Macon v. Paducah St. Ry. Co. (23 Ky. L. R. 46) 349, 353.
Macon City & S. St. Ry. Co., Masterson v. (88 Ga. 436) 145, 146.
Macon Consolidated St. R. Co. v. Barnes (113 Ga. 212) 101, 404.
Cain v. (97 Ga. 298) 213.
Perry v. (101 Ga. 400) 280.
Macon & I. S. St. Ry. Co. v. Holmes (103 Ga. 655) 210, 237.
Madara v. Shamokin & M. C. Electric Ry. Co. (192 Pa. 542) 119.
Madison Electric Ry. Co., Vassau v. (106 Wis. 301) 192, 437.
Magee v. West End St. Ry. Co. (151 Mass. 240) 312.
Mager, Chicago City Ry. Co. v. (185 Ill. 336) 330, 394.
Chicago City Ry. Co. v. (85 Ill. App. 524) 393.
Maguire v. Middlesex R. Co. (115 Mass. 239) 64, 68, 75, 404.
Maher v. Central Park, N. & E. R. R. Co. (67 N. Y. 52) 38, 40.
v. Central Park, N. & E. R. R. Co. (39 Super. Ct. 155) 51.
v. Philadelphia Traction Co. (181 Pa. 391) 284.

[REFERENCES ARE TO PAGES.]

Mahnke v. New Orleans City & Lake R. Co. (104 La. 411) 355.
Mahoney v. Detroit St. Ry. Co. (93 Mich. 612) 204.
v. Metropolitan R. Co. (104 Mass. 73) 366.
v. San Francisco & S. M. Ry. Co. (110 Cal. 471) 313, 314.
Main St. & A. P. R. Co., Sappenfield v. (91 Cal. 48) 382, 406.
Maisels v. Dry Dock, E. B. & B. R. Co. (16 App. Div. [N. Y.] 391) 139, 140, 147.
Malarin, Perry v. (107 Cal. 363) 118, 132, 135.
Malden & M. R. Co., Wright v. (4 Allen [Mass.] 283) 251, 254, 263, 282, 408.
Malecek v. Tower Grove & L. Ry. Co. (57 Mo. 17) 192, 436.
Mallard v. Ninth Ave. R. Co. (15 Daly [N. Y.] 376) 259, 277.
Maloney v. Brooklyn City R. Co. (18 N. Y. Wkly. Dig. 152) 225.
Malpass v. Hestonville, M. & F. P. R. Co. (189 Pa. 599) 227.
Mammet, Toledo Consol. St. Ry. Co. v. (2 Ohio Dec. 532) 406.
Manayunk & R. Boarding & Livery Stable Co. v. Union Traction Co. (7 Pa. Super. Ct. 104) 299.
Mangam v. Brooklyn R. Co. (38 N. Y. 455) 250, 251, 254, 267, 275.
Manhattan Ry. Co., Benson v. (31 Misc. [N. Y.] 723) 61.
Brown v. (81 N. Y. Supp. 755) 56.
Buck v. (15 Daly [N. Y.] 550) 167.
Clark v. (77 App. Div. [N. Y.] 284) 246.
Diabola v. (8 N. Y. Supp. 334) 103.
Donivan v. (49 N. Y. St. Rep. 722) 192, 193, 437.
Graham v. (149 N. Y. 336) 15, 65, 67, 74, 106.
McQuade v. (53 N. Y. Super. Ct. 91) 53.
Merwin v. (48 Hun [N. Y.] 608) 65, 67, 114.
Oppenheimer v. (18 N. Y. Supp. 411) 185.
Palmeri v. (133 N. Y. 261) 188, 190.
Smith v. (18 N. Y. Supp. 759) 11.
Mann v. Philadelphia Traction Co. (175 Pa. 122) 73.
Manning, West Chicago St. R. Co. v. (70 Ill. App. 239; affirmed 170 Ill. 417) 20, 142, 143.
v. West End St. Ry. Co. (166 Mass. 230) 367.
Manor v. Bay Cities Consol. Ry. Co. (118 Mich. 1) 302, 314, 315.
Mantel v. Chicago, M. & St. P. Ry. Co. (33 Minn. 62) 379.
Manville, Galesburg Elec. Motor & Power Co. v. (61 Ill. App. 490) 334, 336.
Mapes v. Union Ry. Co. (56 App. Div. [N. Y.] 508) 327.
Marchal v. Indianapolis St. Ry. Co. (28 Ind. App. 133) 299, 319, 325.
Marion City Ry. Co. v. Dubois (23 Ind. App. 342) 335.
Marion St. R. Co. v. Carr (10 Ind. App. 200) 337.
v. Schaffer (9 Ind. App. 486) 77.
Sirk v. (11 Ind. App. 680) 162.
Market St. Cable Ry. Co., Bailey v. (110 Cal. 320) 217, 227, 233, 234.
Driscoll v. (97 Cal. 553) 209, 214, 215, 233, 235, 237, 238.
Market St. Ry. Co., Barrett v. (81 Cal. 296) 175.
Kernan v. (137 Cal. 326) 209, 217.

[REFERENCES ARE TO PAGES.]

Market St. Ry. Co., Kerrigan v. (138 Cal. 506) 391.
Seller v. (72 Pac. [Cal.] 1006) 65, 76.
Wahlgren v. (132 Cal. 656) 211, 220, 243, 427.
Markowitz v. Dry Dock, E. B. & B. R. Co. (12 Misc. [N. Y.] 412) 365, 408.
Marks v. Rochester Ry. Co. (41 App. Div. [N. Y.] 66) 24, 387.
West Chicago St. R. Co. v. (82 Ill. App. 185) 83, 87.
Marsullo v. Metropolitan St. Ry. Co. (30 App. Div. [N. Y.] 505) 397.
Martin v. Interurban St. Ry. Co. (84 N. Y. Supp. 921) 331.
North Chicago St. R. Co. v. (51 Ill. App. 247) 220.
Omaha St. Ry. Co. v. (48 Neb. 65) 38-40, 60.
v. Second Ave. R. Co. (3 App. Div. [N. Y.] 448) 144, 151.
v. Third Ave. R. Co. (27 App. Div. [N. Y.] 52) 213, 237.
West Chicago St. R. Co. v. (154 Ill. 523) 126.
Martineau v. Rochester Ry. Co. (81 Hun [N. Y.] 263) 251, 264.
Marvil, Citizens' St. R. Co. v. (67 N. E. [Ind.] 921) 358.
Marysville & Y. C. St. R. Co., Nye v. (97 Cal. 461) 33, 171, 182.
Mascheck v. St. Louis R. Co. (3 Mo. App. 600) 251, 272.
v. St. Louis R. Co. (71 Mo. 276) 279.
Mason v. Atlantic Ave. R. Co. (4 Misc. [N. Y.] 291) 252, 284.
Birmingham Ry. & Elec. Co. v. (34 So. [Ala.] 207) 191.
v. Metropolitan St. Ry. Co. (30 Misc. [N. Y.] 108) 292.
v. Minneapolis St. Ry. Co. (54 Minn. 216) 250, 253, 277.
Montgomery St. Ry. Co. v. (133 Ala. 508) 157.
Mason City & C. L. Traction Co., Fitch v. (116 Iowa, 716) 406.
Masterson v. Macon City & S. St. R. Co. (88 Ga. 436) 145, 146
Mathes v. Lowell, L. & H. St. Ry. (177 Mass. 416) 212.
Matthews v. Delaware, L. & W. Ry. Co. (56 N. J. Law, 34) 127
Mathieson v. Omaha St. Ry. Co. (92 N. W. [Neb.] 639) 328.
Mattis v. Philadelphia Traction Co. (6 Pa. Dist. Ct. R. 94) 417, 438.
Matz v. St. Paul City Ry. Co. (52 Minn. 159) 77-79.
Mauer v. Brooklyn Heights R. Co. (87 App. Div. [N. Y.] 119) 218.
Maurer, Indiana Ry. Co. v. (66 N. E. [Ind.] 156) 150.
Maverick v. Eighth Ave. R. Co. (36 N. Y. 378) 79, 102.
Maxey v. Metropolitan St. R. Co. (95 Mo. App. 303) 50, 58.
Maxwell v. Wilmington City Ry. Co. (1 Marv. [Del.] 199) 313, 314, 316, 321, 392, 409, 440.
May v. Metropolitan St. Ry. Co. (26 Misc. [N. Y.] 748) 292.
North Hudson County Ry. Co. v. (48 N. J. Law, 401) 411.
Mayberry v. Second & Third Sts. Ry. Co. (15 Phila. [Pa.] 253) 361.
Maynard, Muncie St. Ry. Co. v. (5 Ind. App. 372) 336.
Mayor of Macon v. Dykes (103 Ga. 847) 339.
Maysville Gas Co., Thomas' Adm'r v. (21 Ky. L. R. 1690) 349.
Mazetti v. New York & H. R. Co. (3 E. D. Smith [N. Y.] 98) 361.
Meade v. Brooklyn Heights R. Co. (3 App. Div. [N. Y.] 432) 431.
Meadows, Evansville St. Ry. Co. v. (13 Ind. App. 155) 23, 25, 76.
Mechler, San Antonio St. Ry. Co. v. (87 Tex. 628) 269, 270.
Medcalf v. St. Paul City Ry. Co. (82 Minn. 18) 342.

[REFERENCES ARE TO PAGES.]

Medinger v. Brooklyn Heights R. Co. (6 App. Div. [N. Y.] 42) 440.
Medlenka, Houston City St. Ry. Co. v. (17 Tex. Civ. App. 621) 407, 418.
Medler v. Atlantic Ave. R. Co. (12 N. Y. Supp. 930) 92, 131, 159.
Meehan, Chicago City Ry. Co. v. (77 Ill. App. 215) 140, 148, 154.
Meesel v. Lynn & B. R. Co. (8 Allen [Mass.] 234) 64, 65, 71, 106.
Meisch v. Rochester Elec. Ry. Co. (72 Hun [N. Y.] 604) 347.
Meixner, Cicero & P. St. Ry. Co. v. (160 Ill. 320) 6. 38-43, 57.
Memphis City Ry. Co. v. Logue (13 Lea [Tenn.] 32) 269, 270, 286.
Memphis St. Ry. Co. v. Graves (75 S. W. [Tenn.] 729) 200.
v. Kartwright (75 S. W. [Tenn.] 719) 349, 351.
v. Norris (108 Tenn. 632) 123.
v. Riddick (75 S. W. [Tenn.] 924) 294.
v. Shaw (75 S. W. [Tenn.] 713) 144, 153.
v. Wilson (108 Tenn. 618) 320, 324.
Mendenhall, Cameron v. (80 Minn. 150) 311.
Currie v. (77 Minn. 179) 92, 143, 159.
Fewings v. (93 N. W. [Minn.] 127) 114.
Holdridge v. (108 Wis. 1) 256, 262, 279.
Warren v. (77 Minn. 145) 311.
Mentz v. Second Ave. R. Co. (2 Rob. [N. Y.] 356) 256.
Mercer, Louisville City Ry. Co. v. (11 Ky. L. R. 810) 187, 192, 426, 436.
Mercier v. New Orleans & C. R. Co. (23 La. Ann. 264) 291.
Meriden Electric R. Co., Budd v. (69 Conn. 272) 250, 274, 411.
Meriden S. & C. Tramway Co., Hesse v. (54 Atl. [Conn.] 299) 83, 87.
Meriwether v. Kansas City Cable Ry. Co. (45 Mo. App. 528) 53, 54.
Merl, Citizens' St. Ry. Co. v. (26 Ind. App. 284) 6, 38, 39, 41, 55, 57, 89.
Merrill v. Metropolitan St. Ry. Co. (73 App. Div. [N. Y.] 401) 103, 130.
Mewin v. Manhattan Ry. Co. (48 Hun [N. Y.] 608) 65, 67, 114.
Messenger v. St. Paul City Ry. Co. (77 Minn. 34) 137.
Metcalf v. Rochester Ry. Co. (12 App. Div. [N. Y.] 147) 309.
Metropolitan El. Ry. Co., Lynch v. (90 N. Y. 77) 171, 182, 184, 189.
Metropolitan R. Co., Bunyea v. (19 D. C. 876) 434, 438.
v. Collins (1 App. D. C. 383) 411.
Commonwealth v. (107 Mass. 236) 263, 275.
Cook v. (98 Mass. 361) 331.
Cram v. (112 Mass. 38) 147, 152.
Eads v. (43 Mo. App. 536) 32, 176, 182, 188.
v. Falvey (5 App. D. C. 176) 97, 101.
Geddes v. (103 Mass. 391) 91, 108.
v. Hammett (13 App. D. C. 370) 120.
Harbison v. (9 App. D. C. 60) 83, 84, 86, 95.
v. Jones (1 App. D. C. 200) 143, 394.
McDonough v. (137 Mass. 210) 6, 7, 38-40, 42, 59.
McKenna v. (112 Mass. 55) 354.
Mahoney v. (104 Mass. 73) 366.

[REFERENCES ARE TO PAGES.]

Metropolitan R. Co., Moore v. (2 Mackey [D. C.] 437) 253, 254.
Redwood v. (6 D. C. 302) 192, 437.
Smith v. (137 Mass. 61) 397.
v. Snashall (3 App. D. C. 420) 77, 78.
Stanton v. (14 Allen [Mass.] 485) 104.
Woodman v. (149 Mass. 335) 357.
Metropolitan St. R. Co., Atwood v. (25 Misc. [N. Y.] 758) 96.
Hoyt v. (73 App. Div. [N. Y.] 249) 241.
Maxcy v. (95 Mo. App. 303) 50, 58.
Moore v. (83 Ga. 453) 23, 25, 77, 421.
v. Powell (89 Ga. 601) 334.
Sciurba v. (73 App. Div. [N. Y.] 170) 272, 275.
Metropolitan St. Ry. Co., Adams v. (60 App. Div. [N. Y.] 188) 251, 264, 275.
Adams v. (81 N. Y. Supp. 553) 368.
v. Agnew (65 Kan. 478) 291.
Anderson v. (30 Misc. [N. Y.] 104) 310, 325.
Armstrong v. (23 App. Div. [N. Y.] 137) 93, 160.
Armstrong v. (36 App. Div. [N. Y.] 525) 161.
v. Arnold (72 Pac. [Kan.] 857) 345.
Bartley v. (148 Mo. 124) 129.
Baumann v. (21 Misc. [N. Y.] 658) 305.
Beers v. (84 N. Y. Supp. 785) 225.
Bello v. (2 App. Div. [N. Y.] 313) 261.
Benjamin v. (133 Mo. 274) 368.
Bessenger v. (79 App. Div. [N. Y.] 32) 145.
Bigelow v. (48 Mo. App. 367) 403.
Blum v. (80 N. Y. Supp. 157) 302.
Blum v. (79 App. Div. [N. Y.] 611) 327.
Boggess v. (118 Mo. 328) 414, 437.
Boston & P. Dispatch Exp. Co v. (14 Misc. [N. Y.] 25) 202.
Brady v. (33 Misc. [N. Y.] 793) 143.
Brennan v. (60 App. Div. [N. Y.] 264) 310, 325.
Brown v. (60 App. Div. [N. Y.] 184) 345.
Bruss v. (66 App. Div. [N. Y.] 554) 297, 319.
Bryant v. (28 Misc. [N. Y.] 532) 304.
Burns v. (71 Pac. [Kan.] 244) 289, 293.
Cardonner v. (26 App. Div. [N. Y.] 8) 344.
Cardonner v. (38 App. Div. [N. Y.] 597) 344.
Casper v. (84 App. Div. [N. Y.] 639) 224.
Cattano v. (173 N. Y. 565) 64, 106.
Clegg v. (1 App. Div. [N. Y.] 207) 402.
Cohen v. (63 App. Div. [N. Y.] 165) 258, 269, 285.
Cohen v. (34 Misc. [N. Y.] 186) 302, 315, 317.
Coleman v. (81 N. Y. Supp. 836) 148.
Conlon v. (34 Misc. [N. Y.] 394) 432, 433.
Connelly v. (84 N. Y. Supp. 205) 233.
Connor v. (77 App. Div. [N. Y.] 384) 302, 331.

[REFERENCES ARE TO PAGES.]

Metropolitan St. Ry. Co., Connor v. (48 App. Div. [N. Y.] 580) 366.
Copeland v. (78 App. Div. [N. Y.] 418) 218.
Cosgrove v. (74 App. Div. [N. Y.] 166) 243.
Coulahan v. (28 App. Div. [N. Y.] 394) 124.
Crowley v. (24 App. Div. [N. Y.] 101) 308.
Csatlos v. (70 App. Div. [N. Y.] 606) 272.
Culbertson v. (140 Mo. 35) 292, 325.
Curtin v. (22 Misc. [N. Y.] 83) 218, 219.
Davidson v. (75 App. Div. [N. Y.] 426) 260, 284.
De la Torre v. (48 App. Div. [N. Y.] 126) 415.
De Ioia v. (37 App. Div. [N. Y.] 455) 280.
DeRozas v. (13 App. Div. [N. Y.] 296) 53.
Devine v. (29 Misc. [N. Y.] 301) 289.
Devlin v. (17 App. Div. [N. Y.] 491) 390.
DeWardener v. (1 App. Div. [N. Y.] 240) 429.
Dise v. (22 Misc. [N. Y.] 97) 298, 320.
Donoho v. (30 Misc. [N. Y.] 433) 80.
Downer v. (54 App. Div. [N. Y.] 315) 430.
Doyle v. (29 Misc. [N. Y.] 331) 155.
Du Frane v. (83 App. Div. [N. Y.] 298) 213.
Eberhardt v. (69 App. Div. [N. Y.] 560) 131, 415.
Ellick v. (15 App. Div. [N. Y.] 556) 253, 259, 274, 283.
Farrell v. (51 App. Div. [N. Y.] 456) 401.
Fay v. (62 App. Div. [N. Y.] 51) 53.
Feary v. (162 Mo. 75) 110, 394.
Flanagan v. (31 Misc. [N. Y.] 820) 143.
Flynn v. (10 App. Div. [N. Y.] 258) 280.
Foley v. (80 App. Div. [N. Y.] 262) 425.
Frank v. (44 App. Div. [N. Y.] 243) 281.
Frank v. (58 App. Div. [N. Y.] 100) 211, 220, 221.
Freeman v. (95 Mo. App. 94) 102.
Fremont v. (82 N. Y. Supp. 307) 49.
Fullerton v. (37 App. Div. [N. Y.] 386) 283.
Fullerton v. (63 App. Div. [N. Y.] 1) 266.
Geary v. (84 App. Div. [N. Y.] 514) 309, 311.
Geary v. (73 App. Div. [N. Y.] 441) 311.
Gildea v. (58 App. Div. [N. Y.] 528) 219, 240.
Goetz v. (54 App. Div. [N. Y.] 365) 390.
Goldwasser v. (32 Misc. [N. Y.] 682) 59, 85.
Goodman v. (63 App. Div. [N. Y.] 84) 271.
Grabenstein v. (84 N. Y. Supp. 261) 163.
Green v. (42 App. Div. [N. Y.] 160) 285.
Green v. (60 App. Div. [N. Y.] 317) 395.
Green v. (65 App. Div. [N. Y.] 54) 285.
Griffiths v. (63 App. Div. [N. Y.] 86) 238, 259, 284.
G'Sell v. (35 Misc. [N. Y.] 387) 224, 243.
Gumby v. (65 App. Div. [N. Y.] 38) 265, 283.
Gumby v. (29 App. Div. [N. Y.] 335) 282.

[REFERENCES ARE TO PAGES.]

**Metropolitan St. Ry. Co. v. Hanson** (72 Pac. [Kan.] 773) 142.
**Hauser v.** (27 Misc. [N. Y.] 538) 356.
**Hill v.** (30 Misc. [N. Y.] 440) 304.
**Hite v.** (130 Mo. 132) 101, 102, 130.
**Hollahan v.** (73 App. Div. [N. Y.] 164) 117.
**Holzman v.** (31 Misc. [N. Y.] 644) 306.
**Honick v.** (71 Pac. [Kan.] 265) 293.
**Irwin v.** (25 Misc. [N. Y.] 187) 394.
**James v.** (80 N Y. Supp. 710) 184.
**Kaplan v.** (52 App. Div. [N. Y.] 296) 431.
**Kappus v.** (82 App. Div. [N. Y.] 13) 213.
**Kantrowitz v.** (63 App. Div. [N. Y.] 65) 125.
**Kay v.** (29 App. Div. [N. Y.] 466) 119.
**Kelly v.** (25 Misc. [N. Y.] 194) 362.
**Kennedy v.** (11 Misc. [N. Y.] 320) 315.
**Kennedy v.** (82 Fed. 158) 381.
**Kimber v.** (69 App. Div. [N. Y.] 353) 39, 40.
**Koues v.** (83 N. Y. Supp. 380) 143.
**Kraemer v.** (51 App. Div. [N. Y.] 475) 429.
**Kuhlman v.** (30 Misc. [N. Y.] 417) 139, 148.
**Lang v.** (26 Misc. [N. Y.] 754) 290.
**Lawson v.** (40 App. Div. [N. Y.] 307) 315-317, 319.
**Levin v.** (140 Mo. 624) 266, 267.
**Levine v.** (78 App. Div. [N. Y.] 426) 265.
**Lezinsky v.** (88 Fed. 437) 190.
**Lobsenz v.** (72 App. Div. [N. Y.] 181) 39, 40.
**Loder v.** (84 App. Div. [N. Y.] 591) 224.
**Lowy v.** (30 Misc. [N. Y.] 775) 296.
**Lucas v.** (56 App. Div. [N. Y.] 405) 74.
**Ludecke v.** (32 Misc. [N. Y.] 635) 316, 329.
**Ludwig v.** (71 App. Div. [N. Y.] 210) 351.
**Lurie v.** (18 Misc. [N. Y.] 81) 341.
**Lynch v.** (112 Mo. 420) 253, 257, 262.
**McDonald v.** (80 App. Div. [N. Y.] 233) 253.
**McKinley v.** (77 App. Div. [N. Y.] 256) 213.
**McQuade v.** (17 Misc. [N. Y.] 154) 210, 214, 237.
**Marsullo v.** (30 App. Div. [N. Y.] 505) 397.
**Mason v.** (30 Misc. [N. Y.] 108) 292.
**May v.** (26 Misc. [N. Y.] 748) 292.
**Merrill v.** (73 App. Div. [N. Y.] 401) 103, 130.
**Monroe v.** (80 N. Y. Supp. 177) 8, 55, 58.
**Moore v.** (84 App. Div. [N. Y.] 613) 297.
**Morris v.** (51 App. Div. [N. Y.] 512) 415, 440.
**Morris v.** (63 App. Div. [N. Y.] 78) 296, 309, 325.
**Muessman v.** (76 App. Div. [N. Y.] 1) 213.
**Mulligan v.** (85 N. Y. Supp. 791) 8, 55, 58.
**Murphy v.** (19 Misc. [N. Y.] 194) 142.
**Nolan v.** (65 App. Div. [N. Y.] 184) 232.

[REFERENCES ARE TO PAGES.]

Metropolitan St. Ry. Co., Nugent v. (17 App. Div. [N. Y.] 582) 275.
Oates v. (168 Mo. 535) 337.
O'Callaghan v. (69 App. Div. [N. Y.] 574) 299, 325.
Parker v. (69 Mo. App. 54) 102, 123.
Parkes v. (76 N. Y. Supp. 983) 358.
Pechesky v. (30 Misc. [N. Y.] 432) 304.
Pelletreau v. (74 App. Div. [N. Y.] 192) 225, 242.
Percy v. (58 Mo. App. 75) 194, 412.
Piercy v. (30 Misc. [N. Y.] 612) 320.
Pollak v. (28 Misc. [N. Y.] 791) 413.
Poole v. (83 App. Div. [N. Y.] 235) 211.
Pryor v. (85 Mo. App. 367) 129, 137.
Raming v. (157 Mo. 477) 28, 29.
Ramson v. (78 App. Div. [N. Y.] 101) 117.
Reed v. (84 N. Y. Supp. 454) 225.
Reed v. (58 App. Div. [N. Y.] 87) 310.
Reidy v. (27 Misc. [N. Y.] 527) 8, 49.
Reilly v. (26 Misc. [N. Y.] 814) 297, 320.
Reilly v. (30 Misc. [N. Y.] 110) 320.
Reiss v. (28 Misc. [N. Y.] 198) 291.
Rippe v. (35 App. Div. [N. Y.] 321) 422.
Robinson v. (31 Misc. [N. Y.] 171) 427.
Roedecker v. (84 N. Y. Supp. 300) 74.
Rohan v. (59 App. Div. [N. Y.] 250) 384.
Roth v. (13 Misc. [N. Y.] 213) 290.
v. Rouch (71 Pac. [Kan.] 257) 302, 314, 315.
Rouse v. (41 Mo. App. 298) 192, 437.
Schilling v. (47 App. Div. [N. Y.] 500) 301.
Schnell v. (50 App. Div. [N. Y.] 616) 361.
Schoener v. (72 App. Div. [N. Y.] 23) 297, 324.
Schoenfeld v. (40 Misc. [N. Y.] 201) 51, 53.
Schroder v. (84 N. Y. Supp. 371) 344.
Sciurba v. (84 N. Y. Supp. 85) 279.
Seelig v. (18 Misc. [N. Y.] 383) 64, 71, 131, 132.
Seggerman v. (38 Misc. [N. Y.] 374) 292.
Sesselman v. (65 App. Div. [N. Y.] 484) 219, 225, 235, 242.
Sexton v. (40 App. Div. [N. Y.] 26) 39, 40.
Shankenberry v. (46 Fed. 177) 125, 127.
Simon v. (29 Misc. [N. Y.] 126) 355.
Sims v. (65 App. Div. [N. Y.] 270) 163.
Slaughter v. (116 Mo. 269) 167, 435.
Slayman v. (64 Kan. 722) 296.
Smith v. (7 App. Div. [N. Y.] 253) 293.
Smith v. (59 App. Div. [N. Y.] 60) 109.
Smith v. (15 Misc. [N. Y.] 158) 441.
Sophian v. (38 Misc. [N. Y.] 787) 326.
Sternfels v. (73 App. Div. [N. Y.] 494) 416.

[REFERENCES ARE TO PAGES.]

Metropolitan St. Ry. Co., Steuer v. (46 App. Div. [N. Y.] 500) 149, 163.
Stewart v. (20 Misc. [N. Y.] 605) 206.
Stillings v. (84 App. Div. [N. Y.] 201) 219.
Sullivan v. (53 App. Div. [N. Y.] 89) 382.
Sullivan v. (63 App. Div. [N. Y.] 46) 402.
Suse v. (80 App. Div. [N. Y.] 24) 124.
Swenson v. (78 App. Div. [N. Y.] 379) 391.
Tarler v. (21 Misc. [N. Y.] 684) 306, 330.
Thal v. (76 N. Y. Supp. 918) 219, 231.
Thompson v. (140 Mo. 125) 98, 101.
Tracey v. (49 App. Div. [N. Y.] 197) 402.
Vonelling v. (35 Misc. [N. Y.] 301) 289, 294.
Wagner v. (79 App. Div. [N. Y.] 591) 321, 426.
Webb v. (89 Mo. App. 604) 437.
Weinberg v. (139 Mo. 286) 428.
Weingarten v. (62 App. Div. [N. Y.] 364) 228.
Weiss v. (29 Misc. [N. Y.] 332) 142.
Weiss v. (33 App. Div. [N. Y.] 221) 253, 260.
Westerman v. (84 N. Y. Supp. 501) 294, 309.
Wigton v. (38 App. Div. [N. Y.] 207) 436.
Williamson v. (29 Misc. [N. Y.] 324) 292, 325.
Willis v. (63 App. Div. [N. Y.] 332) 139-142.
Woods v. (48 Mo. App. 125) 196, 199.
Metropolitan West Side El. R. Co. v. Fortin (203 Ill. 454) 389.
v. Kersey (80 Ill. App. 301) 254, 425.
v. Skola (83 Ill. App. 659) 387, 391.
Mettlestadt v. Ninth Ave. R. Co. (27 N. Y. Super. Ct. 377) 147.
Metz v. St. Paul City Ry. Co. (92 N. W. [Minn.] 502) 218.
Meyer v. Brooklyn Heights R. Co. (9 App. Div. [N. Y.] 79) 292.
v. Brooklyn, Q. C. & S. R. Co. (47 App. Div. [N. Y.] 286) 303.
v. Lindell Ry. Co. (6 Mo. App. 27) 210, 235, 238.
v. Pittsburgh, A. & M. Traction Co. (189 Pa. 414) 226.
v. Second Ave. R. Co. (8 Bosw. [N. Y.] 305) 188, 189.
Meyers v. St. Louis Transit Co. (73 S. W. [Mo. App.] 379) 321, 328.
Middlesex R. Co., Feital v. (109 Mass. 398) 105, 115, 137.
Lapointe v. (144 Mass. 18) 90.
Maguire v. (115 Mass. 239) 64, 68, 75, 404.
Nichols v. (106 Mass. 463) 163.
Valentine v. (137 Mass. 28) 133.
Vinton v. (11 Allen [Mass.] 304) 33, 178.
Wilton v. (107 Mass. 108) 23, 26.
Wilton v. (125 Mass. 130) 76.
Middlesex & S. Traction Co., Gilliland v. (67 N. J. Law, 542) 220.
Norman v. (68 N. J. Law, 728) 386.
Milford, H. & E. St. Ry. Co., Joslyn v. (67 N. E. [Mass.] 866) 157.
Millard v. West End St. Ry. Co. (173 Mass. 512) 386.
Miller v. Lebannon & A. St. Ry. Co. (186 Pa. 190) 356.

[REFERENCES ARE TO PAGES.]

Miller, New Jersey Elec. Ry. Co. v. (59 N. J. Law, 423) 318.
v. St. Louis R. Co. (5 Mo. App. 471) 99, 407.
v. St. Paul City Ry. Co. (42 Minn. 454) 48.
v. St. Paul City Ry. Co. (62 Minn. 216) 402.
v. St. Paul City Ry. Co. (66 Minn. 192) 6, 53, 55, 424.
v. Union Traction Co. (198 Pa. 639) 279.
Mills v. Brooklyn City R. Co. (10 Misc. [N. Y.] 1) 218, 241.
Chicago West Div. Ry. Co. v. (91 Ill. 39) 163.
Chicago West Div. Ry. Co. v. (105 Ill. 63) 142, 143, 162.
v. Wilmington City Ry. Co. (1 Marv. [Del.] 269) 247, 400.
Milwaukee City Ry. Co., Dahl v. (62 Wis. 652) 268, 277.
Dahl v. (65 Wis. 371) 275.
Ellis v. (67 Wis. 135) 194.
Geitz v. (72 Wis. 307) 83, 84, 87.
Heicke v. (69 Wis. 401) 103, 124, 422.
Knowlton v. (59 Wis. 278) 104, 150, 428.
White v. (61 Wis. 536) 118, 132, 400.
Milwaukee Elec. Ry. & Light Co., Bading v. (105 Wis. 480) 393, 426.
Dummer v. (108 Wis. 589) 289, 293.
Forrestal v. (97 N. W. [Wis.] 182) 273.
Hanlon v. (95 N. W. [Wis.] 100) 311, 326.
Smith v. (96 N. W. [Wis.] 823) 118.
Tesch v. (108 Wis. 593) 289, 293, 299, 315, 316.
Tishacek v. (110 Wis. 417) 279.
Milwaukee St. Ry. Co., Block v. (89 Wis. 371) 350, 402.
Deuster v. (89 Wis. 191) 232, 244, 426.
Hardy v. (89 Wis. 183) 393.
McCoy v. (82 Wis. 215) 394, 396.
McCoy v. (88 Wis. 56) 421, 436.
Mueller v. (86 Wis. 340) 322, 331.
Schmitt v. (89 Wis. 195) 393, 396, 433.
Slensby v. (95 Wis. 179) 267, 277.
Mingea, Elyton Land Co. v. (89 Ala. 521) 309.
Mingle, Chattanooga Elec. Ry. Co. v. (103 Tenn. 667) 345, 351.
Minneapolis St. Ry. Co., Anderson v. (42 Minn. 490) 275.
Beardsley v. (54 Minn. 504) 406.
Briggs v. (52 Minn. 36) 179.
Dahlberg v. (32 Minn. 404) 99.
Ekman v. (34 Minn. 24) 368.
Gagne v. (77 Minn. 171) 342.
Lowe v. (37 Minn. 283) 413, 421.
Mason v. (54 Minn. 216) 250, 253, 277.
Moldenhauer v. (80 Minn. 426) 408.
Peterson v. (95 N. W. [Minn.] 751) 216, 218, 243.
Piper v. (52 Minn. 269) 160.
Reed v. (34 Minn. 557) 254, 265.
Riley v. (80 Minn. 424) 293.
Watson v. (53 Minn. 551) 319, 405, 420.

[REFERENCES ARE TO PAGES.]

**Minneapolis** St. Ry. Co., Weiner v. (80 Minn. 312) 432.
Williams v. (92 N. W. [Minn.] 479) 361.
Wilson v. (74 Minn. 436) 320.
**Minster** v. Citizens' Ry. Co. (53 Mo. App. 276) 373, 377.
**Missouri** Pac. R. Co., Dougherty v. (9 Mo. App. 478) 128.
**Missouri** R. Co., Boland v. (36 Mo. 484) 253, 254, 263, 270, 278.
Dougherty v. (81 Mo. 325) 128.
Dougherty v. (97 Mo. 647) 406, 417.
Fortune v. (10 Mo. App. 252) 139, 140, 168.
Hunt v. (14 Mo. App. 160) 77, 79, 392.
Nissen v. (19 Mo. App. 662) 111.
Mitchell v. Broadway & S. A. R. Co. (70 Hun [N. Y.] 387) 413.
v. Electric Traction Co. (12 Pa. Super. Ct. 472) 92, 159.
v. Rochester Ry. Co. (151 N. Y. 107) 434.
v. Rochester Ry. Co. (4 Misc. [N. Y.] 575) 10.
v. Tacoma Ry. & Motor Co. (9 Wash. 120) 253, 256, 277, 395.
v. Tacoma Ry. & Motor Co. (13 Wash. 560) 256, 402, 412, 428.
v. Third Ave. R. Co. (62 App. Div. [N. Y.] 371) 216, 219, 235.
Mobile St. Ry. Co. v. Watters (135 Ala. 227) 174.
Mock v. Los Angeles Traction Co. (73 Pac. [Cal.] 455) 286.
Mogk v. Chicago City Ry. Co. (80 Ill. App. 411) 190.
Moldenhauer v. Minneapolis St. Ry. Co. (80 Minn. 426) 408.
Moll & Citizens' Ry. Co., Padgitt v. (159 Mo. 143) 28-30, 86.
Molyneux v. Southwest Missouri Elec. Ry. Co. (81 Mo. App. 25) 335
Monongahela St. Ry. Co., Mulhause v. (201 Pa. 237) 114.
Monroe v. Metropolitan St. Ry. Co. (80 N. Y. Supp. 177) 8, 55, 58.
Montgomery v. Buffalo Ry. Co. (165 N. Y. 139) 133, 180.
v. Johnson (22 Ky. L. R. 596, 58 S. W. 476) 324, 428.
v. Lansing City Elec. Ry. Co. (103 Mich. 46) 435.
Montgomery St. Ry. Co., Armstrong v. (123 Ala. 233) 92, 159.
v. Hastings (35 So. [Ala.] 412) 307, 333.
McDonald v. (110 Ala. 161) 147, 404.
v. Mason (133 Ala. 508) 157.
Moody v. Springfield St. Ry. Co. (182 Mass. 158) 85.
Moore v. Charlotte Elec. St. Ry. Co. (128 N. C. 455) 296, 315-317.
v. Kansas City & I. Rapid Transit Co. (126 Mo. 265) 314-317
319, 333.
Lincoln Traction Co. v. (97 N. W. [Neb.] 605) 335.
v. Lindell Ry. Co. (75 S. W. [Mo.] 672) 213.
v. Metropolitan R. Co. (2 Mackey [D. C.] 437) 253, 254.
Metropolitan St. R. Co. v. (83 Ga. 453) 23, 25, 77, 421.
v. Metropolitan St. Ry. Co. (84 App. Div. [N. Y.] 613) 297.
Moore's Adm'r, Richmond & M. Ry. Co. v. (94 Va. 493) 247.
Moores, City & Suburban Ry. Co. v. (80 Md. 348) 339.
Moran v. Detroit, Y. & A. A. Ry. Co. (124 Mich. 582) 296.
v. Versailles Traction Co. (188 Pa. 557) 152.
Morey v. Gloucester St. Ry. Co. (170 Mass. 164) 260.
Morgan, Jersey City & B. R. Co. v. (52 N. J. Law, 60) 174.

[REFERENCES ARE TO PAGES.]

Morhart v. North Jersey St. Ry. Co. (64 N. J. Law, 236) 343, 344, 366, 440.
Moritz v. Interurban St. Ry. Co. (84 N. Y. Supp. 162) 188.
Morris v. Atlantic Ave. R. Co. (116 N. Y. 552) 180.
v. Eighth Ave. R. Co. (68 Hun [N. Y.] 39) 61, 429.
v. Metropolitan St. Ry. Co. (51 App. Div. [N. Y.] 512) 415, 440.
v. Metropolitan St. Ry. Co. (63 App. Div. [N. Y.] 78) 296, 309, 325.
Morris' Adm'x, Norfolk & A. Terminal Co. v. (44 S. E. [Va.] 719) 53.
Morrissey v. Bridgeport Traction Co. (68 Conn. 215) 305, 323.
v. Westchester Elec. Ry. Co. (18 App. Div. [N. Y.] 67) 228, 245.
v. Westchester Elec. Ry. Co. (30 App. Div. [N. Y.] 424) 415.
Morrison v. Broadway & S. A. R. Co. (130 N. Y. 166) 38-40, 46.
Morrow v. Delaware County & P. Elec. Ry. Co. (199 Pa. 156) 293.
v. St. Paul City Ry. Co. (74 Minn. 480) 404.
v. Westchester Elec. Ry. Co. (54 App. Div. [N. Y.] 592) 407.
Morvilius, Ft. Wayne Traction Co. v. (68 N. E. [Ind. App.] 304) 13, 141, 157.
Moser v. South Covington & C. St. Ry. Co. (74 S. W. [Ky.] 1090) 74.
v. Union Traction Co. (205 Pa. 481) 291.
Moses v. Newburgh Elec. Ry. Co. (91 Hun [N. Y.] 278) 400.
Moss v. Philadelphia Traction Co. (180 Pa. 389) 278.
Motel v. Sixth Ave. R. Co. (2 How. Pr. [N. S.; N. Y.] 30) 261.
Mound City St. Ry. Co., Watson v. (133 Mo. 246) 210, 213, 235.
Mt. Adams & E. P. R. Co. v. Cavagna (6 Ohio Cir. Ct. R. 606) 274.
v. Wysong (2 Ohio Dec. 65) 143.
Mt. Adams & E. P. I. Ry. Co. v. Doherty (8 Ohio Cir. Ct. R. 349) 182, 185.
v. Lowery (74 Fed. 463) 124.
v. Lowry (68 Fed. 827) 419.
v. Reul (4 Ohio Cir. Ct. R. 362) 98, 106.
Mt. Auburn Cable Co., Brooks v. (29 Wkly. Law Bul. [Ohio] 50) 10, 45.
Mowbray v. Brooklyn Heights R. Co. (59 App. Div. [N. Y.] 239) 422.
Moylan v. Second Ave. R. Co. (128 N. Y. 583) 38, 39, 49, 59, 85.
Mozely, West End & A. St. Ry. Co. v. (79 Ga. 463) 144.
Muckle v. Rochester Ry. Co. (79 Hun [N. Y.] 32) 192, 195, 197, 201, 437.
Muehlhausen v. St. Louis R. Co. (91 Mo. 332) 23, 25.
Mueller v. Milwaukee St. Ry. Co. (86 Wis. 340) 322, 331.
West Chicago St. R. Co. v. (165 Ill. 499) 393.
West Chicago St. R. Co. v. (64 Ill. App. 601) 392.
Muessman v. Metropolitan St. Ry. Co. (76 App. Div. [N. Y.] 1) 213.
Muhlhause v. Monongahela St. Ry. Co. (201 Pa. 237) 114.
Mulcahy v. Electric Traction Co. (185 Pa. 427) 279.
Muldoon v. Seattle City Ry. Co. (7 Wash. 528) 22, 65, 66, 68, 70.
v. Seattle City Ry. Co. (10 Wash. 311) 22.

[REFERENCES ARE TO PAGES.]

Muldowney v. Pittsburgh & B. Traction Co. (8 Pa. Super. Ct. 335) 175, 176.
Mulhado v. Brooklyn City R. Co. (30 N. Y. 370) 142, 150.
Mulhair v. West Philadelphia Pass. Ry. Co. (5 Wkly. Notes Cas. [Pa.] 190) 241.
West Philadelphia Pass. Ry. Co. v. (6 Wkly. Notes Cas. [Pa.] 580) 241.
Mullady v. Brooklyn Heights R. Co. (65 App. Div. [N. Y.] 540) 430.
Mullane v. Houston, W. St. & P. Ferry R. Co. (21 Misc. [N. Y.] 10) 388.
Mullen v. Central Park & E. R. R. Co. (1 Misc. [N. Y.] 216) 306, 330.
v. Philadelphia Traction Co. (19 Phila. [Pa.] 441) 354.
v. Springfield St. Ry. Co. (164 Mass. 450) 261.
Muller v. Brooklyn Heights R. Co. (18 App. Div. [N. Y.] 177) 252, 276.
Mulligan v. Metropolitan St. Ry. Co. (85 N. Y. Supp. 791) 8, 55, 58.
v. Third Ave. R. Co. (87 App. Div. [N. Y.] 320) 219.
v. Third Ave. R. Co. (61 App. Div. [N. Y.] 214) 242.
Mumford, Chicago City Ry. Co. v. (97 Ill. 560) 139, 140, 143.
Muncie St. Ry. Co. v. Mayard (5 Ind. App. 372) 336.
Munroe v. Third Ave. R. Co. (50 N. Y. Super. Ct. 114) 139, 140, 143, 152.
Murdock v. Oakland, S. L. & H. Elec. Ry. Co. (128 Cal. 22) 373, 374.
Murphy v. Central Park, N. & E. R. R. Co. (48 N. Y. Super. Ct. 96) 192, 437.
v. Coney Island & B. R. Co. (65 App. Div. [N. Y.] 546) 390.
v. Coney Island & B. R. Co. (36 Hun [N. Y.] 199) 128.
v. Derby St. Ry. Co. (73 Conn. 249) 254.
v. Lindell Ry. Co. (153 Mo. 252) 246.
v. Metropolitan St. Ry. Co. (19 Misc. [N. Y.] 194) 142.
v. Nassau Elec. R. Co. (19 App. Div. [N. Y.] 583) 300.
v. Ninth Ave. R. Co. (6 Misc. [N. Y.] 298) 88, 95.
v. Suburban Rapid Transit Co. (60 N. Y. Super. Ct. 9) 361.
v. Union Ry. Co. (118 Mass. 228) 33, 178, 186.
Murray v. Brooklyn City R. Co. (7 N. Y. Supp. 900) 111, 131.
Cincinnati St. Ry. Co. v. (53 Ohio St. 570) 126.
v. Forty-Second St., M. & St. N. Ave. R. Co. (9 App. Div. [N. Y.] 610) 240.
v. Paterson Ry. Co. (61 N. J. Law, 301) 270.
v. Pawtuxet Valley St. Ry. Co. (55 Atl. [R. I.] 491) 113.
v. Salt Lake City R. Co. (16 Utah, 356) 411.
v. St. Louis Cable & W. Ry. Co. (98 Mo. 573) 386.
v. St. Louis Transit Co. (75 S. W. [Mo.] 611) 293, 325.
Musa, West Chicago St. R. Co. v. (80 Ill. App. 223) 432.
Muskegon Ry. Co., Cowan v. (84 Mich. 583) 365.
Musser v. Lancaster City St. Ry. Co. (176 Pa. 621) 367, 412.
v. Lancaster City St. Ry. Co. (15 Pa. Co. Ct. R. 430) 429.
Muth, San Antonio St. Ry. Co. v. (7 Tex. Civ. App. 443) 395.
Myers v. Brantford St. Ry. (27 Ont. App. 513) 335.
v. Brooklyn Heights R. Co. (10 App. Div. [N. Y.] 335) 21.

[REFERENCES ARE TO PAGES.]

## N.

Nash, West Chicago St. R. Co. v. (166 Ill. 528) 394.
West Chicago St. R. Co. v. (64 Ill. App. 548) 102.
Nashua St. Ry. Co., Smith v. (69 N. H. 504) 365.
Nashville St. Ry. Co. v. Norman (108 Tenn. 324) 320, 328.
Nashville St. Ry. Co. v. Griffin (104 Tenn. 81) 192, 194, 424, 437.
v. O'Bryan (104 Tenn. 28) 427, 437.
Nassau Elec. R. Co., Adams v. (41 App. Div. [N. Y.] 334) 279.
Adams v. (51 App. Div. [N. Y.] 241) 283.
Bachrach v. (54 N. Y. Supp. 958) 49.
Bergold v. (30 App. Div. [N. Y.] 438) 310.
Bossert v. (40 App. Div. [N. Y.] 144) 301.
Braham v. (72 App. Div. [N. Y.] 456) 351.
Brainard v. (44 App. Div. [N. Y.] 613) 83, 84.
Clarke v. (9 App. Div. [N. Y.] 151) 350.
Ehrmann v. (23 App. Div. [N. Y.] 21) 264.
Flack v. (41 App. Div. [N. Y.] 399) 157.
Hanna v. (18 App. Div. [N. Y.] 137) 22, 68, 180, 196.
Harvey v. (35 App. Div. [N. Y.] 307) 236, 237.
Hassen v. (34 App. Div. [N. Y.] 71) 83, 84, 132.
Henderson v. (46 App. Div. [N. Y.] 280) 83, 85.
Hickman v. (36 App. Div. [N. Y.] 376) 214, 238.
Hickman v. (41 App. Div. [N. Y.] 629) 218.
Hicks v. (47 App. Div. [N. Y.] 479) 257.
Huber v. (22 App. Div. [N. Y.] 426) 319, 325.
Keiffert v. (51 App. Div. [N. Y.] 301) 424.
Levitt v. (14 App. Div. [N. Y.] 83) 431.
McCormack v. (16 App. Div. [N. Y.] 24) 297, 329.
McCormack v. (18 App. Div. [N. Y.] 333) 311.
Murphy v. (19 App. Div. [N. Y.] 583) 300.
O'Flaherty v. (34 App. Div. [N. Y.] 74) 351.
Poulsen v. (18 App. Div. [N. Y.] 221) 102, 108.
Poulsen v. (30 App. Div. [N. Y.] 246) 108.
Regensburg v. (58 App. Div. [N. Y.] 566) 104, 125.
Robson v. (80 App. Div. [N. Y.] 301) 125.
Savage v. (42 App. Div. [N. Y.] 241) 379.
Schlitz v. (44 App. Div. [N. Y.] 542) 292.
Smith v. (57 App. Div. [N. Y.] 152) 426.
Snediker v. (41 App. Div. [N. Y.] 628) 121.
Stemmerman v. (36 App. Div. [N. Y.] 218) 414.
Still v. (32 App. Div. [N. Y.] 276) 73.
Taylor v. (32 App. Div. [N. Y.] 486) 195.
Vitelli v. (53 App. Div. [N. Y.] 639) 296.
Weitzman v. (33 App. Div. [N. Y.] 585) 264, 285.
Wilson v. (56 App. Div. [N. Y.] 570) 411.
Neal v. Wilmington & N. C. Elec. Ry. Co. (3 Pen. [Del.] 467) 349.
Nealand v. Lynn & B. R. Co. (173 Mass. 42) 384.

[REFERENCES ARE TO PAGES.]

Neff v. Harrisburg Traction Co. (192 Pa. 501) 146.
Nein v. La Crosse City Ry. Co. (92 Fed. 85) 343.
Nelson v. Crescent City R. Co. (49 La. Ann. 491) 276.
Little Rock Traction & Electric Co. v. (66 Ark. 494) 23, 25, 27, 58.
North Chicago St. R. Co. v. (79 Ill. App. 229) 217.
Nesbit, Denver Tramway Co. v. (22 Colo. 408) 371, 373, 376.
Neslie v. Second & Third Sts. Pass. Ry. Co. (113 Pa. 300) 106, 151, 156, 164.
Neversink Mountain R. Co., Fleishman v. (174 Pa. 510) 279.
Newark Pass. Ry. Co. v. Block (55 N. J. Law, 605) 209, 217, 219, 220, 234.
Newark & S. O. R. Co. v. McCann (58 N. J. Law, 642) 104, 136.
Newburgh Elec. Ry. Co., Leyh v. (41 App. Div. [N. Y.] 218) 112.
Moses v. (91 Hun [N. Y.] 278) 400.
Strauss v. (6 App. Div. [N. Y.] 264) 309, 329.
Newburyport & A. Horse R. Co., Quested v. (127 Mass. 204) 137.
New Castle Electric St. Ry. Co., Kroesen v. (198 Pa. 26) 275.
Kroesen v. (198 Pa. 30) 264.
Newhart v. St. Paul City Ry. Co. (51 Minn. 42) 376.
New Haven St. Ry. Co., Nugent v. (73 Conn. 139) 88.
Newman v. Phillipsburg Horse Car Co. (52 N. J. Law, 446) 251, 254.
New Jersey Elec. Ry. Co. v. Miller (59 N. J. Law, 423) 318.
New Jersey R. & T. Co., Bennett (36 N. J. Law, 225) 125.
New Jersey Traction Co., Danbeck v. (57 N. J. Law, 463) 23, 24, 26, 77.
v. Gardner (58 N. J. Law, 176) 141.
v. Gardner (60 N. J. Law, 571) 139, 140.
New Orleans City R. Co., Campbell v. (104 La. 183) 279.
Childs v. (33 La. Ann. 154) 227.
Palmicano v (108 La. 243) 281.
Wardle v. (35 La. Ann. 202) 142, 153.
New Orleans, C. & L. R. Co., Bemiss v. (47 La. Ann. 1671) 94.
Byrd v. (43 La. Ann. 822) 477.
Conway v. (51 La. Ann. 146) 243.
Dieck v. (51 La. Ann. 262) 293.
Gannon v. (48 La. Ann. 1002) 270, 272.
Hemingway v. (50 La. Ann. 1087) 328.
Kramer v. (51 La. Ann. 1689) 223, 240.
Lafitte v. (43 La. Ann. 34) 190.
Lott v. (37 La. Ann. 337) 114.
Mahnke v. (104 La. 411) 355.
O'Rourke v. (51 La. Ann. 755) 272.
Sibley v. (49 La. Ann. 588) 87.
Webster v. (51 La. Ann. 299) 213.
New Orleans & C. R. Co., Barksdull v. (23 La. Ann. 180) 262.
Canedo v. (52 La. Ann. 2149) 216.
Conway v. (46 La. Ann. 1429) 142.
De Lucas v. (38 La. Ann. 930) 195.

[REFERENCES ARE TO PAGES.]

New Orleans & C. R. Co., Farrar v. (52 La. Ann. 417) 216, 237.
Forman v. (40 La. Ann. 446) 172.
Govan v. (35 So. [La.] 484) 372.
Gretzner v. (105 La. 266) 150.
Holzab v. (38 La. Ann. 185) 125.
Kaiser v. (107 La. 539) 260.
McLaughlin v. (48 La. Ann. 23) 279.
Mercier v. (23 La. Ann. 264) 291.
Schneidau v. (48 La. Ann. 866) 279.
v. Schneider (60 Fed. 210) 425.
Schwartz v. (34 So. [La.] 667) 243.
Weber v. (104 La. 367) 61.
Weeks v. (32 La. Ann. 615) 212, 223.
New Orleans & L. S. R. Co., Nivette v. (42 La. Ann. 1153) 363.
New Orleans & N. R. Co., Erslew v. (49 La. Ann. 86) 363.
Newport News & O. P. Ry. Co. v. Bradford (40 S. E. [Va.] 900) 425.
Newport St. R. Co. v. Johnson (2 Ky. L. R. 225) 121.
Newport St. Ry. Co., Elliott v. (18 R. I. 707) 83, 84, 87, 103, 420.
Newton St. Ry. Co., Creavin v. (176 Mass. 529) 296.
New York Condensed Milk Co., Hobson v. (25 App. Div. [N. Y.] 111) 373.
New York & B. Brew. Co., Hurley v. (13 App. Div. [N. Y.] 167) 124.
New York & H. R. Co., Mazetti v. (3 E. D. Smith [N. Y.] 98) 361.
Oldfield v. (14 N. Y. 310) 256.
New York & Q. C. Ry. Co., Clancy v. (81 N. Y. Supp. 875) 351.
Koehne v. (32 App. Div. [N. Y.] 419; affirmed 165 N. Y. 603) 102.
Schmedding v. (82 N. Y. Supp. 1034) 320.
Totarella v. (53 App. Div. [N. Y.] 413) 285.
New York & S. B. Ry. Co., Kelly v. (109 N. Y. 44) 96, 112, 164.
New York Steam Co., Francis v. (114 N. Y. 380) 99.
Niagara Gorge R. Co., True v. (70 App. Div. [N. Y.] 383) 375, 377.
Niagara Junction Ry. Co., Einsfeld v. (49 App. Div. [N. Y.] 470) 379.
Nichols v. Brooklyn City R. Co. (30 Hun [N. Y.] 437) 401.
v. Lynn & B. R. Co. (168 Mass. 528) 404.
v. Middlesex R. Co. (106 Mass. 463) 163.
v. Sixth Ave. R. Co. (38 N. Y. 131) 93, 160.
Nicholsburg v. Second Ave. R. Co. (11 Misc. [N. Y.] 432) 311.
Nieboer v. Detroit Electric Ry. Co. (128 Mich. 486) 91.
Nies v. Brooklyn Heights R. Co. (68 App. Div. [N. Y.] 259) 84, 130.
Nilson, West Chicago St. R. Co. v. (70 Ill. App. 171) 209, 225.
Ninth Ave. R. Co., Hill v. (109 N. Y. 239) 123.
Mallard v. (15 Daly [N. Y.] 376) 259, 277.
Mettlestadt v. (27 N. Y. Super. Ct. 377) 147.
Murphy v. (6 Misc. [N. Y.] 298) 88, 95.
Nissen v. Missouri R. Co. (19 Mo. App. 662) 111.
Nivette v. New Orleans & L. S. R. Co. (42 La. Ann. 1153) 363.
Noble v. St. Joseph & B. H. St. Ry. Co. (98 Mich. 249) 135.
Noe v. Rapid Ry. Co. (94 N. W. [Mich.] 743) 386, 388.

[REFERENCES ARE TO PAGES.]

Nolan v. Brooklyn City & N. R. Co. (87 N. Y. 63) 64, 68, 70, 131.
Calumet Elec. St. Ry. Co. v. (69 Ill. App. 104) 359.
Galveston City Ry. Co. v. (53 Tex. 139) 363.
v. Metropolitan St. Ry. Co. (65 App. Div. [N. Y.] 184) 232.
Noll v. St. Louis Transit Co. (73 S. W. [Mo. App.] 907) 302, 327.
Noonan v. Consolidated Traction Co. (64 N. J. Law, 579) 309.
Norfolk & A. Terminal Co. v. Morris' Adm'x (44 S. E. [Va.] 719) 53.
Norfolk Ry. & Light Co. v. Corletto (41 S. E. [Va.] 740) 235.
Norman v. Middlesex & S. Traction Co. (68 N. J. Law, 728) 386.
Nashville Ry. Co. v. (108 Tenn. 324) 320, 328.
Norris v. Brooklyn City R. Co. (4 Misc. [N. Y.] 294) 79.
Memphis St. R. Co. v. (108 Tenn. 632) 123.
Northampton St. Ry. Co., Robinson v. (157 Mass. 224) 163.
North Baltimore Pass. Ry. Co. v. Arnreich (78 Md. 589) 210, 235.
North Beach & M. R. Co., Pleasants v. (34 Cal. 586) 181, 432.
Turner v. (34 Cal. 594) 181, 432.
Schierhold v. (40 Cal. 447) 262, 270, 409.
Wheaton v. (36 Cal. 590) 413, 425.
North Birmingham Ry. Co. v. Liddicoat (99 Ala. 545) 2, 3, 27, 38, 40, 42.
North Birmingham St. Ry. Co. v. Calderwood (89 Ala. 247) 158, 163, 169.
v. Calderwood (96 Ala. 318) 146.
v. Wright (130 Ala. 419) 382.
North Chicago City Ry. Co. v. Gastka (27 Ill. App. 518) 393.
v. Gastka (128 Ill. 613) 171, 183, 187, 189, 190.
North Chicago Elec. Ry. Co. v. Peuser (190 Ill. 67) 313, 314, 316.
North Chicago St. R. Co. v. Allen (82 Ill. App. 128) 324.
v. Anderson (176 Ill. 635) 393.
v. Anderson (70 Ill. App. 336) 413, 418.
v. Barber (77 Ill. App. 257) 435.
v. Barger (54 Ill. App. 284) 20.
v. Baur (179 Ill. 126) 79.
v. Baur (79 Ill. App. 121) 92, 159.
v. Boyd (57 Ill. App. 535) 119, 395.
v. Broms (62 Ill. App. 127) 432.
v. Brown (178 Ill. 187) 93, 160.
v. Brown (76 Ill. App. 654) 421.
v. Conway (76 Ill. App. 621) 385.
v. Cook (145 Ill. 551) 52, 54, 60, 401.
v. Cook (43 Ill. App. 634) 5, 6, 54, 401.
v. Duehner (85 Ill. App. 602) 434.
v. Dudgeon (69 Ill. App. 57) 375, 377.
v. Dudgeon (83 Ill. App. 528) 377, 394, 417.
v. Eldridge (151 Ill. 542) 96.
v. Eldridge (51 Ill. App. 430) 413, 417.
v. Fitzgibbons (180 Ill. App. 466) 393, 396.
v. Fitzgibbons (79 Ill. App. 632) 393, 396, 418.

[REFERENCES ARE TO PAGES.]

North Chicago St. R. Co. v. Gillow (166 Ill. 444) 403.
v. Harms (59 Ill. App. 374) 339.
v. Hoffart (82 Ill. App. 539) 277, 413, 414.
v. Irwin (202 Ill. 345) 343.
v. Kaspers (186 Ill. 246) 12, 404.
v. Kaspers (85 Ill. App. 316) 12, 38, 40.
Kirton v. (91 Ill. App. 554) 184, 436.
v. Lehman (82 Ill. App. 238) 433, 435.
v. Louis (35 Ill. App. 477) 211, 244.
v. Martin (51 Ill. App. 247) 220.
v. Nelson (79 Ill. App. 229) 217.
v. Olds (40 Ill. App. 421) 32, 171, 186.
v. Olds (64 Ill. App. 595) 32, 171.
v. Polkey (67 N. E. [Ill.] 793) 89.
v. Rodert (67 N. E. [Ill.] 812) 325.
Schaefer v. (82 Ill. App. 473) 186.
Schneider v. (80 Ill. App. 306) 48.
v. Schwartz (82 Ill. App. 493) 128.
v. Shreve (70 Ill. App. 666) 414.
v. Smadraff (89 Ill. App. 411) 313, 314, 421.
v. Southwick (66 Ill. App. 241) 92, 159.
Wallen v. (82 Ill. App. 103) 237.
v. Williams (140 Ill. 275) 2, 11, 20, 21, 38-40, 42, 83, 88.
v. Williams (40 Ill. App. 590) 88.
v. Wiswell (168 Ill. 613) 38, 40, 45.
v. Wiswell (68 Ill. App. 443) 431.
v. Wrixon (150 Ill. 532) 414.
v. Wrixon (51 Ill. App. 307) 112, 141, 146, 430, 434, 438, 440.
v. Zeiger (78 Ill. App. 463) 317.
v. Zeiger (182 Ill. 9) 396, 413.
North Chicago St. Ry. Co., Basch v. (40 Ill. App. 583) 10, 49.
v. Brodie (156 Ill. 317) 440.
v. Brodie (57 Ill. App. 564) 413, 440.
v. Cotton (140 Ill. 486) 119, 405.
v. Cotton (41 Ill. App. 311) 119, 435.
v. Hudson (44 Ill. App. 60) 407.
v. Johnson (68 N. E. [Ill.] 463) 273.
v. Thurston (43 Ill. App. 587) 28, 29.
North Hudson County Ry. Co. v. Anderson (61 N. J. Law, 248) 175.
Dusenbury v. (66 N. J. Law, 44) 115, 118.
v. Flanagan (57 N. J. Law, 696) 279.
McKenna v. (64 N. J. Law, 106) 413, 429.
v. May (48 N. J. Law, 401) 411.
Rochat v. (49 N. J. Law, 445) 129.
Schwanewede v. (67 N. J. Law, 449) 291.
Spurr v. (56 N. J. Law, 346) 137.
North Jersey St. Ry. Co., Daniel v. (64 N. J. Law, 603) 180.
Daum v. (54 Atl. [N. J. Law] 221) 229, 246.

[REFERENCES ARE TO PAGES.]

North Jersey St. Ry. Co., Dennis v. (64 N. J. Law, 439) 293, 294.
Fielders v. (67 N. J. Law, 76) 358.
Feuig v. (64 N. J. Law, 715) 142.
Grieve v. (65 N. J. Law, 409) 91.
Hansen v. (64 N. J. Law, 686) 102.
McGrath v. (66 N. J. Law, 312) 209, 213, 217.
Morhart v. (64 N. J. Law, 236) 343, 344, 366, 440.
Perrine v. (54 Atl. [N. J. Law] 799) 196, 201.
Schmidt v. (66 N. J. Law, 424) 38, 39, 49.
Sickler v. (46 Atl. [N. J. Law] 779) 330.
Vogel v. (54 Atl. [N. J. Law] 563) 252.
Woodland v. (66 N. J. Law, 455) 297, 319.
Zeliff v. (55 Atl. [N. J. Law] 96) 100.
North Kankakee St. Ry. Co. v. Blatchford (81 Ill. App. 609) 251.
North Park St. Ry. Co., Knottnerus v. (93 Mich. 348) 247.
Rouser v. (97 Mich. 565) 196, 202.
North & South St. R. Co., Outen v. (94 Ga. 662) 147.
North Side St. Ry. Co. v. Tippens (4 Willson, Civ. Cas. Ct. App. [Tex.] § 160) 336.
v. Want (4 Willson, Civ. Cas. Ct. App. [Tex.] § 168) 322.
Northern Texas Traction Co., Shelton v. (75 S. W. [Tex. Civ. App.] 338) 354.
Northridge v. Atlantic Ave. R. Co. (15 Misc. [N. Y.] 66) 315, 319, 326.
Norton v. Third Ave. R. Co. (26 App. Div. [N. Y.] 60) 158.
Norton & T. St. Ry. Co., Vincent v. (180 Mass. 104) 302, 327.
Norwalk Tramway Co., Horton v. (66 Conn. 272) 104.
Nugent, Baltimore City Pass. Ry. Co. v. (86 Md. 349) 101, 102, 110, 403.
v. Metropolitan St. Ry. Co. (17 App. Div. [N. Y.] 582) 275.
v. New Haven St. Ry. Co. (73 Conn. 139) 88.
v. Philadelphia Traction Co. (181 Pa. 160) 218, 226.
Nusshaum v. Louisville Ry. Co. (28 Ky. L. R. 271, 57 S. W. 249) 182, 397.
Nye v. Marysville & Y. C. St. R. Co. (97 Cal. 461) 33, 171, 182.

## O.

Oakland & B. Rapid Transit Co., Donovan v. (102 Cal. 245) 356.
Oakland Consol. St. Ry. Co., Fox v. (118 Cal. 55) 255, 266, 267, 392, 430, 434, 438.
Howland v. (110 Cal. 513) 413, 417.
Redfield v. (110 Cal. 277) 136, 413, 417, 438.
Oakland Ry. Co. v. Fielding (48 Pa. 320) 358.
Oakland, S. L. & H. Elec. Ry. Co., Johnsen v. (127 Cal. 608) 117, 133, 408.
Murdock v. (128 Cal. 22) 373, 374.
Siemsen v. (134 Cal. 494) 119.
Oates v. Metropolitan St. Ry. Co. (168 Mo. 535) 337.

[REFERENCES ARE TO PAGES.]

Ober v. Crescent City R. Co. (44 La. Ann. 1059) 139, 148, 158.
O'Brien, Denver Tramway Co. v. (8 Colo. App. 74) 384, 387, 388.
v. West End St. Ry. Co. (173 Mass. 105) 383.
O'Bryan, Nashville St. Ry. Co. v. (104 Tenn. 28) 427, 437.
O'Callaghan v. Metropolitan St. Ry. Co. (69 App. Div. [N. Y.] 574) 299, 326.
O'Connell v. St. Louis Cable & W. Ry. Co. (106 Mo. 482) 52, 53, 101, 102, 421.
v. St. Paul City Ry. Co. (64 Minn. 466) 291.
O'Connor v. Union Ry. Co. (67 App. Div. [N. Y.] 99) 230, 245.
West Chicago St. R. Co. v. (85 Ill. App. 278) 366.
Oddy v. West End St. Ry. Co. (178 Mass. 341) 163.
O'Flaherty v. Nassau Elec. R. Co. (34 App. Div. [N. Y.] 74) 351.
v. Union Ry. Co. (45 Mo. 70) 251, 253, 255, 264, 266, 270.
Ogden City St. Ry. Co., Hall v. (13 Utah, 243) 299, 315-317, 321, 328, 408.
Ogier v. Albany Ry. Co. (88 Hun [N. Y.] 486) 280.
O'Keefe v. Eighth Ave. R. Co. (33 App. Div. [N. Y.] 324) 419.
v. St. Louis & S. R. Co. (81 Mo. App. 386) 210, 235, 238.
Old Colony St. Ry. Co., Cassady v. (68 N. E. [Mass.] 10) 108.
Foster v. (182 Mass. 378) 165.
Timms v. (66 N. E. [Mass.] 797) 79, 129.
Oldfield v. New York & H. R. Co. (14 N. Y. 310) 256.
Olds, North Chicago St. R. Co. v. (40 Ill. App. 421) 32, 171; 186.
North Chicago St. R. Co. v. (64 Ill. App. 595) 32, 171.
Olfermann v. Union Depot R. Co. (125 Mo. 408) 167, 392.
O'Leary v. Brockton St. Ry. Co. (177 Mass. 187) 331.
Olis, Chicago City Ry. Co. v. (94 Ill. App. 323) 396.
Oliver v. Denver Tramway Co. (13 Colo. App. 543) 210, 235.
Olsen v. Citizens' Ry. Co. (152 Mo. 426) 123.
Omaha Horse Ry. Co. v. Doolittle (7 Neb. 481) 421.
Haman v. (35 Neb. 74) 182, 183.
Omaha St. Ry. Co. v. Baker (44 Neb. 511) 58.
v. Cameron (43 Neb. 297) 320.
v. Clair (39 Neb. 454) 244.
v. Craig (39 Neb. 601) 92, 151, 159.
v. Duvall (40 Neb. 29) 346.
v. Emminger (57 Neb. 240) 401, 433.
v. Larson (97 N. W. [Neb.] 824) 321.
Leigh v. (36 Neb. 131) 381, 383.
v. Loehneisen (40 Neb. 37) 225, 233, 235.
v. Martin (48 Neb. 65) 38-40, 60.
Mathieson v. (92 N. W. [Neb.] 639) 328.
Pray v. (44 Neb. 167) 80, 81, 106.
U. P. Steam Baking Co. v. (94 N. W. [Neb.] 533) 305.
Omaha & C. B. R. & B. Co., Bryant v. (98 Iowa, 483) 422.
v. Levinston (49 Neb. 17) 144.
Wilkins v. (96 Iowa, 668) 302, 327, 408, 424.

[REFERENCES ARE TO PAGES.]

O'Malley v. Scranton Traction Co. (191 Pa. 410) 229.
O'Mara v. St. Louis Transit Co. (76 S. W. [Mo. App.] 680) 6, **38**, 39, 55, 57.
Omnibus Cable Co., Doolin v. (125 Cal. 141) 414.
  Doolin v. (73 Pac. [Cal.] 1060) 118.
  Finkledey v. (114 Cal. 28) 6, 38-40, 42, 57, 60.
  Sutter v. (107 Cal. 369) 285.
Omnibus R. Co., Robbins v. (32 Cal. 472) 363.
Omslaer v. Pittsburgh & B. Traction Co. (168 Pa. 519) 290, 294.
O'Neil v. Dry Dock, E. B. & B. R. Co. (59 N. Y. Super. Ct. 123) 402, 405.
  v. Dry Dock, E. B. & B. R. Co. (129 N. Y. 125) 319.
  Edgerton v. (4 Kan. App. 73) 311, 314, 319, 435.
  v. Lynn & B. R. Co. (180 Mass. 576) 166.
O'Neill v. Lynn & B. R. Co. (155 Mass. 371) 71, 412.
  v. Third Ave. R. Co. (3 Misc. [N. Y.] 521) 315, 316.
Oppenheimer v. Manhattan Ry. Co. (18 N. Y. Supp. 411) 185.
Orbann, Philadelphia Traction Co. v. (119 Pa. 37) 28, 35, 436.
  v. Philadelphia Traction Co. (19 Phila. 413) 416.
Orleans R. Co., Dominguez v. (35 La. Ann. 751) 355.
  Stucke v. (50 La. Ann. 172) 376.
O'Reilly v. Brooklyn Heights R. Co. (85 N. Y. Supp. 572) 215.
O'Rourke v. Lindell Ry. Co. (142 Mo. 312) 119.
  v. New Orleans, C. & L. R. Co. (51 La. Ann. 755) 272.
  v. Street Railway Co. (103 Tenn. 124) 197, 199, 410.
  v. Yonkers R. Co. (32 App. Div. [N. Y.] 8) 319.
Orr v. Cedar Rapids & M. C. R. Co. (94 Iowa, 423) 293, 321, 409, **412**.
Ortlip v. Philadelphia & W. C. Traction Co. (198 Pa. 586) 378, 381.
Osborn, Cleveland City Ry. Co. v. (66 Ohio St. 45) 125.
Osgood v. Los Angeles Traction Co. (137 Cal. 280) 119.
Oster v. Schuylkill Traction Co. (195 Pa. 320) 283.
Oswego St. Ry. Co., Watson v. (7 Misc. [N. Y.] 562) 181.
O'Toole v. Central Park, N. R. & E. R. R. Co. (12 N. Y. Supp. 347) 223.
  v. Pittsburg & L. E. R. Co (158 Pa. 99) 125, 127.
Ottawa Electric Ry. Co., Davis v. (28 Ont. 654) 180.
Outen v. North & South St. R. Co. (94 Ga. 662) 147.
Ovington v. Lowell & S. St. R. Co. (163 Mass. 440) 365.
Owen, Selma St. & S. Ry. Co. v. (132 Ala. 420) 125, 126.
Owens, Denver Tramway Co. v. (20 Colo. 107) 146, 393, 404.
  v. People's Pass. Ry. Co. (155 Pa. 334) 229, 245.
Owensboro City R. Co. v. Hill (21 Ky. L. R. 1638) 236, 237.
  v. Lyddane (19 Ky. L. R. 698, 41 S. W. 578) 337, 408.
Owings, Atlanta Consol. St. Ry. Co. v. (97 Ga. 663) 349, 421, 439.

## P.

Packer, Covington St. Ry. Co. v. (9 Bush [Ky.] 455) 434, 438.
Padgitt v. Moll & Citizens' Ry. Co. (159 Mo. 143) 28-30, 86.

[REFERENCES ARE TO PAGES.]

Paducah Ry. & Light Co., Floyd v. (73 S. W. [Ky.] 1122) 210, 235.
Paducah St. Ry. Co. v. Adkin's Adm'r (14 Ky. L. R. 425) 252, 253, 272, 397.
Macon v. (23 Ky. L. R. 46) 349, 353.
v. Walsh (22 Ky. L. R. 532) 142.
Palmer v. Warren St. Ry. Co. (56 Atl. [Pa.] 49) 119, 121.
v. Winona Ry. & Light Co. (78 Minn. 138) 168.
Palmeri v. Manhattan Ry. Co. (133 N. Y. 261) 188, 190.
Palmisano v. New Orleans City Ry. Co. (180 La. 243) 281.
Park, Louisville R. Co. v. (96 Ky. 580) 14, 102, 142, 165, 423.
Parker v. Metropolitan St. Ry. Co. (69 Mo. App. 54) 102, 123.
Parkes v. Metropolitan St. Ry. Co. (76 N. Y. Supp. 983) 358.
Parkinson v. Concord St. Ry. Co. (71 N. H. 28) 210, 236.
Pasadena P. Ry. Co., Holloway v. (130 Cal. 177) 65, 68, 106, 131.
Pascoshell v. Twenty-Third St. R. Co. (23 N. Y. Wkly. Dig. 200) 276.
Passamaneck's Adm'r v. Louisville Ry. Co. (98 Ky. 195) 250, 255, 268, 270.
Passenger R. Co. v. Young (21 Ohio St. 518) 188.
Smith v. (13 Phila. 6) 97.
Paterson v. Inclined Plane Ry. Co. (5 Ohio S. & C. P. Dec. 665) 155.
Paterson Ry. Co., Murray v. (61 N. J. Law, 301) 270.
Patterson v. Townsend (91 Iowa, 725) 314.
Washington & G. R. Co. v. (9 App. D. C. 423) 12.
v. Westchester Elec. Ry. Co. (26 App. Div. [N. Y.] 336) 139, 148.
Patton v. Philadelphia Traction Co. (132 Pa. 76) 307, 328.
Paulson v. Brooklyn City R. Co. (13 Misc. [N. Y.] 387) 40, 47.
Pawtucket St. Ry. Co., Sanford v. (19 R. I. 537) 356, 365.
Pawtuxet Valley St. Ry. Co., Murray v. (55 Atl. [R. I.] 491) 113.
Payne, Danville St. Car Co. v. (24 S. E. [Va.] 904) 133.
v. Forty-Second St. & G. St. Ferry R. Co. (40 N. Y. Super. Ct. 8) 98.
v. Spokane St. Ry. Co. (15 Wash. 522) 103.
Peacock, Central Ry. Co. v. (69 Md. 257) 14.
Pearson, Pittsburg, A. & M. Ry. Co. v. (72 Pa. 169) 266, 267.
State v. (34 So. [La.] 575) 181.
v. Union Ry. Co. (14 Mo. App. 579) 271.
Pechesky v. Metropolitan St. Ry. Co. (30 Misc. [N. Y.] 432) 304.
Peetz v. St. Charles St. R. Co. (42 La. Ann. 541) 360, 395.
Pelletier, Chicago City Ry. Co. v. (134 Ill. 120) 32, 171, 177, 182, 184.
Chicago City Ry. Co. v. (33 Ill. App. 455) 32, 176.
Pelletreau v. Metropolitan St. Ry. Co. (74 App. Div. [N. Y.] 192) 225, 242.
Pelzer, South Covington & C. St. Ry. Co. v. (19 Ky. L. R. 88, 39 S. W. 496) 425.
Pendleton St. R. Co. v. Rahmann (22 Ohio St. 446) 414.
v. Shires (18 Ohio St. 255) 233, 235.
v. Stallman (22 Ohio St. 1) 320.
Pendergast v. Union Ry. Co. (10 App. Div. [N. Y.] 207) 112.

[REFERENCES ARE TO PAGES.]

Pendril v. Second Ave. R. Co. (34 N. Y. Super. Ct. 481) 259, 270, 283.
Penny v. Rochester Ry. Co. (7 App. Div. [N. Y.] 595) 252, 253, 262.
Pennsylvania Traction Co., Bard v. (176 Pa. 97) 91.
Harman v. (200 Pa. 311) 346.
People v. Detroit United Ry. (97 N. W. [Mich.] 36) 383.
People's Elec. St. R. Co., Bensing v. (9 Pa. Super. Ct. 142) 162.
People's Pass. Ry. Co., Flanagan v. (163 Pa. 102) 278.
Fry v. (17 Phila. 61) 150.
v. Green (56 Md. 84) 53, 406.
Hazel v. (132 Pa. 96) 335, 338.
Kane v. (181 Pa. 358) 328.
v. Lauderbach (4 Pennyp. [Pa.] 406) 99.
Owens v. (155 Pa. 334) 229, 245.
Phillips v. (190 Pa. 222) 346.
v. Weiller (17 Wkly. Notes Cas. [Pa.] 306) 103, 126.
People's Ry. Co., Bertram v. (154 Mo. 639) 54, 423.
Bischoff v. (121 Mo. 216) 125.
Davies v. (159 Mo. 1) 231.
Davies v. (67 Mo. App. 598) 219, 235.
Kleiber v. (107 Mo. 240) 125, 410.
McAllister v. (54 Atl. [Del.] 743) 111.
Snyder v. (53 Atl. [Del.] 433) 295, 313, 317.
Wilman v. (55 Atl. [Del. Sup.] 332) 294, 313, 317.
People's St. Ry. Co., Henne v. (1 Pa. Super. Ct. 311) 267, 274.
Hudson v. (175 Mass. 23) 379.
Jagger v. (180 Pa. 436) 143, 146, 157.
Pitcher v. (154 Pa. 560) 10, 59.
Warner v. (141 Pa. 615) 213, 333, 234.
People's St. Ry. & E. L. & P. Co., Buck v. (46 Mo. App. 555) 23, 25, 77.
Buck v. (108 Mo. 179) 23, 25, 153, 423.
Mackin v. (45 Mo. App. 32) 133.
Van Natta v. (133 Mo. 13) 253.
Percy v. Metropolitan St. Ry. Co. (58 Mo. App. 75) 194, 412.
Perrine v. North Jersey St. Ry. Co. (54 Atl. [N. J. Law] 799) 196, 201.
Perry v. Macon Consol. St. R. Co. (101 Ga. 400) 280.
v. Malarin (107 Cal. 363) 118, 132, 135.
v. Pittsburg Union Pass. Ry. Co. (153 Pa. 236) 172, 433.
Peters, Calumet Elec. St. Ry. Co. v. (88 Ill. App. 112) 377.
Peterson v. Minneapolis St. Ry. Co. (95 N. W. [Minn.] 751) 216, 218, 243.
v. Seattle Traction Co. (23 Wash. 615) 35, 384, 390.
Petri v. Third Ave. R. Co. (30 Misc. [N. Y.] 254) 291, 320.
Petters, West Chicago St. R. Co. v. (196 Ill. 298) 324.
Peuser, North Chicago Elec. Ry. Co. v. (190 Ill. 67) 313, 314, 317.
Peyser v. Coney Island & B. R. Co. (81 Hun [N. Y.] 70) 396.
Pfeffer v. Buffalo Ry. Co. (4 Misc. [N. Y.] 465) 43, 51, 53.
Pfeiffer v. Chicago City Ry. Co. (96 Ill. App. 10) 253, 270, 409.
Phalen v. Rochester Ry. Co. (31 App. Div. [N. Y.] 448) 427, 439.

[REFERENCES ARE TO PAGES.]

Phelan v. Forty-Second St., M. & St. N. Ave. Ry. Co. (79 App. Div. [N. Y.] 548) 211, 236.
Philadelphia v. St. Charles St. R. Co. (106 La. 592) 93, 147, 160.
Philadelphia City Pass. Ry. Co. v. Hassard (75 Pa. 367) 77, 112, 154.
 v. Henrice (92 Pa. 431) 274.
Philadelphia Traction Co. v. Bernheimer (125 Pa. 615) 335.
 Buzby v. (126 Pa. 559) 14, 17, 224.
 Comey v. (175 Pa. 133) 331, 332.
 Dixey v. (180 Pa. 401) 128.
 Downey v. (14 Pa. Co. Ct. R. 251) 125, 127.
 Evers v. (176 Pa. 376) 251, 264, 266, 269, 275.
 Farley v. (6 Pa. Co. Ct. R. 347) 98.
 Feingold v. (21 Pa. Co. Ct. R. 183) 152.
 Fletcher v. (190 Pa. 117) 374.
 Furguson v. (20 Phila. 249) 231.
 Harper v. (175 Pa. 129) 303, 327.
 Harvey v. (26 Wkly. Notes Cas. [Pa.] 231) 400.
 Jackson v. (182 Pa. 104) 91.
 Jones v. (185 Pa. 75) 390.
 Kierzenkowski v. (184 Pa. 459) 279.
 Lightcap v. (60 Fed. 212) 337.
 v. Lightcap (61 Fed. 762) 337.
 Lumis v. (181 Pa. 268) 357.
 McCauley v. (13 Pa. Super. Ct. 354) 213, 215, 216.
 McLaughlin v. (175 Pa. 565) 358, 408.
 Maher v. (181 Pa. 391) 284.
 Mann v. (175 Pa. 122) 73.
 Mattis v. (6 Pa. Dist. Ct. R. 94) 417, 438.
 Moss v. (180 Pa. 389) 278.
 Mullen v. (19 Phila. 441) 354.
 Nugent v. (181 Pa. 160) 218, 226.
 v. Orbann (119 Pa. 37) 28, 35, 436.
 v. Orbann (19 Phila. 413) 416.
 Patton v. (132 Pa. 76) 307, 328.
 Rauscher v. (176 Pa. 349) 218.
 Reddington v. (132 Pa. 154) 47.
 Reilley v. (176 Pa. 335) 275.
 Reinike v. (31 Wkly. Notes Cas. [Pa.] 471) 267.
 Smith v. (3 Pa. Super. Ct. 129) 315, 317, 323.
 Steiner v. (134 Pa. 199) 335.
 Walters v. (161 Pa. 36) 39, 40, 55, 57.
 Wetzel v. (184 Pa. 407) 375, 376.
 Wheelahan v. (150 Pa. 187) 290, 295.
Philadelphia & G. F. Ry. Co., Hagen v. (10 Wkly. Notes Cas. [Pa.] 360) 147.
Philadelphia & R. R. Co. v. Boyer (97 Pa. 91) 103, 126.
Philadelphia & W. C. Traction Co., Ortlip v. (198 Pa. 586) 378, 381.
Philadelphia & W. C. Turnpike Road Co., Hanlon v. (182 Pa. 115) 337.

[REFERENCES ARE TO PAGES.]

Philadelphia & W. E. Pass. Ry. Co., Bradwell v. (139 Pa. 404) 415.
Phillips v. Duquesne Traction Co. (183 Pa. 255) 343, 344.
Louisville Ry. Co. v. (22 Ky. L. R. 842) 253.
v. People's Pass. Ry. Co. (190 Pa. 222) 346.
Phillipsburg Horse Car R. Co., Newman v. (52 N. J. Law, 446) 251, 254.
Picard v. Ridge Ave. Pass. Ry. Co. (147 Pa. 195) 39, 51, 55, 60.
Pieper v. Union Traction Co. (202 Pa. 100) 291.
Pierce, Baltimore Consol. Ry. Co. v. (89 Md. 495) 387.
v. Camden, G. & W. Ry. Co. (58 N. J. Law, 400) 374.
Piercy v. Metropolitan St. Ry. Co. (30 Misc. [N. Y.] 612) 320.
Pikesville, R. & E. G. R. Co. v. State (88 Md. 563) 377.
Pinckard, Birmingham Ry. & Elec. Co. v. (124 Ala. 372) 322.
Pinder v. Brooklyn Heights R. Co. (173 N. Y. 519) 257.
Pine v. St. Paul City Ry. Co. (50 Minn. 144) 192, 194, 436.
Piper v. Minneapolis St. Ry. Co. (52 Minn. 269) 160.
West Chicago St. R. Co. v. (165 Ill. 325) 122.
West Chicago St. R. Co. v. (64 Ill. App. 605) 310.
Pitcher v. People's St. Ry. Co. (154 Pa. 560) 10, 59.
Pittsburg, A. & M. P. Ry. Co. v. Caldwell (74 Pa. 421) 26, 76, 77, 412.
v. Donahue (70 Pa. 119) 188, 433.
Pittsburg, A. & M. Ry. Co. v. Pearson (72 Pa. 169) 266, 267.
Pittsburg, A. & M. Traction Co., Boehmer v. (194 Pa. 313) 305.
Buente v. (2 Pa. Super. Ct. 185) 268, 283, 286.
Cleary v. (179 Pa. 526) 219.
Dunseath v. (161 Pa. 124) 267, 283.
Haney v. (159 Pa. 395) 300, 330.
Harkins v. (173 Pa. 146) 264, 275.
Jackson v. (159 Pa. 399) 303, 327.
Julius v. (184 Pa. 19) 327.
McCullough v. (183 Pa. 241) 277.
Meyer v. (189 Pa. 414) 226.
Pittsburg Elec. Ry. Co. v. Kelly (57 Kan. 514) 228, 245.
Pittsburg Traction Co., Clow v. (158 Pa. 410) 128.
Kingan v. (5 Pa. Super. Ct. 436) 389.
Laird v. (166 Pa. 4) 182, 197, 200.
Linch v. (153 Pa. 102) 92, 159.
Pittsburg Union Pass. Ry., Perry v. (153 Pa. 236) 172, 433.
Pittsburg & B. P. Ry. Co., Butler v. (139 Pa. 195) 73, 76.
Pittsburg & B. Traction Co., Bamford v. (194 Pa. 17) 368, 433.
Cannon v. (194 Pa. 159) 303, 330.
Kelly v. (10 Pa. Super. Ct. 644) 336.
Kestner v. (158 Pa. 422) 325.
Muldowney v. (8 Pa. Super. Ct. 335) 175, 176.
Omslaer v. (168 Pa. 519) 290, 294.
Reber v. (179 Pa. 339) 78, 80, 132.
Schenkel v. (194 Pa. 182) 365, 433.
Pittsburg & L. E. R. Co., O'Toole v. (158 Pa. 99) 125, 127.

[REFERENCES ARE TO PAGES.]

Pittsburg & W. E. Pass. Ry. Co., Bradwell v. (139 Pa. 404) 415.
Bradwell v. (153 Pa. 105) 360.
Wagner v. (158 Pa. 419) 356.
Plant v. Heraty (92 N. W. [Mich.] 284) 299.
Platt v. Albany Ry. (170 N. Y. 115) 287.
v. Forty-Second St. & G. St. Ferry R. Co. (2 Hun [N. Y.] 124) 14, 236.
Pleasants v. North Beach & M. R. Co. (34 Cal. 586) 181, 432.
Pletcher v. Scranton Traction Co. (185 Pa. 147) 279.
Ploof v. Burlington Traction Co. (70 Vt. 509) 254, 262.
Poe, Louisville R. Co. v. (24 Ky. L. R. 1700, 72 S. W. 6) 217.
Polkey, North Chicago St. R. Co. v. (67 N. E. [Ill.] 793) 89.
Pollak v. Metropolitan St. Ry. Co. (28 Misc. [N. Y.] 791) 413.
Pollock v. Brooklyn & C. T. R. Co. (15 N. Y. Supp. 189) 115.
Pomaski v. Grant (119 Mich. 675) 83, 394.
Poole v. Consolidated St. Ry. Co. (100 Mich. 379) 158, 165.
v. Metropolitan St. Ry. Co. (83 App. Div. [N. Y.] 235) 211.
Pope v. Kansas City Cable Ry. Co. (99 Mo. 400) 321.
Portland & C. E. Ry. Co., Watson v. (91 Me. 584) 64, 66, 74.
Portsmouth, K. & Y. St. Ry., Call v. (69 N. H. 562) 56.
Posch v. Southern Elec. R. Co. (76 Mo. App. 601) 102.
Post v. Hartford St. Ry. Co. (72 Conn. 362) 53, 54.
Posten v. Denver Consol. Tramway Co. (11 Colo. App. 187) 139-141, 168.
Potrero & B. V. R. Co. v. Shea (44 Cal. 414) 233-235.
Potter v. Scranton Traction Co. (38 Wkly. Notes Cas. [Pa.] 453) 339.
Potts v. Chicago City Ry. Co. (33 Fed. 610) 124.
v. Shreveport Belt Ry. Co. (34 So. [La.] 103) 300.
Poulin v. Broadway & S. A. R. Co. (61 N. Y. 621) 142.
v. Broadway & S. A. R. Co. (34 N. Y. Super. Ct. 296) 155.
Poulsen v. Nassau El. R. Co. (18 App. Div. [N. Y.] 221) 102, 108.
v. Nassau El. R. Co. (30 App. Div. [N. Y.] 246) 108.
Powell v. Hudson Valley Ry. Co. (84 N. Y. Supp. 237) 109.
Metropolitan St. R. Co. v. (89 Ga. 601) 334.
Powelson v. United Traction Co. (204 Pa. 474) 8, 42, 43, 53, 55, 58.
Powers v. City of Boston (154 Mass. 60) 375.
v. Quincy & B. St. Ry. Co. (163 Mass. 5) 267.
v. Union Ry. Co. (60 Mo. App. 481) 102.
Pratt, State v. (52 Minn. 131) 366.
Pray v. Omaha St. Ry. Co. (44 Neb. 167) 80, 81, 106.
Preston, Camden, G. & W. Ry. Co. v. (59 N. J. Law, 264) 314, 315, 317, 319.
Price v. Charles Warner Co. (1 Pen. [Del.] 462) 295, 313, 314, 316, 324, 380, 401, 404.
Priest, Cicero & P. St. Ry. Co. v. (190 Ill. 592) 403.
Prince v. Third Ave. R. Co. (84 N. Y. Supp. 542) 297.
Prothero v. Citizens' St. Ry. Co. (134 Ind. 431) 98, 102.
Pryor v. Metropolitan St. Ry. Co. (85 Mo. App. 367) 129, 137.

[REFERENCES ARE TO PAGES.]

Pueblo Electric St. Ry. Co. v. Sherman (25 Colo. 114) 152, 154, 402.
Purtell v. Ridge Ave. Pass. Ry. Co. (3 Pa. Co. Ct. R. 273) 149.
South Chicago City Ry. Co. v. (193 Ill. 454) 406.
Putnam v. Broadway & S. A. R. Co. (55 N. Y. 108) 33, 113, 114, 178, 179.
Pyne v. Broadway & S. A. R. Co. (19 N. Y. Supp. 217) 404.

Q.

Quayle, Washington A. & M. V. Electric Ry. Co. v. (95 Va. 741) 182.
Quested v. Newburyport & A. Horse R. Co. (127 Mass. 204) 137.
Quincy Horse Ry. & Carrying Co. v. Gnuse (38 Ill. App. 212) 256, 270, 276, 282.
v. Gruse (26 Ill. App. 397) 253.
v. Gruse (137 Ill. 264) 410.
Quincy & B. St. Ry. Co., Powers v. (163 Mass. 5) 267.
Spaulding v. (69 N. E. [Mass.] 217) 163.
Quinlan v. Sixth Ave. R. Co. (4 Daly [N. Y.] 487) 135.
Quinn v. Atlantic Ave. R. Co. (12 N. Y. Supp. 223) 301.
v. Brooklyn City R. Co. (40 App. Div. [N. Y.] 608) 301.
v. Dubuque St. Ry. Co. (94 N. W. [Iowa] 476) 313.
v. Shamokin & M. C. Electric Ry. Co. (7 Pa. Super. Ct. 19) 121, 122.
Quirk v. Rapid Ry. Co. (90 N. R. W. [Mich.] 673) 257.

R.

Rack v. Chicago City Ry. Co. (173 Ill. 289) 272.
v. Chicago City Ry. Co. (69 Ill. App. 656) 282.
Rack's Adm'r, Richmond Pass. & P. Co. v. (44 S. E. [Va.] 709) 233.
Raftery v. Central Park, N. & E. R. R. Co. (14 Misc. [N. Y.] 560) 391.
West Chicago St. R. Co. v. (85 Ill. App. 319) 304.
Rahenkamp v. Traction Co. (14 Pa. Super. Ct. 635) 354.
Rahmann, Pendleton St. R. Co. v. (22 Ohio St. 446) 414.
Railway Co., Dix v. (15 Pa. Super. Ct. 350) 222.
Gress v. (14 Pa. Super. Ct. 87) 325.
v. Harrell (58 Ark. 454) 125, 126, 404.
Machen v. (13 Pa. Super. Ct. 642) 156, 433.
Stein v. (10 Phila. 440) 410.
Raming v. Metropolitan St. Ry. Co. (157 Mo. 477) 28, 29.
Rammaker, Louisville Ry. Co. v. (21 Ky. L. R. 250, 51 S. W. 175) 162, 405.
Ramson v. Metropolitan St. Ry. Co. (78 App. Div. [N. Y.] 101) 117.
Randall, Atlanta Ry. Co. v. (43 S. E. [Ga.] 412) 141, 142.
Augusta & S. R. Co. v. (85 Ga. 297) 403.
Augusta & S. R. Co. v. (79 Ga. 304) 411, 436.
v. Frankford, S. & P. C. P. R. Co. (139 Pa. 464) 113, 114.
v. Frankford & S. Pass. Ry. Co. (8 Pa. Co. Ct. R. 277) 107.

[REFERENCES ARE TO PAGES.]

Randell, Denison & S. Ry. Co. v. (69 S. W. [Tex. Civ. App.] 1013) 193.
Randolph, Dallas Consol. Traction Co. v. (8 Tex. Civ. App. 213) 103.
Ranstead, West Chicago St. R. Co. v. (70 Ill. App. 111) 212.
Rapid Ry. Co., Beath v. (119 Mich. 512) 401, 433, 435.
Noe v. (94 N. W. [Mich.] 743) 386, 388.
Quirk v. (90 N. W. [Mich.] 673) 257.
Rapid Transit Ry. Co. v. Lusk (66 S. W. [Tex. Civ. App.] 799) 143.
Rascher v. East Detroit & G. P. Ry. Co. (90 Mich. 413) 302, 314, 317, 327, 332.
Rathbone v. Union R. Co. (13 R. I. 709) 162.
Raulston v. Traction Co. (13 Pa. Super. Ct. 412) 299, 329.
Rauscher v. Philadelphia Traction Co. (176 Pa. 349) 218.
Ray v. Cortland & H. Traction Co. (19 App. Div. [N. Y.] 530) 182, 197, 202.
Read v. Brooklyn Heights R. Co. (32 App. Div. [N. Y.] 503) 293, 294, 319.
v. City & Suburban Ry. Co. (115 Ga. 366) 364.
Reading City Pass. Ry. Co., Barre v. (155 Pa. 170) 28, 185.
Beard v. (38 Pa. Super. Ct. 171) 282.
v. Eckert (1 Pa. Sup. Ct. Dig. 55) 115, 407.
Johnson v. (160 Pa. 647) 268, 275.
Reading & L. St. Ry. Co., Harriman v. (173 Mass. 28) 15, 395.
Reardon v. Third Ave. R. Co. (24 App. Div. [N. Y.] 162) 318, 319.
Reber v. Pittsburg & B. Traction Co. (179 Pa. 339) 78, 80, 132.
Reddington v. Philadelphia Traction Co. (132 Pa. 154) 47.
Redfield v. Oakland Consol. St. Ry. Co. (110 Cal. 277) 136, 413, 417, 438.
Redford v. Spokane St. Ry. Co. (15 Wash. 419) 306, 397.
Redwood v. Metropolitan St. Ry. Co. (6 D. C. 302) 192, 437.
Reed, Denver Tramway Co. v. (4 Colo. App. 500) 187.
v. Metropolitan St. Ry. Co. (58 App. Div. [N. Y.] 87) 310.
v. Metropolitan St. Ry. Co. (84 N. Y. Supp. 454) 225.
v. Minneapolis St. Ry. Co. (34 Minn. 557) 254, 265.
Reem v. St. Paul City Ry. Co. (77 Minn. 503) 411.
Regensburg v. Nassau Electric R. Co. (58 App. Div. [N. Y.] 566) 104, 125.
Reger v. Rochester Ry. Co. (2 App. Div. [N. Y.] 5) 428, 439.
Regner v. Glens Falls, S. H. & F. E. St. R. Co. (74 Hun [N. Y.] 202) 179.
Reich v. Union Ry. Co. (78 Hun [N. Y.] 417) 278.
Reichart, Houston City St. Ry. Co. v. (87 Tex. 539) 360.
Reichenberg v. Interurban St. Ry. Co. (81 N. Y. Supp. 523) 305.
Reid Denver Tramway Co. v. (4 Colo. App. 53) 109, 402.
Denver Tramway Co. v. (22 Colo. 349) 139, 140, 148, 152.
Reidy v. Metropolitan St. Ry. Co. (27 Misc. [N. Y.] 527) 8, 49.
Reilley v. Philadelphia Traction Co. (176 Pa. 335) 275.

[REFERENCES ARE TO PAGES.]

Reilly v. Brooklyn Heights R. Co. (65 App. Div. [N. Y.] 453) 319, 320.
v. Green & C. St. P. Ry. Co. (4 Wkly. Notes Cas. [Pa.] 273) 151.
v. Metropolitan St. Ry. Co. (26 Misc. [N. Y.] 814) 297, 320.
v. Metropolitan St. Ry. Co. (30 Misc. [N. Y.] 110) 320.
v. Third Ave. R. Co. (16 Misc. [N. Y.] 11) 297, 320.
v. Troy City Ry. Co. (32 App. Div. [N. Y.] 131) 331.
Reiners v. Washington & G. R. Co. (9 App. D. C. 19) 275.
Reinig v. Broadway R. Co. (49 Hun [N. Y.] 269) 383.
Reinike v. Philadelphia Traction Co. (31 Wkly. Notes Cas. [Pa.] 471) 267.
Reiss v. Metropolitan St. Ry. Co. (28 Misc. [N. Y.] 198) 291.
Rend v. Chicago West Div. Ry. Co. (8 Ill. App. 517) 122, 332.
Renken, San Antonio St. Ry. Co. v. (15 Tex. Civ. App. 229) 232, 235, 238, 421, 438, 439.
Rennard, Atlantic Coast Elec. R. Co. v. (62 N. J. Law, 773) 320.
Renz, Augusta & S. R. Co. v. (55 Ga. 126) 64, 68, 104, 407.
Reul, Mt. Adams & E. P. I. Ry. Co. v. (4 Ohio Cir. Ct. R. 362) 98, 106.
Reynolds v. Larchmont Horse Ry. Co. (83 App. Div. [N. Y.] 189) 304.
v. Richmond & M. Ry. Co. (92 Va. 400) 6, 46, 47, 60, 103.
v. Third Ave. R. Co. (8 Misc. [N. Y.] 313) 289.
Rice v. Crescent City R. Co. (51 La. Ann. 108) 251, 274, 276, 429, 439.
v. Detroit, Y. & A. A. Ry. Co. (122 Mich. 677) 206.
Richard v. Detroit, R. R. & L. O. Ry. Co. (89 N. W. [Mich.] 52) 137.
Richmond v. Chicago & W. M. Ry. Co. (87 Mich. 374) 381, 432.
v. Second Ave. R. Co. (76 Hun [N. Y.] 233) 149, 156.
Richmond City Ry. Co. v. Scott (86 Va. 902) 142, 157.
Richmond Passenger & Power Co. v. Rack's Adm'r (44 S. E. [Va.] 709) 233.
v. Steger (43 S. E. [Va.] 612) 210, 236.
Richmond Ry. & Elec. Co. v. Bowles (92 Va. 738) 109, 407.
v. Garthwright (92 Va. 627) 321, 413, 427.
v. Hudgins (41 S. E. [Va.] 730) 334, 338.
v. Second Ave. R. Co. (76 Hun [N. Y.] 233) 149, 156.
Richmond Traction Co. v. Clarke (43 S. E. [Va.] 618) 297.
v. Hildebrand (98 Va. 22) 213.
v. Wilkinson (43 S. E. [Va.] 622) 182, 185, 186.
v. Williams (46 S. E. [Va.] 292) 142.
Richmond & M. Ry. Co. v. Moore's Adm'r (94 Va. 493) 247.
Reynolds v. (92 Va. 400) 6, 46, 47, 60, 103.
Richter v. Cicero & P. St. Ry. Co. (70 Ill. App. 196) 337.
Ricketts v. Birmingham St. Ry. Co. (85 Ala. 600) 156.
Riddick, Memphis St. Ry. Co. v. (75 S. W. [Tenn.] 924) 294.
Riddle v. Forty-Second St., M. & St. N. Ave. Co. (173 N. Y. 327) 231.
Ridenhour v. Kansas City Cable Ry. Co. (102 Mo. 270) 142, 152, 153.
Rider v. Syracuse Rapid Transit Ry. Co. (171 N. Y. 139) 291.
Ridge Ave. Pass. Ry Co., Dickson v. (19 Phila. [Pa.] 430) 77, 412.
Picard v. (147 Pa. 195) 39, 51, 55, 60.
Purtell v. (3 Pa. Co. Ct. R. 273) 149.

[REFERENCES ARE TO PAGES.]

Ridge Ave. Pass. Ry. Co., Stager v. (119 Pa. 70) 39, 40, 61.
Riegelman v. Third Ave. R. Co. (9 Misc. [N. Y.] 51) 296, 326.
Ries v. St. Louis Transit Co. (77 S. W. [Mo.] 734) 211.
Rifcowitz, Baltimore Consol. Ry. Co. v. (89 Md. 338) 209, 210, 216, 217, 235.
Riley v. Galveston City Ry. Co. (13 Tex. Civ. App. 247) 389.
v. Minneapolis St. Ry. Co. (80 Minn. 424) 293.
v. Salt Lake Rapid Transit Co. (10 Utah, 428) 253, 262, 282, 431, 440.
Ripley v. Second Ave. R. Co. (8 Misc. [N. Y.] 449) 90, 132.
Rippe v. Metropolitan St. Ry. Co. (35 App. Div. [N. Y.] 321) 422.
Rittenhouse v. Wilmington St. Ry. Co. (120 N. C. 544) 381, 397.
Roach, Chicago City Ry. Co. v. (76 Ill. App. 496) 241.
Robards v. Indianapolis St. Ry. Co. (66 N. E. [Ind. App.] 66) 342.
v. Indianapolis St. Ry. Co. (67 N. E. [Ind. App.] 953) 345.
Robbins v. Omnibus R. Co. (32 Cal. 472) 363.
v. Springfield St. Ry. Co. (165 Mass. 30) 293, 311.
Roberts v. Indianapolis S . R. Co. (158 Ind. 634) 371.
v. Spokane St. Ry. Co. (23 Wash. 325) 342.
Robinson, Chicago City Ry. Co. v. (127 Ill. 9) 252, 255, 256, 259, 284.
Chicago City Ry. Co. v. (27 Ill. App. 26) 284.
Houston Elec. Co. v. (76 S. W. [Tex. Civ. App.] 209) 371.
v. Louisville Ry. Co. (112 Fed. 484) 313, 314, 408.
v. Metropolitan St. Ry. Co. (31 Misc. [N. Y.] 171) 427.
v. Northampton St. Ry. Co. (157 Mass. 224) 163.
v. Rockland, T. & C. St. Ry. Co. (87 Me. 387) 32, 178.
Robson v. Nassau Elec. R. Co. (80 App. Div. [N. Y.] 301) 125.
Rochat v. North Hudson County Ry. Co. (49 N. J. Law, 445) 129.
Roche v. Brooklyn City & N. R. Co. (105 N. Y. 294) 401.
Rochester City & B. R. Co., Alexander v. (128 N. Y. 13) 124.
Birmingham v. (137 N. Y. 13) 137.
Dintruff v. (10 N. Y. Supp. 402) 286.
Ganiard v. (50 Hun, 22; affirmed 121 N. Y. 661) 6, 51, 53, 61.
Herdt v. (20 N. Y. Supp. 346) 83, 84, 86.
Rochester City & B. St. R. Co., Gray v. (61 Hun [N. Y.] 212) 86.
Rochester Elec. Ry. Co., Meisch v. (72 Hun [N. Y.] 604) 347.
Ward v. (17 N. Y. Supp. 427) 289.
Rochester Ry. Co., Ayers v. (156 N. Y. 104) 130.
Bernhard v. (68 Hun [N. Y.] 369) 314, 315, 317, 319.
Brooks v. (156 N. Y. 244) 438.
Curry v. (90 Hun [N. Y.] 230) 213.
Howell v. (24 App. Div. [N. Y.] 502) 283.
Johnson v. (61 App. Div. [N. Y.] 12) 319.
Marks v. (41 App. Div. [N. Y.] 66) 24, 387.
Martineau v. (81 Hun [N. Y.] 263) 251, 264.
Metcalf v. (12 App. Div. [N. Y.] 147) 309.
Mitchell v. (151 N. Y. 107) 434.
Mitchell v. (4 Misc. [N. Y.] 575) 10.

[REFERENCES ARE TO PAGES.]

Rochester Ry. Co., Muckle v. (79 Hun [N. Y.] 32) 192, 195, 197, 201, 437.
Penny v. (7 App. Div. [N. Y.] 595) 252, 253, 262.
Phalen v. (31 App. Div. [N. Y.] 448) 427, 439.
Reger v. (2 App. Div. [N. Y.] 5) 428, 439.
Saperstone v. (25 App. Div. [N. Y.] 285) 415.
Schrank v. (83 Hun [N. Y.] 290) 365.
Sias v. (18 App. Div. [N. Y.] 506) 73.
Snell v. (64 Hun [N. Y.] 476) 356.
Walls v. (92 Hun [N. Y.] 581) 211, 221.
Rockford City Ry. Co. v. Blake (173 Ill. 354) 408, 412.
Rockland, T. & C. St. Ry. Co., Robinson v. (87 Me. 387) 32, 178.
Rodert, North Chicago St. R. Co. v. (67 N. E. [Ill.] 812) 325.
Roedecker v. Metropolitan St. Ry. Co. (84 N. Y. Supp. 300) 74.
Rogers v. Galveston City Ry. Co. (76 Tex. 502) 378.
Rohan v. Metropolitan St. Ry. Co. (59 App. Div. [N. Y.] 250) 384.
Rohe v. Third Ave. R. Co. (10 Misc. [N. Y.] 740) 290.
Rohner, Street Ry. Co. v. (3 Ohio Dec. 570) 325, 393, 423.
Roller v. Sutter St. R. Co. (66 Cal. 230) 268.
Rollins, Cicero & P. St. R. Co. v. (95 Ill. App. 497) 393.
Rombach v. Crescent City R. Co. (50 La. Ann. 473) 328.
Rome St. R. Co., Duncan v. (99 Ga. 98) 276.
Hill v. (101 Ga. 66) 338.
v. McGinnis (94 Ga. 229) 328.
Rood, Chicago City R. Co. v. (62 Ill. App. 550) 123.
Chicago City Ry. Co. v. (163 Ill. 477) 123.
Rooks v. Houston, W. S. & P. Ferry R. Co. (10 App. Div. [N. Y.] 98) 342.
Root v. Des Moines City Ry. Co. (113 Iowa, 675) 139, 140, 142, 143.
Rose, Central Pass. Ry. Co. v. (15 Ky. L. R. 209) 38, 39, 60.
Rosecrans, East Cleveland R. Co. v. (24 Wkly. Law Bul. [Ohio] 220) 408.
Rosenberg v. Third Ave. R. Co. (47 App. Div. [N. Y.] 323) 22.
v. West End St. Ry. Co. (168 Mass. 561) 258.
Rosenblatt v. Brooklyn Heights R. Co. (26 App. Div. [N. Y.] 600) 314-316.
Rosenkranz v. Lindell Ry. Co. (108 Mo. 9) 266, 267, 275.
Ross, Elwood Electric St. Ry. Co. v. (26 Ind. App. 258) 251, 270, 276
Rost v. Brooklyn Heights R. Co. (10 App. Div. [N. Y.] 477) 399.
Roth v. Metropolitan St. Ry. Co. (13 Misc. [N. Y.] 213) 290.
Rott v. Forty-Second St. & G. St. Ferry R. Co. (56 N. Y. Super. Ct 151) 59.
Rouch, Metropolitan St. Ry. Co. v. (71 Pac. [Kan.] 257) 302, 314, 315
Rouse v. Metropolitan St. Ry. Co. (41 Mo. App. 298) 192, 437.
Rouser v. North Park St. Ry. Co. (97 Mich. 565) 196, 202.
v. Washington & G. R. Co. (13 App. [D. C.] 320) 142, 146, 149 163.
Rowe v. Brooklyn Heights R. Co. (71 App. Div. [N. Y.] 474) 390.

[REFERENCES ARE TO PAGES.]

Rowell v. Stamford St. R. Co. (64 Conn. 376) 357, 406.
Rown v. Christopher & T. St. R. Co. (34 Hun [N. Y.] 471) 188, 189.
Roxborough, C. H. & N. Ry. Co., Bland v. (13 Pa. Super. Ct. 93) 357.
Rush, Denver Consol. Tramway Co. v. (73 Pac. [Colo. App.] 664) 142.
Russell v. Shreveport Belt Ry. Co. (50 La. Ann. 501) 127.
Russell's Adm'r, Louisville Ry. Co. v. (20 Ky. L. R. 1246) 110.
Ruth v. St. Louis Transit Co. (71 S. W. [Mo. App.] 1055) 174, 191.
Ryan, Chicago West Div. Ry. Co. v. (131 Ill. 474) 250, 255, 263.
v. Detroit Citizens' St. Ry. Co. (123 Mich. 597) 296, 325.
v. La Crosse City Ry. Co. (108 Wis. 122) 250, 260, 393.

## S.

Saare v. Union Ry. Co. (20 Mo. App. 211) 77, 130.
Sacramento City Ry. Co., Fernandes v. (52 Cal. 45) 228.
Saffer v. Dry Dock, E. B. & B. R. Co. (5 N. Y. Supp. 700) 147.
v. Westchester Elec. Ry. Co. (22 Misc. [N. Y.] 555) 329.
Sahlgaard v. St. Paul City Ry. Co. (48 Minn. 232) 6, 38, 40, 43, 45, 53, 55, 57.
Saiko v. St. Paul City Ry. Co. (67 Minn. 8) 146.
St. Charles St. R. Co., Hearn v. (34 La. Ann. 160) 280.
Peetez v. (42 La. Ann. 541) 360, 395.
Philips v. (106 La. 592) 93, 147, 160.
Welty v. (109 La. 733) 241.
St. Joseph & B. H. St. Ry. Co., Bush v. (113 Mich. 513) 311, 402.
Noble v. (98 Mich. 249) 135.
Westphal v. (96 N. W. [Mich.] 19) 325.
St. Louis Cable & W. Ry. Co., Griveaud v. (33 Mo. App. 458) 362.
Keitel v. (28 Mo. App. 657) 362.
Lamb v. (33 Mo. App. 489) 331.
Murray v. (98 Mo. 573) 386.
O'Connell v. (106 Mo. 482) 52, 53, 101, 102, 421.
St. Louis R. Co., Byington v. (147 Mo. 673) 136.
Glenville v. (51 Mo. App. 629) 332.
Grace v. (156 Mo. 295) 142.
Haderlein v. (3 Mo. App. 601) 102, 115.
Hayes v. (15 Mo. App. 584) 186, 404, 437.
Kennedy v. (43 Mo. App. 1) 279.
Keown v. (141 Mo. 87) 381, 382.
Liddy v. (40 Mo. 506) 234, 242.
Maschech v. (3 Mo. App. 600) 251, 272.
Maschek v. (71 Mo. 276) 279.
Miller v. (5 Mo. App. 471) 99
Muelhausen v. (91 Mo. 332) 23, 25.
Schmidt v. (149 Mo. 269) 253, 282.
Schreiner v. (5 Mo. App. 596) 48.
St. Louis Transit Co., Aldrich v. (74 S. W. [Mo. App.] 141) 210, 214, 235, 239.

[REFERENCES ARE TO PAGES.]

St. Louis Transit Co., Barrie v. (76 S. W. [Mo. App.] 706) 291, 321.
Brazis v. (76 S. W. [Mo. App.] 708) 150.
Dawson v. (76 S. W. [Mo. App.] 689) 152.
Degel v. (74 S. W. [Mo. App.] 156) 321.
Ellerman v. (76 S. W. [Mo. App.] 661) 329.
Fillingham v. (77 S. W. [Mo. App.] 314) 14.
Frank v. (73 S. W. [Mo. App.] 239) 293, 332.
Gebhardt v. (71 S. W. [Mo. App.] 448) 136, 246, 299, 332.
Ledwidge v. (73 S. W. [Mo. App.] 1008) 291.
Meyers v. (73 S. W. [Mo. App.] 379) 321, 328.
Murray v. (75 S. W. [Mo.] 611) 293, 325.
Noll v. (73 S. W. [Mo. App.] 907) 302, 327.
O'Mara v. (76 S. W. [Mo. App.] 680) 6, 38, 39, 55, 57.
Pies v. (77 S. W. [Mo.] 734) 211.
Ruth v. (71 S. W. [Mo. App.] 1055) 174, 191.
Sanitary Dairy Co. v. (71 S. W. [Mo. App.] 726) 293.
Scamell v. (76 S. W. [Mo. App.] 660) 142.
Septowsky v. (76 S. W. [Mo. App.] 693) 321.
Sonnen v. (76 S. W. [Mo. App.] 691) 184.
Twelkemeyer v. (76 S. W. [Mo. App.] 682) 302.
St. Louis & M. R. R. Co., Klockenbrink v. (72 S. W. [Mo.] 900) 302.
Klockenbrink v. (172 Mo. 678) 317, 327.
Schafstette v. (74 S. W. [Mo.] 826) 302.
St. Louis & S. Ry. Co., Campbell v. (75 S. W. [Mo.] 86) 311, 325.
Fleming v. (74 S. W. [Mo. App.] 382) 169.
Holwerson v. (157 Mo. 216) 210, 235, 246.
Lesser v. (85 Mo. App. 326) 171, 180, 182.
McAndrews v. (83 Mo. App. 233) 321, 332.
McLain v. (73 S. W. [Mo. App.] 909) 136, 247, 332, 383.
O'Keefe v. (81 Mo. App. 386) 210, 235, 238.
Schaefer v. (128 Mo. 64) 2, 3, 10, 28, 39.
St. Paul City Ry. Co., Appleby v. (54 Minn. 169) 205.
Baly v. (95 N. W. [Minn.] 757) 213.
Bishop v. (48 Minn. 26) 115, 416.
Blondel v. (66 Minn. 284) 92, 159.
Boyer v. (54 Minn. 127) 225.
Brace v. (87 Minn. 292) 397.
Broderick v. (74 Minn. 163) 384.
Brusch v. (52 Minn. 512) 106, 402, 427.
Cooper v. (54 Minn. 379) 399, 418.
DeFoe v. (65 Minn. 319) 148.
Delude v. (55 Minn. 63) 386, 424.
Donnelly v. (70 Minn. 278) 402, 425.
Downs v. (75 Minn. 41) 260.
Edlund v. (78 Minn. 434) 133, 402.
Flannagan v. (68 Minn. 300) 300.
Fonda v. (71 Minn. 438) 226, 395, 404.
Fonda v. (77 Minn. 336) 233, 416.

[REFERENCES ARE TO PAGES.]

St. Paul City Ry. Co., Fulmore v. (72 Minn. 448) 424.
Funk v. (61 Minn. 435) 389.
Gaffney v. (81 Minn. 459) 5, 6.
Gray v. (87 Minn. 280) 276.
Greengard v. (72 Minn. 181) 226.
Hafner v. (73 Minn. 252) 231.
Herbert v. (85 Minn. 341) 164.
Hickey v. (60 Minn. 119) 212.
Jackson v. (74 Minn. 48) 27, 28, 80, 97, 427.
Johnson v. (67 Minn. 260) 310, 311, 313, 431.
Joyce v. (70 Minn. 339) 402, 427.
Kennedy v. (59 Minn. 45) 432.
Koch v. (45 Minn. 407) 327, 426.
Laschinger v. (84 Minn. 333) 229.
Lorimer v. (48 Minn. 391) 376.
Matz v. (52 Minn. 159) 77-79.
McBride v. (72 Minn. 291) 404.
Messenger v. (77 Minn. 34) 137.
Medcalf v. (82 Minn. 18) 342.
Metz v. (92 N. W. [Minn.] 502) 218.
Miller v. (42 Minn. 454) 48.
Miller v. (62 Minn. 216) 402.
Miller v. (66 Minn. 192) 6, 53, 55, 424.
Morrow v. (75 Minn. 480) 404.
Newhart v. (51 Minn. 42) 376.
O'Connell v. (64 Minn. 466) 291.
Pine v. (50 Minn. 144) 192, 194, 436.
Reem v. (77 Minn. 503) 411.
Sahlgaard v. (48 Minn. 232) 6, 38, 40, 43, 45, 53, 55, 57.
Saiko v. (67 Minn. 8) 146.
Schacherl v. (42 Minn. 42) 139.
Schmeltzer v. (80 Minn. 50) 61.
Shea v. (50 Minn. 295) 293, 314, 315, 318, 325.
Skelton v. (92 N. W. [Minn.] 960) 142.
Smith v. (32 Minn. 1) 6, 119.
Smith v. (79 Minn. 254) 346.
Steeg v. (50 Minn. 149) 52-54.
Stewart v. (78 Minn. 85) 157.
Strutzel v. (47 Minn. 543) 254, 267, 273, 425, 439.
Terien v. (70 Minn. 522) 212, 215-217.
Watson v. (42 Minn. 46) 102.
Weber v. (67 Minn. 155) 401.
Weissner v. (47 Minn. 468) 267, 276.
Winchell v. (90 N. W. [Minn.] 1050) 239.
Wosika v. (80 Minn. 364) 289, 295, 309, 310.
Salem & S. D. R. Co., Lovett v. (9 Allen [Mass.] 557) 185.
Salt Lake City R. Co., Burgess v. (17 Utah, 406) 224.
Dederichs v. (13 Utah, 34) 326.

[REFERENCES ARE TO PAGES.]

Salt Lake City R. Co., Dickert v. (20 Utah, 394) 131.
Murray v. (16 Utah, 356) 411.
Shaw v. (21 Utah, 76) 321, 397.
Salt Lake Rapid Transit Co., Riley v. (10 Utah, 428) 253, 262, 282, 431, 440.
Thompson v. (16 Utah, 281) 257, 269, 271, 286.
Saltzman v. Brooklyn City R. Co. (73 Hun [N. Y.] 567) 80, 81.
Sample v. Consolidated Light & Ry. Co. (50 W. Va. 472) 270.
Sampson, Highland Ave. & B. R. Co. v. (91 Ala. 560) 289, 290, 293, 321.
Highland Ave. & B. R. Co. v. (112 Ala. 425) 289, 408.
Samuels v. California St. Cable Ry. Co. (124 Cal. 294) 131.
San Antonio St. Ry. Co. v. Cailloutte (79 Tex. 341) 277.
v. Mechler (87 Tex. 628) 269, 270.
v. Muth (7 Tex. Civ. App. 443) 395.
v. Renken (15 Tex. Civ. App. 229) 233, 235, 238, 421, 438, 439.
San Antonio Traction Co. v. Crawford (71 S. W. [Tex. Civ. App.] 306) 191.
v. Court (71 S. W. [Tex. Civ. App.] 777) 270, 273, 275.
v. De Rodriguez (77 S. W. [Tex. Civ. App.] 420) 384.
v. Upson (71 S. W. [Tex. Civ. App.] 565) 296, 325.
Sanders v. Southern Elec. Ry. Co. (147 Mo. 411) 332.
Sandford v. Hestonville, M. & F. P. R. Co. (136 Pa. 84) 64, 74, 75, 108.
Sandusky, Chicago City Ry. Co. v. (198 Ill. 300) 296, 325.
Sanford v. Eighth Ave. R. Co. (23 N. Y. 343) 22, 32, 171, 184, 187.
v. Union Passenger Ry. Co. (16 Pa. Super. Ct. 393) 358.
San Francisco & S. M. Ry. Co., Mahoney v. (110 Cal. 471) 313, 314.
Sanitary Dairy Co. v. St. Louis Transit Co. (71 S. W. [Mo. App.] 726) 293.
San Jose & S. C. R. Co., Jamison v. (55 Cal. 593) 13, 100.
Santa Ana, O. & T. St. Ry. Co., McFadden v. (87 Cal. 464) 357.
Sappenfield v. Main St. & A. P. R. Co. (91 Cal. 48) 382, 406.
Saperston v. Rochester Ry. Co. (25 App. Div. [N. Y.] 285) 415.
Sauers v. Union Traction Co. (193 Pa. 602) 344.
Saunders v. City & Suburban R. Co. (99 Tenn. 130) 298, 320, 403.
Savage v. Nassau Elec. R. Co. (42 App. Div. [N. Y.] 241) 379.
v. Third Ave. R. Co. (29 App. Div. [N. Y.] 556) 6, 38, 40, 55, 57.
Savannah, T. & I. of H. Ry. v. Beasley (94 Ga. 142) 324.
Savannah St., etc., R. Co. v. Bryan (86 Ga. 312) 187, 189, 425.
Savannah St. R. Co. v. Jackson (95 Ga. 366) 326.
Sundy v. (96 Ga. 819) 385.
Savannah, T. & G. of H. Ry. v. Williams (43 S. E. [Ga.] 751) 391.
Scamell v. St. Louis Transit Co. (76 S. W. [Mo. App.] 660) 142.
Scanlan West Chicago St. R. Co. v. (68 Ill. App. 626) 264, 432, 440.
Scannell v. Boston El. Ry. Co. (176 Mass. 170) 317.
Schacherl v. St. Paul City Ry. Co. (42 Minn. 42) 139.
Schaefer v. Central Crosstown R. Co. (30 Misc. Rep. [N. Y.] 114) 143, 151, 156, 162.

[REFERENCES ARE TO PAGES.]

Schaefer v. City of Fond du Lac (99 Wis. 333) 354.
v. North Chicago St. R. Co. (82 Ill. App. 473) 186.
v. St. Louis & S. Ry. Co. (128 Mo. 64) 2, 3, 10, 38, 39.
v. Union Ry. Co. (29 App. Div. [N. Y.] 261) 80, 81.
Schafstette v. St. Louis & M. R. R. Co. (74 S. W. [Mo.] 826) 302.
Schalska v. Third Ave. R. Co. (19 Misc. Rep. [N. Y.] 141) 53.
Schapierer v. Third Ave. R. Co. (14 N. Y. Supp. 921) 428.
Schausten v. Toledo Consol. St. Ry. Co. (7 Ohio Cir. Dec. 389) 289.
Schenectady St. Ry. Co., Van Patten v. (80 Hun [N. Y.] 494) 289.
Schenkel v. Pittsburg & B. Traction Co. (194 Pa. 182) 365, 433.
Schepers v. Union Depot R. Co. (126 Mo. 665) 2, 6, 9, 10, 38-40, 45, 54.
Schick v. Brooklyn City R. Co. (10 N. Y. Supp. 528) 393.
Schierhold v. North Beach & M. R. Co. (40 Cal. 447) 262, 270, 409.
Schild v. Central Park, N. & E. R. Co. (16 N. Y. Supp. 701) 361.
Schiller v. Dry Dock, E. B. & B. R. Co. (26 Misc. Rep. [N. Y.] 392) 153.
Schilling v. Metropolitan St. Ry. Co. (47 App. Div. [N. Y.] 500) 301.
Schlitz v. Nassau Electric R. Co. (44 App. Div. [N. Y.] 542) 292.
Schmedding v. New York & Q. C. Ry. Co. (82 N. Y. Supp. 1034) 320.
Schmeltzer v. St. Paul City Ry. Co. (80 Minn. 50) 61.
Schmidt v. Coney Island & B. R. Co. (26 App. Div. [N. Y.] 391) 91.
v. Interurban St. Ry. Co. (81 N. Y. Supp. 832) 289.
v. North Jersey St. Ry. Co. (66 N. J. Law, 424) 38, 39, 49.
v. St. Louis R. Co. (149 Mo. 269) 253, 282.
v. Steinway & H. P. Ry. Co. (132 N. Y. 566) 246.
Schmitt v. Dry Dock, E. B. & B. R. Co. (3 N. Y. St. Rep. 257) 404.
v. Milwaukee St. Ry. Co. (89 Wis. 195) 393, 396, 433.
Schneidau v. New Orleans & C. R. Co. (48 La. Ann. 866) 279.
Schneider v. New Orleans & C. R. Co. (60 Fed. 210) 425.
v. North Chicago St. R. Co. (80 Ill. App. 306) 48.
v. Second Ave. R. Co. (133 N. Y. 583) 110, 127.
v. Second Ave. R. Co. (59 N. Y. Super. Ct. 536) 64, 71, 122, 137.
Schnell v. Metropolitan St. Ry. Co. (50 App. Div. [N. Y.] 616) 361.
Schnur v. Citizens' Traction Co. (153 Pa. 29) 251, 274.
Schoener v. Metropolitan St. Ry. Co. (72 App. Div. [N. Y.] 23) 297, 324.
Schoenfeld v. Metropolitan St. Ry. Co. (40 Misc. Rep. [N. Y.] 201) 51, 53.
Scholl v. Broadway R. Co. (63 Hun [N. Y.] 629, 17 N. Y. Supp. 755) 393.
Schrank v. Rochester Ry. Co. (83 Hun [N. Y.] 290) 365.
Schreiner v. St. Louis R. Co. (5 Mo. App. 596) 48.
Schroder v. Metropolitan St. Ry. Co. (84 N. Y. Supp. 371) 344.
Schron v. Staten Island Elec. R. Co. (16 App. Div. [N. Y.] 111) 300, 310.
Schuler v. Third Ave. R. Co. (1 Misc. Rep. [N. Y.] 351) 102, 111.
v. Third Ave. R. Co. (17 N. Y. Supp. 834) 428.
Schulman v. Houston, W. St. & P. Ferry R. Co. (15 Misc. Rep. [N. Y.] 30) 233, 235, 244.

[REFERENCES ARE TO PAGES.]

Schultz v. Third Ave. R. Co. (89 N. Y. 242) 188.
Schuster, Erie City Passenger Ry. Co. v. (113 Pa. 412) 251, 254.
Schutt v. Shreveport Belt R. Co. (109 La. 500) 346.
Schuylkill Traction Co., Davidson v. (4 Pa. Super. Ct. 86) 315, 328.
Karahuta v. (6 Pa. Super. Ct. 319) 267, 284.
Oster v. (195 Pa. 320) 283.
Walbridge v. (190 Pa. 274) 284.
Schwanewede v. North Hudson County Ry. Co. (67 N. J. Law, 449) 291.
Schwartz v. Cincinnati St. Ry. Co. (1 Ohio Dec. 197) 30, 82.
v. Crescent City R. Co. (30 La Ann. 15) 212.
v. New Orleans & C. R. Co. (34 So. [La.] 667) 243.
North Chicago St. R. Co. v. (82 Ill. App. 493) 128.
West Chicago St. R. Co. v. (93 Ill. App. 387) 270, 274.
Schwartzbaum v. Third Ave. R. Co. (54 App. Div. [N. Y.] 164) 24, 221, 237.
v. Third Ave. R. Co. (60 App. Div. [N. Y.] 274) 211, 221.
Sciacca, Houston City St. Ry. Co. v. (80 Tex. 350) 425, 439.
Sciortino v. Crescent City R. Co. (49 La. Ann. 7) 278.
Sciurba v. Metropolitan St. R. Co. (73 App. Div. [N. Y.] 170) 272, 275.
v. Metropolitan St. Ry. Co. (84 N. Y. Supp. 85) 279.
Scott v. Bergen County Traction Co. (63 N. J. Law, 407) 92, 151, 159.
v. Central Park, N. & E. R. R. Co. (53 Hun [N. Y.] 414) 183.
Consolidated Traction Co. v. (58 N. J. Law, 682) 256, 259, 269, 284.
Richmond City Ry. Co. v. (86 Va. 902) 142, 157.
v. Third Ave. R. Co. (59 Hun [N. Y.] 456) 210, 236.
v. Third Ave. R. Co. (16 N. Y. Supp. 350) 226.
Scranton Traction Co., Keator v. (191 Pa. 102) 12.
O'Malley v. (191 Pa. 410) 229.
Pletcher v. (185 Pa. 147) 279.
Potter v. (38 Wkly. Notes Cas. [Pa.] 453) 339
Stanton v. (11 Pa. Super. Ct. 180) 367.
Thane v. (191 Pa. 249) 78, 80.
Seagriff v. Brooklyn Heights R. Co. (31 App. Div. [N. Y.] 595) 300.
Sears v. Seattle Consol. St. Ry. Co. (6 Wash. 227) 123, 404, 416.
Seattle & R. Ry. Co., Gilmore v. (29 Wash. 150) 393.
Seattle City Ry. Co., Brown v. (16 Wash. 465) 140, 142.
Muldoon v. (7 Wash. 528) 22, 65, 66, 68, 70.
Muldoon v. (10 Wash. 311) 22.
Seattle Consol. St. Ry. Co., Sears v. (6 Wash. 227) 123, 404, 416.
Seattle Electric Co., Blakney v. (28 Wash. 607) 163.
Seattle Electric Ry. & Power Co., Cunningham v. (3 Wash. 471) 190, 432.
Woo Dan v. (5 Wash. 466) 39, 40, 42, 45.
Seattle Traction Co., Gustafson v. (28 Wash. 227) 388.
Peterson v. (23 Wash. 615) 35, 384, 390.
Seccombe v. Detroit Elec. St. Ry. Co. (94 N. W. [Mich.] 747) 378, 382.

[REFERENCES ARE TO PAGES.]

Second & Third Sts. Passenger Ry. Co., Fineburg v. (182 Pa. 97) **397.**
Hall v. (14 Wkly. Notes Cas. [Pa.] 242) 173.
Neslie v. (113 Pa. 300) 106, 151, 156, 164.
Second & Third Sts. Ry. Co., Mayberry v. (15 Phila. [Pa.] 253) **361.**
Second Ave. R. Co., Aaron v. (2 Daly [N. Y.] 127) 251, **277.**
Akersloot v. (131 N. Y. 599) 53.
Akersloot v. (59 N. Y. Super. Ct. 555) **417.**
Barry v. (1 Misc. Rep. [N. Y.] 502) 405.
Barry v. (16 N. Y. Supp. 518) 267.
Baxter v. (3 Rob. [N. Y.] 510) **221.**
Bradley v. (34 App. Div. [N. Y.] 284) 64, 70, **131.**
Bradley v. (8 Daly [N. Y.] 289) 211.
Burns v. (21 App. Div. [N. Y.] 521) 228, **245.**
Coleman v. (114 N. Y. 609) 87, 95.
Fenton v. (126 N. Y. 625) 269, 274, 280.
Furst v. (72 N. Y. 542) 411.
Ginna v. (67 N. Y. 596) 64, 67, 72.
Gray v. (65 N. Y. 561) 307, 334.
Hadencamp v. (31 N. Y. Super. Ct. 490) 64, 68, **103.**
Jackson v. (47 N. Y. 274) 182, 188.
King v. (75 Hun [N. Y.] 17) 402, 403.
Lavin v. (12 App. Div. [N. Y.] 381) **280.**
Lundy v. (1 Misc. Rep. [N. Y.] 100) **243.**
Lyons v. (89 Hun [N. Y.] 374) 420, **439.**
McMahon v. (75 N. Y. 231) 355.
Martin v. (3 App. Div. [N. Y.] 448) 144, **151.**
Mentz v. (2 Rob. [N. Y.] 356) 256.
Meyer v. (8 Bosw. [N. Y.] 305) 188, 189.
Moylan v. (128 N. Y. 583) 38, 39, 49, 57, 85.
Nicholsburg v. (11 Misc. Rep. [N. Y.] 432) 311.
Pendril v. (34 N. Y. Super. Ct. 481) 259, 270, 283.
Richmond v. (76 Hun [N. Y.] 233) **149,** 156.
Ripley v. (8 Misc. Rep. [N. Y.] 449) 90, 132.
Schneider v. (133 N. Y. 583) 110, 127.
Schneider v. (59 N. Y. Super. Ct. 536) 64, 71, 122, **137.**
Stevenson v. (35 App. Div. [N. Y.] 474) 117.
Wihnyk v. (14 App. Div. [N. Y.] 515) 252, 273.
Winterfeld v. (20 N. Y. Supp. 801) 279.
Second Ave. Ry. Co., Akersloot v. (56 Hun [N. Y.] 640, 8 N. Y. **Supp.** 926) 425.
Second Ave. Traction Co., Collins v. (7 Pa. Super. Ct. 318) **372.**
Gaughan v. (189 Pa. 408) 303.
Kern v. (194 Pa. 75) 291.
Levin v. (194 Pa. 75) 291.
Levin v. (201 Pa. 58) 28, 77.
Todd v. (192 Pa. 587) 247.
Waechter v. (198 Pa. 129) 438.
Willis v. (189 Pa. 430) 109, 422, 434.

[REFERENCES ARE TO PAGES.]

Sedalia Electric Ry. Co., Hansberger v. (82 Mo. App. 566) 38-40, 45.
Seelig v. Metropolitan St. Ry. Co. (18 Misc. Rep. [N. Y.] 383) 64, 71, 131, 132.
Seggerman v. Metropolitan St. Ry. Co. (38 Misc. [N. Y.] 374) 292.
Seidlinger v. Brooklyn City R. Co. (28 Hun [N. Y.] 503) 124.
Seifter v. Brooklyn Heights R. Co. (55 App. Div. [N. Y.] 10) 301.
Seigel v. Eisen (41 Cal. 109) 77, 99, 121.
Seigrist, Citizens' Rapid Transit Co. v. (96 Tenn. 119) 298, 320.
Seipp v. Dry Dock, E. B. & B. R. Co. (45 App. Div. [N. Y.] 489) 411.
Seitz v. Dry Dock, E. B. & B. R. Co. (16 Daly [N. Y.] 264) 39.
Selby v. Detroit Ry. (122 Mich. 311) 142, 153.
Seller v. Market St. Ry. Co. (72 Pac. [Cal.] 1006) 65, 76.
Selma St. & Suburban Ry. Co. v. Owen (132 Ala. 420) 125, 126.
Senn v. Southern Ry. Co. (108 Mo. 142) 275, 399, 411.
Septowsky v. St. Louis Transit Co. (76 S. W. [Mo. App.] 693) 321.
Serfass, Central Ry. Co. v. (153 Ill. 379) 433.
Sesselman v. Metropolitan St. Ry. Co. (65 App. Div. [N. Y.] 484) 219, 225, 235, 242.
Sexton v. Metropolitan St. Ry. Co. (40 App. Div. [N. Y.] 26) 39, 40.
Seymour v. Citizens' Ry. Co. (114 Mo. 266) 80, 82.
Shadford v. Ann Arbor Ry. Co. (121 Mich. 224) 386.
Shaffer, Marion St. R. Co. v. (9 Ind. App. 486) 77.
Shamokin & M. C. Electric Ry. Co., Madara v. (192 Pa. 542) 119.
  Quinn v. (7 Pa. Super. Ct. 19) 121, 122.
Shankenberry v. Metropolitan St. Ry. Co. (46 Fed. 177) 125, 127.
Shanks v. Springfield Traction Co. (74 S. W. [Mo. App.] 386) 210, 223, 235.
Shanley v. Union R. Co. (14 Misc. Rep. [N. Y.] 442) 320.
Sharp v. Kansas City Cable Ry. Co. (114 Mo. 94) 110, 403.
Shaw, Memphis St. Ry. Co. v. (75 S. W. [Tenn.] 713) 144, 153.
  v. Salt Lake City R. Co. (21 Utah, 76) 321, 397.
Shea v. Potrero & B. V. R. Co. (44 Cal. 414) 233, 234, 235.
  v. Sixth Ave. R. Co. (62 N. Y. 180) 185, 188.
  v. St. Paul City Ry. Co. (50 Minn. 395) 293, 314, 315, 318, 325.
Shedden Cartage Co., La Pontney v. (116 Mich. 514) 379.
Sheehan v. Citizens' Ry. Co. (72 Mo. App. 524) 300, 321.
Sheeron v. Coney Island & B. R. Co. (78 App. Div. [N. Y.] 476) 83, 84, 132.
Sheets v. Connolly St. Ry., etc., Co. (54 N. J. Law, 518) 250, 260.
Shelton, Electric Ry. Co. v. (89 Tenn. 423) 350.
  v. Northern Texas Traction Co. (75 S. W. [Tex. Civ. App.] 338) 354.
Shenners v. West Side St. Ry. Co. (78 Wis. 383) 276.
Shepherd, Citizens' St. R. Co. v. (29 Ind. App. 412) 155.
  Citizens' St. R. Co. v. (107 Tenn. 444) 323.
Sheridan v. Brooklyn City & N. R. Co. (36 N. Y. 39) 76, 77, 104, 114.
Sherman, Pueblo Electric St. Ry. Co. v. (25 Colo. 114) 152, 154, 402.
Shiplett, West Chicago St. R. Co. v. (85 Ill. App. 683) 244, 413.

[REFERENCES ARE TO PAGES.]

Shires, Pendleton St. R. Co. v. (18 Ohio St. 255) 233, 235.
Shreve, North Chicago St. R. Co. v. (70 Ill. App. 666) 414.
Shreveport Belt Ry. Co., Bland v. (48 La. Ann. 1057) 386.
Cowden v. (106 La. 236) 289, 328.
Crisman v. (34 So. [La.] 718) 346.
Flournoy v. (50 La. Ann. 635) 127, 414.
Leverett v. (34 So. [La.] 579) 62.
Potts v. (34 So. [La.] 103) 350.
Russell v. (50 La. Ann. 501) 127.
Schutt v. (109 La. 500) 346.
Shreveport City R. Co., Barnes v. (47 La. Ann. 1218) 251, 255, 270.
Shropshire, City Electric Ry. Co. v. (101 Ga. 33) 183.
Shuart v. Traction Co. (15 Pa. Super. Ct. 26) 53, 54.
Shugard v. Union Traction Co. (201 Pa. 562) 375.
Sias v. Lowell, L. & H. St. Ry. Co. (179 Mass. 343) 352.
v. Rochester Ry. Co. (18 App. Div. [N. Y.] 506) 73.
Sibley v. New Orleans City & L. R. Co. (49 La. Ann. 588) 87.
Sickler v. North Jersey St. Ry. Co. (46 Atl. [N. J. Law] 779) 330.
Siemsen v. Oakland, S. L. & H. Electric Ry. (134 Cal. 494) 119.
Silberstein v. Houston, W. St. & P. F. R. Co. (4 N. Y. Supp. 843) 257, 277.
Simmons, Jackson & S. St. R. & Tel. Co. v. (107 Tenn. 392) 352.
Simon v. Metropolitan St. Ry. Co. (29 Misc. Rep. [N. Y.] 126) 355.
Sims v. Metropolitan St. Ry. Co. (65 App. Div. [N. Y.] 270) 163.
Sinclair v. Washington & G. R. Co. (MacArthur & M. [D. C.] 13) 414, 427.
Sioux City Ry. Co., Douglass v. (91 Iowa, 94) 102, 137.
Sioux City & H. P. Ry. Co., Curtis v. (87 Iowa, 622) 182, 433.
Sirk v. Marion St. Ry. Co. (11 Ind. App. 680) 162.
Sixth Ave. R. Co., Amato v. (9 Misc. Rep. [N. Y.] 4) 29, 171, 183.
Archer v. (52 N. Y. Super. Ct. 373) 400.
Burgess v. (13 N. Y. Wkly. Dig. 499) 298.
Colt v. (33 N. Y. Super. Ct. 189) 142, 153, 155.
Dillon v. (48 N. Y. Super. Ct. 283) 388.
Drew v. (26 N. Y. 49) 59.
Hendricks v. (44 N. Y. Super. Ct. 8) 113.
Hoyt v. (1 Daly [N. Y.] 528) 172.
Langley v. (48 N. Y. Super. Ct. 542) 430.
Nichols v. (38 N. Y. 131) 93, 160.
Notel v. (2 How. Pr. [N. S.; N. Y.] 30) 261.
Quinlan v. (4 Daly [N. Y.] 437) 135.
Shea v. (62 N. Y. 180) 185, 188.
Wolfkiel v. (38 N. Y. 49) 45, 53, 54.
Skelton v. St. Paul City Ry. Co. (92 N. W. [Minn.] 960) 142.
Skola, Metropolitan West Side El. R. Co. v. (83 Ill. App. 659) 387, 391.
Slaughter v. Metropolitan St. Ry. Co. (116 Mo. 269) 167, 435.
Slayman v. Metropolitan St. Ry. Co. (64 Kan. 722) 296.

Slayton v. West End St. Ry. Co. (174 Mass. 55) 357, 358.
Slensby v. Milwaukee St. Ry. Co. (95 Wis. 179) 267, 277.
Sly v. Union Depot R. Co. (134 Mo. 681) 38-40, 42, 45.
Smadraff, North Chicago St. R. Co. v. (89 Ill. App. 411) 313, 314, 421.
Smedley v. Hestonville, M. & F. P. Ry. Co. (184 Pa. 620) 103, 128, 134.
Smith v. Bailey (14 App. Div. [N. Y.] 283) 230.
Birmingham Union Ry. Co. v. (90 Ala. 60) 143.
v. Brooklyn Heights R. Co. (81 N. Y. Supp. 838) 350.
v. Chicago General Ry. Co. (86 Ill. App. 647) 292.
v. Citizens' Ry. Co. (52 Mo. App. 36) 289, 293, 295, 321.
v. City Ry. Co. (29 Or. 539) 14, 213, 217.
v. Crescent City R. Co. (47 La. Ann. 833) 222.
v. Electric Traction Co. (187 Pa. 110) 292, 316.
v. Hestonville, M. & F. P. Ry. Co. (92 Pa. 450) 251, 254, 263.
v. Hestonville, M. & F. P. R. Co. (17 Phila. [Pa.] 184) 188, 189.
v. Hoemesburg, T. & F. Elec. Ry. Co. (187 Pa. 451) 335.
v. Kingston City R. Co. (55 App. Div. [N. Y.] 143) 142, 154, 155.
Louisville & P. R. Co. v. (2 Duv. [Ky.] 556) 101, 102, 115, 436.
v. Manhattan Ry. Co. (18 N. Y. Supp. 759) 11.
v. Metropolitan R. Co. (137 Mass. 61) 397.
v. Metropolitan St. Ry. Co. (7 App. Div. [N. Y.] 253) 293.
v. Metropolitan St. Ry. Co. (59 App. Div. [N. Y.] 60) 109.
v. Metropolitan St. Ry. Co. (15 Misc. Rep. [N. Y.] 158) 441.
v. Milwaukee Elec. Ry. & Light Co. (96 N. W. [Wis.] 823) 118.
v. Nashua St. Ry. (69 N. H. 504) 365.
v. Nassau Elec. R. Co. (57 App. Div. [N. Y.] 152) 426.
v. Passenger Ry. Co. (13 Phila. [Pa.] 6) 97.
v. Philadelphia Traction Co. (3 Pa. Super. Ct. 129) 316, 317, 323.
v. St. Paul City Ry. Co. (32 Minn. 1) 6, 119.
v. St. Paul City Ry. Co. (79 Minn. 254) 346.
State v. (58 Minn. 35) 383.
v. Third Ave. R. Co. (10 App. Div. [N. Y.] 409) 429.
v. Union Trunk Line (18 Wash. 351) 225.
v. Union Ry. Co. (61 Mo. 588) 360.
Wiley v. (25 App. Div. [N. Y.] 351) 361.
Snashall, Metropolitan R. Co. v. (3 App. D. C. 420) 77, 78.
Snediker v. Nassau Electric R. Co. (41 App. Div. [N. Y.] 628) 121.
Snell, Cincinnati St. Ry. Co. v. (54 Ohio St. 197) 19, 224, 242.
v. Rochester Ry. Co. (64 Hun [N. Y.] 476) 356.
Snyder v. People's Ry. Co. (53 Atl. [Del.] 433) 295, 313, 317.
Solatinow v. Jersey City, H. & P. St. Ry. Co. (56 Atl. [N. J. Sup.] 235) 290.
Solomon v. Central Park, N. & E. R. R. Co. (31 N. Y. Super. Ct. 298) 76.
Somerset Traction Co., Withee v. (56 Atl. [Me.] 204) 375.
Somerville v. City R. Co. (17 N. Y. Supp. 719) 365.

[REFERENCES ARE TO PAGES.]

Somerville Horse R. Co., Braslin v. (145 Mass. 64) 137.
Sonnem v. St. Louis Transit Co. (76 S. W. [Mo. App.] 691) 184.
Sophian v. Metropolitan St. Ry. Co. (38 Misc. [N. Y.] 787) 326.
South Boston Horse R. Co., Hanlon v. (129 Mass. 310) 282.
South Boston R. Co., Bradshaw v. (135 Mass. 407) 196, 197.
Collins v. (142 Mass. 301) 264, 276.
Wakefield v. (117 Mass. 544) 203.
South Chicago City Ry. Co., Gross v. (73 Ill. App. 217) 365.
v. Kinnare (96 Ill. App. 210) 342.
v. McDonald (94 Ill. App. 612) 414.
v. Purvis (193 Ill. 454) 406.
South Chicago R. Co. v. Dufresne (200 Ill. 456) 38-40.
South Covington & C. St. R. Co., Taylor's Adm'r v. (14 Ky. Law Rep. 355) 261.
v. Beatty (20 Ky. Law Rep. 1845) 19.
v. Berry (93 Ky. 43) 133.
v. Constans (74 S. W. [Ky.] 705) 118.
v. Enslen (18 Ky. Law Rep. 921) 291.
McCleave v. (18 Ky. Law Rep. 1036) 100.
Moser v. (74 S. W. [Ky.] 1090) 74.
v. Pelzer (19 Ky. Law Rep. 88, 39 S. W. 496) 425.
v. Ware (84 Ky. 267) 161, 431, 435.
Wise v. (17 Ky. Law Rep. 1359) 183.
Southern Bell Tel. Co., McKay v. (111 Ala. 337) 350.
Southern Elec. R. Co., Chouquette v. (152 Mo. 257) 415.
Chouquette v. (80 Mo. App. 515) 425.
Guiney v. (167 Mo. 595) 312.
Kupferschmid v. (70 Mo. App. 438) 302.
Posch v. (76 Mo. App. 601) 102.
Southern Elec. Ry. Co., Sanders v. (147 Mo. 411) 332.
Southern New England Tel. Co., Bergin v. (70 Conn. 54) 352.
Southern R. Co., Stamm v. (1 Abb. N. C. [N. Y.] 438) 338.
Southern Ry. Co., Chartrand v. (57 Mo. App. 425) 96, 155, 433.
Senn v. (108 Mo. 142) 275, 399, 411.
South Middlesex St. R. Co., Kearns v. (181 Mass. 587) 358.
Southside Passenger Ry. Co. v. Cox (2 Mona. [Pa.] 140) 358.
South Shore & B. St. Ry. Co., Cox v. (182 Mass. 497) 223.
South Side Passenger Ry. Co., McManigal v. (181 Pa. 358) 328.
v. Trich (117 Pa. 390) 62, 130.
Southwest Electric Ry. Co., Holt v. (84 Mo. App. 443) 61.
Southwest Missouri Electric Ry. Co., Krone v. (71 S. W. [Mo. App.] 712) 166.
Molyneux v. (81 Mo. App. 25) 235.
Tanger v. (85 Mo. App. 28) 188, 189, 193.
Southwick, North Chicago St. R. Co. v. (66 Ill. App. 241) 92, 159.
Sowash v. Consolidated Traction Co. (188 Pa. 618) 134.
Spade v. Lynn & B. R. Co. (168 Mass. 285) 434.
Spahr, Citizens' St. R. Co. v. (7 Ind. App. 23) 6, 38, 39, 42, 43, 45, 55, 57, 404.

Spaulding v. Jarvis (32 Hun [N. Y.] 621) 307.
v. Quincy & B. St. Ry. Co. (69 N. E. [Mass.] 217) 163.
Spellman v. Lincoln Rapid Transit Co. (36 Neb. 890) 115.
Spokane St. Ry. Co., Helber v. (22 Wash. 319) 290, 315, 316.
Payne v. (15 Wash. 522) 103.
Bedford v. (15 Wash. 419) 306, 397.
Roberts v. (23 Wash. 325) 342.
Washington v. (13 Wash. 9) 112.
Spooner v. Brooklyn City R. Co. (54 N. Y. 230) 83.
Sprenger v. Tacoma Traction Co. (15 Wash. 660) 173.
Springfield Consol. Ry. Co. v. Ankrom (93 Ill. App. 655) 337.
v. Flynn (55 Ill. App. 600) 191.
v. Hoeffner (175 Ill. 634) 139, 143, 400.
v. Hoeffner (71 Ill. App. 162) 92, 159.
McCauley v. (169 Mass. 301) 372.
v. Welsch (56 Ill. App. 196) 250, 253, 410.
Springfield St. Ry. Co., Moody v. (182 Mass. 158) 85.
Mullen v. (164 Mass. 450) 261.
Robbins v. (165 Mass. 30) 293, 311.
Springfield Traction Co., Shanks v. (74 S. W. [Mo. App.] 386) 210, 223, 235.
Spurr v. North Hudson County R. Co. (56 N. J. Law, 346) 137.
Spurrier v. Front St. Cable Ry. Co. (3 Wash. 659) 318, 401, 427.
Spyzchalski, Hammond, W. & E. C. Electric Ry. Co. v. (17 Ind. App. 7) 102, 127, 401.
Squire v. Central Park, N. & E. R. R. Co. (36 N. Y. Super. Ct. 436) 278.
Stabenau v. Atlantic Ave. R. Co. (155 N. Y. 511) 280, 281.
Stafford v. Chippewa Valley Electric R. Co. (110 Wis. 331) 291.
Stager v. Ridge Ave. Passenger Ry. Co. (119 Pa. 70) 39, 40, 61.
Stallman, Pendleton St. R. Co. v. (22 Ohio St. 1) 320.
Stamford St. R. Co., Rowell v. (64 Conn. 376) 357, 400.
Stamm v. Southern R. Co. (1 Abb. N. C. [N. Y.] 438) 338.
Stammers, Louisville Ry. Co. v. (20 Ky. Law Rep. 688) 317.
Standard L. & A. Ins. Co., Sutherland v. (87 Iowa, 505) 77.
Stanley v. Union Depot R. Co. (114 Mo. 606) 270, 279.
Stanton v. Metropolitan R. Co. (14 Allen [Mass.] 485) 104.
v. Scranton Traction Co. (11 Pa. Super. Ct. 180) 367.
Stapleton v. Citizens' Traction Co. (5 Pa. Super. Ct. 253) 386.
State, Baltimore Consol. Ry. Co. v. (91 Md. 506) 134.
Baltimore Traction Co. v. (78 Md. 409) 2, 7, 46, 47, 60.
v. Foley (31 Iowa, 527) 319.
v. Lake Roland El. Ry. Co. (84 Md. 163) 87, 88, 95.
v. McDonald (7 Mo. App. 510) 192.
v. Pearson (34 So. [La.] 575) 181.
Pikesville R. & E. G. R. Co. v. (88 Md. 563) 377.
v. Pratt (52 Minn. 131) 366.
v. Smith (58 Minn. 55) 383.

[REFERENCES ARE TO PAGES.]

State, Sternberg v. (36 Neb. 307) 206.
United Rys. & Elec. Co. v. (54 Atl. [Md.] 612) 290.
United Rys. & Elec. Co. v. (93 Md. 619) 113.
Western Union Tel. Co. v. (82 Md. 293) 351.
v. Whitaker (160 Mo. 59) 383.
Staten Island Elec. R. Co., Black v. (40 App. Div. [N. Y.] 238) 307, 314, 317.
McCready v. (51 App. Div. [N. Y.] 338) 422.
Schron v. (16 App. Div. [N. Y.] 111) 300, 310.
Staten Island Midland R. Co., McCambley v. (32 App. Div. [N. Y.] 346) 306.
Whitaker v. (65 App. Div. [N. Y.] 451) 97.
Steeg v. St. Paul City Ry. Co. (50 Minn. 149) 52-54.
Steen, Citizens' St. Ry. Co. v. (42 Ark. 321) 282, 317, 321, 329, 436.
Steger, Richmond Passenger & Power Co. v. (43 S. E. [Va.] 612) 210, 236.
Stein v. Railway Co. (10 Phila. 440) 410.
Steiner v. Philadelphia Traction Co. (134 Pa. 199) 335.
Steinhart, Lombard & S. Sts. Pass. Ry. Co. v. (2 Pennyp. [Pa.] 358) 251, 278.
Steinman v. Interurban St. Ry. Co. (84 N. Y. Supp. 231) 292.
Steinway & H. P. R. Co., Lehr v. (118 N. Y. 556) 80, 81, 106.
Schmidt v. (132 N. Y. 566) 246.
Steinway Ry. Co., Brozek v. (10 App. Div. [N. Y.] 360) 293, 300, 314, 315, 319, 325.
Butler v. (87 Hun [N. Y.] 10) 33, 180, 183.
Fishback v. (11 App. Div. [N. Y.] 152) 302, 327.
Geipel v. (14 App. Div. [N. Y.] 551) 303, 330, 338.
Grotsch v. (19 App. Div. [N. Y.] 130) 113, 131.
McKeon v. (20 App. Div. [N. Y.] 601) 210, 236.
Wells v. (18 App. Div. [N. Y.] 180) 14, 358.
Stelk v. McNulta (99 Fed. 138) 241.
Stemmerman v. Nassau Electric R. Co. (36 App. Div. [N. Y.] 218) 414.
Stephens, West Chicago St. R. Co. v. (66 Ill. App. 303) 134.
Sternberg v. State (36 Neb. 307) 206.
Sternfels v. Metropolitan St. Ry. Co. (73 App. Div. [N. Y.] 494) 416.
Stetson, Camden & S. Ry. Co. v. (177 U. S. 172) 400.
Steuer v. Metropolitan St. Ry. Co. (46 App. Div. [N. Y.] 500) 149, 163.
Stevens v. Union Ry. Co. (75 App. Div. [N. Y.] 602) 225, 242.
Stevens Co. v. Brooklyn Heights R. Co. (59 App. Div. [N. Y.] 23) 300.
Stevenson v. Second Ave. R. Co. (35 App. Div. [N. Y.] 474) 117.
Stewart v. Brooklyn & C. R. Co. (90 N. Y. 588) 188, 189.
Johnson v. (62 Ark. 164) 306, 322.
v. Metropolitan St. Ry. Co. (20 Misc. [N. Y.] 605) 206.
v. St. Paul City Ry. Co. (78 Minn. 35) 157.

[REFERENCES ARE TO PAGES.]

Stierle v. Union Ry. Co. (156 N. Y. 70) 101, 103.
v. Union Ry. Co. (156 N. Y. 684) 103.
Still v. Nassau Elec. R. Co. (32 App. Div. [N. Y.] 276) 73.
Stillings v. Metropolitan St. Ry. Co. (84 App. Div. [N. Y.] 201) 219.
Stiver, West Chicago St. R. Co. v. (69 Ill. App. 625) 161.
Stoddard, Citizens' St. R. Co. v. (10 Ind. App. 278) 251, 253, 254, 262, 411.
Stoltenberg, West Chicago St. R. Co. v. (62 Ill. App. 420) 253, 277.
Stone v. Dry Dock, E. B. & B. R. Co. (115 N. Y. 104) 252, 253, 259.
Union St. Ry. Co. v. (54 Kan. 83) 355.
Stovers v. Citizens' St. Ry. Co. (21 Ind. App. 434) 224.
Strauss v. Brooklyn Heights R. Co. (82 N. Y. Supp. 767) 326.
v. Newburgh Elec. Ry. Co. (6 App. Div. [N. Y.] 264) 309, 329.
Streator Ry. Co., Godfrey v. (56 Ill. App. 378) 349.
Street R. Co., Boddy v. (105 Tenn. 666) 14, 16.
Dan v. (99 Tenn. 88) 255.
v. Howard (102 Tenn. 474) 233-235, 411.
Street Ry. Co., Bindbeutal v. (43 Mo. App. 463) 321.
v. Bolton (43 Ohio St. 224) 35, 387.
Britton v. (90 Mich. 159) 142.
Duffy v. (3 Ohio Dec. 678) 322.
v. Eadie (43 Ohio St. 91) 250, 309.
Laughlin v. (62 Mich. 220) 365, 402, 407.
Laughlin v. (80 Mich. 154) 401.
Little v. (78 Mich. 205) 228.
O'Rourke v. (103 Tenn. 124) 197, 199, 410.
v. Rohner (3 Ohio Dec. 570) 325, 393, 423.
Strutt v. Brooklyn & R. B. R. Co. (18 App. Div. [N. Y.] 134) 99.
Strutzel v. St. Paul City Ry. Co. (47 Minn. 543) 254, 267, 273, 425, 439.
Stuart v. West End St. Ry. Co. (163 Mass. 391) 384.
Stucke v. Orleans R. Co. (50 La. Ann. 172) 376.
Stutler, Fairmount & A. C. P. Ry. Co. v. (54 Pa. 375) 143.
Suburban Ry. Co. v. Balkwill (94 Ill. App. 454) 345.
Finseth v. (32 Or. 1) 14, 19.
Hedin v. (26 Or. 155) 264, 266, 270, 275.
Wallace v. (26 Or. 174) 253.
Suburban Rapid Transit Co., Murphy v. (60 N. Y. Super. Ct. 9) 361.
Sullivan, Chicago City Ry. Co. v. (76 Ill. App. 505) 45.
v. Consolidated Traction Co. (198 Pa. 187) 213.
v. Jefferson Ave. Ry. Co. (133 Mo. 1) 114, 397.
v. Metropolitan St. Ry. Co. (53 App. Div. [N. Y.] 89) 382.
v. Metropolitan St. Ry. Co. (63 App. Div. [N. Y.] 46) 402.
v. Third Ave. R. Co. (19 App. Div. [N. Y.] 195) 390.
v. Union Ry. Co. (81 App. Div. [N. Y.] 596) 260, 262.
v. Union Ry. Co. (7 App. Div. [N. Y.] 238) 386, 389.
West Chicago St. R. Co. v. (64 Ill. App. 628) 253, 256, 277.
Summers v. Crescent City R. Co. (34 La. Ann. 139) 99.

[REFERENCES ARE TO PAGES.]

Sundy v. Savannah St. R. Co. (96 Ga. 819) 385.
Superior Rapid Transit Ry. Co., Johnson v. (91 Wis. 233) 310, 392.
Little v. (88 Wis. 402) 396.
Suse v. Metropolitan St. Ry. Co. (80 App. Div. [N. Y.] 24) 124.
Sutherland v. Standard L. & A. Ins. Co. (87 Iowa, 505) 77.
Sutro R. Co., Bosqui v. (131 Cal. 390) 101, 115, 408.
Sutter v. Omnibus Cable Co. (107 Cal. 369) 285.
Sutter St. Ry. Co., Harrison v. (116 Cal. 156) 404, 430, 439.
Roller v. (66 Cal. 230) 268.
Suydam v. Grand St. & N. R. Co. (41 Barb. [N. Y.] 375) 318.
Swain, Continental Pass. Ry. Co. v. (13 Wkly. Notes Cas. [Pa.] 41) 91, 131.
v. Fourteenth St. R. Co. (93 Cal. 179) 312, 317, 324, 413, 419.
Sweeney v. Kansas City Cable Ry. Co. (150 Mo. 385) 86, 92, 159, 397.
Toledo Consol. St. R. Co. v. (8 Ohio Cir. Ct. R. 298) 378.
v. Union Traction Co. (199 Pa. 293) 92, 159.
Sweetland v. Lynn & B. R. Co. (177 Mass. 574) 65, 70, 131, 132.
Swenson v. Brooklyn Heights R. Co. (15 Misc. [N. Y.] 69) 402.
v. Metropolitan St. Ry. Co. (78 App. Div. [N. Y.] 379) 391.
Swope, Highland Ave. & B. R. Co. v. (115 Ala. 287) 412.
Syracuse Rapid Transit Ry. Co., Eddy v. (50 App. Div. [N. Y.] 109) 182, 192, 197, 201, 437.
Hoffman v. (50 App. Div. [N. Y.] 83) 308.
Rider v. (171 N. Y. 139) 291.
Walters v. (64 App. Div. [N. Y.] 150) 344, 352.

T.

Taborn Consolidated Traction Co. v. (58 N. J. Law, 1) 182, 193, 206.
Tacoma Ry. & Motor Co., Jennings v. (7 Wash. 275) 372.
Mitchell v. (9 Wash. 120) 253, 256, 277, 395.
Mitchell v. (13 Wash. 560) 256, 402, 412, 428.
Weideman v. (7 Wash. 517) 389.
Tacoma Ry. & Power Co., Hays v. (106 Fed. 48) 296.
v. Hays (110 Fed. 496) 293, 296.
Lawshe v. (29 Wash. 681) 197, 200.
Tacoma Traction Co., Bailey v. (16 Wash. 48) 65, 67, 68, 73.
Sprenger v. (15 Wash. 660) 173.
Taft v. Brooklyn Heights R. Co. (14 Misc. [N. Y.] 390) 65.
Tait v. Buffalo Ry. Co. (55 App. Div. [N. Y.] 507) 303, 330.
Tama & T. Elec. Ry. & Light Co., Beem v. (104 Iowa, 563) 212, 214, 237.
Tanger v. Southwest Missouri Elec. Ry. Co. (85 Mo. App. 28) 188, 189, 193.
Tanner, Baltimore City Passenger Ry. Co. v. (90 Md. 315) 401.
Tarler v. Metropolitan St. Ry. Co. (21 Misc. [N. Y.] 684) 306, 330.
Tashjian v. Worcester Consol. St. Ry. Co. (177 Mass. 75) 302.
Taunton St. Ry. Co., Hewitt v. (167 Mass. 483) 267, 404.
Wallace v. (119 Mass. 91) 394.

[REFERENCES ARE TO PAGES.]

Taylor's Adm'r v. South Covington & C. St. R. Co. (94 Ky. Law Rep. 355) 261.
Taylor, Chicago City Ry. Co. v. (170 Ill. 49) 433, 434.
Chicago City Ry. Co. v. (68 Ill. App. 613) 416.
v. Grand Ave. Ry. Co. (137 Mo. 363) 120, 121, 137.
v. Nassau Elec. R. Co. (32 App. Div. [N. Y.] 486) 195.
v. Union Traction Co. (184 Pa. 465) 343.
Telle v. Leavenworth Rapid Transit Ry. Co. (50 Kan. 455) 391.
Temple, Commonwealth v. (14 Gray [Mass.] 69) 319.
Tenner, Indianapolis St. Ry. Co. v. (67 N. E. [Ind. App.] 1044) 14, 224.
Terien v. St. Paul City Ry. Co. (70 Minn. 532) 212, 215-217.
Terre Haute Elec. Ry. Co. v. Lauer (21 Ind. App. 466) 77, 79, 434.
v. Yant (21 Ind. App. 486) 335.
Tesch v. Milwaukee Electric Ry. & Light Co. (108 Wis. 593) 289, 293, 299, 315, 316.
Texarkana St. Ry. Co. v. Hart (26 S. W. [Tex. Civ. App.] 435) 135, 416.
Texas & P. Ry. Co. v. Doherty (4 Willson, Civ. Cas. Ct. App. § 164) 137, 432.
Thal v. Metropolitan St. Ry. Co. (76 N. Y. Supp. 918) 219, 231.
Thalheimer, Consolidated Traction Co. v. (59 N. J. Law, 474) 92, 102, 128, 159.
Thane v. Scranton Traction Co. (191 Pa. 249) 78, 80.
Thatcher v. Central Traction Co. (166 Pa. 66) 327.
Third Ave. R. Co., Ackman v. (52 App. Div. [N. Y.] 483) 435.
Barrett v. (45 N. Y. 628) 120, 122.
Borry v. (51 App. Div. [N. Y.] 385) 191.
v. Barton (107 Fed. 215) 89, 96.
Blate v. (44 App. Div. [N. Y.] 163) 296, 325.
Brachfeld v. (29 Misc. [N. Y.] 586) 302.
Brachfeld v. (30 Misc. [N. Y.] 425) 435.
Bresky v. (16 App. Div. [N. Y.] 83) 319.
Buckbee v. (64 App. Div. [N. Y.] 360) 109.
Buys v. (45 App. Div. [N. Y.] 11) 313.
Cady v. (29 Misc. [N. Y.] 741) 432.
Cambeis v. (1 Misc. [N. Y.] 158) 315, 317.
Cass v. (20 App. Div. [N. Y.] 591) 310, 329.
Cords v. (56 N. Y. Super. Ct. 319) 278.
Costello v. (161 N. Y. 317) 253, 259.
Cowan v. (1 N. Y. Supp. 612) 213.
Cowan v. (9 N. Y. Supp. 610) 218.
Coyle v. (18 Misc. [N. Y.] 9) 325.
Dean v. (34 App. Div. [N. Y.] 220) 55.
Dipaolo v. (55 App. Div. [N. Y.] 566) 230.
Duggan v. (9 Misc. [N. Y.] 158) 386.
Duggan v. (8 Misc. Rep. [N. Y.] 89) 402.
Duygan v. (6 Misc. [N. Y.] 66) 396.

[REFERENCES ARE TO PAGES.]

Third Ave. R. Co., Falke v. (38 App. Div. [N. Y.] 49) 119.
Fandel v. (15 App. Div. [N. Y.] 426) 234, 243.
Fash v. (1 Daly [N. Y.] 148) 361.
Fisselmayer v. (2 N. Y. St. Rep. 75) 250, 268.
Floettl v. (10 App. Div. [N. Y.] 308) 246.
Franklin v. (52 App. Div. [N. Y.] 512) 188, 189.
Geoghegan v. (51 App. Div. [N. Y.] 369) 435.
Greenberg v. (35 App. Div. [N. Y.] 619) 278.
Halpin v. (40 N. Y. Super. Ct. 175) 48, 227.
Hamilton v. (53 N. Y. 25) 192, 205.
Hamilton v. (6 Misc. [N. Y.] 382) 291.
Hamilton v. (40 N. Y. Super. Ct. 376) 428.
Hoes v. (5 App. Div. [N. Y.] 151) 394.
Hoffman v. (45 App. Div. [N. Y.] 586) 130.
Hunter v. (21 Misc. [N. Y.] 1) 298, 315, 320.
Hunter v. (20 Misc. [N. Y.] 432) 402, 436.
Isaacs v. (47 N. Y. 122) 188-190.
Jacobs v. (71 App. Div. [N. Y.] 199) 197, 202.
Keegan v. (34 App. Div. [N. Y.] 279; affirmed 165 N. Y. 622) 102, 124.
Kelly v. (25 App. Div. [N. Y.] 603) 139, 148.
Kennedy v. (31 App. Div. [N. Y.] 30) 319.
Kleiner v. (162 N. Y. 193) 435.
Knoll v. (46 App. Div. [N. Y.] 527) 325.
v. Krausz (112 Fed. 379) 228, 233, 235.
Lafferty v. (85 App. Div. [N. Y.] 592) 252-254, 284.
Lasker v. (27 Misc. [N. Y.] 824) 173.
Lhowe v. (14 Misc. [N. Y.] 612) 252, 258.
Little v. (83 App. Div. [N. Y.] 330) 226.
McMahon v. (47 N. Y. Super. Ct. 282) 197, 203.
McCabe v. (22 Misc. [N. Y.] 707) 403.
McDermott v. (44 Hun [N. Y.] 107) 223.
McDonald v. (16 Misc. [N. Y.] 52) 298.
McFarland v. (29 Misc. [N. Y.] 121) 315.
Macer v. (47 N. Y. Super. Ct. 461) 68.
Martin v. (27 App. Div. [N. Y.] 52) 213, 237.
Mitchell v. (62 App. Div. [N. Y.] 371) 216, 219, 235.
Mulligan v. (87 App. Div. [N. Y.] 320) 219.
Mulligan v. (61 App. Div. [N. Y.] 214) 242.
Munroe v. (50 N. Y. Super. Ct. 114) 139, 140, 142, 152.
Norton v. (26 App. Div. [N. Y.] 60) 158.
O'Neill v. (3 Misc. [N. Y.] 521) 315, 316.
Petri v. (30 Misc. [N. Y.] 254) 291, 320.
Prince v. (84 N. Y. Supp. 542) 297.
Reardon v. (24 App. Div. [N. Y.] 163) 318, 319.
Reilly v. (16 Misc. [N. Y.] 11) 297, 320.
Reynolds v. (8 Misc. [N. Y.] 313) 289.

[REFERENCES ARE TO PAGES.]

Third Ave. R. Co., Riegelman v. (9 Misc. [N. Y.] 51) 296, 326.
Rohe v. (10 Misc. [N. Y.] 740) 290.
Rosenberg v. (47 App. Div. [N. Y.] 323) 22.
Savage v. (29 App. Div. [N. Y.] 556) 6, 38, 40, 55, 57.
Schalscha v. (19 Misc. [N. Y.] 141) 53.
Schapierer v. (14 N. Y. Supp. 921) 428.
Schuler v (17 N. Y. Supp. 834) 428.
Schuler v. (1 Misc. [N. Y.] 351) 102, 111.
Schultz v. (89 N. Y. 242) 188.
Schwartzbaum v. (54 App. Div. [N. Y.] 164) 211, 221, 237.
Schwartzbaum v. (60 App. Div. [N. Y.] 274) 211, 221.
Scott v. (59 Hun [N. Y.] 456) 210, 236.
Scott v. (16 N. Y. Supp. 350) 226.
Smith v. (10 App. Div. [N. Y.] 409) 429.
Sullivan v. (19 App. Div. [N. Y.] 195) 390.
Trauber v. (80 App. Div. [N. Y.] 37) 211, 226, 236, 239.
Tyler v. (18 Misc. [N. Y.] 165) 380.
Wallace v. (36 App. Div. [N. Y.] 57) 38, 40, 53, 55.
v. Weber (12 App. Div. [N. Y.] 512) 441.
Weidinger v. (40 App. Div. [N. Y.] 197) 319.
Weldon v. (3 App. Div. [N. Y.] 370) 309.
Winch v. (12 Misc. [N. Y.] 403) 290.
Wolf v. (67 App. Div. [N. Y.] 605) 157.
Wood v. (91 Hun [N. Y.] 276) 368.
Zimmer v. (36 App. Div. [N. Y.] 265) 120.
Third Ave. Ry. Co., Gilbert v. (54 N. Y. Super. Ct. 270) 39.
Wright v. (5 N. Y. Supp. 707) 276.
Zimmer v. (36 App. Div. [N. Y.] 273) 396.
Thirteenth & F. St. Pass. Ry. v. Boudrou (92 Pa. 475) 121.
Tholen v. Brooklyn City R. Co. (10 Misc. [N. Y.] 283) 273.
Thomas v. Altoona & L. V. Elec. Ry. Co. (191 Pa. 361) 356.
v. Citizens' Passenger Ry. Co. (132 Pa. 504) 290, 315, 316, 328.
v. Consolidated Traction Co. (62 N. J. Law, 36) 358.
v. Union Ry. Co. (18 App. Div. [N. Y.] 185) 167.
Thomas' Adm'r v. Maysville Gas Co. (21 Ky. L. R. 1690) 349.
Thompson v. Buffalo Ry. Co. (145 N. Y. 196) 253, 261, 269.
v. Citizens' St. Ry. Co. (152 Ind. 461) 384.
City Ry. Co. v. (20 Tex. Civ. App. 16) 323.
v. Holyoke St. Ry. Co. (170 Mass. 365) 334.
v. Lowell, L. & H. St. Ry. Co. (170 Mass. 577) 248.
v. Metropolitan St. Ry. Co. (140 Mo. 125) 98, 101.
v. Salt Lake Rapid Transit Co. (16 Utah, 281) 257, 269, 271, 286.
v. United Traction Co. (193 Pa. 555) 282.
Thoresen v. La Crosse City Ry. Co. (87 Wis. 597) 296, 317, 324.
v. La Crosse City Ry. Co. (94 Wis. 129) 299.
Thorsell v. Chicago City Ry. Co. (82 Ill. App. 375) 224.
Thurber v. Harlem Bridge, M. & F. R. Co. (60 N. Y. 326) 253, 256.
Thurston, North Chicago St. Ry. Co. v. (43 Ill. App. 587) 28, 29.

[REFERENCES ARE TO PAGES.]

Timms v. Old Colony St. Ry. Co. (66 N. E. [Mass.] 797) 79, 129.
Timony v. Brooklyn City & N. R. Co. (10 Misc. [N. Y.] 261) 259, 282.
Tippens, North Side St. Ry. Co. v. (4 Willson, Civ. Cas. Ct. App. [Tex.] § 160) 336.
Tishacek v. Milwaukee Electric Ry. & Light Co. (110 Wis. 417) 279.
Todd v. Second Ave. Traction Co. (192 Pa. 587) 247.
Toledo Consol. St. R. Co. v. Fuller (17 Ohio Cir. Ct. R. 562) 22.
v. Sweeney (8 Ohio Cir. Ct. R. 293) 378.
Toledo Consol. St. Ry. Co., Dominick v. (3 Ohio Dec. 22) 405.
Foy v. (3 Ohio Dec. 22) 278.
v. Lutterbeck (11 Ohio Cir. Ct. R. 279) 224.
McDonald v. (74 Fed. 104) 339, 365.
v. Mammet (2 Ohio Dec. 532) 406.
Schausten v. (7 Ohio Cir. Dec. 389) 289.
Ulrich v. (10 Ohio Cir Ct. R. 635) 309, 310.
Ulrich v. (5 Ohio Circ. Dec. 111) 409.
Tomlin, Belt El. Line Co. v. (19 Ky. L. R. 433) 142.
Tompkins v. Clay St. R. Co. (66 Cal. 163) 119, 122.
Topeka City Ry. Co. v. Higgs (38 Kan. 375) 83, 87, 102, 107.
Toronto Ry. Co., Coll v. (25 Ont. App. 55) 191.
Toronto St. Ry. Co., Blackmore v. (38 U. C. Q. B. 172) 28.
Cornish v. (23 U. C. C. P. 355) 72.
Torpe, West Chicago St. R. Co. v. (187 Ill. 610) 409.
Totarella v. New York & Q. C. Ry. Co. (53 App. Div. [N. Y.] 413) 285.
Tower Grove & L. Ry. Co., Fath v. (105 Mo. 537) 136, 273.
Fath v. (39 Mo. App. 477) 272.
Malecek v. (57 Mo. 17) 192, 436.
Townsend, Patterson v. (91 Iowa, 725) 314.
Tracey v. Metropolitan St. Ry. Co. (49 App. Div. [N. Y.] 197) 402.
Traction Co., Breary v. (5 Pa. Dist. Ct. 95) 315, 316.
Brown v. (14 Pa. Super. Ct. 594) 291, 292.
Cupps v. (13 Pa. Super. Ct. 630) 291, 315.
Kaechele v. (15 Pa. Super. Ct. 73) 326.
Kissock v. (15 Pa. Super. Ct. 103) 322.
McCurdy v. (15 Pa. Super. Ct. 29) 53, 60.
Rahenkamp v. (14 Pa. Super. Ct. 635) 354.
Raulston v. (13 Pa. Super. Ct. 412) 299, 329.
Shuart v. (15 Pa. Super. Ct. 26) 53, 54.
Trainer, Little Rock Traction Co. v. (68 Ark. 106) 206.
Transfer Co. v. Kelly (36 Ohio St. 86) 123.
Trauber v. Third Ave. R. Co. (80 App. Div. [N. Y.] 37) 211, 226, 236, 239.
Tregear v. Dry Dock, E. B. & B. R. Co. (14 Abb. Pr. [N. S.; N. Y.] 49) 74, 107.
Trenton Pass. Ry. Co., Connelly v. (56 N. J. Law, 700) 209, 217, 219.
v. Cooper (60 N. J. Law, 219) 350, 410.
Trich, South Side Pass. Ry. Co. v. (117 Pa. 390) 62, 130.

[REFERENCES ARE TO PAGES.]

Tri-City Ry. Co. v. Killeen (92 Ill. App. 57) 352.
Trout v. Altoona & L. V. Elec. Ry. Co. (13 Pa. Super. Ct. 17) 289, 294, 316.
Troy City Ry. Co., Dobert v. (91 Hun [N. Y.] 28) 225, 242.
Reilly v. (32 App. Div. [N. Y.] 131) 331.
Windover v. (4 App. Div. [N. Y.] 203) 378.
Troy & L. R. Co., Benoit v. (154 N. Y. 233) 285, 287.
Clancy v. (88 Hun [N. Y.] 496) 291.
Francisco v. (78 Hun [N. Y.] 13) 133.
Francisco v. (88 Hun [N. Y.] 464) 66, 71, 72, 131.
True v. Niagara Gorge R. Co. (70 App. Div. [N. Y.] 383) 375, 377.
Trumbo's Adm'r v. City St. Car Co. (89 Va. 780) 252, 254, 279.
Tucker v. Atlanta St. R. Co. (77 Ga. 61) 6.
v. Buffalo Ry. Co. (53 App. Div. [N. Y.] 571) 99.
Tuerk, West Chicago St. R. Co. v. (90 Ill. App. 105) 124, 419.
West Chicago St. R. Co. v. (193 Ill. 385) 124.
Tullis v. Brooklyn Heights R. Co. (71 App. Div. [N. Y.] 494) 206.
Tunison v. Weadock (89 N. W. [Mich.] 703) 327.
Tuohy, Chicago City Ry. Co. v. (196 Ill. 410) 254, 274, 284.
Turner v. North Beach & M. R. Co. (34 Cal. 594) 181, 432.
Twelkemeyer v. St. Louis Transit Co. (76 S. W. [Mo. App.] 682) 302.
Twenty-Third St. R. Co., Conroy v. (52 How. Pr. [N. Y.] 49) 358.
Berke v. (4 N. Y. Supp. 905) 346.
Brown v. (56 N. Y. Super. Ct. 356) 215, 217, 241.
Corbett v. (42 Hun [N. Y.] 587) 172.
Gumb v. (114 N. Y. 411) 435.
Lockwood v. (15 Daly [N. Y.] 374) 429.
McCaffrey v. (47 Hun [N. Y.] 404) 369.
McKelvey v. (5 Misc. [N. Y.] 424) 231, 233, 234.
Pascoshell v. (23 N. Y. Wkly. Dig. 200) 276.
White v. (20 N. Y. Wkly. Dig. 510) 188, 189.
Zlotovsky v. (8 Misc. [N. Y.] 463) 250, 261.
Twin City Rapid Transit Co., Holmgren v. (61 Minn. 85) 253, 256.
Twiname, Citizens' St. Ry. Co. v. (111 Ind. 587) 102, 134.
Twomley v. Central Park, N. & E. R. R. Co. (69 N. Y. 158) 125.
Tyler v. Third Ave. R. Co. (18 Misc. [N. Y.] 165) 380.
Tyson v. Union Traction Co. (199 Pa. 264) 292.

## U.

Udell v. Citizens' St. R. Co. (152 Ind. 507) 31, 89.
Uggla v. West End St. Ry. Co. (160 Mass. 351) 367.
Ulrich v. Toledo Consol. St. Ry. Co. (10 Ohio Cir. Ct. R. 635) 309, 310.
v. Toledo Consol. St. Ry. Co. (5 Ohio Cir. Dec. 111) 409.
Unger v. Forty-Second St. & G. St. Ferry R. Co. (51 N. Y. 497) 239.
Union Depot Co., Didionsen v. (129 Mo. 392) 131, 132, 420.

Union Depot Co., Olfermann v. (125 Mo. 408) 167, 392.
Sly v. (134 Mo. 681) 38-40, 42, 45.
Union Depot R. Co., Schepers v. (126 Mo. 665) 2-6, 9, 10, 38-40, 45, 54,
Stanley v. (114 Mo. 606) 270, 279.
Union Elec. Ry. Co., Curry v. (86 Hun [N. Y.] 559) 294, 299.
Union Pass. Ry. Co., Clutzbeher v. (1 Atl. [Pa.] 597) 163.
Sanford v. (16 Pa. Super. Ct. 393) 358.
Union R. Co., Beerman v. (52 Atl. [R. I.] 1090) 289.
Bishop v. (14 R. I. 314) 27, 97.
Bosworth v. (55 Atl. [R. I.] 490) 103.
Goldrick v. (20 R. I. 128) 315-317, 322.
Rathbone v. (13 R. I. 709) 162.
Shanley v. (14 Misc. [N. Y.] 442) 320.
Wright v. (21 R. I. 554) 185.
Union Ry. Co., Adams v. (80 App. Div. [N. Y.] 136) 117.
Brown v. (51 Mo. App. 192) 428.
Campbell v. (9 Misc. [N. Y.] 484) 289, 294.
Carvanio v. (84 N. Y. Supp. 246) 290.
Cook v. (125 Mass. 57) 360, 361.
Doller v. (7 App. Div. [N. Y.] 283) 213.
Dunican v. (39 App. Div. [N. Y.] 497) 295, 318.
Fisher v. (86 App. Div. [N. Y.] 365) 133.
Fleck v. (134 Mass. 480) 77, 79, 92.
Garduhn v. (50 App. Div. [N. Y.] 602) 408.
Harris v. (69 App. Div. [N. Y.] 385) 139, 161.
Hergert v. (25 App. Div. [N. Y.] 218) 319.
Jackson v. (77 App. Div. [N. Y.] 161) 226, 239.
Jones v. (18 App. Div. [N. Y.] 267) 351.
Kerr v. (20 Misc. [N. Y.] 171) 415.
Kuhnen v. (10 App. Div. [N. Y.] 195) 242.
Legare v. (61 App. Div. [N. Y.] 202) 259, 283.
Lynam v. (114 Mass. 83) 302, 303.
Mapes v. (56 App. Div. [N. Y.] 508) 327.
Murphy v. (118 Mass. 228) 33, 178, 186.
O'Connor v. (67 App. Div. [N. Y.] 99) 230, 245.
O'Flaherty v. (45 Mo. 70) 251, 253, 255, 264, 266, 270.
Pearson v. (14 Mo. App. 579) 271.
Pendergast v. (10 App. Div. [N. Y.] 207) 112.
Powers v. (60 Mo. App. 481) 102.
Reich v. (78 Hun [N. Y.] 417) 278.
Saare v. (20 Mo. App. 211) 77, 130.
Schaefer v. (29 App. Div. [N. Y.] 261) 80, 81.
Smith v. (61 Mo. 588) 360.
Stevens v. (75 App. Div. [N. Y.] 602) 225, 242.
Stierle v. (156 N. Y. 70) 101, 103.
Stierle v. (156 N. Y. 684) 103.
Sullivan v. (7 App. Div. [N. Y.] 238) 386, 389.
Sullivan v. (81 App. Div. [N. Y.] 596) 260, 262.

[REFERENCES ARE TO PAGES.]

Union Ry. Co., Thomas v. (18 App. Div. [N. Y.] 185) 167.
Warren v. (46 App. Div. [N. Y.] 517) 302.
Zimmerman v. (3 App. Div. [N. Y.] 219) 298, 319.
Zimmerman v. (28 App. Div. [N. Y.] 445) 309.
Zingrehe v. (56 App. Div. [N. Y.] 555) 419.
Union Ry. & Transit Co., Kelly v. (95 Mo. 279) 408.
Union St. R. Co., Edgerly v. (67 N. H. 312) 33, 178, 184.
Union St. Ry. Co., Briggs v. (148 Mass. 72) 38-40.
Brightman v. (167 Mass. 113) 147, 153.
Holman v. (114 Mich. 208) 402, 410.
Howland v. (150 Mass. 86) 257.
Humbird v. (110 Mo. 76) 275.
v. Stone (54 Kan. 83) 355.
Union Traction Co., Ackerman v. (205 Pa. 477) 271.
Anderson v. (7 Pa. Dist. R. 41) 196, 197.
Bainbridge v. (55 Atl. [Pa.] 836) 84.
v. Barnett (67 N. E. [Ind. App.] 205) 359.
Barry v. (194 Pa. 576) 107.
Buehler v. (200 Pa. 177) 134.
Burke v. (198 Pa. 497) 291, 294, 315.
Darwood v. (189 Pa. 592) 289.
Foster v. (199 Pa. 498) 92, 159.
Gould v. (190 Pa. 198) 344.
Holmes v. (199 Pa. 229) 214.
Howard v. (195 Pa. 391) 137.
Howell v. (202 Pa. 338) 164.
Hunterson v. (55 Atl. [Pa.] 543) 8, 43, 55, 58.
Jennings v. (55 Atl. [Pa.] 765) 93.
Keenan v. (202 Pa. 107) 291.
Manayunk & R. Boarding & Livery Stable Co. v. (7 Pa. Super. Ct. 104) 299.
McCaw v. (54 Atl. [Pa.] 893) 68, 108.
McGovern v. (192 Pa. 344) 218.
Miller v. (198 Pa. 639) 279.
Moser v. (205 Pa. 481) 291.
Pieper v. (202 Pa. 100) 291.
Sauers v. (193 Pa. 602) 344.
Shugard v. (201 Pa. 562) 375.
Sweeney v. (199 Pa. 293) 92, 159.
Taylor v. (184 Pa. 465) 343.
Tyson v. (199 Pa. 264) 292.
Watkins v. (194 Pa. 564) 213.
Wimmer v. (12 Pa. Super. Ct. 467) 173.
Union Trunk Line, Cameron v. (10 Wash. 507) 221, 243.
Christensen v. (6 Wash. 75) 292, 404, 409.
Smith v. (18 Wash. 351) 225.
United Rys. & Elec. Co., Garrison v. (55 Atl. [Md.] 371) 173, 195.
v. Hertel (55 Atl. [Md.] 428) 143.

[REFERENCES ARE TO PAGES.]

Union Rys. & Elec. Co., McNab v. (94 Md. 719) 291.
State v. (54 Atl. [Md.] 612) 290.
State v. (93 Md. 619) 113.
v. Woodbridge (55 Atl. [Md.] 444) 143.
United Traction Co., Allen v. (67 App. Div. [N. Y.] 363) 112,
Bliss v. (75 App. Div. [N. Y.] 235) 405.
Bumbear v. (198 Pa. 198) 83, 84, 86.
Dunlay v. (18 Pa. Super. Ct. 206) 109.
Henderson v. (202 Pa. 527) 219, 243.
Jones v. (201 Pa. 344) 277.
Jones v. (201 Pa. 346) 268.
Powelson v. (204 Pa. 474) 8, 42, 43, 53, 55, 58.
Thompson v. (193 Pa. 555) 282.
Welsh v. (202 Pa. 530) 286.
Upham v. Detroit City Ry. Co. (85 Mich. 12) 64, 66, 68.
Upson, San Antonio Traction Co. v. (71 S. W. [Tex. Civ. App.] 565) 296, 325.
U. P. Steam Baking Co. v. Omaha St. Ry. Co. (94 N. W. [Neb.] 533) 305.
Uransky v. Dry Dock, E. B. & B. R. Co. (59 Hun [N. Y.] 626, 13 N. Y. Supp. 670) 394.
Urbana & C. Elec. St. Ry. Co., Hanson v. (75 Ill. App. 474) 14, 183, 404, 415.
Utica & Belt Line St. R. Co., Berry v. (76 App. Div. [N. Y.] 490) 89.
Utica & M. R. Co., Griffith v. (17 N. Y. Supp. 692) 89.

## V.

Vail v. Broadway R. Co. (147 N. Y. 377) 64, 66, 67, 70.
v. Cincinnati Inclined Plane Ry. Co. (7 Ohio Circ. Dec. 28) 117.
Valentine v. Broadway & S. A. R. Co. (14 Daly [N. Y.] 540) 39.
v. Middlesex R. Co. (137 Mass. 28) 133.
Valley City St. & Cable Ry. Co., Finn v. (86 Mich. 74) 14, 142.
Van de Venter v. Chicago City Ry. Co. (26 Fed. 32) 52, 53.
Van Dyke v. Atlantic Ave. R. Co. (67 Fed. 296) 391.
Atlantic Ave. R. Co. v. (72 Fed. 458) 391.
Van Natta v. People's St. Ry., E. L. & P. Co. (133 Mo. 13) 253.
Van Patten v. Schenectady St. Ry. Co. (80 Hun [N. Y.] 494) 289.
Van Pelt, Calumet Elec. St. Ry. Co. v. (68 Ill. App. 582) 256, 277.
Van Sickle v. Atlantic Ave. R. Co. (12 Misc. [N. Y.] 217) 385, 390.
Van Vleck, Chicago City Ry. Co. v (143 Ill. 480) 403.
Van Winkle v. Brooklyn City R. Co. (46 Hun [N. Y.] 564) 98.
Vasele v. Grant St. Elec. Ry. Co. (16 Wash. 602) 49, 57.
Vassau v. Madison Elec. Ry. Co. (106 Wis. 301) 192, 437.
Versailles Traction Co., Moran v. (188 Pa. 557) 152.
Vicksburg R. Power & Mfg. Co., White v. (31 So. [Miss.] 709) 327.
Vincent v. Norton & T. St. Ry. Co. (180 Mass. 104) 302, 327.

[REFERENCES ARE TO PAGES.]

Vinton v. Middlesex R. Co. (11 Allen [Mass.] 304) 33, 178.
Vitelli v. Nassau Elec. R. Co. (53 App. Div. [N. Y.] 639) 296.
Vogel v. North Jersey St. Ry. Co. (54 Atl. [N. J. Law] 563) 252.
Volk, Chicago Ry. Co. v. (45 Ill. 175) 127.
Vonelling v. Metropolitan St. Ry. Co. (35 Misc. [N. Y.] 301) 289, 294.
Vroman v. Houston & W. St. Ferry R. Co. (7 Misc. [N. Y.] 234) 88, 95.

## W.

Wachtel, East St. Louis & St. L. Elec. St. Ry. Co. v. (63 Ill. App. 181) 335, 336.
v. East St. Louis & St. L. Elec. St. Ry. Co. (77 Ill. App. 465) 337.
Wade v. Columbia Elec. St. Ry., L. & P. Co. (51 S. C. 296) 121, 436.
v. City Ry. Co. (36 Or. 311) 408, 409.
Waechter v. Second Ave. Traction Co. (198 Pa. 129) 438.
Wagner v. Metropolitan St. Ry. Co. (79 App. Div. [N. Y.] 591) 321, 426.
v. Pittsburgh & W. E. Pass. Ry. Co. (158 Pa. 419) 356.
Wahlgren v. Market St. Ry. Co. (132 Cal. 656) 211, 220, 243, 427.
Wakefield v. South Boston R. Co. (117 Mass. 544) 203.
Wakefield & S. St. Ry. Co., Hall v. (178 Mass. 98) 372.
Kelly v. (175 Mass. 331) 290.
Kelly v. (179 Mass. 542) 299.
Walbridge v. Schuylkill Elec. Ry. Co. (190 Pa. 274) 284.
Waldhaur, City & Suburban Ry. Co. v. (84 Ga. 706) 343, 424.
Walker, Atlanta Ry. & Power Co. v. (112 Ga. 725) 210, 235.
Atlanta St. R. Co. v. (93 Ga. 462) 360, 401, 410.
v. Dry Dock, E. B. & B. R. Co. (33 How. Pr. [N. Y.] 327) 193.
Little Rock Traction & Electric Co. v. (65 Ark. 144) 191.
Wall, Chicago City Ry. Co. v. (93 Ill. App. 411) 308, 409.
v. Helena St. Ry. Co. (12 Mont. 44) 242.
Wallace, Baltimore Traction Co. v. (77 Md. 435) 210, 235, 236, 238, 433.
v. Detroit City R. Co. (58 Mich. 231) 365.
v. Suburban Ry. Co. (26 Or. 174) 253.
v. Taunton St. Ry. Co. (119 Mass. 91) 394.
v. Third Ave. R. Co. (36 App. Div. [N. Y.] 57) 38, 40, 53, 55.
Wallen, North Chicago St. R. Co. v. (82 Ill. App. 103) 237.
Walling, Germantown Pass. Ry. Co. v. (97 Pa. 55) 80, 81.
Walls v. Rochester Ry. Co. (92 Hun [N. Y.] 581) 211, 221.
Walsh v. Atlantic Ave. R. Co. (23 App. Div. [N. Y.] 19) 220, 298.
Paducah St. Ry. Co. v. (22 Ky. L. R. 532) 142.
West Chicago St. R. Co. v. (78 Ill. App. 595) 14, 247.
Walters, Highland Ave. & B. R. Co. v. (91 Ala. 435) 373.
v. Philadelphia Traction Co. (161 Pa. 36) 39, 40, 55, 57.
v. Syracuse Rapid Transit Ry. Co. (64 App. Div. [N. Y.] 150) 344, 352.

[REFERENCES ARE TO PAGES.]

Walton, Indianapolis St. Ry. Co. v. (29 Ind. App. 368) 359.
Waniata, West Chicago St. R. Co. v. (68 Ill. App. 481) 142, 165, 423, 439.
Want, North Side St. Ry. Co. v. (4 Willson, Civ. Cas. Ct. App. [Tex.] § 168) 322.
Wanzer v. Chippewa Valley Elec. R. Co. (108 Wis. 319) 123, 124.
Ward, Birmingham Ry. & Elec. Co. v. (124 Ala. 409) 432, 433.
v. Central Park, N. & E. R. R. Co. (33 N. Y. Super. Ct. 392) 64, 72.
v. Charleston City Ry. Co. (19 S. C. 521) 405.
v. Lakeside Ry. Co. (20 Pa. Co. Ct. R. 494) 321.
v. Rochester Elec. Ry. Co. (17 N. Y. Supp. 427) 289.
Wardle v. New Orleans City R. Co. (35 La. Ann. 202) 142, 153.
Ware, Collins Park & Belt R. Co. v. (112 Ga. 663) 427.
South Covington & C. St. Ry. Co. v. (84 Ky. 267) 161, 431, 435.
Warner v. People's St. Ry. Co. (141 Pa. 615) 213, 233, 234.
Warren v. Mendenhall (77 Minn. 145) 311.
v. Union Ry. Co. (46 App. Div. [N. Y.] 517) 302.
Warren St. Ry. Co., Palmer v. (56 Atl. [Pa.] 49) 119, 121.
Washington v. Spokane St. Ry. Co. (13 Wash. 9) 112.
Washington, A. & M. V. Elec. Ry. Co. v. Quayle (95 Va. 741) 182.
Washington & G. R. Co., Adams v. (9 App. D. C. 26) 65, 68, 72, 75, 112, 129.
Adams v. (11 App. D. C. 396) 392.
Brown v. (11 App. D. C. 37) 38, 39, 392.
Carpenter v. (121 U. S. 474) 196, 203.
Converse v. (2 MacArthur [D. C.] 504) 179, 182, 187.
v. Dashiel (7 App. D. C. 507) 433.
v. Gladmon (15 Wall. [U. S.] 401) 253, 275.
v. Grant (11 App. D. C. 107) 143, 162.
v. Harmon's Adm'r (147 U. S. 571) 92, 141, 159.
Harmon v. (6 Mackey [D. C.] 57) 147.
v. Hickey (166 U. S. 521) 126.
v. Hickey (12 App. D. C. 269) 127.
Holohan v. (19 D. C. 316) 46, 57.
Hurdle v. (8 App. D. C. 120) 227.
Lemont v. (1 Mackey [D. C.] 180) 33, 178.
McDade v. (5 Mackey [D. C.] 144) 388.
v. McLane (11 App. D. C. 220) 410, 411.
v. Patterson (9 App. D. C. 423) 12.
Reiners v. (9 App. D. C. 19) 275.
Rouser v. (13 App. D. C. 320) 142, 146, 149, 163.
Sinclair v. (MacArthur & M. [D. C.] 13) 414, 427.
Washington Water Power Co., Gray v. (27 Wash. 713, 30 Wash. 665) 361.
Waterbury Horse R. Co., Farrell v. (60 Conn. 239) 228.
Waterloo & C. F. Rapid Transit Co., Ames v. (95 N. W. [Iowa] 161) 219.

[REFERENCES ARE TO PAGES.]

Watermolen v. Fox Rixer Elec. Ry. & Power Co. (110 Wis. 153) 292.
Watervliet Turnpike & R. Co., Higgins v. (46 N. Y. 23) 33, 178, 188.
Losee v. (63 Hun [N. Y.] 404) 142, 163.
Watkins v. Atlantic Ave. R. Co. (20 Hun [N. Y.] 237) 124, 329.
v. Birmingham R. & E. Co. (120 Ala. 147) 92, 140, 159.
Danville St. Car Co. v. (97 Va. 713) 363.
v. Union Traction Co. (194 Pa. 564) 213.
Watson v. Brooklyn City Ry. Co. (14 Misc. [N. Y.] 405) 359.
v. Interurban St. Ry. Co. (84 N. Y. Supp. 556) 307.
v. Minneapolis St. Ry. Co. (53 Minn. 551) 319, 405, 420.
v. Mound City St. Ry. Co. (133 Mo. 246) 210, 213, 235.
v. Oswego St. Ry. Co. (7 Misc. [N. Y.] 562) 181.
v. Portland & C. E. Ry. Co. (91 Me. 584) 64, 66, 74.
v. St. Paul City Ry. Co. (42 Minn. 46) 102.
Watters, Mobile St. Ry. Co. v. (135 Ala. 227) 174.
Weadock, Tunison v. (89 N. W. [Mich.] 703) 327.
Weams, Louisville City Ry. Co. v. (80 Ky. 420) 102, 142.
Weaver v. Benton-Bellefontaine Ry. Co. (60 Mo. App. 207) 292.
Webb v. Chicago City Ry. Co. (83 Ill. App. 565) 223.
v. Metropolitan St. Ry. Co. (89 Mo. App. 604) 437.
v. Yonkers R. Co. (51 App. Div. [N. Y.] 194) 403.
Weber v. Brooklyn, Q. C. & S. R. Co. (47 App. Div. [N. Y.] 306) 32, 33, 183.
v. Buffalo Ry. Co. (20 App. Div. [N. Y.] 292) 356.
v. Kansas City Cable Ry. Co. (100 Mo. 194) 133, 140, 142.
v. New Orleans & C. R. Co. (104 La. 367) 61.
v. St. Paul City Ry. Co. (67 Minn. 155) 401.
v. Third Ave. R. Co. (12 App. Div. [N. Y.] 512) 441.
Webster v. New Orleans City & L. R. Co. (51 La. Ann. 299) 213.
Weeks v. New Orleans & C. R. Co. (32 La. Ann. 615) 212, 228.
Weideman v. Tacoma Ry. & Motor Co. (7 Wash. 517) 389.
Weidinger v. Third Ave. R. Co. (40 App. Div. [N. Y.] 197) 319.
Weil v. Dry Dock, E. B. & B. R. Co. (113 N. Y. 147) 267.
Weiller, People's Pass. Ry. Co. v. (17 Wkly. Notes Cas. [Pa.] 306) 103, 126.
Weinberg v. Metropolitan St. Ry. Co. (139 Mo. 286) 428.
Weiner v. Minneapolis St. Ry. Co. (80 Minn. 312) 432.
Weingarten v. Metropolitan St. Ry. Co. (62 App. Div. [N. Y.] 364) 228.
Weiser v. Broadway & N. St. R. Co. (2 Ohio Dec. 463) 293.
Weiss v. Metropolitan St. Ry. Co. (29 Misc. [N. Y.] 332) 142.
v. Metropolitan St. Ry. Co. (33 App. Div. [N. Y.] 221) 253, 260.
Weissner v. St. Paul City Ry. Co. (47 Minn. 468) 267, 276.
Weitzman v. Nassau Elec. R. Co. (33 App. Div. [N. Y.] 585) 264, 285.
Weldon v. Third Ave. R. Co. (3 App. Div. [N. Y.] 370) 309.
Wellesley & B. St. Ry. Co., Healey v. (176 Mass. 440) 397.
Wells v. Brooklyn City R. Co. (58 Hun [N. Y.] 389) 218, 219, 236.
v. Brooklyn Heights R. Co. (34 Misc. [N. Y.] 44) 246.

[REFERENCES ARE TO PAGES.]

Wells v. Steinway Ry. Co. (18 App. Div. [N. Y.] 180) 14, 358.
Welsch v. Jackson County Horse R. Co. (81 Mo. 466) 271.
Springfield Consol. Ry. Co. v. (56 Ill. App. 196) 250, 253, 410.
Welsh v. United Traction Co. (202 Pa. 530) 286.
Welty v. St. Charles St. R. Co. (109 La. 733) 241.
Werbowlsky v. Ft. Wayne & E. Ry. Co. (86 Mich. 236) 142, 147, 164.
Werner v. Citizens' Ry. Co. (81 Mo. 368) 210, 235, 240.
West Asheville & S. S. Ry. Co., Witsell v. (120 N. C. 557) 118, 410.
Westchester Elec. Ry. Co., D'Arcy v. (81 N. Y. Supp. 952) 109.
Kennealy v. (86 App. Div. [N. Y.] 293) 349, 353.
Kilbane v. (19 Misc. [N. Y.] 184) 296, 325.
Morrissey v. (30 App. Div. [N. Y.] 424) 415.
Morrissey v. (18 App. Div. [N. Y.] 67) 228, 245.
Morrow v. (54 App. Div. [N. Y.] 592) 407.
Patterson v. (26 App. Div. [N. Y.] 336) 139, 148.
Saffer v. (22 Misc. [N. Y.] 555) 329.
West Chicago St. R. Co. v. Binder (51 Ill. App. 420) 9, 233, 235, 239, 270, 281.
v. Bode (51 Ill. App. 440) 417.
v. Boeker (70 Ill. App. 67) 291.
v. Cahill (165 Ill. 496) 403.
v. Camp (46 Ill. App. 503) 271.
v. Carr (170 Ill. 479) 124, 403.
v. Coit (50 Ill. App. 540) 233, 235, 237.
v. Dedloff (92 Ill. App. 547) 297, 308, 408.
v. Dooley (76 Ill. App. 424) 397, 433, 438.
v. Dougherty (89 Ill. App. 362) 313, 314, 316.
v. Dudzik (67 Ill. App. 681) 38, 40.
v. Dwyer (162 Ill. 482) 381.
v. Dwyer (57 Ill. App. 440) 381.
Eastman v. (79 Ill. App. 585) 393.
v. Eagan (74 Ill. App. 442) 256.
v. Estep (162 Ill. 130) 394.
v. Feldstein (69 Ill. App. 36) 332.
Finley v. (90 Ill. App. 368) 278.
v. Fishman (68 Ill. App. 445) 414.
v. Foster (175 Ill. 396) 433.
v. Grenell (90 Ill. App. 30) 398.
Hope v. (82 Ill. App. 311) 150, 393.
v. James (69 Ill. App. 609) 5, 6.
v. Johnson (69 Ill. App. 147) 414.
v. Johnson (180 Ill. 285) 90, 101, 107.
v. Johnson (77 Ill. App. 142) 90, 107, 423.
Kean v. (75 Ill. App. 38) 72, 392.
v. Kennelly (170 Ill. 508) 401, 403.
v. Kennelly (66 Ill. App. 244) 128.
v. Klecka (94 Ill. App. 346) 347.
Kornazsewska v. (76 Ill. App. 366) 392, 396.

[REFERENCES ARE TO PAGES.]

West Chicago St. R. Co. v. Kromshinsky (185 Ill. 92) 102, 412.
v. Levy (182 Ill. 525) 435.
v. Levy (82 Ill. App. 202) 317, 435.
v. Liderman (187 Ill. 463) 232.
v. Liderman (87 Ill. App. 638) 232.
v. Liebig (79 Ill. App. 567) 434.
Lieserowitz v. (80 Ill. App. 248) 396.
v. Luka (72 Ill. App. 60) 141-143.
v. Luleich (85 Ill. App. 643) 32, 33, 171, 178, 189, 413, 427.
v. Lups (74 Ill. App. 420) 38, 40, 424, 433.
v. Lyon (57 Ill. App. 536) 141.
v. Manning (70 Ill. App. 239; affirmed 170 Ill. 417) 20, 142, 143.
v. Marks (82 Ill. App. 185) 83, 87.
v. Martin (154 Ill. 523) 126.
v. McCallum (169 Ill. 240) 241, 324.
McGary v. (85 Ill. App. 610) 137.
v. McNulty (166 Ill. 203) 123.
v. McNulty (64 Ill. App. 549) 83, 86.
v. Mueller (165 Ill. 499) 393.
v. Mueller (64 Ill. App. 601) 392.
v. Musa (80 Ill. App. 223) 432.
v. Nash (166 Ill. 528) 394.
v. Nash (64 Ill. App. 548) 102.
v. Nilson (70 Ill. App. 171) 209, 225.
v. O'Connor (85 Ill. App. 278) 366.
Petters v. (196 Ill. 298) 324.
v. Piper (165 Ill. 325) 122.
v. Piper (64 Ill. App. 605) 310.
v. Raftery (85 Ill. App. 319) 394.
v. Ranstead (70 Ill. App. 111) 212.
v. Scanlan (68 Ill. App. 626) 264, 432, 440.
v. Schwartz (93 Ill. App. 387) 270, 274.
v. Shiplett (85 Ill. App. 683) 244, 413.
v. Stephens (66 Ill. App. 303) 134.
v. Stiver (69 Ill. App. 625) 161.
v. Stoltenberg (62 Ill. App. 420) 253, 277.
Sullivan v. (64 Ill. App. 628) 253, 256, 277.
v. Torpe (187 Ill. 610) 409.
v. Tuerk (193 Ill. 385) 124.
v. Tuerk (90 Ill. App. 105) 124, 419.
v. Walsh (78 Ill. App. 595) 14, 247.
v. Waniata (68 Ill. App. 481) 142, 165, 423, 439.
v. Wheeler (73 Ill. App. 368) 414.
v. Whittaker (72 Ill. App. 48) 277.
v. Williams (87 Ill. App. 548) 123, 426.
v. Wizemann (83 Ill. App. 402) 320.
v. Yund (68 Ill. App. 609) 120, 122.
West Chicago St. Ry. Co. v. Annis (62 Ill. App. 180) 243.

[REFERENCES ARE TO PAGES.]

West Chicago St. Ry. Co. v. Cahill (64 Ill. App. 539) 157.
Cohen v. (60 Fed. 698) 53, 54.
v. Craig (57 Ill. App. 411) 101, 102, 413.
v. Fishman (169 Ill. 196) 403.
Hagestrom v. (78 Ill. App. 574) 27, 30.
West End & A. St. Ry. Co. v. Mozely (79 Ga. 463) 144.
West End St. Ry. Co., Bigelow v. (161 Mass. 393) 14, 158.
Brittain v. (168 Mass. 10) 386.
Corlin v. (154 Mass. 197) 38-40, 44.
Creamer v. (156 Mass. 320) 14, 15, 17, 139, 140, 225.
Dickinson v. (177 Mass. 365) 22, 34.
Driscoll v. (159 Mass. 142) 297, 314, 315, 317, 325.
Galbraith v. (165 Mass. 572) 296, 325.
Gallagher v. (156 Mass. 157) 50.
Gargan v. (176 Mass. 106) 14, 367.
Gilbert v. (160 Mass. 403) 141, 142, 163, 399.
Glazebrook v. (160 Mass. 239) 323.
Gordon v. (175 Mass. 181) 6, 38, 39, 41.
Hall v. (168 Mass. 461) 212, 214.
Hamilton v. (163 Mass. 199) 135, 136.
Holland v. (155 Mass. 387) 75.
Hurley v. (180 Mass. 370) 289.
Jacobs v. (178 Mass. 116) 14, 163, 399.
Kane v. (169 Mass. 64) 361.
Kenneson v. (168 Mass. 1) 382.
Kerrigan v. (158 Mass. 305) 300, 330.
Magee v. (151 Mass. 240) 312.
Manning v. (166 Mass. 230) 367.
Millard v. (173 Mass. 512) 386.
O'Brien v. (173 Mass. 105) 383.
Oddy v. (178 Mass. 341) 163.
Rosenberg v. (168 Mass. 561) 258.
Slayton v. (174 Mass. 55) 357, 358.
Stuart v. (163 Mass. 391) 384.
Uggla v. (160 Mass. 351) 367.
Whelton v. (172 Mass. 555) 372, 407.
White v. (165 Mass. 522) 146, 147.
Widmer v. (158 Mass. 49) 239.
Westerman v. Metropolitan St. Ry. Co. (84 N. Y. Supp. 501) 294, 309.
Western Union Tel. Co. v. State (82 Md. 293) 351.
West Jersey & S. R. Co., Blackman v. (68 N. J. Law, 1) 411.
Westphal v. St. Joseph & B. H. St. Ry. Co. (96 N. W. [Mich.] 19) 325.
West Philadelphia Pass. Ry. Co., Colgan v. (4 Wkly. Notes Cas. [Pa.] 400) 149.
v. Gallagher (108 Pa. 524) 80, 81, 112.
v. Mulhair (6 Wkly. Notes Cas. [Pa.] 508) 241.
Mulhair v. (5 Wkly. Notes Cas. [Pa.] 190) 241.
Whipple v. (2 Wkly. Notes Cas. [Pa.] 559) 90, 413, 420.

[REFERENCES ARE TO PAGES.]

West Philadelphia Pass. Ry. Co. v. Whipple (5 Wkly. Notes Cas. [Pa.] 68) 90.
West Side R. Co., Boerth v. (87 Wis. 288) 290.
Burnell v. (87 Wis. 387) 384.
Hart v. (86 Wis. 483) 23, 26, 36, 185.
Will v. (84 Wis. 42) 303.
West Side St. Ry. Co., Shenners v. (78 Wis. 383) 276.
Woodard v. (71 Wis. 625) 60.
West St. & N. E. Elec. Ry. Co., Cogswell v. (5 Wash. 46) 21, 83, 84, 430.
Wetzel v. Philadelphia Traction Co. (184 Pa. 407) 375, 376.
Whalen v. Consolidated Traction Co. (61 N. J. Law, 606) 84, 89, 102.
Wheaton v. North Beach & Mission R. Co. (36 Cal. 590) 413, 425.
Wheelahan v. Philadelphia Traction Co. (150 Pa. 187) 290, 295.
Wheeler, West Chicago St. R. Co. v. (73 Ill. App. 368) 414.
Wheeling & E. G. R. Co., Dimmey v. (27 W. Va. 32) 135, 406, 421, 439.
Whelton v. West End St. Ry. Co. (172 Mass. 555) 372, 407.
Whipple v. West Philadelphia Pass. Ry. Co. (2 Wkly. Notes Cas. [Pa.] 559) 90, 413, 420.
West Philadelphia Pass. Ry. Co. v. (5 Wkly. Notes Cas. [Pa.] 68) 90.
Whitaker v. Eighth Ave. R. Co. (51 N. Y. 295) 318, 411.
State v. (160 Mo. 59) 383.
v. Staten Island Midland R. Co. (65 App. Div. [N. Y.] 451) 97.
Whitbeck v. Atlantic Ave. R. Co. (4 N. Y. Supp. 100) 409.
Whitcomb, Cincinnati St. Ry. Co. v. (66 Fed. 915) 293, 313, 321.
White v. Albany Ry. (35 App. Div. [N. Y.] 23) 278, 284.
v. Atlanta Consol. St. Ry. Co. (92 Ga. 494) 47.
v. Milwaukee City Ry. Co. (61 Wis. 536) 118, 132, 400.
v. Twenty-Third St. R. Co. (20 N. Y. Wkly. Dig. 510) 188, 189.
v. Vicksburg R. Power & Mfg. Co. (31 So. [Miss.] 709) 327.
v. West End St. Ry. Co. (165 Mass. 522) 146, 147.
v. Worcester Consol. St. Ry. Co. (167 Mass. 43) 314, 315, 317.
Whittaker, West Chicago St. R. Co. v. (72 Ill. App. 48) 277.
Whittemore, Kankakee Elec. Ry. Co. v. (45 Ill. App. 484) 353, 412.
Widmer v. West End St. Ry. Co. (158 Mass. 49) 239.
Wigton v. Metropolitan St. Ry. Co. (38 App. Div. [N. Y.] 207) 436.
Wihnyk v. Second Ave. R. Co. (14 App. Div. [N. Y.] 515) 252, 273.
Wilbrand v. Eighth Ave. R. Co. (3 Bosw. [N. Y.] 314) 317.
Wilcox, Chicago City Ry. Co. v. (138 Ill. 370) 249, 254, 259.
Chicago City Ry. Co. v. (33 Ill. App. 450) 416.
v. Wilmington City Ry. Co. (2 Pen. [Del.] 157) 411, 440.
Wilde v. Lynn & B. R. Co. (163 Mass. 533) 80, 81.
Wildman, Birmingham R. & E. Co. v. (119 Ala. 547) 144.
Wiley v. Smith (25 App. Div. [N. Y.] 351) 361.
Wilkerson v. Corrigan Consol. St. Ry. Co. (26 Mo. App. 144) 102, 115.
Wilkes-Barre, etc., St. Ry. Co., Gibbons v. (155 Pa. 279) 303, 315, 317, 330, 334, 338.

[REFERENCES ARE TO PAGES.]

Wilkes-Barre & W. S. Ry. Co., Central Pennsylvania Tel. Co. v. (1 Pa. Dist. Ct. 628) 349.
Wilkes-Barre & W. V. Traction Co., Davison v. (10 Pa. Super. Ct. 442) 335.
Fenner v. (202 Pa. 365) 307, 326.
Le Grand v. (10 Pa. Super. Ct. 12) 247.
Wilkins v. Omaha & C. B. Ry. & Bridge Co. (96 Iowa, 668) 302, 327, 408, 424.
Wilkinson, Baltimore City Pass. Ry. Co. v. (30 Md. 224) 50.
Richmond Traction Co. v. (43 S. E. [Va.] 622) 182, 185, 186.
Will v. West Side R. Co. (84 Wis. 42) 303.
Willamette St. Ry. Co., Coughtry v. (21 Or. 245) 336.
Williams v. Minneapolis St. Ry. Co. (92 N. W. [Minn.] 479) 361.
North Chicago St. R. Co. v. (140 Ill. 275) 2, 11, 20, 21, 38-40, 42, 83, 88.
North Chicago St. R. Co. v. (40 Ill. App. 590) 88.
Richmond Traction Co. v. (46 S. E. [Va.] 292) 142.
Savannah T. & G. of H. Ry. v. (43 S. E. [Ga.] 751) 391.
West Chicago St. R. Co. v. (87 Ill. App. 548) 123, 426.
Williamson v. Brooklyn Heights R. Co. (53 App. Div. [N. Y.] 399) 416.
v. Cambridge R. Co. (144 Mass. 148) 411.
v. Metropolitan St. Ry. Co. (29 Misc. [N. Y.] 324) 292, 325.
Willis v. Metropolitan St. Ry. Co. (63 App. Div. [N. Y.] 332) 139, 140, 142.
v. Second Ave. Traction Co. (189 Pa. 430) 109, 422, 434.
Willmott v. Corrigan Consol. St. Ry. Co. (106 Mo. 535) 82, 102.
Willoeby, Citizens' St. R. Co. v. (134 Ind. 563) 187, 189, 192, 398, 436.
Will's Adm'x, Louisville Ry. Co. v. (66 S. W. [Ky.] 628) 243.
Wills v. Ashland L. P. & St. Ry. Co. (108 Wis. 255) 260.
v. Lynn & B. R. Co. (129 Mass. 351) 71.
Wilman v. People's Ry. Co. (55 Atl. [Del. Sup.] 332) 294, 313, 317.
Wilmington City Ry. Co., Betts v. (53 Atl. [Del.] 358) 139, 143.
Brown v. (1 Pen. [Del.] 332) 295, 313, 314, 316, 321.
Cox v. (53 Atl. [Del.] 569) 295, 313, 314, 321.
Higgins v. (1 Marv. [Del.] 352) 305, 313, 314, 316, 317, 323, 392.
Karkzewski v. (54 Atl. [Del.] 746) 386, 388.
Maxwell v. (1 Marv. [Del.] 199) 313, 314, 316, 321, 392, 409, 440.
Mills v. (1 Marv. [Del.] 269) 247, 400.
Wilcox v. (2 Pen. [Del.] 157) 411, 440.
Wilmington St. Ry. Co., Rittenhouse v. (120 N. C. 544) 381, 397.
Wilmington & N. Elec. Ry. Co., Adams v. (3 Pen. [Del.] 512) 313, 314.
Farley v. (52 Atl. [Del.] 543) 309, 310.
Farley v. (3 Pen. [Del.] 581) 310, 313, 314.
Wilmington & N. C. Elec. Ry. Co., Neal v. (3 Pen. [Del.] 467) 349.
Wilson v. Broadway & S. A. R. Co. (8 Misc. [N. Y.] 450) 423.
v. Citizens' St. Ry. Co. (105 Tenn. 74) 294, 324.
v. Cunningham (3 Cal. 241) 322.

[REFERENCES ARE TO PAGES.]

Wilson v. Duluth St. Ry. Co. (64 Minn. 363) 331.
Elgin City Ry. Co. v. (56 Ill. App. 364) 115, 132.
Indianapolis St. Ry. Co. v. (66 N. E. [Ind.] 950) 196, 203.
Memphis St. Ry. Co. v. (108 Tenn. 618) 320, 324.
v. Minneapolis St. Ry. Co. (74 Minn. 436) 320.
v. Nassau Elec. R. Co. (56 App. Div. [N. Y.] 570) 411.
Wilton v. Middlesex Ry. Co. (107 Mass. 108) 23, 26.
v. Middlesex Ry. Co. (125 Mass. 130) 76.
Wimmer v. Union Traction Co. (12 Pa. Super. Ct. 467) 173.
Winch v. Third Ave. R. Co. (12 Misc. [N. Y.] 403) 290.
Winchell v. St. Paul City Ry. Co. (90 N. W. [Minn.] 1050) 239.
Windover v. Troy City Ry. Co. (4 App. Div. [N. Y.] 203) 378.
Winn, Highland Ave. & B. R. Co. v. (93 Ala. 306) 182.
Winnegar's Adm'r v. Central Pass. Ry. Co. (85 Ky. 547) 187, 189, 190.
Winnipeg Elec. St. Ry. Co., Lines v. (11 Manitoba, 77) 336.
Winona Ry. & Light Co., Palmer v. (78 Minn. 138) 168.
Winter v. Crosstown St. Ry. Co. (8 Misc. [N. Y.] 362) 304.
v. Federal St. & P. V. Pass. Ry. Co. (153 Pa. 26) 294, 308, 321.
Winterfield v. Second Ave. R. Co. (20 N. Y. Supp. 801) 279.
Winters v. Kansas City Cable Ry. Co. (99 Mo. 509) 254, 269, 277.
Wise v. Brooklyn Heights R. Co. (46 App. Div. [N. Y.] 246) 225.
v. South Covington & C. St. Ry. Co. (17 Ky. L. R. 1359) 183.
Wiswell, North Chicago St. R. Co. v. (168 Ill. 613) 38, 40, 45.
North Chicago St. R. Co. v. (68 Ill. App. 443) 431.
Withee v. Somerset Traction Co. (56 Atl. [Me.] 204) 375.
Witherington v. Lynn & B. R. Co. (182 Mass. 596) 98.
Witsell v. West Asheville & S. S. Ry. Co. (120 N. C. 557) 118, 410.
Witten, Ft. Worth St. R. Co. v. (74 Tex. 202) 419.
Wizeman, West Chicago St. R. Co. v. (83 Ill. App. 402) 320.
Woeckner v. Erie Elec. Motor Co. (176 Pa. 451) 251, 277.
v. Erie Elec. Motor Co. (182 Pa. 182) 264, 434.
v. Erie Elec. Motor Co. (187 Pa. 206) 412.
Woelfel v. Federal St. & P. V. P. Ry. Co. (183 Pa. 213) 329.
Wolf v. City & Suburban Ry. Co. (72 Pac. [Or.] 329) 213, 216, 237.
v. Third Ave. R. Co. (67 App. Div. [N. Y.] 605) 157.
Wolfkiel v. Sixth Ave. R. Co. (38 N. Y. 49) 45, 53, 54.
Woo Dan v. Seattle Elec. Ry. & P. Co. (5 Wash. 466) 39, 40, 42, 45.
Wood, Henderson St. Ry. Co. v. (21 Ky. L. R. 808, 53 S. W. 116) 413, 426.
v. Detroit City St. Ry. Co. (52 Mich. 402) 289, 319.
Louisville City Ry. Co. v. (2 Ky. L. R. 387) 238.
v. Third Ave. R. Co. (91 Hun [N. Y.] 276) 368.
Woodard v. West Side St. Ry. Co. (71 Wis. 625) 60.
Woodbridge, United Rys. & Elec. Co. v. (55 Atl. [Md.] 444) 143.
Woodley v. Baltimore & P. R. Co. (19 D. C. 542) 125.
Woodland v. North Jersey St. Ry. Co. (66 N. J. Law, 455) 297, 319.
Woodlock, Houston City St. Ry. Co. v. (29 S. W. [Tex. Civ. App.] 817) 230, 246.

[REFERENCES ARE TO PAGES.]

Woodman v. Metropolitan R. Co. (149 Mass. 335) 357.
Woods v. Metropolitan St. Ry. Co. (48 Mo. App. 125) 196, 199.
Wooley v. Grand St. & N. R. Co. (83 N. Y. 121) 360, 366, 407.
Wooster v. Broadway & S. A. R. Co. (72 Hun [N. Y.] 197) 404.
Worcester Consol. St. Ry. Co., Gleason v. (68 N. E. [Mass.] 223) 231.
Kane v. (182 Mass. 201) 304.
Tashjian v. (177 Mass. 75) 302.
White v. (167 Mass. 43) 314, 315, 317.
Worcester, L. & S. St. Ry. Co., Cummings v. (166 Mass. 220) 82.
Wormsdorf v. Detroit City Ry. Co. (75 Mich. 472) 111, 406, 411.
Worster v. Forty-Second St. & G. St. Ferry R. Co. (50 N. Y. 203) 361, 362.
Worthington v. Lindell Ry. Co. (72 Mo. App. 162) 49.
Wosika v. St. Paul City Ry. Co. (80 Minn. 364) 289, 295, 309, 310.
Wrasse, Citizens' Traction Co. v. (146 Pa. 417) 149.
Wright, Cincinnati St. Ry. Co. v. (54 Ohio St. 181) 310, 311.
v. Glens Falls, S. H. & F. E. St. R. Co. (24 App. Div. [N. Y.] 617) 173, 191, 437.
v. Malden & M. R. Co. (4 Allen [Mass.] 283) 251, 254, 263, 282, 408.
North Birmingham St. Ry. Co. v. (130 Ala. 419) 382.
v. Third Ave. Ry. Co. (5 N. Y. Supp. 707) 276.
v. Union R. Co. (21 R. I. 554) 185.
Wrixon, North Chicago St. R. Co. v. (150 Ill. 532) 414.
North Chicago St. R. Co. v. (51 Ill. App. 307) 112, 141, 146, 430, 434, 438, 440.
Wyatt v. Citizens' Ry. Co. (55 Mo. 485) 139, 152.
Park Ry. Co., Duncan v. (48 Mo. App. 659) 139, 140, 146, 164.
Wynn v. Central Park, N. & E. R. R. Co. (133 N. Y. 575) 110, 111.
v. City & Suburban Ry. Co. (91 Ga. 344) 21, 31, 75-77, 411.
Wynne v. Atlantic Ave. R. Co. (14 Misc. [N. Y.] 394) 120.
Wysong, Mt. Adams & E. P. Ry. Co. v. (2 Ohio Dec. 65) 143.

## Y.

Yant, Terre Haute Elec. Ry. Co. v. (21 Ind. App. 486) 335.
Yingst v. Lebanon & A. St. Ry. Co. (167 Pa. 438) 335.
Yonkers R. Co., Daub v. (69 Hun [N. Y.] 138) 134.
Delaney v. (13 App. Div. [N. Y.] 114) 303.
Gillespie v. (83 N. Y. Supp 1043) 163.
Guntzer v. (51 App. Div. [N. Y.] 222) 144.
Hyland v. (4 N. Y. Supp. 305) 267, 276.
O'Rourke v. (32 App. Div. [N. Y.] 8) 319.
Webb v. (51 App. Div. [N. Y.] 194) 403.
Young v. Atlantic Ave. R. Co. (10 Misc. [N. Y.] 541) 258.
Camden, G. & W. Ry. Co. v. (60 N. J. Law, 193) 232, 238, 244.
Chicago City Ry. v. (62 Ill. 238) 106, 392.
v. Citizens' St. R. Co. (148 Ind. 54) 216, 222, 232.

[REFERENCES ARE TO PAGES.]

Young, Passenger Ry. Co. v. (21 Ohio St. 518) 188.
Yund, West Chicago St. R. Co. v. (68 Ill. App. 609) 120, 122.

## Z.

Zanesville St. Ry. Co., Chapman v. (27 Wkly. Law Bul. [Ohio] 70) 335.
Zanger v. Detroit City Ry. Co. (87 Mich. 646) 365.
Zeiger, North Chicago St. R. Co. v. (182 Ill. 9) 396, 413.
North Chicago St. R. Co. v. (78 Ill. App. 463) 317.
Zeliff v. North Jersey St. Ry. Co. (55 Atl. [N. J. Sup.] 96) 100.
Zimmer v. Fox River Valley Elec. Ry. Co. (95 N. W. [Wis.] 957) 74, 130.
v. Third Ave. R. Co. (36 App. Div. [N. Y.] 265) 120.
v. Third Ave. R. Co. (36 App. Div. [N. Y.] 273) 396.
Zimmerman v. Denver Consol. Tramway Co. (72 Pac. [Colo. App.] 607) 286.
Zimmermann v. Union Ry. Co. (3 App. Div. [N. Y.] 219) 298, 319.
v. Union Ry. Co. (28 App. Div. [N. Y.] 445) 309.
Zingrebe v. Union Ry. Co. (56 App. Div. [N. Y.] 555) 419.
Zlotovsky v. Twenty-Third St. Ry. Co. (8 Misc. [N. Y.] 463) 250, 261.
Zolpher v. Camden & S. Ry. Co. (55 Atl. [N. J. Err. & App.] 249) 343, 344.

# INDEX.

[REFERENCES ARE TO PAGES.]

## A.

ACT WITHIN SCOPE OF EMPLOYMENT (see "Master and Servant").

AGE (see "Infirm Person").

AGENCY (see "Master and Servant").

AGGRAVATION OF INJURIES (see "Damages").

ALIGHTING FROM CAR,

person a passenger while alighting, 13.
person not a passenger after alighting, 13-17.
a passenger if carrier controls premises, 17-19.
may be passenger if alighting for temporary purpose, 14, 15.
due care in alighting from moving car generally a question of fact, 139, 140.
carrier must furnish reasonable opportunity for alighting, 142.
carrier not an insurer of safety, 141.
carrier must use high degree of care, 141.
slackening speed may constitute invitation to alight, 142.
carrier must know that no one is alighting before starting, 143.
special circumstances may show passenger's lack of due care,
speed of car, 145-148.
manner of alighting,
passenger stepping off moving car backwards cannot recover, 148.
omitting to grasp handles not lack of due care, 150, 151.

[REFERENCES ARE TO PAGES.]

ALIGHTING FROM CAR—Cont'd.

age and physical condition, 152.
children, 152.
aged and infirm persons, 153.
sex of passengers, 154.
wearing trailing dress or hoopskirt not lack of due care, 154, 155.
encumbered with bundles, 156.
place of alighting,
carrier must furnish reasonably safe place for alighting, 157.
carrier must use ordinary care in selecting place for alighting, 157, 158.
preparatory to alighting, 159, 160.
standing on platform, steps, or running board not lack of due care, 159, 160.
notice of desire to alight, 161.
need not be express, 161.
carrier is not negligent when passenger gives no notice, 163.
alighting in spite of warning, 164.
condition of car, 164, 165.
injury by fellow passenger, 166.
carrier must use reasonable care to prevent, 166.
miscellaneous negligence in operation of car, 167.

ANIMALS RUN OVER,

dog, 347.
cow, 347.

ARM,

due care in putting arm outside car window usually for jury, 99.

ARREST (see "Master and Servant").

ASSAULT (see "Master and Servant").

ASSUMPTION OF RISK,

passenger assumes ordinary dangers incident to position assumed,
riding on front platform, 73.

[REFERENCES ARE TO PAGES.]

ASSUMPTION OF RISK—Cont'd.
riding on rear platform, 78, 79.
riding on steps, 82.
riding on running board, 84.
passenger assumes risk from usual movement of street car, 129, 130.
employe assumes risks naturally incident to his employment,
conductors, 371-373.
motormen and drivers, 378.
miscellaneous, 383, 384.
employe may continue working a reasonable time after notice of defect, unless danger evident, 373, 378.

B.

BANANA PEEL,
on stairway of elevated railroad, does not show negligence, 61.

BAR (see "Driving Bar").

BELL (see, also, "Gong"),
unauthorized passenger ringing, 60.

BICYCLE RIDER,
due care in crossing tracks and riding on tracks, 341-343.
negligence of company, 344, 345.

BLIND MAN (see "Infirm Person").

BOARDING CAR,
person boarding car when car stops on signal, a passenger, 5, 6.
person boarding with due care when speed slackened on signal of a passenger, 6, 7.
person boarding when signal unrecognized, not a passenger, 8, 9.
person boarding without signal, not a passenger, 10, 11.
person boarding in violation of rule may be a passenger, 11, 12.
due care in boarding moving car generally a question of fact, 38-42.
special circumstances may show lack of due care,
speed of car, 45.

[REFERENCES ARE TO PAGES.]

BOARDING CAR—Cont'd.

age and physical condition, 46.
incumbered with bundles, 46, 47.
condition of car, 47, 48.
condition of track, 48, 49.
boarding without signal, 49.
boarding against rule of warning, 50.
manner of boarding car, 50, 51.
boarding car not in motion, 51.
carrier must furnish reasonable opportunity for boarding,
carrier not an insurer, 52.
must use high degree of care, 52.
must allow reasonable time for boarding, 53.
must consider age and physical condition of person boarding, 54.
must consider incumbrances of person boarding, 54.
must see that all intending passengers are safe before starting, 54.
slackening speed may be invitation to board, 55.
not negligence to start before passenger is seated, 55.
must use reasonable care in selecting stopping place, 56.
no duty to look out for boys trying to steal ride, 58.
miscellaneous negligence in operating car, 59-62.

BRAKE,

no negligence when passenger injured by, 61.
negligence arising from defect in brake, for jury, 110, 111.

BUMPER,

riding on, lack of due care, 91.
conductor standing on, assumes risk of accident, 372.

BUNDLES (see "Incumbered with Bundles").

C.

CABLE,

where spliced cable broke, negligence for jury, 109.
where city cable killed passenger, no negligence of company, 134.
negligence in operation of, for jury, 367.

CABLE CAR,

same rules in boarding govern cable and electric cars, 45.
same rules as to standing on front platform govern horse, cable, and electric cars, 66, 67.
cable cars resemble steam cars more nearly than horse cars, 148.
cable cars more dangerous than horse cars, 294.

CAR (see "Street Car").

CAR LEAVING TRACK (see "Derailment").

CARRIER (see "Passenger").

CHANGING POSITION ON CAR,

usually held lack of due care, 94, 95.

CHECK (see "Transfer").

CHILD,

invited to ride free, a passenger, 23-26.
  if sui juris, not a passenger, 24, 25.
stealing ride, a trespasser, 27, 28.
stealing ride, employes need not look out for, 28, 58.
newsboy a licensee, 28-30.
not bound by notice forbidding riding on front platform, 72.
age and capacity of child count in determining due care, 75.
carrier must use more care towards children, 76.
  on car, 76.
  alighting from car, 153.
  in street, 270.
capacity of child for exercising due care, 249-251.
standard of care for child, 252, 253, 311.
whether negligence of parent may be imputed to child, 254, 255.
due care of child run over, for jury, 256-260.
lack of due care of child run over, 260, 261.
due care of parent in allowing child in street, 262-264.
due care of parent in leaving child alone in or near house, 265-268.

CITY,

liability for defects in tracks, 355.

[REFERENCES ARE TO PAGES.]

COLLISION,

passenger on running board,
colliding with post, 87-89.
colliding with wagon, 85.
colliding with other car, 86.
passenger on car,
collision between two street cars, 119-122.
collision between street car and wagon, 122-124.
collision between street car and steam railroad, 125-127.
collision between street car and wagon,
wagon crossing tracks, 289-300.
wagon on or near tracks, 301-307.
imputed negligence, 308, 309.
age and occupation of driver, 311, 312.
right of way, 313-320.
negligence in operation of car, 320-332.

COLOR,

passenger may not be ejected on account of, 181.
separate equal accommodations for white and colored persons constitutional, 181.

CONDITION OF CAR (see "Street Car").

CONDITION OF TRACK (see "Track").

CONDUCTOR (see "Employe").

CONTRACT,

relation of passenger and carrier created by, 2.

CONTRACTOR (see "Independent Contractor").

CONTRIBUTORY NEGLIGENCE (see "Passenger"; "Traveler"; "Employe"; "Negligence").

CONTROLLER (see "Electric Car").

COW (see "Animals Run Over").

CROSSING (see "Street Crossing").

CROSSING TRACK (see "Traveler on Highway").

CROWDED CAR,

a circumstance bearing on due care,
passenger on front platform, 68, 69.
passenger on rear platform, 78.
passenger on steps, 80.
passenger on running board, 83.
not negligence on part of company to crowd cars, 106, 107.
company must use greater care when car is crowded, 108.
negligence to run crowded car near obstruction, 87.

CURTAIN HOOK,

no negligence of company when accident from, 112.

CURTAIN ROD,

no negligence of company when accident from, 112.

CUSTOM,

of allowing passengers to ride on front platform, a circumstance bearing on due care, 70.
of requiring passengers to smoke on front platform an express permission for them to ride there, 70.

CUSTOMARY STOPPING PLACE,

relation of carrier and passenger may be established at, 3, 4.

## D.

DAMAGES,

excessive and inadequate damages, 413.
excessive verdict may be set aside when, 413.
excessive verdict may be reduced when, 414.
inadequate verdict may be set aside, 414.
verdicts held not excessive, 416-428.
verdicts held excessive, 428-432.
mental suffering may be recovered for when, 433, 434.
special damages must be specially pleaded, 435.
vindictive damages allowed when, 436.
aggravation of injuries, 437.
damages for death, 438-441.

[REFERENCES ARE TO PAGES.]

DEAF MAN (see "Infirm Person").

DEATH, DAMAGES FOR (see "Damages").

DEFECT IN CAR (see "Street Car").

DEFECT IN TRACK (see "Track").

DERAILMENT,

usually raises presumption of negligence, 115-117.

DISORDERLY CONDUCT (see "Ejection").

DOG (see "Animals Run Over").

DOOR,

no negligence when injury from swinging door in elevated station, 62.
no negligence when passenger injured by placing hand on door of car, 94.
driver negligent in not examining broken door, 111.
conductor negligent in closing, 133.

DOUBLE TRACK,

person, after alighting, ceases to be a passenger, 15-18.
due care of person standing between tracks to board car, 48.
pedestrian crossing may be barred from recovery, 224, 225.

DRESS,

negligence of company when passenger caught dress, 96.

DRIVER OF CAR (see "Employe").

DRIVER OF WAGON (see "Traveler on Highway").

DRIVING BAR,

lack of due care to ride upon, 73.

DRUNKENNESS (see "Intoxication").

DUE CARE (see, also, "Passenger"; "Traveler on Highway"; "Employe"),

even if plaintiff lacking in, he may recover if defendant could have prevented accident, 60, 210, 235, 320, 333, 345.

## E.

EJECTION,

passenger may be ejected for misconduct,
refusal to pay fare, 171-173.
unreasonable tender of fare, 174, 175.
language or conduct likely to cause annoyance, 176-178.
refusal to obey reasonable rule, 179, 180.
no ejection on account of color, 181.
actual force not necessary to ejection, 181.
actual contact not necessary to ejection, 182.
must be performed in reasonable manner, 183.
must be performed at reasonable place and time, 184-186.
carrier liable for acts of servant in course of employment, 187-190.
may be liable in exemplary damages, 192.
passenger must obey reasonable rules as to time and place of transfer, 193-195.
whether transfer bad on face gives right to ride, 196-205.

ELECTRIC CAR,

rules in boarding, compared with those governing other cars,
horse cars, 42-44.
cable cars, 45.
rules regarding riding on platform applied to,
plied to,
horse cars, 66.
cable cars, 67.
occupies position midway between steam car and horse car 80, 83.
more dangerous than horse car, 80, 83, 294.
more like steam car than horse car, 148.
defect in appliances, 108, 109.
not a defect in the highway, 367.

ELECTRICITY,

high degree of care must be used in management of, 109, 349.

[REFERENCES ARE TO PAGES.]

ELECTRIC SHOCK,
presumption of negligence may arise from,
boarding car, 61.
passenger on car, 108, 110.
traveler on foot, 350, 351.
traveler in team, 350.
due care and negligence for jury, 352, 353.

ELEVATED RAILWAY,
person on platform of, a passenger, 4.
no negligence when banana peel on steps of, 61.
no negligence when passenger injured by swinging door, 62.
no negligence when passenger injured by placing hand on door of car, 94.

EMBANKMENT,
carrier must use reasonable care to warn passengers alighting near, 157.

EMPLOYE,
employe riding free held a passenger, 34, 35.
accidents to conductors,
assumption of risk, 371-373.
lack of due care, 373, 374.
due care, for jury, 374, 375.
who are fellow servants of, 375, 376.
negligence of company, 376, 377.
accidents to motormen, gripmen, and drivers,
assumption of risk, 378.
lack of due care, 379.
due care for jury, 380.
who are fellow servants of, 381.
negligence of company, 381-383.
accidents to miscellaneous employes,
assumption of risk, 383, 384.
lack of due care, 385.
due care for jury, 385, 386.
who are fellow servants of, 387, 388.
negligence of company, 389-391.
rights and duties of conductor in operating car (see, also, "Ejection"),

[REFERENCES ARE TO PAGES.]

EMPLOYE—Cont'd.

inviting child to ride free, within scope of authority, 23.
negligence in starting car while passenger boarding, for jury, 59.
conductor not necessary as matter of law, 61, 168.
ordinance requiring, is proper regulation, 133.
not bound to remember passenger's notice of desire to alight, 163.
evidence of negligence when conductor caused passenger to fall, 168, 169.
negligence in operation of car, 60.

rights and duties of motormen, gripmen, and drivers in operating car,
inviting child to ride free, within scope of authority, 23.
duty to keep lookout, 236-241, 272-281, 323, 324.
duty to run at proper speed, 241-243, 282-284, 325-330.
duty to give warning, 242, 243, 284, 285, 325.
duty when horse frightened at car, 335-338.
need not come to full stop when signaled, 57.
duty to avoid collisions, 123.
negligence in operation of car, 134.

EVIDENCE,

value of evidence,
credibility of witness for jury, 392, 393.
credibility as affected by interest or bias, 393-395.
credibility as affected by corroboration, 396.
credibility as affected by contradictory statements, 397.

admissibility of evidence,
plaintiff himself as evidence, 398.
physical examination of plaintiff, 399, 400.
exclamations and statements of plaintiff, 400, 401.
medical testimony, 402.
evidence of other witnesses, 403.
competency of employes, 404.
starting and stopping cars, 405.
condition of car, 406.
condition of track, 407.
speed of car, 408, 409.
general negligence in operation of road, 409-412.

[REFERENCES ARE TO PAGES.]

EXCAVATION,

carrier must use reasonable care to warn passengers alighting near, 157.
passenger alighting near, may be guilty of lack of due care, 158.
excavations may be sufficient warning to pedestrians or drivers of wagons, 357.

EXEMPLARY DAMAGES (see "Damages").

## F.

FALLING FROM CAR,

due care of passenger, 97.
negligence of company, 97.

FARE,

actual payment of, not necessary to establish relation of passenger and carrier, 20-22.
person riding free under rule, a passenger, 22.
person riding on pass limiting liability cannot recover, 22.
child invited to ride free, a passenger, 23-26.
if sui juris, not a passenger, 24, 25.
child stealing ride, a trespasser, 27, 28.
newsboy a licensee, 28-30.
passenger forfeits rights by refusal to pay, 32.
passenger may be ejected for refusal to pay, 171-173.
taking fare a circumstance bearing on question of due care when passenger occupies unusual position,
front platform, 68.
rear platform, 78.
steps, 80.
running board, 83.

FELLOW PASSENGERS,

carrier must use reasonable care to protect passengers from injury by,
on car, 113, 114.
alighting from car, 165, 166.

FELLOW SERVANTS,

who are, 375, 376, 381, 387, 388.

[REFERENCES ARE TO PAGES.]

FENDER,

company not negligent in not providing, 287.
car with fender projecting, not an obstruction of highway, 367.

FIRE EXTINGUISHER,

falling in car, raises presumption of negligence, 112.

FIREMAN,

permitted by his occupation to take unusual risks, 311, 312.

FIRE WAGON,

driver of, has right of way in the streets, 313, 318.

FOOT BOARD (see "Running Board").

FORCE (see "Ejection").

FREE PASS (see "Pass")

FREE PASSENGER (see "Fare")

FRIGHTENING HORSE (see "Horse")

FRONT PLATFORM,

not lack of due care to board moving car by, 40.
more dangerous to board by, than by rear platform, 40.
person boarding by, against rule, cannot recover, 50.
not lack of due care to ride upon, 64, 65.
circumstances bearing on due care in riding on,
taking fare, 68.
no objection made, 68.
custom of carrier to permit, 70.
passenger directed to so ride, 70.
position on platform, 72-74.
holding on, 72.
riding on driver's stool, 73.
riding on driving bar, 73.
passenger on front platform assumes ordinary, but not unusual, risks of position, 73.
passenger disobeying reasonable rule cannot recover, 71.
intoxication does not necessarily prevent recovery, 74.
more care must be used towards children, 76.

FUSE,
usually only flash of light when fuse blows out, 108.

GATE,
defective, evidence of negligence, 112.
negligence in failing to provide, 112.

GONG (see, also, "Warning"),
ringing when horse is frightened, 335, 336.

GRATUITOUS PASSENGER (see "Fare").

GUARD (see "Street Car").

## H.

HANDLE BAR,
no recovery by passenger when handle bar broke, 83.

HEADLIGHT,
not necessary as matter of law, 332.

HOLDING ON,
a circumstance affecting due care of passenger,
boarding car, 50, 51.
riding on front platform, 72.
riding on rear platform, 79.
alighting, 151.

HOLE (see "Excavation").

HORSE,
care in selection and use, 135, 247, 287.
frightening horses,
due care of driver, 333, 334.
negligence of company, 335-340.

HORSEBACK RIDERS,
accidents to, 346.

HORSE CAR,
rules in boarding compared with those governing electric cars, 42-44.
rules regarding riding on front platform applied to.
electric cars, 66.
cable cars, 67.
electric car more dangerous than horse car, 80, 83, 148, 294.
cable car more dangerous than horse car, 148.

## I.

ICE,
negligence for jury when ice on steps, 164.

IMPUTED NEGLIGENCE,
whether negligence of parent may be imputed to child, 254, 255.
whether negligence of driver may be imputed to person in team, 308.
negligence of employe in charge of car cannot be imputed to passenger, 121, 123, 125.

INCUMBERED WITH BUNDLES,
a circumstance bearing on due care of passenger,
boarding car, 46, 47.
alighting from car, 156.
carrier must use more care towards person when boarding, 54.

INDEPENDENT CONTRACTOR,
company not liable for negligence of, 247, 356, 369, 377.
company may be liable for negligence of, 247, 248, 339, 356, 377.

INFANT (see "Child").

INFIRM PERSON,
a circumstance bearing on due care of passenger,
boarding car, 46.
alighting from car, 152, 168.
carrier must use more care towards,
boarding car, 54.

INFIRM PERSON—Cont'd.

on car, 153.
a circumstance bearing on due care of person crossing tracks, 212, 223, 311.
deaf man must have other senses more alert, 212, 311, 343.

INSURER,

carrier is not an insurer of safety of passenger,
boarding car, 52.
on car, 101.
alighting from car, 141.

INTOXICATION,

rule forbidding intoxicated passengers' riding on front platform is reasonable, 71.
will not necessarily prevent recovery by passenger, 74, 80, 88.
may do so, 75.
company liable for injury to fellow passenger by, 113.
mere fact of, will not always justify expulsion, 178.
will not necessarily prevent recovery by pedestrian crossing tracks, 212.
intoxication no excuse, 211.
lack of due care, 222, 223, 342.

INVITATION,

stopping car on signal, invitation to board, 5.
slackening speed on signal may be invitation to board, 6.
to child to ride free, within scope of employe's authority, 23.

## J.

JAR (see "Jerk").

JERK,

passenger on platform assumes risks of ordinary jerk,
on front platform, 73.
on rear platform, 78, 79.
on steps, 82.
on running board, 84.
unusual jerk raises presumption of negligence, 128.

JOINT TORT FEASORS,

may be sued jointly, 122, 127, 137, 332, 354.
who are not, 137.
satisfaction from one, a bar, 137.

JOLT (see "Jerk").

## L.

LABORER,

due care of, working on or near track, 227-233.
negligence of company towards, 245, 246.

LANGUAGE (see "Ejection").

LAW OF ROAD (see "Rule of Road").

LEASE,

lessee company held liable, 137, 354.
lessor company held liable, 137, 354.

LEAVING CAR (see "Alighting from Car").

LISTENING (see "Looking and Listening").

LOOKING (see "Looking and Listening").

LOOKING AND LISTENING,

pedestrian crossing tracks without looking cannot recover, 212-214.
stopping, looking, and listening not necessary as matter of law, 215.
whether looking and listening necessary as matter of law, 216.
whether looking necessary as matter of law, 217.
child not bound to look as matter of law, 256, 257.
usually barred from recovery, 260, 261.
driver of team not looking before crossing track barred from recovery, 289.
driver need not stop, look, and listen, as matter of law, 293.
whether driver must look and listen, as matter of law, 293.
whether driver must look, as matter of law, 294.

[REFERENCES ARE TO PAGES.]

LOOKOUT,

scope and extent of motorman's duty, 236-241, 272-281, 323, 324.

## M.

MASTER AND SERVANT,

company liable when employe invites child to ride free, 23, 24.
company liable for acts of employe within scope of authority, 62, 187, 190.
assault, 189.
ejection, 189.
arrest, 189.
whether company may be held in exemplary damages without authorization or ratification, 192.

MENTAL SUFFERING (see "Damages").

MISCONDUCT (see "Ejection").

MOTORMAN (see "Employe").

## N.

NEGLIGENCE (see "Passenger"; "Traveler"; "Employe"; "Imputed Negligence"),

even if plaintiff is lacking in due care, company may be liable if accident could have been prevented, 60, 210, 235, 320.

NEWSBOY,

a licensee, 28-30.
duty of carrier towards, 29, 30.
not an employe, 35.

NOTICE,

forbidding riding on front platform, reasonable, 71, 72.
may be waived, 70.
person able to read held bound to know, 71.
child not bound, 72.
passenger alighting without notice, in general, cannot recover, 163.

## O.

OBJECTIONABLE PASSENGER (see "Ejection").

OBSTRUCTION OF TRACK (see "Track").

ORDINANCE,

whether company liable without accepting ordinance, 246.
regulating speed, not permission to run up to limit on all occasions, 281.
in absence of any speed not dangerous, proper, 282.
whether violation of, regulating speed, negligence as matter of law, 328.

OVERLOADING CAR (see "Crowding Car").

## P.

PARALLEL TRACK (see "Double Track").

PARENT AND CHILD (see "Child").

PASS,

passenger riding on, limiting liability, cannot recover, 22.

PASSENGER,

relation of passenger and carrier, 2.
is a contractual one, 2.
may be established at station or customary stopping place, 3, 4.
may be established while boarding car in street, 4, 5.
stopping car on signal, an invitation to board, 5.
person thus boarding, a passenger, 5, 6.
slackening speed on signal may be invitation to board, 6-8.
unrecognized signal creates no relation, 8, 9.
signal and answer insufficient to create relation, 9, 10.
boarding without signal creates no relation, 10, 11.
violation of rule in boarding does not prevent relation, 11, 12.
relation continues during transfer, 12, 13.

[REFERENCES ARE TO PAGES.]

PASSENGER—Cont'd.

continues while passenger is alighting, 13.
terminates after passenger has alighted, 13-17.
continues if carrier controls premises, 17-19.
may continue if alighting for temporary purpose, 14, 15.
payment of fare not necessary to establish, 20-22.
person riding free, under rule, a passenger, 22.
person riding on pass limiting liability cannot recover, 22.
child invited to ride free, a passenger, 23-26.
if child sui juris, not a passenger, 24, 25.
child stealing ride, a trespasser, 27, 28.
newsboy a licensee, 28-30.
person occupying unusual position, a trespasser, 30-32.
terminates on refusal to pay fare, 32.
terminates on improper conduct, 32, 33.
reasonable anticipation of improper conduct enough, 33.
refusal to obey reasonable rule terminates, 33.
employe riding free under rule, a passenger, 34, 35.
passenger assisting employe, not fellow servant, 35, 36.
boarding car,
due care in boarding moving car generally a question of fact, 38-42.
special circumstances may show lack of due care,
speed of car, 45.
age and physical condition, 46.
incumbered with bundles, 46, 47.
condition of car, 47, 48.
condition of track, 48, 49.
boarding without signal, 49.
boarding against rule of warning, 50.
manner of boarding car, 50, 51.
boarding car not in motion, 51.
carrier must furnish reasonable opportunity for boarding.
carrier not an insurer, 52.
must use high degree of care, 52.
must allow reasonable time for boarding, 53.
must consider age and physical condition of person boarding, 54.
must consider incumbrances of person boarding, 54.
must see that all intending passengers are safe before starting, 54.

[REFERENCES ARE TO PAGES.]

PASSENGER—Cont'd.

slackening speed may be invitation to board, 55.
not negligence to start before passenger is seated, 55.
must use reasonable care in selecting stopping place, 56.
no duty to look out for boys trying to steal ride, 58.
miscellaneous negligence in operating car, 59-62.

on car,

not lack of due care to ride on platforms, steps, or running board, 64, 65, 77, 80, 82.
circumstances of each case to be considered,
consent of those in charge of car, 67-71, 78, 81, 83.
crowded condition of car, 68, 69, 78, 81, 83.
position on platform, 72-74.
intoxication, 74, 75.
children, 75, 76.
collision with post, 81, 87-89.
collision with wagon, 85.
collision with other car, 86.
standing in car, not lack of due care, 89, 90.
riding on bumper, lack of due care, 91.
standing in car preparatory to alighting, not lack of due care, 92-94.
changing position on car may be lack of due care, 94, 95.
due care under other conditions, generally for jury,
catching dress, 96.
falling from car, 97.
tripping in car, 98.
putting arm outside car, 99.
transferring, 100.
carrier not an insurer, 101.
must use high degree of care, 101.
traveling on Sunday no defense to carrier, 104, 105.
negligence in crowding cars, 106, 107.
condition of car, 108.
must reasonably protect from injury by fellow passengers, 113, 114.
derailment prima facie evidence of negligence, 115-117.
collision between two street cars, 119-122.
collision between car and wagon, 122-124.
collision between steam and street railroad, 125-127.
unusual jerk prima facie evidence of negligence, 128.
negligent speed of car, 132.

[REFERENCES ARE TO PAGES.]

PASSENGER—Cont'd.
miscellaneous negligence in operation, 133-137.
alighting from car,
due care in alighting from moving car generally a question of fact, 139, 140.
carrier must furnish reasonable opportunity for alighting, 142.
carrier not an insurer of safety, 141.
carrier must use high degree of care, 141.
slackening speed may constitute invitation to alight, 142.
carrier must know that no one is alighting before starting, 143.
special circumstances may show passenger's lack of due care,
speed of car, 145-148.
manner of alighting,
passenger stepping off moving car backwards cannot recover, 148.
omitting to grasp handles not lack of due care, 150, 151.
age and physical condition, 152.
children, 152.
aged and infirm persons, 153.
sex of passengers, 154.
wearing trailing dress or hoop skirt not lack of due care, 154, 155.
incumbered with bundles, 156.
place of alighting,
carrier must furnish reasonably safe place for alighting, 157.
carrier must use ordinary care in selecting place for alighting, 157, 158.
preparatory to alighting, 159, 160.
standing on platform, steps, or running board not lack of due care, 160.
notice of desire to alight, 161.
need not be express, 161.
carrier is not negligent when passenger gives no notice, 162, 163.
alighting in spite of warning, 164.
condition of car, 164, 165.

[REFERENCES ARE TO PAGES.]

PASSENGER—Cont'd.

injury by fellow passenger,
carrier must use reasonable care to prevent, 165, 166.
miscellaneous negligence in operation of car, 167-169.
ejection,
passenger may be ejected for misconduct,
refusal to pay fare, 171-173.
unreasouable tender of fare, 174, 175.
language or conduct likely to cause annoyance, 176-178.
refusal to obey reasonable rule, 179, 180.
no ejection on account of color, 181.
actual force not necessary to ejection, 181.
actual contact not necessary to ejection, 182.
must be performed in reasonable manner, 183.
must be performed at reasonable place and time, 184-186.
carrier liable for acts of servant in course of employment, 187-190.
may be liable in exemplary damages, 192.
passenger must obey reasonable rules as to time and place of transfer, 193-195.
whether transfer bad on face gives right to ride, 196-205.

PEDESTRIAN (see "Traveler on Highway").

PHOTOGRAPH (see "Evidence").

PHYSICAL CONDITION (see "Infirm Person").

PLATFORM (see "Front Platform"; "Rear Platform").

POSITION ON CAR,

person occupying unusual position not a passenger, 30-32.

POSITION PREPARATORY TO ALIGHTING (see "Standing in Car").

POST,

passenger colliding with, 81, 87-89.

PRESUMPTION OF NEGLIGENCE,

defect in electrical appliances, 61, 108, 110, 350.

[REFERENCES ARE TO PAGES.]

PRESUMPTION OF NEGLIGENCE—Cont'd.

derailment, 115-117.
collision, 119, 126.
jerk, 128.

R.

RAIL (see "Track").

REAR PLATFORM,

not lack of due care to board moving car by, 40.
less dangerous to board by, than by front platform, 40.
riding on, not lack of due care, 77.
circumstances of each case to be considered,
consent of those in charge of car, 78.
crowded condition of car, 78.
holding onto car, 79.
rule forbidding riding on, reasonable, 78.
passenger assumes risk of ordinary movements of car, 78, 79.

RIDING ON PLATFORM (see "Front Platform"; "Rear Platform").

RIGHT OF WAY,

street car has superior, but not exclusive, right of way, 233, 234, 269, 313-318.
at street crossings, car and wagon have equal rights, 235, 269, 319, 320.

RING,

defective ring in floor of car, negligence, 112.

RULE,

person boarding car in violation of, may be passenger, 11, 12.
person riding free under, a passenger, 22.
passenger refusing to obey reasonable rule forfeits rights, 33.
person boarding in violation of, held unable to recover, 50.
rule forbidding backing car held unreasonable, 56.
taking fare waives rule forbidding riding on front platform, 68.
prohibiting smoking except on front platform waives rule forbidding riding on platform, 69.
prohibiting riding on front platform reasonable, 71.

RULE—Cont'd.

prohibiting intoxicated persons from riding on front platform reasonable, 71.
prohibiting riding on rear platform reasonable, 78.
person violating, cannot recover, 79.
rules as to fares held reasonable, 171, 172, 175.
various rules of carrier held reasonable, 179, 180.

RULE OF ROAD,

does not apply to wagon meeting car, 317, 318.

RUNNING BOARD,

not lack of due care to board moving car by, 40.
not lack of due care to ride upon, 82.
circumstances of each case to be considered, 83.
consent of those in charge of car, 83.
crowded condition of car, 83.
collision by passenger on running board,
with post, 87-89.
with wagon, 85.
with other car, 86.

S.

SIGNAL,

stopping car on signal an invitation to board, 5.
slackening speed on signal may be invitation to board, 6-8.
unrecognized signal does not establish relation of passenger and carrier, 8, 9.
signal and answer insufficient to create relation of passenger and carrier, 9, 10.
person boarding car without signal, not a passenger, 10, 11.
not negligence to fail to stop car on signal, 57.
liability of company where passenger gives signals, 60.
right to give, when horse frightened, 335, 336.

SLACKENING SPEED OF CAR,

on signal, may be invitation to board, 6-8.

SMOKING,

rule prohibiting, except on front platform, waives rule forbidding riding on front platform, 69.

[REFERENCES ARE TO PAGES.]

SMOKING—Cont'd.

custom of permitting, on front platform, a circumstance bearing on passenger's due care, 70.

SNOW,

negligence in obstructing steps with, 164.
duty to remove from tracks, 365, 366.

SPECIAL DAMAGES (see "Damages").

SPEED,

of car, as affecting passenger's due care,
boarding, 45.
alighting, 145, 146.
negligence of company in running car at high speed, 131-133, 241-243, 282-284, 325-330.

STANDING IN CAR,

not lack of due care as matter of law, 89, 90.
must hold on, if possible, 88.
preparatory to alighting, 92-94.

STATION (see, also, "Elevated Railway"),

relation of passenger and carrier may be established at, 3.

STEALING RIDE (see "Trespasser").

STEAM RAILROAD,

rules governing are not applicable to street railroads,
boarding car, 42.
riding on front platform, 66.
riding on rear platform, 77.
outside city limits, same rules govern, 78.
alighting from car, 148.
due care in crossing tracks, 215, 293.

STEP,

when obviously unsafe, person boarding by, cannot recover, 47.
not lack of due care to ride upon, 80-82.
circumstances of each case must be considered, 81, 82.

STEP—Cont'd.

consent of those in charge of car, 81.
crowded condition of car, 81.
negligence in condition of, 164, 165.

STOPPING CAR,

on signal, invitation to board, 5.

STOPPING, LOOKING, AND LISTENING (see "Looking and Listening").

STREET CAR (see, also, "Cable Car"; "Horse Car"; "Electric Car"),

condition of, may make attempt to board lack of due care, 47, 48.
defects in condition of car, 59, 60, 79, 98, 108-112, 164, 165, 286, 287, 320.

STREET CROSSING,

rights of car and public equal, 235, 269, 319, 320.

STREET RAILROAD,

rules governing are not applicable to steam railroad,
boarding car, 42.
riding on front platform, 66.
riding on rear platform, 77.
outside city limits, same rules govern, 78.
alighting from car, 148.
due care in crossing tracks, 215, 293.

STREET SWEEPER,

held unable to recover when run over, 230.

SUNDAY,

riding on, will not prevent recovery, 104, 105.

## T.

TENDER OF FARE,

what is reasonable, 174, 175.

TRACK,

wagon must not unnecessarily obstruct, 319.
must be kept in reasonably safe condition, 361.
accidents from excavations near or between, 357, 358.
accidents from obstructions near, 359.
accidents from defects in, 360-362.
obstructing by snow, dirt, etc., 365, 366.

TRANSFER,

person transferring is a passenger, 12, 13.
person receiving must obey reasonable rules, 193-195.
rights under transfer bad on face, 196-205.

TRAP DOOR,

passenger's knowledge of, no defense for company, 112.

TRAVELER ON HIGHWAY,

adults run over,
must use ordinary care in crossing tracks, 209.
must use ordinary care in walking on or near tracks, 222, 223.
circumstances bearing on due care,
intoxication, 211.
infirmity, 212.
pedestrian crossing tracks without looking cannot recover, 212-215.
stopping, looking, and listening not necessary, as matter of law, 215.
whether looking and listening necessary, as matter of law, 216.
whether looking necessary, as matter of law, 217.
speed of car, 218.
failure to give warning, 219.
more care necessary when view obstructed, 219.
no recovery if traveler takes chance of crossing ahead of car, 219.
traveler may be barred from recovery when crossing double tracks, 224-227.
laborer working on or near track,
due care of, 227-232.

[REFERENCES ARE TO PAGES.]

TRAVELER ON HIGHWAY—Cont'd.
negligence of company towards, 245, 246.
street car has superior, but not exclusive, right of way, 233.
at street crossings, rights of cars and pedestrians are equal, 235.
rights and duties of employes in charge of cars,
lookout, 236-240.
warning, 242, 243.
speed, 241.
children run over,
capacity of child for exercising due care, 249-251.
standard of care for child, 252, 253.
whether negligence of parent may be imputed to child, 254, 255.
due care of child run over, for jury, 256-260.
lack of due care of child run over, 260, 261.
due care of parent in allowing child in street, 262-264.
due care of parent in leaving child alone in or near house, 265-268.
street car has superior, but not exclusive, right of way, 269.
at street crossings, rights of cars and pedestrians are equal, 269.
company must use more care towards children than towards adults, 270.
rights and duties of employes in charge of cars,
lookout, 272-281.
warning, 284, 285.
speed, 282-285.
accidents to drivers of teams,
driver of team not looking before crossing track, barred from recovery, 289, 290.
driver need not stop, look, and listen, as matter of law, 293.
whether driver must look and listen, as matter of law, 293.
whether driver must look, as matter of law, 294.
no recovery where driver takes chance of crossing ahead of car, 291.
circumstances bearing on questions of due care,
obstruction of view, 290, 299.
character of locality, 295.
speed of car, 296-298.
distance of car from team, 296-298.

[REFERENCES ARE TO PAGES.]

TRAVELER ON HIGHWAY—Cont'd.
failure to give warning, 298.
due care of driver of team in driving on or near tracks,
may be barred from recovery, 304, 305, 307.
due care for jury, 301-303, 306.
whether driver's lack of due care can be imputed to person driving with him, 308-310.
age and occcupation, as bearing on question of due care,
children, 311.
aged persons, 311.
infirm persons, 311.
firemen, 311-313.
street car has superior, but not exclusive, right of way, 313.
rights of cars and wagons at street crossings are equal. 313.
rights and duties of employes in charge of cars,
lookout, 323, 324, 328.
speed, 325-327.
warning, 325.
accidents from frightened horses,
due care of driver, 333, 334.
negligence of company, 335-340.

TRESPASSER,
child stealing ride is, 27, 28.
person occupying unusual position is, 30-32.

TRIPPING IN CAR,
due care of passenger, 98.
negligence of company, 98.

V.

VINDICTIVE DAMAGES (see "Damages").

W.

WAGON,
passenger on street car injured by collision with wagon, 122-124.
passenger on running board colliding with wagon, 85.

[REFERENCES ARE TO PAGES.]

WAGON—Cont'd.

driver of wagon injured by collision with street car, 289-325.

WALKING ON TRACK (see "Traveler on Highway").

WARNING,

person boarding in spite of, cannot recover, 50.
person alighting in spite of, cannot recover, 164.
duty of motorman or driver to give, 242, 243, 284, 285, 325.
right to give, when horse frightened, 335, 336.

WIRE,

accidents from contact with, 349, 350, 363, 364, 369

WITNESS (see "Evidence").